Footprint **Kenya**

Lizzie Williams
1st edition

W9-AUF-183

*I had seen a herd of elephant travelling
through the dense native forest, pacing
along as if they had an appointment
at the end of the world.*

Isak Dinesen (aka Karen Blixen)

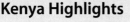

Kenya Highlights

See colour maps at back of book

1 Lamu
Steeped in Swahili history, with intriguing alleyways and Arabian houses

2 Malindi
A hugely popular European holiday destination with excellent facilities

3 Fort Jesus Museum, Mombasa
Learn the history of the coast

4 Tamarind, Mombasa
Eat delicious seafood on a romantic white-sailed dhow

5 Diani Beach
One of the finest stretches of white sand beach in the country

6 Tsavo National Park
The largest game park in East Africa, famous for its herds of big tuskers

7 Amboseli National Park
With a backdrop of snow-capped Mount Kilimanjaro, watching wildlife here is very scenic

8 Carnivore
Nairobi's top eating place for a gut-busting meat extravaganza

9 Nairobi National Park
View all of the Big Five except elephant

10 Langata Giraffe Centre
Eyeball a giraffe at giraffe height

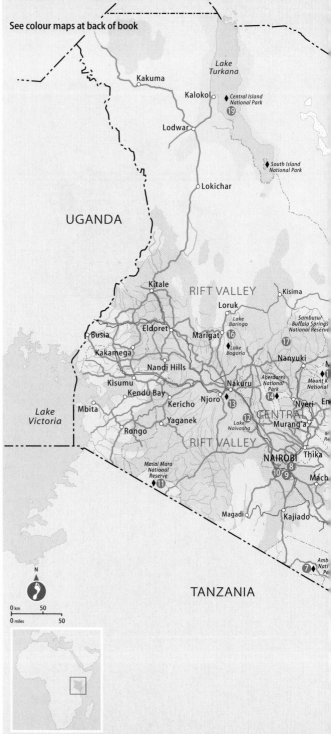

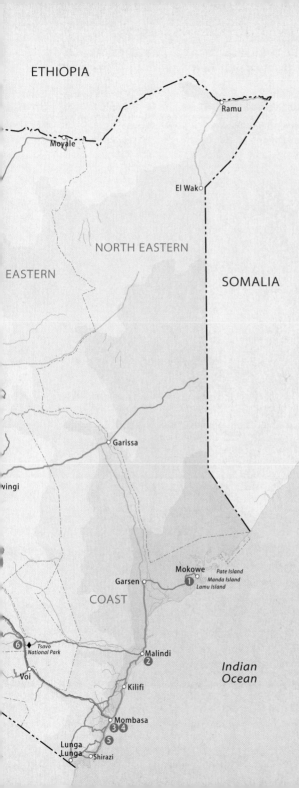

11 Masai Mara Game Reserve
The plains are trampled by up to three million mammals during the annual wildebeest migration

12 Lake Naivasha
Rift Valley freshwater lake surrounded by feathery papyrus, marshy lagoons and grassy shores

13 Lake Nakuru National Park
Famous for its healthy rhino population and pink flamingos

14 Aberdares National Park
Treetops and the Arc are the famous park lodges

15 Mount Kenya
Climb Africa's second tallest peak

16 Lakes Bogoria and Baringo
Lovely lakes with one of the highest densities of birds in East Africa

17 Laikipia Plateau
Kenya's newest wildlife destination and conservation success story

18 Samburu and Buffalo Springs National Reserves
Unusual wildlife in an arid environment

19 Lake Turkana
Difficult to access but the parched desert environment and dazzling waters make the journey worthwhile

Basket with a view
A balloon ride over the Masai Mara must rank as one of the best safari experiences, especially during the wildebeest migration, the world's biggest natural movement of large animals.

A foot in the door

To move through Kenya is to experience a motion picture of landscapes from rolling savannah, where the Masai tend their herds, to mountain forests full of birds, stony parched deserts and a tropical coast fringed by white-sand beaches and clear blue sea. It is these habitats that draw many visitors, harbouring, as they do, some of the world's most incredible species.

Safari means journey in Kiswahili, but this is something of an understatement for many visitors. It is an opportunity to get close to zebra, leopard, cheetah, lion, tiger, elephant, giraffe, crocodile, rhino, hippo, to name a few. The Masai Mara is probably the most famous game reserve in the country and one of Kenya's biggest attractions. Along with the Serengeti National Park in neighbouring Tanzania, this important eco-system contains over three million large mammals that move around the plains of East Africa on a continuous annual migration – the world's single biggest natural movement of large animals. Along with wildlife on the plains, there are the coral reefs of the coast, teeming with life and colour, and the Rift Valley lakes, home to thousands of flamingos.

For all its scenic beauty and wildlife, Kenya isn't just a land to be viewed through a disc of glass. For centuries it has been occupied by myriad different people and today there are over 70 traditional ethnic groups. The majestic Masai and Samburu still stalk the plains dressed in their trademark red and purple robes, and the legacies of the European white settlers, who came in search of pristine farming land and hunting trophies, can still be seen. Kenya's two major cities – the high-altitude, colonial-built capital Nairobi and the steamy trading port of Mombasa – have a vibey African feel and, along the coast, are testaments to the Swahili civilization that has lived in East Africa for hundreds of years.

1 *Elephants get friendly in the harsh environment of Samburu National Reserve in Kenya's northern region.* ▸▸ *See page 294.*

2 *Diani Beach is the longest beach in Kenya with some 20 km of bright white sand, coconut trees, clear sea and a coral reef.* ▸▸ *See page 224.*

3 *In the dry, arid area around Buffalo Springs, camels are a common sight.* ▸▸ *See page 295.*

4 *Tea is one of Kenya's biggest exports. The brilliant green plantations also make a lovely landscape.* ▸▸ *See page 145.*

5 *The coral reefs off the coastline are an underwater paradise. Here, a whale shark rears its head.* ▸▸ *See page 42.*

6 *Eyeball to eyeball with a giraffe at Langata Giraffe Centre, one of a few great excursions from Kenya's capital, Nairobi.* ▸▸ *See page 71.*

7 *Step back in time on the atmospheric island of Lamu, where there is only one car and the most popular way of getting around is by donkey.* ▸▸ *See page 264.*

8 *Lake Bogoria, one of the famous Rift Valley lakes, is home to some spectacular wildlife including hundreds of flamingos.* ▸▸ *See page 118.*

9 *Islam arrived along the East African coast in the eighth century, as part of the trade routes from the Persian Gulf and Oman. Today mosques are a common sight in this region.* ▸▸ *See page 311.*

10 *A lion finds a better viewpoint in the Masai Mara National Reserve.* ▸▸ *See page 123.*

11 *A Masai women decoratively adorned.* ▸▸ *See page 320.*

12 *Wildebeest in the shadow of Kilimanjaro in Amboseli National Park.* ▸▸ *See page 202.*

On the road
The dramatic landscape will take your mind off the bumpy ride when travelling around the country. Here, a road cuts through the countryside towards Kitale.

Park life

Aside from tracking the Big Five or following the wildebeest migration in the Masai Mara, walking, cycling, birdwatching, fishing or trekking safaris are available to explore the ever-changing terrain to its full advantage. The options are as varied as climbing Mount Kenya to traversing the thirstlands of northern Kenya with a camel train, or tracking elephant on foot. The Masai Mara is famous for its cats. Tsavo is especially known for elephants with very big tusks and Amboseli has the dramatic backdrop of snow-capped Mount Kilimanjaro. Buffalo Springs, Samburu and Shaba in the north offer a different environment for game viewing with a more parched landscape and unusual animals. In Lake Nakuru visitors can just about trip over rhino and this park can be easily combined with visits to lakes Baringo and Bogorio to witness the spectacular birdlife. For those looking for something a little more intimate, the superb game lodges on the Laikipia Plateau are a fine bet.

Lazy days

On the coast are magnificent swathes of white-sand beaches, bordered with coconut palms, where it is impossible not to relax. In the far north are the islands of Lamu, a flat mangrove creek paradise with miles of deserted white beach. These islands are so culturally preserved that there is only one car and life hasn't changed much for hundreds of years. A walk through the narrow, twisting passageways and Arabic architecture of Lamu town plunges you into the past. Veiled women with hennaed hands haggle for coconuts in markets, while old men sit on crumbling walls to drink chai and idly gossip. South of Mombasa are a string of unobtrusive resorts catering for the upmarket European holidaymaker. Diani is easily the best beach in Kenya, with fine white sand, bordered by forests and lapped by the azure Indian Ocean. If swaying in a hammock gets too much, there are plenty of activities from diving and snorkelling to deep-sea fishing, windsurfing and jet skiing.

Close encounters

Urban Africa has style and excitement and the towns and cities are densely packed centres of burgeoning commerce. The teeming markets, crowded roadside stalls and frantic ports and bus stations are great places to get a feel for Kenyan life. A visit to Nairobi, with its diverse mix of inhabitants and good shopping, restaurants and nightlife, can be great fun and offers some insight into what makes the country tick. Predominantly Muslim, Mombasa has a completely different atmosphere to the skyscrapers of Nairobi; here you will find old forts, bustling markets and crumbling mosques. There are also more intimate opportunities to meet Kenyans. You can visit a Masai village (*manyatta*) around Amboseli and the Masai Mara, go trekking with the Samburu on camel trains in the north, or visit the Pokot people from the Marich Pass Field Studies Centre or the Sirikwa people from Sirikwa Safaris.

Contents

Introducing
Kenyan highlights 2
A foot in the door 5

Essentials 11
Planning your trip 12
Before you travel 19
Money 22
Getting there 23
Touching down 26
Getting around 30
Sleeping 34
Eating 36
Entertainment 38
Festivals and events 39
Shopping 39
Sport and activities 40
Parks and safari 43
Health 51
Keeping in touch 57

Guide

Nairobi 59
Sights 65
Excursions 70
Listings 76

Rift Valley 95
**Naivasha
and around 98**
Naivasha 99
Lake Naivasha 99
Hell's Gate
National Park 102
Nakuru and around 107
Lake Elementeita 107
Nakuru 107
Lake Nakuru
National Park 109
Nyahururu and
Thompson's Falls 114
Further north 118
Lake Bogaria
National Reserve 118
Lake Baringo 119
Northern Rift Valley 121

**Masai Mara
National Reserve 123**

Western Kenya 131
Kisumu 134
South of Kisumu 141
Kisumu to the
Tanzanian border 141
Kisii and the Western
Highlands 144
Kakamega 148
The far north 153
Ugandan border 153
Kitale 153
Saiwa Swamp
National Park 154
Mount Elgon
National Park 155

Central Highlands 159
Nyeri and around 163
Solio Game Ranch 165
Aberdares
National Park 166
**Mount Kenya
and around 172**
Nanyuki 172
Mount Kenya
Biosphere Reserve 172
Laikipia Plateau 179
Moving east 184

Southern Kenya 189
**Heading south
from Nairobi 192**
Nairobi to
Lake Magadi 192
Mombasa road 192
Tsavo National Park 195
**Amboseli and the
Tanzanian border 201**

The coast 207
Mombasa 211
South coast 223
Tiwi Beach 223
Diani Beach 224

Shimba Hills National
Reserve 225
South of Diani 227
North coast 237
Mombasa to Kilifi 237
Kilifi 240
Arabuko Sokoke
Forest Reserve 241
Watamu 242
Gedi Ruins 244
Malindi 246

Lamu Archipelago 261
Lamu 264
Pate Island 277
Kiunga Marine
National Reserve 279
Dodori and Boni
national reserve 280

Northern Kenya 283
**Kitale to
Lake Turkana 287**
Isiolo and around 293
**Isiolo to
Lake Turkana 298**
Marsabit to Moyale 304

Background 309
History 310
Modern Kenya 314
Economy 316
Culture 318
Land and environment 324
Books 334

Footnotes 335
Language 336
Index 337
Complete title listing 340
Map index 342
Advertisers' index 342
Map symbols 343
Credits 344
Author biography 345
Acknowledgements 345
Colour maps 346

Essentials

Planning your trip	12
Before you travel	19
Money	22
Getting there	23
Touching down	26
Getting around	30
Sleeping	34
Eating	36
Entertainment	38
Festivals and events	39
Shopping	39
Sport and activities	40
Parks and safari	43
Health	51
Keeping in touch	57

Footprint features

Touching down	25
How big is your footprint?	28
Hotel price codes explained	35
Restaurant price codes explained	37
How big is your flipper?	43
On the up	44
What's what?	45
Rules of the game	48

Planning your trip

Where to go

Kenya is a country of enormous diversity. Most people come to go on a safari in one or several of the excellent game reserves and national parks in pursuit of the Big Five. Safari means journey in Kiswahili and, whilst the journey may be rough on the parks' bumpy and slippery roads, there is no denying that there is a wide range of locations in which to see an array of game. Not so well known is Kenya's bird life; the country has a huge range of species in the forests of the highlands and the Rift Valley lakes. Some of the game lodges are not as luxurious as in other regions of Africa, but they are improving, and some first-rate small establishments that match the luxury of lodges in southern Africa are beginning to appear on the safari circuit. In the Masai Mara alone there are almost 40 game lodges and tented camps, and in the other parks, such as Tsavo, tourism facilities are growing to match the demand of visitors. Kenya's coastal attractions include palm-fringed, white sandy beaches and coral reefs surrounding the off-shore islands, some of which drop off forming steep underwater cliffs that plunge to depths of over 600 m. There are a number of marine national parks along the coast that form a veritable playground for a wide range of marine species. Most visitors on package holidays combine time on the beach with a safari to see the animals. Independent visitors have the added opportunity to explore the areas away from the normal tourist circuit: the impossibly pretty forests and highlands in the interior, the arid northern deserts, the stately Mount Kenya or the ancient lifestyle of the islands of Lamu.

None of the circuits below is a complete itinerary in itself, and they are not set in stone. Rather, they are regional suggestions for travellers wishing to explore a certain part of the country. Nairobi or Mombasa are the usual arrival points into Kenya for international travellers, so what you do rather depends on where you arrive.

One week

If you arrive in **Mombasa**, the beaches around offer week-long (or more) affordable beach holidays with good air travel and transfers directly to the resorts. From the beach resorts there is the opportunity to take day trips along the coast to see the various attractions, such as **Wasini Island** to the south, the **old town** of Mombasa itself, or the **marine parks** along the northern beaches. Not far away from the beach is the **Shimba Hills National Reserve**, a very popular day trip where there is an excellent chance of spotting elephant. **Tsavo East** and **West National parks** are also within striking distance of the coast, less than a two-hour drive away, and a beach holiday can be combined with one or two nights in a game lodge within the parks. There is also the possibility of heading up to the north of the coast for a night or two to the islands of **Lamu**, less than an hour's flight from Malindi, to experience a very different atmosphere from the beachside hotels. Lamu is underdeveloped for tourism and, in addition to beautiful beaches, there is the wonderfully friendly ancient stone town of Lamu with its intriguing narrow alleyways, superb museum and Arabic houses.

If flying into **Nairobi**, there are parks and reserves just a few hours' drive away. The closest is **Nairobi National Park**; it has the city as its backdrop and can easily be visited on a half day trip. Tour operators in Nairobi can organize safaris to the **Masai Mara**, **Amboseli**, **Tsavo**, the **Aberdares**, **Lake Nakuru** and the other **Rift Valley lakes** and **Mount Kenya**. How many you visit and how long you stay depends on personal preference and there are any number of combinations. A popular circuit from Nairobi is two to three nights in the Masai Mara with one night in the Naivasha region to see Lake Naivasha, and one night in Nakuru to visit Nakuru National Park. Another is the

on offer from Nairobi are two nights in either Amboseli or the Masai Mara. Nairobi
itself is worth making at least a day for as there are some very interesting wildlife
centres and attractions on the edge of the city. These include the **Langata Giraffe
Centre**, the **David Sheldrick Elephant Orphanage** and the **Karen Blixen Museum**.

Two to three weeks
The above options can be combined as a two-week tour of Kenya offering some time
relaxing on the beach and some time watching the wildlife. Transport links between
Nairobi and the coast are very good; there are several flights and buses and also there
is the option of taking the overnight train. For those with more time, an interesting
excursion from Nairobi, which shouldn't take more than three to four days, is to drive
around **Mount Kenya**, with perhaps a night or two at the **Aberdares National Park**. The
road is good and goes completely around the circumference of the mountain. Here in
the highlands are atmospheric colonial country hotels with the ever-present view of
brooding Mount Kenya. If you want to climb the mountain allow four to five additional
days. Another three- to four-day alternative is to explore the **Rift Valley**. **Naivasha** is a
short drive from Nairobi where there is a fine selection of lakeshore accommodation to
choose from and plenty of interesting things to do including walking or cycling in **Hell's
Gate National Park** or visiting one of the new wildlife conservancies in the region. From
here, **Nakuru** and **Nakuru National Park** can easily be explored in half a day, and **Lake
Bogoria** and **Baringo**, where you can see excellent bird life, are not far away.

A month
As well as the above, from the Rift Valley you can head west into the **Kenyan
highlands** towards **Lake Victoria** and the provincial towns of **Kisumu**, **Kericho** and
Kitale. The towns themselves won't keep your interest for long but the countryside is
extraordinarily pretty, especially at the **Kakamega Forest** and the verdant hillsides
around Kericho that are covered in tea plantations. This is also the region of the
Mount Elgon and **Saiwa Swamp national parks** which are very different to the
southern reserves. In Mount Elgon there is the opportunity to see the unusual
elephants that seek salt in the mountain's caves; Saiwa is home to the rare sitatunga
antelope. North of the **Aberdare Mountains** is the newly established **Laikipia Plateau**,
an applauded conservation effort by the ranch owners in this region to use their land
for the protection of, and in many cases the breeding of, wildlife. This has been
Kenya's greatest conservation success story in recent years and there are now some
wonderful lodges and safari companies offering a huge range of safari activities. Here
guests will receive more intimate and educational wildlife encounters than in the
main parks (though at a price). For those with a penchant for adventurous travel,
northern Kenya is a wild and untamed region of parched deserts, spectacular
mountain ranges, and the turquoise waters of Kenya's largest lake, Turkana. Travel in
this region is challenging and difficult, and has in recent years been marred by
security problems. It is best to explore this region on a tour.

When to go

Straddling the equator, Kenya's daytime temperatures average between 20°C and
25°C, though it is cooler in the highlands and hotter along the coast. Humidity varies,
being high along the coastal strip but much lower in the interior highlands. On the
coast, high temperatures are cooled by ocean breezes so it is rarely overpoweringly
hot. Away from the coast, it is much drier and the rains are a little kinder. On peaks
above 1,500 m the climate is cooler with permanent snow on the highest peaks, such
as Mount Kenya where nighttime temperatures drop to below zero. There are two

rainy seasons in the country, the long rains fall in March to April and the short rains fall in October to December. Even in these months, however, there is an average of four to six hours of sunshine each day. Bear in mind that malaria peaks during the rainy seasons, when the mosquitoes are prolific.In terms of avoiding the rains, the driest times are between May-September and January-February when the weather is hot and dry, encouraging wild animals to the nearest waterholes. Travelling by road, especially in the more remote areas or through the national parks, is easier during the dry months, as road conditions deteriorate significantly in the rainy seasons.

If you are on a budget, bear in mind that most of the game lodges and beach resorts drop their rates significantly, sometimes by as much as 50%, during low season which is usually from the beginning of April to the beginning of June.

High season along the coast is from September to January and it gets especially busy around the Christmas and New Year period, whilst high season in the safari regions is July to November, especially in the Masai Mara as this is when the wildebeest have arrived from the Serengeti in Tanzania on their annual migration. There are a number of events throughout the year, such as the Safari Rally or Lewa Marathon, which visitors can watch or participate in and can be combined with a safari or beach holiday. For sheer numbers of birds the best time for birdwatching in Kenya is between October and April when more than 120 migrant species arrive from the northern hemisphere, mostly from the Palearctic but with some African migrants too. If you're interested in bird ringing, towards the end of the season is a large bird ringing exercise **Ngulia Lodge** in Tsavo National Park. The coast is particularly good during this period with large flocks of water birds congregating at Mida Creek and Sabaki Estuary, while the Rift Valley lakes and Amboseli attract a lot of northern waterfowl. From April to October the Northern Migrants are replaced by birds from the southern hemisphere and Madagascar, but these are much fewer in number.

Tour operators

Africa
Africa Travel Co, T021-556 8590, www.africa travelco.com.
Easy Travel & Tours Ltd, T+255 222-123 526, www.easytravel.co.tz.
Predators Safari Club, T+255 272-506 471, www.predators-safaris.com.
Wild Frontiers, T011-702 2035, www.wildfrontiers.com.

Australia and New Zealand
Classic Safari Company, T1300-130218, www.classicsafaricompany.com.au.
Peregrine Travel, T303-96638611, www.peregrine.net.au.

North America
Adventure Centre, T800-2288747, www.adventure-centre.com.
Africa Adventure Company, T800-8829453, T954-4918877, www.africa-adventure.com.
Distant Horizons, T800-3331240, T562-9838828, www.distant-horizons.com.

Hoopoe Safaris, T800-4083100, www.hoopoe.com.
Legendary Adventure Co, T303-4131182, www.legendary adventure.com.

UK
Abercrombie & Kent, T0800-5547016, www.abercrombiekent.com.
Acacia Adventure Holidays, T020-77064700, www.acacia-africa.com.
The Africa Travel Centre, T0845-4501520, www.africatravel.co.uk.
African Odyssey, T01242-224482, www.africanodyssey.co.uk.
Africa Travel Resource, T01306-880770, www.africatravelresource.com.
Alpha Travel/Ranger Safaris, T020-84230220, www.rangersafaris.com.
Footprint Adventures, T01522-804929, www.footprint-adventures.co.uk.
Global Village, T0870-999484, www.globalvillage-travel.com.

Essentials Planning your trip

Hoopoe Safaris, T01923-255462,
www.hoopoe.com.
Predators Safari Club, T020-83710042,
www.predators-safaris.com. Based in Tanzania
with an office in London.
Safari Consultants, T01787-228494,
www.safari-consultants.co.uk.

Safari Drive, T01488-71140,
www.safaridrive.com.
Sherpa Expeditions, T020-85772717,
www.sherpa-walking-holidays.co.uk.
Somak, T020-84233000, www.somak.co.uk.
Steppes Africa, T01285-650011,
www.steppesafrica.co.uk.

Finding out more

Tourist information

Apart from **Kenya Tourist Board** on Langata Road in Nairobi, T020-604245, www. magicalkenya.com, which will send you brochures on request and has an excellent website, there are other sources of useful information. In Kenya the free publication *Tourist's Kenya* is published fortnightly and offers a rundown on things going on. There is another publication called *What's On*, which comes out monthly. **Kenya Tourism Federation,** on Langata Road in the Kenya Wildlife Services Complex in Nairobi, offers a **tourist help line**, T020-604767, safetour@wananchi.com, and a Safety and Communication Centre which advises tourists on most things including road conditions or emergency help. If you want to go off the beaten track, get advice from them first.

There is of course a wealth of information in print. The authoritative and inspirational *Travel Africa Magazine*, available in the UK, is well worth a read when planning a trip. See page 334 for background reading.

Kenyan tourist offices overseas

Canada, 1599 Hurontario St, Ontario, T905-8913909, contact@kenyatourism.ca.
France, 11 Rue Blanche, Paris 75009, T01-53251207, Kenya@interfacetourism.com.
Germany, Schwarz Bach Strasse 32, Mettman, T02-2104 832919, kenia@travelmarketing.de.

Italy, Via Salaino 12, Milan 20144, T+39 (0)2 48102361, kenya@adams.it.
Netherlands, Leliegracht 20, Amsterdam 1015, T20-4212668, kenia@travelmc.com.
UK, 36 Southwark Bridge Rd, London, SE1 9EU, T0207 2026373, Kenya@hillsbalfour.com.
USA, PO Box 59159, Minneapolis, T+1866 4453692, infousa@magiacalkenya.com.

Useful websites

www.africaonline.com Comprehensive website covering news, sport and travel all over Africa.
www.esok.org Website for the Ecotourism Society of Kenya, a forum founded in 1996 to provide support for small community ecotourism projects.
www.go2africa.com Booking service for East Africa, with useful practical information.
www.katokenya.org Website for the Kenya Association of Tour Operators.
www.kenyalastminute.com Bargain last-minute holidays to Kenya, excellent site and service.

www.kenyalogy.com General tourism information.
www.kws.org Kenya Wildlife Services.
www.magicalkenya.com Official website of the Kenya Tourist Board, comprehensive and detailed information.
www.mombasacoast.com Tourist information, reservation service.
www.overlandafrica.com Sells a variety of overland tours throughout East Africa.
www.statehousekenya.go.ke Website for the Kenya government.
www.watamu.net Information and booking services for coastal hotels.

Essentials Planning your trip

Kenya is a welcoming country and the first word that you will hear and come to know is the Kiswahili greeting 'Jambo' – 'hello', often followed by 'Hakuna matata' – 'no problem'! There are a number of local languages but most people in Kenya, as in all East Africa, speak Kiswahili and some English. Kiswahili is the official language of Kenya and is taught in primary schools. English is generally used in business and is taught in secondary schools. Only in the remote rural regions will you find people that only speak in their local tongues. A little Kiswahili goes a long way, and most Kenyans will be thrilled to hear visitors attempt to use it. Although Kiswahili is a Bantu language in structure and origin, its vocabulary draws on a variety of sources including Arabic and English. The word for tea, *chai*, is the same in East Africa as it is in China and India for example. On the coast, Kiswahili is a little more grammatically developed. In other parts of the country, a more simplified version is spoken, known as 'kitchen swahili'. Since the language was originally written down by the British colonists, words are pronounced just as they are spelt. ▶▶ *For useful words and phrases in Kiswahili, see page 336.*

'Poa' is a verb in Kiswahili slang meaning chill out, relax, be cool.

Specialist travel

Disabled travellers
Wheelchairs are very difficult to accommodate on public road transport, so Kenya would need to be visited on an organized tour or in a rented vehicle. Most operators are accommodating and being disabled should not deter you from visiting Kenya. With the exception of the most upmarket hotels there are few designated facilities for disabled travellers. However, a few of the game park lodges have ground-floor bedrooms, in contrast to most hotels where the bedrooms are upstairs and there are no lifts. Safaris should not pose too much of a problem given that most of the time is spent in the vehicle, and wheelchair-bound travellers my want to consider a camping or tented safari which provides easy access to a tent at ground level. One leading safari company that deals with disabled travel to Kenya is **Southern Cross Safaris**, Mombasa, T041-475074, www.southerncrosssafaris.com.

Gay and lesbian travellers
Homosexuality is illegal in Kenya so extreme discretion is advised. Gay clubs and bars are conspicuous by their absence.

Student travellers
There are generally no discounts for students in Kenya and student rates advertised for museums and parks will usually only apply to local residents. There are a few hostels affiliated to the YHA network, but you do not need to produce a card to either stay there or hope for a discount.

Travelling with children
Kenya has a great appeal to children because of the animals, and safaris are very exciting for children (and their parents) when they catch their first glimpse of an elephant or lion. However, small children may get bored driving around a hot game park or national park all day if there is no animal activity. Some game lodges do not permit children at all, whereas others are completely child-friendly and are aimed at families. If you travel in a group, think about the long hours inside the vehicle sharing little room with other people. Noisy and bickering children can annoy your travel

mates and scare the animals away. Many travel agencies organize family safaris that are especially designed for couples travelling with children. There are considerable discounts on accommodation at the beach for children, especially in the family orientated resorts, when often children under 12 get a sizeable reduction and those under 6 go free. Many hotels have either specific family rooms or adjoining rooms suitable for families. This is always worth asking about when enquiring about accommodation. Africans are child-friendly. However, items such as disposable nappies, formula milk powders and puréed foods are only available in the major cities and they are expensive, so you may want to bring enough with you. It is important to remember that children have an increased risk of gastro-enteritis, malaria and sunburn and are more likely to develop complications, so care must be taken to minimize risks. See the health section for more details.

Women travellers

Women do have to be more wary than men, although Kenya seems to be a more pleasant place for lone women travellers than many other countries. If you are hassled, it is best to ignore the person totally, whatever you feel, as expressions of anger are often taken as acts of encouragement. Women in Kenya dress very decorously, and it is wise to follow suit particularly in small towns and rural areas. Kenyan women will generally be very supportive if they see you are being harassed and may well intervene if they think you need help, but the situation is very rarely anything more than a nuisance. You are more likely to be approached at the coast, as the number of women coming to Kenya for sexual adventure has encouraged this type of pestering. The key is to keep patient and maintain a sense of humour.

Working in the country

Whilst there is a fairly large expatriate community in Nairobi and Mombasa working in construction, telecommunications and the import/export industry, there are few opportunities for travellers to obtain casual paid employment in Kenya and it is illegal for a foreigner to work there without an official work permit. A number of NGOs and voluntary organizations can arrange placements for volunteers, usually for periods ranging from six months to two years, see www.volunteerafrica.org.

Before you travel

Visas and immigration

Almost all nationalities require a visa, with the exception of the Irish. A transit visa valid for seven days costs US$20 per person; a single-entry visa valid for three months costs US$50; a multi-entry visa valid for 12 months costs US$100. Visas are issued at the following entry points: Namanga, Moyale, Taveta, Busia, Lunga Lunga, Malaba and Migori border posts and at Jomo Kenyatta International Airport in Nairobi, Moi International Airport in Mombasa and Eldoret International Airport. Multi-entry visas are not available on arrival but only through embassies. Visas can be paid for in US dollar, euros or UK pounds sterling. Visas are usually valid for three months and as long as your single-entry visa remains valid you are allowed to move freely between Kenya, Tanzania and Uganda without the need for re-entry permits. If you want to get an extension you can stay a maximum of six months in the country fairly easily, but at extra cost. In Nairobi this can be done at Nyayo House, corner of Kenyatta Avenue and Uhuru Highway (Monday-Friday 0830-1230 and 1400-1530); it can also be done at the Provincial Commissioner's Offices in Embu, Garissa, Kisumu,

> : *Visa application forms can be downloaded from www.kenyaembassy.com. Visas are available on arrival at the airport and all land borders, but there are often lengthy queues.*

Mombasa and Nakuru. Do check your visitor's pass as it has been known for people who have overstayed their time in the country to be fined quite heavily. Your passport must be valid for a minimum of six months after your planned departure date from Kenya; this is a requirement whether you need a visa or not.

Embassies and consulates

Australia, 33 Ainstie Av, Canberra, T026-2474788, kenrep@dynamite.com. au.

Canada, 415 Laurier Av East, Ottawa, T0613-5631773, kenrep@on.aibn.com.

Ethiopia, Hiher 16, Kebelle 01, Fikre Mariam Rd, Addis Ababa, T180033.

European Union, 208 Winston Churchill Av, Brussels, Belgium, T02-3401040, kenbrussels@ hotmail.com.

France, 3 Rue Frey Cinet, Paris, T1-56622525, kenparis@wanadoo.fr.

Germany, Markgrafen Str 63, Berlin, T030-259266, embassy-kenya.bn@wwmail.de.

Italy, Via Archimede 164, Rome, T6-8082714/17/18, kenroma@linet.it.

Netherlands, Nieuwe Park Laan 21, The Hague, T070-3504215, kenre@dataweb.nl.

RD Congo, Plot 5002, av de l'ouganda, BP 9667 Zone Gombe, Kinshasa, T12-30117.

Rwanda, PO Box 1215, Kigali, T250- 82774/5.

South Africa, 302 Brooks St, Melo Park, Pretoria, T012-3622249, kenp@pta.lia.net.

Sudan, Street 3, Amarat, Khartoum, T011-460386.

Tanzania, 4th floor, NIC Investment House, Samora Av, PO Box 5231, Dar es Salaam, T51-31502.

Uganda, 60 Kira Rd, PO Box 5220, Kampala, T41231861.

UK, 45 Portland Place, London W1N 4AS, T020-7632371/5, kcomm45@aol.com.

USA, 2249 R St, Washington DC, T202-3876101, KLQY53A@prodigy.com.

Zambia, 5207 United Nations Av, Lusaka, T01-250722, kenhigh@zamnet.zm.

Zimbabwe, 95 Park Lane, Harare, T04-704820, kenhicom@ africaonline.co.zw.

Customs

You are expected to pay duty on items bought as gifts or for sale in Kenya, though not if they are for your personal use. You are more likely to be asked if you have anything to declare at airports than at the border crossings from neighbouring countries. There is now no requirement to change currency on entry. A litre of spirits or wine and 200 cigarettes are permitted to be taken in duty free. There is no duty on any equipment for your own use (such as a laptop computers or cameras). Narcotics, pornography and firearms are prohibited. The CITIES Convention was established to prevent trade in endangered species. Attempts to smuggle controlled products can result in confiscation, fines and imprisonment. International trade in elephant ivory, sea turtle products and the skins of wild cats, such as leopard, is illegal. Casual vendors and small stalls can offer prohibited products – sea-shells can be a particular problem. If you were to buy such items, you should always consider the environmental and social impact of your purchase. Removal of coral, shells from turtles or any other kind of marine animal also causes a tremendous upset to the balance of marine life which is more often than not impossible to correct.

Vaccinations

No vaccinations are required by law but if you are entering the country overland, you may be asked for a yellow fever and/or a cholera certificate. You should have these done before arrival as a sensible health precaution anyway. The following other vaccinations are recommended: typhoid, poliomyelitis, tetanus, hepatitis A and B: BCG (against tuberculosis), meningitis, and rabies. In addition, children should be protected against whooping cough, mumps, measles and diphtheria, and teenage girls if they haven't already had it, should be given the rubella vaccination. Seek advice from your local doctor about six weeks before your departure. See also page 51.

Before departure, it is vital to take out comprehensive travel insurance. There are a wide variety of policies to choose from, so shop around. At the very least, the policy should cover medical expenses, including repatriation to your home country in the event of a medical emergency. If you are going to be active in Kenya, ensure the policy covers trekking or diving for example. There is no substitute for suitable precautions against petty crime, but if you do have something stolen whilst in Kenya, report the incident to the nearest police station and ensure you get a police report and case number. You will need these to make any claim from your insurance company. Kenya is covered by the **Flying Doctors' Society of Africa**, based at Wilson Airport in Nairobi. For an annual tourist fee of US$50, it offers free evacuation by air to a medical centre or hospital. This may be worth considering if you are visiting more remote regions, but not necessary if visiting the more popular parks in the north as adequate provision is made in the case of an emergency.

What to take

A good rule of thumb is to take half the clothes you think you'll need and double the money. Laundry services are generally cheap and speedy in Kenya and you shouldn't need to bring too many clothes. A backpack or travelpack (a hybrid backpack/suitcase) rather than a rigid suitcase, covers most eventualities and survives the rigours of a variety of modes of travel. A lock for your luggage is strongly advised – there are cases of pilfering by airport baggage handlers the world over.

Light cotton clothing is best, with a fleece or woollen clothing for evenings. Also pack something to change into at dusk – long sleeves and trousers (particularly light coloured) help ward off mosquitoes, which are at their most active in the evening. During the day you will need a hat, sunglasses and high-factor sun cream for protection against the sun. Modest dress is advisable for women, particularly on the coast, where men too should avoid revealing shoulders. Kenya is a great place to buy sarongs – known in East Africa as *kikois*, which in Africa are worn by both men and women and are ideal to cover up when, say, leaving the beach. Footwear should be airy because of the heat: sandals or canvas trainers are ideal. Trekkers will need comfortable walking boots, and if you are climbing Mount Kenya, ones that have been worn in. Those going on camping safaris will need a sleeping bag, towel and torch, and budget travellers may want to consider bringing a sleeping sheet in case the sheets don't look too clean in a budget hotel.

Before you leave, send yourself an email with details of travellers' cheques, passport, driving licence, credit cards and travel insurance numbers. Be sure that someone at home also has access to these details.

Checklist Essentials: air tickets; camera; camera film (if you don't have a digital); cash; chequebook; credit cards; passport including visa; passport photographs; photocopies of main documents (keep separate); travellers' cheques. Apart from these everybody has their own list. **Toiletries**: comb; concentrated detergent; contact lens cleaner; deodorant; adhesive bandages; insect repellent; nailbrush; razor and blades; shampoo; soap; sun protection cream; talcum powder; tissues and toilet paper; toothbrush; toothpaste; Vaseline/moisturiser. **Other**: binoculars; ear plugs; electric insecticide vaporizer and tablets; eye mask; folding umbrella; inflatable cushion; lock and chain (securing luggage at night); money belt; multiple outlet adaptor; plastic bags; sewing kit; short-wave radio and batteries; small torch plus batteries; sunglasses; Swiss army knife; traveller's heating jug; water bottle; universal washbasin plug.

Lotions and potions often leak out of their containers during a flight. This is because aeroplane holds are not always pressurized, and so the air in a bottle expands, forcing out the liquid. To avoid, carry bottles that do not have screw tops, in your hand luggage.

Money

Currency

The currency in Kenya is the Kenyan shilling (the written abbreviation is either KSh or using /= after the amount, ie 500/=). Notes are 50, 100, 200, 500 and 1000 KSh, coins are 5, 10 and 20 KSh. As it is not a hard currency, it cannot be brought into or taken out of the country, however there are no restrictions on the amount of foreign currency that can be brought into Kenya. There are banks with ATMs and bureaux de change at both Nairobi and Mombasa airports. There are inevitable queues but at Nairobi it is marginally quicker to change your money after you go through customs. The easiest currencies to exchange are US dollars, UK pounds and euros. If you are bringing US dollars in cash, try and bring newer notes – because of the prevalence of forgery, many banks and bureaux de changes do not accept US dollar bills printed before 1995. Travellers' cheques are widely accepted, and many hotels, travel agencies, safari companies and restaurants accept credit cards. Most banks in Kenya are equipped to advance cash on credit cards, and increasingly most now have ATM machines that accept Visa and Mastercard. Departure taxes can be paid in local or foreign currency.

Exchange

Visitors to Kenya should change foreign currency at banks, bureaux de change or authorized hotels, and under no circumstances change money on the black market which is highly illegal. All banks have a foreign exchange service, and bank hours are

❖ *Lower denomination dollar bills attract a lower exchange rate than higher denomination bills.*

Monday-Friday 0830-1500, Saturday 0830-1100, although in Mombasa they open and close half an hour earlier. The government has authorized bureaux de change known as forex bureaux to set rates for buying foreign currency from the public. Forex bureaux are open longer hours and offer faster service than

banks and, although the exchange rates are only nominally different, the bureaux usually offer a better rate on travellers' cheques. In the large private hotels, rates are calculated directly in US dollars, although they can be be paid in foreign or local currency. Airline fares, game park entrance fees and other odd payments to the government (such as the airport international departure tax) are also quoted in dollars, though again these can be paid for in both foreign or local currency. Just ensure that you are getting a reasonable exchange rate when the hotel or airline etc converts US dollars to Kenyan shillings.

Credit cards and travellers' cheques

Credit cards are now accepted by large hotels, airlines, major tour operators and travel agencies, upmarket shops and the better restaurants, but of course will not be taken by the smaller hotels and cheaper restaurants and so on. Almost all banks around the country have ATMs that allow you to withdraw cash from Visa, Mastercard, Plus and Cirrus cards. Diners Club and American Express are, however, limited. Increasingly, many of the large petrol stations, such as Caltex and Mobil, are starting to install ATMs, especially in Nairobi and Mombasa. Your bank will probably charge a small fee for withdrawing cash from an ATM overseas. These days is is quite feasible to travel around Kenya with just a credit or debit card, although it is always a good idea to bring some cash or travellers' cheques as a back-up.

Cost of travelling

In first-rate luxury lodges and tented camps expect to pay in excess of US$150 per night for a double, rising to US$500 per night per person in the most exclusive establishments. There are half a dozen places aimed at the very top-of-the-range tourist or honeymooner that charge nearer US$1,000 per person per night! For this you will get impeccable service, cuisine and decor in fantastic locations either in the parks or on the coast. In four- and five-star hotels and lodges expect to spend US$150-200 a day. Careful tourists can live reasonably comfortably on US$60 a day staying in the mid-range places, however, to stay in anything other than campsites on safaris, they will have to spend a little more for the cheapest accommodation in the national parks. Budget travellers can get by on US$20 utilizing the cheap guest houses and going on a basic camping safari. However, with additional park entry fees and related costs, organized camping safari costs are at the bare minimum US$200 for a three-day/two-night excursion to the Masai Mara for example. The cost of living and the favourable exchange rate in Kenya is attractive to tourists spending US dollars, pounds and euros. A bottle of water costs in the region of US$0.50, a soda US$0.30 and a beer US$1. Commodities such as camera film, chocolate and toiletries are on the expensive side as they are imported but are readily available. Restaurants vary widely from side-of-the-road local eateries where a simple meal of chicken and chips will cost no more than US$2-3 to the upmarket restaurants in the cities and tourists spots that can charge in excess of US$60 for two people with drinks.

Getting there

Air

From Europe

Kenya is the cheapest country in East Africa to get to by air and consequently is a good place to start off a tour of the region. There are several airlines that fly into Kenya from most various cities in the world and airfares are very competitively priced. The main point of arrival is Nairobi's Jomo Kenyatta International Airport, though there are also a substantial number of scheduled and charter flights from Europe to Moi International Airport in Mombasa. Nairobi's Jomo

www.kenyaairports. co.ke has up to the minute information on flight arrivals and departures.

Kenyatta International Airport was built in 1978. Originally constructed to handle 2.8 million passengers per year, today it handles over 3.4 million, with an average of 15,000 passengers passing through each day and 58,000 landings and take-offs each year. It is an important hub for air travel in Africa and the third busiest airport after Johannesburg and Cairo. There are currently plans to begin a major refurbishment of the airport thanks to a loan from the World Bank of US$35 million topped up to US$42 million by the Kenya Airports Authority. The complete makeover should include state-of-the-art check-in and baggage handling systems, refurbished public areas, and duty-free shops, a new car park and a 200-room hotel.

London is by the far the cheapest place in the western world from which to get to Kenya and there are loads of discounted flights and package holidays. In the past, the only discounts were for unsold seats but now there is an enormous range of deals for students, academics or people under a certain age (usually either 26 or 32). Although not all the deals may mean cheaper flights, they usually do mean flexible flight arrangements and flight dates, which is very helpful if you are planning a longish trip and do not know when you want to return. A very good idea is to look for a package deal to Mombasa and travel on from there. All flights either go to Nairobi, the capital (about nine hours from London), or Mombasa on the Indian Ocean coast (about 11 hours).

The cheapest plane tickets are in the 'offseason', from February to June and again from October to early December. If you do have to go during peak times, book as far in advance as you can, particularly if you aim to get there in mid-December when flights get full very quickly. **EgyptAir** offers very good deals and a stopover in Cairo for as long as you like at no extra cost. **KLM** and **British Airways** have surprisingly good deals as do **Emirates**, **Saudia** and **Ethiopian Airlines**. **Kenya Airways**, the national airline of Kenya, handles most internal routes as well as regular flights to Europe.

If you are short of time, a package holiday could well be a useful option, particularly if you go out of the peak season when you can get excellent deals. Beach holidays are far cheaper than safaris. It is a good idea to find out as much as you can about the hotel in the package deal before going, although you can always stay elsewhere if necessary. It is sometimes the case that a package trip to the coast will be cheaper than a flight alone.

From Africa
You can fly to Kenya direct from: **Abidjan** (Ivory Coast); **Accra** (Ghana); **Addis Ababa** (Ethiopia); **Antananarivo** (Madagascar); **Bujumbura** (Burundi); **Cairo** (Egypt); **Dakar** (Senegal); **Dar es Salaam** (Tanzania); **Douala** (Cameroon); **Dzaoudzi** (Comoros); **Entebbe** (Uganda); **Gaborone** (Botswana); **Harare** (Zimbabwe); **Johannesburg** (South Africa); **Khartoum** (Sudan); **Kigali** (Rwanda); **Kinshasa** (RD Congo); **Lagos** (Nigeria); **Lome** (Togo); **Luanda** (Angola); **Lusaka** (Zambia); **Moroni** (Comoros); **Ouagadougou** (Burkina Faso); **Zanzibar** (Tanzania).

From the rest of the world
There are no direct flights from the USA to Kenya. Americans have to change flights in Europe or the Middle East depending on which carrier they choose. It is usual to fly via London, Amsterdam or Dubai if travelling from the USA.

Airlines

Air Zimbabwe, T020-74910009 (UK), www.airzimbabwe.com.
British Airways, T0870-8509850 (UK), www.britishairways.com.
Emirates, T0870-2432222 (UK), www.emirates.com.
Ethiopian Airlines, T020-89877000 (UK), wwww.flyethiopian.com.
Gulf Air, T020-74114221, www.gulfairco.com.
Kenya Airways, T01784-888222 (UK) reservations, T01784 888233 (UK) sales, www.kenya-airways.com.
KLM, T0870-5074074 (UK), www.klm.com.
South African Airways, T011-9785313 (South Africa), www.flysaa.com.
Swiss International, T0845-6010956 UK, www.swiss.com.

Discount flight agents

UK and Ireland
Bridge the World, T0870-4432399, www.bridgetheworld.com.
Flightbookers, T0870-0107000, www.ebookers.com.

Flight Centre, T0870-4990040, www.flightcentre.co.uk.
STA Travel, T0870-1600599, www.statravel.co.uk.
Trailfinders, T020-79383939, www.trailfinders.co.uk.
Travelbag, T0870-9001351, www.travelbag.co.uk.

North America
Air Brokers International, T800-883 3273, www.airbrokers.com.
STA Travel, T800-7814040, www.statravel.com.
Travel Cuts, T866-2469762 (Canada), www.travelcuts.com.
Worldtek, T800-2421723, www.worldtek.com.

Australia and New Zealand
Flight Centre, T133-133, www.flightcentre.com.au.
Skylinks, T02-9234277, www.skylink.com.au.
STA Travel, T300-733035 (Australia), T09-3099723 (New Zealand), www.statravel.com.au.
Travel.com.au, T02-9246000, www.travel.com.au.

Touching down

Business hours Banks:
Monday-Friday 0830-1330, Saturday
0830-1100. **Embassies**: usually
mornings only. **Post offices**:
Monday-Friday 0800-1300 and
1400-1630. Some are also open on
Saturday. **Shops**: generally
0800-1700 or 1800, and on Saturday.
Kiosks: often open all hours, as the
owner frequently lives on site.

IDD code T+254.
Official time Kenya is three hours
ahead of GMT.
Voltage 220-240 volts supply.
Square three-pin plugs in modern
buildings. Great variety in older
places. An adapter is advised.
Weights and measures Metric.
In country areas items are often
sold by the piece.

Road

Border crossings between Kenya and its neighbours can be laborious or simple, depending on your preparation and the state of your vehicle's paperwork. If you are in your own vehicle you will require a Carnet de Passage issued by a body in your own country (such as the Automobile Association), vehicle registration, and you will also be required to take out third party insurance for Kenya from one of the insurance companies who have kiosks at the border posts. Most car hire companies will not allow you to take a rented vehicle out of the country, but some may consider it if you only want to go to Tanzania.

Ethiopia The crossing is at **Moyale**, between Marsabit and Addis Ababa. The road from Isiolo up to the border is rough, particularly in the wet. Also, because of armed robberies in recent years, vehicles are required to travel in armed convoys on part of this road between Isiolo and Moyale. There is no public transport north of Isiolo so the only option is to hitch a lift from truck drivers on the route, but trucks are very infrequent.

Somalia In more tranquil times it has been possible to take a bus from Kismayo to the border at **Liboi**, and then on to Garissa, or from Mogadishu to **Mandera**, and then on to Wajir. These crossings are currently not an option for travellers as a result of the civil war in Somalia and public transport on this route has been largely suspended.

Sudan In principle it has in the past been possible to cross from Lodwar to Juba, although there was never any public transport on this route, and it was a matter of hiring rides from truck drivers. This is not currently an option for travellers as a result of civil war in the south of Sudan.

Tanzania The main road crossing is at **Namanga**, see page 202, on the road between Arusha and Nairobi. As this border receives thousands of tourists on safari each week en route between the Kenyan and Tanzanian parks, it is reasonably quick and efficient. There are also regular shuttle buses connecting the two cities, which takes about four hours on fairly good roads all the way. The shuttle services pick up and drop off at the major hotels in Nairobi and Arusha and cost in the region of US$25 each way. A cheaper alternative is to do the journey in stages by taking a *matatu* from Ronald Ngala Road in Nairobi to Namanga, crossing the border on foot, then catching another *matatu* to Arusha. This will take a little longer than the shuttle, but will cost half the price. Other crossings are at **Lunga Lunga**, see page 229, between Mombasa and Dar es Salaam on a recently improved road. There are daily buses between the cities. There is also a crossing at **Taveta**, see page 204; there are frequent buses. The border crossing from **Masai Mara Park** into the Serengeti is currently closed.

Uganda There are buses that run from Nairobi to Kampala, crossing at **Malaba** and **Busia**, taking about 15 hours and costing around US$15. Standards of service vary. It is possible to do the journey in stages in *matatus* but buses are more comfortable and quicker. There is also a border crossings at **Suam** to the north of Mount Elgon, but this is rarely used.

Touching down

Airport information

Departure tax is frequently incorporated into the air fare in international air tickets. It is advisable to check when purchasing your ticket. For international flights the charge is US$20, for domestic flights KSh100. ▶▶ *For further information, see pages 62 and 210.*

Local customs and laws

Codes of conduct

Stand for the national anthem and show respect if the national flag is being raised or lowered. Do not take photographs of military or official buildings or personnel, especially the president. *Always* ask before photographing local people. In some regions, the Masai are so used to tourists wanting to take pictures of them, a fee is most definitely expected. Respect the national currency (do not tear it) and the currency laws of the country, and if you have to have any dealings with the police be polite. Importing or possession of drugs and guns is prohibited and punished severely. The attitude to cannabis (*bhangi* – which is readily available) and *miraa* is ambivalent: both are illegal but appear to be tolerated by the authorities. However, if you are caught your embassy is unlikely to be sympathetic. If you do get in trouble with the law or have to report to the police – from a minor driving offence, being robbed, to something a lot more serious – *always* be exceptionally polite and relatively humble, even if you are reporting a crime against yourself. The Kenyan police generally enjoy their authoritative status; to rant and rave and demand attention will get you absolutely nowhere. Calling a policeman 'sir' is also customary. Respect is accorded to elderly people, usually by the greeting *Shikamoo, mzee* to a man and *Shikamoo, mama* to a woman. In English, it is common for people to use the terms 'my sister' or 'my aunt', 'my brother' or 'my uncle' (depending on how old they think you are) as greetings. For anyone spending any length of time in Kenya, or returning over a period of a few years, it is a sad day indeed when you have reached the status of aunt or uncle – it simply means you are getting old!

Dress

Travellers are encouraged to show respect by adhering to a modest dress code in public places, especially in the predominantly Muslim areas like Mombasa or Lamu. In the evening at social functions there is no particular dress code although hosts will feel insulted if you arrive for dinner in shorts, sandals or bare feet, and you will be expected to dress up a little in the more upmarket lodges and hotels. Long hair on men makes local people uneasy. On safari, clothes in muted brown and khaki colours are the best. This is certainly true of the more remote parks where seeing unexpected bright colours may startle the animals. But in the Masai Mara, the animals here are so used to seeing a hoard of minibuses of tourists each day, it is not so important.

Bargaining

Whilst most prices in the shops are set, the exception to this is shops selling typically tourist-related items such as curios, when a little good-natured bargaining is possible, especially if you are buying a number of things. Bargaining is very much expected in the street markets whether you are buying an apple or a Masai blanket. Generally traders will attempt to overcharge tourists who are unaware of local prices. Start lower than you would expect to pay, be polite and good humoured, and if the final price doesn't suit – walk away. You may be called back for more negotiation if your final price was too high, or the trader may let you go, in which case your price was too low. Ask about the prices of taxis, excursions, souvenirs and so on at your hotel. Once you have gained confidence, try bargaining with taxi drivers and at hotels when negotiating a room.

Tipping

It is customary to tip around 10% for good service, which is greatly appreciated by hotel and restaurant staff, most of whom receive very low pay. Some of the more upmarket establishments may add a service charge to the bill. It is also expected to tip safari guides. What you give rather depends on the level of service you have received and the enjoyment level of your tour. Roughly a tip of US$10-15 a day for drivers and guides is about right, but remember excessive tipping can make it difficult for the next customer. If in any doubt, ask the company that you booked the tour through for advice on how much to tip.

Begging

This is most common in Nairobi and Mombasa. Many Kenyans give money to beggars who are clearly destitute and or disabled and, in a country with no social welfare, have few alternative means of livelihood. A fairly recent phenomenon has been the rise of street children in Nairobi and Nakuru. If you feel the need to do something constructive about street children, consider making a donation to **Street Kids International** (SKI), based in Toronto, Canada, www.streetkids.org.

Responsible tourism

Much has been written about the adverse impacts of tourism on the environment and local communities. It is usually assumed that this only applies to the more excessive end of the travel industry. However, travellers can have an impact at almost any density and this is especially true in areas 'off the beaten track', where local people may not be used to western conventions and lifestyles and where natural environments are sensitive.

Of course, tourism can have a beneficial impact and this is something to which every traveller can contribute. The tourism industry in Kenya is very important for the country's economy, and creates many thousands of jobs. In recent years there has been a well-applauded effort to initiate tourism projects that involve and benefit the local communities and the wildlife. Both people and animals share and rely on Kenya's wide open spaces and Kenya really has embraced the age of ecotourism in these projects through effective community-run wildlife management.

Many national parks are part-funded by receipts from people who come to see exotic plants and animals. Similarly, travellers can promote protection of valuable archaeological sites and heritages through their interest and entrance fees. However,

⁞ How big is your footprint?

The point of a holiday is, of course, to have a good time, but if it's relatively guilt-free as well, that's even better. Perfect ecotourism would ensure a good living for local inhabitants, while not detracting from their traditional lifestyles, encroaching on their customs or spoiling their environment. Perfect ecotourism probably doesn't exist, but everyone can play their part. Here are a few points worth bearing in mind:

→ Think about where your money goes, and be fair and realistic about how cheaply you travel. Try and put money into local people's hands; drink local beer or fruit juice rather than imported brands and stay in locally owned accommodation wherever possible.

→ Haggle with humour and not aggressively. Remember that you are likely to be much wealthier than the person you're buying from.

→ Think about what happens to your rubbish. Take biodegradable products and a water bottle filter. Be sensitive to limited resources like water, fuel and electricity.

→ Help preserve local wildlife and habitats by respecting rules and regulations, such as sticking to footpaths, not standing on coral and not buying products made from endangered plants or animals.

→ Don't treat people as part of the landscape; they may not want their picture taken. Ask first and respect their wishes.

→ Learn the local language and be mindful of local customs and norms. It can enhance your travel experience and you'll earn respect and be more readily welcomed by local people.

→ And finally, use your guidebook as a starting point, not the only source of information. Talk to local people, then discover your own adventure.

where visitor pressure is high and/or poorly regulated, damage can occur. In Kenya, many of the most popular destinations are in ecologically and culturally sensitive areas which are easily disturbed by extra human pressures.

It is worthwhile noting the major areas in which travellers can take a more responsible attitude to the countries they visit. These include changes to natural ecosystems (air, water, land, ecology and wildlife), cultural values (beliefs and behaviour) and the built environment (sites of antiquity and archaeological significance). At an individual level, travellers can reduce their impact if greater consideration is given to their activities. Canoe trips up the headwaters of obscure rivers make for great stories but how do local communities cope with the sudden invasive interest in their lives? Similarly, have the environmental implications of increased visitor pressure been considered? Where do the fresh fish that feed the trip come from? Hand caught by line is fine but dynamite fishing causes a great deal of damage and waste.

Some factors, such as the management and operation of a hotel chain, are beyond the direct control of individual travellers. However, it is possible to voice concern about damaging activities. An increasing number of hotels and travel operators are taking 'green concerns' seriously, even if it is only to protect their share of the market. Be wary of the 'eco' label, however; all too often companies use the word to refer to outdoor adventure activities, not environmentally protective practices.

Environmental legislation, too, plays its role in protecting destinations. The **Convention on International Trade in Endangered Species of Wild Fauna and Flora** and also 'recognisable parts or derivatives' of protected species. If you feel the need to purchase souvenirs and trinkets derived from wildlife, it would be prudent to check whether they are protected. Importation of CITES protected species can lead to heavy fines, confiscation of goods and even imprisonment.

Safety

The majority of the people you will meet are honest and ready to help you so there is no need to get paranoid about your safety. However, Nairobi and Mombasa do have reputations for crime, and the most popular national parks have their fair share of robberies. There is a high rate of street crime not just in Nairobi and Mombasa but also in Kisumu and the coastal beach resorts, most especially bag-snatching crimes. Basically, you just have to be sensible and not carry expensive cameras, open bags or valuable jewellery and be careful about carrying large sums of money when you are rubbing shoulders with local people. Waist pouches ('bum-bags' or 'moon-bags') are very vulnerable as the belt can be cut easily. Day packs have also been known to be slashed, with their entire contents drifting out on to the street without the wearer knowing. Carry money and any valuables in a slim belt under clothing. Also, do not automatically expect your belongings to be safe in a tent. Avoid walking around after dusk, particularly in the more run-down urban areas – take a taxi – and walking alone at night, even on beaches, is dangerous. In built-up areas, lock your car, and if there is a security guard (*askari*) nearby, pay him a small sum to watch over it, although you should still be careful as con-artists have been known to impersonate hotel employees and even police officers. There is no need to pay street children to guard a vehicle. Also be wary of someone distracting a driver in a parked vehicle, whilst an accomplice gets into the car on the opposite side. Always keep car doors locked and windows wound up, and lock room doors at night as noisy fans and air-conditioning can provide cover for sneak thieves. Crime and hazardous road conditions make travel by night dangerous.

⚱ In 2004, the Tourist Police Unit was set up under the direction of the Ministry of Tourism and Wildlife. A team of 300 officers will target key tourist areas, especially the beaches from Malindi to the south coast.

Car-jacking has occurred in both rural and urban areas and is a particular problem in Nairobi. You also need to be vigilant of thieves on buses and trains and guard your possessions fiercely. For petty offences (driving without lights switched on, for example) police will often try to solicit a bribe, masked as an 'on-the-spot' fine. Establish the amount being requested, and then offer to go to the police station to pay, at which point you will be released with a warning. For any serious charges, immediately contact your embassy or consulate. The British High Commission strongly advise against travel in Northeast Kenya (Moyale, Mandera, Wajit and Garissa), because of difficulties with the Somalian unrest. The road from Mombasa to Lamu has also been targeted by Somalian robbers, who have hijacked buses and robbed the passengers. Armed police escorts are now on buses to cope with this problem with the *Shiftas*.

It's not only crime that may affect your personal safety; you must also take safety precautions when visiting the game reserves and national parks. If camping, it is not advisable to leave your tent or banda during the night. Wild animals wander around the camps freely in the hours of darkness, and a protruding leg may seem like a tasty take-away to a hungry hyena. This is especially true at organized campsites, where the local animals have got so used to humans that they have lost much of their inherent fear of man. Exercise care during daylight hours too – remember wild animals can be dangerous.

Getting around

Kenya has an efficient transport network linking its towns and cities. There are regular flights between Nairobi and the coast and Kisumu, and further afield to Tanzania and Zanzibar. There is an excellent overnight train service between Nairobi and Mombasa that is a very enjoyable experience, and in recent years there have been great improvements of standards of the bus and *matatu* (minibus) services. It is quite feasible for a visitor to move around by public transport, which is cheap and efficient, but be aware of petty theft not only on the vehicles but in the bus stands and stations.

Air

Air transport started in Kenya with the formation of the **East African Airways** in 1946 under the then East African High Commission, an economic union linking Kenya, Uganda and Tanzania. Kenya Airports Authority, established by the government, oversees the management and administration of the airports which include freight services for horticultural and agricultural goods, for example the flowers and vegetables flown out of Eldoret International Airport daily headed for European supermarkets, though this airport is not used for passenger services. Today internal travel in Kenya is quite cheap and efficient. There are daily flights between Nairobi and Mombasa, Lamu and Kisumu on **Kenya Airways**, T020-32074747 (reservations), www.kenya-airways.com. There are also several flights daily from Wilson Airport, with **Air Kenya**, Nairobi, T020-605745 (reservations), www.airkenya.com, from Nairobi to the Masai Mara, Lamu, Kiwayu, Amboseli, Nanyuki, Samburu, Meru and Malindi. **Mombasa Air Safari**, Moi International Airport, Mombasa, T041-433061, www.mombasaairsafari.com, has daily flights between Mombasa, Malindi and Lamu. **Safarilink**, Wilson Airport, Nairobi, T020-600777, res@safarilink.co.ke, is a new company that was established in 2004; at the time of writing it was establishing a scheduled service around Kenya as well as links to Tanzania. Flights will go between Nairobi and Nanyuki, Samburu, Lewa Downs, Amboseli, Tsavo West, Masai Mara, Samburu, and Kilimanjaro in Tanzania. In addition there are many charter flight services supported by over 150 airstrips spread all over the country: **C H S Aviation Ltd**, Wilson Airport, Nairobi, T020-501408; **Capital Airlines**, Wilson Airport, Nairobi, T020-502280; **Eagle Aviation**, Wilson Airport, T020-606015; **Equator Airlines Ltd**, Wilson Airport, T020-501360; **Ibis Aviation Ltd**, Wilson Airport, T020-602257.

‡ *www.kenyaairports.co.ke has up to the minute information on flight arrivals and departures.*

‡ *Internal flights incur a departure tax of KSh100 (approximately US$1.50).*

Rail

Taking the **Nairobi-Mombasa** overnight train is a splendid experience. It is a narrow-gauge railway and so is able to to to climb up the steep escarpments. As it gets dark, the train begin its journey across the plains and looking out of the window you can get a real feeling of emptiness with just a glimpse of the occasional pair of glowing eyes. First-class cabins are two-berth with washbasins. The second class are four-berth with washbasins that are pretty unreliable as the carriages are around 85 years old. The train covers 530 km and goes through Tsavo National Park, so look out for game whilst taking breakfast in the restaurant car in the Mombasa to Nairobi direction. The train can run late, so to be on the safe side, don't plan any tight connections at the other end. **First class** costs US$38 per person sharing a two-bed compartment, and includes dinner and breakfast in the restaurant car. **Second class** costs US$26 per person sharing a four-bunk compartment. **Third class** is seated, and can get very crowded. Sexes are separated in first- and second-class sections, unless you book the whole compartment. Children under three years travel for free, three years to 11 years pay half fare, 12 years and over pay adult fares. Historically, this train has always run daily, but a few years ago it was reduced to running three days a week. One train departs each way at 1900 and the journey takes about 13 hours. It departs from Nairobi on Monday, Wednesday and Friday and in the other direction it departs from Mombasa on Saturday, Tuesday and Thursday. It is essential to make reservations in advance and this can be done personally at the stations or through a tour operator or travel agent. See under Transport for Nairobi and Mombasa.

Road

The present road transport network comprises a variety of roads ranging from forest and farm tracks to multi-lane urban and suburban highways. The system is divided into classified and unclassified roads, with a total network of 151,000 km. Out of the classified network of 62,667 km, 7,943.2 km are tarred (compared with 1,811 km at independence), 26,180.8 km are gravel and the rest are dirt.

Bus and *matatu*

Safety records for public transport have been pretty awful in the past with many road accidents involving overcrowded buses and *matatus* and some large derailments on the railways. However, since 2002 public transport in Kenya has gone under quite a transformation since the new government instigated new regulations, which have already seen positive results on getting the accident rate down. All buses, *matatus*, taxis and any vehicle carrying paying passengers, now have a yellow stripe around them, and *matatus*, which were once famously painted in lots of bright colours and murals, are now mostly uniformly white and quite new. Buses are still different colours, although each company has smartened up their image and many of the buses from the same fleet are in the same colour. Brand new Metro red buses have been introduced to Mombasa, and new green City Hoppers in Nairobi, which are gradually taking over the old fleet of city buses. All public buses and *matatus* now have to be speed governed at 80 km per hour. Every single vehicle has been fitted with seat belts and it is now law for every passenger in any vehicle to buckle up. Police issue on-the-spot fines to passengers who haven't got seat belts on. The number of passengers has been governed to stop the overcrowding. In *matatus* this has been restricted to 15 passengers, all with their own seat, with a seat belt. The police also frequently stop the vehicles and count how many people are on board. The same goes for larger buses where standing is no longer permitted and everyone gets their own seat. Where once public transport was very dangerous and uncomfortable in Kenya, these regulations mean that it is now not unreasonable for independent travellers to move around Kenya on buses and *matatus*. There are lots of private bus companies operating in Kenya, and the system is very good on the whole, being reliable, running on time and offering cheap fares. In addition, the accident rate on the roads has fallen dramatically in recent years. The larger buses cover the long-distance routes and you will be able to reserve a seat a day in advance, whilst the *matatus* do the shorter distances and link the major towns and usually go when full. If you have problems locating the bus station, alternatively called bus stand or bus stage in Kenya, or finding the right bus in the bus station, just ask around and someone will direct you.

Driving conditions The key roads are in good condition; away from the main highways the majority of roads are bad and hazardous. The minor roads of unmade gravel with potholes can be rough going and they deteriorate further in the rainy season. Road conditions in the reserves and national parks of Kenya are extremely rough. During the rainy season, many roads are passable only with four-wheel-drive vehicles. Even some of the tarred roads are in poor shape: cracked, crumbling and littered with small and not so small potholes. There is little road maintenance and when re-tarring of the roads does occur, the new tar that is laid is so thin it deteriorates within months. On hills, heavy vehicles with hot tyres curve the tar into steep ridges, making the roads very bumpy. Added to this are Kenya's speed bumps (hardly necessary when the potholes do a fine job of slowing traffic down), which are in place every few metres wherever there is any kind of settlement and are prolific all over the towns. It is still possible to drive on Kenya's main roads in a normal saloon car, although the going is slow and you will have to take extra care to avoid the deeper potholes. A four-wheel drive is recommended as the high clearance is better for the potholes, and is essential if you are going off the tarred roads or into the game parks.

● When you park in any Kenyan town on the side of the street, you have to pay a small fee of KSh40-60 to the Muncipality. A parking attendant will approach you when you park, and issue you with a parking ticket which you must display in the windscreen.

Car hire Renting a car has certain advantages over public transport, particularly if you intend visiting any of the national parks or remoter regions of the country, or there are at least four of you to share the costs. You should be able to rent either a fixed price per day or by mileage. If you are organizing your own safari by hire car, it requires careful planning, and you need to be confident about driving on the poor roads. A four-wheel drive is essential, such as a Land Rover, Pajero or Suzuki. Minimum engine size should be 1300cc, as anything smaller cannot cope with the rough roads in the game parks. Make sure that the car is not more than two years old. Driving is on the left side of the road.

To hire a car you generally need to be over 23, have a full driving licence (it does not have to be an international licence, your home country one will do – with English translation if necessary), and to leave a large deposit (or sign a blank credit card voucher). Always take out the collision damage waiver premium as even the smallest accident can be very expensive. Costs vary between the different car hire companies and are from around US$40-80 per day for a normal saloon car, rising to US$80-100 for a four-wheel drive. Deals can be made for more than seven days' car hire. It is important to shop around to get the best-value rates. Things to consider include whether you take out a limited mileage package or unlimited mileage depending on how you many kilometres you think you willdrive. For example, a company may offer a package for US$60 per day, with 200 km free per day, and any mileage after that at US$0.25 per km. If you think you are going to be driving for more than 200 km a day then a more expensive unlimited mileage package may be better. Also check the insurance policies. Some of the companies that offer the cheapest rates have policies where in the event of an accident or the car gets stolen, the excess on the policy that the client must pay is sometimes as high as US$1,200, where as the better but more expensive companies offer policies where the excess is as little as US$25. Finally some of the companies add 16% VAT. It is essential to shop around and ask questions of the companies about what is and what is not included in the rates.

● If you break down, the common practice throughout Africa is to leave a bundle of leaves some 50 m behind and in front of the vehicle to warn oncoming motorists.

Taxi

Hotels and town centres are well served by taxis, some good and some very run-down but serviceable. Hotel staff, even at the smallest locations, will rustle up a taxi even when there is not one waiting outside. If you visit an out-of-town centre location, it is wise to ask the taxi to wait – it will normally be happy to do so for the benefit of the return fare. Up to 1 km should cost US$1. Very few of the cabs have meters, and you should establish the fare (*bei gani?* – how much?) before you set off.

Tuk tuks A tuk tuk is a motorized three-wheeled buggy; cheap and convenient, they are starting to feature in many Kenyan towns and cities. The driver sits in the front whilst two to three passengers can sit comfortably on the back seat. They are still quite a novelty and as yet there are few around, but the idea is catching on quickly and in the future they should offer a service that is at least half the price of regular taxis. They do not however, go very fast so for longer journeys stick to taxis.

Boda boda A *boda boda* is a bicycle taxi with one padded seat on the back, and so named as they were first popular in the border towns to transport people across no man's land between the border posts of East Africa and the cyclist would shout out '*boda boda*' offering his services. They are very popular along the coast and in the smaller towns, although not in Nairobi and Mombasa, and cost next to nothing. The driver/cyclist does an excellent job of cycling and keeping the bike balanced with you on the back of it, although you are still advised to hang on to the seat. A word of warning to the ladies, however, if you are wearing skirt you will have to sit side saddle, which makes the bike far more wobbly.

Trucks

Overland truck safaris are a popular way of exploring Kenya by road. They demand a little more fortitude and adventurous spirit from the traveller, but the compensation is usually the camaraderie and life-long friendships that result from what is invariably a real adventure, going to places the more luxurious travellers will never visit. The standard overland route most commercial trucks take through East Africa (in either direction) is from Nairobi a two-week circuit into Uganda to see the mountain gorillas via some of the Kenya national parks, then crossing into Tanzania to Arusha for the Ngorongoro Crater and Serengeti, before heading south to Dar es Salaam, for Zanzibar. There are several overland companies and there are departures almost weekly from Nairobi throughout the year.

Overland truck safari operators
Dragoman, T01728-861133, www.dragoman.com.
Encounter, T01728-861133, www.encounter.co.uk.
Exodus Travels, T020-87723822, www.exodus.co.uk.

Explore, T0125-239448, www.explore.co.uk.
Kumuka Expeditions, T020-79378855, www.kumuka.com.
Oasis Overland, T01258-471155, www.oasisoverland.co.uk.
Phoenix Expeditions, T01509-881341, www.phoenix-expeditions.co.uk.

Maps

The best map and travel guide store in the UK is **Stanfords**, 12-14 Long Acre, Covent Garden, London WC2 9LP, T020-78361321, www.stanfords.co.uk, with branches in Manchester and Bristol. **The Map Studio**, T0860-105050, www.mapstudio.co.za, produces a wide range of maps covering much of Africa. **The Nation**, on Kenyatta Avenue in Nairobi, next to the Thorn Tree Café, has a good selection of maps.

Sleeping

There is a wide range of accommodation on offer from top-of-the-range game lodges and tented camps that charge US$150-1,000 per couple per day to mid-range safari lodges and beach resorts with self-contained double rooms with air conditioning for around US$25-100, and those used by local people (and budget travellers) at under US$10 a day. At the top end of the market, Kenya now boasts some accommodation options that would rival the luxurious camps in southern Africa – intimate safari camps with unrivalled degrees of comfort and service in stunning settings. The beach resorts too have improved considerably in recent years, and there are some highly luxurious and romantic beach lodges and hotels that again are in commanding positions. At the budget end there's a fairly wide choice of cheap accommodation. A room often comprises a simple bed, shared toilet and washing facilities, and may have an irregular water supply; it is always a good idea to look at a room before deciding to ensure it's clean and everything works. It is also imperative to ensure that your luggage will be locked away securely for protection against petty theft especially in shared accommodation. For the more expensive hotels, the airlines, game park entrance and camping fees, a system operates where tourists are charged approximately double the rate locals are charged– resident and non-resident rates – although these can be paid in foreign currency as well as KSh. Note that the word hotel (or in Kiswahili, *hoteli*) means food and drink only, rather than lodging. It would be better to use the word guesthouse (or in Kiswahili, *guesti*).

Generally accommodation booked through a European agent will be more expensive than if you contact the hotel or lodge directly. Kenya's hoteliers are embracing the age of the internet, and an ever-increasing number can take a reservation by email or through their websites. Low season in East Africa is from the beginning of April to the end of June, when most room rates drop considerably. Some establishments even close during this period.

Hotels

There are roughly 75,000 hotel beds in over 2,000 licensed hotels within the country. A large majority of these are found in the coastal region, thanks to the rapid development of tourism infrastructure and beach resorts in the late 1970s and early 1980s. Some of the beach hotels are full-on resorts with a range of watersports and activities where guests stay for their entire holiday, whilst some are of the small, simple beach cottage variety in splendid locations and excellent value. A few international hotel chains, such as **Hilton International** and **Intercontinental Hotels** among others, have hotels in Nairobi. Most local town and city hotels tend to be bland with poor service, although there are a number of characterful hotels that have been around since the colonial days, such as Nairobi's **The Norfolk** or the **Country Club** in Naivasha. Prices of hotels are not always a good indication of their quality, and it is sensible to check what you will get before committing yourself, though prices are often negotiable, even in large hotels. On the coast and in the game parks, you can expect to pay more in the high season, particularly mid-December to mid-February. Low season in Kenya is generally 1 April-30 June (excluding Easter weekend). The town and city hotels tend to keep their rates the same year round.

Self catering and homestays

Renting a private property is a good way to gain a new perspective on Kenya and to get away from lodges, camps and hotels and relax on your own. The real advantage of a Kenyan homestay is the opportunity to spend time with Kenyans and their families, and to share the benefit of their many years of local experience. These are often

Hotel price codes explained

L	Over US$150	D	US$11-20
A	US$101-150	E	US$5-10
B	US$51-100	F	Under US$5
C	US$21-50		

Prices refer to the cost of a double room, not including service charge or meals unless otherwise stated.

surprisingly good value if you intend to stay for a while. They vary from rustic cottages in the bush, historic Swahili mansions on the coast to serviced city apartments. Many of the homes used as homestays are in the highland areas of Kenya, legacies of the pre-independence settlers, and the coastal belt; very few are near the game parks. Homestays tend to be more expensive than hotels and are often built into the more expensive, individually tailored itineraries. Such properties can either be booked privately or through a travel agent or safari operator. There is also an increasing number of self-catering apartments for rental especially at the coast. Often assistance with cleaning and cooking is available. Whilst some of these facilities are custom built, many are holiday homes leased out when not in use by the owners. These range from quite simple and basic beach cottages to sophisticated villas. For more information contact **Kenya Holiday Villas**, www.kenyaholidayvillas.com, or **Kenya Safari Homes**, www.kenyasafarihomes.com. Each website has a full description including photographs of each property.

When sleeping, be prepared for insects – mosquitoes in particular. Sleep under a net treated with insecticide; smear exposed skin with insect repellent; use an electric heat-pad insecticide tablet vapourizer at night; and buy a can of insecticide to spray your room.

Hostels

The youth hostel in Nairobi is not only an excellent place to stay, but also a good place to meet other travellers. Apart from this one, there are very few hostels around the country, although there are a number of YMCAs and YWCAs, most of which are clean and safe and, of course, very cheap. The ones in Nairobi tend to cater for long-term residents and many people from the university stay at the YMCA, so it is a good place to meet Kenyans. The Naivasha YMCA also has a deservedly good reputation.

Camping

There are many campsites all over Kenya. They are usually very cheap with basic amenities and some are very good. Camping can be a very useful option as it allows you to stay wherever you want. It is essential if you are on a tight budget but want to explore the national parks. You should always have your own tent and basic equipment as these cannot always be hired at the sites. You should also carry adequate supplies of fresh water, food, fuel and emergency supplies. Do not rely on local water supplies or rivers and streams for potable water. Any water taken from a stream should be filtered or boiled for several minutes before drinking. If you are trekking and planning to wild camp outside of official or designated campsites, seek local advice in advance. The land on which you are planning to camp may be privately owned or be traditional lands under the control of a nearby village. In some instances, advance permission and/or payment is required. If camping in the vicinity of a village, as you may be asked to do, remember to be culturally sensitive.

All safari companies offer basically the same safari but at different prices, which is reflective on what accommodation is booked. For example, you can choose, say, a two-day safari of the Masai Mara and the options would be camping (the companies provide the equipment) or a lodge safari, making it considerably more expensive. For those that want to spend more, there is the option of adding flights between destinations or staying at one of the luxury private tented camps in the private concession areas on the edges of the parks. Everyone is likely to have the same sort of game viewing experiences, but the level of comfort you want on safari, rather depends on where you stay and how much you spend.

Hotels and lodges These vary and may be either typical hotels with rooms and facilities in one building or individual bandas or rondavels (small huts) with a central dining area. Standards vary from the rustic to the modern, from the simply appointed to the last word in luxury. Efforts are usually made to design lodges that blend into their environment, with an emphasis on natural local building materials and use of traditional art and decoration. Most lodges serve meals and have lounges and bars, often with excellent views or overlooking waterholes or salt licks that attract game. Many have resident naturalists, as well as guides for organized walks or game drives.

Tented camps A luxury tented camp is really the best of both worlds. They are usually built with a central dining area. Each tent will have a thatched roof to keep it cool inside, proper beds and a veranda and they will often have a small bathroom at the back with solar-heated hot water. But at the same time you will have the feeling of being in the heart of Africa and at night you will hear animals surprisingly close by. Tented camps can be found in many of Kenya's national parks and game reserves, as well as on private game ranches and sanctuaries.

Campsites There are campsites in most national parks. They are extensively used by camping safari companies. Vehicles, guides, tents and equipment, as well as food and a cook, are all provided. They are often most attractively sited, perhaps in the elbow of a river course but always with plenty of shade. Birds are plentiful and several hours can be whiled away birdwatching. Some campsites have attached to them a few bandas or huts run by the park where you may be able to shower. Toilet facilities can be primitive – the 'long drop', a basic hole in a concrete slab being very common. Most camps are guarded but despite this you should be careful to ensure that valuables are not left unattended. If you are camping on your own, you will almost always need to be totally self-sufficient with all your own equipment. The campsites usually provide running water and firewood. Camping should always have minimal impact on the environment. All rubbish and waste matter should be buried, burnt, or taken away with you. Do not leave food scraps or containers where they may attract and harm animals. Campers should also take care of wildlife. Do not leave fruit or other food inside tents, it can attract monkeys, baboons, and even in some areas elephants, resulting in destruction.

Eating

Food

Kenyans are largely big meat eaters and a standard meal is *nyama choma* – roasted beef or goat meat, usually served with a spicy relish, although some like it with a mixture of raw peppers, onions and tomato known as *kachumbari*. This is usually prepared on simple charcoal grills outside in beer gardens. The main staple or starch in Kenya is *ugali*, a mealie meal porridge eaten all over Africa. In Kikuyu areas you will

Restaurant price codes

🍴🍴🍴	Expensive	Over US$10
🍴🍴	Mid-range	US$5-10
🍴	Cheap	Under US$5

Price includes at least one main course with either a soft drink or a beer.

find *irio* of potatoes, peas and corn mashed together. A popular Luo dish is fried *tilapia* (fish) with a spicy tomato sauce and *ugali*. *Githeri* is a bean stew. Cuisine on mainland Kenya is not one of the country's main attractions. There is a legacy of uninspired British catering (soups, steaks, grilled chicken, chips, boiled vegetables, puddings, instant coffee). Small town hotels and restaurants tend to serve a limited amount of bland processed food, omelette or chicken and chips, and perhaps a meat stew but not much else. Asian food is extremely good in Kenya and cheap, and an important option for vegetarians travelling in the country. Many Indian restaurants have a lunchtime buffet where you can eat as much as you want for less than US$8 a head. Other cuisines include Italian, French, Chinese, Japanese and even Thai, though only in the larger towns and in the upmarket coastal hotels. Also on the coast, the Swahili style of cooking features aromatic curries using coconut milk, fragrant steamed rice, grilled fish and calamari, and delicious bisques made from lobster and crab. Some of the larger beach resorts offer breakfast, lunch and dinner buffets for their all-inclusive guests, some of which can be excellent. Restaurant prices are low; it is quite possible to eat a meal in a basic restaurant for US$3 and even the most expensive places will often not be more than US$20 per person. The quality, standard and variety of food depends on where you are and what you intend to pay. Various western-style fast foods are becoming ever more popular such as chips, hamburgers, sausages and fried chicken. Finally, the service in Kenyan restaurants can be somewhat slower than you are used to and it can take hours for something to materialize out of a kitchen. Rather than complain just enjoy the laid-back pace and order another beer.

A variety of items can be purchased from **street vendors** who prepare and cook over charcoal, which adds considerably to the flavour, at temporary roadside shelters (kiosks). Street cuisine is pretty safe despite hygiene methods being fairly basic. Most of the items are cooked or peeled, which deals with the health hazard. Savoury items include chips, omelettes, barbecued beef on skewers (*mishkaki*), roast maize (corn), samosas, kebabs, hard-boiled eggs and roast cassava (looks like white, peeled turnips) with red chilli-pepper garnish. Roadside stalls selling *mandazi* (a kind of sweet or savoury doughnut), roasted maize, grilled, skewered meat, or samosas are popular and very cheap. Fruits variously in season include oranges (peeled and halved), grapes, pineapples, bananas, mangoes (slices scored and turned inside-out), paw-paw (papaya) and watermelon. These items are very cheap and are all worth trying, and when travelling, are indispensable.

Most food produce is purchased in open-air markets. In the larger towns and cities these are held daily and, as well as selling fresh fruit and vegetables, sell eggs, bread and meat. In the smaller villages, a market will be held on one day of the week when the farmers come in to sell their wares. Markets are very colourful places to visit and just about any fruit or vegetable is available. Other locally produced food items are sold in supermarkets, often run by Asian traders, whilst imported products are sold in the few upmarket supermarkets in the larger cities such as Nakumatt.

Sodas (soft drinks) are available everywhere and are very cheap, the bottles are refundable. The other common drink throughout the country is *chai*, milky sweet tea, which is surprisingly refreshing. When available, fresh fruit juices are very good as they are freshly squeezed. Bottled water is expensive, around US$1 per 1½ litres and is available in all but the smallest villages. Tap water is reportedly safe in many parts of the country. However, it is far more prudent to avoid drinking any tap water, and do not use it to brush your teeth without prior sterilization. Place your glass on ice cubes to cool drinks unless the ice cubes are made of purified water. It is also best to avoid borehole or rainwater unless your stomach is quite hardy.

Kenyan beer is very good: *Tusker*, *White Cap* and *Pilsner* are the main brands sold in half-litre bottles. Fruit wines are also popular; they come in a variety of different flavours but tend to be sweet. Papaya wine is widely available, but is a little harsh.

Spirits tend to be extremely expensive and most local people will buy them in tiny sachets. Local alternatives are *Kenya Cane*, a type of rum, and the sweet *Kenya Gold* coffee liqueur.

Traditional Kenyan drinks include **chang'aa**, a fierce spirit made from maize and sugar and then distilled. Sentences for distilling and possessing **chang'aa** are severe and it is sometimes contaminated. It has been known to kill so think twice before tasting any. Far more pleasant and more common are **pombe** (beer), brewed from sugar and millet or banana depending on the region. It is quite legal, tastes a bit like flat cider and is far more potent than it appears at first. **Palm wine** is drunk at the coast.

Entertainment

Nairobi and the coast have a wide selection of bars, nightclubs, cinemas, casinos and live music venues. Much musical entertainment is in hotels where traditional dance programmes are staged for tourists, and there are live bands and discos.

Bars and clubs
Kenyans themselves love to party and in Nairobi and Mombasa there are some raucous nightclubs, some of which can hold thousands of people. Prostitutes abound in many, and these girls aren't shy – it doesn't take much to work out what the term 'the Nairobi handshake' comes from! These places are fun and a real eye opener, but it is best to visit in a group and always take a taxi. Less visited areas tend to have more basic establishments, but even the smallest town will usually have a bar – the exception being Lamu, which is strongly Muslim and there are few places to buy an alcoholic drink.

Cinema
Cinemas are found in most large towns, and show mostly Indian, Kung Fu and western action films. The larger, more modern cinema complexes in Nairobi and Mombasa show up to date Hollywood and Bollywood movies.

Music and dance
Displays of dancing are put on for the tourists all over the country including the **Bomas of Kenya** just outside Nairobi. The best known are the **Masai** and **Samburu** dances. Traditional Kenyan music is most likely to be performed by the drummers of **Akamba** and the **Mijinkenda** peoples.

Congolese music (*Lingala*) is extremely popular and the type you are most likely to hear on *matatus*, in the streets, in bars and clubs, in fact anywhere and everywhere. Many of the more upmarket discos and clubs play western or reggae music.

Festivals and events

The **Islamic calendar** is followed and festivals are celebrated all along the coast and in the northeast. These include the beginning and end of **Ramadan** (variable); **Jun, Islamic New Year** and **Aug, Prophet's birthday**. On Lamu the Islamic **Maulidi Festival** is held each year (see box, page 281).

Calendar

Jan New Year's Day Dhow Race, Shela Beach on Lamu, is an important event on the island. Only 8 captains are invited to race, so winning the race is a great honour. *Dhows* are brightly decorated and festivities last well into the night. See box, page 270.

Jun Rhino Charge, normally held on 1 Jun and the course changes each year. This is an off-road 4WD motor rally and fund-raising event to raise money for the fencing of the Aberdares National Park. The winner is the car that visits all of the 10 control points along the course and has the lowest mileage within the allocated 10 hrs of driving time. **Rhino Ark**, T020-604246, www.rhinoark.org.

Lewa Marathon, usually held in Jun (but check dates) at Lewa Wildlife Conservancy. A fund-raising event to support the conservancy on the Laikipila Plateau amongst other good community causes. Both the half and full marathons attract runners from all over the world, including many of the world-class Kenyan long-distance runners. They are hard runs at altitude and the course is held within the game conservancy. Helicopters are used to keep an eye out for elephant and predators along the course. It is a unique experience! You can take part or watch. Contact **Lewa Wildlife Conservancy**, page 181, or the **Tusk Trust** in the UK, T020-79787100, www.tusk.org.

Jul Safari Rally has been going since 1953 and was first run to celebrate the queen's coronation. It runs for 3 days over a course of about 3,000 km. It goes all over the country on some of the worst roads and often in appalling weather. Watching is exciting especially from a good vantage point in the Rift Valley where the cars go charging up and down the escarpments. Safari Rally, Nairobi, T020-891124, www.safarirally.com.

Aug Maralal International Camel Derby has been operating since 1990, and from 1998 the event has been coupled with the Kenya Amateur Cycling Association Race. These races are held over the first weekend of Aug each year. See box, page 299 or visit www.yaresafaris.com.

Dec Craft Fair, Ngong Racecourse, Nairobi, is held in early Dec. A large craft fair with many home-made items from all over Kenya: curios, home-made soaps, jams, furniture, toys, embroidery and quilted items.

Shopping

Kenya has several unique souvenirs on offer including ebony wood carvings, soapstone carvings, musical instruments, basket ware and textiles. Also look out for fantastic women's hand-made leather sandals with Masai beading on them, especially at the coast. Other Masai crafts such as beaded jewellery, decorated gourds and spears are available to buy in southern Kenya as well as the distinctive red checked Masai blankets. Brightly coloured sarongs called *kangas* are worn by women all over Tanzania. They're sold in pairs and emblazoned with a traditional proverb. Woven with vertical stripes, *kikois* are similar but are traditionally worn by the men of the Swahili Coast as wrap-around sarongs. There are many other items made from these clothes including trousers, tops and skirts, cushion covers and bags. Kenyan **baskets**, made from sisal and leather, are also popular and cheap.

Prices in tourist shops are largely fixed, though in the depths of the quiet low season, can be negotiable. Prices at roadside stalls or markets are always negotiable. See Local customs and laws, page 26, for tips on bargaining.

Sport and activities

Kenya has good opportunities to get active, and trekking, cycling or horse or camel riding safaris are popular alternatives to being ferried around in zebra camouflaged vehicles in the national parks. Diving, snorkelling and deep-sea fishing are favourite pastimes on the coast and climbing Mount Kenya remains a popular challenge. There are also a number of spectator sports to enjoy. Details about local operators are given in the activities and tours sections of each chapter.

Ballooning

The Masai Mara is the top spot for a gentle float over the animals from a balloon and for many this excursion is the highlight of a visit to the reserve (albeit expensive). Most of the lodges and camps offer this activity, which always works in a similar way. Tourists are picked up around 0530 and driven to the site where the lift-off will take place. The balloon blow-up is part of the experience. Once the balloon rises, passengers have the chance to watch the sunrise high above the plains when the sun comes up and turns the grasslands from blue to gold. Especially during the months of the migration, this is quite a spectacular experience. The flight lasts 60-90 minutes.

Birdwatching

Kenya is well renowned as a birdwatching destination and there are over 1,000 species of birds. This puts the country into the top of the world's birding destinations as this number represents over 10% of the world's listed species. Birds are abundant countrywide but serious twitchers should head for the lakes in the Rift Valley, the Arabuko Sokoke Forest on the coast, the Kakamega Forest National Reserve in the Western Highlands, Tsavo National Park, and even the Ngong Forest just outside of Nairobi. Many of the tour operators run specialized birding tours. World Birdwatch is held every two years usually over a weekend in October and is a worldwide event. Birdwatchers all over Kenya count bird species and Kenya has consistently won this event with over 700 species counted over the weekend. The next World Birdwatch is due to be held in 2007. Contact **Nature Kenya** for details, Nairobi T020-749957, www.naturekenya.org. Also visit www.kenyabirds.org.uk.

Bungee jumping

There is a bungee jump on the Tana River just south of Sagana on the road around Mount Kenya at the Savage Wilderness whitewater rafting base camp. It is from a 60-m tower over the Tana River and costs US$50, though to operate the jump there needs to a minimum of three people. You can jump on your own or with a friend tandem style, weight limits are minimum of 40 kg and maximum of 110 kg. **Savage Wilderness Safaris**, Sarit Centre, Nairobi, T020-521590, www.whitewaterkenya.com, or **Bungeewalla**, Village Market Shopping Centre, Nairobi, T020-523094, reblin@mit suminet.com. See page 86.

Caving

Whilst still a fledgling activity, caving has been growing in popularity and there is enormous potential for it in Kenya. There are many infrequently explored cave networks in the Chyulu Hills, Tsavo East, Cherangani Hills and Mount Elgon as well as many other sites. Shimoni Caves on the south coast near to the Tanzania border are probably most accessible for non-experienced cavers, see page 228. Serious cavers should contact **Cave Exploration Group of East Africa**, Nairobi, T020-520883, fajo@kenyaweb.com.

Climbing

Climbing is extremely popular among visitors to Kenya, particularly for the climb up **Mount Kenya** but other lesser known treks include the **Aberdares Mountains, Cheranganis Hills, Mathew's Mountains, Hell's Gate** and **Rift Valley volcanoes**. Each is described in the relevant section. The Mountain Club of Kenya, which is based at Wilson Airport in Nairobi, T020-501747, www.mck.or.ke, has lots of maps and books in its library, non-members can attend the open night on Tuesdays at the club house at Wilson Airport, and the website is an excellent resource for information.

Fishing

Not a particularly popular pastime in Kenya's rivers, but it is a very popular pastime at either the coast or on Lake Victoria. The latter attracts big game fisherman after the weighty Nile Perch that reach up to 100 kg, though the fishing camps around Lake Victoria are only in the top price category for accommodation. Kenya has excellent deep-sea fishing on the coast and there are a number of operators listed in the relevant chapters. Websites to check out include www.biggame.com and www.kenyadeepseafishing.com. Marlin, tuna, sailfish, shark, swordfish and yellowfin are caught on a tag and release system. The best destinations to head for are Watamu, Shimoni, Malindi and Kilifi.

Golf

Quite surprisingly, and presumably because of Kenya's colonial legacy, there are over 35 golf courses in Kenya, and some are of a very high standard. Most permit temporary membership and allow visitors to play and some hire out golf clubs. The most prestigious event in the golfing year is the **Kenya Open Golf Tournament** held annually in February or March at the Muthaiga Country Club in Nairobi. For more information on courses and events see the relevant chapters or visit www.kenya open.co.ke or www.golfingkenya.com.

Kite surfing

This is the latest craze on the Kenya coast, particularly at Diani Beach where almost all of the 12 km of smooth sand can be surfed along in good wind conditions. Kite surfing involves flying a large kite which pulls you along on the sand or shallows of the ocean on a small surf board. A number of resorts listed in the relevant chapters hire out equipment and offer lessons. Alternatively visit www.kitebeachkenya.com.

Mountain climbing

Although not as famous as Kilimanjaro in neighbouring Tanzania, Mount Kenya is a popular climb although fairly technical. Tour operators and trekking companies will happily put together an itinerary that suits your preferences. It is advisable, especially when climbing at higher altitudes, to take things slowly and allow your body to acclimatize. There are no mountaineering or outdoor outfitters in Kenya, so when preparing for a trek in the country, bear in mind that you'll need to bring most of your own gear. Sleeping bags, good hiking boots, many layers and waterproof outer clothing is essential for keeping warm and comfortable at high altitudes. Bring a few refillable plastic water bottles and a good day pack as well – although porters will carry the heavier equipment, you'll want to have a few things easily available throughout the day. Tour operators offering climbs are listed in the relevant chapters.

Riding

Horse and camel riding can be experienced on a day trip from Nairobi. Horse riding is available in the Ngong Hills and camel riding south of Nairobi towards Lake Magadi. See pages 86 and 194. There are many horse and camel treks on offer on the game ranches of the Laikipia Plateau and in Northern Kenya. Although in some cases you can ride camels, they are usually used as pack animals on walking safaris. It is thanks to these creatures that safaris can go well off the beaten track into some real areas of wilderness areas. These excursions mostly use local guides, especially the Samburu in the north.

Scuba diving

Undoubtedly one of East Africa's greatest tourism assets are the vast areas of fringing coral reef that stretch south from the equator hugging the coastline and surrounding islands. These huge living coral formations, which in the past were a mariners' worst nightmare, have now become the playground for the tourist and house at least 3,000 different species of marine animals and plants. The infamous El Niño has been to blame for much of the coral bleaching and damage to many top reefs of East Africa but the positive signs of regrowth are definitely in place, and for divers the visible damage shouldn't detract from the splendour and abundance of the fish life. The best time to dive in Kenya is between October and April before the long rains and subsequent river outflows affect visibility but check individual locations in this section for more details. Plankton blooms are reasonably common and can reduce the visibility drastically. Out of season many dive centres/resorts close. Average visibility in the diving season ranges between 10 m and 30 m.

If you are a qualified diver and have your own kit, take it. If you do not have your own equipment everything is available for hire.

The warm waters and colourful reefs provide an exciting training ground for first-timers wishing to explore the underwater realm. Most dive centres run PADI courses up to Divemaster level. BSAC, NAUI, CMAS and SSI centres also exist but are not as common. Five-day entry level courses include theory, pool sessions and four or five ocean training dives. Medical questionnaires must be completed prior to a course; medical certificates might be required. Costs average US$50 per dive, though if you book more than one dive at a time costs come down. The beginner's PADI Open Water course takes four to five days and costs US$320-500 depending on marine park fees, day excursions including lunch, and whether you get to keep the expensive training manual after the course. Check with your dive centre for local marine hazards.

There are many excellent spots for diving along the coast and most of the reefs and marine life are protected in the marine national parks. The offshore reefs are alive with coral, myriad fish, sea turtles and dolphins. Both outer and inner reef walls offer world-class diving with spectacular coral gardens and drop offs. None of the dive sites are more than a 30-minute boat ride away from the beaches. The marine parks include Kisite to the south of Mombasa around beautiful Wasini Island, an ideal day trip for divers and snorkellers, and Watamu and Malindi marine parks to the north of Mombasa. Recently a wreck was purposely sunk off the coast just north of Mombasa, which is fast becoming a successful artificial reef (see box, page 239). There are many dive schools along the coast and almost every hotel and resort offers diving. Most schools offer single dives or learn to dive courses, often in Italian, German and French as well as English. Dive schools are listed in the relevant chapters and all their websites are a very good resource for more information about diving in Kenya.

Watersports

Watersports are widely available at the coast and any of the hotels and resorts can organize wind surfing, kite surfing, scuba diving (see above), snorkelling, jet skiing, sailing and deep-sea fishing. For the less active the superb coral reefs can be explored by glass-bottomed boat. An especially recommended day excursion is to Wasini Island to the south of Diani Beach for snorkelling and the delicious seafood lunch at the famous **Charlie Claw's Restaurant**. Here there is also the opportunity to spot whales and dolphins. This can be arranged all along the coast. See page 229.

⁝ How big is your flipper?

All divers should be aware of the potential threat they pose to reefs and should help to sustain this delicate ecosystem by doing a few simple things. These diving tips are adapted from the Marine Conservation Society 'Coral Code'. For further information visit www.mcsuk.org or contact the Communications Officer, T01989-566017.

→ Review your skills. If you haven't dived for a while, practise in the pool or sandy patch before diving around the reef.

→ Choose your operator wisely. Report irresponsible operators to relevant diving authorities (PADI, NAUI, SSI).

→ Control your fins. Deep fin kicks around coral can cause damage.

→ Practise buoyancy control. Through proper weighting and practice, you should not allow yourself or any item of your equipment to touch any living organism.

→ Never stand on the reef. Corals can be damaged by the slightest touch. If you need to hold on to something, look for a piece of dead coral or rock.

→ Avoid kicking up sand, which can smother corals and other reef life.

→ Know your limits. Don't dive in conditions beyond your skills.

→ Do not disturb or move things around (eg for photography).

→ Do not collect or buy shells or any other marine curios (eg dried pufferfish).

→ Do not feed fish.

→ Do not ride turtles or hold on to any marine animal as this can easily cause heart attacks or severe shock to the creature.

Whitewater rafting

The base for the rafting operator, **Savage Wilderness Safaris**, Sarit Centre, Nairobi, T020-521590, www.whitewaterkenya.com, is on the Tana River just south of Sagana on the road around Mount Kenya. It offers whitewater rafting on the river; a one-day trip from Nairobi costs US$95, including transport from Nairobi. Longer three-day, 80-km rafting trips on the Athi River further south can be arranged that go through Tsavo National Park.

Parks and safari

National parks and reserves

During the 1970s and 1980s the country's parks suffered at the hands of poachers and whole populations of wildlife – particularly rhino and elephant – were wiped out. But thanks to gallant efforts by the well-organized Kenya Wildlife Services and many private ranch owners, the animals are better protected and today the many national parks and game reserves are home to a dazzling array of animals, birds, reptiles and plant species. Kenya's wildlife is one of its greatest assets and many of the parks and reserves offer a glimpse of a totally unspoilt, peaceful world. Marine life is also excellent and is preserved in the marine national parks off Malindi, Watamu and Kisite.

:: On the up

Kenya Wildlife Service has proposed an increase of its park fees that would take effect on 1 July 2006, once approved by the Minister of Tourism and Wildlife. The park fees given throughout guide are those current at the time of publication. (November 2005).

Category A
Aberdares, Amboseli, Lake Nakuru, Tsavo, Meru, Nairobi.
US$40 adults per day.
US$20 children per day.

Category B
Shimba Hills, Arabuko Sokoke Forest,

Kakamega Forest.
US$20 adults per day.
US$10 for children per day.

Category C
Marine Park and Reserves.
US$10 for adults per day.
US$5 for children per day.

Category D
Nairobi Safari Walk, Animal Orphanage, Impala Sanctuary
US$10 for adults per day.
US$5 for children per day.

Mara and Samburu are expected to follow suit.

Along with the wildlife, some of the parks have been gazetted to preserve the vegetation and unique locations such as Mount Kenya or the Kakamega Forest. Some of the parks and reserves are world famous, such as the **Masai Mara** and **Amboseli**, and have excellent facilities and receive many visitors. Many others rarely see tourists and make little or no provision in the way of amenities for them. The difference between a 'national park' and a 'national reserve' depends on the access given to local people. In national parks the animals have the parks to themselves. In national reserves the local people, in particular pastoralists such as the Masai, are allowed rights of grazing. Reserves are often found adjoining national parks and have usually been created as a result of local pressure to return some of the seasonal grazing lands to pastoralists.

The Kenyan government has long been aware that the principal attraction of the country to tourists is its wildlife, and since 1989 has been keen to ensure it is available in abundance for tourists to see. Richard Leakey was appointed head of the Ministry of Wildlife in 1989 and put in force some drastic methods to reduce poaching. Poaching patrols are well trained and well equipped with Land Rovers and guns and there are extremely stiff penalties for anyone caught poaching. In 1990, 200 US-trained paramilitary personnel were deployed on shoot-to-kill patrols. The Kenyan government's policies have been controversial, and it has struggled to strike a balance between the demands of conservation and the needs of local people. However, in recent years there have been excellent initiatives that have involved the community in wildlife management and tourism which have helped to resolve the human/wildlife conflict. It is essential to tour the parks by vehicle and walking is prohibited in most of the parks. The exceptions to this are Hell's Gate, parts of Nakuru and Saiwa Swamp National Park near Kitale. You will either have to join an organized tour by a safari company, or hire or have your own vehicle. Being with a guide is the best option as without one, you will miss a lot of game.

Costs

The Kenyan park entry fees haven't changed since 1996, when a differential pricing structure was implemented. The environmentally fragile parks with an overload of visitors, such as Amboseli and Lake Nakuru, charge higher park fees, while those parks with low tourist volume and not threatened with environmental damage charge

⁞ What's what?

National parks
National parks are wildlife and botanical sanctuaries and form the mainstay of Kenya's tourist industry. They are conservation points for educational and recreational enjoyment and are managed by Kenya Wildlife Services.

National reserves
National reserves are similar to the national parks but under certain conditions the land may be used for purposes other than nature conservation. Some controlled agriculture may be permitted or pastoralists such as the Masai may be allowed to graze their livestock. In marine reserves there may be monitored fishing permitted.

Biosphere reserves
Set up in 1989, these are protected environments which contain unique land-forms, landscapes and systems of land use. There are four in Kenya; 271 in the rest of the world. Specific scientific research projects are attached to them, funded by UNESCO. They are protected under national and international law.

World Heritage Sites
World Heritage Sites are even more strictly protected under international law. Kenya signed the convention in 1989; as yet only three sites have been scheduled: Mount Kenya, Sibiloi/Central Island national parks, as well as Lamu old town. Other sites being considered are the Gede ruins, Hell's Gate and the Masai Mara.

Essentials Parks & safari

less, to encourage a wider spread of tourists within the national parks. See box, 'On the up' for the price rises due. Current prices are given throughout the text. The national reserves, such as the Masai Mara and the Samburu-Buffalo Springs-Shaba complex, are not administered by Kenya Wildlife Services and are managed by local councils who set their own prices.

In recent years, Kenya Wildlife Services has introduced the electronic entry ticketing system to the national parks known as a Smartcard. This initiative has curbed corruption by greatly reducing the opportunity for unscrupulous employees to siphon off admission fees, but the disadvantage is that it has caused frustrating delays at the entrance gates of the national parks. If you are on an organized safari your tour operator will organize Smartcards, but if you are visiting the parks independently, you need to go to a point of sale and 'load' the card. Assess how much your park entry fees, vehicle costs (there are also fees if you are flying into a national park) and camping fees are going to be, depending on how long you will spend in the parks, and how many parks you want to visit, and load up the Smartcard with the relevant amount of money. Anyone over the age of 18 must have their own Smartcard. Young people under 18 years can be paid for with a parent's Smartcard, but always check receipts as it has happened that teenagers have been charged for as adults. At the main gates of the parks, you will slide the Smartcard through a machine which will deduct your entry fees etc off the amount loaded on to the card. You need to get amounts of money loaded on to the card right, because if you do not have the correct amount of money on arrival at the gate of the parks then you will not be permitted to enter and will have to return to a point of sale, which are few and far between, to reload. Kenya Wildlife Services Smartcards can be obtained and loaded at the Kenya Wildlife Services headquarters at the Main Gate of Nairobi National Park on Langata Road in Nairobi, where the Safari Walk and Animal Orphanage are located; from the Lake Nakuru National Park headquarters at the Main Gate; at the Main Gate of the Aberdares National Park; and at the Voi Gate of Tsavo East National Park. They can also be reloaded (but not obtained) at the Mtito Andei Gate of Tsavo West. When the money has run out on your Smartcard, it will be retained at one of the park gates. Money on the cards is not refundable. For further details contact Kenya Wildlife Service, Nairobi, T020-600800, www.kws.org.

Park entry and the relevant costs to the national reserves such as the Masai Mara that are not under the jurisdiction of Kenya Wildlife Services are paid for on arrival at the main gates or lodges in cash, or will be included in the price of an organized safari.

Major parks and reserves

Aberdares National Park, west of Mount Kenya; **Amboseli National Park,** close to the Tanzanian border in the shadow of Mount Kilimanjaro; **Lake Nakuru National Park,** 3 km south of Nakuru town in Kenya's Rift Valley; **Masai Mara National Reserve,** contiguous with the Serengeti, scene of the wildebeest migration; **Mount Elgon National Park,** in the western Rift Valley on the Ugandan border; **Mount Kenya National Park,** a World Heritage Site containing Africa's second-highest mountain; **Tsavo National Parks East and West,** jointly the largest national park in Kenya; and **Chyulu Hills National Park,** largely incorporated into Tsavo West National Park.

Other parks and reserves

Nairobi region Nairobi National Park, a central location that offers a good chance of seeing black rhino; **Olorgesailie Prehistoric Site; Lake Magadi,** famed for its pink soda pools and graceful flamingos.

Central region Ol Doinyo Sapuk National Park; Solio Game Ranch, famed for its rhino conservation.

Rift Valley region Lake Naivasha and **Hell's Gate National Park,** located to the south of Lake Naivasha in the Rift Valley; **Mount Longonot National Park; Lake Bogoria National Reserve,** in the Rift Valley near Baringo, 80 km north of Nakuru; **Lake Baringo National Reserve.**

Western Kenya Ndere Island National Park; Thimlich Ohinga Prehistoric Site; Lambwe Valley National Reserve; Ruma National Park, 10 km east of Lake Victoria in the South Nyanza district; **Rusinga Island,** rich in fossils; **Mfangano Island** has rock paintings and with wonderful fishing; **Kakamega Forest National Reserve,** a remnant of equatorial rainforest; **Saiwa Swamp National Park,** home of the rare sitatunga antelope.

Northern Kenya Samburu/Buffalo Springs National Reserve, 325 km from Nairobi and 50 km from Isiolo town; **Shaba National Park,** also in Isiolo District, 70 km north of Mount Kenya; **Maralal Game Reserve; Nasolot and South Turkana national reserves,** in Turkana District in the Rift Valley; **Losai National Reserve,** situated in the northern territory; **Marsabit National Park,** in Eastern Province 560 km north of Nairobi; **Mount Kulal Biosphere Reserve,** southeast of Lake Turkana; **Central Island National Park,** a World Heritage Site in Lake Turkana; **Sibiloi National Park,** adjacent to Lake Turkana.

East of Mount Kenya Meru National Park, 85 km east of Meru town, surrounded by several reserves; **Bisanadi National Reserve,** adjacent to the northeast boundary of Meru National Park; **Kora National Reserve,** on the Tana River, adjacent to Meru National Park; **North Kitui National Reserve,** southeast of and adjacent to Meru National Park; **Rahole National Reserve,** northeast of Kora National Reserve; **Mwea National Reserve,** southeast of Embu; **South Kitui National Reserve,** located north of Tsavo East National Park.

Shimba Hills National Reserve, a small reserve 30 km southwest of Mombasa; **Mwalunganje Elephant Sanctuary,** adjacent to Shimba Hills National Reserve; **Kisite-Mpunguti Marine National Park,** located close to the Tanzanian border; **Arabuku-Sokoke Forest Reserve,** a remnant of coastal forest close to Kilifi; **Malindi and Watamu Marine national parks; Malindi Marine Biosphere Reserve; Tana River Primate National Reserve,** 120 km north of Malindi on the Tana River; **Arawale National Reserve,** north of Malindi not far from Tana River Primate National Reserve; **Kiunga Biosphere National Park,** a marine national park in the northeast coastal border district of Lamu; **Boni and Dodori national reserves,** very remote, located in the far northeast of the country close to the Somali border north of Lamu.

When to visit

You are likely to see more animals during the dry season as they will congregate round waterholes. Also, driving during the wet season becomes far harder in deep mud as none of the park roads are paved. However, prices can be up to a third lower in lodges during the rainy seasons.

Going on safari

Seeing the animals – going on safari – can be a most rewarding experience at any time of year. However, for the vast majority of travellers it is something to be prepared for, as it will almost certainly involve a degree of discomfort and long journeys. Some of the roads in Kenya can be very exhausting for travellers, the unsealed roads are bumpy and dusty, and it will be hot. It is also important to remember that, despite the expert knowledge of the drivers, no one can guarantee that you will see any animals, though the drivers will try very hard. When they do spot one of the rarer animals – a leopard or rhino perhaps – their pleasure is almost as enjoyable as actually seeing the animal. To get the best from your safari, approach it with humour, look after the driver as well as you are able (a disgruntled driver will quickly ruin your safari), and do your best to get on with and be considerate to your fellow travellers.

The rules of the national parks are really just common sense and are aimed at visitor safety and conservation.The parks are open from 0600-1900 and at other times driving in the parks is not permitted. The speed limit is 40 kph but you will probably want to go much slower most of the time as at 40 kph you will miss a lot of game.

There are a huge number of companies offering safaris which are listed in the relevant chapters. Safaris can be booked either at home or once in Kenya – if you go for the latter it may be possible to obtain substantial discounts. If you elect to book in Kenya avoid companies offering cheap deals on the street especially in Nairobi – they will almost always turn out to be a disaster and may appear cheap because they do not include national park entrance fees. Safaris do not run on every day of the week. In the low season you may also find that they will be combined. If you are on a four-day safari you can expect to join another party. This can be awkward as the 'six-dayers' will already have formed into a coherent group and you may feel that you are an outsider.

Food and drink

Standards at lodges and tented camps are the same as at normal hotels. Camping safaris usually have a cook. Food is wholesome and surprisingly varied. You can expect eggs, bacon and sausages and toast for breakfast, salads at midday and meat/pasta in the evening with perhaps a fruit salad for dessert. Companies will cater for vegetarians, and you must tell the cooks if you have specific allergies such as

Rules of the game

→ **Never harass the animals** Do not make any noise, flash lights or make sudden movements to scare them away. Never try and attract the animals' attention by calling out or whistling. For wildlife photography, silence is golden. Your vehicle serves as a blind or hide, since animals usually will not identify it with humans. As long as you remain inside the car you do not mean any danger to them, so it is unlikely that you will be attacked. Never chase the animals and always give way, as they have the right of way under any circumstance.

→ **Keep on the well-marked roads and tracks** Off-road driving is harmful to the environment because of smoke, oil and destruction of the grass layer, causing soil erosion and altering the drainage patterns. Also, do not drive through closed roads or park areas. These may have been closed off because of obstacles on the road, such as flooding, falling rock etc, or perhaps because there is a film crew shooting a wildlife documentary. If on safari do not try and persuade your driver to go off-road to get closer to the animals by, for example, offering him a bigger tip. It is mandatory to enter and exit the parks through the authorized gates; otherwise you will be violating the parks regulation and driving off-road.

→ **Do not feed the animals** The food you provide might produce illness. Even more, this practice alters the behaviour patterns and makes the animals become beggars and can cause them to react aggressively when they do not get what they want. This is especially true of baboons. If camping at night in the parks, ensure that the animals cannot gain access to any food you are carrying.

→ **Do not leave any litter, used matches or cigarette butts** This not only increases fire risk in landscapes that in the dry season are exceptionally brittle and arid, but also some animals will eat whatever they find.

→ **Do not disturb other visitors** They have the same right as you to enjoy nature. If you discover a stopped vehicle and you want to check what they are looking at, never hinder their sight or stop within their photographic field. If there is no room for another car, wait patiently for your turn. They will leave and the animals will still be there. If there is a group of vehicles most drivers will take it in turns to occupy the prime viewing spot. Always turn the engine off when you are watching game up close.

→ **Do not speed in the parks** The speed limit is usually 40 kph. Speeding damages road surfaces, increases noise and raises the risk of running over animals sitting in the road or crossing, some of which can be very small and hard to spot at high speed.

→ **Wild animals are dangerous** Despite their beauty and the ease in which they let you watch them, unless you are an expert, there is no way of

peanuts which are used a lot in east African cuisine. Tea and coffee are on hand at all times of the day. Insects are a fact of life and despite valiant attempts by the cook it is virtually impossible to avoid flies (as well as moths at night) alighting on plates and uncovered food. Notwithstanding this, hygiene standards are high.

judging their behaviour and wild animals' reactions are unpredictable. Do not expose yourself to unnecessary risks. Severe accidents have occurred due to an excess of confidence. Very rarely are these accidents the animals' fault, but if they cause serious injury to someone who they have attacked, they often have to be destroyed.

→ **For your own safety, stay in your vehicle at all times** In all the parks that are visited by car, it is forbidden to leave the vehicle except in designed at places, such as picnic sites or walking trails.

→ **Stick to the parks' opening hours** It is usually forbidden to drive from dusk to dawn unless you are granted special authorization. Overnight you are requested to stay at your lodge or campsite. Some of the parks provide evening or night drives with specialist guides and drivers.

→ **Do not take or purchase anything that is a bi-product of an animal** Most curio shops no longer sell any items manufactured with animal materials, although there may be rare occasions that you might be approached by someone at petrol stations or markets trying to merchandise such products; ostrich eggs for example. Never buy anything in this situation: it is an offence and is heavily fined and encourages the trade to continue.

→ **Do not bring pets** It is not allowed to bring pets of any kind into the parks and reserves. They could attract predators and can communicate diseases to the wild animals.

→ **In marine parks** Stick to the same behaviour rules. Do not take or harm coral, shells, starfish or any other living organisms as it is illegal and hazardous for the ecosystems. Also, do not purchase any shells or other products made from living things. This promotes looting in reefs around the protected areas. Obviously, do not throw litter. Sea turtles can mistake plastic bags for jellyfish and they will certainly die if they swallow them. Do not feed the fish, some species can be dangerous and this also disrupts the traditional feeding patterns. Line and bait fishing is allowed in certain regions but not in the marine parks. Harpoons are forbidden everywhere.

→ **Travelling with small children** Keep in mind some special considerations. For children, seeing animals is very exciting but they usually get bored quickly of looking at the same thing for a long time and get tired travelling by car, especially if there is not much animal action, and their feeding is often an issue. At some game lodges children are not permitted at all whereas others are completely child-friendly. If you travel in a group, think about the long hours inside the vehicle sharing little room with other people. Noisy and bickering children can annoy your travel mates and scare the animals away. Many tour operators organize family safaris that are especially designed for couples travelling with children.

Game drives

There are usually two game drives each day. The morning drive sets off at about 0700 and lasts until midday. The afternoon drive starts at about 1600 and lasts until the park closes (roughly 1830-1900). In addition you may have an early morning drive which will mean getting up well before dawn at about 0500.

Essentials Parks & safari

Safaris vary in cost and duration. On the whole you get what you pay for. Obviously the longer you spend actually in the parks, rather than just driving to and from them, the better. The costs will also vary enormously depending on where you stay and how many of you there are in a group. For an all-inclusive **tented camp** or **lodge safari** the cost will average out at about US$150-250 per person per day, although at the very top end of the scale, staying in the most **exclusive tented camps and lodges** and flying between destinations, expect to pay US$500-600 per day. At the lower end of the market, a **camping safari** using the basic national park campsites is about US$80-100 per person per day. These rates include park entrance fees, cost of vehicle and driver, and food.

Organizing your own safari

An alternative to going on an organized safari is to self-drive on a do-it-yourself safari. However, because of the entry fees for vehicles this does not necessarily work out cheaper but it is a good option if you are confident about driving on the poorly maintained tracks within the parks and are prepared to camp. Costs can be favourable compared to an organized safari for a family or group. The obvious benefit is that you can go wherever you please and are not restricted to the safari company's agenda or timetable, and you are not confined in a vehicle with other passengers. Some of the parks are better for self-drive than others. For example, Lake Nakuru and Nairobi national parks are easily negotiable in a car and are a pleasure to drive around, whilst others, such as the Masai Mara or Tsavo, have rough roads and there are some remote areas where you certainly do not want to get stuck in the event of a breakdown or emergency. On your own safari remember that you will need to budget for vehicle, camping and entry fees and load your Smartcard with the relevant costs. It is a good idea to discuss your itinerary with the staff at the Kenya Wildlife Services head office in Nairobi and they will advise on the fees. In the parks themselves there is also the option to hire a guide from the park HQ for half or a full day to accompany you in your own vehicle.

Special interest safaris

There are a number of alternative safari options in Kenya aside from the usual herding around the national parks in pop-up minibuses. Whilst historically Kenya has always involved the local communities in park management – the Masai Mara for example is managed by the Masai – in recent years there have been some excellent conservation initiatives in Kenya that have involved and benefited local communities and have proved instrumental in the protection of the wildlife. An excellent example is the Laikipia Plateau where commercial ranches have turned their land into successful game farms and where new tourist lodges provide employment and other benefits to the local people. Many tour operators and lodges have also adopted cultural or environmental policies – supporting local communities, schools or empowerment projects – worth thinking about when choosing a safari operator. There are a range of tours and establishments to visit away from the national parks that offer more unusual wildlife watching activities, such as tracking rhino and elephant, walking and trekking safaris with camels and Masai or Samburu guides, or horse or mountain bike safaris.

Tipping

How much to tip the driver and guide on safari is tricky. It is best to enquire from the company at the time of booking what the going rate is. As a rough guide you should perhaps allow about US$10-15 per adult per night (half this for a child). Always try to come to an agreement with other members of the group and put the tip into a common kitty. Again remember that wages are low and there can be long lay-offs tipping which can cause problems for future clients being asked to give more than they should. If you are on a camping safari and have a cook, give all the money to the guide and leave him to sort out the split.

Transport

It is worth emphasizing that most parks are some way from departure points. If you go on a three-day safari, you will often find that at least one day is taken up with travelling to and from the park – leaving you with a limited amount of time in the park itself. You will be spending a lot of time in a vehicle. On most safaris these will almost certainly be a Land Rover, Land Cruiser or minibus accommodating six to eight people. Leg room can be very limited. They will have a viewing point through the roof (the really upmarket ones will also have a sun shade). In practice this means that only three to four people can view out through the roof at any one time – passengers usually take turns to stick their heads and cameras out of the top.

What to take

Room is very limited in the vehicles and you will be asked to limit the amount you bring with you. There is very little point in taking too much clothing – expect to get dirty, particularly during the dry season when dust can be a problem. Try to have a clean set of clothes to change into at night when it can also get quite cold. Comfortable, loose clothing and sensible footwear is best. Few safari companies provide drinking water and it is important to buy enough bottles to last your trip before you set off. It is surprising how much you get through and restocking is not easy.

The other important items are binoculars, a camera with a telephoto lens (you will not get close enough to the animals without one) and plenty of film. Take twice as much as you think you will need. Film can be purchased at the lodges but it will cost you three times as much.

The wildlife colour section and text (see page 324) in this handbook will enable you to identify many animals. However, you may wish to take a more detailed field guide. The **Collins** series is particularly recommended. The drivers are usually a mine of information. Take a notebook and pen as it is good fun to write down the number of species of animals and birds that you have spotted – anything over 100 is thought to be pretty good.

Health

Local populations in Kenya are exposed to a range of health risks not encountered in the western world. Many of the diseases are major problems for the local poor and destitute and although the risk to travellers is more remote, they cannot be ignored. Obviously five-star travel is going to carry less risk than backpacking on a minimal budget.

Remember that it is risky to buy medicinal tablets abroad because the doses may differ and there may be a trade in false drugs.

The health care in the region is varied. There are many excellent private and government clinics/hospitals. As with all medical care, first impressions count. If a facility is grubby then be wary of the general standard of medicine and hygiene. It's worth contacting your embassy or consulate on arrival and asking where the recommended (ie those used by diplomats) clinics are. Providing embassies with information of your whereabouts can also be useful if a friend/relative gets ill at home and there is a desperate search for you around the globe. You can also ask them about locally recommended medical dos and don'ts. If you do get ill, and you have the opportunity, you should also ask your medical insurer whether they are satisfied that the medical centre or hospital that you have been referred to is of a suitable standard.

Before you go

Ideally, you should see your GP or travel clinic at least six weeks before your departure for general advice on travel risks, malaria and vaccinations. Make sure you have travel insurance, get a dental check (especially if you are going to be away for more than a month), know your own blood group and if you suffer a long-term condition such as diabetes or epilepsy make sure someone knows or that you have a Medic Alert bracelet/necklace with this information on it.

Basic vaccinations recommended for almost anywhere other than Western Europe, North America, Australia and New Zealand include: **Polio** if none in last 10 years; **Tetanus** again if you haven't had one last 10 years (after five doses you have had enough for life); Diphtheria if none in last 10 years; **Typhoid** if none in last three years; **Hepatitis A** as the disease can be caught easily from food/water. If you are entering the country overland, you may be asked for a yellow fever certificate.

On the road

Altitude sickness

Symptoms Acute mountain sickness can strike from about 3,000 m upwards and in general is more likely to affect those who ascend rapidly (for example by plane) and those who over-exert themselves. Teenagers are particularly prone. On reaching heights above 3,000 m, heart pounding and shortness of breath, especially on exertion, are almost universal and a normal response to the lack of oxygen in the air. Acute mountain sickness takes a few hours or days to come on and presents with heachache, lassitude, dizziness, loss of appetite, nausea and vomiting. Insomnia is common and often associated with a suffocating feeling when lying down in bed. You may notice that your breathing tends to wax and wane at night and your face is puffy in the mornings – this is all part of the syndrome.

Cures If the symptoms are mild, the treatment is rest, painkillers (preferably not aspirin-based) for the headaches and anti-sickness pills for vomiting. Should the symptoms be severe and prolonged it is best to descend to a lower altitude immediately and reascend, if necessary, slowly and in stages. The symptoms disappear very quickly with even a few 100 m of descent.

Prevention The best way of preventing acute mountain sickness is a relatively slow ascent. When trekking to high altitude, some time spent walking at medium altitude, getting fit and getting adapted, is beneficial. On arrival at places over 3,000 m a few hours' rest and the avoidance of alcohol, cigarettes and heavy food will go a long way towards preventing acute mountain sickness. Other problems experienced at high altitude are sunburn, excessively dry air causing skin cracking, sore eyes (it may be wise to leave your contact lenses out) and sore nostrils. Treat the latter with Vaseline. Do not ascend to high altitude if you are suffering from a bad cold or chest infection and certainly not within 24 hours following scuba diving.

Diarrhoea and intestinal upset

Symptoms Diarrhoea can refer either to loose stools or an increased frequency; both of these can be a nuisance. It should be short lasting but persistence beyond two weeks, with blood or pain, requires specialist medical attention.

Cures Ciproxin (Ciprofloxacin) is a useful antibiotic for traveller's bacterial diarrhoea. It can be obtained by private prescription in the UK. You need to take one

500 mg tablet when the diarrhoea starts and, if you do not feel better in 24 hours, the diarrhoea is likely to have a non-bacterial cause and may be viral (in which case there is little you can do apart from keep yourself rehydrated and wait for it to settle on its own). The key treatment with all diarrhoeas is rehydration. Try to keep hydrated by taking the right mixture of salt and water. This is available as Oral Rehydration Salts (ORS) in ready-made sachets or can be made up by adding a teaspoon of sugar and a half teaspoon of salt to a litre of clean water. Drink at least one large cup of this drink for each loose stool. You can also use flat carbonated drinks as an alternative. Immodium and Pepto-Bismol provide symptomatic relief.

Prevention The standard advice is to be careful with water and ice for drinking. Ask yourself where the water came from. If you have any doubts then boil it or filter and treat it. There are many filter/treatment devices now available on the market. Food can also transmit disease. Be wary of salads (what were they washed in, who handled them), re-heated foods or food that has been left out in the sun having been cooked earlier in the day. There is a simple adage that says wash it, peel it, boil it or forget it. Also be wary of unpasteurized dairy products, these can transmit a range of diseases from brucellosis (fevers and constipation), to listeria (meningitis) and tuberculosis of the gut (obstruction, constipation, fevers and weight loss).

Bites and stings

Mosquitoes and other insects such as tsetse flies can administer a wicked bite and of course can carry diseases such as malaria. It is essential to wear long sleeves and trousers in the evening when mosquitoes are at their most prevalent and use a mosquito repellent (see under Malaria below). Rooms with air conditioning or fans also help ward off mosquitoes at night. If you do get bitten try not to scratch as an inflamed bite can easily become infected, although antiseptic cream or ointment should sort out an infected bite fairly quickly.

It is a very rare event indeed for travellers but, if you are unlucky (or careless) enough to be bitten by a venomous snake, spider, scorpion or sea creature, try to identify the creature, without putting yourself in further danger (do not try to catch a live snake). Snake bites in particular are very frightening, but in fact rarely poisonous – even venomous snakes bite without injecting venom. Victims should be taken to a hospital or a doctor without delay. Commercial snake bite and scorpion kits are available but are usually only useful for specific types of snake or scorpion. Most serum has to be given intravenously so it is not much good equipping yourself with it unless you are used to making injections into veins. It is best to rely on local practice in these cases, because the particular creatures will be known about locally and appropriate treatment can be given.

Certain tropical sea fish when trodden upon inject venom into bather's feet. This can be exceptionally painful. Wear plastic shoes if such creatures are reported. The pain can be relieved by immersing the foot in hot water (as hot as you can bear) for as long as the pain persists. The citric acid juice in fruits such as lemon can be useful.

Symptoms Fright, swelling, pain and bruising around the bite and soreness of the regional lymph glands, perhaps nausea, vomiting and a fever. Symptoms of serious poisoning would be: numbness and tingling of the face, muscular spasms, convulsions, shortness of breath or a failure of the blood to clot, causing generalized bleeding.

Treatment of snake bite Reassure and comfort the victim frequently. Immobilize the limb by a bandage or a splint and get the person to lie still. Do not slash the bite area and try to suck out the poison because this sort of heroism does more harm than good. If you know how to use a tourniquet in these circumstances, you will not need this advice. If you are not experienced, do not apply a tourniquet.

Precautions Do not walk in snake territory in bare feet or sandals – wear shoes or boots. If you encounter a snake stay put until it slithers away – do not investigate a wounded snake. Spiders and scorpions may be found in the more basic hotels. If stung, rest and take plenty of fluids and call a doctor. The best precaution is to keep beds away from the walls and look inside your shoes and under the toilet seat each morning.

Dengue fever

Unfortunately there is no vaccine against this and the mosquitoes that carry it bite during the day. You will feel like a mule has kicked you for two to three days, you will then get better for a few days and then feel that the mule has kicked you again. It should all be over in seven to 10 days. Heed all the anti-mosquito measures that you can.

Hepatitis

Symptoms Hepatitis means inflammation of the liver. Viral causes of the disease can be acquired anywhere in the world. The most obvious symptom is a yellowing of your skin or the whites of your eyes. However, prior to this all that you may notice is itching and tiredness.

Cures Early on, depending on the type of hepatitis, a vaccine or immunoglobulin may reduce the duration of the illness.

Prevention Pre-travel hepatitis A vaccine is the best bet. Hepatitis B (for which there is a vaccine) is spread through blood and unprotected sexual intercourse: both of these can be avoided. Unfortunately there is no vaccine for hepatitis C or the increasing alphabetical list of other Hepatitis viruses.

Malaria

Symptoms Malaria is present in Kenya and epidemics do occur so protect yourself. Malaria can cause death within 24 hours. It can start as something just resembling an attack of flu. You may feel tired, lethargic, headachy, feverish; or, more seriously, develop fits, followed by coma and then death. Have a low index of suspicion because it is very easy to write off vague symptoms, which may actually be malaria. If you have a temperature, go to a doctor as soon as you can and ask for a malaria test. On your return home if you suffer any of these symptoms, get tested as soon as possible, even if any previous test proved negative, the test could save your life.

Cures Treatment is with drugs and may be oral or into a vein depending on the seriousness of the infection. Remember ABCD: Awareness (of whether the disease is present in the area you are travelling in), Bite avoidance, Chemoprohylaxis, Diagnosis.

Prevention This is best summarized by the B and C of the ABCD: bite avoidance and chemoprophylaxis. Wear clothes that cover arms and legs and use effective insect repellents in areas with known risks of insect-spread disease. Use a mosquito net dipped in permethrin as both a physical and chemical barrier at night in the same areas. Guard against the contraction of malaria with the correct anti-malarials (see above). Some would prefer to take test kits for malaria with them and have standby treatment available. However, the field tests of the blood kits have had poor results: when you have malaria you are usually too ill to be able to do the tests correctly enough to make the right diagnosis. Standby treatment (treatment that you carry and take yourself for malaria) should still ideally be supervised by a doctor since the drugs themselves can be toxic if taken incorrectly. Note that the Royal Homeopathic Hospital in the UK does not advocate homeopathic options for malaria prevention or treatment.

Mosquito repellents Remember that DEET (Di-ethyltoluamide) is the gold standard. Apply the repellent every four to six hours but more often if you are sweating heavily. If a non-DEET product is used check who tested it. Validated products (tested at the London School of Hygiene and Tropical Medicine) include Mosiguard, Non-DEET Jungle formula and non-DEET Autan. If you want to use citronella remember that it must be applied very frequently (ie hourly) to be effective. If you are a popular target for insect bites or develop lumps quite soon after being bitten, carry an Aspivenin kit. This syringe suction device is available from many chemists and draws out some of the allergic materials and provides quick relief.

Rabies

Remember that rabies is endemic throughout certain parts of the world, so avoid dogs that are behaving strangely and cover your toes at night from the vampire bats, which also carry the disease. If you are bitten by a domestic or wild animal, do not leave things to chance: scrub the wound with soap and water and/or disinfectant, try to at least determine the animal's ownership, where possible, and seek medical assistance at once. The course of treatment depends on whether you have already been satisfactorily vaccinated against rabies. If you have (this is worthwhile if you are spending lengths of time in developing countries) then some further doses of vaccine are all that is required. If not already vaccinated then an anti-rabies serum (immunoglobulin) may be required in addition. It is important to finish the course of treatment.

Schistosomiasis (bilharzia)

Symptoms The mansoni form of this flat worm occurs in Suriname and Venezuela. The form that penetrates the skin after you have swum or waded through snail infested water can cause a local itch soon after, fever after a few weeks and much later diarrhoea, abdominal pain and spleen or liver enlargement.

Cures A single drug cures this disease.

Prevention Avoid infected waters, check the CDC, WHO websites and a travel clinic specialist for up to date information. Lake Victoria and many smaller lakes are infected.

Sexual health

The range of visible and invisible diseases is awesome. Unprotected sex can spread HIV, Hepatitis B and C, Gonorrhea (green discharge), chlamydia (nothing to see but may cause painful urination and later female infertility), painful recurrent herpes, syphilis and warts, just to name a few. You can cut down the risk by using a condom, a femidom or avoiding sex altogether.

Sun protection

Symptoms White Britons are notorious for becoming red in hot countries because they like to stay out longer than everyone else and do not use adequate sun protection. This can lead to sunburn, which is painful and followed by flaking of skin. Aloe vera gel is a good pain reliever for sunburn. Long-term sun damage leads to a loss of elasticity of skin and the development of pre-cancerous lesions. Years later a mild or a very malignant form of cancer may develop. The milder basal cell carcinoma, if detected early, can be treated by cutting it out or freezing it. The much nastier malignant melanoma may have already spread to bone and brain by the time that it is first noticed.

Prevention Sun screen. SPF stands for Sun Protection Factor. It is measured by determining how long a given person takes to 'burn' with and without the sunscreen product on. So, if it takes 10 times longer to burn with the sunscreen product applied, then that product has an SPF of 10. If it only takes twice as long then the SPF is 2. The higher the SPF the greater the protection. However, do not use higher factors just to stay out in the sun longer. 'Flash frying' (desperate bursts of excessive exposure), as it is called, is known to increase the risks of skin cancer. Follow the Australians' with their Slip, Slap, Slop campaign referred to below under 'What to take'.

Ticks and fly larvae

Ticks usually attach themselves to the lower parts of the body often after walking in areas where cattle have grazed. They take a while to attach themselves strongly, but swell up as they start to suck blood. The important thing is to remove them gently, so that they do not leave their head parts in your skin because this can cause a nasty allergic reaction some days later. Do not use petrol, vaseline, lighted cigarettes etc to remove the tick, but, with a pair of tweezers remove the beast gently by gripping it at the attached (head) end and rock it out in very much the same way that a tooth is extracted. Certain tropical flies which lay their eggs under the skin of sheep and cattle also occasionally do the same thing to humans with the unpleasant result that a maggot grows under the skin and pops up as a boil or pimple. The best way to remove these is to cover the boil with oil, vaseline or nail varnish so as to stop the maggot breathing, then to squeeze it out gently the next day.

Underwater health

Symptoms If you go diving make sure that you are fit do so. The **British Sub-Aqua Club** (BSAC), Telford's Quay, South Pier Road, Ellesmere Port, Cheshire CH65 4FL, UK, T01513-506200, www.bsac.com, can put you in touch with doctors who do medical examinations. Protect your feet from cuts, beach dog parasites (larva migrans) and sea urchins. The latter are almost impossible to remove but can be dissolved with lime or vinegar. Keep an eye out for secondary infection.

Cures Antibiotics for secondary infections. Serious diving injuries may need time in a decompression chamber.

Prevention Check that the dive company knows what it is doing, has appropriate certification from BSAC or Professional Association of Diving Instructors (PADI), Unit 7, St Philips Central, Albert Road, St Philips, Bristol, BS2 OTD, T0117-3007234, www.padi.com, and that the equipment is well maintained.

Water

This is one of the main culprits for illness whilst overseas. There are a number of ways of purifying water. Dirty water should first be strained through a filter bag and then boiled or treated. Bringing water to a rolling boil at sea level is sufficient to make the water safe for drinking, but at higher altitudes you have to boil the water for a few minutes longer to ensure all microbes are killed. There are sterilizing methods that can be used and there are proprietary preparations containing chlorine (eg *Puritabs*) or iodine (eg *Pota Aqua*) compounds. Chlorine compounds generally do not kill protozoa (eg Giardia). There are a number of water filters now on the market available in personal and expedition size. They work either on mechanical or chemical principles, or may do both. Make sure you take the spare parts or spare chemicals with you and do not believe everything the manufacturers say.

What to take

The Australians have a great campaign, which has reduced skin cancer. It is called Slip, Slap, Slop. Slip on a shirt, Slap on a hat, Slop on **sun screen**. **Painkillers** Paracetomol or a suitable painkiller can have multiple uses for symptoms but remember that more than eight paracetomol a day can lead to liver failure. **Ciproxin (Ciprofloxacin)** A useful antibiotic for some forms of travellers' diarrhoea. **Immodium** A great standby for those diarrhoeas that occur at awkward times (ie before a long coach/train journey or on a trek). It helps stop the flow of diarrhoea and in my view is of more benefit than harm. (It was believed that letting the bacteria or viruses flow out had to be more beneficial. However, with Immodium they still come out, just in a more solid form.) **Pepto-Bismol** Used a lot by Americans for diarrhoea. It certainly relieves symptoms but like Immodium it is not a cure for underlying disease. Be aware that it turns the stool black as well as making it more solid. **MedicAlert** These simple bracelets, or an equivalent, should be carried or worn by anyone with a significant medical condition.

For longer trips involving jungle treks, it is common sense to take a clean needle pack, clean dental pack and water filtration devices.

Further information

Websites

Blood Care Foundation (UK), www.bloodcare.org.uk Blood Care Foundation is a Kent-based charity "dedicated to the provision of screened blood and resuscitation fluids in countries where these are not readily available". They will dispatch certified non-infected blood of the right type to your hospital/clinic. The blood is flown in from various centres around the world.

British Travel Health Association (UK), www.btha.org This is the official website of an organization of travel health professionals.

Department of Health Travel Advice (UK), www.doh.gov.uk/traveladvice This excellent site is also available as a free booklet, the T6, from post offices. It lists the vaccine advice requirements for each country.

Fit for Travel (UK), www.fitfortravel.scot.nhs.uk This site from Scotland provides a quick A-Z of vaccine and travel health advice requirements for each country.

Foreign and Commonwealth Office (FCO) (UK), www.fco.gov.uk This is a key travel advice site, with useful information on the country, people and climate and lists of the UK embassies/consulates. The site also promotes the concept of 'Know Before You Go' and encourages travel insurance and appropriate travel health advice. It has links to the Department of Health travel advice site, see below.

Health Protection Agency (UK) www.hpa.org.uk. This site has up to date malaria advice guidelines for travel around the world. It gives specific advice about the right drugs for each location. It also has useful information for those who are pregnant, suffering from epilepsy or planning to travel with children.

Medic Alert (UK), www.medicalert.co.uk This is the website of the foundation that produces bracelets and necklaces for those with existing medical problems, where key medical details are engraved, so that if you collapse, a medical person can identify you as someone with epilepsy or allergy to peanuts etc.

Travel Screening Services (UK), www.travelscreening.co.uk This is the author's website. A private clinic dedicated to integrated travel health. The clinic gives vaccine, travel health advice, email and SMS text vaccine reminders and screens returned travellers for tropical diseases.

World Health Organization, www.who.int The WHO site has links to the WHO Blue Book on travel advice. This lists the diseases in different regions of the world. It describes vaccination schedules and makes clear which countries have Yellow Fever Vaccination certificate requirements and malarial risk.

Books

Travellers' Good Health Guide by Dr Ted Lankester, ISBN 0-85969-827-0. *Expedition Medicine (The Royal Geographic Society)*, editors David Warrell and Sarah Anderson, ISBN 1-86197-040-4. *International Travel and Health*, World Health Organization, Geneva, ISBN 9-24158-026-7. *The World's Most Dangerous Places* by Robert Young Pelton, Coskun Aral and Wink Dulles, ISBN 1-566952-140-9.

Keeping in touch

Communications

Internet Internet cafés and email facilities are plentiful in the major towns, and range from the upmarket hotels, cybercafés with fast connections to small shops and business centres, that may just have a single computer. The cost of access has fallen considerably over the last few years and is available from about US$1 per hour, although the use of more modern equipment is likely to cost US$1 per 15 minutes.

Post Sending post out of the country is cheap and efficient; it generally takes a week to Europe and about 10 days to Australia and the USA. There are post offices and post boxes in most towns. Many shops in tourist lodges and hotels sell stamps. Receiving post is also easy, although not parcels. All parcels need to be checked by officials for import duty and it is not uncommon for them to go astray unless they have been sent by registered post or by courier. If you are sending things out of the country they must be wrapped in brown paper with string. There is no point doing this before getting to the post office as you will be asked to undo it to be checked for export duty. Parcels must not weigh more than 20 kg seamail or 30 kg airmail or be more than 100 cm long.

Telephone Generally speaking, the telephone system in Kenya is very good. You should be able to make international calls from public call boxes and the easiest way of doing this is if you get a phone card (available from most post offices). If this is not possible, you can book your call through post offices where you get your money back if you fail to get through. If you dial through the operator, there is a three-minute minimum. Most hotels and lodges offer international telephone and fax services, though they will usually charge you double the price for the privilege. In larger towns, private telecommunication centres also offer international services. Telephone calls from Kenya to Tanzania and Uganda are charged at long-distance tariffs rather than international. If you have a mobile phone with a roaming connection, then you can make use of Kenya's cellular networks, which cover most larger towns and tourist areas. Top-up cards for the pay-as-you-go mobile providers are available just about everywhere; in the towns and cities these often have their own shops, but you can buy cards from roadside vendors anywhere, even in the smallest of settlements. Indeed, mobile phones are now such a part of everyday life in Kenya, many establishments have abandoned the less reliable local landline services and use the mobile network instead. You will see from listings such as hotels and restaurants in this book, mobile numbers are offered instead of landline numbers.

❖ IDD code T+254.

Media

Newspapers and magazines Kenya has several English-language newspapers. The most popular are the *Daily Nation* (www.nationaudio.com) and *The East African Standard* (www.eastandard.net). *The East African* is a weekly newspaper sold throughout Kenya, Tanzania and Uganda. There are two seperate Swahili news- papers, *Taifa Leo* and *Kenya Leo*. *The Kenya Times* is the government-owned paper. Of the international press, *Time* and *Newsweek* are regularly available, as is the *International Herald Tribune*. UK daily newspapers arrive a day or two late in larger towns.

Radio This is the most common method with which Kenyans keep themselves informed. **Kenya Broadcasting Corporation** (KBC) broadcasts in Kiswahili, English and some local languages. **BBC World Service** is broadcast to Kenya on short wave and also on the FM frequency 93.7 in Nairobi and 93.9 in Mombasa.

Television There are two television channels: **Kenya Broadcasting Corporation (KBC)**, which replaced **Voice of Kenya**, broadcasts in Kiswahili and English with a considerable number of imported foreign programmes; and **Kenya Television News**, based on CNN material. Many hotels will have satellite TV. This is usually DSTV (Digital Satellite Television), South African satellite TV, with several channels. The most popular are the sports channels, especially Supersport, which provides extensive coverage of European football.

Nairobi

Ins and outs	62
Background	64
Sights	65
Excursions	70
Listings	**76**
Sleeping	76
Eating	80
Bars and clubs	83
Entertainment	84
Shopping	84
Activities and tours	86
Transport	90
Directory	93

᛫ Footprint features

Don't miss...	61
Arriving at night	63
Rhino rescue	68
Elephants never forget	72
Planes, training and autobiographies	74

Introduction

Nairobi, capital of Kenya, is a lively, cosmopolitan and bustling city. The centre is modern and prosperous; services are well organized and efficient. Businessmen and women talking on mobile phones walk the pavements alongside Masai warriors with long, ochre-stained hair, tourists mingle with busy traders and commuters, markets sell traditional handicrafts in the shadow of office towers, and life goes on at a frenetic pace. The city never stops moving, and the streets throng with pedestrians, cars, *matatus* and *mkokoteni* (hand-drawn carts used to carry goods to market). However, the combination of Kenya's rising population and migration to the towns has resulted in the size of Nairobi increasing at an enormous rate. Housing and other facilities have failed to keep up and shanty towns in the outskirts are the inevitable result. The population is still officially estimated at 2,200,000, but the realistic estimate as used by the Urban Planning Department is about 3,000,000. Nairobi has also unfortunately attracted fame for its high crime rate, and visitors should at all times exercise caution. Nevertheless, you can see the full spectrum of society here, and there are also a number of interesting things to do and see. Nairobi National Park is in sight of the city, there are a number of other wildlife attractions within a stone's throw and Nairobi itself is home to some of the best restaurants and shops in East Africa. It's worthwhile making time for Nairobi at the beginning or end of a trip to Kenya. The city sits at 1,870 m above sea level – from here it is a long and steady fall to the coast 500 km away.

★ Don't miss...

1 **Karen Blixen Museum** Visit this museum and evoke the *Out of Africa* atmosphere, page 70.

2 **Nairobi National Park** See the wildlife here; it has all the Big Nine except elephant. Early morning and just before dusk are the best times, page 71.

3 **David Sheldrick Elephant Orphanage** Watch baby elephants at play at this important sanctuary for lost, orphaned and abandoned elephants, page 72.

4 **Carnivore** Have a night out at this famous restaurant and attached nightclub, the Simba Saloon. Here you can eat a banquet of meat including game meat, but it caters well for vegetarians too, page 80.

5 **Lord Delamere's Bar** Have a drink in this atmospheric bar in the Norfolk which has been serving gin and tonics to Kenya's settlers for over 100 years, page 83.

6 **Ngong Racecourse** Go at the weekend to watch the horse racing, scene of Beryl Markham's greatest triumphs, page 86.

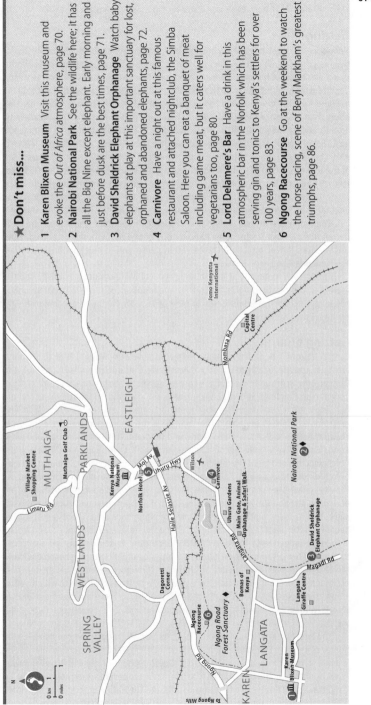

Ins and outs → *Phone code: 020. Colour map 1, grid A/B4. Population: 2,200,000.*

Getting there

Nairobi is the most important transport hub for East Africa. International flights for neighbouring East African countries touch down at **Jomo Kenyatta International Airport**, 15 km southeast of Nairobi. There are good road connections into the city. The airport departure tax is fairly hefty at US$40, although this is usually included in the cost of the airline ticket. There are several banks, most with ATMs, which have longer banking hours than the rest of the country. A taxi from the airport into the centre should cost around US$12 (negotiate first). Most hotels and tour operators provide transport inclusive of a holiday package or at the very least can arrange a shuttle bus. There is also a bus service to and from the airport, number 34 (to get on it ask for the bus stand at the airport), and to the airport board outside the **Hilton Hotel** in the city, US$0.50, journey time 40 minutes. Nairobi's second airport is **Wilson Airport**, 6 km south of the city on the Langata Road. This airport is used for internal, charter and some international flights, as well as being the base for AMREF – the Flying Doctor Service.

The long-distance bus station is on Landhies Road from where there are daily departures to most destinations. **Akamba Bus** is one of the better organized, safer bus services, travelling long distance within Kenya and to neighbouring countries. The terminus is in Lagos Road.

The railway station is at the southern end of Moi Avenue. It is easily spotted thanks to the coloured lights around the main entrance. There is currently only a passenger rail service from Nairobi to Mombasa, with the train travelling overnight through Tsavo National Park.

Getting around

Central Nairobi is bounded by Uhuru Highway to the west, Nairobi River to the north and east and the railway to the south. Across the Uhuru Highway is Uhuru Park and Central Park. In the southwest of this central triangle of about 5 sq km are most of the government buildings, offices, banks, hotels and shops. In the northern section the buildings are closer together and there are many less expensive shops and restaurants, while to the east of the triangle is the poorer section where there are cheaper hotels and restaurants, shops and markets. This is the area around River Road, which is very lively, full of character and has the authentic atmosphere of the African section of a great city (although it is an area in which visitors should take care over their personal safety). Walking around Nairobi is relatively straightforward, as the city centre is small and accessible. Taxis are widely available, convenient and are parked on just about every street corner. Any make of car can serve as a taxi, although all Nairobi taxis are marked with a yellow line along each side. There is also a large fleet of London black taxis operating within the city. Taxis are not metered, and a price should be agreed with the driver before departure. Buses operate on set routes throughout the city, and can be boarded at any stop and tickets purchased on board. *Matatus* (minibuses) also operate on city routes throughout the day, and are the most popular form of local public transport. Again like taxis most are white with a yellow stripe. Their destination is clearly written on the side. There are countless *matatu* stands throughout Nairobi, with continuous arrivals and departures throughout the day.

The best maps of Nairobi are the *City of Nairobi: Map and Guide*, published by the Survey of Kenya in English, German and French. If you want more detail or are staying a while it may be worth getting *A to Z Guide to Nairobi*, by RW Moss (Kenway Publications), which is clear and easy to use. There are several other maps on offer, so it's just a case of finding one that suits you. Try the **The Nation**, near the Stanley Hotel, or the bookshops in the shopping centres, which all have a good selection.

Arriving at night

Jomo Kenyatta International Airport is very busy with a number of flights arrive and depart late in the evening or very early in the morning. If you arrive after dark the sensible option to get from the airport to the city safely is to take a taxi. Avoid the public bus. There will not be any problem with finding a taxi at the airport; if you have arranged accommodation in one of the upmarket hotels, they will often offer a shuttle service that can be arranged when you book your hotel room. You will need KSh to pay for a taxi, roughly the equivalent of US$12; you will be able to change money at the banks and bureaux de change in the airport.

Best time to visit

Nairobi lies 145 km south of the equator but it's far from hot. The city is 1,870 m high so temperatures are a moderate 15-25°C year-round. September to April are the hottest months, with maximum temperatures averaging 24°C, but falling at night to around 13°C. May-August is cooler, with a maximum average of 21°C, and minimum of 11°C at night. The highest temperature ever reached in Nairobi was only 32°C. The main rainy seasons are March-May and October-December, when it gets slightly humid and Nairobi's streets become flooded and muddy.

Tourist information

There is no tourist information centre in Nairobi, but the tour operators will be able to help, see page 88. Two free publications are available at tour companies and tourist hotels: *Tourist's Kenya*, which is published fortnightly and which gives a rundown on things going on, and *What's On*, which comes out monthly. **Kenya Tourism Federation**, on Langata Road in the Kenya Wildlife Services Complex, near to the Main Gate of Nairobi National Park, offers a **tourist help line**, T020-604767, safetour@wananchi.com, and a Safety and Communication Centre which advises tourists on most things including road conditions or emergency help. If you want to go off the beaten track, get advice from them first. **Kenya Wildlife Services**, T020-600800, www.kws.org, also has a shop here that sells some useful brochures and maps on the national parks, and they are very helpful with advice about visiting the parks.

Safety

Over recent years Nairobi has become one of the poorest, dirtiest and most dangerous cities in Africa. There are increasing reports of muggings, snatchings, car hijackings and robberies. These can certainly be a problem if you are not extremely sensible. If you walk around with a camera hanging from your neck, an obviously expensive watch, jewellery or a money belt showing then you are extremely vulnerable. If you are at all unsure take a taxi that you should lock from the inside if possible, and make it a rule to always do so at night. Places to definitely avoid walking around, especially at night, include River Road, Uhuru Park, Haile Selassie Avenue, along Uhuru Highway and the road past the National Museum. Some thieves specialize in jostling, robbing and snatching from new arrivals on buses and *matatus* from the airport. On buses and *matatus* **do not** take items to eat offered by strangers, even by children, as these have frequently been drugged to aid robbery. Despite all this, things have improved in central Nairobi since the mid-1990s. The Nairobi Central Business District Association (NCBDA), www.ncbdakenya.org, has worked with police to provide better policing of the streets and some CCTV cameras have been installed. As a result there has been a marked decline in petty theft. Nevertheless it is always wise to exercise caution when walking around Nairobi.

Background

The name Nairobi comes from the Masai words *enkare nyarobe* meaning sweet (or cold) water, for originally this was a watering hole for the Masai and their cattle. Just 110 years ago Nairobi hardly existed at all. It began life in 1896 as a railway camp during the building of the railway from the coast to the highlands. It grew steadily and by 1907 had become a town sufficient in size to take over from Mombasa as capital of British East Africa. Its climate was considered healthier than that of the coast and its position was ideal for developing into a trading centre for the settlers who farmed the White Highlands. The fertile farmland around Nairobi attracted some 80,000 British settlers between the 1920 and the 1950s including Karen Blixen of *Out of Africa* fame – her house is now a museum on the outskirts of the city. Nairobi's famous **The Norfolk** opened in 1904, and was once the social meeting place for this privileged community, and today you can still enjoy a G&T in the colonial bar. The local Kikuyu who were losing their land to these great white hunters, moved into Nairobi and the city swelled.

Like many African cities, Nairobi has bustling markets, alarming *matatu* drivers, potholed roads, dusty shanty towns and leafy suburbs. As well as being the seat of government and commerce for Kenya, it is also the most important city in East Africa and is home to many diplomatic agencies, NGOs and multinationals. Over the years it has also attracted many of Kenya's rural poor seeking gainful employment in the big city, which has resulted in large slums developing around the city centre.

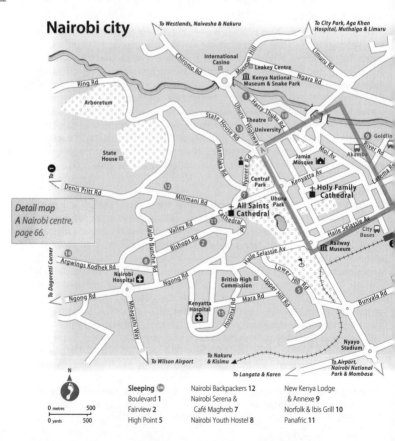

Nairobi city

Detail map
A Nairobi centre, page 66.

N

0 metres 500
0 yards 500

Sleeping
Boulevard **1**
Fairview **2**
High Point **5**

Nairobi Backpackers **12**
Nairobi Serena &
 Café Maghreb **7**
Nairobi Youth Hostel **8**

New Kenya Lodge
 & Annexe **9**
Norfolk & Ibis Grill **10**
Panafric **11**

Sights

Most operators are able to arrange a tour of Nairobi and this is a very useful way of familiarizing yourself with the layout of the city, as well as seeing some of the sites that are further out. The tours will usually include a trip to the City Market, the Parliament buildings and the National Museum. For tour operators, see page 86.

The Norfolk

Anyone with an interest in the growth of the city from its early colonial days should visit this hotel on Harry Thuku Road, a place that played a vital role in Nairobi's history. This was the city's first hotel, built in 1904 to house new arrivals to the colony. The Norfolk became an important meeting point and watering hole for settlers, adventurers and travellers from all over the world. It once looked out across sweeping plains but is now in the heart of the bustling city. The mock Tudor façade and colonial opulence remains intact. Lord Delamere's Bar is a good place for a drink and is the place where the early Nairobi colonial society enjoyed their gin and tonics in the evening.

Kenyatta Avenue

Another hotel with a place in history is the **Stanley** (formerly the **New Stanley**), built in 1913 and named after the great African explorer. This hotel was built as a central landmark on Kenyatta Avenue, and its reputation as an important stopover for African travellers was cemented in 1961, with the creation of the famous **Thorn Three Café**. Here, a single acacia tree in the centre of the café became a notice board for travellers, who would leave notes, letters and messages for fellow travellers pinned to the trunk. This tradition became so popular that the thorn tree became an icon for African travel. Eventually notice boards had to be erected to protect the tree. The original tree died a natural death and has been replaced, but the café remains popular, and these days there is an internet café here for the passing on of messages. Other colonial era monuments include a pair of twin **War Memorials**, dedicated to the fallen members of the Carrier Corps and the King's African Rifles from the two world wars. Opposite the post office, is **Kipande House**, an historic building where Kenyans were once required to be registered and issued with identification cards known as *Kipand*.

Jevanjee Gardens, Biashara Street and around

The small **Jevanjee Gardens**, off Moi Avenue north of the city market, were named after AM Jevanjee, one of Nairobi's first Indian businessmen. A railway contractor by trade, he was also a philanthropist and donated the land to

Silver Springs **14**
Upper Hill Campsite **15**
YMCA **13**

Eating 🍴
Osteria del Chianti **1**
Railway **2**

Nairoi Sights

the city after the small bazaar it housed was burned down. In 1906 a statue of Queen Victoria was unveiled here by her son, the Duke of Connaught. Today the park is a popular place with preachers and each lunchtime people come to sing evangelical hymns. This area is bordered by **Biashara Street**, still a stronghold of Asian enterprise. The influence of Nairobi's Indian community, the descendants of the

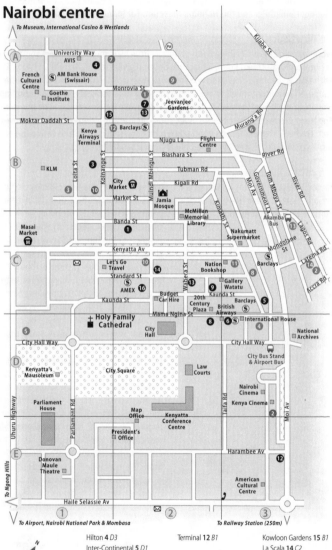

Nairobi centre

Sleeping 🛏
Diplomat **13** C3
Grand Regency **3** B1
Greton **2** C3

Hilton **4** D3
Inter-Continental **5** D1
Iqbal **14** C3
Kenya Comfort **1** A2
Meridian Court **6** B3
Nairobi Safari Club **7** A1
Oakwood **8** C3
Parkside **9** A2
Six Eighty **10** C2
Stanley & Thorn
Tree Café **11** C3

Terminal **12** B1

Eating 🍴
African Heritage
  Café **1** C2
Alan Bobbe's
  Bistro **3** B1
Debonairs **7** A2
Dragon Pearl **16** C2
Hong Kong **4** A1
Java Café **6** D3

Kowloon Gardens **15** B1
La Scala **14** C2
Pasara Café **9** C2
Red Bull **8** D2
Steers **13** B2,C2
Tacos Club **5** C3
Tamarind **12** E3

Bars & clubs 🍸
Florida 2000 **2** D3
New Florida **10** B1

0 metres 100
0 yards 100

original colonial railway labourers and merchants, is undeniable. They play a major role in the economic and social life of the city, and there are a number of Indian shops along this street. There are several Hindu and Sikh temples throughout Nairobi, one of the most impressive being the recently constructed **Swami Narain Temple** on Forest Road, a massive temple complex with fine external statuary. At the centre of the city near the market is the large **Jamia Mosque** with attractive twinned minarets.

Kenya National Museum

ⓘ *On Museum Hill off Chiromo Rd, www.museums.or.ke, 0930-1800, US$3.*

This museum presents an overview of Kenya's history, culture and natural history. Construction of the present site began in 1929 after the government set aside the land for it. It was originally named Coryndon Museum, in honour of Sir Robert Coryndon, one-time governor of Kenya and a staunch supporter of the Uganda Natural History Society. After the opening of the museum, the society moved its extensive library into the museum complex. In the 1950s the late Doctor Louis Leakey made a public appeal for funds to enlarge the Museum's galleries. The result was the construction of all the present galleries to the right of the main entrance: the Mahatma Gandhi Hall, the Aga Khan and the Churchill Gallery among others. In 1964 the Coryndon Museum changed its name to the National Museum of Kenya. The Leakey Memorial building was opened in 1976 and houses the administration, archeology and palaeontology departments. The Casting Department sells casts of important fossil discoveries to other museums worldwide, both for study and for exhibition. The section on prehistory is particularly strong with exhibits of archaeological findings made so famous by the work of the Leakeys. The museum also has an excellent collection of butterfly and bird species found in Kenya. The **Kenya Museum Society** offers guided tours of certain exhibitions and these are recommended. There's a bird walk every Wednesday at 0845 from the museum car park returning at about 1230 (US$1.50). There are also craft shops here and the museum shop sells a range of interesting books on animals and plants. Linked to the museum is an excellent new arts project founded by the **Kuona Trust**. The trust provides studio space in a building next to the museum where artists can walk in off the street and use the space to paint and sculpt. Not only does it offer artists studio space free of charge but it also gives them an opportunity to exhibit (and sell) their work in one of the galleries. This is a great place to meet and talk to young people from Nairobi in a very welcoming atmosphere.

Snake Park and Aquarium

ⓘ *Opening hours and charges are the same as for the National Museum.*

This place houses examples of most of the snake species found in Kenya as well as crocodiles and tortoises. There are many live snakes including puff adders and black and green mambas; some are in glass tanks and others in open pits.

Railway Museum

ⓘ *T020-221211, 0815-1645, US$3.*

Located next to the railway station on Station Road, in the rail compound at the corner of Haile Selassie and Uhuru Highway, it can be seen from Uhuru Highway where the railway line crosses it. Visitors should approach from Uhuru Highway, avoiding the two blocks of muddy footpath from the post office. Among the exhibits are a number of the old steam trains from the colonial era. There is also a model of *MV Liemba*, the vessel built by the Germans and which still plies up and down Lake Tanganyika in Tanzania. One of the best known is the carriage that was used during the hunt for the Maneater of Kima in 1900. In a case not unlike the earlier tale of the *Maneaters of Tsavo* a lion halted

🟢 *In just over 100 years Nairobi has been transformed from a humble railway camp to a*
⚫ *modern commercial centre and the largest city between Cairo and Johannesburg.*

⠿ Rhino rescue

Within the decades of 1970-1990 Kenya lost 98% of its wild rhino population due to poaching. The black rhino, *Diceros bicornis*, was classified as Critically Endangered in the IUCN 1996 Red List of Threatened Animals. The southern white rhino, *Ceratotherium simum*, was rescued from virtual extinction 100 years ago when remaining numbers in South Africa were estimated at less than 100. By 1999 the numbers were estimated to be over 10,000. Figures released by the WWF in August 2000 showed that the current conservation measures have proved successful with the total number of rhinos up to 13,000 in 1999 from 8,300 in 1992.

However, these improved figures disguise the fact that two of the six African sub-species remain at critically low numbers. The western black rhino is estimated to be reduced to about 10 animals scattered across northern Cameroon and the remaining northern white rhino is estimated at around 25 animals in the Democratic Republic of Congo. The measures required to conserve rhino habitat are expensive: estimated by

IUCN/WWF at US$1,000 per sq km per annum.

The demand for rhino horn used in traditional Chinese medicine, not as is commonly believed as an aphrodisiac, and for making ornately decorated dagger handles for oil-rich wealthy Middle East clients continues to pose a threat to the African rhino. A single horn can earn up to US$15,000 on the black market, a major economic incentive for an impoverished people.

There are a number of rhino conservation initiatives in Kenya. David Sheldrick Trust has played a pivotal role in the reversal of the near extinction of rhinos by financing several conservation initiatives and co-ordinating a joint approach through the Rhino Action Group. The Trust runs a sanctuary in Nairobi National Park hand-rearing orphaned rhino and elephant calves, later releasing them back into secure sanctuaries. The first high-security rhino sanctuary was set up in Lake Nakuru National Park, followed by a second electrically enclosed sanctuary at Tsavo West. Nairobi National Park has been successful in providing a safe

the construction of the line with repeated attacks on the labour camps. A colonial officer, Captain Charles Ryall, and some other men positioned themselves in a rail carriage one night in an effort to shoot the man-eater. Unfortunately they all fell asleep, and the lion slipped into the carriage under cover of darkness, took Ryall into his mouth and sprang through a window. The museum is still connected to the railway allowing steam locomotives on to the main railway line on excursions. Kenya Railway Corporation sometimes operates a train ride to Naivasha which usually goes on the second Saturday of every month.

National Archives

ⓘ *To20-228959, www.kenyarchives.go.ke, Mon-Fri 0815-1615, Sat 0815-1300, free.*
This is more interesting than it might sound to the non-historian. The building originally served as the **Bank of India** and is located on Moi Avenue opposite the **Hilton Hotel**. It contains various exhibitions of arts and crafts as well as photographs and, of course, hundreds of thousands of documents.

Holy Family Cathedral

Nairobi's population is predominantly Christian, and there are countless churches throughout the city. In the city centre is the large Catholic **Holy Family Cathedral**. Also rhino environment and Tsavo East has the only unfenced sanctuary in the country run by Kenya Wildlife Service, containing an estimated 50 rhino. These animals are provided with armed game rangers for 24-hour protection. Most of Kenya's wildlife lives outside the national parks and the Ngare Sergoi Rhino Sanctuary, now incorporated into the Lewa Wildlife Conservancy near Isiolo, and the Sweet Waters Rhino Sanctuary within Laikipia Ranch near Nanyuki, have also developed successful breeding programmes. Solio Game Ranch, a private sanctuary close to Nyeri, contains the highest density of black rhino in the world. Its conservation and breeding programme has been so successful that Solio Game Ranch has provided stock that has been moved to other sanctuaries, such as Nakuru and Tsavo national parks, and it is planned to stock the new Salient sanctuary in Aberdares National Park – currently under construction.

Solio Game Ranch, a private sanctuary close to Nyeri, contains the highest density of black rhino in the world. Its conservation and breeding programme has been so successful that Solio Game Ranch has provided stock that has been moved to other sanctuaries such as Nakuru, Tsavo and the Salient Sanctuary in the Aberdares National Park. The Rhino Charge off-road four-wheel drive motor rally is an annual fund-raising event towards the cost of constructing a rhino sanctuary with a solar-powered electrified enclosure fence in the Salient area of the Aberdares National Park. The aim of the project is to provide a safe haven for the black rhino as well as other endangered species, while conserving the rainforest that is also under threat by human habitation. The object of the Rhino Charge competition is to complete the challenging course, calling at the 10 control points, while recording the lowest overall mileage within the allocated period of 10 hours. The race is held in rocky terrain and the vehicles are customized, reinforced with steel plates to withstand the rigors of the course. For further details, contact **Rhino Ark**, T020-604246 (in Kenya) or T020-7610 6118 (in UK), www.rhinoark.org.uk.

of interest is **All Saints' Cathedral**, a Gothic style Anglican church that was founded in 1917 and consecrated in 1952.

Parliament House

Parliament House on Parliament Road is recognizable by its clock tower and was built in the 1950s. When Parliament is in session you can watch the proceedings from the public gallery, otherwise you can usually arrange to be shown around the building – ask at the main entrance. Directly beside Parliament the republic's first president, Jomo Kenyatta, rests in a respectfully landscaped Mausoleum.

Kenyatta Conference Centre

The Kenyatta International Conference Centre overlooks a large amphitheatre, built in the traditional shape of an African hut, with a central plenary hall that resembles the ancient Roman Senate. This building is the tallest in the city with 33 floors and was built in 1972. At the top is the revolving restaurant, which functions only periodically. However, you can usually go up to the viewing level from where you can take photos – ask at the information desk on the ground floor. There can be stunning views of Mounts Kenya and Kilimanjaro on a clear day. It is free but it is usual to tip the guard.

Excursions

Uhuru Gardens

Near Wilson Airport, on Langata Road, the Uhuru Gardens, are Nairobi's largest memorial to the struggle for Independence and were built on the spot where freedom (*Uhuru*) from colonial rule was declared at midnight on 12 December 1963. The monument is a 24-m-high triumphal column, supporting a pair of clasped hands and the dove of peace, high over a statue of a group of freedom fighters raising the flag.

Karen Blixen Museum

① *To20-882779, www.karenblixen.com, 0900-1800, US$3. From Nairobi take the No 111 bus from the front of the Hilton. Journey time 1 hr, costs US$0.50. Change at Karen village to No 24 matatu or walk for half-an-hour. Once there guided tours are offered continuously. A museum shop offers handicrafts and books.*

The museum is found in the house of Karen Blixen (Isak Dinesen), in the suburb of Karen, about 10 km from the city centre. Many people who have read her books or seen *Out of Africa* will want to savour the unique atmosphere. The house was originally a coffee plantation out in the country (she wrote, "I had a farm in Africa, at the foot of the Ngong Hills...") but now finds itself on the outskirts of Nairobi. The quiet, tree-lined roads and older homes with large yards make this a pleasant place to visit. The author lived in the house known as *Bogani* from 1914 until 1931. Efforts have been made to decorate all of the rooms of the house in their original style, and it is furnished with a mixture of original decor and props from the 1985 film production that was filmed here. Exhibits include many photographs of Karen Blixen, Denys Finch Hatton and various agricultural implements used to grade and roast coffee beans. The house was bought by the Danish government in 1959 and presented to the Kenyan government at Independence, along with the nearby agricultural college. The house is surprisingly small and dark but the gardens are quite special. Karen Blixen Coffee Gardens restaurant is just up the road, adjacent to a particularly interesting old settler's house.

Nairobi Arboretum

① *Off State House Rd and the Uhuru Highway, To20-3749957, www.naturekenya.org.*

Nairobi Arboretum covers 30 ha and is home to many species of indigenous plants and over 100 species of birds, as well as Sykes and vervet monkeys and butterflies. There are picnic places, jogging trails and nature trails, and at the entrance you can buy a booklet on tree identification. On the last Monday and the second Saturday of every month, guided morning tree walks are held, meet at the gate at 0930, US$1.50.

Ngong Road Forest Sanctuary

① *Ngong Rd, 6 km from the city centre, To20-3749957, www.naturekenya.org.*

This sanctuary is a 620-ha piece of forest carved out of the larger Ngong forest characterized by indigenous trees interspersed with grassy patches. Here there are 120 bird species, 35 mammals and numerous insects and reptiles. There have been incidents of mugging in the forest before, though it was recently fenced with an electric fence which should stop the problem. You can visit on one of the guided group forest walks which are held on the first and third Saturday of each month, meet outside the restaurant at the Ngong Racecourse at 0900, US$1.50.

Bomas of Kenya

① *1½-hr shows begin at 1430 Mon-Fri, 1530 Sat and Sun, and cost US$10. Take a matatu from outside Development House on Moi Av which takes about 30 mins.*

Bomas of Kenya are found in the Nairobi suburb of Langata, 2 km past the main gate of Nairobi National Park (see below). A boma is a traditional homestead. Here programmes based on traditional dances of the different tribes of Kenya are presented. They are not in fact performed by people of the actual tribe but by a professional group called the **Harambee Dancers**. The dancers finish with a lively display of acrobatics and tumbling. The bomas form an open-air museum that shows the different lifestyles of each tribe. There is also a bar and a restaurant that serves *nyama choma* (grilled meat).

Langata Giraffe Centre

ⓘ *To20-890952, www.giraffecentre.org, 0900-1730, US$7 for adults and US$3.50 for children. If you do not have transport you can get there on the No 24 bus.*

Set in 6 ha of indigenous forest, this centre is 20 km out of the city near the Hardy Estate Shopping Centre. It is funded by the African Foundation for Endangered Wildlife and houses a number of Rothschild's giraffes. To date, the centre has rescued, hand-reared and released about 500 orphaned giraffes back into the wild. The Rothschild's giraffe is no longer threatened with imminent extinction, having tripled in number and been successfully reintroduced to four of Kenya's national parks. Money raised by ticket sales is used to fund an education centre promoting conservation, visited by school children from all over Kenya. There is information about the giraffes on display, designed to be interesting to children. The young visitors' artistic interpretations of East African wildlife adorn the walls. You can watch and feed the giraffes from a raised wooden structure. The centre is also an excellent spot for birdwatching.

Nairobi National Park

ⓘ *Daily 0600-1900, entry fee US$23 plus vehicle fee, you can buy and reload Smartcards at the Main Gate. Situated to the south of the city and to the west of Jomo Kenyatta Airport. The main point of entrance is through Main Gate, at the Safari Walk and Animal Orphange on the Langata Rd, although there are 4 other gates through which visitors can access the park: East Gate on the northeast of the park on the Embakasi Plain; Cheetah Gate at the far eastern edge of the park; Banda Gate on the western edge of the park; Masai Gate at the south of the park near the Oloonjua Ridge. See page 86 for details of tours from Nairobi.*

❖ *The roads within the park are good and during the dry season, with the exception of the one leading from the Masai Gate entrance, are negotiable in a normal car.*

Nairobi National Park is so close to Kenya's capital city, it's not unusual to take a photo of a rhino browsing peacefully amongst the acacia thorn with a background of high-rise office buildings. The park covers 117 sq km and was established in 1946 and is the oldest in the country. It's only 7 km or a 20-minute drive from the city centre and most of its fences border Nairobi's suburbs with only the southern perimeter unfenced where some of the animals migrate into Masai grazing areas. Despite its proximity to the city, it is home to over 100 recorded species of mammal. Animals include all the Big Five, except for elephant – the park is too small to sustain them, though you can see baby elephants at the David Sheldrick Elephant Orphanage at the edge of the park (see page below). You are also very likely to see zebra, giraffe, gazelle, baboons, buffalo, ostrich, vultures, hippos and various antelope. This is one of the best parks for spotting black rhinos – the area is not remote enough for poachers, and Nairobi National Park has proved to be one of the most successful rhino sanctuaries in Kenya.

The concentration of wildlife is greatest in the dry season when areas outside the park have dried up. Water sources are greater in the park as a number of small dams have been built along the Mbagathi River. There are also many birds, up to 500 permanent and migratory species in a year. The park is small, only 117 sq km, but is well worth visiting if you are staying in Nairobi. To the south of the national park is the Kitengela Game Conservation Area and Migration Corridor leading to the Athi and Kaputiei plains. The herbivores disperse over these plains following the rains and return to the park during the dry season.

⁙ Elephants never forget

David Sheldrick Wildlife Trust was set up in 1977 and was named after the late naturalist who created Kenya's vast Tsavo East National Park. It is administered by his pioneering wife Daphne who developed the first formula milk that can be given to baby elephants (within 24 hours of becoming orphaned, a calf less than two years old will die without milk). It took years for Daphne to perfect the formula – a combination of milk powder designed for sensitive and premature human babies, coconut, vegetable oils and cereals. It has proved to be a massive success and brought new hope for survival of Kenya's vulnerable milk-dependent calves. Most of the infants that are brought to the nursery are between a few days and three months old. It's not easy to hand-rear an elephant, they are complex feeders and it's difficult to duplicate a natural mother's nurturing and support in captivity. Elephants need to be taught, and it takes endless patience by the trained keepers at the orphanage to teach a baby to suckle (the very young ones need to suckle every 12 minutes). These keepers become mother substitutes, providing all the care and attention a baby

elephant needs whilst growing up. The calves are bottle-fed on demand, and the keeper provides a back or arm for the baby to rest its trunk while feeding. They also need to be taught how to use their trunks and ears, roll in the dust, bathe and cover their stools. (They have to learn to control their bowels, which can move up to 300 times a day!) In the wild the herd shelters the baby from the elements, but keepers provide hanging blankets for shade and as something warm to rub up against as if it was a mother's belly. They even apply sunscreen when necessary. The foster parents remain with the babies 24 hours a day and provide a close physical relationship and constant companionship. The extraordinary dedication and amount of man hours it takes to raise an elephant by these people is remarkable. A sense of family is crucial, as is mental stimulation – play and communication amongst the other orphans is encouraged. Keepers are employed for the full two years that it takes a calf to be weaned off milk and at one year the formula is changed. Skimmed milk, fat producing components, and antibodies needed to build up the immune system are

Animal Orphanage ① *T020-500622, 0830-1730, US$5*, located close to the main entrance of the Nairobi National Park, opened in 1963. Orphaned and sick animals are brought from all over Kenya to be cared for, the aim being release back into the wild. The centre is most popular at about 1430 when it is feeding time. There is also a Wildlife Conservation Education Centre, which has lectures and video shows about wildlife and guided park and orphanage tours, primarily but not exclusively to educate schools and local communities. In response to criticism, the animals are now housed in more spacious accommodation in a more natural environment. In 2000, Kenya Wildlife Services created a **Safari Walk**, a raised wooden platform to highlight the variety of plants and animals in Kenya and how they affect local people.

David Sheldrick Orphanage for Rhinos and Elephants
① *T020-891996, www.sheldrickwildlifetrust.org. 1100-1200. Phone before visiting or book on a tour through one of the tour operators. Access is via the Maintenance Gate (normally closed to the public) on Magadi Rd. Entry is by (hopefully generous) donation.*
On the edge of the Nairobi National Park lies this remarkable rescue centre for lost, abandoned and orphaned elephants. Daphne Sheldrick lives in the national park

added – stimulants for a stomach that will process a diet of greens later in life. Like humans, calves go through the upsetting and painful period of teething when their first molars appear at four months. When the calves are no longer dependent on milk they are transported to Tsavo National Park and gradually released back into the wild. (Nairobi National Park is too small to accommodate elephant.) In the beginning the keepers remain nearby, keeping a safe distance so the elephants can return to them at any time. Elephants are naturally sociable animals and integrate well both with the wild herds of Tsavo, and the ex-orphans who are led by a wild matriarch named Catherine. Since the project started, several of the orphans have given birth in Tsavo. Daphne Sheldrick has been involved in elephant conservation for over 30 years. Previous orphans of her nursery still recognize her decades later, and she has known some as long as her own children. Not only has she developed the milk formula, but recognized the sophisticated, almost human like, emotions and social needs of the calves. Some arrive at the trust severely traumatized and confused,

having often witnessed their mother being killed by poachers or farmers, becoming irretrievably trapped, deserted by the herd, or suffering severely from drought or sunburn. They go through an intense period of grieving for many months, and are known to suffer depression and even cry. Survival depends on an individual's personality and willpower, but it is essential that the elephant is happy and feels safe and cared for – emotions necessary for the welfare of any baby. With her milk formulas and sensitivity for elephant's emotional needs, Daphne Sheldrick has contributed greatly towards conservation in Africa. All her elephants now in Tsavo retain a deep fondness for her and the keepers who acted as a foster family in their childhood. It seems that it is true when they say 'an elephant never forgets'.

"Animals are indeed more ancient, more complex, and in many ways more sophisticated than man… perhaps the most respected and revered should be the elephant, for not only is it the largest land mammal on earth, but also the most emotionally human." – Daphne Sheldrick

Nairobi Excursions

on Magadi Road and set up this orphanage following the death of her husband, David Sheldrick, the anti-poaching warden of Tsavo National Park, with the emphasis on hand-rearing orphaned elephants with her unique milk formula. The hand-rearing of orphaned elephants and the later relocation and release back into secure sanctuaries requires great expertise, which the trust has perfected over the years. They have constructed night stockades for orphaned elephants in Tsavo National Park, as part of their programme to reintroduce them to wild herds. (See box for more information). The Trust also plays an active role in de-snaring game in the national parks and in treating the injured animals. This morning excursion involves visiting the sanctuary when the baby elephants are brought out by their keepers into an enclosure for perhaps a bath or a play with each other and visitors can watch. It is quite an endearing experience and thoroughly recommended. It is a real treat to see a baby elephant trot along, trunk and ears flopping this way and that as they discover what they are supposed to do with them. It is like watching a playground full of kids – tearing around, chasing each other, playing, arguing and even standing in a corner and visibly sulking! Visitors are encouraged to adopt an elephant.

Planes, training and autobiographies

Beryl Markham was a champion horse trainer, record-breaking aviator, author and celebrated beauty, with two members of the British royal family among her many lovers. Her style was formed by a unique childhood which embraced both traditional African and European ways of life.

Beryl was born in Leicestershire in 1902 and, when Beryl was two, the family sold up and sailed for East Africa where her father took a job as dairy manager for Lord Delamere at Equator Ranch near Njoro in Kenya. Home was a rondavel – a mud hut with a thatched roof and sacking covering the windows.

Beryl grew up with local Nandi house servants and farm workers and their children with whom she formed an enduring bond, going barefoot, eating with her hand and wearing a shulen, an African shirt. Kiswahili was Beryl's first language.

At nine Beryl was sent to board at Nairobi European School, but she ran away after less than a year, returning to Njoro, the stables and her Kipsigis companions.

Ten years later Beryl began training horses, first for a neighbour, Ben Birkbeck, and then for Delamere at his nearby estate, Soysambu.

In 1928 Kenyan society was in a frenzy of anticipation for the visit of Edward, Prince of Wales, and his younger brother Henry, Duke of Gloucester. Beryl and her then husband, the sophisticated, very well-off but rather frail Mansfield Markham, took up residence for the duration at the Muthaiga Club. In next to no time Beryl had secured both royal trophies.

When the royal tour ended at the end of November, cut short by the illness of King George V, Beryl, although six months pregnant, travelled to London where the Duke of Gloucester met her on the quay side and installed her in a suite at the Grosvenor Hotel, close to Buckingham Palace. When the Duke was out of town she would tryst with the Prince of Wales. Mansfield Markham came from Kenya for the birth of Gervaise Markham in February.

In the London of 1929 flying became a very fashionable pastime. Both of Beryl's royal lovers became aviators and Beryl took some flying lessons before returning to Kenya in 1930. The Prince of Wales revisited. Karen Blixen's coffee farm was failing and about to be sold, and Denys Finch-Hatton, adored lover of both Karen Blixen and Beryl, was killed when his plane crashed at Voi.

This tragedy did not deter Beryl, and under the tutelage of her instructor and lover, Tom Campbell-Black, she gained a pilot's licence in July 1931. In 1933 she got her 'B' licence which allowed her to work as a commercial pilot – the first woman in Kenya to do so.

One evening in the bar of the White Rhino in Nyeri a wealthy local flying enthusiast JC Carberry dared Beryl to fly solo across the Atlantic from east to west, 'against the wind'. Carberry offered to bankroll the flight. The feat had never been achieved in 39 previous attempts. Beryl ordered the recently designed Percival Vega Gull, a single-engined monoplane, from De Havillands at Gravesend. At the end of 1935 she flew to London in her Leopard Moth, hopping across Africa and Europe with Bror Blixen, a former lover and white hunter husband of Karen, as passenger. *The Daily Express* bought exclusive rights to Beryl's story and the audacity of the attempt allied to Beryl's beauty created a fever of interest as she waited patiently for fair weather. On 4 September the winds had dropped. Beryl, in a white leather flying suit and helmet, squeezed into the cramped cockpit with five flasks of coffee, some cold meat, dried fruit, nuts and fruit pastilles and a hip flask of brandy. There was no room for a life jacket. Edgar Percival, the plane's designer, swung the propeller. With a wave, Beryl rumbled down the runway and climbed slowly into the air. It was close to twilight, just before 1900. Edgar Percival shook his head and observed to onlookers: "Well, that's the last we shall see of Beryl".

After a flight of over 21 hours Beryl saw land, but she was on the last tank of fuel and the engine began to splutter. She selected a landing field but ditched in a Nova Scotia bog.

The Atlantic flight made Beryl a sensation in America – a crowd of 5,000 awaited her flight to New York – there were press conferences, radio interviews, banquets and guest spots on comedy shows. This was all cut short when she learned that Tom Campbell-Black, her flying instructor, had been killed in a flying accident. Beryl sailed back to England. She filled in time with an affair with Jack Doyle, the Irish heavyweight boxer.

In 1937 she returned to America to do some screen tests for a film of her epic flight – which were not a success. While in California she met Raoul Schumacher, five years younger than Beryl, tall, born in Minneapolis, comfortably off, and good company, who was working as a writer in Hollywood. They produced *West with the Night*, a memoir of Beryl's childhood and transatlantic flight. Although Beryl was credited as author, it seems clear that Raoul provided the structure and style. It was published in 1942 to excellent reviews and was on the bestseller lists. Ernest Hemingway judged it a 'bloody wonderful book'.

Raoul and Beryl married in 1942 but Beryl took a string of lovers and in 1946 Raoul moved out. Beryl continued to amuse herself in her accustomed manner, had a farewell fling with the singer Burl Ives, and in 1949 moved back to Kenya.

She stayed in the guest cottage of Forest Farm near Nanyuki, owned by the Norman family. Forest Farm was managed by a Dane, Jorgen Thrane, who became Beryl's lover. Beryl bought a small farm nearby and Jorgen managed that as well.

A trip to see her father in South Africa got her in the mood for training horses again. Back in Kenya she set to with a purpose, and over the next 15 years she was outstandingly successful, training winners for all the Kenyan Classic Races, and winning the Derby four times.

In 1965, the relationship with Jorgen waning, Beryl found a property in South Africa going for a song and she relocated her training stables there, but the move was not a success. Returning to Kenya in 1970, Beryl managed to get her trainer's licence back and she had some triumphs including a fifth Derby win. She carried on training until 1983, although the latter part of this period was marred by continual squabbles with jockeys, owners and the stewards.

The Jockey Club made her an honorary member and allocated her a cottage on the Ngong Racecourse. Interest in her book was revived and a reissue in 1983 sold over a million copies. Beryl enjoyed a revival of her fame as a celebrity and she was the subject of considerable television and newspaper interest. Greeting well-wishers with a cigarette in one hand and a tumbler of vodka in the other, however, she could be less than gracious to visitors.

Beryl died in 1986 and her ashes were scattered at Cemetery Corner on Ngong Racecourse.

As well as elephants, the David Sheldrick Trust has also taken a primary role in protecting the remaining rhinos on private land and has co-ordinated a joint approach through the **Rhino Action Group**, comprising all the conservation groups in Kenya. The trust has played a pivotal role by financing several initiatives, such as the construction of holding enclosures, travelling crates and a loading sledge, veterinary costs and equipping the Kenya Wildlife Services with radio communication links. To date, several infant black rhinos have also been re-released from the sanctuary. They are easier than elephants as they are only milk-dependent for one year and can take full cream human baby formula, but it takes longer to rehabilitate them in the wild as they are territorial.

Ngong Hills

These undulating hills with four peaks, said to resemble knuckles, commonly numbered one to four – north to south – are located about 25 km to the southwest of Nairobi on the edge of the Great Rift Valley. Masai legend has it that the hills were created from a handful of earth that a giant clutched after falling over Mount Kilimanjaro. Partly wooded, the hills are no longer rich in animals, but zebra, giraffe and bush-buck remain in large numbers. Plan for at least a half-day round trip. It is advisable to go in a group and to take care over security as muggings have occurred here in the past. Take the Langata Road out through the suburbs of Langata and Karen until you reach the town of Ngong. Just after this town turn right up the Panorama Road, which should be well signposted. The road winds up fairly steeply in places, and to reach Lamwia, the highest peak (No 4), requires a four-wheel-drive vehicle. The route is about 100 km in all and you climb up 1,000 m. It is possible to walk along the four peaks, allow two to three hours for this. From the top you can look back from where you have come to see the skyline of Nairobi. The city centre with its skyscrapers is clearly visible and gradually peters out to the suburbs and farms. On a very clear day you can see Mount Kenya in the distance. Looking over in the other direction, towards the Great Rift Valley, is a view of about 100 km.

● Sleeping

There is an enormous range of hotels from the most expensive to the most basic. Those at the top of the range have all the facilities that you would expect of any international 5-star hotel. The hotels out of town are more peaceful than those in the centre.

L **Giraffe Manor**, Koitobos Rd, T020-891078, www.giraffemanor.com. Profits go to support the Giraffe Centre. The red-brick, ivy-covered house is redolent of an English country manor house, set in beautiful wood- land and gardens. A family home with 4 double bedrooms with bathrooms on offer, and excellent food. It is perhaps the only place in the world that you can feed giraffe from your 2nd floor bedroom window, over the lunch table, and at the front door. A double costs US$595 and includes all meals prepared by a gourmet chef, tea, wine and cocktails. Mick Jagger, Jerry Hall, Johnny Carson and Brooke Shields have all stayed here.

L **Grand Regency**, Loita St, T020-211199, www.grandregency.co.ke. A profusion of marble and gilt. 194 rooms, with a/c, satellite TV, internet access, several restaurants including the **Sitah** which is a very good Indian, cocktail lounges, bars, ballroom, gym, swimming pool and a shopping arcade.

L **Hilton**, Mama Ngina St, T020-250000, www.hilton.com. The 287-room **Hilton** is very centrally located and the circular building a landmark in the city centre. All rooms have a/c, satellite TV, electronic safes, electronic locks and mini bar. 4 restaurants, 1 pub with live entertainment, a heated pool, gym, sauna, steam bath and massage.

L **Inter-Continental**, City Hall Way and Uhuru Highway, T020-320000, www.ichotel sgroup.com. About 400 rooms on 6 floors, non-smoking rooms, a/c, 4 restaurants, several bars, business/conference facilities, gym, sauna, jacuzzi and swimming pool.

L **Muthaiga Country Club**, Nguruwe Rd, Langata, near the Giraffe Centre, T020-3767754, www.muthaigacountryclub nairobi.com. Small charming hotel with 6 lovely rooms that opened on New Year's Eve 1913. 4-poster beds and unusual and interesting decor, each with a sitting room and terrace. In the evenings, you can dine in the wood-panelled splendour of the dining room – the original silver carvery trolley still makes its stately rounds – and finish off the evening with a rubber of bridge in the card room or a spot of snooker in the games room. Swimming pool, 6 tennis courts, 2 squash courts and an immaculate bowling green with its own pavilion.

L **Nairobi Safari Club**, Lillian Towers, University Way, Koinage St, T020-251333, www.nairobisafariclub.com. One of the newest of the Nairobi hotels, perhaps the priciest and one of the few places where you are expected to wear a tie and jacket. It does not welcome children under the age of 12. Palatial with marble, fountains and lots of greenery, 2 restaurants, a swimming pool, sauna, health centre, hairdresser and meeting rooms; you have to pay temporary membership to use these facilities.

L **Nairobi Serena**, Kenyatta Av and Nyerere Rd, close to All Saints' Cathedral, T020-2725111, www.serenahotels.com. Set in beautiful gardens it has plenty of parking space and runs a shuttle service into town. The Serena has a good reputation and is generally considered the finest hotel in central Nairobi. Wonderful views of the city, especially at sunset. 183 rooms including 7 suites, a swimming pool, health club, meeting rooms, shops and fine restaurant.

L **Ngong House**, in Karen at the base of the Ngong Hills, T020-891856, www.ngong house.com. 5 rooms in attractive treehouses in the forest and 1 room in the main house. Built entirely from wood, the treehouses are on 2 levels with a bedroom area upstairs and a living area on the lower floor, raised 5 m from the ground to gain an uninterrupted view of the Ngong Hills. Hand-woven rugs and bedcovers, stained-glass windows, paintings and objects d'art. Superb 4-course dinners are on offer eaten with the family

and the other guests or at the small dining area in the treehouses. Rates are in the region of US$300 per person half board.

L **The Norfolk**, Harry Thuku Rd, T020-216940, www.lonrhohotels.com. Built in 1904, this is a world-famous hotel and as a result many people who cannot afford to actually stay drop in for a drink. Theodore Roosevelt, Lord Baden-Powell and the Baron and Baroness von Blixen have all been part of the hotel's history. It suffered some damage in 1980 when a bomb, believed to be being carried by a terrorist in transit, went off in the hotel. However it was repaired and in 1991 it underwent extensive renovations. 129 rooms, 18 suites and 6 luxury cottages. **Lord Delamere's Bar** is a popular drinking spot. You can also sit on the terrace or in the gardens. Swimming pool, shops, 2 restaurants and bars and a ballroom.

L **Safari Park Hotel and Casino**, 15 km north in Kasarani on the Thika Rd, T020-3633000, www.safaripark-hotel.com. 204 rooms, 7 restaurants, 3 bars, a swimming pool, tennis and squash courts, a casino and meeting rooms, all set in 64 acres of lush gardens. All rooms have 4-poster beds, satellite TV, a/c and a balcony with a view.

L **Stanley** (previously the **New Stanley**), corner of Kenyatta Av and Kimathi St, T020-228830, Sarova Group, reservations, T020-271444, www.sarova.co.ke. The oldest hotel in Nairobi though not originally located here. The celebrated outdoor **Thorn Tree Café** is found here as well as the **Nation Bookshop**. It has recently been renovated. 240 rooms, meeting rooms, valet parking, gym and health club, shops, bars and 2 restaurants.

L **Windsor Golf and Country Club**, 9 km north of Nairobi on Garden Estate Rd, T020-862300, www.windsorgolfresort.com. Built in 1991, this is one of Nairobi's newer hotels. 130 rooms and 15 luxury cottages without a/c. It is modelled on a Victorian-style English country hotel and has extensive facilities including 3 restaurants, meeting rooms, a health club, an 18-hole golf course (located in a forest), squash and tennis courts and riding facilities.

A **Holiday Inn**, Parklands Rd, Westlands, T020-3740920, www.holiday-inn.com.

🔵 *For an explanation of sleeping and eating price codes used in this guide, see inside the*
🔵 *front cover. Other relevant information is found in Essentials, see pages 34-38.*

Standard set-up, modern functional, little atmosphere. Housed in a fairly attractive double-storey mock tudor house with a red-tiled roof surrounded by pretty gardens. Bar, sauna, swimming pools, a **Spur Steakhouse** restaurant (South African chain) and the **Oasis** restaurant next to the pool serving buffets (dinner US$20). 171 rooms, a few equipped for the disabled, TV.

A Panafric, Kenyatta Av, T020-720822, Sarova Group, reservations, T020-271444, www.sarova.co.ke. A modern practical hotel, 153 rooms, 40 apartments, no atmosphere. Swimming pool, hairdressers, shop. A café by the pool and the **Simba Grill** is popular.

A-B Fairview, Bishops Rd, T020-2713991, www.fairviewkenya.com. Very peaceful with 5 acres of well-kept and extensive tropical gardens. A wonderful hotel that is extremely popular with overseas visitors and Kenyans alike. It caters both for business people and families. Has conference rooms, and an excellent terrace restaurant. New swimming pool and health club. Highly recommended.

B Boulevard, Harry Thuku Rd, T020-227567, www.hotelboulevardkenya.com. 500 m from city centre and near the museum, this represents good value. 70 rooms, each with its own balcony. Swimming pool, tennis courts, gardens, bar, restaurant and internet room. Virtually all the overland companies begin and end their tours here.

B High Point Hotel, Lower Hill Rd, T020-2724312, www.highpointcourt.com. Set in 2.5 acres with well-manicured gardens and exotic trees are 2 very modern blocks of apartments and hotel rooms around a large swimming pool (shaped like a fish). Comfortably furnished, satellite TV, cocktail bar, laundry, internet café and beauty parlour.

B Oakwood Hotel, Kimathi St opposite the Stanley Hotel, T020-220592, www.madahotels.com. Good value, just 23 rooms, price includes breakfast. Bar, restaurant and a roof terrace. Well-furnished single, double and triple rooms with TVs and excellent en suite bathrooms. Laundry service available.

B Silver Springs Hotel, 2 km from the city centre in Hurlingham, T020-2722451, www.silversprings-hotel.com. 124 rooms with satellite TV, internet access, electronic door locks and safes and room service. Restaurant with buffet meals, Indian and Chinese dishes from the **Pool Terrace** restaurant, bar with

satellite TV for sports, a new fully equipped modern gym and aerobics studio. Steam room, sauna, jacuzzi and massages, pool.

B Six Eighty, Muindi Mbingu St, T020-315680, www.680-hotel.co.ke. Very central with an unprepossessing appearance. 380 clean rooms, those at the back of the hotel are the best option as the noise from a disco across the road can sometimes be heard. Underground car park, shops, 2 restaurants, one is Japanese, a bar, casino, coffee shop and business centre. The staff are very helpful.

B Utalii, 8 km on the Thika Rd, T020-802540, www.utalii.co.ke. *Utalii* is the Kiswahili word for tourism and this is the government-run training centre for hotel and catering students (the service is very good). 50 rooms with TV, private bathroom and balcony. Swimming pool, lovely gardens, tennis courts, cocktail lounge and a restaurant.

C Kenya Comfort Hotel, corner of Muindi Mbingu/Monrovia sts, T020-317606, www.kenyacomfort.com. Good location in one of the quieter sections of the centre opposite Jeevanjee Gardens, friendly set-up and well used to budget travellers, single, double, triple and quad rooms, 90 en suite rooms in total, more expensive ones have wardrobes and TVs, the **Sokoni** restaurant is open 24 hrs and the **Blue Spirits Bar** is open until late and there is an internet café. Recommended.

C Meridian Court Hotel, Murang'a Rd, T020-2313991, www.meridianhotelkenya.com. Good value, includes breakfast, 85 rooms with satellite TV, the more expensive suites have a small kitchen and a sitting room, 1st-floor restaurant serving buffet meals, the **Khyber Restaurant** specializes in authentic Chinese and Indian cuisine, rooftop swimming pool with bar, and a sports bar with widescreen TV and pool tables.

D Diplomat Hotel, Tom Mboya St, T020-246114. Extraordinarily good value and pretty slick for the price, with wall-to-wall carpeting, self catering, modern rooms, breakfast included. The rooms that face the street can be very noisy.

D Hotel Greton, Tsavo Rd, T020-336648, 331865. Good value and very secure hotel in a smart brick block with 52 rooms. Clean, decent-sized, furnished rooms with hot water and breakfast is included in the tariff. Has a relaxed restaurant that is better for drinks than food.

D Parkside, Monrovia St, T020-333348. 60 rooms have bathrooms and hot water and the price includes breakfast. It is friendly and clean but relatively expensive for what you get and there is a restaurant attached.

D-E Karen Camp, in Karen, Marula Lane (the turning after the **Karen Blixen Restaurant** on Karen Rd), T0733-703510 (mob), www.karen camp.com. Fairly new establishment set up by Dougie, an ex overland driver, good and lively bar, home-cooked food, comfortable self-catering doubles in the main house, dorms with shared bathrooms in the outside buildings, plenty of grass for camping and overland vehicles. Satellite TV and good music, excursions to local attractions.

D-E Jungle Junction, 6 km from the centre in the quiet suburb of Lavington, off the James Gichuru Rd and Gitanga Rd, T0722-752 865, c_handschuh_68@yahoo. com. New budget place, comfortable and very clean rooms, 2 doubles with en suite, and 2 doubles and 1 single with shared bathroom, a dormitory is in the planning, full use of kitchen, lounge and washing machine. Set in lush gardens providing shady camping, room for overlanders though not big trucks.

D-E Nairobi Park Services Campsite, Magadi Rd, off Langata Rd, T/F020-289261, nps@swiftkenya.com. Excellent budget facilities, internet and email, pool table, bars and restaurant. Dorms are US$6, self-catering doubles are US$15, camping is US$4. Hot showers, laundry facilities, camping, parking for overland vehicles in a secure, fenced compound. Can organize airport pick-ups.

D-E YMCA, State House Rd, T020-713599, kenyaymca@net2000ke.com. Dormitories and en suite rooms. Safe and reasonable value single rooms but overpriced shared rooms. It caters mostly for long-term visitors; many of the residents are Kenyan students. Swimming pool. Alcohol is not allowed.

E Iqbal, Latema Rd, T020-220914. One of the most popular places in central Nairobi, so arrive early. Sometimes hot water in the mornings and although only basic it is very friendly and you will meet lots of travellers here. All 36 rooms have shared bathrooms. Baggage storage facilities, laundry, TV room and a notice board. However, it is reported to survive mostly on past reputation.

E Nairobi Backpackers, T020-2724827, www.nairobibackpackers.com. A small,

intimate hostel in an old colonial house. Comfortable dormitory rooms, twins, singles and a family room in a friendly and secure atmosphere, dorms US$7 and rooms from US$13, bedding only supplied in the rooms so you will need a sleeping bag. Hot showers, breakfast room with TV, storage room and a travel desk.

E Nairobi Youth Hostel, 2 km out of town on Ralph Bunche Rd (which runs between Ngong Rd and Valley Rd), T020-721765. You must be a member of the International Youth Hostels Association to stay here but can join on the spot (costs 100KSh per day). The shared bathrooms pump out hot water all day. Clean, friendly and safe. Take No 8 *matatu* from outside the **Hilton** or at the junction of Kenyatta Av and Uhuru Highway and ask to be dropped off at Ralph Bunche Rd. Do not walk back to the hostel at night.

E New Kenya Lodge and Annex, River Rd by the junction of Latema St, T020-222202. (The annex is just around the corner). A very popular budget hotel. Very basic, bathrooms are shared and there is only hot water in the evenings, except in the Annex, which only has cold water. Reasonably clean and friendly and has baggage storage facilities and a notice board. Travellers have reported that the associated safari company, **Neo-KL Tours and Safaris**, offers very poor service.

E Orchid Hotel, previously *Dolat*, Mfangano St, T020-222797. Great location, very secure, friendly staff. Very good value for money. Relatively quiet and friendly, very clean, all rooms have a bath and lots of hot water. Used by **Venture Africa** along with the **Iqbal** to accommodate Gap Year school leavers.

E Terminal, Moktar Daddah St, in the northwest of town, T020-228817. Popular, although it has seen better days. Clean and safe with friendly, helpful staff. Can be noisy, especially early in the morning and at night. Rooms have bathrooms with hot water, but breakfast is not included.

E Upper Hill Campsite, Menengai Rd/Upper Hill, Nairobi, T020-720290. Opened in 1995, 5 dormitory bedrooms, 2 double rooms and 1 single rooms, plus tent space and tents for hire. It can get muddy here in the wet. Good clean amenities, bar and restaurant, with good security, and is reasonably central, only 30 mins' walk from city centre. The food is cheap but good and the staff are friendly.

Most of the hotels have restaurants, the top ones also have bars. There are also a number of superb individual restaurants but most of these tend to be out in the upmarket suburbs so you will need to take a taxi. Increasingly, many of the good restaurants have relocated from the city centre to the shopping centres and malls on the outskirts. For cheap eats in the city centre there are numerous food kiosks around River Rd and Tom Mbeya St selling African and Indian food and snacks, and around the business district of the city between Kenyatta Av and City Hall Way there are plenty of coffee bars.

International

TTT Alan Bobbe's Bistro, Cianda House Arcade, Koinange St, T020-226027. Small and intimate restaurant established in 1962. Sadly the affable Alan Bobbe died in 2005, but the restaurant remains open. It specializes in French cuisine and very good wines, the food and atmosphere are both excellent, very personalized service, reservations are recommended. Open 1200-1500, 1830-2230, closed Sat lunch and all day Sun. In the evening ensure you get a taxi here, or arrange a free pick-up with the restaurant; Koinange St is Nairobi's red-light district after dark.

TTT Café Maghreb, Serena Hotel, T020-2822000. A popular hotel buffet, this has Moroccan decor and is next to the swimming pool and is particularly busy on Fri evenings. Has themed evenings including Mongolian stir fries, seafood and pasta. Open daily 1230-1500, 1900-2400.

TTT Carnivore, Langata Rd, about 20 mins out of town past the Wilson Airport, T020-602990, www.carnivore.com. This is large complex of bars, restaurants and dance floors that was set up by the owners of the Tamarind. It has been incredibly successful and has frequently appeared in listings as one of the world's top restaurants. As is clear from the name, it specializes in meat dishes including game (wart-hog, giraffe, zebra, gazelle, crocodile, wildebeest and water-buck) which are grilled over a huge charcoal fire. The waiters bring the skewer (a Masai spear) of meat to your table and keep carving the various meats until you say stop!

You do this by lowering the little white flag of surrender that is placed on the table. There is also a vegetarian menu, and in general portions are huge and it works out as fairly good value. It is also a drinking venue and a nightclub. Open daily 1200-1430 and 1900-2230 for eating, much later for the bars (see under Bars and clubs).

TTT Ibis Grill, The Norfolk, T020-250900, specializes in nouvelle cuisine and the food is very good. It has a lovely setting and a good atmosphere, jacket and tie recommended. A great Nairobi experience. The Norfolk also does a wonderful buffet breakfast that is open to non-residents. Open Mon-Fri 1230-1400 for lunch, daily 1930-2200 for dinner.

TTT Karen Blixen Coffee Gardens, up the road from the Karen Blixen Museum, Karen Rd, T020-882508, www.blixencoffeegarden.com. With an outstanding setting, this charming restaurant is set in what was Blixen's farm manager's house and it oozes with colonial atmosphere. There is a formal dining room and bar, and at lunchtime, tables are laid out in the pretty grounds. Very good food and service. Daily 0700-2200.

TTT Lord Erroll, Ruaka Rd, off Limuru Rd, T020-7122433, www.lord-erroll.com. Taking its name from the famous unsolved murder in colonial times of the 22nd Lord Erroll, a member of Kenya's Happy Valley set in the 1930s, this smart restaurant offers an exceptional garden setting and gourmet food. Mongolian stir fry or BBQ prepared at your table, Italian and Oriental dishes. A pianist performs on Sun when there is a special and good-value buffet for US$20. One of the most atmospheric places to eat in Nairobi with fine champagnes, wines and coffees, crowned cranes stalk the grass, very special and highly recommended. Open 1200-1430, 1800-2100, closed Mon.

TTT Macushla House, Nguruwe Rd, Langata, T020-891987. The food here will leave you in no doubt that you are in a private home. Meals are prepared with the freshest of ingredients with particular care being given to presentation. Lovely terrace, gardens and pool. Open daily 1230-1500 and 1730-2130.

TTT Pasara Café, Kaunda St, ground floor of Lonrho House, T020-338247. Not cheap but good, build your own sandwiches from baguettes, French bread and pittas, plus make-your-own omelettes, pastries, coffee, soups, some hot meals, very good atmosphere, with newspapers and magazines available, movie posters on the wall. Recommended for lunch.

††† **The Pavement**, Westview Centre off the ring road, T020-441711, is a pavement-café style that is light and bright, reflected in a varied menu of Thai, Japanese and Italian dishes or just steak and chips. Nightclub too.

††† **Rangers**, Main Gate Nairobi National Park, T020-607329. Set on the edge of the park on a veranda that overlooks a waterhole (floodlit in the evenings). This is a unique restaurant that offers diners the opportunity to spot animals in the park as they eat. Good *nyama choma* plus western dishes. Free entry offered to the nearby Safari Walk at the Animal Orphanage during its opening hours if you eat here. 0830-2230.

††† **Red Bull**, Silopark House, Mama Ngina St, T020-224718, has long been one of Nairobi's most popular restaurants – for residents, business people and tourists alike. Portions are generous, the food is of high quality, the speciality is steak.

††† **Tamambo**, in the Westlands Mall, T020-4448064, has very high standards. Stylish, decorated in African antiques, cocktails and wines, very good gourmet food and gooey chocolate desserts, plus light meals at lunch including salads and wraps. 1200-2230.

††† **The Tamarind**, National Bank building on Harambee Av, T020-251811. Nairobi's finest seafood restaurant where seafood is brought up from the coast daily. Popular with Kenyan business people, and can get unexpectedly lively, excellent ambience and service. Highly recommended. Mon-Sat 1200-1400, 1830-2200, reservations required.

†† **Horseman**, Ngong Rd in Karen, near the Karen Blixen Museum T020-882033, is highly recommended for meat lovers. You can also eat burgers and other snacks outside in the garden and at the bar for considerably less than the cost of a meal in the restaurant. Has a rather English ambience. Intermittent power supply problems. This has recently lost some of its popularity and it is nearly empty on quieter nights. 1000-2300.

†† **Java Café**, branches at Adam's Arcade, Ngong Rd, Mama Ninga St, and at the

airport. This is a friendly, alcohol-free hang-out, with a modern bistro atmosphere. Offers generous portions of chilli con carne, salads, omelettes and burgers. Does excellent coffee and the breakfasts are good. 0700-2100.

†† **Outside Inn**, a fair way out of town in Karen on Karen Rd. Popular and friendly expat haunt with good bar with fireplace and a great atmosphere, a huge variety of food from snacks such as brie samosas, fish goujons and chicken spring rolls to full meals including steaks and very good home-made pies. Good value, popular with expats.

†† **Tacos Club**, Kimathi St. This is popular with business people for quick cheap lunches. Informal downstairs bar and upstairs balcony overlooking the traffic, TV showing sport, shakes and juices as well as booze, fajitas, tacos, quesaidillas and the like.

†† **Thorn Tree Café**, Stanley Hotel, T020-228830. Very popular place to meet people although the service is notoriously slow. Trendy coffees, pizzas and continental dishes, sometimes has live music in the evenings. Valet parking. 0600-2200.

† **Debonairs and Steers**, Muindi Mbingu St. Quality South African chains. Debonairs serves pizza and salads, while Steers offers burgers, ribs and chips. Not the cheapest but good quality.

† **Railway Restaurant**, at the station. OK food but the setting is everything, decor as it always has been, and the atmosphere when a train is getting ready to depart is fantastic.

† **Steers**, Mutual House, Wabera St. Quality South African fast food chain selling ribs, burgers and shakes.

African

††† **Nyama Choma**, Safari Park Hotel, about 15 km north of Nairobi in Kasarani on the Thika Rd, T020-3633000. A similar concept to **Carnivore** (see above), all-you-can-eat grilled meat is served at your table, including game meat, entertainment is from the Safari Cats band. Open daily 1900-2300.

††† **Pool Garden**, Panafric Hotel, Kenyatta Av, T020-720822. Varied Kenyan buffets of trad-itional local food such as grilled tilapia fish, beef and matoke, offal and kachumbari, sauted spinach and sweet potatoes. Inter-national dishes also available, as the name suggests next to the swimming pool, popular with families. Daily 1200-1500, 1900-2300.

♔ **African Heritage Café**, Banda St, T020-222010. African food with Ethiopian in the evening. Offers a selection of dishes from a buffet. Also a garden. Highly recommended.
♔ **Kariokor Market**, Racecourse Rd. Good and cheap African local food, you eat with your hands, although utensils are provided on request. A specimen menu is goats' ribs, *ugali*, chopped spinach, *irio* made with peas, potatoes and sweetcorn, cost around US$1.

Chinese

♔♔♔ **China Plate**, Chancery Building, Valley Rd, T020-2719194, and Mpaka Centre Westlands, T020-4446144. Very good but expensive. Decor is authentic Chinese and the service attentive. Has been running successfully for 25 years. Best known for Szechwan cuisine and seafood: crab, calamari, langustine, lobster, scampi. Rotisserie chicken, steaks, Indian dishes also. Open daily 1230-2230.
♔ **Bangkok**, Amee Arcade, T020-3751312. Very authentic and specializing in seafood. Ginger garlic crab and pepper sautéed prawns are especially good, full bar and takeaway service. Deservedly popular. Open daily 1100-1500 and 1800-2230.
♔ **Dragon Pearl**, Bruce House, Kenyatta Av/Standard St, T020-338863. Rightly popular, full range of dishes including seafood, duck, lamb and pork, attentive chefs who make requests.
♔ **Hong Kong**, Koinange St, T020-288612. Chinese lanterns and bright red walls, specializes in Cantonese dishes and has a good reputation, good and filling noodle soups and spring rolls at lunchtime. Open daily 1200-1430 and 1800-2230.
♔ **Kowloon Garden**, Nginyo Towers, Koinange St, T020-318885. Standard but authentic food, good service, Peking duck and steamed chicken, some wines and spirits in the bar, also does takeaway and delivers.
♔ **Mr Wok**, Capital Centre, Mombasa Rd, T020-318885. Stylish with black and red simple decor and Chinese lanterns. Good food that you can watched being cooked in woks in the open kitchen, try the fish in hot garlic sauce or very good beef with green pepper. Open daily 1200-2200.
♔ **Panda**, located Fedha Towers, Kaunada, T020-213018. Good food especially the Peking duck, lots of vegetarian options, Chinese chefs and friendly staff. Open daily 1200-1500, 1800-2200.

Indian

♔♔♔ **Haandi**, Westlands Mall, T020-448294, www.haandi-restaurants.com. Excellent northern Indian cuisine. Very authentic dishes prepared by imported chefs, each dish is prepared with the utmost of attentiveness and the emphasis here is very much to relish the gourmet food and service, one of the best Indian restaurants in Africa. Open daily, 1230-1500, 1830-until late.
♔♔♔ **Haveli Restaurant**, Capital Centre, Mombasa Rd, T020-531607, www.haandi-restaurants.com. Excellent quality, very authentic food, huge with modern decor, parking. Open daily 1200-1500, 1800-late.
♔♔♔ **Minar**, Barclays Plaza in the city, T020-3743741, and ABC Place, Westlands, T020-650403. Northern Indian food, good for vegetarians, the tandoori dishes are very good, buffet lunches, friendly service. Must book ahead. Open 1230-1430, 1900-2230.
♔ **Pepper's**, Parklands Rd, opposite the Holiday Inn, T020-3755267. Specializes in Indian Tawa cuisine, also have a chicken rotisserie and shwarma machines, stylish decor with wooden chairs and tables, it's in a big house so you can eat inside or outside, full bar though drinks are served with meals only. Open daily 1200-1530, 1900-2230.

Italian

♔♔♔ **Il Casale**, Mpaka Rd, Westlands, T020-4440892. Authentic Italian atmosphere, run by an Italian, Bruno, decorated in lots of dark wood and bottles of red wine, imported parma ham and cheese, home-made pasta, pizzeria, seafood and meat, desserts.
♔♔♔ **Le Prugna D'oro**, Intercontinental Hotel, City Hall Way and Uhuru Highway, T020-32000000, nairobi@interconti.com. Superb Italian with real Italian chefs, pasta, meat, seafood dishes, lovely decor with drapes and paintings, white table cloths and fine china. Open Mon-Sat 1200-1500, 1900-2245.
♔♔♔ **Osteria del Chianti**, Nyangumi Rd, off Lenana Rd, T020-2723173. Cosy and intimate Italian with a friendly atmosphere, some outside tables under umbrellas, elegant decor, a vast range of food from melon and parma ham or fish carpaccio to start, followed by pasta, and huge slices of creamy tiramisu. Open daily 1200-1600, 1900-2400.
♔♔♔ **Salumeria**, Valley Arcade, Lavington, T020-575226. A small place with tables

outside that serves very good home-made pasta and antipasta, excellent reputation, Italian wines. Sun-Fri 1200-late, Sat 1700-late.

Café Latino, Village Market, Limaru Rd, T020-7122661. High-quality food, home-made pastas and good range of wines, some seafood, attractive outside terrace with large umbrellas. Open 1100-2200, closed Mon.

La Scala, Phoenix House Arcade, Standard St, T020-332130.Ignore the dark and forbidding external appearance. Quiet at lunchtime but gets lively with a local crowd in the evenings. Trendy, friendly, good pizza, pasta, steaks and cakes, cappuccino and shakes.

Lebanese

Phoenician, Karuna Rd, behind the Sarit Centre, Westlands, T020-3744279. Lebanese and continental dishes, pitta bread and pizzas cooked in a wood-burning oven, plenty of vegetarian options, mezzes, also has a delicatessen for olives, hummus and the like, inside and outside tables and children's play area in the garden. Open Tue-Sun, 1130-late.

◑ Bars and clubs

Bars

Eating, drinking and dancing are the most popular evening entertainments in Nairobi. There are a number of popular bars and clubs, and a number of casinos. Single men should expect a lot of attention from girls and prostitutes. As with most establishments in Kenya, dress is casual with the exception of bars in the upmarket hotels.

Aksum, Nairobi Serena Hotel. Cocktail bar with an Ethiopian theme, expensive but atmospheric, snacks, specialist coffees, salsa on Sat, jazz on Tue. Open daily 0800-2400.

The Cork, Village Market Shopping Centre, Limuru Rd. Live music, modern interior, snacks, dance floor, modern paintings, live jazz on Sat and open mike on Thu, nice atmosphere. Open daily 0830-late.

Gypsy Bar, Woodvale Grove, opposite Barclays Bank, Westlands. Consistently popular, especially with expats, lots of atmosphere, infectious Latin and flamenco music, delicious tapas, packed on weekend nights. Open daily 1200-1500, and 1800-late.

Hidden Agenda, Sarit Centre, Westlands. Cosy pub, continental dishes and grills, extensive bar, popular. Open daily 1200-late.

Jockey Club, Hilton Hotel. Very popular, all dark wood and booths, very English, beer on tap, smoky. Open daily until about 0200.

Lord Delamere's Bar, The Norfolk, T020-250900. A popular spot for Kenya's white settlers from 1904 who used to come to the terrace bar for gin and tonics. Very atmospheric, continental food served too.

Modern 24-Hour Green Bar, Latema Rd. This is the authentic African city side of Nairobi. If you want to drink all day and night and are not too fussy about your surroundings try here but its pretty rough.

Safari Bar, Intercontinental Hotel, City Hall Way. Comfortable pub atmosphere, different music each night, jazz on Mon, karaoke on Tue, Salsa on Wed and Fri, R'n'B on Thu, rock on Sat, and DJ on Sun. Open daily 1700-0045.

Shooters Cocktail Restaurant, Murang'a Rd, opposite Meridian Ct. Tastefully modern and spacious cocktail bar. Open day and night with good food, drinks and music.

Thorn Tree, Stanley, is a good meeting place but the service is slow. If you are there at lunchtime (1100 to 1400) or dinner time (1700 to 1900) you must order food too.

Clubs

Many of the bars already listed have dance floors, and many of the hotels have clubs.

K1 and K2 Klub House, 2 adjacent venues on Ojijo Rd, Parklands, T020-751310. **K1** has pool tables, dance floors on 2 floors. Wed night is salsa night with free salsa lessons. **K2** is a stylish modern pub with big TV screens for watching sport, pool tables, disco, Wed is Kenyan music and Sun is Soul Nite. Open daily from 0800 till the early hours.

Mambo Club, Westlands Rd, International Casino, large and flashy club, up to date music, snacks at the casino, open until 0600.

The New Florida and **Florida 2000**, at Chai House, Koinange St, T020-334870, and Moi Av, T020-226457, respectively, are both very popular and they are heaving at the weekends. They have fairly good sound systems and lights and stay open until 0600.

These are fun places to visit and are certainly real eye openers, but it is best to visit in a group and don't take anything valuable with you. Prostitutes abound and they will think nothing of putting hands in trousers and have been known to rob tourists so watch out! **The Florida** is probably where the term 'the Nairobi handshake' comes from!

The Pavement Club 'n' Cafe, Westview Centre, Ring Rd, Westlands, T020-4441711, is a trendy club venue, also serves excellent and expensive international and Thai food until 2300 (see under Eating), very colourful decor, popular with a wide range of ages and groups, predominantly Nairobi residents. Fri and Sat nights are the liveliest. US$5, open Wed, Fri, Sat and Sun until late.

Simba Saloon, Carnivore, see Eating, Langata Rd, T020-501709. Live bands every Wed popular with expats, and Sun draws in the Asian community. Very large dance floor and good modern music, a fun night out after eating at the restaurant. Entry US$4, open until about 0400.

● Entertainment

Arts centres
Mzizi Cultural Centre, T020-245364/6, 6th Floor Sonalux House, Moi Av, close to Hilton Hotel, is a gallery and houses works of Kenyan contemporary artists, as well as offering daily performances of music, story telling and poetry reading. You can pick up the latest copy of its magazine, *SANAA* (meaning 'art' in Kiswahili), which lists theatre performances, shows, film screenings etc.

Casinos
The oldest is the **International Casino**, T020-744477, also housing Mambo nightclub. **RKL Casino**, in the Intercontinental, on Uhuru Highway. **Casino de Paradise**, in the Safari Park on Thika Rd. **Florida Casino**, corner Uhuru Highway and University Way. **Mayfair Casino**, in the Holiday Inn on Parklands Rd. **Celebrities Casino**, in the Esso Plaza, Muthaiga; and one in the **680 Hotel**.

Cinemas
Fox, Thika Rd, T020-802293, a drive-in; **Nairobi**, Uchumi House, Moi Av, T020-241614; **Kenya**, on Moi Av, T020-227822; **20th Century**, the most expensive on Mama Ngina St, T020-338070;

Sarit Centre Cinema, Westlands; **Casino Cinema**, Ndumberi Rd, T020-229492.

Music
African Heritage Café, Banda St, has live bands most weekends.
Carnivore, Langata Rd, has a live band, usually rock, every Wed.
Nairobi Music Society, choral concerts are held at All Saints' Cathedral.
Nairobi Orchestra gives occasional shows.
Simba Grill, Panafric Hotel, Kenyatta Av, has resident bands playing Thu, Fri and Sat.

Theatre
The local papers have notices of what's on. **Kenya National Theatre**, opposite the Norfolk, Harry Thuku Rd, T020-220536, and **National Theatre**, have productions. **Professional Centre** has performances at the **Phoenix Theatre**, Parliament Rd, T020-212661. Although a small group they are the most active and produce a range of drama of a very high standard.
There are 2 high standard amateur groups, **Lavington Players** and **Nairobi Players**, who present a range of comedies, musicals and pantomimes, all of which are very popular.

○ Shopping

Bookshops
Books First, Nakumatt, Monrovia St, and at the Ukay Centre in Westlands, is an excellent new chain. They have a good selection of imported books and cafés with good coffee, alcoholic drinks, internet access. 0700-late.

The Nation, Kenyatta Av, next to the Thorn Tree Café, has a good selection of fiction and non-fiction, as well as maps and helpful staff. **Select**, Kimathi St, opposite the Stanley, is larger although rather run-down. There is a good but small antique East African section.

Other bookshops that stock a fairly good African selection include the **Book Corner** and **Prestige**, both located on Mama Ngina St, while the **Text Book Centre**, at the Sarit Centre in Westlands, has text books as well as fiction. There's also a number of book stalls along **Tom Mboya St** and **Latema Rd** where you may be able to pick up a few bargain second-hand books.

Clothing

There is a cluster of shops selling material and cloth squares (*kangas* and *kikois*) on Biashara St quite close to the market. Here you can also watch tailors on their foot-propelled machines sewing clothes, cushions etc and stitching some of the most elaborate embroidery at amazing speed. There are lots of places that will kit you out in safari gear. **Colpro** on Kimathi St is recommended as good quality and reliable.

Kikois (cotton sarongs) are popular all over the world today, and are also made into brightly coloured clothes, though their traditional home is East Africa, check out www.kikoy.com.

Handicrafts and souvenirs

There are a huge number of souvenir shops in Nairobi. They vary enormously in terms of price and quality. Be sure to have a good look – wood that may look like ebony may in fact just have been polished with black shoe polish. Also cracks may appear in the wood (particularly when it is placed in a centrally heated room) if it has not been properly seasoned. At stalls you will be able to bargain the prices down to between a third and a half of the original asking price.

African Heritage, Banda St, and Libra House, Mombasa Rd, T020-530054, www.africanheritage.ne. A vast collection of original works of art and tribal sculptures from all parts of Africa, and authentic artefacts from Kenya. There are 6 lines of jewellery and hand-painted beads. Banda St branch has a café for snacks and drinks, and at Libra House, there is a salad and juice bar.

Antique Gallery, Kaunda St, T020-227759, and **Antique Auction**, Moktar Daddah St, T020-336383, have antique East African artefact collections.

Gallery Watatu, first floor, Lonhro House, Standard St, T020-218737, www.gallerywat

atu.com. Showcases contemporary African paintings, a formal art gallery with spacious and well-lit exhibition space. 1000-1700.

Kariakor Market, Ring Rd at Ngara, is perhaps the best place for baskets.

Persian Bazaar, Barclays Plaza, Market St. Persian carpets, kilims, hand-blown glassware and African curios.

Rupas, T020-224417, has an outstanding selection of gift purchases, good quality, courteous staff and competitve prices.

Spinners Web, Kijabe St close to **The Norfolk**, is a good craft shop, in particular for fabrics and baskets. Its merchandise comes from various self-help groups around the country and the staff are very helpful.

Zanzibar Curio Shop, Moi Av, has the best prices on curios, the prices are marked and there's no haggling. Established in 1936, it sells batiks, jewellery, safari wear, Arabian chests, sisal baskets, ebony carvings and African semi-precious stones.

Markets and supermarkets

City Market, Muindi Mbingo St, sells fruit and vegetables, curio stalls stock armies of wooden giraffes amongst other crafts. Around the market and the Jamia Mosque stalls sell baskets, wooden and soapstone carvings, bracelets and lots of other souvenirs. Be prepared to bargain and go in late afternoon, as prices are lowest just before they close.

Masai Market, where over 350 traders and artists sell their work. This is held near the Globe Cinema, on Tue, and at the **Village Market Shopping Centre**, Limuru Rd, on Fri.

Photography

There are a number of camera shops and places to get film developed along Mama Ngina St, so it is worth shopping around. Recommended is **Camera Experts**, Mama Ngina St, T020-337750. Also try **Elite Camera House**, opposite the Stanley, for repairs and and equipment.

Supermarkets and shopping centres

Nakumatt chain of shops is a good source of household goods and processed food. One on Nanyuki Rd and Uhuru Highway. Sell some camping equipment too. Another big chain is Uchumi, with branches in the Sarit Centre in Westlands and the Village Market.

▲▲ Activities and tours

Cricket

Nairobi Gymkhana Simba Union Club, off Forest Rd, in Parklands, T020-741310. **Aga Khan**, Matam Ln, off Parklands Av, Parklands, T020-742930. Exciting league games played on Sat and Sun, with good crowds. Take taxi from town centre, US$4.

Golf

There are a number of very well-kept golf courses in the suburbs of Nairobi, although you will need to take out temporary membership. All of Kenya's 35 golf courses are listed at www.golfinginkenya.com.

Karen Country Club, Karen Rd, T020-882801, generalmanager@karen.or.ke. This is famous for its beautiful 18-hole championship course and lawn terrace. Many of the trees seen on the fairways are indigenous to Kenya. The sophisticated irrigation system, the maintenance of the fairways and the flowering bushes and trees give the course the look of a lovingly cared for garden. Founded in 1933 by the Karen Estates Company Ltd.

Muthaiga Golf Club, Muthaiga Rd, T020-2762414. 18-hole golf course first laid out in 1912, home to the Kenya Golf Union and plays host to the most prestigious golfing event in the country, the Kenya Open.

Railway Golf Club, Ngong Rd, T020-728920, is bisected by the railway, which can put you off your game when trains are coming through, as they do 6 times a day.

Windsor Golf & Country Club, T020-862300, 9 km north of Nairobi on Garden Estate Rd, T020-862300, www.windsorgolf resort.com. Another stunning well-tended course, the resort is best suited for people on specific golfing holidays.

Horse racing

Jockey Club of Kenya Race Tracks, at **Ngong Racecourse**, Ngong Rd, T020-573923, jck@karibunet.com, which holds meetings most Sun except Aug. The Delamere Gold is on 28 Nov. It is a wonderful setting as well as being a great place to observe all sections of Nairobi society. It's also good for children with extra activities include face painting and bouncy castles. Entry fee is US$4 to the Main Enclosure and US$0.75 to the Gold Ring. A new addition is the 9-hole golf course and driving range in the middle of the racecourse. Green fees start from US$8.

Polo

Weather permitting, polo is played on Sat and Sun at **Jamhuri Club**, Dagoretti Corner, Ngong Rd. In Kenya, polo is a relatively popular sport, although it is considered a sport of the elite. A number of tournaments are held in Nairobi, and have attracted top polo players and international teams.

Riding

Hardy Stud, Hardy Estate, Karen, T020-722737, www.hoofbeat.biz. This stud offers horse riding in the countryside around Karen, including daily rides to Lenana, Ngong and Olalua forests. There is a weight limit of up to 95 kg and you have to know how to ride, US$12.50 per hr.

Sporting clubs

British settlers introduced sporting clubs to their colonies and Kenya still maintains a strong legacy of sporting clubs suitable for individuals and families. Most clubs offer standard facilities such as swimming pools, squash and badminton courts and field sports. In addition, there are recreational bars and restaurants. Other clubs offer golf, cricket, rugby, hockey, tennis or sailing. Indoor games and sports include snooker, pool, billiards and darts. Club membership costs vary but most offer temporary membership to visitors.

Nairobi Railways Club, Haile Selassie Av, T020-725125; **Ruaraka Sports Club**, Thika Rd, T020-860280; **United Kenya Club**, State House Rd, T020-725638; **Parklands Sports Club**, Ojijo Rd, Parklands, T020-745164.

Swimming

Most of the big hotels have swimming pools that can also be used by non-residents for a daily fee of about US$2. The pool at **YMCA** is particularly good.

DRIVE YOUR
MOUSE WILD!

UNIGLOBE
beyond expectation **Travel**

Head Office, Nairobi.
Tel: (254-20) 4447151/4441030.
E-mail:info@letsgosafari.com
www.letsgosafari.com

With 400 lodges, hotels, community
lodges and 200 safaris to choose from,
click your mouse onto www.letsgotravel.com
and you can find yourself on a comprehensive
journey in East Africa. Let our experienced travel
advisors help you find that special place in Kenya.

Ten-pin bowling
Cosmic Bowling and Pool Centre,
The Village Market, T020-522488/9.

Tours

There are a number of minibus tours for either a morning or an afternoon, arranged by any of the tour companies in Nairobi. The cost can vary; if you are lucky you may be able to negotiate a price of less than US$40 per person, although you are more likely to be quoted a price upwards of US$45. See tour operators below for recommended companies and Excursions, page 70, for details of the surrounding parks.

Tour operators

There are numerous tour operators based in Nairobi where you should be able to get fairly reliable information, book safaris etc. It is important to find an operator that you like, offers good service, and does not pressurize you into booking something that is not what you are looking for.
Especially recommended are:
Bunson Travel Service, Pan Africa House, Standard St, T020-221992-4, www.bunson. co.ke. Good, reliable, well-established travel and tour agent. Does flight and rail bookings, car hire, safaris and hotel bookings.
Gametrackers, 5th floor, Nginyo Towers, Moktar Daddah St, T020-222703, www. game trackers.com. Well-established company organizing camping safaris with both vehicles and camels to Lake Turkana and the Ndoto Mts, as well as biking and walking safaris. Its 8- and 10-day trips to northern Kenya are probably the best and most affordable on offer. They go to the Kalacha Desert, Lake Turkana and Maralal, including a camel safari. Recommended.
Hoopoe Safaris, inside Wilson Airport, T020-604303-4, UK address: PO Box 278, Watford WD19 4WH, T01923-255462, www.hoopoe.com, has been consistently recommended by a number of travellers. Condé Nast Traveler (USA) magazine voted them the best Eco Tourism Operator in the World for 2004. This is the first time any African company has won this prestigious award. It has an excellent commitment to the local communities and conservation.

A range of safaris and climbs and unusual trekking itineraries.
Origins Safaris, www.originsafaris.info. A special interest safari operator with 40 years' experience based in Kenya but covering much of east and central Africa. Main areas of expertise are safaris using a combination of private lodges, tented camps and its own mobile tented camps, cultural expeditions and tours to emerging destinations especially in central Africa. It supports a wildlife research and conservation education centre in Tsavo. Here volunteers pay a nominal amount to cover costs and spend weeks or months with scientists and researchers or volunteering their skills to assist the development of local communities in the area to enhance their economic status and reduce human/wildlife conflict. One of Africa's best tour operators, but not cheap, arrangements are between US$5,000-8,000 per person. It does not take direct bookings; you need to go through an agent, if you email, it will send a list of its agents.
SunTrek Tours and Travel, Safari Centre, Waiyaki Way, T020-4442982, T0722-758171 (mob), www.suntreksafaris.com. Excellent tour operator that organizes tailormade lodge safaris, plus adventure activities such as whitewater rafting, trekking, including Mt Kenya climb, scuba diving on the coast, also can combine with safaris to Tanzania, has an impressive fleet of 25 smart safari landcruisers, 4WD vehicle hire, the sample itineraries on the website can be adapted to suit what you want to do and your budget. Very professional.
UNIGLOBE Let's Go Travel, 1st floor, ABC Place, Waiyaki Way, Westlands, T020-4447151, Caxton House, Standard St, in the city centre, T020-4441030, Karen Shopping Centre, T020-882505 (as well as offices in Uganda), www.letsgosafari. com. Very professional tour operator offering reasonably priced balloon safaris, camel safaris, horseback safaris, fishing, golf, walking, trekking and climbing, diving, water sports and whitewater rafting. A well-organized company, it acts as agents for several other companies, and publishes price and information lists of hotels, camps and lodges. Well recommended. Organizes travel all over East Africa.

Other highly recommended operators include:

Abercrombie and Kent, Mombasa Rd, T020-6950000, www.abercrombiekent.com, arranges some of the most luxurious safaris in Kenya. It has good relations with top wildlife photographers, writers, historians, anthropologists and other specialists who can host dinners and lead safari and excursion groups.

Acacia Trails, T020-501858/608487, www.africantravelreview.com. Established operator with over 40 years of experience, offers fully guided safaris utilizing two superbly designed luxury tented camps of its own, in addition to a collection of other tented camps and bush homes.

Across Africa Safaris, Bruce House, Standard St, T020-315535, www.acrossafricasafaris. co.ke. A variety of safaris with a big fleet of vehicles, also has an office in Mombasa.

Adventure Naturetrek Safaris, Vedic House, Mama Ngina St, opposite International Life House, T020-341188, www.naturetreksafaris. com.

Adventure Penfam Tours & Travel, Trust Building, Moi Av, T0722 877149 (mob), www.penfamtours.com.

AustralKen Tours & Travel, Sonalux House, 8th floor, Moi Av, T020-222297, www.australken.com.

Basecamp Explorer, Ole Odume, T020-572139, www.basecampexplorer.com.

Best Camping Tours and Safaris Ltd, corner of Kenyatta Av and Muindu Mbingu St, opposite Six Eighty Hotel, T020-229667.

Bike Treks, T020-446371, www.biketreks. co.ke. Organizes reasonably priced walking/ cycling tours, supported by a back-up vehicle, including a 3-day Masai Mara safari. Excellent value.

Breakaway Expeditions Africa, Mama Ngina St, T020-342974, www.breakaway expedition.com.

Bush and Beyond/Bush Homes of East Africa Ltd, T020-600457, www.bush-and -beyond.com and www.bush-homes.co.ke. Reservations for some of the more exclusive camps, all over US$500 per person per night in the Masai Mara, Lewa Conservancy and Amboseli.

Call of Africa Safaris, Uganda House, 3rd Floor, T020-229729 www.call-of-africa-safaris. com. Lodge safaris, beach accommodation and car hire. Recommended for its quality of service.

Cheli and Peacock Safaris, Parklands, T020-604053, www.chelipeacock.com.

Dallago Tours and Safaris, Othaya Rd, Kileleshwa, T020-572845, www.dallago tours.com. New and expanding company receiving good reviews, all safaris, cultural tours, mountain climbing and hotel reservations.

Den and Burrows Safaris, 2nd floor, Beaver House, Tom Mboya St, T0720-770575 (mob), www.denburrowssafaris.com.

Derviv Tours & Car Hire, Standard Building, Standard St, T020-230557, www.dervivtours.com.

Express Travel Group, 2nd floor, Middle East Bank Tower, T020-334722, www.etg-safaris.com.

East African Wildlife Safaris, T020-605350, www.eaws.kenyaweb.com. Very upmarket safaris on offer, all tailormade to the best lodges and camps, the company was originally started by Richard Leakey in 1966.

Gamewatchers, Village Market, T020-7123129, www.porini.com.

Going Places, Westlands Centre, Mapaka Rd, Westlands, T020-4442312, www.goingplaceskenya.com.

Kenya & Beyond Safaris, 5th floor, Norwich Union House, Mama Ngina St, T020-607014, www.kenyaandbeyondsafaris.com.

Kenyun Tours Company, Masaba Rd, T020-2728540, www.kenyunafrica.com.

Mountain Rock Kenya, Jubilee Insurance House, junction of Wabera and Kaunda sts, T020-242133, www.mountainrockkenya.com.

Oasis Sunset Travel, K.C.B Bldg, Jogoo Rd, T020-537605, www.oasissunset-travel.com. Predators Safari Club, www.predators-safaris. Com, offers good safari options throughout Kenya and Tanzania.

Safari Camp Services, corner of Koinange and Moktar Daddah sts, T020-228936, www.safaricampserv.com. This company is famous for its long-established and well-recommended *Turkana Bus* and *Wildlife Bus* services, which offer excellent value to the budget traveller. Camel trekking options are also available in combination with the *Turkana Bus* trip.

Savage Wilderness Safaris Ltd, Thigiri Rd, T/F020-521590, whitewater@alphanet.co.ke, (also 22 Wilson Av, Henley, Oxon, UK,

T01491-574752, and 925 31 St Av, Seattle, WA 98122, T206-3231220). Whitewater river rafting on several Kenyan rivers.

Savuka Tours and Safaris Ltd, Pan Africa House, 4th Floor, Kenyatta Av, T020-215256, www.savukatravels.com. Offers very good value for budget travellers, including student card reductions. Open to negotiation on prices.

Shoor Safaris, PO BOX 13908, T733-736131, T203740407, www.shoortravel.com. Good safari operator (also has an office in Nakuru).

Sights of Africa Safari Company, 4th floor, Asili Co-operative Building, Moi Av/Muranga Rd, T020-247439. Highly recommended.

Sights of Africa Tours & Travel, Gilfillan House, Kenyatta Av, T020-249967, www.sightsofafricaea.com.

Somak Safaris, Mombasa Rd, T020-535508, www.somak-nairobi.com.

Tobs Golf Safaris, T020-721722, www.kenya-golf-safaris.com. Golf specialist.

🚌 Transport

For getting around the city there are plenty of buses, *matatus* and taxis, all of which are very cheap. Both buses and *matatus* are almost always full and you should beware of pickpockets when travelling in them. The most popular form of public transport in Kenya is the *matatu*, which has become a national icon and a large part of Kenyan modern culture. A *matatu* is a minibus, usually a Nissan, with a 3 tonne capacity, hence the name *Matatu – tatu* is 3 in Kiswahili.

Air

The main airport is Jomo Kenyatta International Airport, T020-822111, 15 km southeast of the city, connected by a good dual carriageway. There is a small fee of US$0.75 per car to get into the airport and you may have to pay this on top of the taxi fare. There is also Wilson Airport, 6 km south of the city, on Langata Rd, T020-501943, from which smaller planes, including many internal charter flights, leave. See Ins and outs, page 62, for details regarding transport to and from the airports.

Kenya Airways, www.kenya-airways.com, has daily flights to **Kisumu**, **Malindi**, **Lamu** and **Mombasa** from Jomo Kenyatta Airport.
Air Kenya, based at Wilson Airport, T020-605745, www.airkenya.com, has scheduled flights between Nairobi and **Amboseli**, **Kilimanjaro**, **Kiwayu**, **Lamu**, **Malindi**, **Nanyuki**, **Masai Mara** and **Samburu**. Specific schedules are detailed under each relevant chapter.

Airlines

Air India, Jeevan Bharati Building, Harambee Av, T020-334662, www.airindia.com.
Air Kenya, Wilson Airport, T020-605745, www.airkenya.com. **Air Malawi**, International House, Mama Ngina St, T020-240965, www.airmalawi.com. **Air Mauritius**, International House, Mama Ngina St, T020-229166, kirui@airmauritius.co.ke. **Air Seychelles**, Lonrho House, Standard St, T020-229359. **Air Zimbabwe**, Chester House, Koinanage St, T020-339522, www.airzimbabwe.com.
British Airways, International House, Mama Ngina St, T020-3277000, www.britishairways.com. **EgyptAir**, Hilton Hotel Arcade, City Hall Way, T020-226821. **Emirates**, Viewpark Towers, T020-211900. **Ethiopian Airlines**, Standard St, T020-822285, www.flyethiopia.com. **Gulf Air**, International House, Mama Ngina St, T020-241133, www.gulfairco.com. Offers very competitive prices to Europe.
Kenya Airways, Barclays Plaza, 5th floor, Loita St, T020-32074100, airport office T020-32823535, www.kenya-airways.com.
KLM/Northwest Airlines, Barclays Bank Plaza, Loita St, T020-3274747, www.klm.com.
Lufthansa, Ambank House, University Way, T020-226271, www.lufthansa.com. **Qantas Airways**, Rehema House, Kaunda St, T020-213221, www.quantas.co.au. **Saudia Arabian Airlines**, Anniversary Towers, University Way, T020-230337. **South African Airways**, International House, Mama Ngina St, T020-229663, www.flysaa.com. **Swiss International**, Caltex Plaza, Limuru Rd, T020-3746663. **Uganda Airlines**, Uganda House, Kenyatta Av, T020-221354.

Bus

Local

Central Bus Station, T020-2246067. The main city bus terminal is located at the end of River Rd and there are main bus stops outside the **Hilton Hotel** on Moi Av, outside Nation House on Tom Mboya St, outside the Railway Station at the end of Moi Av, and outside the General Post Office on Kenyatta Av. The buses cover all the routes and operate as early as 0600 and as late as midnight, and each bus has an assigned route number. Useful numbers are 34 to the airport from the Hilton stop, and 111 to Karen from in front of the Railway Station. Most buses are pale blue city buses, but increasingly newer City Hoppers are appearing on the streets that are green.

Long distance

The long-distance bus station is on Landhies Rd. Buses go from Nairobi to a variety of long-haul destinations both within Kenya and in neighbouring countries. There are at least daily departures to almost every destination. The timetable is fairly flexible. For a long journey you will be told to arrive at 0700 or earlier, but the bus will not go until it is full. For information and bookings there are a number of coach company offices along Accra Rd. Remember the area around River Rd where the bus station and bus offices are located is renowned for being unsafe. Beware of robbery and look after your luggage at all times.

Recommended for long-distance journeys is **Akamba Bus**, a private company offering a very good level of service. It is not the cheapest option but the buses are well maintained and have a good safety record. There are many companies to choose for buses between **Nairobi** and **Mombasa** and they go frequently, taking 7-8 hrs, the standard services costing around US$10. There are daily bus services between Nairobi and the Ugandan capital, **Kampala**.

There are daily shuttle services to **Arusha** and **Moshi** in Tanzania. The operators utilize 20- to 30-seat buses with comfortable, individual seating. They pick up at the major hotels and depart Nairobi each day at 0800 and 1400, and take about 4½ hrs to Arusha, and 5½ hrs to Moshi. These services cost

US$25 and can be arranged through the hotel receptions, or through a tour operator.

Akamba Bus has 2 departures, one during the day and an overnight service. The first service leaves Nairobi at 0700, arriving at Kampala at around 1800. The overnight service departs at 2100, arriving the following morning at 1000. Akamba also operate a 'Royal Service' on this route where the buses carry less passengers, have slightly bigger seats and are generally more comfortable. The border posts normally used are Busia and Malaba where immigration procedures are completed. Visas for most nationalities can be obtained at the border. Passengers departing for **Jinja** can also use this service. Travellers can also travel from Nairobi to **Dar es Salaam** on a same day service via Arusha in Tanzania.

Two companies, **Akamba** and **Scandinavian Express** (an equally good Tanzanian company), operate on a daily basis departing Nairobi at 0700 and arriving in Dar around 2030, US$20-25. The border at Lunga Lunga is again efficient and visas can be purchased.

Akamba Bus, Lagos Rd, off Latema Rd, T020-221779. **City Link Express**, River Rd, T020-218605. **Coastline Safaris**, Accra/Duruma Rd, T020-245840. **Garex**, General Waruinge St, T020-760011. **Goldline**, Cross Rd, T020-225279. **Gusii Deluxe**, Temple Rd, T020-220059. **Kenya Bus Service**, General Waruinge St, T020-229707. **Malindi Bus Services**, Duruma/Kumasi Rd, T020-229662. **Riverside Shuttle**, Pan Africa Insurance House, Kenyatta Av, T020-229618, www. riverside-shuttle.com. As well as Moshi and Arusha, **Riverside** can organize transfers from Nairobi to Kilimanjaro International Airport in Tanzania. **Scandi navaian Express**, River Rd, T020-242523, www.scanindaviangroup.com. **Sunbird Services**, Accra Rd, T020-251310. **Tawfiq Bus Services**, Duruma Rd, T020-338920.

Car

Cars can be rented easily in Kenya, with or without a driver. You will usually need to be over 25 years of age and have a drivers' licence. Driving in Nairobi is a bit of an art and you will have to get used to a large number of roundabouts with rather bizarre

lane systems. The right of way is usually (but not always) given to traffic already on the roundabout. Be prepared for a lot of hooting, traffic-light jumping and the odd pothole. Parking is a problem and you will be pestered by parking boys. Policies towards these vary although there is no evidence that it is necessary to pay them to ensure the safety of your vehicle. There is a multi-storey car park at the Intercontinental Hotel (around US$1 per hr). Car hire rates obviously vary, but try **Central Hire a Car** for the best deal. For more information see Getting around, page 30. Companies include:
Avis Rent a Car, University Way, T020-316061, Karen office, T020-883791, Village Market shopping centre, T020-522080, airport, T020-333082 (24 hrs), www.aviskenya.com.
Budget, Muindi Mbingu St, T020-223581, T020-223582, Airport, Arrivals Terminal, T020-822370, www.budget-kenya.com.
Central Hire a Car, Six Eighty Hotel, Muindi Mbingu St, T020-222888, www.carhirekenya.com.
Crossways, Banda St, T020-223949, F214372, can arrange hire cars suitable for organizing your own safari.
Europ Car, Airport, Arrivals Terminal, T020-822625, www.europcar.com.
Glory Car Hire Ltd, Hilton Hotel building, T020-352476, www.glorycarhire.com.
Hertz, at the Stanley Hotel on Standard St, T020-311143, www.hertz.co.ke.
UNIGLOBE Let's Go Travel, ABC Place, Waiyaki Way, Westlands, T020-447151, Karen Shopping Centre, T020-882505, www.letsgosafari.com.

Matatu

Local
Matatus are assigned to set routes within the city. They are usually Nissan 14-seater minibuses. They collect as many passengers as possible both from the outset and along the way, and passengers board and alight whenever and wherever they choose. Matatus normally have a crew of two, a driver and a 'tout' who tries to encourage as many passengers as possible to board, and collects their fares, using an impressive cash handling and management system in which notes of different denominations are wedged between separate fingers. Until a

few years ago, the vehicles were often spectacularly painted, but these days they are mostly uniform white with a yellow stripe and their destination painted along the side. Also these days they are only permitted to carry a maximum of 14 passengers on seats with seat belts, so overcrowding is a thing of the past. Most matatu rides within Nairobi cost US$0.20.

Long distance
Matatus do run on certain routes within a couple of hours from Nairobi such as Nakuru, Naivasha, and the Namanga border with Tanzania. There are regular departures and they go when full. For longer distances you need to swap matatus in the regional centres to get any further.

Taxi

Available outside cinemas, restaurants, hotels and at official taxi stands. Your hotel will order one for you. They cannot be hailed in the street but are easy enough to find on street corners. It is recommended that you should always take a taxi if you want to get around at night. A taxi to the airport costs approximately US$12, but you may be charged more on arrival. The taxis are usually metered, although this is not always the case so you need to agree a price with the driver before setting off. A short journey within the city centre should cost US$3-5. Like matatus, Nairobi taxis are marked with a yellow line along each side. There is also a large fleet of large black London taxis operating within the city.

Train

Nairobi Railway Station, T020-221211, is to the south of Haile Selassie Av, at the very end of Moi Av. The overnight train that runs between Nairobi and **Mombasa** is an historic and authentic rail experience and is an excellent way of getting to the coast. It departs Nairobi at 1900 on Mon, Wed and Fri and arrives in Mombasa at 0830. In the other direction it departs Mombasa on Sat, Tue and Thu at 1900 and arrives in Nairobi at 0900. Bear in mind delays do occur and sometimes the train maybe a few hours late, so do not arrange onward travel arrangements too close to the scheduled arrival times. First class is in cabins that sleep 2 people in bunks and includes bedding and a sink, 2nd class is 4 people in bunks but with no bedding, and 3rd class is seating in carriages that take up to 80 people. First class is very comfortable and recommended. There is a good restaurant car where 1st- and 2nd-class passengers can have dinner and drinks, though you may want to bring additional drinks and snacks with you. Tickets; 1st class, US$40; 2nd class, US$30; and 3rd class, US$6. It is essential to make reservations in advance and this can be done personally at the stations or through a tour operator or travel agent.

Tuk tuk

The 3-wheel Bajaj auto-rickshaw or tuk tuk of southeast Asia are becoming increasingly popular as taxis in Nairobi. Once again, fares need to be negotiated in advance.

🛈 Directory

Banks

There are banks all over central Nairobi. Most now have ATM machines although some only accept VISA cards. Best bet for other cards such as Mastercard is the numerous branches of **Barclays** and **Standard Chartered**. The largest Barclays is at the corner of Kenyatta and Moi Ave, where it is possible to withdraw US dollars, and another large branch is on Mama Ngina St near the **Hilton Hotel**.

There are also numerous **bureaux de change**, also known as forex bureaux, far too many to list. Exchange rates are just about the same in most, though commission is charged on changing travellers' cheques so shop around for the best deal. The hotels will also change money but at excessive exchange rates.

Courier companies

DHL, Longonot Place, Kijabe St, T020-223063, **DHL Express centre**, International House, Mama Ngina St, T020-6925120, booking@nbo-co.ke.dhl.com. **Federal Express**, Bruce House, Standard St, T020-240106, www.fedex.com. **United Parcel Service**, Fedha Towers, Kaunda St, T020-252200, www.ups.com. **TNT**, Kiambere Rd, T020-723554, www.tnt.com.

Cultural centres

Other places that have films, concerts and talks, and in some libraries and language courses, include the **Alliance Française**, ICEA Building, Kenyatta Av, T020-336264; **American Cultural Centre**, National Bank Building, Harambee Av, T020-337877; **British Council**, ICEA Building, Kenyatta Av,

T020-334855, www.britishcouncil.org/kenya; **French Cultural Centre**, Maison Française, Loita St, T020-336263, director@alliance frnairobi.org; **Goethe Institute**, Maendeleo House, Monrovia St, T020-211381, nbo-spl @goethe.or.ke; **Italian Cultural Institute**, Prudential Building, Wabera St, T020-340966, iicnbi@iicnairobi.org; **Japan Information Centre**, Kumbu Drive, T020-566262.

Embassies and consulates

Algerian Embassy, Comcraft House, Haile Selassie Av, T020-213866. **Australia**, ICIPE House, Riverside Drive, T020-445034. **Austria**, 2nd floor, City House, Corner Wabera St/ Standard St, T020-247365, austria@africa online.co.ke. **Belgium**, Limuru Rd, T020-741565, nairobi@diplobel.org. **British High Commission**, Upper Hill Rd, T020-714699, information@nairobi.mail.fco.gov.uk. **Burundi**, Development House, Moi Av, opposite the Milimani Police Station, T020-335973. **Canada**, Comcraft House, Haile Selassie Av, T020-226987. **Denmark**, HFCK Building, Koinange St, T020-331088. **Djibouti**, Comcraft House, Haile Selassie Av, T020-339633. **Egypt**, Harambee Plaza, Haile Selassie Av, T020- 225992. **Eritrea**, Rhapta Rd, T020-443164. **Ethiopia**, State House Av, T020-723035. **France**, Barclays Plaza, Loita St, T020-339783. Issues visas for Togo, Senegal, Burkina Faso, Mauritania and the Central African Republic. **Germany**, Williamson House, Ngong Av, T020-712527. **India**, Jeevan Bharati Building, Harambee Av, T020-222566, hcindia@form-net.com. **Ireland**, Waumini House, Chiromo Rd, T020-444367. **Israel**, Bishops Rd, T020-724021. **Italy**, International Life House,

Mama Ngina St, T020-337357. **Japan**, ICEA Building, Kenyatta Av, T020-332956. **Malawi**, Mvuli/Church Rd, Westlands, T/F020-440568. **Morocco**, Diamond Trust House, Moi Av, T020-222264. **Netherlands**, PO Box 41537, Uchumi House, Nkrumah Av, T020-332420, holland@Form-net.com. **Norway**, Rehani House, Kenyatta Av, T020-337121. **Rwanda**, International Life House, Mama Ngina St, T020-212345. **Saudi Arabia**, Muthaiga Rd, T020-762782. **South African High Commission**, Lonrho House, Standard St, T020-215616. **Spain**, Bruce House, Standard St, T020-226568. **Sudan**,Minet ICDC House, T020-720883. **Sweden**, International House, Mama Ngina St, T020-229043. **Switzerland**, International House, Mama Ngina St, T020-228736. **Tanzania**, Continental House, T020-331104. **Uganda**, Uganda House, Kenyatta Av, T020-330814. **United States**, Mombasa Rd, T020-334142, consularnairob@ state.gov. **Zambia**, Nyerere Rd, T020-724799. **Zimbabwe**, Minet ICDC House, Mamlaka Rd, T020-721045.

Internet

A vast number of places now offer internet access all over the city centre. As well as some of the more expensive hotels, options range from smart internet cafés with fast reliable connections, to tiny corner shops that have just one computer and erratic connections. There is little point in listing them as they would fill a fair few pages, but be assured you will come across internet access on just about every street. Costs have come down considerably in recent years, expect to pay about US$1 per hr.

Medical services

Hospitals There are 2 private hospitals, both with good facilities and staff: **Nairobi Hospital**, Argwings Kodhek Rd, T020-2722160, www.nairobihospital.org; **Aga Khan Hospital**, Parklands Ave, Parklands, T020-746309. Avoid the **Kenyatta Hospital**, if you can; although it is free it is not worth trying to save the money as the wait can be so long. If you are planning to travel in more isolated areas, consider the **Flying Doctors' Society of Africa**, based at Wilson Airport.

For an annual tourist fee of US$50, it offers free evacuation by air to a medical centre or hospital. This may be worth considering if you are visiting more remote regions, but not necessary if visiting the more popular parks in the north as adequate provision is made in the case of an emergency. The income goes back into the service and the African Medical Research Foundation (AMREF) behind it. You can contact them in advance; membership/ information on T020-501301, www.amref.org.

Pharmacies These are found all over downtown Nairobi and in all shopping centres but are generally expensive. The major hospitals (see above) have 24-hr pharmacies. Vaccinations are available from **City Hall Clinic** on Mama Ngina St, open mornings only.

Post office

Moi Av, half-way between Kenyatta Av and Tubman Rd on the east side, T020-227401. There is also a post office on Haile Selassie Av, T020-228441, where you will find the fairly reliable, and free, poste restante. Post offices are open 0800-1230 and 1400-1700.

Telephone

Almost opposite the post office on Haile Selassie Av, is the **Extelcoms** office from which you can make international phone calls (3 min minimum period of use) or send faxes. You can also make calls from the **Kenyatta Conference Centre** – the telephone exchange is on the ground floor and it is usually much quieter than the post office. If you are using a Kenya service provider for your cell phone, top up cards for Kenya's two cell networks, Cellnet and Safaricom, are available from their specific shops all around the city and from just about every street vendor. You can only buy phonecards from the Extelcoms office.

Useful numbers

Police Central Police Station, University Way, T020-222222, Nairobi, T020-717777. Always inform the police of any incidents – you will need a police form for any insurance claims. In emergencies dial 999.

Rift Valley

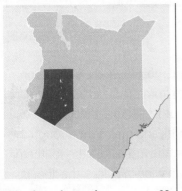

Naivasha and around	98
Nairobi to Naivasha	98
Naivasha	99
Lake Naivasha	99
Hell's Gate National Park	102
Kigloi Wildlife Conservancy	102
Mount Longonot	103
Listings	103
Nakuru and around	**107**
Lake Elementeita	107
Nakuru	107
Lake Nakuru National Park	109
Hyrax Hill Prehistoric Site	111
Rongai	112
Menengai Crater	113
Nyahururu and Thompson's Falls	114
Listings	114
Further north	**118**
Lake Bogaria National Reserve	118
Lake Baringo	119
Northern Rift Valley	121
Listings	121
Masai Mara National Reserve	**123**
Listings	126

⁑ Footprint features

Don't miss...	97
Dwindling flocks	111
Born to run	120

Introduction

The Great Rift Valley is one of the most dramatic features on earth, stretching some 6,000 km from the Dead Sea in Jordan down to Mozambique in the south. In Kenya, the Rift Valley starts at Lake Turkana in the north, and runs right through the centre of the country to Lake Natron just across the southern border in Tanzania. Up to 100 km wide in places, the floor is littered with the famous Rift Valley lakes, such as Nakuru, Naivasha, Baringo and Bogoria, which are surrounded by fascinating cliffs, escarpments, rivers and arid plains. These support an enormous diversity of wildlife, birds, trees and plants. The valley floor rises from around 200 m at Lake Turkana to about 1,900 m above sea level at Lake Naivasha to the south. The walls rise where the valley floor is at its highest, and reach their peak in the Aberdares, above Naivasha. In the south of the region the Masai Mara, bordering the Serengeti in Tanzania, is one of the most exciting game parks in the world, teeming with wildlife and the site of the quite spectacular wildebeest migration. It is also the most likely place to see lions in Kenya.

No visit to Kenya is complete without spending some time in the Rift Valley. The scenery here is wonderful, with Mount Kilimanjaro in the background acting as the perfect backdrop to miles and miles of arid savannah plains covered with fragile grasslands and scrub bush. Evaporation has left a high concentration of alkaline volcanic deposits in the remaining water. The algae and crustaceans that thrive in the soda lakes are ideal food for flamingos and many of these beautiful birds are attracted here, making a truly spectacular display.

★ Don't miss...

1 **Viewpoints on the Rift Valley** Stop and stare at the Rift Valley from the escarpment that leads from Nairobi to Naivasha, page 98.

2 **Lake Naivasha** Stay in one of the many country lodges on the shores of the lake, shaded by trees and offering boat trips and bike rides, page 99.

3 **Hell's Gate National Park** Explore this park by foot, one of the few in Kenya where you can spot raptors, antelope, zebra and giraffe, page 102.

4 **Lake Nakuru National Park** Spend only half a day here and you are bound to trip over rhino. It's also good for leopard, who inhabit the giant yellow acacia trees near the main gate, page 109.

5 **Masai Mara** Balloon over the park at dawn, an expensive activity but highly recommended during the wildebeest migration, page 123.

6 **Masai Mara's Governors' Camps** Stay in one of the camps. The BBC's TV series *The Big Cat Diary* was filmed from here and you may have the opportunity to see the stars of the show, page 126.

Rift Valley

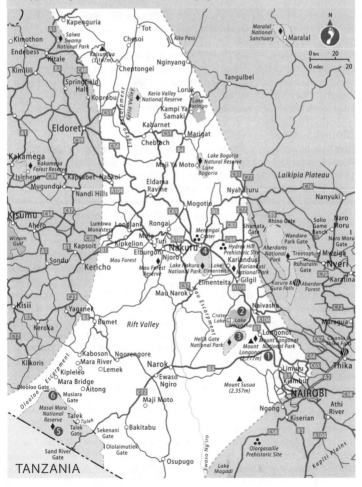

Naivasha and around

Nairobi to Naivasha

There are two roads connecting Nairobi and Navaisha, the A104 and the B3. Both roads are tarred, although potholed, and are very busy routes, since they are the main artery between the country's capital, the Rift Valley and ultimately Uganda. The A104 Nairobi-Nakuru road is the starting route for many safaris. Therefore, plenty of visitors get their first sight of the Kenyan landscape from here. Your first glimpse of the huge Rift Valley emptiness is likely to be from the viewpoints just past Limuru, at the top of the escarpments of the valley. Below, the acacia-scattered Kedong Valley bed conveys a neat and archetypal snapshot of the African landscape. Further away, you get a glimpse of Mount Longonot, Hell's Gate National Park and Lake Naivasha, while the plains seem to sweep on forever to the south. ▶▶ *For Sleeping, Eating and other listings, see pages 103-106.*

Ins and outs

Vehicles of 10 tonnes and over are not permitted on the A104 and instead are routed along the lower B3 road before joining the B4 to the north of Naivasha. This heavy traffic makes it a dangerous route with a high accident rate, so take care if driving. From the old Nairobi-Naivasha road (B3 – the more westerly road) which forks to the left at Rironi, the road continues in a northwesterly direction for approximately 6 km then turns left on a sealed tarmac road in a southwesterly direction around Mount Longonot. The road leads to the small town of Narok, see page 123, the main access point to the Mara. Some interesting diversions along this route are listed below.

Mount Suswa

From Nairobi, after a drive of about 17 km, a small dirt road leads to the south towards Mount Suswa, 2,356 m, an easily accessed volcano in the heart of Masai country, only 50 km from Nairobi. It is not as well known as Mount Longonot to the north. The outer crater has been breached on the southern and eastern sides by volcanoes, and numerous lava flows are visible. This whole area is honeycombed with lava caves and there are many examples of obsidian pebbles and rocks. One of the caves, over 20 km deep, is believed to be the longest in Kenya. The caves are home to several small mammals and birds including bats, snake owls, rock hyrax and squirrels.

‼ If you visit the caves, take care as there are some concealed drops in the cave floor.

It is possible to drive up to the floor of the outer of the two craters, approximately 10 km in diameter. The outer caldera floor is richly covered with grasses, from which the volcano takes its name. The Masai graze their cattle in this peaceful enclosure, also home to a variety of game. The inner crater, which is ring shaped, has a diameter of approximately 5 km, and is covered with dense vegetation. There is a large central lava plug. The inner crater edge offers a good ridge walk of about 1½ hours to the main summit, **Ol Donyo Onyoke**. Circumnavigation of the crater rim is possible, but can take up to eight hours because of the difficulty going over the sharp lava blocks and fields in the southeast section of the crater. It is possible to camp in the caves, but you must bring all supplies, including water, with you.

Kiambu → *Colour map 1, grid A4.*

The most straightforward way to get to Naivasha is along either the main A104 or B3 from Nairobi. Amore interesting route to Naivasha, which need not add more than an hour to your overall journey time (if in your own car), is via Kiambu, a one-way commuter town, and **Limuru**, a lively market town. The drive to Kiambu is hilly but

smooth, through corridors of high trees and past the **Windsor Golf and Country Club.**
Although neither town is particularly attractive, the Kiambu-Limuru road provides a quite beautiful half-hour drive through lush, fertile land full of rich tea and coffee plantations, and dotted with the elegant, umbrella-like thorn trees.

This area is on the lower slopes of the Aberdares, and the soil and climate are ideal for growing coffee, which was introduced in 1902. The action of water from many streams flowing southeast from the Kinangop Mountain (3,900m) to join the Athi River has divided the area into sheer ridges and deep valleys. There are several waterfalls in the higher areas.

It is also the centre of one of the main Kikuyu clans (the other is based on Nyeri). The Kiambu Kikuyu were particularly powerful during the presidency of Jomo Kenyatta, who came from this clan. Many displaced Masai refugees settled in this area after the Masai civil wars at the end of the 19th century, and in time intermarried with the Kikuyu people.

Kiambethu/Mitchell's Farm

① *T0154-40756. Not open all year; visitors must book (usually at least 1 week in advance). US$25 includes food and drinks. Day trips from Nairobi can be organized through the tour operators for US$55.*

This place offers an unusual opportunity to tour one of the first tea farms in Kenya. Two English families, Mitchell & McDonnell, in the early 1900s, built the estate. These families are said to be the first to have ventured into the tea business. The farm is about 30 km northwest of Nairobi, towards Limuru, and your friendly host will be Mrs Evelyn Mitchell, the daughter of Mr McDonnell. You can visit for lunch and afternoon tea. The Kiambethu Estate is located at an altitude of 7,000 ft above sea level, and has lush acres of tea plantations that appear to vanish in the horizon. You will also have a lecture on the area and about the production of tea. In the afternoon, a walk through the tea plantations and forests will display the conditions needed for the growth of tea.

Naivasha → *Phone code: 050. Colour map 1, grid A4.*

The most likely reason for stopping in Naivasha town is en route to either Lake Naivasha or Hell's Gate. There are a few accommodation options in town but it is far nicer to stay near the lake, where there are resorts, campsites and hotels catering to all budgets. The main road through town is horrendous and the heavy truck traffic has chewed the tar up beyond recognition. Naivasha is a small trading centre just off the main road from Nairobi to Nakuru. It was traditionally used as grazing land by Masai, until they were displaced by European settlers at the turn of the 20th century. The best reason to stop is for the excellent **Belle Inn** fruit juices and pastries.

Lake Naivasha → *Phone code: 050. Colour map 1, grid A4.*

Lake Naivasha is one of the few fresh water lakes in the Rift Valley and is 170 sq km lying at about 1,890 m above sea level. It is a lovely place to come for a weekend if you are staying in Nairobi as it is only a 1½-hour drive away. Strong afternoon winds cause the lake to get suddenly very rough and the local Masai called the lake *Nai'posha* meaning 'rough water', which the British later mis-spelt as Naivasha. Much of the lake is surrounded by forests of the yellow-barked acacia tree, full of birds and black and white colobus monkeys, once called 'yellow fever trees' after explorers who camped under them caught malaria. It has no apparent outlet, but it is believed to be drained by underground. The lake itself is quite picturesque with floating islands of papyrus.

There are hippos that come out onto the shore at night to graze, and there are many different types of waterbirds. The lake is dominated by the overshadowing Mount Longonot (2,880 m), a partially extinct volcano in the adjacent national park (52 sq km). On the southern lakeshore, the road goes through a major flower-growing area. Owned by Brooke Bond, it is an important exporter and employs thousands of local people. The flowers are cut, chilled and then air freighted to Europe from the new international airport at Eldoret. ➤ *For Sleeping, Eating and other listings, see pages 103-106.*

Ins and outs

The first 20-30 km of road around the southern lakeshore is in an appalling condition with deep potholes and ruts and clouds of dust. Beyond that it is remarkably OK until it meets the back road to Nakuru at Kongoni where it turns into a dirt track that is only suitable for four-wheel drive vehicles. If you are in a saloon car you will have to turn back from here and backtrack to the main Nairobi-Nakuru road despite the bad 20-km stretch to Naivasha town. It is possible to come to spend a day at one of the lakeside hotels without staying the night (there may be a small charge or it may be free if you eat there). The lake itself is best explored by boat (a number of the hotels

Lake Naivasha & Hell's Gate

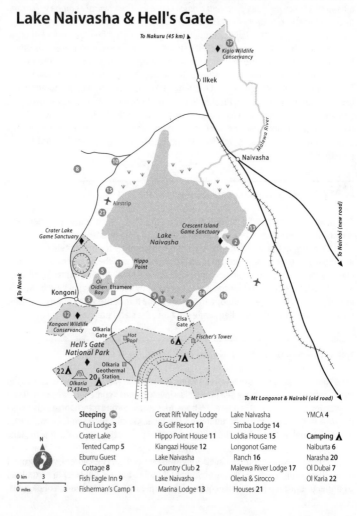

Sleeping	Great Rift Valley Lodge	Lake Naivasha	YMCA 4
Chui Lodge 3	& Golf Resort 10	Simba Lodge 14	
Crater Lake	Hippo Point House 11	Loldia House 15	Camping ▲
Tented Camp 5	Kiangazi House 12	Longonot Game	Naiburta 6
Eburru Guest	Lake Naivasha	Ranch 16	Narasha 20
Cottage 8	Country Club 2	Malewa River Lodge 17	Ol Dubai 7
Fish Eagle Inn 9	Lake Naivasha	Oleria & Sirocco	Ol Karia 22
Fisherman's Camp 1	Marina Lodge 13	Houses 21	

listed rent vessels out for hire). A motorboat can be hired for US$20 per hour; a rowing boat for about US$7 per hour. There are fish eagle nests near the Yacht Club. The twin-hulled launch from the Country Club on its 'ornithological cruise' often tries to entice the birds with fish. The evening cruise at about 1800 is a good time to see them. Alternatively you could work your way around the shore by bicycle, and there are a few places that rent out bikes.

Background

The region was first settled in the 1930s by the notorious British 'Happy Valley' set who bought all the neighbouring farmland – much of which is still owned by white Kenyans. Around this time Lake Naivasha was also Kenya's international airport. Flying boats from Europe used to land on the water and even today, when the water is low, you can see the wooden posts that mapped out the runway. The lake is about 13 km across, but its waters are shallow with an average depth of 5 m. At the beginning of the 20th century, Naivasha inexplicably completely dried up and the land was farmed, until heavy rains a few years later caused the lake to return.

Sights

Crescent Island Game Sanctuary ① *US$8-10 plus boat across the lake.* Morning and evening walks can be made here, a protected reserve where you can walk amongst zebra, antelope and giraffe that come to the water's edge to drink. It is located at the eastern shore of the lake near the Lake Naivasha Country Club, and it is not actually an island, as it is connected to the mainland by a slither of land. There are no predators so this is one of the few places in Kenya offering the opportunity to walk amongst the animals. Trips can be arranged at the **Lake Naivasha Country Club**, **Fisherman's Camp** or **Fish Eagle Inn**.

Elsamere ① *1500-1800, US$8 includes copious amounts of tea, see also Sleeping.* A few kilometres past **Fisherman's Camp** and **Fish Eagle Inn** is Elsamere, the former home of George and Joy Adamson (see box, page 322). It is easy to miss, so look out for the sign to the Olkaria Gate of Hell's Gate; it is a few hundred metres further on the right-hand side. There is a small **museum** with first editions of her books, her typewriter, her dress that she wore for the premier of *Born Free* in London and a selection of her paintings (although the best of her paintings of the various tribes of Kenya hang in the National Museum in Nairobi). The gardens are very pleasant with lots of birds and black and white colobus monkeys flying among the trees, though in recent years some of the giant acacia trees have had to be felled because of disease. It is open daily in the afternoon for afternoon tea and a video. The aged film shows the life (and death) of Joy. Beware though it lasts well over one hour! Worth sitting through though for the tea – tables in the house are laden with scones, jam and cream, dainty sandwiches, home-made cookies, slices of cake, and pots of tea and coffee.

Kongoni Wildlife Conservancy Further south of Elsamere the road passes around Oidien Bay, a bottleneck in the extreme southwest corner of the lake, and reaches the village of Kongoni and the turn-off to **Chui Lodge** and **Crater Lake Tented Camp**. For a few kilometres before Kongoni, the road passes through the Oserian Game Corridor, part of the private Kongoni Wildlife Conservancy, where the fences on the private land have been removed allowing the game in the area free access to the lakeshore. You are likely to see zebra and antelope from the road. The Kongoni Wildlife Conservancy (also known as Oserian) is a private reserve that was formed in 1997 on what was formerly a dairy and beef ranch of 3,500 acres. The revised management plan was to create a wildlife sanctuary with emphasis on protection of all biodiversity and to create a sustainable ecotourism destination. Wildlife was present on the land but numbers were declining. There are three accommodation options within the conservancy.

Crater Lake Game Sanctuary ① *US$2.50.* West of Lake Naivasha, one hour's walk from Kongoni and approximately 17 km past **Fisherman's Camp** is Crater Lake. Its often jade-coloured waters are quite breathtaking. There is an animal sanctuary, but some of the tracks in this area are only manageable by foot or with a four-wheel drive. There is a nice two-hour nature trail to the lake, and you are allowed to walk around by yourself and it's easy to see the rare black and white colobus monkey. It is possible to cycle to the game park, although the soft, dusty track after Kongoni is hard going.

Hell's Gate National Park → *Colour map 1, grid A4.*

① *Access is south of the YMCA at Lake Naivasha, through Elsa Gate and Olkaria Gate, south of Elsamere. Park entry fee is US$15 per day.*

About 90 km from Nairobi and 14 km southeast of Lake Naivasha is this national park, a major attraction in the Rift Valley. It is one of the few parks you are allowed to explore on foot, with bicycles and motorcycles allowed too, all offering excellent ways of exploring its 68.25 sq km. The flora is mainly grasslands and shrubland with several species of acacias. It is famous for its water geysers, as well as being a breeding area for Verreaux's eagles and Ruppell's vultures. Lammergeyers have also been spotted hovering over the dramatic cliffs of Hell's Gate Gorge. A feature of this landscape is the lustrous acid-resistent volcanic glass, usually black or banded, called obsidian, formed from cooled molten lava. When fractured it displays curved shiny surfaces.

Two extinct volcanoes are to be found here – **Olkaria** and **Hobley's**. The route through the park is spectacular, leading through a gorge lined with sheer red cliffs and containing two volcanic plugs – **Fischer's Tower** and **Central Tower**. The park is small and, although there is a wide variety of wildlife – including eland, giraffe, zebra, impala and gazelle – you may not see many of them as they are few in number. What you will see though is the incredibly tame hyrax that looks like a type of guinea-pig but is actually more closely related to the elephant, and a host of different birds of prey.

Within the park is the substantial **Olkaria Geothermal Station** generating power from underground – lots of large pipes and impressive steam vents in the hills. Near Central Tower is a smaller lower gorge that extends out of the park to the south. Here is a ranger post where drinks and sodas can be purchased, and a path that descends steeply into the gorge. The path skirts along the river in the bottom, into which hot springs in the cliffs flow, and then climbs back to the ranger post. While in the gorge branch off into an even smaller gorge that has high, water-eroded walls that are so narrow in places that the sky is almost blocked out. After about 700 m there is a high wall that will force you to turn back, but on your return you will get a great view of Central Tower rising above the gorge.

In the park, close to the ranger post mentioned above, is **Oloor Karia Masai Cultural Centre**, where Masai people demonstrate singing, dancing and jewellery making. There is no extra charge on top of the park entrance fee. The opening times vary. Ask at the information centre at Elsa Gate for details. The information centre sells some food and soft drinks, and also has a good, inexpensive guide to the park.

Kigoi Wildlife Conservancy

① *Open daily, US$1.50 entry fee.*

Located in the hills to the northeast of Naivasha off the road to Nakuru, is this 3,500-acre wildlife sanctuary with breathtaking views of the Rift Valley, Mount Longonot and Lake Naivasha. Visitors can walk or cycle amongst the wildlife and birds, or enjoy a splash in the Malewa River that runs through the conservancy.

The last remaining giraffe in the Naivasha region died as a result of poaching in 1996. Following an application by the management to the Kenya Wildlife Service to reintroduce giraffe, the request to relocate Rothschild's giraffe to the conservancy was granted, provided the property was fenced. Funding for this was sourced amongst others, from the European Union, and the Born Free Foundation. With these facilities in place, eight Rothschild's giraffe were relocated from Lake Nakuru in 2002. Subsequently another young male giraffe was moved from Giraffe Manor in Nairobi to join the herd. The entire episode was filmed by the BBC for the *Born to be Wild* series narrated by Joanna Lumley. The giraffe have settled well and there have already been five births since 2003. Morley, the young giraffe from the Giraffe Manor, is very approachable and many visitors have had the unique experience of feeding him by hand. The conservancy also has around 300 identified bird species, including the reputedly largest population of grey crested helmet shrikes in the world, and is home to 45 different mammals, including leopard, buffalo, topi, hippo, spotted hyena, and most of the plains game. In 1996, the large mammal count was only about 100 in this area, but these days it is up to 1,500, so the conservancy has been a success. According to the lodges that operate in this area, none other than Danny De Vito and Jim Carrey have visited the conservancy.

Mount Longonot → *Colour map 1, grid A4.*

ⓘ *US$15 fee to climb Mt Longonot.*

Mount Longonot is a dormant volcano standing at 2,886 m. The mountain cone is made up of soft volcanic rock that has eroded into deep clefts, v-shaped valleys and ridges. There is little vegetation on the stony soil. However, the crater is very lush and green, with fairly impenetrable trees. There are fine views over the Rift Valley on one side and into the enormous crater on the other. Longonot Park covers an area of 52 sq km, predominantly filled by the mountain. To climb Mount Longonot you need to get to Longonot village, about 12 km south of Naivasha town along the old road; from there it is about 6 km to the base of the mountain. There is a marked gate, where there is a secure parking area. You can be escorted up by Kenya Wildlife Service rangers and the fairly straightforward climb takes about an hour, but be prepared for the last section which is quite steep. A wander round the rim of the mountain takes a further two or three hours.

🖢 Sleeping

There is plenty of excellent accommodation in this popular and expanding weekend retreat for Nairobians, although there is little of attraction in the town itself except for **La Belle Inn**; its far nicer to stay near the lake-shore. Some of the places to stay are quite exceptional and thanks to a number of conservation projects in the region, game numbers have increased considerably which has caused a mushrooming of game lodges.

Lake Naivasha is home to several hundred hippo. At the lakeshore hotels, lodges and campsites, be very wary of the hippos that feed in the grounds at night. There have been accidents, including a fatality in 2005, from people getting too close.

Naivasha *p99*

C **La Belle Inn**, Moi Av, T050-2021007, labelleinn@kenyaweb.com. Popular place with very attentive staff and a selection of comfortable rooms at different prices, all including huge and very good breakfast (fresh fruit juice, croissants, home-made jam, butter, bacon, eggs and lots of coffee). This is a relative institution in Kenya and the large terrace restaurant is an excellent place to stop for a break from driving for the selection of pastries, sandwiches, pies, cakes and full meals (many vegetarian which is unusual for Kenya). The hotel also has 3 lively bars, and contains the Naivasha Business Centre, with internet access.

D Ken-Vash Hotel, Posta Lane, just up from Moi Av, T050-2030049. Enormous white building, the tallest in town, with spacious and comfortable rooms with balconies, and friendly staff. It has a good, cheap restaurant and a lively bar.

D Malewa Garden Hotel, Moi Av, north of **Wambuku Hotel**. Very new, had only been open a month on our visit, 19 rooms with hot water and mosquito nets, bar and restaurant, decor a little plain, best budget option as everything is so new. A double goes for US$12, although breakfast is extra.

D Naivasha Silver Hotel, Kenyatta Av, T050-2020580. Above the **Jolly Café**, basic but clean and comfortable rooms with hot water, relatively expensive for what you get, serves African staples and beer.

Lake Naivasha *p99, map p100*

L Chui Lodge, Kongoni Wildlife Conservancy, T050-2020792, www.kongoni.com. Exclusive lodge overlooking a waterhole with the dramatic Mau Escarpment as a backdrop, crafted from simple bush stone, local acacia and olive woods, African antiques. The 5 individual and well-spaced cottages are built in the same fashion as the main building. Each room has a veranda with its own view, log fire, marble bathroom and 4-poster beds. Heated swimming pool and Japanese Teppanyaki hot plate.

L Crater Lake Tented Camp, near Hippo Point, east of the Crater Lake Game Sanctuary, reservations though **Pride of Africa Safaris**, Nairobi, T020-884258, www.prideofafricasafaris.com. At over US$300 a night, this exclusive camp has a great position on the shores of the lake, the 11 tents sit in secluded clearings in the lakeside forest with sweeping views, fine dining, a very romantic and relaxing spot.

L Great Rift Valley Lodge and Golf Resort, about 11 km from Naivasha on the northern lakeshore road, best accessed from the main Nairobi-Nakuru road, reservations through **Heritage Hotels**, Nairobi, T020-4442115, www.heritage-eastafrica.com. Perched on the panoramic shoulder of the Eburu Escarpment overlooking Lake Naivasha and home to Kenya's newest championship 18-hole golf course. Private airstrip, 2 clay tennis courts, swimming pool, activities include walking and horse-riding safaris and

fishing. 30 twin and double rooms with private balconies, 4-poster beds, luxurious furnishings, 2 bars, very good food.

L Hippo Point House, at Hippo Point to the southwest of the lake, T0733-333014 (mob), www.hippo-pointkenya.com, is one of the most expensive places to stay in Kenya, there are 2 private homes, the unusual 115-ft-high Hippo Point Tower, which has room for up to 9 guests on 8 floors, and Hippo Point House, an old colonial house with 8 rooms for up to 14 guests. Built in 1933 and lovingly restored in 1998 to the highest standards. The cuisine is superb, game drives are included, horse riding, sailing, water-skiing and day trips are also available.. Swimming pool.

L Lake Naivasha Country Club, reservations **Block Hotels**, Nairobi, T020-650500, www.blockhotelske.com. The 55-acre property boasts green lawns shaded by mature acacias and spreading fever trees that stretch down to the lakeshore. The rooms are quite good with all amenities including a swimming pool, one of the cheaper options on the lakeshore at around US$190 for a double. Children are welcome and there is a small adventure playground for them. Good food with an excellent buffet lunch on Sun (on lawns if the weather is good) – eat as much as you like for around US$10 – only drawback is it often gets crowded with tour groups from Nairobi.

L Loldia House, a prestigious Governors' Camp, book through an agent or at www.governorscamp.com. One of Kenya's oldest farms on the western shore, with lush lawns that run down to the lakeshore. 8 en suite rooms in the main house or in garden cottages, colonial style with original furniture. Very atmospheric and here you'll experience the life of Kenya's early settlers – the ranch was established by a family who trekked by ox-wagon from South Africa a century ago, and the property is still owned by the descendants.

L Longonot Game Ranch, reservations, Nairobi, T020-890435, www.safarisun limited.co.ke. A local home-stay situated on the 80,000-acre Kedong Game Ranch, overlooking Lake Naivasha off the South Lake Rd. Beautiful and rustic, small groups of up to 6 people are catered for. Rooms are very comfortable with en suite bathrooms. If you want to see some wildlife on horseback, this would be a good option.

L Malewa River Lodge, T050-203031, www.malewariverlodge.com. Situated within the private Kigio Wildlife Conservancy to the northeast of the lake off the road to Nakuru. A small exclusive 12-bed 'eco friendly' lodge, cottages are nestled in the shade of huge acacia trees, full board with very good cuisine, horse riding, walking or cycling on offer. The beds, tables and chairs are constructed using the timbers from old fencing posts taken from the former cattle ranch that was on this site. The open-plan main building offers a large sitting room, open fire, spacious veranda, bar and dining area with views over the Malewa River.

L Oleria and Sirocco Houses, about 19 km from Naivasha on the north lake shore road near the airstrip and Loldia House, reservations Nairobi T020-334868, www.olerai.com. Oleria and Sirocco are the homes of Iain Douglas-Hamilton and his wife Oria. Iain is a leading conservation specialist who has been instrumental in protecting elephants in Kenya for decades (see also Elephant Watch Safari Camp at Samburu on page 296). The houses have been the family's home for many years. Accommodation is in very tranquil garden cottages decked with crawling vines and flowers, or in superbly luxurious rooms in the main houses. Rates are in the region of US$500 per person per day, and are all inclusive of drinks and food. Activities include pirogue trips on Lake Naivasha with the Masai.

A Elsamere, T050-21055, www.elsatrust.org, is Joy and George Adamson's house (see above). The conservation centre provides accommodation for 16 people in cottages set in the gardens around the main house. The rooms are bright and attractive and all have en suite bathrooms. Guests may also choose to stay in the main house in the Joy Adamson bedroom (has easy wheelchair access). Dinner is hosted each night and it is the perfect opportunity to get to know other guests, many of whom may be visiting researchers and conservationists, no bar but guests are invited to bring their own alcohol.

A Kiangazi House, also in Kongoni Wildlife Conservancy, same reservation details as the **Chui Lodge** above. Delightful lush gardens, rolling lawns, swimming pool, private country house with 3 double rooms in the house and 2 doubles and 1 single room in the garden, satellite TV lounge and library, tennis court. A salt lick and waterhole is excellently located at the bottom of the garden and attracts the local game.

A Lake Naivasha Simba Lodge, reservations Nairobi, T020-4444401, www.marasimba. com. Opened in 2003, this is a large modern lodge built in expansive grounds full of giant acacia trees. 70 rooms in several blocks of stone buildings with slate roofs, disabled rooms and facilities, non-smoking rooms, French and German spoken, heated swimming pool, restaurant and pub, bike hire, tennis courts, and a health club with gym, massage and sauna. A good set-up but primarily a conference venue so give it a miss if there is a large conference on.

C-D Fish Eagle Inn, T050-2030306, www.fish -eagle.com. Decent bandas available, as well as small but clean dormitories (with electricity) made with local materials. Also has camping facilities, but the food and hospitality is not the best. There is an excellent swimming pool but only those staying in the most expensive bandas can use it without extra charge (US$1, US$2 for visitors). Steam room, sauna and gym available at extra cost. Hippos come out of the water at night and graze a stone's throw away. Recommended despite the shortfalls. Hot water available 24 hrs, can get a bit crowded during holiday peak periods. At the time of writing, it was changing hands.

D Eburru Guest Cottage, North Lake Rd, 30 km from Naivasha. Reservations through **UNIGLOBE Let's Go Travel**, Nairobi T020-4447151, www.letsgosafari.com. On Green Park development at an altitude of 2,132 m up Eburru Hill – be warned it can get extremely cold up here at night. 2 small buildings close to the main house, self-catering, accommodates 4 adults, and has an electricity supply, bring all provisions.

D Fisherman's Camp, T050-2030088, next door to **Fish Eagle Inn**, is set in beautiful surroundings, deeply shaded by huge acacia trees. There are comfortable bandas with reasonable facilities including showers,

For an explanation of sleeping and eating price codes used in this guide, see inside the front cover. Other relevant information is found in Essentials, see pages 34-38.

bedlinen and electricity. There are also cheaper spartan dormitory-type bunks. Camping is on springy grass beneath the huge arms of the trees, with showers and toilets in tin sheds, and a communal washing-up area. Hot water is available in the evenings. There is also a bar and restaurant in a rustic thatched shed, and drinks and food are available. Motor boat trips to Crescent Island can be arranged with plenty of time for walking before the ride back. Recommended budget option.

D-E Lake Naivasha Marina Lodge, roughly 3 km down the lakeshore road from the turn-off, T050-2021010. Simple campsite and bandas next to the lake although the reeds mean you can't get too close to the shore. Bandas are self catering and equipped with utensils, but you will need to bring all food and water with you, the shared ablution block has hot showers in the evening. You can organize boat trips from here.

E-F YMCA, T020-2050109, is the closest accommodation to the main gate of Hell's Gate National Park. A good 15 mins from the lakeside, set in beautiful gardens. It is sometimes possible to buy provisions here and you can also camp in the grounds.

Hell's Gate National Park *p102, map p100*
There are a few campsites within the park; Naiburta, Ol Karia, Ol Dubai, and Narasha, see map. Each has water and pit latrines. Contact the warden, T050-2020284, hellsgatenp@africaonline.co.ke, or Kenya Wildlife Services, Nairobi, T020-600800, www.kws.org.

🍴 Eating

All the hotels have their own restaurants, many are extremely good. In Naivasha itself **La Belle Inn** is easily the best place to eat whatever your budget. There is a stall opposite that sells fresh fish and crayfish. See Sleeping above for more information.

🚌 Transport

Mount Suswa *p98*
Matatus serve the B3 Narok road, but there is little traffic or hitching opportunities along

the last 12 km south on rough unmade roads. The road skirts the northeast flank of the mountain until it reaches a crossroad. Turn right here along a rough track until you reach a group of *manyattas* (Masai villages) that extend over a distance of 1½ km. From here a rough track leads up to the caldera. The only identifying marks are the deeply grooved water channels lying to the sides of the track. The distance to the caldera is approximately 7 km. Turn left for the caves or right to reach the inner crater, a distance of another 8 km.

Lake Naivasha *p99, map p100*
If you are coming by road from Nairobi there are 2 routes. The first is along the old road that nowadays is the preserve of hundreds of lorries driving between Mombasa and Uganda. The road is poor, although the views are great and you are likely to see herds of zebra and other wildlife roaming the vast valley floors. The other route is along the new A104 road that does not come into Naivasha town itself. It is in good condition and has the added advantage of having the most wonderful views of the Rift Valley, particularly at the equator.

There is regular public transport between Naivasha and **Nairobi** and **Nakuru**. Buses and *matatus* arrive and depart at the bus stand on Kariuki Chotara Rd in Naivasha.

There are also regular *matatus* from the centre of town along the southern lakeshore road as far as **Kongoni**.

There is cycle hire available from various places from around US$10 a day, greatly increasing your options for exploration, particularly to Hell's Gate National Park. Try **Fisherman's Camp** and **Fish Eagle Inn**, or the stall at the turn-off to the Elsa Gate of Hell's Gate National Park.

🗂 Directory

Lake Naivasha *p99, map p100*
Banks Barclays Bank, on Moi Av, will change money and has an ATM. **Internet** From **Naivasha Business Centre** at La Belle Inn. **Post office** On Moi Av. Securicor, along Moi Av, offers DHL parcel services.

Nakuru and around

Lake Elementeita → *Colour map 1, grid A3/4.*

From Naivasha the road continues towards Nakuru, a 1½-hour drive, via the uninspiring town of Gilgil. The small 18-sq-km lake is the notable attraction on this route. Elementeita lies in the shadow of an impressively peaked hill known locally as the 'Sleeping Masai' and is roughly half-way between Naivasha and Nakuru, just off the main road. It is a shallow soda lake, similar to Lake Nakuru, although it does not attract such enormous numbers of flamingos which apparently fled due to encroachment by pelicans. Elmenteita is now one of Kenya's main breeding grounds for the great white pelican. As it is not a national park, you can walk around it and you don't have to pay. Most of the safaris covering the trip from Naivasha to Nakuru only stop at the viewpoint overlooking the lake on the main road.

Near the lake are several prehistoric sites, indicating that this area was once densely populated. The best-known archaeological site is **Gambles Cave**, 10 km southwest of Elmenteita. There are few facilities at the lake or in Elmenteita town, but it is an easy day trip from Nakuru with direct *matatus* (one hour) or 30 minutes from Gilgil. It is an easy walk from the main road down to the edge of the lake, but fairly steep coming back up. **Kariandusi** ① *0800-1800, US$3*, is a prehistoric site of the Acheulean period to the right of the Naivasha-Nakuru road (A104) discovered by Dr L Leakey in 1928 and excavated from 1929 to 1947. Studies suggest that it was not an area of permanent habitation and the findings indicate that the people who lived here were of the genus *Homo erectus*. There is a small museum housing obsidian knives, Stone Age hand axes and a molar of the straight-tusked elephant, a variety which roamed in Northern Europe before extinction. The nearby diatomite mine (a type of algae) produces a white stuff used for paints, insulation and as a face paint by the Masai.

Nakuru → *Phone code: 051. Colour map 1, grid A3.*

The next major town along from Naivasha, Nakuru is Kenya's fourth largest town and is in the centre of some of the country's best farming land. It is a pleasant, slightly dusty agricultural town with many supermarkets, and shops mostly selling farming equipment and supplies. Nakuru came into existence in 1900 when the building of the railway opened up access to the surrounding lush countryside attracting hundreds of white settlers to the area. Lord Delamere, one of the most famous figures in colonial times, collected around 600 sq km of land here and developed wheat and dairy farming. ▶▶ *For Sleeping, Eating and other listings, see pages 114-120.*

Ins and outs
There are frequent buses and *matatus* from just about everywhere in the highlands region of Kenya to and from Nakuru. The main road from Nairobi passes by Naivasha and Gilgil and Lake Elementeita on the way. Nakuru town itself is compact enough to walk around, though *boda bodas* (bicycle taxis), regular taxis and the odd tuk tuk are available to get around. Many of the more upmarket hotels and lodges in the region can arrange transfers to and from Nairobi.

Sights
On the corner of Kenyatta Avenue and Mburu Gichua Road is an area where street performers demonstrate their skills, including dancing, music and juggling. An

interesting structure is the **Eros Cinema**, an example of functional post-war architecture, with slender columns and glass walls. **Breaker's Music Centre**, on the corner of Kenyatta Avenue and Club Road, has an unusual cupola room on the corner. **Nyayo Garden** is well kept and central with a war memorial. **Nakuru Station** is another fine example of post-war architecture. A mural dominates the booking hall. The two artists, M Ginsburg and R McLellan-Sim, depict settlers looking out over the Rift Valley showing the Masai, cattle and rolling wheatfields. A notable Hollywood film star is said to have been the model for the male settler – he subsequently had a successful career in politics. The station itself has a slender clocktower with slim columns and delicate iron screens. And the clock still keeps time.

The other notable building is the **Rift Valley Sports Club** (T051-2212085). This was formerly the Nakuru Club, and was first built in 1907, was burnt down in 1924 and then restored. A patio restaurant looks out over the cricket pitch. The cricket pavilion has photos of past teams and the ground is prettily surrounded by jacarandas and mango trees. In the Men's Bar (women still not allowed) there are sporting prints and etchings. Tennis, squash and a small swimming pool are available as well as cricket nets on Tuesday and Thursday. There is also a small library here. It is possible to stay here (see Sleeping, below). Visitors need to pay a temporary daily membership of US$4, or be signed in as a guest by another member.

Nakuru

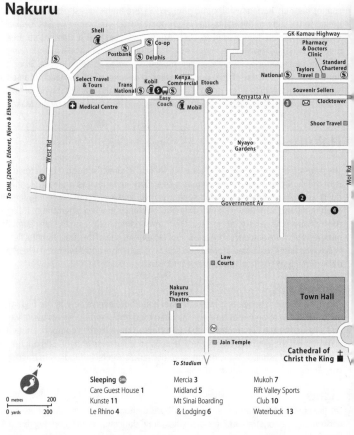

Sleeping		
Care Guest House 1	Mercia 3	Mukoh 7
Kunste 11	Midland 5	Rift Valley Sports
Le Rhino 4	Mt Sinai Boarding	Club 10
	& Lodging 6	Waterbuck 13

0 metres 200
0 yards 200

Lake Nakuru National Park → *Colour map 1, grid A3.*

ⓘ *0600-1900, US$30 per day.*

This national park is just 3 km south of Nakuru town in central Kenya and 140 km northwest of Nairobi. It was established in 1960 as the first bird sanctuary in Africa to protect the flamingos and the other birds in the hills and plains around the lake. It is about 199 sq km and the lake is fringed by swamp, and surrounded by dry savannah. The upper areas within the national park are forested. The lake itself is in the centre of the park surrounded by huge white salt crusts, whose surface area varies from five to 40 sq km. ▸▸ *For Sleeping, Eating and other listings, see pages 114-120.*

Ins and outs

Game viewing is very easy and rewarding here, and the whole park can be driven around in half a day. You will need to be in a vehicle, although you are allowed to get out at the lakeside. The most frequent way of accessing the park is through the Main Gate, 4 km south of Nakuru centre, next to the park's headquarters, where you can also obtain and reload your Smartcard. From Kenyatta Avenue, take Moi Road and turn left to Stadium Road, which will lead you right to the gate. Here there is also a map on a board showing the spots of the latest animal sightings. If you come from

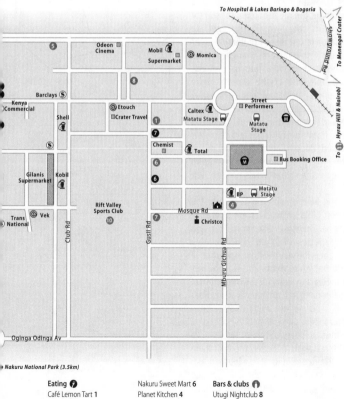

▶ Nakuru National Park (3.5km)

Eating 🍴	Nakuru Sweet Mart 6	Bars & clubs 🍸
Café Lemon Tart 1	Planet Kitchen 4	Utugi Nightclub 8
Courtyard 2	Plovers 5	
Nakuru Coffeehouse 3	Tipsy 7	

Nairobi and you want to avoid Nakuru altogether, you can enter the park through Lanet Gate, although this is not very well signposted off the main road. The turn-off is about 3 km before you reach town. Finally, Nderit Gate lies at the east side of the park, close to **Lake Nakuru Lodge**. This is a suitable way for visitors arriving from Mau Narok or Lake Elmenteita on the back road. The park's tracks are usually well kept, although you may find some mud during the rains. The main road circles the lake completely. The north drive is very busy and is hence less interesting for wildlife viewing. The biggest stretch of land in the park is located south of the lake. There is a track network here which is much less visited and where you will have the chance to see some of the park's herbivores, such as Rothschild's giraffe, black and white rhino and eland.

Sights

The blue-green algae *Spirulina Platensis* flourishes in the alkaline waters and is a primary food source for the **flamingo** population. Recently there have been unexpectedly high death rates of these graceful birds, see box. In 1958 alkaline-tolerant *Tilapia grahami* were introduced to the lake to try to curb the problem of malaria in the nearby town. **Fish eagles** appeared in this area shortly afterwards thanks to the abundant supply of these fish. There is a wide variety of wildlife: **bat, colobus monkey, spring hare, otter, rock hyrax, hippo, buffalo, waterbuck, lion, hyena**, and **giraffe**, but the most popular reason for visiting is the wonderful sight of hundreds of thousands of flamingos. At one time there were thought to be around two million flamingos here, about one third of the world's entire population, but the numbers have considerably diminished in recent years. These days the number of flamingos varies from several thousand to a few hundred, depending on the level of the water and their frequent migration between the other lakes in the Rift Valley.

The best viewing point is from the **Baboon Cliffs** on the western shores of the lake. There are also more than 450 other species of birds here. Another highlight is the very healthy population of **black** and **white rhino**, and Nakuru was declared a sanctuary for the protection of these endangered animals in 1987. Both black and white rhino have been reintroduced, and the park has become the most successful refuge for rhino in East Africa – you'll literally trip over them here. There are quite a few **leopard** too, which are often, and unusually, spotted during daylight hours in the acacia forest at the very entrance to the park. In 1974 the endangered Rothchild's **giraffe** was ntroduced from the Soy plains of Eldoret

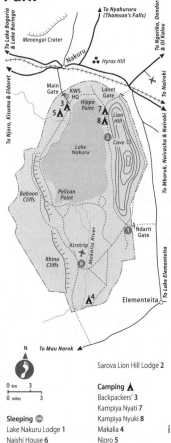

Lake Nakuru National Park

To Nyahururu (Thomson's Falls)
To Lake Bogoria & Lake Baringo
To Ngorika, Dondori & Ol Kalou
Menengai Crater
Nakuru
Hyrax Hill
To Njoro, Kisumu & Eldoret
Main Gate
KWS HQ
Lanet Gate
To Nairobi
Hippo Point
Lion Hill
Cave
Lake Nakuru
Baboon Cliffs
Pelican Point
To Mbaruk, Naivasha & Nairobi
Ndarit Gate
Airstrip
Makalia River
Rhino Cliffs
To Lake Elementeita
Elementeita

N
To Mau Narok

0 km 3
0 miles 3

Sleeping
Lake Nakuru Lodge **1**
Naishi House **6**

Sarova Lion Hill Lodge **2**

Camping
Backpackers' **3**
Kampiya Nyati **7**
Kampiya Nyuki **8**
Makalia **4**
Njoro **5**

i

Dwindling flocks

In recent years, an alarming rise in the number of flamingo deaths has been noted at several of the Rift Valley lakes. Around 30,000 died within a three-month period in 1993 and two years later in 1995 another 15,000 flamingos perished at Lake Nakuru. In 2000 the number of deaths was estimated at 30,000, and the following year there were again a very large number of sick birds. The current deaths have been occurring at lakes Bogoria, Nakuru and Elementeita. Post-mortems appear to show that the flamingos are dying from heavy metal poisoning (cadmium, lead, arsenic and nickel), in addition to pesticide accumulation. However, analysis of the fish stocks shows no significant changes in the concen-trations of these metals. The water level of Lake Nakuru has decreased by about 60% from its normal level due to recent droughts. The debate continues as to whether the drought has altered the alkalinity of the waters or whether the birds are dying after consuming toxic waste from the nearby sewage plant.

Some of the other lakes, like Magadi and Sonachi, that also have high levels of heavy metal contamination have no surface inflow, a factor that effectively excludes the possibility of man-made pollution in those lakes. As the Rift Valley is volcanic it is possible that the source of these contaminants is natural. Work is currently being undertaken in a Kenyan/Swedish study to determine whether algae toxins may be a co-factor, as many of these deaths have occurred following periods of algae bloom.

The flamingos, a major tourist attraction of Lake Nakuru, have moved to other alkaline lakes including the tiny Lake Simbi Nyaima, 200 km west, close to Lake Victoria. The flamingo has an estimated lifespan of 50 years, and older birds are believed to guide the others. Fortunately, the deaths are not expected to have too great an impact on the overall numbers of flamingos as they are very successful breeders, with 250,000 hatchlings surviving annually.

where they have bred successfully. Because of its proximity to Nakuru town, the park is fenced, to stop the animals wandering into town and, at one time, to stop poachers wandering into the park. It's so close to the city that it's not out of the ordinary to be watching a lion within the park, and at the same time watching a woman doing her washing outside her house beyond the fence! The advantage of being so close is that the local people can get to know the wildlife – the park owns a bus and buses in all the local school children for game drives.

Hyrax Hill Prehistoric Site → Colour map 1, grid A4.

ⓘ www.museums.or.ke, 0930-1800, small entrance fee. Just off the Nairobi road, it is easy to get to. Take a matatu heading for Gilgil and ask to be dropped off at the turning for Hyrax Hill. It is about 1 km from here to the museum. You can camp here if you wish. About 4 km from Nakuru, Hyrax Hill contains Neolithic and Iron Age burial pits and settlements, first investigated by the Leakeys in the 1920s and work has been going on there, periodically, ever since. The excavations have found evidence of seasonal settlements from 3,000 years ago, and there are signs of habitation here up until about 300 years ago. The presence of beach sands is an indicator that Lake Nakuru may have extended right to the base of the hill in former times, turning Hyrax Hill into a peninsula or even an island. It is possible that 9,000 years ago this vast prehistoric lake may have extended as far as Lake Elementeita. The hill was given its name during the early part of the 20th century, reflecting the abundance of hyraxes in the rocky fissures of the hill.

The northeast village has some enclosures where the digging was carried out although only one is not overgrown. It dates back about 400 years and the finds have been pieced together and are exhibited in the museum. There is no evidence of human dwelling suggesting this may have been used for livestock but not humans.

Up at the top of Hyrax Hill are the remains of a stone-walled fort and on the other side of the hill it is possible to see the position of two huts in a settlement which have been dated back to the Iron Age. A series of burial pits with 19 skeletons were found, most of them decapitated, dating back to the same time. The remains are all in a heap and all appear to be young men suggesting they were buried in a hurry – possibly the remains of the enemy after a battle. On the path back to the museum, a bau board has been carved into the rock. One very curious find was six Indian coins dating back 500 years – no one knows how they got here.

Underneath the Iron Age site, a neolithic site was found and the neolithic burial mound has been fenced off as a display, the stone slab which sealed the mound having been removed. Nine female skeletons were found at the site. Unlike the male remains, the female remains have been buried with grave goods including dishes, pestles and mortars. No one can be sure why the women were buried with grave goods and not the men, but it could indicate that women were more politically powerful in former times. Oral history in the region suggests this may have been the case. Why the Iron Age burial site is directly on top of the neolithic one also remains a mystery. Hyrax Hill was gazetted a National Monument in 1943. The **museum**, which contains artefacts from the site, was previously a farmhouse.

Rongai → *Colour map 1, grid A3.*

Rongai is a small, pretty village about 25 km west of the Nakuru in the valley of the Rongai River, which rises in the Elburgon Hills. Originally the area was inhabited by the Tugen and Njembs tribes, before they were driven out by the Masai. But the Masai never settled and there is no record of their ever constructing *manyatta* (Masai villages) in the valley. ▸▸ *For Sleeping, Eating and other listings, see pages 114-120.*

Ins and outs
Rongai is a short diversion off of the A104 Nakuru-Eldoret road. Numerous *matatus* go from Nakuru along the A104 past the turning to Rongai. Here you can swap for another going from the turn off to Rongai. From Nakuru there are also four or five direct *matatus* each day in both directions.

Background
The land was part of the great tract leased to Lord Delamere, who then rented it out to settlers. In the colonial period Rongai grew to prominence as a maize-growing area. This crop was first introduced to Kenya by the Portuguese, but it did not do well. Then an American variety was used to develop a hybrid known as Kenya White, which flourished. The land was tilled by teams of oxen, maize was being exported by 1910, and

Rongai

as part of the line onward from Nairobi to Uganda. A branch line was built from Rongai
northeast to Solai, now disused, although you can still see the tracks. The branch
went entirely through settler country and, as there was no 'native land' along the
route, it was much criticized as an example of the colonial administration favouring
the interests of the settlers over those of the Africans.

Sights

One notable feature of Rongai is the number of churches. **Africa Inland Church** has
arched windows in pairs, glazed in yellow, green and orange, with sunrise airbricks
above each pair. The walls are of grey volcanic stone, and it has a tin roof. The
Catholic Church of St Mary is a modern, neat, functional structure of grey stone with
timber panelling. **Heart of Christ Catholic Seminary**, PO Box 238, dates from 1986,
but is cloistered and quiet, with well-tended flower beds, run by Italian Fathers.

The prettiest of the churches, and a testament to the determination of the settlers
to reproduce rural England on the equator, is **St Walstan's**, built in 1960. It is an exact
replica of an early English (1016) country church at Bawburgh, 6 km east of Norwich in
the UK. St Walstan is known as the 'Layman's Saint'. He came from a wealthy
land-owning family, was fond of farm animals, and he insisted on working in the
fields with the farm labourers. He collapsed and died while working one day, and a
spring bubbled up on the very same spot. The church building has a square tower
with battlements, pointed windows, and a shingle (wooden tile) roof. In the vestibule
is a piece of flint from the church in Bawburgh. Inside there is a tiny gallery with steps
up to it cut into the wall. The saints are depicted in orange, yellow and blue
stained-glass windows. The roof is supported by timber beams and there is a small
bell, about 30 cm across. The approach to the church is bordered by jacarandas that
carpet the path with fallen blue blossoms when the trees are in flower.

Another rather charming building is the **Rongai Railway Station**. It has its name
picked out in white cement on the ground. The platform has street lamps, glass
panelled, lit by oil. The flowerbeds have frangipani and variegated sisal plants. The
rods and wires of the signalling system and the points run over the ground. The
station is of wooden weatherboarding in the cream and brick-red livery of Kenya
Railways with a small veranda in front. Inside is the original control gear, now about
70 years old, with big brass keys for regulation of the traffic on the single line, and
wicker hoops and pouches for collecting mail from non-stopping trains. The original
telegraph system is still in place too, now with the addition of some antique black
bakelite telephones.

Menengai Crater → *Colour map 1, grid A3.*

This extinct volcano on the northern side of town is 2,490 m high and is the second
largest surviving volcanic crater in the world, with a surface area of 90 sq km.
However, it is not easy to see it from the town. A sign erected at the highest point by
the Rotary Club shows the distances and general directions of several places
worldwide. The crater is 8 km from the main road. As you ascend, the views over Lake
Nakuru are excellent, although it is not visible from the top. If walking, leave from the
Crater Climb Road, then Forest Road (it takes a couple of hours but is pleasant
enough). However, recent reports of robberies makes this a less safe option, and an
alternative is to drive along Menengai Drive out through the suburbs. It is fairly well
signposted. There is no public transport from the town to the Menengai Crater, and as
few people visit it there is scant hope of hitching a lift. There are a number of kiosks en
route to the top where you can get a drink and basic local foods but no refreshments
are available at the summit.

In the 19th century the Menengai Crater was the site of a bloody battle between different Masai clans, vying for the pastures of the Rift Valley slopes and Naivasha. The Ilaikipiak Moran (warriors) were defeated by their southern neighbours the Ilpurko Masai, who reputedly threw the former over the crater edge. According to legend the fumaroles rising from the crater bed are the souls of the vanquished seeking to find the way to heaven. The Maa word *Menenga* means 'the dead'.

The views over Lake Nakuru are excellent (although the lake dried up completely in spring 1994 but has now refilled) as are the views towards Lake Bogoria over the other side. The crater itself is enormous, about 12 km across and 500 m deep. The mountain is surrounded by a nature reserve.

Nyahururu and Thomson's Falls

→ *Phone code: 065. Colour map 1, grid A4.*
The small town of Nyahururu lies at high altitude (2,360 m) with a splendid climate and is Kenya's highest town. Surrounded by pretty tracts of forest and agricultural land, the region benefits from high rainfall. It originally served the colonial settler farmers in the area and was boosted when a branch line of the railway reached the town in 1929. This still runs, but only carries freight. In the postwar period the town was prosperous enough to boast a racecourse. Although only a few kilometres north of the equator, nights can be cold here with occasional frosts in the early months of the year.

An explorer, Joseph Thomson, came across the waterfall to the north of the town in 1883 which he named Thomson's Falls after his father. The cascade plunges 75 m, and is a pretty area to walk around. It's more commonly known as 'T-falls'. Upstream on the **Ewaso Narok River** is found one of Kenya's highest altitude hippo pools in an area of marshy bogland, about 2 km from the falls.

● Sleeping

Lake Elementeita *p107*
A **Lake Elementeita Lodge**, 30 km south of Nakuru off the main road to Nairobi, T051-850833, www.lakenakuru lodge.com. Built in 1916, 33 en suite rooms, dining and living rooms, lush tropical gardens, wide terrace overlooking the lake, activities include bird walks and safaris by ox wagon with the Masai. However, it is expensive for what you get and somewhat impersonal.

Nakuru *p107, map p108*
L **Deloraine**, 33 km from Nakuru on the A104 (6 km northwest of the turning to Rongai), T051-2032005, www.offbeatsafaris. com. On the Deloraine Estate, this is an exclusive homestay in a classic colonial house on the lower slopes of Londianin Mountain, set on a 2,000-ha farm. 6 double bedrooms with bathrooms. All meals are taken in the dining room and guests are expected to be part of the family in a house party atmosphere. There are small children

and dogs in the family too. Croquet, lawn tennis, horse-riding safaris. There is no electricity and lighting is by gas and hurricane lamps. The house was built in 1920 and there are some fine antiques.
A **Mercia Hotel**, Kenyatta Av, T051-2216013, www.merciagrouphotels.com. A surprise for dusty little old Nakuru: very modern block with a fabulous atrium-style lobby where all the doors to the rooms look inward on several storeys and are reached by glass elevators. 89 rooms and 4 suites, singles cost US$65, doubles cost US$110, all rates are half board, if you are not staying buffet dinner costs US$13. There's a bar, a good swimming pool at the rear and secure parking.
B-E **Kembu Farm and Camp**,
T051-2343203, www.kembu.com. Take the main A104 road from Nakuru towards Eldoret and after a few kilometres turn-off on to the C56 to Njoro. From Njoro take the Molo road, the farm is 8 km beyond Njoro. *Matatus* from Nakuru to Molo will drop you

off to the turning to the farm. The cottages and campsite are located on a large 900-acre working farm, young children can help feed horses, calves and chickens, mountain biking and horse riding are on offer. Accommodation is in 3 en suite cottages (one of which was built in 1915 and was a former home of Beryl Markham), rooms in the family house, and 1 unique treehouse with double bedroom only, for which guests use toilets and showers in the campsite. The campsite itself is a fantastic swathe of springy green grass surrounded by bushes full of chameleons. There's a lovely rustic bar and restaurant with wood fire and superb farm cuisine.

C Kunste, T051-2212140, about 2 km out on the Nairobi road. Large spacious hotel with secure parking, outside bar with kid's playground, restaurant, 105 comfortable rooms, singles, doubles and triples, the bigger suites also have TV, old-fashioned decor but well run with friendly staff.

C Midland, Geoffery K Kamau Rd, T051-2217222, midland@africaonline.co.ke. The comfortable, well-appointed rooms have en suite bathrooms and satellite TV, breakfast is included, car washing for a small tip, newspapers in the morning. 2 bars with giant screen TV, and an excellent restaurant serving reasonably priced steaks and pork chops, fresh tilapia fish, pasta and delicious filled pancakes. Recommended.

C Rift Valley Sports Club, Club Rd, T051-2212085, rvscnku@wananchi.com. Very central. You need to become a temporary member which costs US$4, 29 very modern and smart rooms in a much newer block in the grounds of the old club, the more expensive executive suites have TV. Eat and drink at the club. Secure parking.

D Hotel le Rhino, Mburu Gichua Rd, T051-2216741. Comfortable and clean, has good rooms with bathrooms plus some cheaper single rooms without bathrooms. Restaurant and pleasant bar where a guitarist plays at the weekends, helpful staff and good views from roof. The price can be negotiated especially in low season.

D Waterbuck, West Rd, T051-2215672. Modern hotel with good facilities, very clean and spacious, the rooms have balconies. The restaurant is affordable and good. Can organize game drives.

E Care Guest House, Gusii Rd, very central, T0721-636447 (mob). The best at the cheapest end of the scale in an umissable bright pink building on several storeys with 70 rooms. A double is only a little over US$5, clean rooms with simple concrete shower and loo, hot water, mosquito nets, very secure and there are additional locked gates at the end of each corridor. First-floor restaurant serves good simple snacks and breakfasts but no booze.

E Mt Sinai Boarding and Lodging, Gusii Rd, T051-2211779. Large building on 5 storeys, very clean in fairly modern rooms, hot water, secure, large restaurant for breakfast and lunch and cold sodas.

E Mukoh, corner of Mosque and Gusii Rd. Popular place offering clean, quiet and comfortable accommodation. It has some rooms with baths, hot water in the morning, and the best breakfast in town. It is a little overpriced, and is also good for snacks. Good view of town and Lake Nakuru from the roof.

Lake Nakuru National Park *p109*
The rates of the accommodation options within the park do not include park entrance fees or vehicle costs.

L Lake Nakuru Lodge, T051-2085446, www.lakenakurulodge.com. Medium-sized lodge situated to the southeast of the park near the Ndarit Gate, with pleasant gardens and pool overlooking the park, can accommodate 176 people in cottages, bandas and suites, friendly service, bar and dining room, and 24-hr room service. The original house was part of Kenya pioneer Lord Delamere's estate.

L Sarova Lion Hill Lodge, close to eastern shore of lake, access from Lanet Gate, T051-2085455, www.sarova.co.ke/lionhill. Each of the 67 chalet-style rooms and suites have a private bathroom and veranda where meals can be served. Swimming pool, sauna, massages and boutique available on site. There are good views and it is popular with group tours. Rates start from US$205 for a double.

For an explanation of sleeping and eating price codes used in this guide, see inside the front cover. Other relevant information is found in Essentials, see pages 34-38.

B Naishi House, Kenya Wildlife Service, Nakuru Warden, T051-2044069, kwslnnp@africanonline.co.ke, Nairobi, T020-600800, www.kws.org. National park self-catering accommodation in the south of the park, near **Makalia Campsite**. The house is furnished with rugs and paintings by local artists and has a fully equipped kitchen (including fridge), lounge, dining room and 2 bedrooms, each with a double and a single bed. There are also 2 single rooms in an adjacent cottage. Bring all food and drinking water. Escorted game drives can be organized from here. The whole house rents for US$200, including the cottage, but other arrangements may be possible.

Camping

E Backpackers' Campsite, just inside the Main Gate. It is possible to camp here even if you do not have a vehicle, and there is no entry fee to the park. However, the park cannot be explored on foot, so to go on a game drive you would have to hitch from the main gate, and if you were lucky enough to get a lift (remember safari companies are unlikely to pick up non-paying passengers), then you would have to pay park entry fees.
E Kampi ya Nyati (Buffalo) and **E Kampi ya Nyuki** (Bee), both lead down to quiet viewpoints on the lakeshore. These 2 campsite are near the northeast entrance. Reservations through Kenya Wildlife Service (see under **Naishi House** above) or simply book and pay for camping when you arrive at the main gate.
E Makalia Campsite, by the southern boundary of the park and close to the waterfall. Exercise caution: lions are often spotted here.
E Njoro Campsite, about 1 km into the park on the northwest side of the lake.

Nyahururu and Thompson's Falls p114
C-E Thomson's Falls Lodge, T065-22006, is the most popular choice, just off the road out of town toward Nyeri and Nanyuki. Built in 1931, it is set in pleasant gardens adjacent to the waterfall. Very charming colonial atmosphere, there is a choice of rooms in the main building or cottages. More people visit to see the falls and have a drink at the bar than actually stay but the rooms are well furnished, if a little cheerless, and all have fireplaces, the restaurant is good and the staff are friendly. There's also a campsite on the grounds, with hot showers, US$4.
E Baron Hotel, Ol Kalou Rd, T065-32056. Some rooms have bathrooms others have showers, it is clean and comfortable although less than lavish. There is a bar-restaurant, disco at weekends. One disadvantage is that it is very noisy from 0600 when the *matatus* get going.

⊘ Eating

Nakuru p107, map p108
The best restaurants are attached to hotels and the **Midland** and the **Mercia** hotels are especially good. There are a number of places for cheap snacks around town. The many supermarkets also sell pies, samosas and pieces of fried chicken. About 2 km outside Nakuru on the road to Nairobi on the left-hand side there is a shopping centre with good snacks for a short stop if you are only driving through.
▦ Courtyard, Government Av, T051-2211585. Formal and very comfortable restaurant that offers an excellent choice of hot and cold starters, salads, Indian food, seafood, pizza or grills, huge varied menu and not unreasonably priced. You can choose to eat inside, on the terrace at the front, or in the lovely courtyard decked with plants to the rear. Full bar including some wines. Open daily until 2200.
▦ Planet Kitchen, Government Av. Very nice terrace with lots of pot plants, snacks and full meals, friendly atmosphere, good place for a cold beer, notice the bike park across the street, where hundreds of tightly packed bicycles are chained up.
▯ Café Lemon Tart, corner of Moi Rd and Kenyatta Av, T051-2213208. Excellent breakfasts and light snacks, simple café environment, good coffee, will make birthday cakes to order.
▯ Nakuru Coffeehouse, Moi Rd, T051-2214596. Serves very good coffee, snacks and ice cream, although the café is a little dim inside and seating is on plastic bucket chairs. However, this is a recommended stop to buy fresh coffee beans and if you so wish they will grind them for you in a wonderful old-fashioned grinder.

🍴Nakuru Sweet Mart, Gusii Rd, and another branch on Moi Rd. Vegetarian Indian food, pastries, proper French bread, cold drinks.
🍴Plovers, Kenyatta Av. Nice terrace outside, popular with bank workers at lunchtime, cold drinks and snacks, plus full meals, good steak and chicken as they have their own butchers next door.
🍴Tipsy Restaurant, Gusii Rd. Popular with local people and is good value, they have western dishes as well as good curries and tilapia (fish).

🎵 Bars and clubs

Nakuru *p107, map p108*
Many of the hotels have discos or live music at the weekends.
Club Lule's, Club Rd, opposite the Rift Valley Sports Club. Popular local disco, open Wed-Sat, sometimes has live bands.
Utugi Nightclub, a block south of the Odean Cinema. Local and lively bar, plenty of cold beer, snacks, stays open late, decorated with Masai blankets and rather unusual leather wall hangings, gets very busy in the evening on the outside terrace.

🔺 Activities and tours

Nakuru *p107, map p108*
It can be cheaper to book a safari in Nairobi.
Crater Travel, T051-2215019, just off Kenyatta Av, 1 block west of the **Care Guest House**, can arrange air tickets.
Menengai Holidays, Hotel Waterbuck, T0720-950500 (mob), www.menengai holidays.com. Local safaris and reservations.
Select Travel and Tours, Kenyatta Av, T051-2214030/1, select@multitechweb. com, arranges hotel bookings, car hire and flight ticketing.
Shoor Safaris, Moi Rd, T051-2211408, www. shoortravel.com. Quality safari operator and travel agent that also has an office in Nairobi. Best in Nakuru with very helpful staff, members of the Kenya Asscociation of Travel Agents, organize local tours as well as packages throughout East Africa. If you haven't arranged tours to lakes Baringo and Bogoria or Nakuru National Park by the time you get to Nakuru head here.

Taylers Travel, Kenyatta Av, near Standard Chartered Bank, T051-2217048, taylers@ multitechweb.com. All airline ticketing, useful and efficient general travel agent.

⊖ Transport

Nakuru *p107, map p108*
There are regular *matatus* and buses to Nakuru from **Nairobi** (3 hrs), **Nyahururu**, **Naivasha** (1½ hrs) and all points west including **Kisumu** (4½ hrs), **Eldoret** (4 hrs) and **Busia** (8 hrs). The main bus station is on the eastern edge of town. **Easy Coach**, which has a terminal in town at the Kobil petrol station on Kenyatta Av, is recommended as all its vehicles are very new. It has services from Nakuru to Nairobi, Eldoret and Kakamega.

Nyahururu and Thompson's Falls *p*
There are regular buses and minibuses linking to **Nakuru** to the west and **Nyeri** to the east.

❻ Directory

Nakuru *p107, map p108*
Banks Most of the big banks have a bureau de change and ATMs including **Barclays** and **Standard Chartered** on Kenyatta Av. The **Postbank** on GK Kamau Highway can arrange Western Union money transfers.
Internet There are a number of internet cafés around town but the best is the **Cyber Café**, Kenyatta Av, which has lots of terminals, is cheap at about US$1 per hr and has surprisingly fast access by Kenya's standards. **Medical services** Pharmacy: there is a well-stocked pharmacy next to a doctor's clinic near the Standard Chartered Bank. **Post office** The post office is close to the clock tower on Kenyatta Av.

Nyahururu and Thompson's Falls *p*
Banks Barclays, Kenya Commercial Bank and Kenya Co-op Bank are all in the vicinity of the post office. **Medical services** Mbaria Centre, opposite the town hall, has a medical centre. **Post office** Securicor, Mbaria Centre, for delivery services.

Further north

The Rift Valley lakes of Baringo and Bogoria are not far from Nakuru and make an interesting diversion away from the game parks. The lakes are in attractive settings with Bogoria being best known for its hot springs and flamingos and Baringo for its large pods of hippos and excellent birdlife. Serious twitchers should head to this region as it offers some of the best birding in East Africa. ►► *For Sleeping, Eating and other listings, see pages 121-122.*

Lake Bogoria National Reserve → *Phone code: 037. Colour map 3, grid C6*

ⓘ *US$15 entrance fee plus US$1.50 per vehicle and US$2 per person for camping.*

This reserve, which covers an area of 107 sq km in the Rift Valley, is 40 km south of Lake Baringo and 80 km north of Nakuru, and is mainly bushland with small patches of riverine forest. The main reason people visit Lake Bogoria is to see the thermal areas with steam jets and geysers and the large number of flamingos that live here.

Ins and outs

It is an easy drive from Nakuru taking less than one hour along the Baringo road. Motorbikes are allowed into the park and the road is paved up to the hot springs, after which it becomes very rough. It is not possible to drive all around the lake as the road is closed on the east side between just north of **Fig Tree Camp** to just east of Loboi Gate. There are three gates, all accessible from by-roads off the B4 main road leading to Baringo. The main gate is Loboi Gate, at the lake's north end. The detour eastward from the B4 is 4 km south of Marigat. A paved road, the E461, heads for Loboi and the gate after a 21 km stretch. The other two gates are to the south of the reserve. Take the east turn-off the B4 at Mogotio, 59 km south of Marigat. This road covers some 20 km up to Mugurin. One kilometre ahead, the road splits into two. The left track heads on for some 20 km until a right turn-off which leads you to Maji Moto Gate, close to the hot springs. The other track at the right is badly damaged and quite steep at some stretches, and covers 14 km before reaching Emsos Gate, the southernmost gate, at the reserve's forest area. ►► *See also Transport, page 122.*

> ❗ *Baringo and Bogoria can be easily visited on a day trip from Nakuru, see page 107.*

Sights

There are now thought to be in excess of two million flamingos, predominantly the lesser flamingo, that feed on *Spirulina platensis*, the blue-green algae. Many of the flamingos have moved here from Lake Nakuru, possibly because the water level there fell so dramatically. Lake Bogoria's geysers are located mostly on the western side of the lake. There are pools with rather foul-smelling sulphurous steam bubbles, some of which send up boiling hot water spumes several metres high. Take care, the water is very hot and you can get badly burnt.

This is the least-visited of all Kenya's Rift lakes, but it can conveniently be included in a visit to Lake Baringo and the Kerio Valley, all of which are in this extremely hot area of the Rift Valley. The lake itself lies at the foot of the Laikipia Escarpment and its bottle-green waters reflect woodlands to the east. It is a shallow soda lake, between 1 m and 9 m in depth, and the shoreline is littered with huge lava boulders, surrounded by

> ● *In 2002 a herd of elephants swam across Lake Baringo, an event never seen at the lake before. It was believed locally that the elephants were on their way from the Kerio Valley National Reserve to the Laikipia Plateau.*

grassland. On the eastern side of the lake are found a number of greater kudu; they can best be seen in the evening when they come down to the lake to drink. The northern and eastern shoreline is swampy and attracts many waders. Along the eastern end of the lake you can see the northernmost part of the Aberdares. Trees including wild fig and acacia grow densely alongside the dry river beds and this is the best place for birdwatching.

❖ The lake area is a malarial zone; use nets, plenty of repellent and cover up.

Lake Baringo

Lake Baringo, 20 km north of Marigat, is a peaceful and beautiful freshwater lake covering about 168 sq km, at an altitude of about 1,000 m. It is a shallow lake with a maximum depth of 12 m. Like Lake Naivaisha, Lake Baringo appears to have no outlet, although it is thought that it drains to the north through an underground series of rocky fissures, possibly reappearing at Kapedo, 80 km away, where steaming water tumbles over a 10-m cliff, having been heated as a result of subterranean volcanic activity. This part of Kenya used to be heavily populated with game, but rinderpest greatly reduced the wildlife numbers in the early part of the 20th century.
➤➤ *For Sleeping, Eating and other listings, see pages 121-122.*

Ins and outs

Some 30 km past Nakuru on the B3 is the right turn-off to the B4, toward Kampi Ya Moto, Bogoria, Marigat and Kampi Ya Samaki, the latter town being at the lakeshore 2 km away from the main road. The road is tarmac up to the north tip of the lake. From Eldoret, take the C51 heading northward to Cherangani Hills. Some 33 km ahead, at the town of Iten, the road turns southeast. From there you will pass the towns of Kamarin, Tambach, Chebloch and Kabarnet and finally reach the junction with the B4 in Marigat, where you will turn left for Kampi Ya Samaki and Lake Baringo. ➤➤ *See also Transport, page 122.*

Sights

It is an extremely attractive lake with small, wooded creeks and little islands white pebble beaches, framed by the mountains to the east and west. The

Lakes Bogoria & Baringo

Rift Valley Further north

Lake Bogoria **8**
Roberts Campsite **5**
Semation Island **7**
Soi Safari Lodge **6**

Sleeping 😴
Island Camp **1**
Lake Baringo Club **2**

Camping ⛺
Acacia Tree **3**
Fig Tree **4**

⁞ Born to run

The Kalenjin people have attracted world-wide attention as they are markedly over-represented in world-class middle- and long-distance running championships. Numbering around three million, or 10% of Kenya's population, the Kalenjins have won about 75% of Kenya's distance running races, and 40% of international honours in the past 10 years. Kalenjin men are the world champions in more than half the sub-marathon distance races. The first of these amazing athletes from this part of Kenya was Kip Keino, who rose to world prominence in the Mexico Olympics in 1968. Despite suffering severe pain from gallstones he competed in the 10,000-m race. With two laps to go, whilst in the lead pack, he collapsed in pain, staggering off the track, but before the stretcher arrived he returned to the track and completed the race, despite having been disqualified. Just four days later he won the silver medal in the 5,000 m, and beat the American Jim Ryun for the gold in the 1,500 m. In the 1972 Games, Kip Keino won the gold in the steeplechase and silver in the 1,500 m. Nowadays Kip Keino helps to run a children's home with his wife Phyllis, and they have set up a school as well as the adjacent Baraka Farm with the aim of making these enterprises self sufficient.

Curiously, Kalenjin women have not enjoyed the same level of athletic success, although Joyce Chepchumba did win the London Marathon in 1999. The reason for the Kalenjins success has been ascribed in part to their 'altitude' training as their homesteads and farms are mostly located above 2,000 m, with its known aerobic benefits, plus their normal diet that contains a high percentage of complex carbohydrates. Whether this group of runners have an inherent genetic advantage is currently being studied. They appear to have an enhanced capacity to rapidly increase aerobic efficiency with training. In addition, an important co-factor is that the Kenya Amateur Athletics Association has actively fostered young athletic talent in the past 25 years. In combination with US scholar-ships, this has enabled many of these promising young Kalenjins to compete at international level.

For more information visit www.kenyaathletics.com.

Njemps fishermen can be seen on the lake, and the imposing Laikipia Escarpment creates a magnificent backdrop. The lake contains large schools of **hippo** and **crocodile,** and the delicious fish, tilapia, is caught here. There are several islands, **Ol Kowkwe** being the biggest of them at approximately 1,200 ha while the other islands include **Parmolok, Willys Island, Devils Island** and many others. The lake's greatest attraction is the huge numbers and varieties of **birds**. There are said to be 450 species of birds here, including the Hemprich's hornbill and Verreaux' eagle. On **Gibraltar Island** there is a very large colony of the Goliath heron, the largest concentration of these magnificent birds in East Africa. Mammals found locally include Grant's gazelle, waterbuck, mongoose and dikdik. The extended area around the lake is very hot and dry.

If you continue driving north past Lake Bogoria you will start noticing large sawn-off tree trunks lying horizontally in the higher branches of many of the trees. This odd sight is in fact a method of honey cultivation (the trunks are hollowed out to the bee's taste); the effort to get the branches up there is quite amazing. The result is the delicious Asilah honey on sale at the roadside.

Northern Rift Valley

Much of the northern part of the Rift Valley remains relatively unexplored by travellers and facilities are few and far between. The landscape is quite different from the central and western parts of the Rift. It is hot and arid, and only sparsely inhabited, but it has a stark beauty and provides an adventurous route to the Cherangani Hills, dealt with in the Northern Kenya chapter. ▸▸ *For Sleeping, Eating and other listings, see pages 121-122.*

Kerio Valley National Reserve → *Colour map 3, grid C6.*

Once past the lakes of Bogoria and Baringo you are heading up into the less-frequented regions of Kabarnet. Marigat to Kabarnet is a torturously slow drive. The extremely steep climb and slow *matatus* make for a trotting pace in first gear. The advantage though is of lingering views back over the Rift Valley and the lakes below. The town of Kabarnet is set in the Tugen Hills, which are virtually impenetrable, and looks 1,500 m down into the **Kerio Valley**, designated a national reserve in 1983 in recognition of its biodiversity. The deep valley covers an area of 66 sq km and is carpeted with lush, semi-tropical vegetation on the slopes, and thorn bush on the dry valley floor.

Isolated *shambas* (small farms) of the **Kalenjin** are dotted around the mountainous countryside. The Kalenjin people are very successful in world-class middle- and long-distance running championships, see box page 120. Apart from the Kalenjin herders and their livestock, there is little else in the Kerio Valley. The unspoilt beauty and quiet of the place is hardly disturbed by vehicles, although this does make it hard to explore except by hiking. It is best to visit in June, July and August after the long rains, when the land is at its greenest and the temperatures are comfortable.

Kabarnet → *Colour map 3, grid C6.*

Kabarnet itself is a quiet, unimposing town despite the fact that it is the capital of Baringo district. Its high altitude means it is cool (especially noticeable if you've come from the heat of Marigat), with an Alpine summer feel and there are great views northwards over the Kerio Valley. It is the hometown of Daniel Arap Moi, ex-president of the Republic of Kenya. The town itself is hardly interesting, but the location and the road that climbs up Tugen Hills, at the edge of Kerio Valley, display magnificent views. In town there are two banks, a post office, petrol station and a good supermarket in the same building as **Sinkoro** restaurant. **Kabarnet Museum** ① *Hospital Rd, www.museums.or.ke, 0900-1800, US$3,* belonging to the National Museums of Kenya, is in the former residence of the District Commissioner and exhibits elements from the local culture and traditions, as well as information on Lake Baringo and its environment. Lush vegetation growing in its broad gardens makes it almost a small botanic park.

✺ Sleeping

Lake Bogoria National Reserve *p118*
A **Lake Bogoria Hotel**, outside of the reserve, T037-40225, www.bogoriasparesort.com. 23 slightly faded, old-fashioned private cosy cottages with en suite bathrooms and a/c, and the only natural heated health spa in Kenya. The spa pool feeds from the hot springs of Bogoria, and the entrance gates to the park are only a 5-min drive away.

Camping
There are 3 campsites in the reserve.

E **Acacia Tree**, on the western shore, has pit latrines but no other facilities, bring all equipment, food and drinking water.
E **Fig Tree Campsite**, on the southern shore, is pleasant and quiet. There is a freshwater stream running through the campsite that is just big enough to get into. Beware of the baboons: secure your property and avoid camping directly under the fig trees as they enjoy the fruit enormously with predictable results. Access to the site is a winding rocky narrow track.

L **Island Camp**, reservations **UNIGLOBE Let's Go Travel**, Nairobi T020-4447151, www.lets gosafari.com, www.island-camp.com. Based on Ol Kokwe Island at the centre of Lake Baringo. This is quite an experience, even if only for a day trip. There is a swimming pool at the highest point of the camp where there are very good views. Winding paths lead down from the pool to the informal dining and bar areas. All 23 tents have own bathroom with flush toilet and shower, as well as a shaded veranda. Activities on offer include water skiing and windsurfing, guided walks and champagne bush breakfasts.

L **Semation Island**, reservations **Bush and Beyond/Bush Homes of East Africa**, Nairobi, T020-600457, www.bush-and-beyond.com and www.bush-homes.co.ke. A small island with breathtaking views, luxury accommodation up to 10 guests in 4 comfortable, airy, open-plan cottages, each with its own bathroom and sitting area. One is a family cottage with an upstairs and downstairs bedroom, sharing bathroom, sitting room and veranda. New swimming pool and very good food, rates are all-inclusive. Closed Apr-May.

L-A **Lake Baringo Club**, reservations **Block Hotels**, Nairobi, T020-650500, www.block hotelske.com. Noted for its 26 acres of colourful gardens, it also has a swimming pool and serves good buffet-style food. 48 rooms spread out in the gardens. Non-residents are welcome to use facilities on payment of a small fee. A resident ornithologist can accompany you on bird walks before breakfast and in the evening. Don't miss the bird boat trip which is highly recommended for birdwatchers. Boats take 8 people, and the tour is 2 hrs to see the lake, islands, crocodiles, hippos and birds.

B **Soi Safari Lodge**, just north of Kampi ya Samaki, T053-51242, www.soisafarilodge. com. Relatively new camp with a/c cottages, the bar and restaurant overlooks the lake and its imposing islands from a double-storey building with a sort of pagoda-style tiled roof. Buffet lunches and BBQ dinners are served, and there is a swimming pool.

B-F **Roberts Campsite**, T053-51431, www. lake-baringo.com. Camping is US$5 per person, shared hot showers, and bandas with kitchens are US$25 for 2 people, larger ones sleeping 4-6 are US$63. Boat hire from US$17 and bird walks from US$3.50. **The Thirsty Goat Pub and Restaurant** prides itself on an astonishing range of ice cold beers, wines, spirits and exotic cocktails, as well as a very good menu that includes vegetarian dishes. Watch out for hippos in this area and don't approach them; although they seem docile they can be dangerous.

Kabarnet *p121*

C **Kabarnet**, a 5-min walk from the post office, T053-22150, is this good modern hotel although furnishings are starting to look faded, set in well-tended gardens, perched on top of a hill for fine views of the valley. It has a lovely cool pool (non-residents US$2), restaurant and bar with set meals.

D **Hotel Sinkoro**, T053-22245. Central, good-value hotel, all rooms have hot water and breakfast included. The restaurant is very good for snacks and meals.

⊖ Transport

Lake Bogoria National Reserve *p118*
Several *matatus* a day run between Nakuru and **Loboi**.

Lake Baringo *p119*
From Nakuru, there are 2 buses daily to Kampi Ya Samaki, but *matatus* only reach Marigat. The boats for Ol Kokwa island, where **Island Camp** is located, may be hired at the jetty north of Kampi Ya Samaki.

Kabarnet *p121*
Buses to **Eldoret** (3 hrs) and **Nakuru** (2 hrs) leave early in the morning. There are regular *matatus* to **Eldoret**, **Nakuru** and **Marigat**. If you are driving, from Baringo, head south from Kampi Ya Samaki along the B4 and turn right in Marigat to the C51 for Eldoret. From Eldoret take the C51, which is a good sealed road, the 20 km or so to Iten and then follow the road as it zigzags up and down the Rift Valley although the Tugen Hills to Kabarnet. The journey to Eldoret, especially down to the valley floor, is very beautiful.

● *For an explanation of sleeping and eating price codes used in this guide, see inside the*
● *front cover. Other relevant information is found in Essentials, see pages 34-38.*

Masai Mara National Reserve

→ *Colour map 1, grid B2/3.*
This is the most popular of Kenya's parks, with very good reason. Almost every species of animal you can think of in relation to East Africa lives on the well-watered plains in this remote part of the country. One of the unique, spectacular and most memorable sights is the annual migration of hundreds of thousands of wildebeest, gazelle and zebra. The landscape is mainly gently rolling grassland with the rainfall in the north being double that of the south. The Mara River runs from north to south through the park and then turns westwards to Lake Victoria. Most of the plains are covered in a type of red-oat grass with acacias and thorn trees. ↠ *For Sleeping, Eating and other listings, see pages 126-130.*

Ins and outs

The Mara is 275 km southwest of Nairobi (five hours by road) in the remote southwestern corner of the country right on the Tanzanian border. The main access to the reserve is through the town of Narok, 141 km to the west of Nairobi. It is the main trading centre for the Masai people in southwestern Kenya and the last place you can get a cold drink or refuel if travelling there. Narok has two banks (one with an ATM), a post office and a museum plus countless souvenir stalls. From Narok, there is no singular major road into the reserve, which makes it advisable to study your route into the Mara depending on what your destination is once there. None of the access roads to the Masai Mara are in good condition and during the wet season they become quagmires, and a 4WD is essential. Because of this a large number of visitors choose to travel to the Mara by plane although it is of course more expensive. Air Kenya offers two scheduled flights a day from Wilson Airport to the park lodge airstrips. The flight lasts around 45 minutes compared to the five or more hours by road. Opening hours are 0630-1900, fees are US$30 per person per day, vehicle 500KSh, which covers entry to the national reserve and the Greater Mara region, which also includes a number of group ranches and conservancy regions. The fees can also be paid at many of the lodges and camps, or will be part of your safari package if you are on an organized tour.

Sights

The Mara covers some 1,510 sq km ranging between 1,500 m and 2,100 m above sea level. The reserve receives a high rainfall as a result of the altitude and humidity of nearby Lake Victoria, 160 km west. It is an extension of Tanzania's Serengeti National Park, a small part of the Serengeti ecosystem covering some 40,000 sq km between the Rift Valley and Lake Victoria.

If you can, time a visit with the annual migration of hundreds of thousands of wildebeest (estimated at 500,000 animals), gazelle and zebra as they move from the Serengeti Plains in January, having exhausted the grazing there, on their way northwards, arriving in the Masai Mara by about July-August. In the Mara, the herbivores are joined by yet another 100,000 wildebeest coming from the Loita Hills, east of the Mara. Once the Mara's new grass has been eaten, the wildebeests, zebra and gazelles retrace their long journey south to Tanzania in October, where their young are born, and where the grasslands have been replenished in their absence. It is estimated that in four or five months, the wildebeest alone deposit 60,000 tonnes of dung which fertilizes the grasslands for the next year's migration. One of the highlights of the migration is seeing the animals crossing the Mara River. Sometimes thousands of animals will mass on the banks, waiting for an opportunity to cross. Below, waiting knowingly in the river, are the enormous Mara crocodiles. First one, then another and then the whole frenetic herd leap into the water. In places, the river banks have been worn down considerably after centuries of crossings. Most make it

124 to the other side but many hundreds are either taken by crocodiles or drown. This lengthy trek costs the lives of many old, young, lame and unlucky animals, picked off by predators like lions, leopards and hyenas.

The reserve is teeming with herbivores – numbering around 2,500,000 including: wildebeest, Thompson's and Grant's gazelle, zebra, buffalo, impala, topi, hartebeest, giraffe, eland, elephant, dik-dik, klipspringer, steinbok, hippo, rhino, warthog and bushpig. There are also large numbers of lion, leopard, cheetah, hyena, wild dog and jackal, as well as smaller mammals and reptiles. In the Mara River hippo and apparently sleepy crocodiles can be seen. The number of animals suited to grasslands living in this area has increased enormously over the last 30 years due to woodland being cleared. In addition to the numerous mammals, over 450 species of birds have been recorded, including 57 species of birds of prey. The Masai Mara has a very high density of lion with about 500 in just over 1,500 sq km. Among the rarer mammals found here are the Roan antelope in the southwest sector, and the

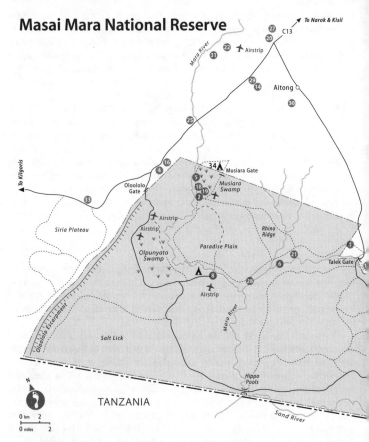

Masai Mara National Reserve

To Narok & Kisii
C13
Mara River
Airstrip
Aitong
To Kilgoris
Musiara Gate
Oloololo Gate
Musiara Swamp
Airstrip
Siria Plateau
Airstrip
Rhino Ridge
Olpunyata Swamp
Paradise Plain
Talek Gate
Airstrip
Oloololo Escarpment
Mara River
Salt Lick
Hippo Pools
TANZANIA
Sand River

0 km 2
0 miles 2

Sleeping 🛏
Acacia Camp **11**
Acacia Valley Camp **14**
Basecamp Masai Mara **15**
Bateleur Camp **16**
Cottars' 1920s Safari Camp **17**
Fig Tree Camp **1**
Governors' Il Moran Camp **18**

Governors' Camp **2**
Governors' Private Camp **19**
Keekorok Lodge **3**
Kicheche Mara Camp **20**
Kichwa Tembo Camp **4**
Little Governors' Camp **5**
Mara Explorer **21**
Mara Intrepids **6**

Mara Safari Club **22**
Mara Serena Lodge **8**
Mara Simba Lodge **23**
Mara Sopa Lodge **9**
Mara Springs Safari
 Camp **24**
Mpata Safari Club **33**
Olarro Camp **32**

Olonana Camp **25**
Olperr Elongo Camp **26**
Rekero Cottages **27**
Rekero Tented Camp **28**
Richard's Camp **29**
Saruni Camp **30**
Sarova Tented Camp **7**
Sekenani Camp **12**

thousands of topi only found here and in the Tsavo National Park. Another shy mammal is the bat-eared fox sometimes seen peering out of their burrows.

The **Oloololo Escarpment** on the western edge of the park is the best place to see the animals, although it is also the hardest part to get around, particularly after heavy rain, when the swampy ground becomes impassable.

The Masai Mara is not a national park but a game reserve, divided into an inner and outer section. The inner section covers an area of 52,000 ha, and the greater conservation area is 181,000 ha. The inner section has no human habitation apart from the lodges. In the outer reserve area the Masai coexist with the game and evidence of their village communities can be seen in the many *manyattas*. The essential difference between a game reserve and a national park is that the indigenous people (the pastoral Masai) have the right to graze their animals on the outer part of the reserve and to shoot animals if they are attacked. However, the game does not recognize these designated boundaries and an even larger area, known as the 'dispersal area' extends north and east contiguous with the reserve, where the Masai people live with their stock. However, the Masai have never hunted wild animals for food but depend on their cows, and effectively live in peace with the wildlife. The reserve is controlled by the Narok and Trans-Mara County Councils and not by Kenya Wildlife Services.

There is increasing concern about the impact that the servicing of the requirements of the tourists is having on the finely tuned ecological balance of the reserve. A couple of the identified concerns are the impact that the off-road driving is having on the flora. Many vehicles criss-cross the area causing soil erosion by churning up the grasslands. However, the animals do not appear to be adversely affected by the huge number of visitors to the reserve. Another concern regards the disposal of waste generated by the tourist industry, as some of the predators like hyenas are discovering an easier food source by rummaging through the garbage.

A community initiative has been established at **Rekero Camp** where you are introduced to the cultural side of the Mara as well as seeing the wildlife. Visits to Masai *manyattas* (homes) are on offer as well as game drives. The money generated by this ecotourism initiative goes directly to the local community. Just outside the Oloolaimutia Gate there is a Masai village, open to the public, which you can wander round taking as many photographs as you wish for about US$7 per person.

Rift Valley Masai Mara National Reserve

Loita Hills

To Narok, Naivasha & Nairobi

Talek River

Airstrip

Sekenani Gate

Park HQ

Oloolaimutia Gate

Sand River

Sand River Gate

Siana Springs Intrepids 13
Voyager Safari Lodge 31

Camping
Musiara Gate 34
Oloolaimutia 35
Sand River 36
Talek River 37

● Sleeping

There is an abundance of luxury lodges and tented camps but the Masai Mara also offers a large number of campsites, really the only option for budget travellers (although almost all are accessed on poor roads).

In the reserve *p123, map p124*
Lodges
L **Keekorok Lodge**, in the southeast of the reserve, reservations **African Mecca Safaris**, www.africanmeccasafaris. com. Oldest lodge in the Mara, set in a grassy plain, swimming pool, wildlife and local culture lectures, game drives arranged. High-standard rooms, cosy lounge, outside dining room, an elevated walkway to a bar overlooking a hippo pool.
L **Mara Serena Lodge**, T050-22253, www. serenahotels. com. Well designed, 74 boma style rooms with balconies with a superb view over the Mara River and plains beyond, restaurant overlooking a waterhole, pool. Two-day packages include return flights from Nairobi or Mombasa, full board and 3 or 4 game drives. Wildlife films, Masai dancing.
L **Mara Sopa Lodge**, reservations, Nairobi, T020-336088, www.sopalodges.com. Well located near to Oloolaimutia Gate, 200-bed lodge: 77 rooms, 12 suites and 1 presidential suite. One of the most popular in the reserve. Rondavel rooms with balconies/verandas, grand African-style public areas, fine food, friendly staff, excellent swimming pool, balloon safaris and night game drives.

Tented camps
A stay in one of the tented camps, with perhaps a dawn hot-air balloon safari (around US$375), is an unforgettable experience (book well in advance). They often include game drives in the price.

There are 5 'Governors' Camps', all different and all expensive although game drives are included. They are unfenced, but patrolled by Masai guards just in case the animals get too curious. All the Governors' Camps are consistently rated in the Gold List of *Condé Nast Traveller*'s 'Best Place to Stay in the World'. Rates vary between US$165 and US$500 per person per night, with Governors' Camp being the cheapest. Reservations, Nairobi, T020-2734000, www.governors camp.com.

L **Governors' Bush Camp**, a traditional mobile camp that moves seasonally and is used for Governors' walking safaris. The standards are as high as the other camps but accommodation is a little simpler. Patrick Reynolds, who has many years of walking safari experience, is the head guide. There are also Masai scouts, who have an intimate knowledge of the flora and fauna of the area, the medicinal properties of the plants and knowledge of Masai culture and customs. 4 double tents with en suites, all the other facilities are under canvas, and there is a nightly campfire. Walking, game drives and visits to Masai villages are all on offer.
L **Governors' Camp**, solid floors for tents , very spacious and nicely decorated, verandas, bar lounge, candlelit dinners, small museum, balloon safaris, no swimming pool, beautiful site by the Mara River and excellent game viewing. The guides on the game drives and walks are very knowledgeable.
L **Governors' Il Moran Camp**, in bush along the Mara River. Small and intimate camp hidden under ancient trees. 10 tents are very private and furnished to a superior standard, with antiques, stunning beds hand-made from olive trees, large bathrooms with showers and Victorian baths, you can take dinner at your tent if you wish. Game drives and game walks are included in the rate and complimentary wine is served with dinner.
L **Governors' Private Camp**, on a bend of the Mara River. A private camp that can only be booked by one family/group at a time, up to 16 people (minimum of 4), and usually for a minimum of 3 nights. The food is delicious, and served on fine china and crystal, and guests can design their own menus.
L **Little Governors' Camp**, access by ferry across the Mara River followed by a short walk with guards. Very special, a splendid site with very high standards. 17 comfortable and tasteful tents with solid floors are tucked around a large watering-hole that teems with animal and bird life. In keeping with safari tradition lighting is by gas and kerosene lantern or candlelight. Flickering lights at dusk make this an atmospheric place.
L **Mara Explorer**, reservations **Heritage Hotels**, Nairobi T020-4442115, www.heritage -eastafrica.com. On a bend of the Talek River,

this is intended to provide ultra-exclusive sophistication and style for couples. 10 tents where a personal butler is on hand at all times, elephants can be watched from the outside bath tubs. Rates upwards of US$500.

L Mara Intrepids, reservations **Heritage Hotels**, Nairobi, T020-4442115, www.heritage -eastafrica.com. By the Talek River, 30 tents with large 4-poster beds, en suite bathrooms, swimming pool. Bar overlooks a leopard bait.

L Rekero Tented Camp, very close to the confluence of the Mara and Talek rivers, www.rekero.com. Mobile camp situated for the annual migration, set up seasonally (Jun-Oct, and Dec-Mar), takes up to 14 guests in 5 spacious tents, farmhouse meals, picnics in the bush and sundowners, very good guides for game activities. Jackson ole Looseyia, the local Masai guide, is quite exceptional.

Greater Mara *p123, map p124*
Lodges

L Mara Simba Lodge, reservations Nairobi, T020-4444401, www.marasimba.com. Over-looking the Talek River just north of the Talek Gate, 84 guest rooms arranged in clusters of 6 natural wood and stone thatched bandas. Each has 4 rooms on the ground floor and 2 interconnecting rooms on the 1st floor, all have en suite bathrooms and verandas overlooking the river. Restaurant and bar. Wildlife and ecology talks. Swimming pool, room service and evening entertainment. The only lodge in Kenya which has installed a waste water treatment plant.

L Mpata Safari Club, Oloololo Escarpment, reservations Nairobi, T020-310867, www.mp ata.com. 5-star lodge with restaurant, library, bar, pool, jacuzzi, very stylish modern decor, very good views, designed by one of Japan's leading architects, 23 cottages with bath-rooms, each with private plunge pool and veranda, game drives, walks, Masai villages.

L Olarro Camp, reservations Archer's Tours & Travel, Nairobi, T020- 3752481, www. olarro.com. Olárrò means buffalo in the Masai language. On 150,000 acres of private land, perched 2,000 m up in the scenic Loita Hills, offering superb views (though some distance from the reserve, 35 km). 8 African-style cottages tucked in the bush, lovely

lounge area, pool, game drives and walking safaris are conducted personally by the camp's manager who is a professional guide.

L Rekero Cottages, www.rekero.com, in Masai Mara Conservation Area. Expensive – only room for 8 guests, thatched bungalows with en suite bathrooms, and a twin-bed fully furnished tent, personally conducted safari walks available, game drives, visits to local communities. Closed Apr-May and Nov.

L Saruni Camp, www.sarunicamp.com. On the Lemek Koyiaki Group Ranch, to the north of the Mara, near Aitong. New, de luxe and intimate lodge with 6 large and very elegant cottages furnished with colonial antiques, Persian carpets and African art, Italian bathroom fittings, polished wooden floors and large bathrooms with a view.

L Voyager Safari Lodge, reservations Heritage Hotels, Nairobi, T020-4442115, www.heritage-eastafrica.com. Located on the banks of the Sante River, which is home to many hippo. Aimed at first-time safari-goers who want luxury. 78 en suite rooms in riverside cottages, bar and breakfast/cocktail terrace, swimming pool, children's safari activities, Masai entertainment.

Tented camps

L Acacia Valley Camp, reservations Acacia Trails, Nairobi, T020-501858, acacia@swift kenya.com. In a valley with en suite bucket showers and a 'short-drop' camp toilet, each has a private, shady veranda and is lit with gas and paraffin lanterns. Large and comfortable dining and lounge tent with a 'self-help' bar for all-inclusive guests, buffet lunches are served outside and dinners are silver service.

L Basecamp Masai Mara, reservations Nairobi, T020-577490, www.basecamp explorer.com. On a peninsula by the Talek River. 15 spacious, comfortable tents shaded by grass roofs, each has own terrace and a hot shower open to the sky. Restaurant, bar, game viewing tower, Masai entertainment. Popular with Scandinavians. Makes use of dry toilets, recycling of waste, solar energy etc. Can organize walking safaris.

L Bateleur Camp, reservations, CC Africa, Johannesburg, T+27-118094300, www.cc

---

🎈 *For an explanation of sleeping and eating price codes used in this guide, see inside the front cover. Other relevant information is found in Essentials, see pages 34-38.*

africa.com. On the Mara River, below the location where *Out of Africa*'s final scene was filmed. Romantic and totally private exuding the ambience of Kenyan safaris of the 1920s and 1930s. 9 exclusive tented suites, with expansive en suite bathrooms, ceiling fans, private butler service. Beautiful antiques. Walking safaris, pool, day/night game drives. US$445-560 per person all-inclusive.

L **Cottars' 1920s Safari Camp**, www.cottars. com. Award-winning unspoilt site, specialist walks and lectures with renowned guide Calvin Cottar, swimming pool. 6 authentic white canvas tents are luxuriously furnished with original safari antiques from the 1920s, private en suite dressing rooms, bathrooms with old-fashioned tubs. Butlers and beauty therapist for massages and treatments.

L **Kicheche Mara Camp**, reservations Nairobi T020-890541, www.kicheche.com, on the Aitong Plains in the northern Koiyaki Lemek region. 11 comfortably furnished tents with en suite bathrooms, most are secluded and overlook the plains and hills, others are closer together for families/groups. Lounge with comfortable seating, library and games, dining is either alone or with the hosts, good fresh food. A 2-night package including meals and game activities costs US$630.

L **Kichwa Tembo Camp**, reservations CC Africa, Johannesburg, T+27-118094300, www.ccafrica.com. At the base of the Oloololo Escarpment, 40 Hemingway-style safari tents, with en suite bathrooms and private verandas. Main thatched guest areas include a bar/sitting area, indoor/outdoor dining areas. Bush breakfasts or dinners, bush walks and night game-drives can be organised. Rates US$185-260 per person.

L **Mara Safari Club**, reservations Lonrho Hotels, The Norfolk, Nairobi, T020-216940, www.lonrhohotels.com. At the foot of the Aitong Hills, positioned on an ox-bow of the Mara River. 50 tents with 4-poster beds, 10 of which have sunken baths and platforms for private dining. Surrounded by well-cultivated gardens, swimming pool. Wildlife slide shows, dancing and talks on Masai culture. Comfortable bar also offering afternoon tea.

L **Olonana Camp**, www.olonana.com. A lavish camp on the Mara River, 12 spacious tents, each tastefully appointed with large, riverview verandas. Superb food in the dining room overlooking the river, comfort-able sitting area, swimming pool. Meals, game drives etc. US$225-450 per person.

L **Richard's Camp**, reservations through **Cheli & Peacock**, Nairobi, T020- 604053, www.chelipeacock.com. Originally built as the Roberts' family home whilst carrying out conservation work, this small and exclusive tented camp has 6 individually decorated tents, with en suite flush loo and heated shower, all meals are taken outside, and there is a cozy sitting room with roaring fire. A Victorian bath has been tucked away in the bush where you can bathe by candlelight.

L **Sekenani Camp**, reservations Nairobi, T020-571597, www.vastray.com. Intimate, luxurious and very charming. 15 tents are raised on wooden platforms and set well apart amid lush vegetation. Polished wooden floors, grand baths, hurricane lamps, fine food. A suspension bridge leads to the dining room serving fresh gourmet meals.

L **Siana Springs Intrepids**, reservations **Heritage Hotels**, Nairobi, T020-4442115, www.heritage-eastafrica.com. At the base of the Ngama Hills, set in a lush indigenous forest watered by the largest natural springs in the Mara ecosystem known as 'Siana' meaning 'the plentiful' in the local language. 38 luxury tents, bar and large dining area, swimming pool, adventure club for kids. Walking safaris, night drives and fly camping along the seasonal streams beneath the Ngama Hills. Rates around US$300 per person.

L-A **Fig Tree Camp**, reservations **Mada Hotels**, Nairobi, T020-218321, www.mada hotels.com. One of the original camps, lately refurbished. 65 units, some tented camp and some timber cabins with electricity, pool, 2 bars and restaurants, and a treehouse coffee deck. Rates US$200 for a double in high season and US$120 in low season.

L-A **Sarova Tented Camp**, reservations, Nairobi T020-2714444, www.sarova.co.ke. Good tents and food, beautiful views, pool, bar with large fireplace, meals can be taken in the restaurant or out bush, large with 75 tents, so rather impersonal. Massages are available.

C-F **Acacia Camp**, reservations, Nairobi, T020-210024, www. acaciacamp.com. Simple and cheap, 34 walk-in tents, built up on wooden platforms under a thatch cover, each tent has 2 single beds and a small table, shared showers and toilets. Without bedding, US$24, with US$32. Camping with own tent

US$5. Fully operational kitchen with gas stoves, but you will need to bring all food.

C-F Mara Springs Safari Camp, reservations Nairobi, T020-242133, www.mountainrock kenya.com. At the foot of Naunare Hills alongside the forested banks of Sekenani River, 3 km from the Sekenani Gate. Very basic with tents with beds and bedding or pitch your own tent on the well-shaded campsite. Self catering in the fully equipped kitchen or meals from the restaurant, shared bathrooms with hot showers and flush toilet. US$15 per person for pre-erected tent, US$5 per person with your own tent, US$40 per person full board, and US$30 per person full board if in your own tent.

D-F Olperr Elongo Camp, www.biketreks. co.ke. Olperr Elongo is Masai for *Albizia gummifera*, a local tree that grows near the spring from where the camp obtains its water. Well-shaded and spacious, the large tents are set up on plinths and contain 2 camp stretcher beds and table with chairs on the veranda. Camping with your own tent too. Shared hot showers and flushing toilets. Meals are taken in a mess tent. A percentage of all fees go to the local community. Cycling in the conservation area can be arranged.

Camping

The Masai Mara hardly caters for budget travellers apart from a few campsites. The total figures usually speak of 25 campsites, but the number varies depending on the source. In theory, they should be booked in advance, but for public campsites it is possible to do this once at the reserve. Camping fees are paid at the gates, but if you want to hire a Masai *askari*, you will pay for his services directly to him. There are campsites close to every gate and one public campsite within the reserve near the **Serena Lodge**. Few have any facilities, although firewood is usually available. Those listed below are recommended.

E Musiara Gate, there are no facilities but you should be able to get water from the wardens. This is very popular for being a safe area, shaded and with plentiful wildlife.

E Oloolaimutia Campsite, at the eastern side of the park, is the most lively place to stay. It is Masai-run and is where most budget safari outfits stay. Water is limited and you have to buy it if you need it. Nearby **Mara Sopa Lodge** serves food and drink (warm beers) and has a lively atmosphere.

E Sand River Gate, with lavatories, water and a shop, which is located by a waterhole usually visited by animals at night.

E Talek River Campsites, close to the Talek Gate, at 10 locations. These are located east of the gate, bordering the river at the north bank, which at the same time is the reserve's limit. Several of them are nearly always booked up by safari companies.

▲ Activities and tours

A very popular activity in the Masai Mara is a balloon flight above the plains to watch the big herds from the air. Most of the lodges and camps offer this activity, which always works in a similar way. Tourists are picked up around 0530 and driven to the site where the lift-off will take place. The balloon blow-up is part of the experience. Once the balloon rises, passengers have the chance to watch the sunrise high above the plains when the sun comes up and turns the grasslands from blue to gold. Especially during the months of the migration, this is often the highlight of visitors' trips to Kenya. The flight lasts 60-90 mins. Finally, the price usually includes a bush breakfast, made on firewood stoves beneath a tree, frequently served with champagne. If your lodge does not offer this service, they can arrange it and book the day before with one of the lodges that does. The following lodges have balloons; **Little Governors' Camp, Keekorok Lodge, Fig Tree Camp** and the **Mara Serena**. Flights cost in the region of US$370-400. **Shoor Safaris**, based in Nairobi and Nakuru, T253-733-736131/203740407, www.shoor travel.com, offers good tours throughout the Masai Mara.

☻ Transport

Air
Air Kenya, Wilson Airport, Nairobi, T020-605745 (reservations), www.airkenya.com, has daily flights between **Nairobi** and the Masai Mara, which cost US$95 one way and US$170 return in the low season, and US$105 one way and US$185 return in the high season. Low season is 1 Apr-15 Jun and 1 Nov-15 Dec. Flights depart Nairobi twice daily (1000 and 1500) and take 45 mins. Return flights leave the Masai Mara at 1100 and 1600. **Air Kenya** also has a daily one-way flight from **Nanyuki**, which leaves at 1000 and arrives about 1130, US$172. Baggage allowance is only 15 kg for **Air Kenya**.

Road
If you are exploring the Masai Mara independently in your own vehicle let someone know where you are going, travel in groups of 2 or more vehicles if possible, seek advice about the state of the roads especially in the wet seasons, and remember, in the event of an emergency mobiles to do not yet get full coverage in the reserve.

Public buses from **Nairobi** only go as far as **Narok** and the chances of hitching a lift to and through the reserve are slim. To get to Narok from the capital take the old Nairobi-Naivasha road (B3 – the more westerly road) that forks to the left at Rironi, the road continues in a northwesterly direction for 6 km then turns left on a sealed

tarmac road in a southwesterly direction south of Mt Longonot. From here it is 82 km to Narok. The route is well served by *matatus* and share-taxis. From Narok to the reserve, if you are driving yourself there are a number of possibilities of accessing the reserve. Some 15-20 km past Narok, the B3 road reaches Ewaso Ng'iro, where there is a crossroads, and from here there are 2 options. The first is the most frequent route, leading to the eastern sector of the park, where **Keekorok Lodge** is located. At Ewaso Ng'iro, there is a left turn on to the C12. Some 40 km ahead the road divides. Both tracks lead to the Masai Mara, but to different gates, and converge within the reserve at **Keekorok Lodge**. The one at the right is the main access, leading to Sekenani Main Gate. The left route reaches Ololamutiek Gate crossing a collapsed bridge, but it is passable for a 4WD vehicle. The second option from Ewaso Nyiro is less used because of its worse condition and abundance of mud after the rains. At Ewaso Ng'iro, go straight ahead along the B3 some 40 km more up to Ngorengore. At this village turn left on to the C13. From here there are two further choices. The first one is driving straight to Oloololo Gate and Kichwa Tembo Camp, at the western side of the reserve. The second option is turning left at Aitong to the E177. This track leads to the eastern sector through Talek Gate. If arriving from Kisii from western Kenya, take the main A1 highway heading south for Tanzania. Past Migori, at Suna, just before reaching the border, there is a left turn-off toward Lolgorien and the Masai Mara. This track crosses the Soit Ololol Escarpment and is very steep in places. You'll enter the reserve through Oloololo Gate, at the western sector of the reserve. There are two bridges that cross the Mara River, the New Mara Bridge is along the reserve's main road, the E176, which connects Keekorok Lodge with Oloololo Gate. The second bridge over the Mara, lies outside the reserve, northwest of the limits shortly after Oloololo Gate. Apart from this main network, there is a web of minor roads in different conditions, some of them passable all the year round and others flooded during the rainy season. Off-track driving over the years has caused wheel-track tangles that are hard to discern from the authorized roads, and the maps available are generally far from perfect.

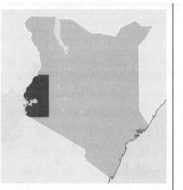

Western Kenya

Ins and outs	134
Kisumu	**134**
Listings	138
South of Kisumu	**141**
Kisumu to the Tanzanian border	141
Kisii and the Western Highlands	144
Listings	146
Kakamega and around	**148**
Kakamega	148
Kakamega Forest National Reserve	148
Eldoret	150
Listings	150
The far north	**153**
Ugandan border	153
Kitale	153
Saiwa Swamp National Park	154
Mount Elgon National Park	155
Listings	157

⦂ Footprint features

Don't miss...	133
Rat tales	135
Lake Victoria	137

Introduction

Western Kenya is the most fertile and populous part of the country, teeming with market towns and busy fishing villages. There are also a number of national parks and reserves in this region. Kakamega Forest National Reserve is the only tract of equatorial rainforest in Kenya that was once linked to the mighty forests of Central Africa. It contains many species of birds, trees and butterflies that are found nowhere else in the country and is a delightful and tranquil place for walking. Saiwa Swamp National Park, near Kitale, is worth a visit to see the rare sitatunga antelope. Mount Elgon National Park has good climbing and is accessed from Kitale and is home to the famous elephants that enter its caves in search of salt. To the south of this region is Kenya's share of Lake Victoria, Africa's largest lake which can be visited from Kisumu, Kenya's third largest town, which is extremely laid back and very friendly. Fishing for tilapia and Nile perch provides a living for many of the Luo who live along the lakeside. Most of the fishing is from small picturesque dugout canoes, equipped with lateen sails, and the fish are sold at local markets or to the processors for sale in Nairobi and for export.

For some reason the region is not that popular with the big tour operators which is all to the benefit of the independent traveller. In fact, conditions for budget travellers are perfect; over half the population of the whole country lives here so public transport is excellent and the road surfaces tend to be above average. There are numerous cheap hotels and restaurants, and there is plenty to see and do. Tourists wanting slightly more upmarket services are not so well catered for, their best bet being to stay in one of the better hotels in Kisumu and hire a car to explore other parts of the region.

★ Don't miss...

1 **Lake Victoria** Fishermen should head for the fishing camps on the islands of Africa's largest lake to try their luck at catching a massive Nile perch, page 137.
2 **Around Kericho** Take a drive through the impossibly pretty hillsides covered with acres of brilliant green tea plantations, page 145.
3 **Kakemega Forest** Walk through the Kakemega Forest, once part of the equatorial forest that spread right across Africa, and home to a variety of birds, monkey, butterflies and rare flowers, page 148.
4 **Saiwa Swamp National Park** Search for the rare and very unusual antelope, the semi-aquatic sitatunga, page 154.
5 **Sirikwa Safaris** Join this family-run business at a rambling old settler home near Kitale and go trout fishing and on guided walks in the hills, page 158.

Western Kenya

Ins and outs

Getting around Western Kenya is pretty straightforward. All the regional towns are linked by a steady stream of buses and *matatus* and most (not all) of the roads are in a reasonable tarred condition with only the occasional pothole. The main A1 that goes to Tanzania is good all the way through to Mwanza, and there are frequent buses to the border and beyond. Indeed Tanzanian long-distance buses between Mwanza to Arusha and Dar es Salaam usually take the route via Kenya. From the border, the Western Corridor of Tanzania's Serengeti National Park is less than 200 km from Kenya, so there is the option of exploring some of Tanzania along with Western Kenya. Self driving is also a good option in this region, and distances between the towns and sights are relatively short and there are plenty of places to stop for petrol and take a break. The towns themselves hold little interest but driving around the region gives a good opportunity to enjoy the countryside, especially the impossibly scenic hills covered in the brilliant green tea plantations around Kericho and Kisii. There are a few tour operators that are doing much to promote this region and a number of safaris are on offer that are way off the normal tourist trail. Kisumu is a four- to five-hour drive from Nairobi or alternatively there are regular flights.

Kisumu → *Phone code: 057. Colour map 1, grid A2. Population 250,000.*

Kisumu, on the shore of Lake Victoria, is the principal town in Western Kenya and the third largest city in the country. It is a very pleasant place with a slow, gentle pace of life, a relaxed ambience, and the whole town coming to a standstill on Sunday. The sleepy atmosphere is as much due to lack of economic opportunities as to the extremely hot dry weather, which makes doing almost anything in the middle of the day quite hard work. The town has been by-passed by post-Independence development, and the signs are all too visible. Warehouses by the docks remain empty and the port does not have the bustling atmosphere you would expect in such an important town. Many of the wealthier people have moved out of Kisumu, hence the number of large houses lying empty or run down. Twitchers will enjoy nearby, Ndere Island National Park. ▸▸ *For Sleeping, Eating and other listings, see pages 138-140.*

Ins and outs

Kisumu is an excellent base for exploring the region with good bus and *matatu* links to nearby towns, as well as to Western Kenya and Uganda. Kisumu has a small airfield, but most people come to and go from here by bus or *matatu*. Despite the hilly terrain, you will have no problem getting around Kisumu as there are literally thousands of *boda bodas* (bicycle taxis) – so much so it is quite difficult to drive through central Kisumu because of the barrage of bikes. ▸▸ *See Transport, page 140, for further details.*

History

Kisumu developed during the colonial era into the principal port in the region. The railway line reached Lake Victoria in 1902, five years after plate laying began 1,000 km away in Mombasa, opening up trade opportunities. It was briefly called Port Florence. By the 1930s it had become the hub of administrative and military activities on the lake. Kisumu was a difficult place at this time, bilharzia was endemic, malaria and sleeping sickness were common and the climate was sweltering. However, the area attracted investment from many different quarters, including Asians ending their contracts to work on the railway.

⁑ Rat tales

Around 1916 or 1917 the plague spread across parts of Kenya and Uganda. It was spread by rats, or rather the fleas that live on the rats, and in an effort to curb the problem the medical authorities in Kisumu had a plan. They offered 10 cents for every dozen rats' tails that were brought in to them. About 18 miles from Kisumu, at Maseno, many dozens were collected – but it was a long walk to take them into Kisumu.

So the collectors approached the missionary authorities and asked whether they could give the rats' tails as collection in church. This was agreed on, and provided they were sun-dried, and correctly bundled, there was no objection. Every Sunday the collection tray was passed around, many bundles were collected and on Monday the mission sent someone to Kisumu with them, for payment.

The Luo felt they were neglected immediately after Independence, and that political life was dominated by Kikuyu who centred development on Central province. The breakdown of trade between Kenya, Uganda and Tanzania and the collapse of the East African Community in 1977 badly affected Kisumu and there has been no compensating expansion of manufacturing in the area.

The murder of Robert Ouko, a Luo, in 1990 led to riots where many people died and much property was destroyed. Later, in the build-up to multi-party elections in Kenya, the nearby area was the scene of outbreaks of ethnic violence and thousands of people fled their *shambas*, coming into Kisumu or heading up to Eldoret.

Sights

Kisumu Museum ① *T035-40804, www.museums.or.ke, 0930-1800, US$3*, is to the east of the town's lively market. Its small yet comprehensive exhibit gallery focuses on displays of material culture of the peoples of the Western Rift Valley and Nyanza Province. This includes traditional clothing and adornment, basketry, fishing gear, agricultural tools and hunting weaponry. There are also a number of stuffed birds, mammals, reptiles and fish. Most impressive is a lion bringing down a wildebeest. A 190-kg Nile perch is exhibited, thought to be the largest ever caught in Kenya. The ethnographic exhibits centre on the customs and traditions of the tribal groups who lived in this area. There is a life-size replica of a traditional Luo homestead, and includes livestock pens and a granary. There is also a giant tortoise, imported to Kenya from the Seychelles in 1930, that is reputedly over 300 years old.

Majority of people here are Christian (mainly Roman Catholics), but there are a significant number of Muslims. **Jamia Mosque**, on Otieno Oyoo Street, is testament to the long tradition of Islam here. Built in 1919, this green and white building has two imams and calls to prayer can be heard in much of the town.

Dunga Swamp is located by following the shoreline road south past the **Sunset Hotel**. It is home to the rare *Papyrus gonolek*, which faces extinction due to the cutting down of papyrus reeds along the shores of Lake Victoria. Dunga Swamp attracts birders from all over the world as it is the only habitat of the *Papyrus gonolek*. Ornithologists have expressed concern that the destruction of the environment combined with frequent hunting of the bird is threatening its survival.

Excursions

Dunga itself is a small village just 3 km outside Kisumu. It is a lovely, peaceful place to visit on the shores of Lake Victoria. **Dunga Refreshments**, where you can get a cold soda and something to eat whilst watching fishermen bring in their catch, has great views over the lake. There are hippos here, but they are elusive. Once night has fallen they come out of the water to graze on land. You can negotiate with a fisherman to

❣ Avoid the temptation to swim in the lake here as bilharzia is rife.

take a rowing boat out to nearby Hippo Point where you can see the hippos in the water. Watching the sun set over the lake is a very pleasant way to end the day.

On the way up the dirt track to Dunga you pass the compact **Impala Sanctuary** ⓘ *0600-1800, US$5*. This tiny sanctuary, only 0.4 sq km of marsh, forest and grassland, was created to protect the few remaining impala in the region, decimated over the last century by hunting. The sanctuary was expanded to act as a holding point for captured animals. Nowadays it has two leopards, a spotted hyena and several vervet monkeys in addition to several reptiles and birds, but they are all in cages and it is nothing more than a sad-looking zoo. Hippos come up to the sanctuary to graze, and in the past there have been sightings of the rare Sitatunga antelope.

Kisumu Bird Sanctuary is off the A1 on the way to Ahero, about 8 km out of Kisumu. You need to follow the track round the marshy areas along the lakeshore for the best viewing sites. This is a nesting and breeding site for hundreds of birds including herons, ibises, cormorants, egrets and storks. The best time to visit is from April to May.

Gazetted in 1986, **Ndere Island National Park** ⓘ *0600-1800, US$15*, covers a small island of just over 4 sq km off the northern shore of Lake Victoria, 30 km from Kisumu. In the local Luo language Ndere means 'meeting place' and, according to

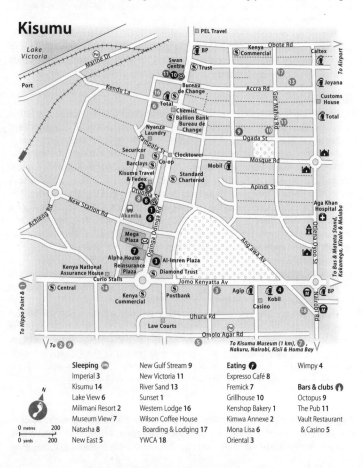

Kisumu

Sleeping 🛏	New Gulf Stream 9	Eating 🍴	Wimpy 4
Imperial 3	New Victoria 11	Expresso Café 8	
Kisumu 14	River Sand 13	Fremick 7	Bars & clubs 🍸
Lake View 6	Sunset 1	Grillhouse 10	Octopus 9
Milimani Resort 2	Western Lodge 16	Kenshop Bakery 1	The Pub 11
Museum View 7	Wilson Coffee House	Kimwa Annexe 2	Vault Restaurant
Natasha 8	Boarding & Lodging 17	Mona Lisa 6	& Casino 5
New East 5	YWCA 18	Oriental 3	

0 metres 200
0 yards 200

Lake Victoria

Lake Victoria is one of the most important natural water resources in the sub-Saharan region of Africa. It is the second biggest fresh water lake in the world, with a surface area of approximately 69,500 sq km. The Tanzania share of the lake is 49%, whilst the Kenyan share of the lake is 6% and Uganda has 45%. The surrounding lake communities in all three countries equal around 30 million people, with a large proportion being totally dependent on the lake for water, food and economic empowerment.

Despite its vast size, Lake Victoria remained one of the last physical features in Africa to be discovered by the 19th-century explorers from Europe. Early charts depict a vague patch of water lying to the north and east of the 'Mountains of the Moon' (today's Rwenzori Mountains in Uganda), but it was not until 1858 that explorers Speke and Burton stumbled on to its southern shore near Mwanza in Tanzania. He said "the lake at my feet is the most elusive of all explorers' dreams, the source of the legendary Nile".

Lake Victoria is relatively shallow and has a gentle slope on the shores hence any slight change in lake level affects a considerably large land area. The lake has a mean depth of about 40 m, with the deepest part at 82 m.

Scientifically, it is puzzling that so many diverse species unique to these waters could evolve in so uniform an environment. Biologists speculate that hundreds of thousands of years ago, the lake may have dried into a series of smaller lakes causing these brilliantly coloured cichlids to evolve differently. These fish are greatly sought after for aquariums. One unique characteristic for which cichlids (tilapia being the best known) are noted for is the female's habit of nursing its fertilized eggs and young in its mouth. To the people of Lake Victoria, the cichlids have been their livelihood. Lake Victoria is also a home to a predator fish, the Nile perch, introduced into the lake 20 years ago as a sport fish. The lake once had abundant hippo and crocodile but these are reduced.

legend, Kit Mikayi, mother of the tribe, rested up near here following her long journey south down the Nile Valley. The island is home to a large bird population including the fish eagle. Hippos and crocodiles are plentiful on the shoreline, and there is also a small herd of impalas. Other animals present include pythons and moniter lizards. Very few visitors make it to Ndere Island, due to its small size and lack of terrestrial wildlife. Bird enthusiasts, however, would find a visit to Ndere Island very rewarding. The island vegetation is primarily glades in the upland areas, with a shoreline fringe of woodland. However, as with other parts of this area of Kenya, tsetse flies are common, along with the ubiquitous malaria-vector mosquitoes. Access to the island is by boat from Kisumu, although the water hyacinth problem in Lake Victoria has proved to be an impediment. **Lake Victoria Environmental Management Project** (LVEMP) has begun a major programme to shred 1,500 ha of the water hyacinth weed. The project has received funds from the **World Bank**, and two 'Swamp Devils' have been purchased to chop, shred and remove the prolific weed that has formed great mats, inhibiting even large boats from using the ports. There is no regular boat service to the park, so transport has to be negotiated with the local fishermen. Small boats can be hired at the fishing villages of Kamuga or Asembo on the nearby mainland for the short distance to Ndere Island. Alternatively you can organize a motorized canoe to take you the 30 km from Kisumu which is quite a good way to explore Lake Victoria. It is possible to camp on the island but you have to be completely self sufficient.

Western Kenya Kisumu

● Sleeping

Kisumu is swarming with mosquitoes. If you don't have a net, get a room with one. Use cover up and repellents. A fan is a boon too.

B Imperial, Jomo Kenyatta Av, T057-202 0002, www.imperialkisumu.com, is the best in this range. Plush carpets and fittings, a/c, very good swimming pool and friendly staff. Two bars (one rooftop), restaurant, coffee shop and internet access. Standard double room is US$85 a night (with rates significantly lower Fr-Sun). Very popular so book.

B Kisumu, Jomo Kenyatta Av, T057-2024155. Very large and grand colonial building that was bought by the Kisumu University who completely refurbished and reopened it in 2004. Despite being very run-down before this, it did have a certain dilapidated colonial charm. Now, with a modern tiled lobby, made-for-hotel furnishings and wall-to-wall carpeting, the atmosphere has been somewhat lost and it's a shame they didn't refurbish it in the style of its era. However, the rooms are neat with brand new bathrooms, phone and TV, bar and restaurant with buffet meals, lovely pool, and car park.

B Sunset, south of the town, T057-202217, hotelsunset1977@yahoo. co.uk. Veranda looks over beautiful lawns, restaurant and bar, secure parking and a good swimming pool. All 50 rooms have views of the lake and sunset, and you can take a good photograph of the lake from the hotel roof.

C Milimani Resort Hotel, T057-2023245, F2023242. Modern hotel with car parking in a quiet location, a fair distance south of the town centre, but signposted from Jomo Kenyatta Av from the **Kisumu Hotel**. Rooms have different prices, are well equipped with fans, nets and TVs but a little on the small side. Breakfast included. Restaurant, bar, pool and conference centre.

C New Gulf Stream, around the corner from the **Millimani Resort Hotel** and clearly signposted in town from Jomo Kenyatta Av, T057-2025460, nghksm@yahoo.com. Big concrete block, adequate rooms, if not a little plain, with satellite TV and fan, tiled floors, pleasant outside restaurant and bar terrace with plants, rates include breakfast.

D Hotel Natasha, Otuoma St, close to the Akamba Bus stop, T057-2020189. Hot water showers and toilet, very clean, friendly, quiet,

though a little gloomy and no mosquito nets but has a fan. Restaurant next door (**Expresso Café**), phone booth outside.

D Museum View, on the same road as the museum, T057-2021149. Clean, large rooms with hot water and mosquito nets, secure parking. Comfortable but a bit out of the way, except for the museum.

D New East, Omollo Ager St, T057-2041871. In a quiet residential area, with a secure car park, reasonably smart block, rooms have very old-fashioned furniture and fixtures, clean though and friendly, dining room for breakfast only, and no bar.

D New Victoria, Gor Mahia Rd, T057-2021067. Excellent value, clean and large rooms with fans and good protection from mosquitoes. In an unmissable building brightly painted green and yellow. Triple rooms available, 2nd-floor rooms have pleasant balconies (rooms 205-207 have views of the lake). Popular TV room, food OK but not to the standard of the rest of the hotel. Muslim-owned, so no alcohol and the rules stress that there should be no 'private meetings' in rooms.

D Western Lodge, Kendu Lane, T057-2042586. Good cheap rooms and good security with an *askari* at the door, and a safe in each room. Nice little upstairs terrace with pot plants and tables for breakfast.

E Lake View, Kendu Lane, T057-2045055. Friendly hotel from where the lake can only just be seen, mirrored exterior, basic rooms are on the 1st floor but the very heavy dark brown curtains make them a little gloomy, the Gatiba Bar is next door.

E River Sand Hotel, tall brick building on Accra Rd. All rooms are comfortable and have bathrooms, the double rooms have a balcony, but the water is cold and better value can be had elsewhere. Has a restaurant and bar.

E Wilson Coffee House Boarding and Lodging, Gor Mahia Rd. Good clean rooms, with hot water, friendly staff and a good view from the restaurant.

F YWCA, off Ang'awa Av, T057-2043192. Reasonable, rooms with 3 or 4 sharing, often full with church groups, small café serving African staples, there is not always water here.

● Eating

It is quite easy to get good cheap food in Kisumu, except on a Sun, when most places are closed. The fish dishes using fresh tilapia from the lake, which is quite delicious, are good value. The large Asian community that has settled here means it is possible to get excellent Indian meals. Cheap kiosks near the bus station sell grilled meat on skewers or tilapia fish with *ugali* (maize dough).

↑↑↑ Sunset Hotel, out of town to the south, T057-202217. Serves good weekend buffets for lunch in slightly grand surroundings, very attractive terrace overlooking the lake with the best views in Kisumu, à la carte dinners and excellent friendly service.

↑↑↑-↑ Grillhouse, Accra Rd, in the Swan Centre. Very good bar and café. Simple baguettes, omelettes, spring rolls, fish, steak, pork chops, or chicken cooked in every way imaginable, try the pan-fried whole tilapia fish fresh from the lake. Outside and indoor tables and good service. Recommended.

↑↑ Fremick, Alpha House, Oginga Odinga Rd. Bar and restaurant with simple but good food, nice terrace area with wrought-iron furniture but it overlooks a car park. Local food such as rice and beans or *ugali* and stew, plus omelettes, burgers, sandwiches.

↑↑ Oriental Restaurant, in the Al-Imren Plaza, Oginga Odinga Rd, excellent value, tasty authentic Chinese dishes, generous meals and good service.

↑ Expresso Café, Otuoma St. Popular with office workers during the day, closes in the evening. Simple café environment, good and cheap grills, curries, burgers and sandwiches, hot and cold drinks, nice fresh fruit juice.

↑ Kenshop Bakery, Oginga Odinga Rd. Very good pastries, bread, pizza and ice cream, open 0900-1500, closed Sun.

↑ Kimwa Annex, Otuona Rd. A clean, tiled local canteen with plastic tables that's very popular for huge plates of cheap local fare, served up self service style from big catering tins, also a bar with pool table, open 24 hrs.

↑ Mona Lisa, Oginga Odinga Rd. Good breakfasts, cheap snacks, hot and cold drinks in a canteen environment.

↑ New Victoria Hotel, Gor Mahia Rd. Does a substantial breakfast from 0700-0900, good Indian menu with lots of vegetarian options, owned by a family from Yemem, very quick

service and large portions. Can get quite busy, the menu states all food will be served within 15 mins.

↑ Wimpy, Jomo Kenyatta Av, towards the market. Burgers, chicken, fries, good fry-up, and coffee, best pineapple milkshake ever.

● Bars and clubs

There are many African bars which play music, mainly Lingala, open till late.

Octopus, Oganda St, plays western music. Sophisticated and good fun. It gets very crowded late in the evening, US$2 entry fee.

Pirate's Den Rooftop Bar, between the **Octopus** restaurant and disco, there are stairs leading up to here. Pleasant, has a dartboard and is a good place to have a drink as the sun goes down.

The Pub, a couple of doors along from the **Grillhouse Restaurant**, on Accra Rd, in the Swan Centre, pleasant bar with tables outside and there's an adjoining casino.

Vault Restaurant and Casino, Oginga Odinga Rd, near **Barclays Bank**. Very long green awning outside and black mirrored exterior. Bar and casino with a good atmosphere, also does excellent pizzas.

● Shopping

Handicrafts

There are many artefacts from other parts of the country available here. Kisii stone is a particularly good buy as are *kikois* (woven cloth). Street vendors are outside the post office and at a line of stalls opposite the **Kisumu Hotel** on Jomo Kenyatta Av. In Kisii stone there are chess boards, bowls, pots, candle holders and sculptures. There are also wooden animals, Masai warriors, drums, spoons/forks, masks and trinkets. These are excellent quality and good value, but you will need to barter hard to get a good price.

Markets

Kisumu's main fruit and vegetable market on Nairobi Rd is one of the largest in Western Kenya, and worth a wander to soak up some of the atmosphere. The market bustles every day, although Sun tends to be quieter. You'll find that most things on offer tend to be quite similar. Look out for *kikois*, some real gems are available if you look hard enough.

Otherwise it's run-of-the-mill stuff: fruit and vegetables, children's clothes, tools, flip-flops, radios, batteries, bags, sheets etc, but also a surprisingly large number of trainers/sneakers along Jomo Kenyatta Av. There are also second-hand clothes and shoes stalls all over town.

Supermarkets

Big Buys, Oginga Odinga St, is slightly larger and cheaper and has a wider array of goods than Nyanza, below. Good spice selection. **Nyanza Supermarket** at Mega Plaza on Oginga Odinga Rd. Ex pat owned, slightly more expensive, but sells 'reassurables' for those feeling a little homesick! (Heinz beans/ketchup/Marmite/Pringles/ Robertson's marmalade). Closes 1245-1400 for lunch.

Three shopping arcades have opened off Oginga Odinga Rd, near the post office: The largest is **Mega Plaza** which, apart from the well-stocked supermarket, has a bag shop, café bar with pool table and pet shop. The others are **Al-Imren Plaza** and **Reinsurance Plaza**.

▲▲ Activities and tours

Swimming

Use pools rather than the lake as bilharzia is rife. There are four; the best is at the **Sunset**. There are also pools at **Kisumu**, **Milimani Resort** and the **Imperial**. Each charges around US$2 for non-guests to use the pool.

Tour operators

Kisumu Travels, Oginga Odinga Rd, T057-2020785. General travel agent.
Pel Travels Ltd, Oginga Odinga Rd, T057-2022780. For transport, hotel bookings and foreign exchange.
Both has a limited number of cars for hire but more expensive than Nairobi.

⊙ Transport

Air

Kenya Airways, Alpha House, Oginga Odinga Rd, T057-2020081, www.kenya-airways.com. There are flights between Kisumu and **Nairobi** taking 1 hr and costing US$73 one way. On Mon, Thu and Fri, there are 2 flights per day and on Sat and Tue 1 flight.

Bus and *matatus*

The main *matatu* and bus stopping point is behind the covered section of the main market. There are regular *matatus* and buses travelling between Kisumu and most major towns in Western Kenya. There are also many leaving for Nairobi passing through **Nakuru** and **Kericho** on the B1. Approximate times: **Nairobi** to Kisumu, express 6 hrs or normal 8 hrs. It takes approximately 2 hrs to **Kericho**, 5 hrs to **Nakuru**, 2 hrs to **Eldoret**, 1 hr to **Kakamega**. The offices of **Akamba Buses** are in the town centre, just off New Station Rd.

Ferry

Small motor ferries running between Kisumu and a number of lakeshore towns were a very cheap and nice way of seeing around Lake Victoria. However, all operations have been suspended until further notice.

⊙ Directory

Banks Barclays, Kampala St, or Standard Chartered, Oginga Odinga Rd, are the most efficient for changing money. Both have ATMs as do **Kenya Commercial Bank** and **Co-op Bank**. Banking hours are Mon-Fri 0900-1500 and Sat 0830-1100. Foreign exchange facilities. There are 2 **forex bureaux** towards the northern end of Oginga Odinga Rd and one in Reinsurance Plaza. **Western Union** money transfer can be organized at the **Post Bank**. **Internet** Access is available at a number of places around town including the **Imperial Hotel**, **Kisimu Hotel**, **Cyber Joint**, next door to the Grillhouse Restaurant on Accra Rd, and **etouch** in Reinsurance Plaza. There are also 2 cyber cafés in the Al-Imren Plaza, Oginga Odinga Rd. The best of the lot is **Cyber Station**, Oginga Odinga Rd, next to the Kenshop Bakery, which is also a coffee shop. It also offers international phone calls via the internet, open Mon-Sat 0830-2000, Sun 1030-1800. All roughly charge US$1 per hr. **Post office** Oginga Odinga Rd, Mon-Fri 0800-1700 and Sat 0900-1200, has a reliable poste restante service. DHL, delivery services from **Securicor**, Fedex from Kisumu Travel, Oginga Odinga Rd. **Telephone** Direct calls from the card phone outside the post office.

South of Kisumu

Kisumu to the Tanzanian border

The main route from western Kenya to Tanzania, the A1, runs from Kisumu via Oyugis and Kisii, and is in excellent condition, except for a few patches around Kisii where there are some potholes. Mgori is the last town along this stretch, on the Tanzanian border. This small town is a transit stop for people travelling to Musoma and Mwanza in Tanzania. The lakeshore region to the south of Kisumu is known as South Nyanza is an easy enough area to explore by *matatu*. However, there is limited accommodation in this region. Self-drive is probably recommended to get to some of the more remote spots, such as the prehistoric site of Thimlich Ohinga, and Ruma National Park you will need your own four-wheel-drive transport. Fishing (a male activity) and the smoking of fish (a female activity) are important occupations around this region. Homa Bay is the biggest town in the area and here there is a branch of Barclays Bank, a post office and a petrol station. Out on the lake are two islands, Rusinga and Mfangano. Rusinga is the burial place of Tom Mboya, a great son of Kenya who was assassinated in Nairobi in 1969. On each of the islands there are fishing camps providing boats for hire and some accommodation in sublime settings. Much of the business comes from the Masai Mara lodges where, every morning, small planes pick up upmarket safari goers that also want to go fishing.

> ‼ If you have arrived from Tanzania, you will need to have a valid certificate to prove vaccination against yellow fever.

Kendu Bay → *Colour map 1, grid A2.*

Kendu Bay is a small town in South Nyanza, now Homa Bay District. It is an hour's drive from Kisumu, on the Homa Bay-Katito road, off the Ahero-Sondu-Kisii road. It has become a fairly important lake port, receiving boats from Tanzania and merchandise from the rich Kisii highlands, in the form of coffee and tea, although this has diminished in recent years.

The main reason for coming here is to visit the curious **Simbi Nyaima Lake** – a deep volcanic lake, steeped in myths and legends. It has bright green opaque water, and is located only a few kilometres from Lake Victoria. No one knows what the source of the lake is and its size is constantly changing. Local people believe it to be unlucky and the surrounding area is certainly devoid of vegetation. It is not fished and the area is uninhabited. According to one legend, a hungry and tired old woman called Ateku arrived in this area, where she found the villagers celebrating by eating, drinking and dancing. Only one caring female villager gave her food and drink and a bed in which to rest her weary bones. To give thanks, Ateku ordered water to spring from the ground, which later went on to flood the area. Another version of the legend was that the old lady was denied food and lodgings and in wrathful vengeance induced a massive flood that swamped the village.

In more recent years, however, Simbi Nyaima Lake has seen the widespread migration of flamingos from Lake Nakuru, 200 km away, see page 110. In 1988 many of the birds flew to other soda lakes, including Lake Simbi, for breeding purposes as Lake Nakuru virtually dried up. Another reason for the transposition of the flamingos is believed to be that the level of algae, *Spiruline Platensis*, part of the flamingo's diet, has diminished in Lake Nakuru. Many of the birds that made the lengthy journey are believed to have guided younger birds back to Lake Simbi. As a result, the lake is becoming a developing tourist attraction. To get there take the road towards Homa Bay and it is a 4-km walk from Kendu Bay. It takes about two hours to walk around the lake. There are no facilities so take food and drink.

Ruma National Park is 10 km east of Lake Victoria in the Lambwe Valley in the Suba District, 140 km from Kisumu. The park was established in 1966 to protect the rare roan antelope, found only in this part of Kenya. However, its isolation and consequent lack of income, ensured a very slow pace of development. With its recent conversion into a national park, game viewing tracks and general park maintenance have been established. The land is a mixture of tall grassland and woodlands of acacia, open savannah and riverine forests interspersed with scenic hills. There are abundant wild flowers, including a varient of the fire lily. In addition to the roan antelope, other mammals found here include the Bohor reedbuck, Jackson's hartebeest, hyena, leopard, buffalo and topi. Rothchild's giraffe, zebra and ostrich have been introduced in recent years. Oribi, one of the smallest of the antelope family, are also present. Birdlife is plentiful and diverse, and Ruma is the only protected area in Kenya where the globally threatened blue swallow, a scarce intra-African migrant, is regularly recorded. Blue swallows arrive from their breeding grounds in southern Tanzania around April and depart in September. They depend on moist grassland for feeding and roosting. The diurnal yellow-eared bat is also found.

≈ *The Lambwe region is infested with tsetse fly that can be fatal to domesticated animals, but not to wild animals.*

This is a delightful park for anyone wishing to achieve isolation on their safari, although there is no accommodation and the roads are pretty rough. From Kisumu, follow the A1 south onto the C18 Homa Bay turn-off. Continue along the C18 past the Homa Bay turn-off to the north (the C20) and access to the park is on a turn-off to the right soon after the town of Mirogi. From the Migori Shopping Centre it is 10 km to the park headquarters along a murram road. Within the park are also unsealed murram roads, which become impassable with black sticky mud, known locally as black cotton, when it rains. A four-wheel drive is needed and is essential during the rainy season. Activities include birdwatching, trekking and fishing.

There are two camping sites here, **Kamato** and **Nyati**. However, facilities are only basic and, given the tsetse fly situation, you may want to give camping a miss.

Rusinga Island → *Colour map 1, grid A2.*

Rusinga Island lies in the northeastern corner of Lake Victoria in Kenyan waters. Ferry access from Homa Bay is restricted due to the water hyacinth problem in Lake Victoria, but the island is now linked to the mainland by a causeway. Rusinga is an austerely scenic island with high crags dominating the desolate goat-grazed landscape. A single dirt road runs around its circumference. The main town on Rusinga Island, Mbita, is unexceptional, but inland foreigners are rare and you are sure of a welcome. Life here is difficult, drought commonplace, and high winds a frequent torment. The occasional heavy rain either washes away the soil or sinks into the porous rock, emerging lower down where it creates swamps. Almost all the trees on the island have been cut down for cooking fuel or been converted into lucrative charcoal. These conditions make farming highly unpredictable and most people rely on fishing to make ends meet.

The island is rich in fossils, and famed for the 1948 discovery by Mary Leakey, the anthropologist, of one of the earliest austrapithecines remains, the skull of *Proconsul Africanus* (*P. heseloni*), a sub-group of *Dryopithecus*, said to be 17.5 million. This anthropoid ape lived on the island three million years ago, and is believed to be a probable ancestor of the chimpanzee. Aside from the public interest it spurred, the discovery of the skull also ensured the Leakeys funding for their next expeditions. Louis and Mary, thrilled at the discovery, decided the best way to celebrate would be by having another child. Their third son, Philip, was born in 1949 almost nine months later to the day that the skull was discovered. The skull can be seen in the National Museum.

Rusinga Island was also the birthplace of Tom Mboya, an important Kenyan political figure during the fight for Independence. A civil rights champion, trade unionist and charismatic young Luo politician, he was gunned down in Nairobi by a Kikuyu policeman in 1969, sparking off a crisis that led to over 40 deaths in widespread rioting and demonstrations. There is a school and a health centre named after him, and Tom Mboya's mausoleum lies on family land at Kasawanga on the north side of the island, about 7 km by the dirt road from Mbita, or roughly 5 km directly across the island. The mausoleum (open most days to visitors) contains various mementoes and gifts Mboya received during his life. The inscription on the grave reads: *Go and fight like this man, Who fought for mankind's cause, Who died because he fought, Whose battles are still unwon.* You don't have to know anything about the man to be impressed. In any other surroundings his memorial might seem relatively modest, but on this barren, windswept shore, it stands out like a beacon. Mboya's family live right next door and are happy to meet foreign visitors, who rarely come here.

If you do intend to walk around the island take plenty of water as it is extremely hot and humid here and mosquitoes are plentiful, although there is little danger of getting lost.

The island is popular with game fishermen and holds the IGFA all-tackle record for the heaviest Nile perch ever caught. Over 80 species of bird are found here, including fish eagles and bee-eaters. On the shores of the island you may see the rare spotted-necked otter, giant monitor lizards or hippo. Lake Victoria is renowned for its glorious sunsets, and after dark the Luo fishermen from the villages scattered along the lakeside can be seen out on the lake in their beautifully painted boats, lit by paraffin lamps. Boat trips to visit other nearby islands can be arranged locally with these fishermen.

Mfangano Island → *Colour map 1, grid A1/2.*

Further along Lake Victoria, slightly bigger than Rusinga Island, Mfangano has shade from giant fig trees, and is much more remote and primitive, with few tourist facilities and no roads. The island is populated by a curious mixture of immigrants from all over Kenya, administered by a chief and three sub-chiefs with help from a trio of policemen. Mfangano's greatest economic resource is still the lake itself and the islanders fish with floating kerosene lamps to draw in the fish to be netted. Hippos are very much in evidence, as are monitor lizards basking in the sun. There are interesting prehistoric rock paintings here showing signs of centuries of habitation. The rock paintings are in a gently scooped cave on the north coast of the island and are reddish coloured shapes. It is not known who drew them, when or why, although one theory is that they were the work of Twa Pygmy hunters from Congo, and could be 8,000 years old. Local people associate the site with supernatural powers and miraculous events, and in some measure fear them too, which has so far helped prevent the vandalism which has afflicted other rock art sites in Kenya. The site is still used for traditional rain-making ceremonies, when elders pray to their ancestors to intercede on their behalf.

A large wooden boat shuttles people between Mbita and surrounding places. It leaves Mbita at 0900 and takes about 90 minutes to Sena on the east of Mfangano. There is one luxury lodge on the island and a government rest house (officially free though ask for permission to stay) and local people are usually willing to put up travellers. The island is completely free of vehicles, and has neither electricity nor piped water, so bear this in mind if you intend to stay. Mfangano's people rely on a network of temporary footpaths which are constantly changing course. If you arrive at Sena by boat, which is the main centre, you can walk all over the island.

Thimlich Ohinga → *Colour map 1, grid A2.*

Some 60 km southwest of Homa Bay or 45 km northwest of the town of Migori on the main A1 to the border with Tanzania, the Thimlich Ohinga Prehistoric Site is one of the most significant archaeological sites in East Africa. The name means 'thick bush' or 'frightening dense forest' in the local DhoLuo language. It was declared a national monument in 1983, and consists of dry stone enclosures of what appears to be one of the earliest settlements in the Lake Victoria area. It is an impressive example of a style of architecture whose remnants are found all over the district. The main structure consists of a compound about 140 m in diameter with five smaller enclosures in each and at least six house pits. The dry stonewalls were constructed without using mortar, and range from 1 to 4 m high and from 1 to 3 m wide. The materials used were collected locally from the nearby hills. Several parts of the enclosing wall have caved in, and conservation work is urgently required. A giant *Euphorbia candelabrum* towers over the site.

The design of these structures would appear to indicate that the dry stone enclosures were built by a cohesive community, thought to date from about the 14th century, believed to be mostly of Bantu origin. It is believed that the Bantu lived here prior to the arrival of the Luo people. Between them, the early Bantu settlers and later Nilotic settlers built about 521 enclosures in over 130 locations in the Lake Victoria region. They are similar to the 17th-century stone ruins in Zimbabwe. Later settlers appear to have carried out repairs to the stonework between the 15th and 19th centuries. It is unclear as to why the area was abandoned by the Ohingnis in the early 20th century. A similar style of dwelling is used in some places by Luos today.

There is no public transport to get here. If driving you need to follow the A1 road to Rongo then head southwest to Karungu where there are signposts to Thimlich Ohinga. There is a small entry fee and the ruins are generally accessible during daylight hours.

Kisii and the Western Highlands

The Western Highlands are the agricultural heartland of Kenya, separating Kisumu and its environs from the rest of the country. The Highlands stretch from Kisii in the south up to the tea plantations around Kericho, through to Kitale, Mount Elgon and Eldoret. Away from the towns other highlights in this region include the Saiwa Swamp National Park. This is one of the few parks that permits walking, and is an ideal place for a day's hike. This wild country is home to many and varied species, the best known being the very rare sitatunga, a semi-amphibious antelope that lives in the depths of these swamps. The Western Highlands have become a major draw for sporting tourists. This is the home of many of Kenya's world-famous runners. This is probably the finest place on earth for high-altitude athletic training, and many international athletes visit training camps around Iten and Kaptagat. There are good bus and *matatu* connections among most towns and villages and it is an easy region to get around, although the roads around Kisii are in a poor shape.

Kisii → *Phone code: 058. Colour map 1, grid A2.*
Set in picturesque undulating hills in some of the most fertile land of the country and with abundant sunshine and rainfall, Kisii is a very lively and fast-growing town. As with so many other towns in agricultural areas, the market here is buzzing and has an excellent array of fresh fruit and vegetables. The town lies on a fault line, so earth tremors are not uncommon. This is the home of the Gusii people, and is famous for its **soapstone**, although you may look to buy some in vain as most of what is locally produced is bought up by traders to stock the tourist shops in Nairobi.

Tabaka → *Colour map 1, grid A2.*
About 25 km from Kisii, this village is the most important producer of soapstone and the centre of carvings in the country. To visit the quarries or the carvers, you need to

go past the Tabaka Mission Hospital to the **Kisii Soapstone Carvers Co-operative**, which is about 5 km from the main road. The local children will be happy to direct you. There are lots of local shops where you can buy soapstone artefacts. The stone comes in a variety of colours from orange (the softest) to deep red (the heaviest).

Kericho → *Phone code: 052. Colour map 1, grid A3.*

Perched on the top of a hill, the tea plantations stretch for miles on either side of the road, their bright green bushes neatly clipped to the same height with paths running in straight lines in between. At 1,800 m above sea level, the tea plantations stretch along the western edge of the Great Rift Valley. An evocative image of this region is of the many hundreds of men and women plucking the tea leaves in the plantations with their distinctive white polythene sacks on their backs. The predictable weather (it rains every afternoon here) and the temperate climate giving a high ground temperature, make this

> ‡ *Tea bushes are trimmed to a certain height so their branches produce more leaves and for ease of 'pluckability'.*

the most important tea-growing region in Africa. Kenya is the world's third largest tea-producing nation, after India and Sri Lanka. This is an orderly part of Kenya, very different from the *shambas* further down the slopes, and very English, exemplified by the **Tea Hotel** with its lovely gardens that used to be owned by Brooke Bond. Kericho is named after Ole Kericho, a Masai chief who perished in battle at the hands of the Gusii in the 18th century. The town's main purpose is to service the enormous tea plantations, so it has most of the basic amenities on the main road, Moi Highway: branches of the main banks, post office, market, library, village green, the English-style Holy Trinity Church, War Memorial, cemetery and a Hindu Temple used by Kericho's large Asian population. For tea tours, where the growing and picking procedures are explained, enquire at the **Tea Hotel**. Peter is the hotel's resident guide and he will take you for a walk to the hotel's own estate and explain all about how tea was introduced into the region and the tea-growing process, tea tasting is included in the excursion. It costs US$2.50 per person. If you would like to visit a tea-processing factory around Kericho, get in touch with the hotel two weeks in advance and they will be able to arrange this.

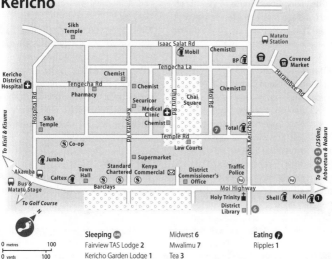

Western Kenya South of Kisumu

Sleeping		Eating
Fairview TAS Lodge 2	Midwest 6	Ripples 1
Kericho Garden Lodge 1	Mwalimu 7	
	Tea 3	

About 8 km to the northeast of Kericho off the road to Nakuru is this exceptionally attractive arboretum. It was established after the Second World War by a Kericho tea planter, John Grumbley, now retired to Malindi on the coast. It houses many tropical and sub-tropical trees surrounded by well-tended lawns running down to the lake's edge. The lake is covered in water lilies and fringed with stands of bamboo. Trout fishing is available in the Kiptariet River. The **Tea Hotel** will arrange for permissions and equipment hire. The river runs closeby the hotel.

● Sleeping

Rusinga Island *p142*

L Rusinga Island Lodge, reservations Private Wilderness, Nairobi, T020-605349, www.rusinga.com. 6 cottages with their own veranda, and 1 family cottage made up of 2 rooms with shared veranda, all overlooking the lake. All rooms are en suite, the cottages are made from stone, wood and grass thatching, decorated with traditional fabrics and baskets. Game drives at Ruma National Park are on offer, as is waterskiing and fishing for Nile perch on the lake. Can collect guests from anywhere in the country with their own light aircraft. 40 mins (130 km) by air from the Masai Mara. Rates are US$370 per person sharing and including meals and drinks and all activities except air transfers.

E Elk Guesthouse, next to the bus stand in Mbita. A very basic local guest house but clean and all beds are fitted with mosquito nets. Does not have a restaurant or bar but there are several cheap eating places nearby.

E The Viking Guest House, to the right of the bus stand is very similar, although with shared bathrooms, and it also has a bar in a bougainvillea shaded courtyard.

Mfangano Island *p143*

L Mfangano Island Camp, set in beautiful gardens that mostly attracts serious (and wealthy, at US$500 a night) fishermen. Reservations Governors' Camp, Nairobi, T020-2734000, www.governorscamp.com. Just 6 rooms made from natural clay and banana thatch, with private verandas and lovely stone bathrooms, beautifully decorated with 4-poster beds with mosquito nets, very good food, bar, swimming pool. All fishing activities are organized, especially for Nile perch, and are included in the price.

Set in a secluded bay surrounded by fig trees. Very high standards here to match the Governors' Camps in the Masai Mara, most guests arrive here by plane from the Mara.

Kisii *p144*

C Zonic Hotel, at the corner of Hospital Rd and Ogemba Rd, T058-30298, is a fairly new and very large hotel on 5 storeys and is easily the best good-value place to stay in town. All rooms have bathrooms and some have balconies, on the roof is a nice terrace, the restaurant does decent food, at the weekends there is sometimes a disco, secure parking, rates include breakfast.

D Kisii, north of town centre on the Kisumu Rd, T058-30134. Probably the best of the budget places, the rooms are spacious with bathrooms but very basic. It is an old slated wooden building in a compound with secure parking, there is a comfortable colonial atmosphere, with attractive gardens and OK food in the restaurant and there's a lively bar.

D Kisii Sports Club, behind Barclays Bank on the main road, has quite spacious rooms within the clubhouse, with nets and bathroom but a little gloomy. Has a bar and restaurant. Price includes breakfast, but the use of the facilities (swimming pool, squash, snooker and pool tables) requires an extra small payment. Club membership fee is necessary to play golf.

Kericho *p145, map p145*

B Tea Hotel, east of town centre, on Moi Highway on road to Nakuru, T052-30004/5, teahotel@africaonline.co.ke. Set in lush gardens and backing directly on to the tea plantations this is the best hotel in Kericho.

 For an explanation of sleeping and eating price codes used in this guide, see inside the front cover. Other relevant information is found in Essentials, see pages 34-38.

It was built in 1958 by Brooke Bond. Although now looking very slightly drab the old colonial building is spacious, comfortable and well appointed. It has a swimming pool and very attentive staff make it a very pleasant place to stay. Some of the rooms have TVs. The hotel offers email facilities, and has a reasonable restaurant with a solid and dependable English-style menu, and some Indian dishes. Standard and superior rooms available, some of the rooms are rather basic so it's overpriced for what you get, but you cannot argue with the colonial ambience. Visa and Mastercard accepted. There's also a very pleasant campsite here (**F**) in the grounds with toilets and hot showers, a tap for filling water tanks for overland vehicles and an electric point for charging batteries.
C Midwest, Moi Highway opposite police station, T052-20611. Relatively modern, central yet with garden, clean, spacious, functional. 2 price categories available, the more expensive rooms have TV. Gym and sauna, good restaurant with a reasonable daily set menu of western dishes.
D Kericho Garden Lodge Hotel, Moi Highway, close to **Tea Hotel**, T052-20878. Fairly basic but very friendly, hot water, breakfast included, very pleasant garden bar, *nyama choma* and basic food, TV room with satellite TV, secure parking in the sweeping drive.
E Fairview TAS Lodge, northwest of town centre, on Moi Highway on road to Nakuru, close to **Tea Hotel**, T052-21112. Clean rooms have loose hanging wires and bathrooms, bar, restaurant, attractive garden setting.
E Mwalimu, Temple Rd, just to north of Chai Sq in town centre, T052-20601. Corridors are quite dark but the rooms are OK, and clean, with own bathroom, and this place has got a good local reputation, restaurant and bar, price includes breakfast.

● Eating

Kericho *p145, map p145*
¶ **Ripples Pub & Restaurant**, at the Kobil petrol station on Moi Highway. Reasonable meals in a modern canteen environment, and not a bad place to stop for refreshments if driving through town, also snacks and cold drinks, and a few plastic chairs outside on the petrol station forecourt.

● Bars and clubs

Kericho *p145, map p145*
This is a town with relatively little to see and do, and it appears to close down at the end of the business day, with not much available in the way of nightlife.
Sunshine Hotel, Kenyatta Rd, is about the size of it (remember *Hotel* in Kiswahili also means bar). Pleasant and clean with friendly staff, popular with locals, the terrace gets fairly busy and there is plenty of cold beer.

● Transport

Kisii *p144*
Kisii is about 115 km from Kisumu on the A1. *Matatus* from **Kisumu**, take 2 hrs and the *matatu* stand is on the main road that runs through town, Moi Highway. There is another *matatu* stand 2 blocks east of the market. Buses to **Nairobi** go via **Kericho** and **Nakuru** and the Akamba Bus office is also on Moi Highway near the post office.

Kericho *p145, map p145*
The *matatu* and bus station is at the northern end of Isaac Salat Rd and is well organized. There is plenty of transport, both buses and *matatus* run regularly throughout the day for **Nakuru** and **Kisumu** where you can pick up onward transport. Akamba Bus has a stand on the corner of Moi Highway and Hospital Rd, and runs a daily service to **Nairobi**.

● Directory

Kisii *p144*
Barclays Bank, Moi Highway, open Mon-Fri 0830-1300 and Sat 0830-1100.

Kericho *p145, map p145*
Banks Barclays and Standard Chartered banks are both on Moi Highway and both have ATMs. **Western Union** money transfer is available at the post office and post bank. **Courier services** Securicor on Kenyatta Rd. **Internet** Email from Tea Hotel. **Medical services** Kericho District Hospital is on (naturally) Hospital Rd. **Police** The main police station is just to the southwest of the Tea Hotel on Moi Highway.

Kakamega and around

Kakamega → *Phone code: 056. Colour map 3, grid C5.*

This pleasant lively place is the main town of the Luhya people. A major attraction is the **Kakamega Forest** (see below), and the town is the place to buy provisions for an excursion there. At the end of November is the **Kakamega Show**, an agricultural festival at the showground just to the north of the town, on the Webuye Road. Most travellers tend to head straight out to the forest reserve and stay there, which is a much more pleasant alternative than staying in town. Kakamega is famous for being the centre of a gold rush in the late 1920s, which attracted huge numbers of hopeful prospectors. The largest nugget found was named the **Elbon Nugget**, so named by reversing the surname of Dan Noble, formerly a postman, who later bought Nairobi's first hotel, the old **Hotel Stanley**. ►► *For Sleeping, Eating and other listings, see pages 150-152.*

Kakamega Forest National Reserve → *Colour map 3, grid C5.*

ⓘ *0600-1800. US$10. Guide fee is US$4 per hour and represents excellent value as the guides are extremely knowledgeable.*

Western Kenya's Kakamega Forest would not look out of place on the set of a Tarzan movie – tangled vines, intermingled branches, and a chorus of screeches and mutterings from a whole host of African creatures. Declared a forest reserve in 1966, Kakamega Forest's headquarters lie 12 km from the town of Kakamega on the Kisumu-Eldoret road, the A1. One of the last remaining (and fast diminishing) tropical rainforests of East Africa, Kakamega is a remnant of the Guineo-Conglian equatorial belt that once covered all land from the Atlantic to the Rift Valley as little as 400 years ago. Its closest relation, to whom it once joined, is Bwindi Impenetrable Forest on Uganda's western border with the DRC. This forest is only 45 sq km and is the sole remnant of tropical rainforest in Kenya and has been a protected area since the 1930s. It is an extraordinarily beautiful forest, with at least 150 species of tree, shrubs and vines, including the Elgon teak, 90 dicotyledenous herbs, 80 monocotyledonous herbs of which 60 are orchids (nine unique to Kakamega), and a further 62 species of fern, making a total of 380 different plants in one small area. The indigenous trees along the trails are identified with small

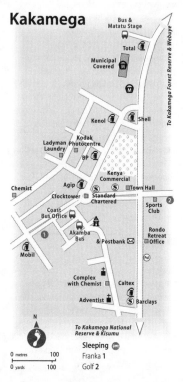

Kakamega

Bus & Matatu Stage

Total

Municipal Covered

Kenol — Shell

Kodak Photocentre
Ladyman Laundry
BP

Kenya Commercial

Chemist

Agip

Clocktower — Standard Chartered

Town Hall

Coast Bus Office

Akamba Bus & Postbank

Mobil

Sports Club

Rondo Retreat Office

Complex with Chemist — Caltex

Adventist — Barclays

To Kakamega National Reserve & Kisumu

To Kakamega Forest Reserve & Webuye

N

0 metres 100
0 yards 100

Sleeping
Franka 1
Golf 2

plaques giving their Latin as well as their local names. Many of these provide a valuable source of fruits and green vegetables for the local people and about 50 herbs are used for medicines and ritual events.

There are a number of animals here that are found in no other part of the country including the grey duiker, bushpig, bush-tailed porcupine, giant water shrew, clawless otter and a few leopards. There are also several primates including the olive baboon, the red-tailed monkey, the black and white colobus and blue monkey. The forest is also home to the hairy-tailed flying squirrel that can 'fly' as far as 90 m, bush babies and the lemur-like potto can be spotted amongst the branches at night, along with the hammer-headed fruit bat – the largest in Africa with a wing span of over 1 m and an exceptionally big head.

❧ *Approximately 20% of the flora and fauna in the Kakamega Forest is not found anywhere else in Kenya.*

The forest is also of great ornithological interest as many birds found here are not seen elsewhere in Kenya. Hornbills, woodpeckers, honeyguides, both Ross's and the great blue turaco, grey parrot and the rare snake-eating bird are among the avian residents. In addition several varieties of barbet including the double-toothed, speckled and grey-throated are found here. Butterflies are abundant, and snakes, normally only found in West Africa, can be seen too. Look out for the Gabon viper, a particularly nasty, deadly but fortunately very shy snake that lives in the forest. Near to the reserve on the Kakamega-Kisumu road is a curiosity called the **Weeping Stone**. This is an 8-m-high rock upon which a smaller rock is balanced, and between the rocks a small trickle of water emanates, and continues to flow even during the dry season.

The most rewarding way to appreciate Kakamega is to walk through the narrow winding paths accompanied by a knowledgeable guide from the forestry station. These dedicated local people, who are often self-taught, make excellent and informative guides and know the flora and the fauna intimately. The enthusiastic welcome by the proud employees of the Forestry Service is almost overwhelming, and if given the chance, they will reel off every species name in Latin. Birdsong and the occasional whoop of a black and white colobus monkey accompany walks ranging from 1 to 6 km through the peaceful interior. If you wish to see the flowers at their best, plan your visit during the rainy season from April to July. Exotic orchids grow in the junctions of the tree branches. There are two areas in the forest that cater for tourists: **Isecheno** towards the south/centre of the forest and **Buyangu** in the north. At Buyangu several walks are possible, the longer of which offers the chance to reach **Buyangu Hill**, from where there is a good view over the tree canopy or to a small waterfall (**Isiukhu Falls**). Here the canopy spreads out like a thick green blanket and on a clear day brooding Mount Elgon can be sighted in the distance. On the banks of the Yala River you can see deep pits, which were dug to extract gold, and occasionally you may see local people panning for the precious metal. It is advisable to wear waterproofs if you plan to visit, as the rain is heavy, regular and predictable, but it is beautiful walking country.

Kakamega Forest National Reserve

To Webuye & Eldoret

Kenya Wildlife Service HQ

Isiukhu Falls

Buyangu

A1

Kakamega

Weeping Stone

Isecheno

Shinyalu

Khayega

Chepsonoi

To Kapsabet

A1

To Kisumu

Kaimosi

Chavakali

N

0 km 5

0 miles 5

Sleeping
Forest Rest House **3**
Isecheno Bandas **2**
Rondo Retreat Centre **1**
Udo's Bandas & Campsite **4**

Eldoret → *Phone code: 053. Colour map 3, grid C5.*

The journey from Kericho due north to Eldoret passes through the Nandi Hills, some of the most spectacular scenery in this part of the country, and the Kano Plains, bleak mountainous scrubland and ravines. Eldoret was originally settled by South African Boers who sailed from the Cape to Mombasa after the Boer War. They then trekked from the coast inland by ox wagon to what was 'plot 64', the number of the farm plot that had a post office on it, which was renamed Eldoret in 1912. This pleasant, busy and fairly prosperous highland town is surrounded by fertile countryside growing a mixture of food and cash crops. There is large-scale maize and wheat farming, and cattle keeping of the Ayrshire breed. The market is good and there are some useful shops if you are stocking up on provisions. Eldoret is dubbed 'home to running' thanks to a number of Olympic medal-winning athletes that have come from the region. An international airport opened at the end of the 1990s used to transport fresh flowers from the Naivasha region directly to the flower markets of Amsterdam and elsewhere in Europe. It is home to **Moi University** and this appears to be benefiting the town and expanding its economic potential. It is also home to a large teaching hospital which attracts many European medical professionals on placements. It is a very busy town, with a banks, supermarkets, trading stores and dozens of internet cafés, but there's no special reason you should stay here, unless en route to the Cherangani Hills.

● Sleeping

Kakamega *p148, map p148*

B **Golf**, just off main road, T056-30150/1/2, T020-330820 Nairobi, for reservations. Rooms have own bathrooms and TV, there is a swimming pool and facilities for golf, tennis and squash at the **Sports Club** next door. The bar is open to non-residents. Modern, very pleasant, excellent service and food, English-style cooking with some Indian dishes, but room rates are fairly expensive, especially considering Kenyan residents pay almost half price.

E **Franka**, southwest of the clocktower, T056-20086. Basic and quite small but clean rooms with hot water. Bar and restaurant, overall this hotel is quite reasonable and this is the best of the basic board and lodgings in town, although the bar can get noisy. Rates include breakfast.

Kakamega Forest National Reserve *p148, map p148*

A **Rondo Retreat Centre**, T056-30268, www.rondoretreat.com, is a religious centre open to the public, in a serene location within the forest. Originally Rondo was owned by a sawmiller who, in 1948, built a house at his wife's request at the base of what was thought to be the biggest tree in the Kakamega Forest, an Elgon olive tree that

still stands today. The sawmiller left Kenya in 1961, leaving the property to the Christian Council of Kenya. It was first used as a youth centre and orphanage, but more recently it has been involved with conservation efforts for the forest and it produces its own field guidebook. The homestead consists of the main house of clapboard and colonial era corrugated iron, and 5 cottages in the same style. Very good wholesome food in the dining room, but you need to be on best behaviour here. It's not suitable for children and there is no alcohol or smoking. Office in Kakamega town is opposite the post office.

D **Isecheno Bandas**, Isecheno Forest Station, 20 km from Kakemega town on Shinyala rd, T0722-619150 mob, reservations **UNIGLOBE Let's Go Travel**, Nairobi, T020-4447151, www.letsgosafari.com. There are 6 bandas that in total can sleep 18 people, a shared kitchen, bathroom and dining area. You need to bring your own bedding, food and firewood, though meals can be arranged on request with notice. This project is owned and run by the Kakamega Environmental Education Program (KEEP) which can provide guides for walks into the forest; you can also visit its resource centre nearby. It is promoted by the Ecotourism of Kenya Society.

D Udo's Bandas and Campsite, just outside the entrance gate in the north of the forest at Buyangu. Reservations **Kenya Wildlife Service Nairobi**, T020-600800, www.kws.org. 7 2-bed bandas, communal cooking area but no utensils, you need to bring firewood and water as well as linen and towels, US$10 per person, bucket showers and long drop loos. You can also camp next to the stream for US$3. A small shop sells a few basic supplies such as bread and soda, and there are small shops and tiny local restaurants in the village.
F Forest Rest House, within the forest reserve not far from the park office at Isecheno. It is a small building on stilts, with 4 bedrooms, all with private bathrooms but its pretty filthy and unkempt with no electricity and an erratic water supply. You will need to bring all food supplies from town although nearby there is a very small shop/restaurant where you can arrange a plate of food in advance.

Eldoret *p150*

C Eldoret Wagon, Elgeyo Rd, T053-62270, www.eldoretwagonhotel.co.ke. Comfortable, some triple and family rooms, has restaurant and bar, there are new and old blocks so some rooms are better than others, secure parking. This started life as a members' club for senior railway staff, notice the dining room was built in the shape of a railway carriage with a hooped roof. Casino too.
C Eldoret White Castle, Uganda Rd, T053-2033095. 120 very pleasant, clean rooms. Good modern facilities: restaurant, bar, health club and disco. However, it is bang slap in the middle of town with no parking save for a few spaces on the street.
C Sirikwa, Elgeyo Rd, reservations Nairobi, T020-224925, sirikwahotel@yahoo.com. Large hotel located in well-tended gardens, impressive entrance hall, a good swimming pool. Rooms are a worn but comfortable with bathrooms, price includes breakfast. Relaxed bar and good food in the restaurant.
D Eldoret New Lincoln, Oloo Rd, T0733-499780 (mob). Colonial-style hotel with some character and helpful staff. The best in this price range in town (but makesure out of the 46 rooms your is not one of the few with a leaking toilet and without hot water).

Good restaurant, pleasant bar, car park, but noisy club next door. Breakfast is US$1.50.
D Soy Safari Lodge, 22 km from Eldoret, close to Soy on the Kitale Rd, T072-350343 (mob). Simple country lodge, with 17 rooms, old fashioned and basic but adequate, Indian food but need to request this in advance, nice swimming pool and pretty gardens, double or single US$12, also camping for US$1 in the grounds and plenty of secure parking.
D-E Overland Stop, T053-2033029, campsite@ africaonline.co.ke. Located about 12 km from Eldoret on the road to the Kerio Valley, the C54 to Kaptagat, this turn-off is a few kilometres south of Eldoret at the Shell petrol station on the Nairobi road. This is Raj's new camp; the old one, Naiberi River Campsite is a further 8 km and will eventually close. Very unique in its design, carrying over many of the styles from the old camp such as a tunnel leading to cool bar with running streams, huge central fire place, glass roof with views of the moon and the setting sun over the forest. Lovely stonework, dorms and some double rooms, and they are in the process of building 20 more, kitchens, spotless ablution blocks and beautiful gardens. A very popular spot for overlanders, the parties here can be huge if there are large groups staying, good food on offer including lots of Indian snacks, run by Raj who owns a big textile factory in Eldoret. Prehistoric remains have recently been discovered here and the site is being developed. Recommended.

● Eating

Eldoret *p150*

† **Arcade**, a new food court type complex on Oloo Rd, which has the **Swiss Restaurant** which serves pizza, a branch of **Paul's Bakery**, for pies, sandwiches and cakes, the **Spree Club**, which is a bright and modern bar and disco, and an internet café.
† **Oriental**, Kenyatta St. Chinese restaurant, large portions, popular and very cheap, actually owned by Chinese people.
† **Paul's Bakery**, to the north of town on Uganda Rd. Good place to stop for fresh

● The story goes that the first bank in Eldoret was built around the bank's safe which had
● accidentally dropped off the back of a wagon and was too heavy to move again.

bread, pies, cakes etc. There is also a good shop at the cheese factory located to the south of the roundabout at the end of Kenyatta St, which sells a surprising range of very good cheeses and excellent ice cream plus other dairy products.

♥ **Sizzlers Cafe**, Kenyatta St. American diner style, good local food, snacks and milk-shakes, good service too.

♥ **Sunjeey**, Kenyatta St. Cheap café serving good-value and tasty Indian dishes with good choices for vegetarians, popular with the local Indian community which is always a good sign that the food is authentic.

⊙ Bars and clubs

Eldoret *p150*
The best and the newest disco is **Cyclone Disco**, on Kenyatta St.
Woodhouse Disco, Oginga Odinga St, is also popular and very lively.
Kutara Club, on Oloo Rd, **Places Disco** on Uganda Rd near the post office (a particularly lively local spot), and the one at **Eldoret White Castle Hotel**, all open their doors to revellers.

▲ Activities and tours

Eldoret *p150*
Eldoret Travel Agency, Kenyatta St, T053-2033351-3, F2032588, can book flights.
Kwa Kila Hali Safaris, PO Box 6793, Eldoret, T/F053-822154, www.kwakilahalisafaris.com. Very good and knowledgeable tour operator for western and northern Kenya, tailormade tours to all the sights, camping or lodge safaris, walking, fishing, and agro-tourism (farms, horticulture and livestock). Has assisted the BBC in making a film about the elephants in Mount Elgon National Park.

⊖ Transport

Kakamega *p148, map p148*
The town is less than 1 hr from **Kisumu** along the excellent though very busy A1 and there are plenty of buses and *matatus* travelling this route. The main bus stand is close to the market. The **Akamba** bus service has its stand opposite the Hindu Temple, off the Mumias Rd, for **Nairobi**.

Kakamega Forest National Reserve *p148, map p148*
For Isecheno take the Kisumu road south of Kakamega for about 10 km and turn left at Khayega. Carry on down this road for about 7 km when you will reach the village of Shinyalu where the forest is signposted. Take a right and after about another 5 km you will reach the forest reserve.

Buyangu is much easier to get to if you do not have your own transport as it is a walk of less than 1 km from the main road, about 20 km north of Kakamega, on the way to Webuye. This route is served by countless *matatus*, but watch out, very few of the drivers or conductors seem to recognize the name Buyangu.

Eldoret *p150*
Some 16 km south from Eldoret on the Eldoret-Kisumu Rd is the airport which, at the time of writing, was only being used for freight. Check though, this may change.

The *matatu* stand is in the centre of town just off Uganda Rd and there are a number of *matatus* and buses throughout the day. The journey direct to **Nairobi** takes just 3½ hrs. Recommended is **Easy Coach** which has its office next to Eldoret Valley Board and Lodging on Uganda Rd. It has a daily service between Eldoret and Nairobi via **Nakuru**. Akamba Bus also offers daily services and the office is on Nandi Rd.

❶ Directory

Kakamega *p148, map p148*
There is internet access at the Kakamega post office, which is in the middle of town.

Eldoret *p150*
Internet Cyber Café, next to Barclays Bank, on Uganda Rd. Cyberhawk, Nandi Rd. Jambo Internet Café, Uganda Rd, next to Standard Chartered Bank, and **Worldwide Information Technology**, Kenyatta St. **Medical services** Hospital, southwest of the centre at the end of Nandi Rd, is very good with a large casualty department. **Post office** The post office is on Uganda Rd, opposite is the Post Bank which offers **Western Union** money transfer. DHL services from **Eldoret Travel Agency**, Nandi Rd/Kenyatta St corner.

The far north

Ugandan border

From Eldoret the A104 passes through **Webuye** and **Bungoma** to reach **Malaba**, the most common border crossing into Uganda. These towns are all geared toward the transit traffic heading for Uganda. **Webuye Falls** are about 5 km from the road, and provide the water for **Panafric Paper Mills. Chetambe's Fort** is a further 8 km from the Webuye Falls, and is the site of the last stand of the Bukusu group of the Luhya people against the British in 1895. The Bukusu had strongly resisted the British incursions into their lands to build the railway during the 1890s. On the lower slopes of Mount Elgon the warriors were grouped together in a fortified stronghold located on the top of a hill. Armed only with spears they proved no match for the British (and sundry other mercenary soldiers) who massacred over 100 of the Bukusu warriors with an early machine gun, known as the Hotchkiss. The Malaba border itself is very busy especially with trucks and if you are in your own vehicle it may be better to cross at **Busia** (see below) some 30 km to the south and more easily accessed from Kisumu. Most of the buses between Nairobi and Kampala also use this border, as well as buses from Mwanza in Tanzania that go to Arusha and Dar es Salaam. It is actually quicker to go via Kenya on this route than to go through central Tanzania on appalling roads. Visas for Uganda and Kenya can be bought at both Malaba and Busia border post and the crossings are quick and efficient. Remember that if you go into Uganda and return to Kenya, the Kenyan visa is still valid and you do not need to get another one. However if you go into Uganda and then into Rwanda or the Democratic Republic of Congo to, say see the mountain gorillas, and then return to Kenya via Uganda, the Kenyan visa will not be valid and you will have to get another one. This visa agreement is only between Kenya, Uganda and Tanzania.

Busia is a small town that primarily consists of one road lined with shops, kiosks and cafés. About 20 km out of town is a small hill, **Got Ramogi**. From the top are great views over Lake Victoria on one side and of *shambas* on the other. The hill is of great significance to the Luo people as it is the site where their ancestors fought for the right to settle here in the 15th century.

Kitale → *Phone code: 054. Colour map 3, grid B3.*

A pleasant, small town, Kitale is in the middle of lush farmland between Mount Elgon and the Cherangani Hills. Originally this was Masai grazing land, but it was taken over by European settlers after the First World War. The town did not really develop until after 1925 and the arrival of a branch line of the railway. The region is known for its fruit and vegetables, including apples which are rare in East Africa. Kitale's main attraction for tourists is as a base from which to explore the Cherangani Hills, see page 123 (and information about guides later on in this section), or Mount Elgon, see page 155, and the Saiwa Swamp National Park, see page 154. It's also a stopping-off point on the route to Lake Turkana in the north.

> ⚫ *The Kitale Show at the beginning of November is a major agricultural festival.*

Sights

Kitale Museum ⓘ *close to the Eldoret Rd, T054-20670, www.museums.or.ke, 0800-1800, US$3,* contains ethnographic displays of the life of the people of Western Kenya with lots of tribal artefacts, and has a section on the evolution of man with special reference to East African and Kenyan discoveries. The museum also contains a very comprehensive insect collection (including butterflies) as well as birds, reptiles and wildlife exhibits. Murals on local life can be viewed in the Museum Hall. The museum buildings are set in spacious gardens, and the indigenous trees are labelled. There is an excellent nature trail through local forest, the remnants of a much larger forest that once clothed this area, that is rich in birdlife and monkeys, terminating at some very pleasant picnic sites. There is also is a **Snake Park**, home to both non-venomous and venomous snakes, in addition to an enclosure containing two crocodiles. Another enclosure contains tortoises. Nearby is a display of traditional homesteads of the Luhya, Nandi, Luo and Sabaot peoples. A biogas generation unit to demonstrate the use of animal waste to produce methane is an unusual exhibit.

Olaf Palme (Vi) Agroforestry Centre ① *T054-20139, viafp@net2000ke.com, free*, next door to the Kitale Museum, has received Swedish funding. It was established to assist and educate local farmers in soil conservation and improvement techniques, with advice and support about methods of tree planting and preventing soil erosion. There is an arboretum, an indigenous tree nursery and an agro-forestry demonstration area, in addition to a conference centre with educational displays.

Excursions

Kitale Nature Reserve ① *T0722-330803 (mob)*, owned by Mr Boniface Ndura, is a private park some 5 km from Kitale on the Lodwar road. The entrance is just before the bridge that crosses the Koitobos River. The small reserve covers about 40 ha of grasslands and acacia woodland, and riverine forest along the Koitobos which becomes swampy after the wet seasons. Orchids can be seen growing on tree trunks in the forests. There are a number of nature trails and you can buy drinks.

> ● *Around Kitale are extensive areas of greenhouses used for growing flowers that are exported to Europe.*

Kaisagat Desert Garden is a unique collection of indigenous and exotic desert plants, about 18 km from Kitale on the Lodwar road. Each one is labelled and, as well as the Kenyan species, there are examples from South Africa, Mozambique and Somalia. The path winds through rock covered mounds of earth where the succulents grow. The garden's creator is John Wilson who has two plants named after him.

Kitale is the nearest town to Saiwa Swamp and Mount Elgon national parks. See below for their descriptions.

Saiwa Swamp National Park → *Colour map 3, grid C5.*

① *0630-1800, US$15. Reached via the sealed well-signposted road, 24 km east of Kitale on the Kitale-Kapenguria road. There is a 5-km murram road linking Saiwa to the main road.*

Kenya's smallest national park, at 2.9 sq km, was established to protect the rare semi-aquatic sitatunga antelope (*Tragelaphus spekei*). The park is a perfect example of how a small area can survive as a complete ecological entity; it encloses the swamp fed by the Saiwa River together with its fringing belts of rainforest. The star of the show, the sitatunga, has widely splayed hooves that have evolved, allowing it to walk on the swamp vegetation. There are a sufficient number here to ensure a sighting. Other animals found here include the giant forest squirrel, bushbuck, Bohor reedbuck, bush duiker, the de Brazza monkey and both the spotted-necked and clawless otter. There is prolific birdlife estimated at over 400 species of birds and includes the great blue turaco, several varieties of kingfisher and the wonderfully named bare-faced go-away-bird. The national park is also home to a very large variety of reptiles, amphibians, butterflies and other insects. There are about three nature

66 99 The El Gonyi people, a Masai tribe, lived in the lava-tube caves for hundreds of years with their cattle, and the caves were used for many of their ceremonies. The mountain peak is considered to be a sacred place of worship, home to the gods...

trails, totalling 10 km, on duckboards traversing the varying habitats, and there are rest areas and picnic areas along the trails. Several tree hides with viewing platforms have been built along the western boundary from where it is possible to view the mammals and birds. The best time to see the Sitatunga is in the early morning or evening, as it rests semi-submerged and very well hidden during the heat of the day. The park has three distinctive vegetation types: wetland vegetation with stands of bullrush, reeds and sedges; wooded grasslands containing shrubs and grasses; indigenous forest as the national park contains remnants of tropical forest including wild fig and banana trees, *Terminalia spp* and *Albizia spp*.

Mount Elgon National Park → *Phone code: 054. Colour map 3, grid C5.*

① *Park entry fee is US$15 per day.*

The brooding flat-topped Mount Elgon which straddles the border with Uganda is a distinctive feature of this region of Western Kenya. Located in the Mount Elgon National Park, the mountain is home to a wide diversity of habitats created by the changing altitude at differing heights. From the base of the mountain to the top are a number of ecological zones going from mixed deciduous and evergreen forest, which include wonderful specimens of the Juniperus procera more commonly known as the East African cedar, as well as the Elgon teak and the great podos. With increasing altitude the vegetation changes to bamboo forest, and then opens up to Afro-alpine moorlands. Several rivers rise in these peaks including the Malakis and the Nzoia that feed Lake Victoria, and the Suam and the Turkwell that feed Lake Turkana to the north. The park also contains several beautiful waterfalls, dramatic cliffs and gorges, as well as hot springs. The name Elgon is said to be derived from the Masai *ol doinyo ilgoon* meaning 'the mountain with the contours of the human breast'. This area is known as Koitoboss meaning 'table rock' by virtue of its flat-topped basalt columns. There are a number of lava-tube caves formed by the action of water on volcanic ash, some are over 60 m wide and attract elephants and other herbivores in search of salt. Some of them can be explored. The El Gonyi people, a Masai tribe, lived in the lava-tube caves for hundreds of years with their cattle, and the caves were used for many of their ceremonies. The mountain peak is considered to be a sacred place of worship, home to the gods.

Ins and outs

The park is about 26 km northwest of Kitale, and the roads are clearly signposted. The most popular entry to the national park is by Chorlim Gate. Two routes to the gate can be used, either via Endebess, about 15 km from Kitale, or take the tarmac road 11 km past Kitale and turn left onto a murrum road leading to the gate. Most roads within the park are in good condition but a four-wheel drive is recommended.

‡ *It is illegal to enter the park zone without a vehicle.*

Mount Elgon National Park is in the Rift Valley on the western border with Uganda, covering 169 sq km on the Kenyan side. The peak of the extinct volcano, which reaches 4,322 m, the second highest mountain in Kenya with a radius of about 100 km, is estimated to be more than 15 million years old. The Kenya/Uganda border cuts through the caldera of this extinct volcano, giving half the mountain to Uganda, including the highest peak Wagagai (4,320 m), with Lower Elgon Peak (also sometimes called Sudek Peak) (4,307 m) in Kenya. The park's boundaries go down to 2,336 m.

Four of the lava-tube caves can be explored. **Kitum** is the largest cave extending to over 180 m in depth with a width of 60 m, and overhanging crystalline walls. This is the cave most favoured by the elephants that weave between the bounders and fallen rocks where the cave roof has collapsed. Using their tusks the elephants scrape away at the rock face and pick up the shards with their trunks. Every night it is possible to see long elephant convoys entering the cave to supplement their diet on the rich salt deposits. Kitum is also home to a large population of fruit bats. **Makingeni Cave** is not far from Kitum, and is favoured by buffalo, and both **Chepnyalil** and **Ngwarisha caves** can also be explored.

⁑ Bring a powerful torch for exploring the caves.

Endebess Bluff offers a panoramic view of the surrounding area. Animals likely to be seen here include black and white colobus monkey, blue monkey, forest elephant (sometimes referred to as cave elephant), leopard, giant forest hog, bushbuck, eland, buffalo, duiker and golden cat.

It is possible to drive up to about 4,000 m – the road passes through forest that is later supplanted by montane bamboo – and then hike over the moorlands with tree heathers up to 6 m tall, to Koitoboss peak. In the Afro-alpine zone are found giant lobelia and groundsels, believed to be survivors from the Ice Age. From there it is possible to climb over the crater rim and descend to the floor of the caldera.

Climbing Mount Elgon

Although it is possible to climb Mount Elgon at any time of year, the crater gets very cold and snow and hail are quite common, so the best times are between December and March. It is possible to reach the summit and back in a day in dry weather when

Mount Elgon National Park

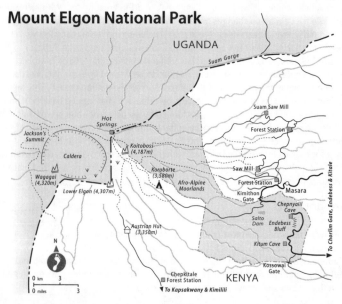

you are able to drive to within a few hours' hike of the highest point. Make sure that you are suitably equipped with warm and waterproof clothing and appropriate footwear. There is not such a severe problem with altitude sickness as on Mount Kenya, but a night spent en route will lessen any problems that might arise. If you do not have a four-wheel drive, the ascent can be hiked in a fairly leisurely manner, spending three days on the way up and two down.

The usual entry to the park is through the main Chorlim Gate and then driving through the park to the end of the road track at Koroborte (3,580 m), where there is a campsite and water. From here it is then about three hours to the Koitoboss summit.

Kimilili route This runs south of the route through the park. Starting from the village of Kimilili, there is a track to Kapsakwany, 8 km away. Another 2 km on is the turning to the forest gate, which is a further 2½ km. It is then 26 km, which can be driven comfortably in dry weather, to the **Austrian Hut** (3,350 m), where it is possible to stay or camp, with water nearby. There is a further 3 km of driveable track. From here it is about a four-hour hike to Koitoboss summit. There are picnic sites at Elephant Platform and Endebess Bluff.

Kimithon route This runs north of the park route. Starting from Endebess, it is 16 km to Masara village. About 1 km further on take the right fork (not the left to the Kimithon Gate). The middle of three tracks leads to Kimithon Forest Station, where it is possible to camp. Koitoboss is then about six hours' hike away. There may be problems with the Forest Station about using this route, but they can usually be negotiated with.

Equipment, porters and guides Camping gear and appropriate clothing can be hired in Nairobi at **Atul's**, Biashara Street, PO Box 43202, T020-225935. Costs are about US$30 per day, with about US$200 in deposits. You should obtain one of the maps of the mountain showing the trails in some detail. Porters for your gear, and guides, cost about US$3 a day, and are a sound investment, and can be recruited at any of the climb departure points. It is wise to ensure that the agreement with any guides or porters is clear. Guides are not obligatory, but if you don't have one, an armed ranger must be hired for the day to take you to the crater rim. *Mount Elgon Map and Guide*, by A Wielochowski, is available at **The Nation** bookshop in Nairobi, see page 84, or from 1 Meadow Close, Goring, Reading, RG8 9AA, England.

Western Kenya The far north Listings

● Sleeping

Kitale *p153*
B-C Kitale Club, Eldoret Rd, T054-31330, F30924, doubles up as a residential establishment for both temporary and permanent residents, in addition to offering sporting facilities. It is said to have been built on the site of the old slave market and has old colonial buildings with a few more modern additions. Range of rooms available: cottages with own bath and shower, or comfortable single rooms with hot water. Restaurant (mid-range) serves solid English fare with some Indian dishes. Satellite TV, swimming pool, tennis,

squash, snooker and an 18-hole golf course set amid clumps of natural forest. It is very pleasant but a little overpriced. Temporary membership (US$6) must be paid.
C-D Sunrise Motel, Kenyatta St. Standard or de luxe rooms, de luxe have nicer furnishings and balconies but both are large and comfortable. Friendly staff. Good restaurant, with a wide menu. Recommended.
D Alakara, Kenyatta St/Post Office Rd corner, T054-20395, F30298. Secure, has hot water all day, rooms are pleasant, although the beds are very short. Restaurant serves fairly simple food but it's good value.

 For an explanation of sleeping and eating price codes used in this guide, see inside the front cover. Other relevant information is found in Essentials, see pages 34-38.

D **Bongo Hotel**, Moi Av, T054-20593. Rooms are clean and pleasant, and have hot water and nets, good but just shaded by **Alakara** and **Sunrise Motel**.

Saiwa Swamp National Park p154
D-E **Sirikwa Safaris**, reservations **Barnley's House**, PO Box 322, Kitale, T/F0325-20061, T0722-767055 (mob), is a small, family-run campsite and safari company 20 km north of Kitale and 6 km past the gate to park (it's signposted on the right-hand side of the road). It has been operating for over 30 years with father and son, Tim and Dick Barnley, taking clients all over the region, including meetings with the remnants of the Sirikwa people. Now run by Jane and Julia Barnley, this is a lovely site, with excellent facilities, including a BBQ, flush toilets, hot showers, firewood, electricity and excellent food. Camping charges US$5 per person. To hire a tent costs US$15 per person, meals US$5. If you don't have a tent you can hire a room in the guest house fairly cheaply. Trout fishing in the Marun River can be arranged from here, as well as day trips to the Saiwa Swamp and Mt Elgon national parks. Guides are available for trekking in the Cherangani Hills. The tour includes the villages of Kapsangar-Tapach and Tamcal. Allow 3-4 days for the trip. Highly recommended.
E **Campsite**, small, near the park entrance at Saiwa Swamp. You need to bring along all your camping equipment and food. Better to stay at **Sirikwa Safaris**.

Mount Elgon National Park p155
L **Lokitela Farm**, 19 km west of Kitale, in the foothills of Mt Elgon, reservations **Bush and Beyond/Bush Homes of East Africa**, Nairobi, T020-600457, www.bush-and-beyond.com and www.bush-homes.co.ke. This farm mainly produces maize and milk and covers an area of 365 ha, of which 30 ha are riverine forest. 350 different species of birds and mammals have been identified here. 3 comfortable rooms and cosy sitting with a fireplace, good wholesome food using farm fare. This is a homestay hosted by the Mills family who are a wealth of information about the Elgon region, they offer nature

walks, trips to Saiwa Swamp National Park, as well as Mt Elgon, also overnight stays in the Cherangani Hide, a shelter built on wooden stilts beside the Suam River.
D-E **Delta Crescent Camp**, T054-31462. www.dcfelgonsafaris.com. Another family-run enterprise, this farm is situated 28 km from Kitale and 6 km from the Chorlim Gate. It covers 60 ha and activities include horse riding, accommodation is in simple bandas or camping and you can hire camping equipment and 4WDs, meals and drinks available, evenings are spent around a large bonfire. Guided mountain safaris can be arranged.
C **Kapkuro Bandas**, reservations **Kenya Wildlife Service**, Nairobi, T020-600800, www.kws.org. 2 semi-detached self-catering cottages with 1 double and 1 single bed, en suite bathrooms and kitchen with gas cooker. Located in a forest glade near the park HQ near Chorlim Gate, utensils in the kitchen are provided but no sheets and towels, although blankets and lanterns are supplied, guests need to bring with them their own firewood and drinking water.
E **Camping** There are 2 public campsites and 1 special campsite in the park, with fresh water and toilets. Reservations through Kenya Wildlife Services as above.

● Transport

Kitale p153
In Kitale there are various bus stands and *matatu* stops at the western end of the road to Mt Elgon. Akamba Bus stand is on the corner of Moi Av and Bank St. Getting to and from Kitale is relatively easy as it is on the A1 heading for Kakamega and Kisumu in the south, and is the main route to Lake Turkana in the north. There are regular buses and *matatus*. The road north from Eldoret to Marich Pass/Lake Turkana is very good.

● Directory

Kitale p153
The **post office** is on Post Office Rd and the main **banks** are pretty close to Bank St, as you might expect!

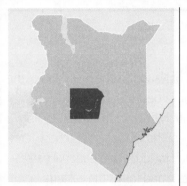

Central Highlands

Ins and outs	162
Nyeri and around	**163**
Thika to Nyeri	163
Nyeri	164
Solio Game Ranch	165
Aberdares National Park	166
Listings	168
Mount Kenya and around	**172**
Naro Moru	172
Nanyuki	172
Mount Kenya Biosphere Reserve	172
Mount Kenya	173
Listings	176
Laikipia Plateau	**179**
Listings	182
Moving east	**184**
Nanyuki to Embu	184
Meru	184
Meru National Park	185
Chogoria	186
Embu	186
Mwea National Reserve	186
Listings	187

⚬ Footprint features

Don't miss...	161
Baden-Powell	162
Treetops	167
Leafy streets	185

Introduction

Central Highlands, to the north of Nairobi, is the heartland of the Kikuyu people who make up the largest tribal group in Kenya. It used to be known as the 'White Highlands' because – being fertile and well watered – many of the white settlers chose it for their farmland. This region, which includes two national parks – Mount Kenya and the Aberdares – and forms the eastern boundary to the Rift Valley, is very densely populated.

A whole network of roads weave their way up into the highlands to Nyeri and on to Nanyuki. There are a number of towns in the Central Highlands – Nyeri, Embu, Meru, Nanyuki and Isiolo to name a few – and these are useful for shops and communications but have few distractions and will not hold the attention of visitors for very long. The real reason people come to the Central Highlands is to visit the Aberdares National Park – home to the famous hotels, the Ark and Treetops – the more remote Meru National Park, and also to climb Mount Kenya. The newest attraction of the region, and one of East Africa's wildlife conservation success stories, is the Laikipia Plateau. Here the many farms and ranches across a vast area have joined forces to protect the wild animals on their land and start up tourism initiatives to support their gallant efforts. This area is over 9,500 sq km and covers not only much of the Central Highlands but also stretches into the Northern Territory and into Western Kenya. It is, however, best accessed from the town of Nanyuki so it is included in this chapter.

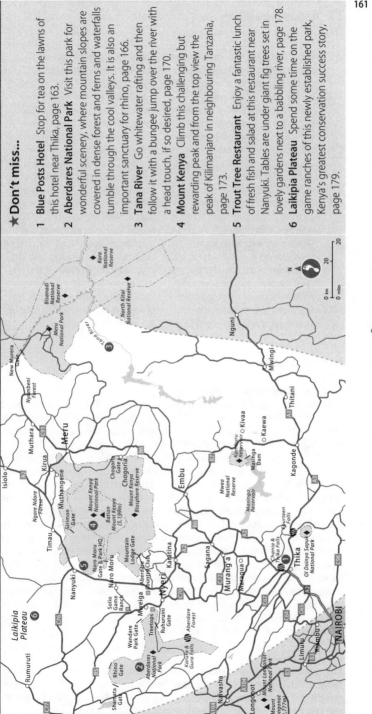

★ Don't miss...

1 **Blue Posts Hotel** Stop for tea on the lawns of this hotel near Thika, page 163.

2 **Aberdares National Park** Visit this park for wonderful scenery, where mountain slopes are covered in dense forest and ferns and waterfalls tumble through the cool valleys. It is also an important sanctuary for rhino, page 166.

3 **Tana River** Go whitewater rafting and then follow it with a bungee jump over the river with a head touch, if so desired, page 170.

4 **Mount Kenya** Climb this challenging but rewarding peak and from the top view the peak of Kilimanjaro in neighbouring Tanzania, page 173.

5 **Trout Tree Restaurant** Enjoy a fantastic lunch of fresh fish and salad at this restaurant near Nanyuki. Tables are under giant fig trees set in lovely gardens next to a babbling river, page 178.

6 **Laikipia Plateau** Spend some time on the game ranches of this newly established park, Kenya's greatest conservation success story, page 179.

Central Highlands

Baden-Powell

Lord Baden-Powell distinguished himself in the Boer War during the seige of Mafeking. At the time he was 45 years old, the youngest General in the British Army.

He is best known as the founder of the Boy Scout movement. Guides were soon to follow and, for younger children, Cubs and Brownies. The movement was very successful, and is still popular around the world.

Baden-Powell once visited a small boarding school in the Rift Valley which was popular amongst British settlers and missionaries. Some of the children there were as young as six, and considered to be too small to join the Brownies or the Cubs. Baden-Powell therefore decided to establish something for the youngest children – and so the 'Chippets' were born. The school remembers Baden-Powell each year. They also have a flag mounted in one of the corridors which was presented to the school by Baden-Powell's wife after his death.

Nyeri was Baden-Powell's great love and he once wrote that "The nearer to Nyeri the nearer to bliss". In the grounds of the Outspan Hotel is the cottage, Paxtu, built with money collected by guides and scouts from around the world, where Baden-Powell spent his final years. He died in 1941 and his obituary states: "No Chief, no Prince, no King, no Saint was ever mourned by so great a company of boys and girls, or men and women, in every land." He is buried in Nyeri cemetery, and his wife's ashes are buried beside him. Lady Baden-Powell was World Chief Guide until her death (in England) at the age of 88 on 25 June 1977.

Ins and outs

Getting there and around

There are a number of towns located along the Kirinyaga Ring Road at the base of Mount Kenya. The route round the mountain is becoming increasingly popular as a tourist circuit, which is not surprising for it is a really beautiful part of the country, and the mountain and the game parks nearby are an added attraction. From Nairobi the main A2 heads north, firstly along a dual carriageway through the outskirts of the city to Thika, a distance of 42 km. It then continues northwards through the lush, verdant countryside. Almost every inch of ground is cultivated and you will see terraces on some of the steeper slopes. You will soon notice that this is pineapple country and many hectares are taken up with plantations. There are a number of routes to choose from: you can go north to Nyeri and the Aberdares National Park, then clockwise round the mountain via Naro Moru, or anti-clockwise via Embu. The following section will cover the clockwise route around Mount Kenya, taking in Nyeri and Naro Moru, to Nanyuki. It is possible to continue on all the way around the mountain via Meru to Embu and rejoin the A2 at Thika. The towns are linked with a steady stream of *matatus* and long-distance buses operate services with Nairobi. There are also bus and *matatu* links across country to Naivasha and Nakuru in the Rift Valley. Main access points to the lodges in the Laikipia Plateau region is from Nanyuki, Isiolo, Nyahuru or Maralal depending on where the lodges are located. See the relevant chapters for transport details.

Best time to visit

This area is very high, with peaks in the Aberdares of up to 4,000 m, and Mount Kenya, which is 5,199 m. You should therefore expect it to get fairly chilly, especially at night. The maximum temperature range is 22-26°C and the minimum 10-14°C. It is also very wet here with annual rainfall of up to 3,000 mm not unusual.

Nyeri and around

Thika to Nyeri

Thika → *Phone code: 067. Colour map 1, grid A4.*

Directly from Nairobi, the four-laned A2 continues up towards Thika, which is actually off the main road. This town was made famous by the book (and later the television series) *The Flame Trees of Thika* by Elspeth Huxley. It is about her childhood when her parents came out to Kenya as one of the first families, and their attempts to establish a farm. However, there is little special about Thika – not even many flame trees to brighten it up. It is primarily a base for manufacturing activity.

The singular attraction is the **Blue Posts Hotel**, a famous colonial landmark. A visit is a must if you're in the area. It is nestled between Chania and Thika Falls with shaded tables in sight of the falls, where all you hear is the crashing water, birdsong and the rustling of leaves. There are also easy trails around the base of the falls, thick with flowers and foliage, teeming with butterflies and dragonflies.

Ol Doinyo Sapuk National Park → *Colour map 1, grid A5..*

① *Park entry fee is US$15 per day, plus vehicle fee.*

The park, 25 km from Thika and 50 km from Nairobi, is named after the extinct volcano, Ol Doinyo Sapuk, 2,150 m, which means the mountain of the buffalo. It can be climbed or you can drive to the summit in a four-wheel drive. From the top are views of Nairobi, Mount Kenya and even Mount Kilimanjaro on clear days. The top of the volcano is covered in dense forest vegetation including the giant lobelia, and the area is home to large number of birds. There is some game but it is difficult to spot in the heavily wooded terrain.

Sir William Northrup MacMillan, a well-heeled gentleman of St Louis, bought the mountain and much of the surrounding land in the early part of the 20th century. This immensely wealthy, 158-kg American came to the protectorate in 1904. He received a knighthood from the British in recognition of his support during the First World War. He was famous among the early settlers for his generous entertainment of most of the people of note who passed through Kenya, including Roosevelt and Churchill. After his death he bequeathed the mountain to the nation and was buried at the 7-km mark along the road to the summit. It had been intended that his remains would be interred at the summit, but they proved to be too heavy for the hearse, supported on skis and pulled by a tractor, to complete its ascent. Oak trees were planted by the graveside.

Fourteen Falls → *Colour map 1, grid A5.*

These falls are particularly splendid during the rainy season. Recently declared a national park (*US$2*), this broad plume of water plummets 30 m over a multi-lipped precipice. There is a path leading from the car park to the base of the falls. The falls derive the name from their 14 successive falls of water along the Athi River.

Murang'a → *Colour map 1, grid A4.*

This small, bustling town is situated just off the main road north. The town has become known as the Kikuyu Heartland because it is close to **Mugeka**, the *Mukuruwe wa Gathanga* (Garden of Eden of the Kikuyu), which has an important place in Kikuyu mythology. The legend is that it was here that N'Gai (God) led Gikuyu to the mountain and told him to build his home there. He was given his wife Mumbi and in time they had several daughters. N'Gai found nine husbands under a fig tree for the nine daughters of Gikuyu and Mumbi, who in mythology are the ancestors of all Kikuyu.

These nine became the forefathers of the nine Kikuyu clans – in alphabetical order: Achera, Agachiku, Airimu, Aithaga, Aitherandu, Ambui, Angare, Angui and Anjiru. There was actually also a tenth daughter. However, the Kikuyu are very superstitious and one of their beliefs is that the number 10 is unlucky, so the term the 'full nine' is often used instead, and is still in use today especially by older Kikuyus. **Church of St James and All Martyrs** is not particularly old but has some interesting decorations painted in 1955 by a Tanzanian artist named Elimo Njau. It shows various scenes from the Bible with an African Christ and in African surroundings. The church was founded in memory of the Kikuyu who died at the hands of the Mau Mau.

From Murang'a the main road continues north towards Nyeri, Naro Moru and Nanyuki. It is possible to take a detour into the **Aberdare Forest**. Follow one of the minor roads from Murang'a, which eventually leads to Othaya and on to Nyeri – the turning for this is to the left just before you get to Murang'a.

Sagana and Karatina → *Phone code: 061. Colour map 1, grid A4.*
The main road road continues north through the small settlement of **Sagana** where **Savage Wilderness Safaris** has its base for whitewater rafting (see under Activities and tours below), to **Karatina** which is the next town you will reach. There are baskets for sale from the Kikuyu women who sit by the road side. It is often the vendors themselves who make the baskets, and they are good value. Worth a visit on market days (Tuesday, Thursday and Saturday), this is one of the biggest fruit and vegetable markets in East Africa, and it attracts buyers from as far away as Mombasa.

Nyeri → *Phone code: 061. Colour map 1, grid A4.*

Nyeri, 120 km from Nairobi, is the administrative capital of the Central Province. The town was named by Richard Meinertzhagen in 1902. He had camped at Nyeri Hill nearby during an expedition against the Tetu (a sub-group of the Kikuyu) who had ambushed an Arab caravan. It is at the base of the Aberdares, close to the boundary of the Aberdares National Park, west of the town. During the British colonial period Nyeri developed as an army base and then as an important trading centre for farmers from the surrounding countryside. The land is very fertile and as you drive into Nyeri you will see the many *shambas* (farms) growing maize, bananas and coffee, as well as many varieties of vegetables. On a clear morning you can see Mount Kenya in the distance.

Ins and outs
Getting there and around There are regular *matatus* from Nairobi and other main towns in the area. The main street, Kimathi Way, is where you will find banks, post office and hotels. A little to the south of this cluster is the market and the bus stand.
Best time to visit It is one of the wettest parts of Kenya and has a cool climate, and can even be cold in the evenings.

Sights
On the main road you can see a **memorial** to those who died during the Mau Mau. It has the inscription: to the Memory of the Members of the Kikuyu Tribe Who Died in the Fight for Freedom 1951-1957.

It is possible to visit **Lord Baden-Powell's home** ① *US$1.50, free to scouts in uniform, pay at the hotel reception*, which contains a small **museum** with a display of memorabilia. The cottage *Paxtu* lies in the grounds of the **Outspan Hotel**. Baden-Powell's home in England was named *Pax*, and the name of his Kenyan home was a pun on the original (*Pax Two*). Baden-Powell died in Nyeri in 1941 and is buried nearby, at the graveyard of St Peter's Church. On his headstone are the words 'Robert Baden Powell, Chief Scout of the World'. His wife Olave, who died in the UK 36 years after her husband, was cremated and her ashes were buried in the same grave. In the living room are some of the greeting cards Baden-Powell drew for friends. Outside, two big scout movement emblems are surrounded by a tropical garden.

After Baden-Powell's death, *Paxtu* was the home of Jim Corbett, famous hunter/destroyer of several man-eating tigers in India in the 1920s and 1930s. In 1947 Jim Corbett and his sister Maggie moved to Nyeri where he wrote most of his books. In 1952 (when aged 80 years) he received a request to meet Princess Elizabeth and Prince Philip at **Treetops**, where he identified animals for the Royals.

Out of town on the D435 road that leads to the Ruhuruini Gate is an enormous **Italian church** built in remembrance of the Italian soldiers who died in East Africa during the Second World War. In front of the main altar lies the grave of Amadeo di Savoia, Duce d'Aosta, the commander of the main Italian armies in Ethiopia, who formally surrendered to the Allied army at Amba Alagi, 20 May 1941, and died in Nairobi in 1942.

Solio Game Ranch → *Colour map 1, grid A4.*

① *To171-55271, eparfet@africa online.com.*
About an hour's drive north of Nyeri, is this private ranch that incorporates one of the most successful rhino breeding programmes in Africa. It contains both black and white rhino and is located a little north of Mweiga, along the B5 towards Nyaharuru, between Solio and Naro Moru. Its conservation and breeding programme has been so successful that Solio Park has provided stock that has been translocated to other sanctuaries, such as Nakuru, Tsavo and the Aberdares national parks. In 2004 six white rhino were also relocated to the Lewa Wildlife Conservancy. Trips to visit the ranch can be arranged at the **Aberdare Country Club**.

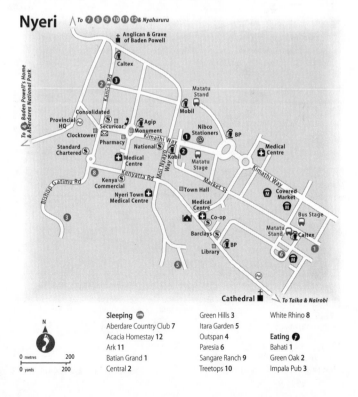

Nyeri

Sleeping 🛏	Green Hills 3	White Rhino 8
Aberdare Country Club 7	Itara Garden 5	
Acacia Homestay 12	Outspan 4	**Eating** 🍴
Ark 11	Paresia 6	Bahati 1
Batian Grand 1	Sangare Ranch 9	Green Oak 2
Central 2	Treetops 10	Impala Pub 3

0 metres 200
0 yards 200

Central Highlands Nyeri & around

Aberdares National Park → *Phone code: 061.*

The national park, established in 1950, encompasses an area of around 715 sq km and is one of Kenya's only virgin forest reserves. The Aberdares are the third highest massif in the country, with dramatic peaks, deep valleys, enormous spectacular waterfalls cascading down the rock face, volcanic outcrops of bizarre proportions and undulating moorlands. There isn't a huge amount of wildlife (comparatively) although birdlife is rich, and the walks around the park offer tremendous views.

Ins and outs

The park is 10 km from Nyeri and 165 km from Nairobi. From Nyeri you can enter the park through three gates: Ruhuruini Gate, Wandare Gate and Kiandongoro Gate. Outspan Hotel is the base hotel for Treetops and visitors usually come here first. From Nyeri there is a road to Mweiga, the town close to the Aberdare Country Club, the base for The Ark. Also in Mweiga is the KWS headquarters, where you can obtain or reload your Smartcard. The lodges and hotels organize transfers and game drives, and there are hiking trails although a ranger guide is compulsory. Gates are open 0600-1900 (no entry after 1815). Park entry fee US$30 per day, plus vehicle fees.

The park is not often visited primarily because of the weather. It rains heavily and frequently, making driving difficult and seeing the game and mountain peaks almost impossible. Set off early in the day, as it frequently clouds over by late morning. It is often closed during the wet season as the roads turn into mudslides.

Aberdares National Park

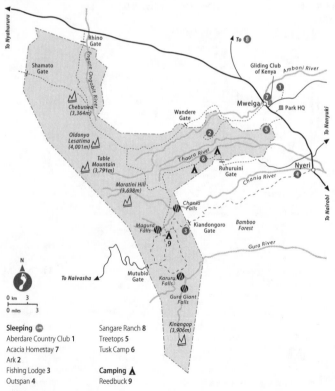

Sleeping 🛏️
Aberdare Country Club **1**
Acacia Homestay **7**
Ark **2**
Fishing Lodge **3**
Outspan **4**

Sangare Ranch **8**
Treetops **5**
Tusk Camp **6**

Camping ⛺
Reedbuck **9**

● Treetops

Originally, Treetops was nothing more than a two-room treehouse sitting on top of a fig tree. Intrepid travellers reached it on foot escorted by armed rangers that protected them from wild animals during the walk. Then guests were left on their own with just a picnic supper and some oil lamps. At dawn, the rangers returned to escort them back, after an exciting and chilling night in the midst of the forest watching the wildlife roaming below their feet. In 1952, Treetops was enlarged for a royal visit from Princess Elizabeth and her husband Philip. A third room was added and a small cabin for the ranger on duty was attached. During their overnight stay, the young princess and her husband witnessed a thrilling fight between two male waterbucks that ended with one killing the other. However, that night would become historical because of a different reason as the princess's father, King George VI, died in London. Although the princess was not aware of the bad news until her next stop at Sagana, the morning she descended from Treetops she had become the Queen of England. The hotel was burnt down by the Mau-Mau two years later, but it was rebuilt in 1957 at the opposite side of the waterhole. The modern building, several times enlarged since then, is a pillared wooden house embracing the branches of a chestnut tree. A second waterhole was artificially opened at the back side of the building, although for some reason the animals prefer the original pond. The lodge's employees spread salt on the soil, which the animals lick.

Sights

The Aberdares is a range of mountains to the west of Mount Kenya, running in a north-south direction between Nairobi and Nyahururu (Thomson's Falls). The Aberdares come to a peak at about 4,000 m and the middle and upper reaches are densely forested with thickets of bamboo, giant heath and tussock grass. The eastern and western slopes in particular are covered with dense forest and tree ferns in places.

The Kikuyu call these mountains Nyandarua ('drying hide') and they were the home to guerrilla fighters during the struggle for Independence. Nowadays the mountains are home to bongo (elusive forest antelope), buffalo, elephant, giant forest hog, red duiker, and Syke's and colobus monkeys. The rare, handsome bongo is most likely to be spotted near The Ark, which is sited close to a swampy glade, waterhole and salt-lick, or up in bamboo zone. Dawn and the following hour is the optimum time to see these elusive forest antelopes. At about 3,500 m, where the landscape opens up, you may see lions, leopards, serval cats and even bushbucks. Caution is required with the lions. Birdlife is prolific here; most obvious are the four species of sunbirds. Among the birds of prey are the crowned hawk eagles, mountain buzzard and the African goshawk. Wildlife is comparatively scarce, but the views in the park are spectacular. Particularly good walks include trekking up the three peaks, **Satima**, 3,998 m, **Kinangop**, 3,906 m, and **Kipipiri**, 3,348 m. You can hire a guide if you wish, but, if walking, an armed guard, costing US$6.50 daily, is obligatory to protect you from the wildlife. Trout fishing is very popular, especially high up in the moors. A fishing licence is required, obtainable from the park headquarters for US$5.

The park is split into two sections, the beautiful high moorland and peaks with sub-alpine vegetation, and the lower Salient which is dense rainforest and where much of the wildlife lives. The Aberdare Salient is closed to the public and the animals can only be viewed from **Treetops** or **The Ark** (details below). Access to these lodges is prohibited to private vehicles; visitors are obliged to use the hotel bus.

Central Highlands Nyeri & around

There are a number of spectacular waterfalls in the park including the **Chania Falls** and the **Karuru Falls** that have a total drop of 273 m in three steps. The more remote and inaccessible **Gura Giant Falls**, to the south, have a higher single drop of over 300 m. There are a few roads traversing the centre of the national park from Nyeri to Naivasha, giving access to most of the waterfalls.

A major project in recent years has been the building of the **rhino sanctuary** here, funded by the Kenya Wildlife Services, the Overseas Aid Agency and conservation organizations including Rhino Ark, www.rhinoark.org. An area has been enclosed by a high-security electrified fence, which extends for 380 km to form a sanctuary for the endangered rhino. Other wildlife also live within the fence including elephant and various members of the cat family. The electricity for the fence is generated locally using waterwheels to harness water from within the forest, a project that also provides power for local people living in the surrounding villages. The local villages support and also raised money for this project, which also protects their livestock and crops from the animals. Various fund-raising activities in support of the project include the 'Rhino Charge' motor rally (see box, page 68).

● Sleeping

Thika p163

C **Blue Posts Hotel**, just north of Thika, to-wards Murang'a (take the first slip road off the main A2 after the main junction for Thika), T067-22241, blueposthotel@africa online.co.ke. Established in 1908 as a stop-over for white settlers who farmed and lived in central Kenya, it is still a popular hotel, with a very good view over the falls (Thika and Chania rivers surround the hotel each with a natural waterfall). Easily the nicest place to stay in the area, rustic, sprawling, safari-style lodge, with large gardens and ostrich farm. 32 rooms, TV, veranda, night-club, good food, buffet lunches on a day trip from Nairobi are recommended. Camping.
E **New Fulilia Hotel**, there are 2: Kwame Nkrumah Rd, T067-31286, the other is 2 blocks east. Go to the first one first and you may be directed to the other one if it's full. Both are good value, clean and basic.
E **White Line**, in the centre of Thika, is not a bad place to stay, the rooms have bathrooms and there is sometimes hot water, usually in the evenings. Good value for the price.

Ol Donyo Sapuk National Park p163

E **Camping**, Kenya Wildlife Service, Nairobi, T020-600800, www.kws.org, in a very basic campsite near the main gate with water and a pit latrine, so you will need to bring everything.

Karatina p164

D **Hotel Ibis**, there are 2 Ibis hotels in town, 1 on the main road, T061-772777, and the other is 1 block back from the BP garage on the main road, T061-772800. In a striking and modern pink and blue tower, both are smart and good value with modern bathrooms, the first one has a restaurant and bar, although there is no parking at either.
D **Tourist Lodge**, T061-71522. Set back from the main road in the centre of town with secure parking, simple rooms, everything is worn and old fashioned but it is well run, rates include breakfast.
E **3 in 1**, near the bus stand, basic lodgings in a tall block, can get noisy but rooms are clean. Very cheap restaurant for African food.

Nyeri p164

L **Aberdare Country Club**, 12 km to the north of Nyeri, reservations The Norfolk, Nairobi, T020-216940, www.lonrhohotels. com. Formerly a farmhouse, it is another old colonial-type country hotel with 46 rooms, very luxurious with tennis courts and a 9-hole golf course. You can arrange game drives into the national park. Rates are per night full board, inclusive of temporary membership and golf, US$200 for a double in high season, US$150 in low season.
L **Outspan Hotel**, 20 mins' walk or a taxi ride away, reservations Aberdare Safari Hotels,

---

● *For an explanation of sleeping and eating price codes used in this guide, see inside the*
● *front cover. Other relevant information is found in Essentials, see pages 34-38.*

Nairobi, T020-4452095, www.aberdaresafari hotels.com. Built in the 1920s, it contains within its grounds a cottage that was the last residence of Lord Baden-Powell. Has a wonderful atmosphere, set in the most beautiful gardens, swimming, tennis, squash, snooker. Very spacious rooms, prices depend on the season. This hotel is also used as a safari base for the Aberdares National Park.

L Sangare Ranch, reservations **Savannah Camps**, Nairobi, T020-331684, www.savannah camps.com. In the foothills of the Aberdare Mountains the 6,500 acres has a private airstrip, and guest rooms in 6 en suite tented units. An attractive cedar wooden cottage is the bar and dining room. Camp overlooks a small lake and is encircled by yellow acacia trees where elephant and buffalo visit. Rates are all-inclusive – food, drinks, laundry, game drives in Solio Game Ranch and horse riding.

C Acacia Homestay, 10 km to the northwest of Nyeri near Mwegia, T0733-760331 (mob), www.acaciahomestay.com. Family- run lodge set on a 2,000-acre natural wild bush ranch where you may see elephant, giraffe, impalas and other wildlife. Comfy rooms in garden cottages, meals in the main house with the family, organize activities including horse riding, game walks and gliding.

C Green Hills, Mumbi Rd, T061-2030604, greenhillshotel@wananchi.com, is on the top of a hill to the southwest of the town. Spread over extensive gardens and is large with 105 rooms with balconies. Also traditional-style thatched cottages. Decor is slightly dated – embroidered 'arm covers' over the sofas, etc. Friendly staff and excellent facilities including restaurant, bar, swimming pool, laundry and parking. Price includes breakfast.

D Batian Grand Hotel, T061-2030783, on the east side of town, near the bus parks. Large modern block with central courtyard, rooms with hot water, restaurant, bar with pool table, and secure parking.

D Central, Kanisa Rd, T061-2034233, is a modern hotel close to the post office in the north of the town, fairly basic but clean, comfortable and good value. All the rooms have bathrooms with hot water, it has secure parking, a restaurant and a pleasant open-air bar and a disco at weekends.

D White Rhino, Kenyatta Rd, T061-2030934. This colonial hotel is located fairly centrally in Nyeri. One of the oldest buildings in the

town and starting to feel its age, the facilities are not that extensive, but the atmosphere, friendly staff and pleasant gardens make it worth while. It has a bar with a pool table, restaurant, lounge and laundry service.

E Itara Garden, T061-2032537. A fairly new hotel with basic but clean rooms in the main modern building or thatched wooden complex. Has a restaurant and good outdoor bar with pool tables.

E Paresia, T061-2032765, is a large block in a run-down area south of the bus station. But clean and bright with hot water and friendly.

Aberdares National Park p166

As accommodation is expensive and limited at the park, an alternative option is to stay at Nyeri (see page 164).Remember it gets freezing at night.

L The Ark, reservations well in advance at The Norfolk, Nairobi, T020-216940, www. lonrhohotels.com. Wooden lodge with 46 double, 5 single and 8 triple rooms with en suite bathrooms, located in the centre of the park. This tree-lodge is uniquely shaped to resemble the actual Ark, designed with decks from which numerous balconies and lounges provide superb vantage points for viewing the animals visiting the salt-lick and waterhole. A ground-level bunker provides excellent photographic opportunities, and the waterhole is floodlit at night. Costs vary between US$150-250 depending on season, rates are full board, and include transfer to the hotel but exclude park entry fees, children under 7 are not allowed.

L Fishing Lodge, T061-55465, or **Kenya Wildlife Service**, Nairobi, T020-600800, www.kws.org. 2 stone-built cottages each with 2 bedrooms (each has a double and single bed), and a third smaller bedroom (has a single bed), plus 2 bathrooms. Everything is provided except for food, firewood (though there is a gas cooker) and drinking water. Facilities are shared by everyone and include a communal eating area. A 4WD is recommended at all times of year to get here because of the steep hills. It is usual for a whole cottage to be rented out for US$200 per night, but it is possible to share.

L Treetops, inside the park entrance, reservations **Aberdare Safari Hotels**, Nairobi, T020-4452095, www.aberdaresafarihotels.com. This is a little more basic than **The Ark**, and has small cabin-type rooms with shared bathroom facilities. There is a roof deck from where you can safely view the animals at night. The original treehouse was actually burnt down in 1955, but at that time this was a facility very much for the élite. Princess Elizabeth was staying at **Treetops** when she became Queen Elizabeth II (see box, page 167). Access is from the **Outspan Hotel** in Nyeri, you need to arrive for lunch at 1130, the bus leaves for the park at 1430.

L **Tusk Camp**, through Kenya Wildlife Service reservations as above, 1 banda with 2 double beds and 1 banda with 4 single beds, sleeps 8 in total for US$100, external bathroom, gas cooker, some kitchen utensils, caretaker on site, guests must provide firewood and drinking water, linen and lanterns supplied.

Camping

There is a site near the fishing lodge though it is extremely basic and you will have to be completely self sufficient. Since the early 1980s, camping is restricted when some campers were attacked by lions. The attacking animals were probably several semi-tame lions used for a film. **Reedbuck** public campsite, relatively new and close to the fishing lodge, is now the only authorized campsite in the high moorlands. It provides water, firewood, toilets and rain shelter, but you need to bring food and other supplies. In the Salient area there are 8 special camp sites, one in Prince Charles, 2 in Kiguri and 5 in Muringato. For reservations contact the Warden, T061-55465, or **Kenya Wildlife Service**, Nairobi, T020-600800, www.kws.org.

⊘ Eating

Thika p163

⊌⊌⊌ **Blue Posts Hotel**, very good food and wide selection of dishes, the buffet lunches even if not staying, say on a day trip from Nairobi, are recommended. Lovely place and very attentive chefs. Kids will enjoy the ostrich farm, pony rides and playground.
⊌ **Prismos Hotel**, Kwane Nkrumah Rd. Large popular restaurant with covered balcony but the usual chicken and chips and the like.
⊌ **Suitable Bar and Restaurant**, next door to the **New Fulilia** on Kwame Nkrumah Rd. Cold drinks, stews and basic grills. Nothing special, name says it all.

Nyeri p164

If you are staying in one of the top range hotels you will probably eat there. Otherwise the **Central** and **White Rhino** have restaurants which are both good value. Many small restaurants offer cheap meals.
⊌⊌⊌ The **Outspan** is a good place to stop for breakfast or lunch – you can admire the gardens and, as long as the clouds are not down, you will get a good view of Mt Kenya and the Aberdare range behind. There is also a pub on site serving good food.
⊌ **Bahati**, opposite **Green Oak**, is very similar and mostly sells chicken dishes.
⊌ **Green Oak**, Kimathi Way. Local restaurant with a covered balcony where you can look down on to the street. Mostly African food, very cheap, and is very popular with office workers at lunch time.
⊌ **Impala Pub**, on the corner opposite the **Central Hotel**, is a popular, relaxed local bar.

▲ Activities and tours

Sagana and Karatina p164

Savage Wilderness Safaris, Sarit Centre, Nairobi, T/F061-521590, www.whitewater kenya. com. Its base is on the Tana River just south of Sagana, which is clearly signposted. It offers whitewater rafting on the river as well as climbs of Mt Kenya. A 1-day trip from Nairobi costs US$95, and includes transport from either the Sarit Centre or **The Norfolk**, tea and coffee on arrival at the river, and a 4-hr rafting trip. Afterwards there is time to relax at the Savage Camp, have a hot shower or a swim in the pool, plus a BBQ lunch. Other options are floats on flat stretches of the Tana River for those who do not want to go through the rapids for birdwatching with an experienced guide for US$80, and a full-moon rafting trip once a month that lasts for 3 hrs, US$125. Longer 3-day, 80-km rafting trips on the Athi River further south can be arranged that go through Tsavo National Park for US$360 – the most exciting rapids on this trip are named *Vietnam* and *Crocodile Burn Up*. Also at the Savage Camp is a new bungee jump from a 60-m tower over the Tana River that costs US$50, although to operate the jump there needs to a minimum of 3 people. You can jump on your own or with a friend tandem style, weight limits are min 40 kg and max 110 kg.

Nyeri *p164*

Gliding

It is possible to hang-glide over the Aberdares National Park with the **Gliding Club of Kenya**, which has its headquarters at Mweiga Air Field, 8 km north of Nyeri and 12 km southwest of Kirinyaga, with Petra and Peter Allmendinger, T0733-760331 (mob), www.acaciahomestay.com (details of gliding can also be found on this website). This German couple, who offer accommodation on an old coffee farm (see **Acacia Homestay** above), run and manage the **Gliding Club of Kenya** on a commercial basis, in addition to offering farm and riding holidays for families and less adventurous guests. The 'Soaring Safaris' offer a wonderful overview of the Aberdares and are well suited for long high-altitude flights due to the convergence of two differing air masses, the moist cumulus weather at Mweiga and the dry hot desert air just 35 km to the north. There is a runway of 1,300 m in length and the Allmendingers also run a gliding school. The gliders are released at an altitude of 1,300 m and the soaring range can be as much as 120 km from the airfield. The best time to visit is from Sep to Apr; Aug is too wet for gliding. A 10-min flight costs around US$50.

Tour operators

Nyeri is the gateway to the Aberdares National Park and you will come here before you go to the park. If you do not already have a trip arranged you can organize one through the **Outspan**. You will need a group of at least 3 people (the more people the cheaper it should work out). They are just for the day and are ideal if you cannot afford the lodges in the park itself. They are also fairly good value and the price varies depending on the season and where you want to go in the park. You can rent self-drive vehicles from the Outspan.

◉ Transport

Thika *p163*

There are frequent *matatus* from **Nairobi** to Thika from Racecourse Rd and Ronald Ngala Roundabout (45 mins). In Thika the *matatu* stand is at the end of Commercial St opposite the **White Line Hotel**. From here *matatus* also go to **Nyeri** and beyond to the

north along the main highway, and across country to **Naivasha** and **Nakuru**. Getting around town is simple enough as there are plenty of taxis, *boda bodas* (bicycle taxis) and the odd tuk tuk. If you arrive in town on public transport and want to go to the **Blue Posts Hotel** you will need to take a taxi, but it's not far.

Ol Donyo Sapuk National Park *p163*

The only route to the park is through the village of Kilima Mbogo, 4 km south of the main A3 Thika – Garissa road. From Kilima Mbogo, a dirt track runs 7 km to the park gate. Buses run regularly from Thika towards Garissa and you can get off at Kilima Mbogo junction. However, from there, transport to the park is irregular and walking within the boundaries of the park is prohibited without an armed escort. Oldonyo Sapuk is best visited by organized tour from Nairobi.

Nyeri *p164*

Matatus ply the route to **Nairobi** and there are good connections with the main towns in the area. The bus and *matatu* stand is on Kimathi Way in the centre of town.

◉ Directory

Thika *p163*

Banks Barclays Bank is on Kenyatta Highway to the south of town, which has an ATM that accepts most cards. **Standard Chartered** is on the corner of Commercial and Uhuru sts. **Internet** Emails can be checked at **Next Net Cyber Café** on Uhuru St north of the post office.

Nyeri *p164*

Banks Money can be changed at most banks, many of which are found near the post office to the west of town, but **Barclays** is opposite the library on Kenyatta Rd, which has an ATM. Western Union money transfers are available at the **Post Bank** next to the bus station. **Internet** Available from **Nibco** stationers on Kimathi Way and several other places in the centre of town including the post office also on Kimathi Way, but service can be slow. **Post** Securicor, near the post office, offers **Omega, Pony** and **DHL** delivery services.

Mount Kenya and around

Naro Moru → *Colour map 1, grid A4.*

The road from Nyeri climbs gradually up to Naro Moru, which is little more than a village located at the base of the mountain. It has a few shops, guest houses and a post office and is clustered around the railway station that no longer functions as a passenger terminal. Bear in mind before you arrive here that there are no banks in the village. There are no restaurants apart from the one at the **Naro Moru River Lodge**, and if you are cooking your own food you would be advised to stock up before you get here. However, the village does receive quite a few visitors as it serves as the starting point of the **Naro Moru Trail**, one of the most popular routes up the Mount Kenya. Before you set off on this route you have to both book and pay for the mountain huts that you will stay in on the way up. This must be done through the **Naro Moru River Lodge**, if you are not already on an organized climb.

Nanyuki → *Phone code: 062. Colour map 1, grid A4*

Nanyuki is a small up-country town, located to the northwest of Mount Kenya, which dates back to about 1907 when it was used by white settlers as a trading centre and for socializing. First settlers arrived to find a few Masai *manyattas* and a great deal of game. The town was established as a trading centre and still has a country atmosphere. Its name means 'place of red water' in the Masai language and today has a population of about 30,000. The town today is home to the Kenyan Air Force as well as a British army base. Despite this it is a fairly sleepy kind of town and retains some of its colonial character. Nanyuki is usually visited by people planning to use the Sirimon or Buguret trails up Mount Kenya. Its good range of shops provides its only interesting diversion. The town serves as the supply centre for ranchers on the Laikipia Plateau (see below), as well as the nearby tourist hotels in the foothills of the mountain. On the main road just to the south of Nanyuki there are signposts marking the equator, and more than a few pushy souvenir sellers.

Mount Kenya Biosphere Reserve

This reserve includes the Mount Kenya National Park, 715 sq km, which straddles the equator about 200 km northeast of Nairobi in Central Province. Mount Kenya, or Kirinyaga – the shining mountain, also sometimes referred to as the black and white striped mountain – is the sacred mountain of the Kikuya (Gikuya) people, who believe that it is where their God 'Ngai' lives. The Kikuyu who live on the slopes always build their homes facing this sacred peak. As you drive around the road that circles Mount Kenya you will spend much of the time looking towards the mountain – however, much of the time it is shrouded in cloud. There are some clear days – otherwise very early in the morning or just before nightfall the cloud will often lift suddenly, revealing the two snow-capped peaks for a few minutes. The upper base of the mountain is nearly 100 km across and has two major peaks, **Nelion** at 5,199 m and **Batian** at 5,189 m. Mount Kenya has a vital role in ecosystems in the area. It is Kenya's most important watershed and its largest forest reserve and the lower slopes make up the country's richest farmlands. The dramatic landscape includes glaciers, moraines, waterfalls, precarious looking rock pinnacles and hanging valleys. At the very top is permanent ice in some 11 glacier lakes. Though due to global warming these are shrinking fast and seven glaciers have already disappeared in the last 100 years.

Mountain flora includes a variety of different vegetations over altitudes ranging from 1,600 m to 5,199 m. From bottom to top, it goes from rich alpine and sub-alpine flora to bamboo forests, moorlands with giant heathers and tundra. Over 4,000 m some extraordinary vegetation is found including the giant rosette plants.

In the lower forest and bamboo zones, giant forest hog, tree hyrax, white-tailed mongoose, elephant, suni, duiker and leopard roam. Further up in the moorlands there are hyrax, duiker and Mount Kenya mouse shrews. In higher altitudes still there are the fairly common mole rat and the very rare golden cat.

Mount Kenya → *Colour map 1, grid A4/5.*

Fewer people go trekking on Mount Kenya than Kilimanjaro in Tanzania, but those that do rate the experience far better than the Kili climb. There are several routes up the mountain. The two most popular routes are described here. They are best taken

Mount Kenya region

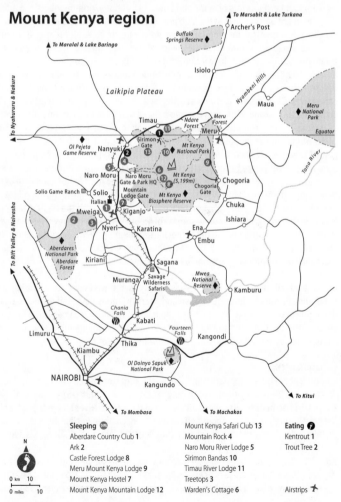

Sleeping		Eating
Aberdare Country Club **1**	Mount Kenya Safari Club **13**	Kentrout **1**
Ark **2**	Mountain Rock **4**	Trout Tree **2**
Castle Forest Lodge **8**	Naro Moru River Lodge **5**	
Meru Mount Kenya Lodge **9**	Sirimon Bandas **10**	
Mount Kenya Hostel **7**	Timau River Lodge **11**	
Mount Kenya Mountain Lodge **12**	Treetops **3**	
	Warden's Cottage **6**	Airstrips

N

0 km   10
0 miles   10

leisurely in six days, although they can be done in four. It is an interesting variation to ascend by one route and descend by another (but make sure you keep the park fee receipts for the exit). Point Lenana at 4,986 m is your destination; it is a strenuous hike, but quite manageable if you are reasonably fit and allow sufficient time to acclimatize to the rarefied atmosphere. It is sometimes called the trekker's or tourist's peak. The trek is an excellent opportunity to enjoy the beautiful scenery on the mountain and the snow on the equator.

Ins and outs

Getting there There are a number of towns located along the Kirinyaga Ring Road at the base of Mount Kenya, which serve as starting points for the various climbs up the mountain. Main road access is via Nanyuki or Naro Moru, from where roads go further into the foothills. Trekkers attempting the Chogoria route access the mountain from the small village of Chogoria on the eastern side.

Getting up Prior to climbing Mount Kenya it is a good idea to get in touch with the **Mountain Club of Kenya**, which is based at Wilson Airport in Nairobi, T020-501747, www.mck.or.ke. It has lots of maps and books in its library, non-members can attend the open night on Tuesdays at the club house at Wilson Airport, and the website is an excellent resource for information. Take great care over equipment and altitude sickness precautions, otherwise the climb can be sheer misery. Trekkers should be aware that sudden storms, heavy cloud cover and fog can lead to climbers getting lost on the mountain, and guides are recommended unless you are very experienced. Guides are especially recommended for trekkers with limited high altitude experience. Climbers without any experience at all are strongly advised to go on an organized tour. Many of the tour operators listed under Nairobi can organize climbs, as well as the lodges in the vicinity of the mountain. Porters and guides cost about US$6 a day, and are a sound investment. Make sure that the agreement with any guides or porters is clear before you set off. Guides and porters can be arranged at **Naro Moru River Lodge** or contact the **Mount Kenya Guides and Porters Association**, T062-62015, www.gotomountkenya.com, located on the road to the main gate of the park from Naro Moru. Evans Mwangi has been voted as one of the top 10 guides for Mount Kenya by the club. Only experienced climbers can climb the highest peaks of Nelion or Batian – 5,199 m and the summit of Mount Kenya, as this involves the use of ropes, ice-axes, crampons and other specialized climbing gear. Kenya Mountain Club owns some of the mountain huts, which are reserved for members only, although there may be reciprocal arrangements with other clubs.

Costs and climate Park entry fee is US$15 per day. Costs for climbing vary depending on which route you choose and over how many days, but expect to pay in the region of US$300-350 for a four-day climb, although the price goes down for larger groups. The best months to climb Mount Kenya are January-March or July-August. Avoid the rainy seasons April-May and November-December.

Equipment

Camping gear and appropriate warm and waterproof clothing can be hired in Nairobi at **Atul's** on Biashara Street, T020-225935. Costs are about US$30 per day, with about US$200 in deposits. Alternatively hire at **Naro Moru River Lodge** (see Sleeping below) although costs are about 50% more expensive than in Nairobi. It is essential to take effective waterproofs, gloves, headgear, spare boots/shoes, as well as

● *The Englishman Sir Halford Mackinder was the first to climb to the top of Mount Kenya in*
● *1899. Kisoi Munyao was the first known African to reach the top in 1959 and again in 1963*
when he carried and raised the newly independent Kenya's flag on the summit.

warm/windproof clothing (several layers are preferable) as many of the huts have no drying facilities. Also ensure that you have at least a three-season sleeping bag and a sleeping mat because 3,000 m the night temperatures can fall to as low as -10°C. Sunglasses are also useful as the glare off the snow and ice can be very uncomfortable. If you are attempting the climb independently, a stove, fuel, food supplies and water must also be carried. You should obtain one of the maps of the mountain showing the trails in some detail.

❖ *The relative ease of climbing to 4,200 m in 48 hourrs makes altitude sickness a common occurrence. Make sure you allow enough time to acclimatize. See Health section, page 51.*

Maps and guides

Mount Kenya Map and Guide, by M Savage and A Wielochowski, is available at **The Nation** bookshop in Nairobi, see page 84, **Stanfords Bookshops** in the UK, from **Amazon.co.uk**, or from **West Col Productions**, 1 Meadow Close, Goring, Reading, RG89 9AA, England. Mountain Club of Kenya has published the excellent detailed *Guide to Mt Kenya and Kilimanjaro*, listing all the routes, edited by Iain Allan. It is available in the Nairobi bookshops or directly from the club.

Naro Moru approach

Naro Moru approaches from the west and is the most direct, popular but least scenic route, and includes trekking through a long vertical bog. Opposite the Naro Moru police station is a signposted road that leads to the park entrance. It is possible to drive as far as the Meteorological Station, although inexperienced climbers are less likely to suffer from altitude sickness if they walk the 26 km.

Day 1 Is best spent travelling from Naro Moru to the **Meteorological Station** at 3,050 m. A ride can be hired from **Naro Moru River Lodge** part or all of the way. There are some bandas here or some permanent tents.

Day 2 Is to **Mackinder's Camp** (sometimes referred to as **Teleki Valley Lodge**), located at an altitude of 4,200 m, through terrain that is often very wet underfoot. An early departure is recommended as fog and rain is more commonplace during the afternoon. This section includes a very tiring climb through a steep vertical bog, and when you've cleared the bog the route then continues along a ridge on the southern side of the Teleki Valley, gradually descending to the valley floor. This section is much more attractive with *Senecio* (giant groundsel), heathers, the broad-leafed *Lobelia keniensis* and the feathery *Lobelia telekii*. The camp, a stone building, has about 40 bunks and some tents. It is possible to visit the Teleki tarn from here, taking about 1-1½ hours, if the weather holds out.

Day 3 It is possible to make the final leg to Point Lenana, although it is more comfortable to spend Day 3 in and around the surrounding area known as Mackinder's, getting acclimatized to the altitude. From here there are some of the best views of the central peaks.

Day 4 Climb to **Point Lenana**. Most trekkers leave Mackinder's at between 0200-0400 to ensure that they reach the summit at sunrise, so a powerful torch is an essential piece of equipment, climbing past the Austrian Hut, 4,790 m, owned by the Mountain Club of Kenya. From here it is about half-an-hour to an hour scramble, depending on fitness, to reach Point Lenana.

Day 5 It is possible to descend all the way to Naro Moru (with a lift from the Meteorological Station), but it is more leisurely to return to Mackinder's Camp for a night, and then on to Naro Moru on **Day 6**. From here there are some of the best views of the central peaks.

Chogoria approach

The Chogoria approach is from the east between Embu (96 km) and Meru (64 km), and is the most scenically attractive of the routes, although it can be wet. Chogoria village, see page 186, is the starting base for the deeply rutted road (four-wheel drive essential) takes you past small, intensively cultivated *shambas* within the lowland forest rising to become bamboo forest. Colobus monkeys can occasionally be seen here. Most trekkers organize the 32-km ride from Chogoria to approximately 6 km beyond the park gate to the roadhead, 3,110 m. However, if you walk this stretch you will greatly reduce the possibility of developing altitude sickness.

Day 1 From village to the roadhead by vehicle and camp there. Alternatively it is possible to stay at the bandas near the park gate. The roadhead is about one hour from the bandas.

Day 2 From the roadhead cross the stream and follow the path going in a southwesterly direction. The route continues along the west side of the Nithi Gorge and it is about a six-hour hike to **Minto's Hut**, 4,300 m, which has only very basic facilities. En route there are spectacular views of the Gorges Valley. The path leads through dramatic rock fields and later through the heather moors to Vivienne Falls, 3,650 m, where you can swim in the bracing waters. As you progress upwards, Lake Michaelson can be seen on the valley floor 300 m below Hall Tarns.

Day 3 It is possible to reach Point Lenana, but it may be more comfortable to spend the day getting acclimatized in and around Minto's Hut, located close to Minto's Tarn, 4,540 m, which is framed by lofty pinnacles, the scree slopes flecked with giant lobelia and senecio.

Day 4 From Minto's Hut it is about a four- to five-hour climb to **Point Lenana**, via the Austrian Hut, close to the Lewis Glacier.

Day 5 It is possible to descend all the way back to Chogoria (with a lift from the park gate), but it is more leisurely to return to Minto's Hut for a night, and then on to Chogoria on **Day 6**.

● Sleeping

Nanyuki *p172*

B-E Sportsman's Arms, T062-31448, www.sportsmansarms.com, located across the river, 500 m east of town, built in the 1930's, but extended more recently so there are new and old parts of the hotel. Probably the best-value hotel in Nanyuki, the cheapest rooms start at US$50, surrounded by gardens and in a lovely setting. Rooms are complete with TVs and fires. Price includes breakfast, and full board is also available. It is clean and friendly. Excellent facilities include fitness centre, swimming pool, sauna, tennis, good restaurant and bar with pool tables and a disco at the weekends. You can also camp here, US$4 with your own tent, US$6 with tent hire.

D Simba Lodge, opposite the **Sportsman's Arms**, 500 m from the main road on a very rough road, T062-31723. Clean, comfortable and secure in a neat compound. 32 rooms with hot water in either a block or individual chalets, TV room, bar with pool tables and *nyama choma*, good set menus in the restaurant, breakfast included, parking.

E Equator Hotel, Kenyatta Av. Newly painted block with an enormous sign, good rooms, patio, above a supermarket, very nice terrace restaurant. Recommended budget option.

E Ibis, close to the *matatu* stand, T062-31536. Comfortable rooms with hot water, nets, above its own bar/restaurant. Secure parking, laundry service available.

E Jambo House Hotel, Bazaar St, T062-22751. Located at west corner of the park, one of several cheap hotels along Bazaar St, and not the worst despite the rather dark, dingy rooms. Hot water, plus a bar with a pool table.

Mount Kenya Biosphere Reserve *p172, map p173*

There are a couple of cheap basic places for board and lodgings in Naro Moru, but for budget travellers it is best to camp at the **Naro Moru River Lodge** or the **Mountain Rock Hotel**, which both hire out tents, and make use of the excellent facilities. There are other accommodation options that provide access to the mountain in Nanyuki itself.

L Mount Kenya Mountain Lodge, 5 km inside the park from the Mountain Lodge Gate, reservations **Serena Hotels**, Nairobi, T020-711077, www.serenahotels.com. Quality lodge of the Serena group situated at 2,194 m on Mt Kenya's slopes overlooking a waterhole, 42 double bedrooms with en suite bathrooms, fireplaces and hot water bottles. A close-up viewing bunker is connected to the hotel by a tunnel, post-climb massages and trout fishing on offer, very good guides for walking and climbing excursions, restaurant and bar built on stilts.

L Mount Kenya Safari Club, reservations **The Norfolk**, T020-216940, www.lonrho hotels.com. 15 km east of Nanyuki in the foothills of the mountain is the region's most exclusive and luxurious hotel. 115 guest rooms set in over 100 acres of landscaped gardens. The club was originally founded by movie star William Holden (of *Bridge Over the River Kwai* fame) and the club's illustrious former members have included Winston Churchill and Bing Crosby. Facilities include horse riding, golf, croquet, a putting green, a bowling green, table tennis, swimming, a beauty salon, an animal orphanage, several restaurants, lounges and bars. Rates start from US$290 for a double in low season.

A-E Naro Moru River Lodge, 2 km from Naro Moru off the main road, reservations **Alliance Hotels**, Nairobi, T020-4443357, www.alliancehotels.com. Overlooking the Naro Moru River which is stocked with trout, this is a popular place to stay for all budgets and it organizes climbs up the mountain. 19 de luxe cottages with 2 double beds, bathrooms, sitting room area with fireplaces, all elegantly furnished in pine, another 12 standard cottages which are a bit cheaper, and 12 self-catering cottages aimed at families. Facilities include a swimming pool, tennis and squash courts, 2 restaurants, bar with roaring log fire. Also a campsite where you can hire the necessary equipment and use all the hotel facilities, US$5 per person.

B Castle Forest Lodge, 2 km from the Forest Gate within the park, on the slopes to the south of Mount Kenya, T0721-422908 (mob), castlelodge@wananchi.com. Set in a natural surrounding of rainforest and rivers with falls on either side of the lodge. The main house was built in 1910 of river stones and wood, and both Queen Elizabeth and President

Jomo Kenyatta stayed here in the past. A charming old building with a cosy dining and bar and a veranda overlooking a waterhole and the valley below. Recently renovated, the main house contains 3 double rooms, in the gardens is a bungalow that sleeps 4, and 8 double cottages, each en suite with a fireplace. Rates are full board. Can organize climbs from US$60 per day.

B Sirimon Bandas Kenya Wildlife Service, reservations **Kenya Wildlife Service**, Nairobi, T020-600800, www.kws.org. Managed self-catering accommodation near Sirimon Gate, which is about 9 km along a turning off the main road, 16 km north of Nanyuki. It has 2 furnished cottages, each has 1 room with a double bed, 1 room with 2 single beds, fitted kitchen and lounge, linen, towels, and kitchen utensils provided but you will need to bring your own food, firewood and drinking water. Each cottage is normally rented out as a whole for US$70.

B Warden's Cottage, as per **Sirimon Bandas** except that there is only 1 cottage, it has 1 bedroom with a double bed and 1 with 2 single beds, and is just inside the park at the main Naro Moru Gate.

B-E Mountain Rock Hotel, T062-62625, www.mountainrockkenya.com. 8 km north of **Naro Moru Lodge**, on the road to Nanyuki (signposted off the main road). Lovely surroundings and a range of self-catering cottages with fireplaces, welcome on cold evenings. The hotel, which arranges a wide range of activities including horse riding, fishing, birdwatching, is known for its very well-run treks up the mountain (taking the Naro Moru, Sirimon or Burguret routes), you can choose an itinerary to suit you. There is also a quiet, secure campsite with toilets, hot showers, kitchen area with firewood available, and if you don't have a tent or equipment you can hire everything here.

D-E Timau River Lodge, 20 km north of Nanyuki towards Isiolo 1 km after Timau, 1 km off the main road, T062-41230, www.timauriverlodge.8m.com. On the forested slopes of Mt Kenya, simple bandas sleeping 2-4 people and campsites located amongst trees at the top of a very pretty waterfall. There is a restaurant and bar serving very good Indian and vegetarian food.

E Mount Kenya Hostel, T062-62414, about 12 km from Naro Moru off the main highway along the dirt road towards the Naro Moru Gate, about 4 km from the park entrance gate. Popular with budget travellers, simple bunk beds, hot showers and cooking facilities, and you can also camp here. Meals are available but you will have to give some notice. The hostel has some equipment for climbing to hire, and it can organize guides and porters.

Eating

Nanyuki *p172*

Apart from the restaurants attached to the hotels there are few places to eat in Nanyuki. **Marina Grill**, opposite the post office, is popular with locals and visiting soldiers, and offers friendly service, an attractive rooftop bar with BBQ and pool table. Convenient for a cold beer and a snack, and has a good selection of desserts. There is also an internet café here.

Mount Kenya Biosphere Reserve *p172, map p173*

There are 2 very good options on the road running around the mountain that also offer accommodation.

Kentrout, clearly signposted, located about 2.5 km down a track from the village of Timau, 35 km north of Nanyuki, T062-41016. Open daily 1200-1700, this is primarily a trout farm that serves delicious buffet lunches to passing visitors, eaten in the very pretty gardens next to the Teleswan River. There are also some comfortable cottages with bathrooms, and you may be able to negotiate camping in the grounds.

Trout Tree Restaurant, about 12 km south of Nanyuki past the Nanyuki airstrip, T062-62059, trouttree@wananchi.com. A similar set-up to **Kentrout** above, fantastic trout lunches served 1100-1600 daily, main courses cost around US$6, the very attractive restaurant is constructed around a giant fig tree and overlooks the fish ponds, the menu is superb and there are steaks and fresh salads and vegetables on offer as well as fish. It also has 1 self-catering cottage for rent for families or groups, with 4 double rooms, 2 bathrooms and fully fitted kitchen. Rates are in the region of about US$90 for the whole house which represents excellent value for a group of people.

Shopping

Nanyuki *p172*

Nanyuki Spinners and Weavers Workshop, 1 km from town on the Nyaharuru road, sells hand-woven rugs and other items. This is run by a women's co-operative group that was established in 1977, who sell to the **Spin and Weave Shop** in Nairobi, but you will get a lower price here. Very interesting place to visit, and the group are pleased to give you a full guided tour. The Kenyan Highlands wool is very good for hand spinning, and there is a good selection of rugs, tablemats, sweaters and shawls.

Settlers Stores, on the main street, is one of the oldest shops in town (founded in 1938) and sells hardware and groceries.

United Stores and **Modern Sanitary Stores**, for all your supplies.

Activities and tours

Nanyuki *p172*

Nanyuki Sports Club, east of Sportsman's Arms, offers tennis, squash, golf, swimming and snooker, but the problem is that you must be sponsored by an existing member.

Sirimon Guides, Porters and Safaris, next to **Barclays Bank**, Kenyatta Av, T0733-247865 (mob), kenyaadventures@hotmail.com. Local operator for Mt Kenya climbs.

Sportman's Arms Hotel has facilities that can be used, including a pool, for a small fee.

Transport

Nanyuki *p172*

Air

The airstrip at Nanyuki is just to the south of town. **Air Kenya**, Wilson Airport, Nairobi, T020-605745 (reservations), www.airkenya. com, has daily flights from Wilson Airport, Nairobi, leaving at 0915 and arriving 45 mins later, US$80 one way, US$135 return. Return journey leaves Nanyuki at about 1130, depending on passenger loads. **Tropic Air**, T062-32890, www.tropicair-kenya.com, is an air charter company operating out of Nanyuki (Kenya's only charter company based outside of Nairobi). Destinations include the airstrips on the Laikipia Plateau, Samburu, Masai Mara, Meru, the Rift Valley lakes, Amboseli and the Chyulus Hills.

Bus and *matatus*
Buses leave from behind Ngumba House next to the **Sirimon**. There are frequent buses and *matatus* running between Nanyuki and **Nairobi**. If you are heading north to Marsabit and Northern Kenya you can get buses and *matatus* from Nanyuki to **Isiolo** (which is the last town on the good road heading north), and from there continue north. The *matatu* station is located next to the park.

Car
Nanyuki is located about 60 km from **Nyeri** and 190 km from **Nairobi** – a drive that will take you about 3 hrs.

✪ Directory

Nanyuki *p172*
Banks On main street there are branches of **Barclays Bank**, **Kenya Commercial Bank** and **Standard Chartered Bank**. Barclays has a bureau de change and an ATM that accepts Mastercard and Visa. **Internet** Services are available at **Global Information Centre** next to Barclays Bank and at the **Marina Grill Restaurant**, a few doors along on Kenyatta Av. **Medical services** District Hospital is located about 1 km out of town to the east. **Post office** On the main street. Securicor, Kimathi Rd, offers secure delivery services.

Laikipia Plateau

Laikipia Plateau has only recently been recognized as a wildlife area in its own right, and this spectacular region is considered the gateway to Kenya's wild northern frontier country. The plateau covers an area of 9,723 sq km – roughly half the size of Wales in the UK. Altitudes range from 1,700 to 2,600 m above sea level. Wild and sparsely populated, much of Laikipia is covered by large privately owned ranches. These ranches cover a wide range of landscapes, and the plateau is dominated by acacia bushland with large areas of open grasslands to the north and south of the district, and dense olive and cedar forests to the east. It is, without doubt, Kenya's greatest conservation success story over the last decade; an area of beautiful wilderness, where protected game roams freely and safely, while preserving traditional farming methods and ways of life. ▸▸ *For Sleeping, Eating and other listings, see pages 182-184.*

Ins and outs

This area of wilderness is a sprawling, rather loosely defined area, accessible by road from Nanyuki, Baringo, Eldoret or Isiolo. The main roads that cross this region are the C76 which connects Nanyuki with Nyaharuru, the C77 that runs between Nyaharuru and Maralal, and the C78 that joins Maralal with Isiolo. It is important to remember that many of the ranches, and the roads therein, are privately owned. Some ranches allow day visitors with their own transport, others do not. Visitors should always make enquiries in advance. If you are visiting a ranch with your own private transport, and it is essential to have a four-wheel drive, ask for directions and preferably a map, in advance. Many ranches and sanctuaries have their own airstrips, which can be used by charter aircraft. Between them, **Air Kenya** and **Safarilink** run scheduled services from Nairobi to Samburu, Nanyuki, and Lewa Downs. **Tropic Air** based at Nanyuki offers a charter service, see page 178. Most ranches will arrange to transfer guests directly by air or road from Nairobi or any other destination, as part of their service. Nanyuki serves as the supply centre for ranchers on the Laikipia Plateau. Many of the ranches and game reserves work closely with the Kenya Wildlife Service in conservation and poaching control. Consequently there is often an additional conservancy fee of US$20-30 per person on top of the accommodation rates.

● *Three-quarters of Kenya's wildlife is found on private land outside the national parks and reserves.*

Central Highlands Laikipia Plateau

Sights

The district is located on the leeward side of Mount Kenya, forming the arid and semi-arid highlands west and northwest of the mountain. The region spreads north from Nanyuki from the northern foothills of Mount Kenya to Maralal, northeast to Isiolo, and west to Nyahururu. The region is dominated by the Ewaso Ng'iro and Ewaso Narok rivers, and it incorporates the entire Ewaso rivers ecosystems, the Laikipia National Reserve and the Lewa Wildlife Conservancy. On most ranches cattle share the land with free-ranging wildlife. In recent years this wildlife has become a valuable asset, with many ranches now establishing guest houses, homestays and private camps within their boundaries. The Laikipia Wildlife Forum (LWF) was formed in 1992 by private and communal landowners with a common interest in preserving the wildlife. This has proven a great success, and many ranches now rely on a thriving tourist trade. There are currently over 50 tourism operations active in the region, and together they promote their region through the LWF.

Importantly, community ranches have also been formed. These are sanctuaries created by local communities, who have combined small-scale farms and grazing land into large group ranches. Once again, the tourist trade has proved infinitely more profitable than agriculture or herding, and this allows them to use their traditional lands in a way that is sustainable and productive. Significantly, they are conserving more than just wildlife, but also a way of life. These ranches have bolstered a sense of local identity and strengthened community ties.

Wildlife

Centred around the original Laikipia National Reserve, this area has become a sanctuary for elephant, lion, leopard, buffalo and a wealth of plains game, including many endemic northern species such as the Grevy's zebra, gerenuk and reticulated giraffe. It has one of the highest diversity of large mammals in all of Kenya, including significant populations of all the major predators and the Big Five. Almost 6,000

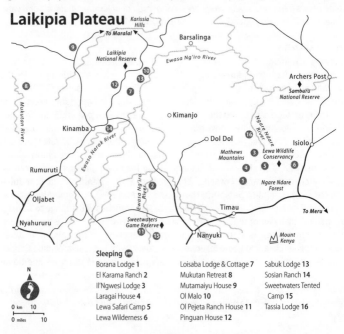

Laikipia Plateau

Sleeping 😴
Borana Lodge **1**
El Karama Ranch **2**
Il'Ngwesi Lodge **3**
Laragai House **4**
Lewa Safari Camp **5**
Lewa Wilderness **6**
Loisaba Lodge & Cottage **7**
Mukutan Retreat **8**
Mutamaiyu House **9**
Ol Malo **10**
Ol Pejeta Ranch House **11**
Pinguan House **12**
Sabuk Lodge **13**
Sosian Ranch **14**
Sweetwaters Tented Camp **15**
Tassia Lodge **16**

0 km 10
0 miles 10

elephants migrate through the region each year. Laikipia has also become a focus for many conservation efforts; some ranches have become breeding sanctuaries for rhino, and now the region protects over 50% of Kenya's population of black and white rhino. Wild dog and the rare sitatunga antelope are also present, and these days the region is widely believed to have an animal diversity second only to the Masai Mara. On Ol Pejeta Ranch, a refuge for chimpanzees rescued from the pet and bush meat trade has also been established. Visiting a private ranch in this region is an ideal way of exploring the Kenyan wilderness while getting off the well-beaten paths of the national parks. The real attraction of Laikipia is a wonderful sense of freedom. Staying on a private ranch gives a wide range of options for both activities and relaxation, and game viewing tends to be more intimate and adventurous.

Lewa Wildlife Conservancy

① *To64-31405, www.lewa.org, entry fee is US$35 by prior arrangement only. To visit here you will need to be staying at Borana Lodge, Lewa Safari Camp, Laragai House, Il Ngwesi Lodge or Lewa Wilderness (see under Sleeping below).*

Lewa Wildlife Conservancy is situated about 15 km southwest of Isiolo on the northern foothills of Mount Kenya on the Laikipia Plateau, approximately 65 km northeast of Nanyuki. It was originally a 18,000-ha cattle ranch. The land comprises savannah, wetland, grassland and indigenous forest. It was officially registered as a Non-Profit Organization in 1995. The conservancy project aims to minimize the conflict between conservation and human settlement and protect and encourage the rhinoceros and other endangered species. The Lewa Downs and later the adjoining state-owned **Ngare Ndare Forest** were fenced to reduce the human/wildlife conflict and loss of smallholders, crops to elephants. It also incorporates the **Ngare Sergoi Rhino Sanctuary**, which no longer exists as a separate entity. Numbers of both black and white rhino have increased, with none lost to poachers. It is possible to see the Big Five here. Grevy's zebra numbers have risen from 81 to over 400. Lewa Downs also contains an archaeological site where Mary Leakey found prehistoric tools and artefacts, some of which are on display in the Meru Museum. Tourism has been expanded to help cover the cost on the conservancy, but has been kept within clear limits: low-impact/high-income tourism with a maximum of 60 tourist beds. The original homestead has been converted into a Conservation Centre. As it is a non-profit organization all tourist-generated income goes to pay for security and management of the wildlife.

Sweetwaters Game Reserve and Chimpanzee Sanctuary

Located on Ol Pejeta Ranch is the 9,700-ha Sweetwaters Game Reserve and Chimpanzee Sanctuary, 17 km northwest of Nanyuki off the road to Nayahururu. To visit here you need to be staying at the **Sweetwaters Tented Camp** (see Sleeping below), although if you are in your own vehicle you can pre-arrange a day visit. This game sanctuary was established in 1988 and is home to all the Big Five, with the highest ratio of game-to-area of any park or reserve in Kenya. It has the fastest growing population of rhino in the country, and visitors can also meet Morani, a tame rhino. The Laikipia Environmental Conservation Centre based at Sweetwaters, is visited by over 100 Kenyan schools each year and teaches the students about ecology, wildlife management and culture. Apart from safaris in vehicles, game walks and horse rides are available, plus camel riding and night game drives.

Sweetwaters Chimpanzee Sanctuary ① *entry fee US$16*, is home to 24 rescued chimps, most of which came from Burundi with help from the Jane Goodall Institute. You can view these from a boat in the Ewaso Ng'iro River.

● Sleeping

Laikipia Plateau *p179, map179*

All the places to stay here are very expensive. However, most rates are full board and include game drives, walks and horse riding. Expect to pay in the region of US$150-500 per person sharing. For this, however, you will get an impeccable and private safari experience a long way from the hoards in the national parks and game reserves.

L Il'Ngwesi Lodge, Mathew's Mountains north of the Lewa Wildlife Conservancy, reservations **Bush and Beyond/Bush Homes of East Africa**, Nairobi, T020-600457, www.bush-and-beyond.com and www.bush-homes.co.ke. This lodge was awarded the prestigious British Airways Best Eco-tourism Destination Award in 1997. Constructed with materials from the local area, it comprises 6 individual bandas which all have adjoining open-air showers. They are thatched, open plan and on high supports to ensure fantastic views and privacy, 2 of them have a platform where you can roll out the double bed and spend the night under the stars. Large sitting area and a strikingly designed swimming pool. Around US$190 per person.

L Laragai House, Borana Ranch, reservations **Bush and Beyond/Bush Homes of East Africa**, Nairobi, T020-600457, www.bush-and-beyond.com and www.bush-homes.co.ke. The private home of the Cecil family is available for rent when they are not in residence. The most opulent home in Laikipia, antiques were brought over from Ireland, china from London and furniture from Rajasthan. The result is an eclectic mixture of styles and textures, totally unique. The house can sleep 10 in extreme comfort and there is plenty more room for children and guides. Exquisite paintings, medieval weapons. The sound system is brilliant and there is a full sized electronic keyboard wired to the amplifier. The house has a full staff. Rates are in the region of US$500 per person.

L Lewa Safari Camp, Lewa Wildlife Conservancy (old rhino sanctuary headquarters), T064-31405, contact Clare Moller, c.moller@lewa.org or **Bush and Beyond/Bush Homes of East Africa**, Nairobi, T020-600457, www.bush-and-beyond.com and www.bush-homes.co.ke. Lush green lawns, swimming pool and tented accommodation, guests get a real insight to conservation and wildlife management. The camp can sleep 26, and comprises 9 twin rooms, 1 double and 2 family/triple tents. The property has a main building with a lounge and dining area and veranda with good views over a waterhole frequented by rhino and elephant. Closed Apr-May. US$270 per person.

L Lewa Wilderness, reservations **Bush and Beyond/Bush Homes of East Africa**, T020-600457, www.bush-and-beyond.com and www.bush-homes.co.ke, on Lewa Wildlife Conservancy, south of Isiolo. One of Kenya's major private conservation successes, **Lewa** has been the Craig family home since 1924 when the family came from England and began raising cattle here. Rhino, Grevy's zebra and the sitatunga are among many other species of game found here. The family home accommodates 16 guests in 8 comfortable thatched cottages with en suite bathrooms, fireplaces and verandas. The food is wholesome and organically grown. There is a cosy sitting room and meals are eaten on a long banquet table in the open-air dining room. Game drives, horseback expeditions and camel safaris are available. US$380 per person.

L Loisaba Lodge, T062-31072, www.loisaba.com, or **Bush and Beyond/Bush Homes of East Africa Ltd**, Nairobi, T020-600457, www.bush-and-beyond.com and www.bush-homes.co.ke. A 150-sq-km private wildlife conservancy in the centre of Laikipia Plateau with a lodge for 14 guests. 4 double and 3 twin bedrooms with en suite bathrooms and verandas are perched over an escarpment, with commanding views of Mt Kenya. This area is especially known for sightings of cats. Swimming pool, tennis court, bocce court and croquet lawn. The spa offers massage and beauty treatments and a romantic open air bubble bath, all with a tranquil view of the unspoilt Karissia Hills. There are also 'skybeds', 4 wooden platforms set against rocky outcrops and partially covered by a thatched roof, with shower and flushing toilet. The first and original set are located amongst a kopje of rocks in one of the eastern valleys overlooking a waterhole. The second and newer set is located about 8 km further south on the banks of the Ewaso

Ng'iro River. Costing over US$400 and still the poor relations of the lodge, the skybeds form part of optional walking, horse or camel safaris.

L **Mukutan Retreat**, reservations, Nairobi, T020-520799, www.mukutan.com. The ranch belonging to the author of *I Dreamed of Africa*. At 400 sq km, it lies at the Mukutan River at the northwestern edge of the plateau, on the slopes and hills where the film was shot starring Kim Basinger. 3 separate large cottages, with a spacious central building provides private, luxurious and romantic accommodation for up to 6 people, swimming pool. Built in elegant, traditional style using local stone, papyrus and native woods, each cottage is original and different in decoration and layout. Fresh, organic ingredients all locally grown on the ranch are used in the restaurant, Italian cuisine and Indian spicy vegetarian food is prepared by Italian and Indian chefs. There is no generator so lighting is powered by solar energy. Meditation and yoga are on offer as well as numerous game activities. There are substantial numbers of black rhino and large herds of buffalo on this ranch. US$350 per person.

L **Mutamaiyu House**, www.mutamaiyu.com, is on Mugie Ranch at the northern end of the plateau. A magnificent family-owned house built in a grove of ancient, twisting olive trees. It is a 49,000-acre working ranch, home to all the Big Five and now the latest private rhino sanctuary in Kenya with the re-introduction of 20 black rhino in Jul 2004; these have not been seen in the area for the last 25 years. Mutamaiyu comfortably accommodates up to 8 people in 4 African-style cottages, built of local stone and traditionally thatched using *makuti* over a vaulted wooden frame. US$320 per person.

L **Ol Malo**, halfway between Archers Post and Loruk, to the west of Samburu National Reserve, reservations Nairobi, T020-2523107, www.olmalo.com. A ranch and game sanctuary with 4 expensive and exclusive guest houses and 2 luxury tents on a hill near the Ewaso Ng'iro River, with en suite bathrooms and verandas offering views towards Mt Kenya. The guest cottages are spread out along the cliff edge and are built out of natural rock and ancient olive wood, with thatched roofs and huge glass windows. You can soak in the bath whilst looking at the animals at the waterhole. There is a dining room, sitting room and swimming pool, most of the food is home grown. US$450 per person.

L **Ol Pejeta Ranch House**, 40 km west from Nanyuki near Sweetwaters, managed by **Lonrho Hotels**, reservations **The Norfolk**, T020-216940, www.lonrhohotels.com. 6 elegantly appointed suites overlooking extensive tropical gardens and 2 swimming pools. **Ol Pejeta** was formerly owned by Lord Delamere and was also one of the holiday homes of the international arms dealer Adnan Kashoggi. An 8-ft basket, which can be winched down by a pulley system, hangs above the main dining room table – it is said that a naked young lady covered in fruit, hidden in the basket, was a treat for guests when Khashoggi owned the ranch! High-season rates are US$360 per person.

L **Pinguan House**, Kamogi Ranch, UK T+44-02891-884780, www.kamogi.com, is beside the ancient springs of the Il Palagani Valley and looks towards the Karissia Hills. It has a wonderful garden, swimming pool and tennis court. The 5,000-acre ranch is farmed with Dorpar sheep and Boran cattle. There are many birds on the ranch and a lot of wildlife. There are 3 cottages all with private bathrooms and own verandas, sleeping 12 in total. The dining room has a roof terrace ideal for evening cocktails and studying the stars with a telescope. They farm their own sheep, ducks and vegetables. US$750 per day for the exclusive rent of the house for 12 people, all inclusive of accommodation, staff, horse riding and game drives. Food and drink is US$50 per person per day.

L **Sabuk Lodge**, reservations **Cheli and Peacock**, Nairobi, T020-604053, www.cheli peacock.com, at the northern edge of the plateau on the banks of the Ewaso Ng'iro River. 5 cottages have stunning views of the river and cliffs, perched on the edge of the gorge overlooking the river. Each thatched rondavel has its own unique design, crafted from local stone and ancient cedar and olive

For an explanation of sleeping and eating price codes used in this guide, see inside the front cover. Other relevant information is found in Essentials, see pages 34-38.

wood. The lodge is the starting/finishing point for camel-assisted walking safaris, when guests are guided through completely deserted tracts of wilderness. Most of the walking is done in the morning, leaving the afternoon free to enjoy the river, swim, fish, or learning bush crafts with the guide. US$280 per person.

L Sweetwaters Tented Camp, reservations **Serena Hotels**, Nairobi, T020-711077, www.serenahotels.com. Located on Ol Pejeta Ranch, 30 luxury tents overlook a waterhole, floodlit by night, swimming pool, restaurant and 2 bars in what was the original homestead. Apart from safaris in vehicles, game walks and horse rides are available, plus camel riding, night game drives and bush lunches or dinners. High season rates are US$310 for a double or twin.

B Tassia Lodge, www.tassiakenya.com, also reservations **UNIGLOBE Let's Go Travel**, Nairobi, T020-4447151, www.letsgosafari. com, is a new community lodge north of **Borana Lodge** where elephants can be observed. The ranch is covered with original cedar forest to the west, it then stretches down the Mokogodo Escarpment onto the plains. 5 double bedrooms and 1 twin room, all with en suite bathrooms. Also a kids' bunkhouse with 3 double bunk beds and a shower room. **Tassia** is designed to be booked on an exclusive-use basis. A comfortable sitting and dining area overlooks a stunning swimming pool, which is built into rocks, and there is also an attractive and well-appointed kitchen.

B-E El Karama Ranch, 40 km to the north of Nanyuki, T062-32526, www. Horsebackin kenya.com, or reservations **UNIGLOBE Let's Go Travel**, Nairobi, T020-4447151, www.lets gosafari.com. 1 cottage and 1 rondavel with bathrooms, sleeping up to 5 in each, with fully equipped kitchen and living area, fridge and kerosene lamps. Also 3 slightly cheaper double bandas, with outside shower and long drop loo, and shared outside cooking facilities. There are also some camping sites near the Uaso Nyiro River. Bring all food and drinking water. Game walks and drives can be arranged. It also offers horse-riding safaris combined with fly camping in lovely wilderness places, accompanied by a pack string of camels. These are really only advised for experienced riders and you must bring your own hat and boots. Home for the duration of the safari is a green canvas tent with a foam mattress, plus a shower tent and long drop latrine. Some of the camps are situated near a ranch coral or boma, in which the horses and camels sleep, at other sites the horses sleep picketed to a rope stretched between trees in the middle of camp, and the camels sleep tied down near their handlers' tent. In either case the animals and the men who look after them are very much a part of camp life.

Moving east

Nanyuki to Embu

Northeast from Nanyuki the road continues around Mount Kenya. The next village that you will reach after Nanyuki is **Timau** – there is very little here except for the excellent **Kentrout**, see Eating page 178. Another 35 km or so down the road is the turning off to the left that goes on up to Marsabit and Northern Kenya. The first town on this road is **Isiolo**, which is located about 30 km off the Nanyuki-Meru road and is where the good road ends, see page 293.

Continuing around the mountain about 30 km on after the turning off to Isiolo, you will reach the town of Meru. The journey from Nanyuki to Meru is very beautiful, and shows the diversity of Kenya's landscape. To the south is Mount Kenya, to the north (on a clear, haze-free day) you can see miles and miles of the northern wilderness of Kenya.

Meru → *Phone code: 064. Colour map 1, grid A5.*

Meru, a thriving and bustling trading centre, is located to the northeast of Mount Kenya, about 70 km from Nanyuki. It stands in a heavily cultivated and forested area

⁞ Leafy streets

Miraa, also known as *qat* and *gatty,* is produced in large quantities around Meru. It is a leaf which is chewed and is a mild stimulant as well as acting as an appetite suppressant. You will see people all over Kenya (but particularly in the north) holding bunches of these leaves and twigs and chewing them. In Meru there is a street corner devoted to the selling of *miraa.* It is a small tree that grows wild here and is also grown commercially. It is produced legally and it is also sold to the northeast of Kenya and exported to Somalia, Yemen and Djibouti.

at an altitude of about 3,000 m and in the rainy season it is cold and damp. However, if you are here on a clear day you may get good views of the mountain peaks. From Meru the road to Embu is good, and about 5 km to the south of town, the road crosses the equator again where there is a sign and a few curio stalls. Although it serves as an important trading centre it does not receive many visits from travellers. As it is not close to any of the trails up the mountain, it has not been developed for this. It is, however, the base for visits to the Meru National Park, the entrance of which is just over 80 km from the town. There is a noticeable military presence here and a good range of shops, banks and internet facilities.

Meru National Museum ① *T064-20482, www.museums.or.ke, Mon-Fri 0930-1800, Sat 0930-1400, US$3, down the road roughly opposite the Meru County Hotel,* is housed in the oldest building in town, built in 1916, formerly a District Commissioner's Office. It has several small galleries, with displays ranging from local geology, stuffed birds and animals, to innovative toys made from scrap materials. The most interesting section of the museum is that related to the customs and culture of the local Meru people: various ethnographic artefacts are exhibited, as well as examples of local timber and stone and tools from the prehistoric site at Lewa Downs. There is a Meru homestead that gives a good idea of how the Meru people live. In the museum shop is a relic of colonial days – a wind-up gramophone made by His Majesty's Voice. This particular model came via Pakistan where the then owner was stationed with the King's African Rifles. There is a small selection of bakelite 78 records which can be played for KSh10. Outside there is a display of various herbs and other medicinal plants, including an example of a *miraa* plant. The museum also has a snake pit and a crocodile pit. A craft shop sells locally produced items.

There are two **markets** at Meru: one on the main road towards Nanyuki and the other on the opposite side of town. The merchandise on sale is very cheap and includes not just agricultural produce from the farms around Meru, but also baskets and household goods.

Meru National Park → *Colour map 1, grid A5.*

① *Entry fee US$20 per day, plus vehicle fees. It has a road system of over 600 km, much of which has recently been upgraded.* With just a few tourist package tours visting Meru National Park, it makes it one of the least trampled and unspoiled of Kenya's parks. Some 85 km away from Meru town and 370 km northeast of Nairobi, straddling the equator, the 1,810 sq km is mainly covered with thorny bushland and wooded grasslands to the west. There are 13 rivers and numerous mountain-fed streams that flow into the Tana River from the south. Dense riverine forests grow along the watercourses surrounded by the prehistoric-looking doum palms. There are hundreds of species of birds including the Somali ostrich, the red-necked falcon and

⁞ *Although Meru National Park is in the Eastern Province it will be described here, as this is the route normally taken by road when visiting the national park.*

Pel's fishing owl, which can be heard at night by the Tana River. Animals include lion, leopard, cheetah, elephant, Grevy's and plains zebra, gerenuk, reticulated giraffe, hippo, lesser kudu, oryx, hartebeest and Grant's gazelle.

The park was opened in 1968 and became famous for its role in the *Born Free* story. The late Joy Adamson hand-reared the orphaned lioness Elsa here, later releasing her into the wild. Elsa died of tick-borne fever and was buried in a forest clearing by Joy. After her death, Joy was also buried at the same site near the Adamson's Falls next to the Tana River, where the grave is marked by a small plaque. For the full *Born Free* story see box, page 322. The national park suffered greatly from lawless poachers during the late 1980s, which resulted in the deaths of several rangers and two French tourists, along with the annihilation of the introduced white rhino population. Following these incidents the option of visiting Meru National Park was effectively withdrawn by all the safari operators. The Kenyan government have now driven out the poachers and restored security. However, much of the wildlife in the park was decimated and it will be some time before numbers are recovered. However, in July 2001 the Kenya Wildlife Service embarked on an elephant translocation initiative and moved 56 elephants (nine different families) from the Laikipia district to Meru National Park. A variety of other game has also been relocated into Meru, including rhino which have since bred successfully.

In recent years, Kenya Wildlife Services built a three-span Bailey bridge across the Tana River. Funded by the World Bank, the 138-m galvanized steel bridge links Meru National Park to Kora National Park. The bridge has been named the Adamson Bridge in honour of George Adamson who lived nearby with his beloved lions at Kampi ya Simba.

Meru National Park is close to several national reserves including Bisanadi, North Kitui and Rahole. They have no tourist facilities at present. Kora was upgraded from reserve to national park following the death of George Adamson and there are plans to open it up in the near future. For further information about these reserves, see Northern Kenya, page 293.

Chogoria and Embu

Between Meru and Embu is the village of **Chogoria**, which is the starting point for the **Chogoria trail**. This is the only eastern approach up the mountain and it is generally considered to be the most beautiful of the routes. It is also supposed to be the easiest as far as gradients are concerned. For the Chogoria trail, see page 175.

Embu is the final town in the clockwise circuit around Mount Kenya, before rejoining the road south to Nairobi. Named after the Embu people who live in this area, it is the provincial headquarters of the Eastern Province. The town is strung out along the main road; it's a busy place, with the bars staying open late. There's not a great deal to see here although the **Isaac Walton Inn** is a very pleasant place to stay. The surrounding area is densely populated and intensively cultivated.

Mwea National Reserve → *Colour map 1, grid A5.*
① *Entry fee is US$15. Check with the Kenya Wildlife Service, Nairobi, T020-600800, www.kws.org, regarding current regulations on camping.*

Mwea National Reserve is a small reserve of 68 sq km, gazetted in 1976, located southeast of Embu. It lies immediately north of the Kamburu Reservoir, constructed at the confluence of the Tana and Thiba rivers, and the Kaburu and Masinga hydro-electric dams are sited in the reserve. The vegetation is mainly thorny bushland with patches of woodland and scattered baobab trees. Part of the park has recently been enclosed with an electrified fence; it provides a home for elephant, buffalo, impala, lesser kudu, baboon, vervet and Sykes' monkeys, hippos and crocodiles in the rivers, and a profusion of birdlife.

The adjacent rice-growing paddies and fields have attracted large number of waders and waterbirds and this area is also rich in birds of prey. A dispute between local rice farmers and the National Irrigation Board (NIB), who process and market the crop, but who were accused of exploitation and of leaving the farmers with insufficient rice to feed their families, resulted in the shooting of two of the farmers by police in 2000 at Ngarubani, a local market. The Kenyan Human Rights Commission has expressed concern at the violations of the farmers' human rights.

The most direct route from Embu is to follow the infrequently used B7 road towards Kangonde, south of Mount Kaniro, 1,549 m, and branch off to the right on a small road approximately 10 km before Iriamurai. Alternatively, travellers coming from Nairobi, 180 km away, can take the A3 towards Garissa, branching north on the B7 as far as the town of Kaewa where you can branch left onto the same small road to Mwea but approaching from the south.

There are two picnic sites at Hippo Point and Gichuki Island, but no other visitor facilities. The nearest mid-range accommodation is at Embu.

● Sleeping

Meru *p184*

D Meru County, T064-20432, F31264, is situated on the main road and is probably the best hotel in the town centre. It is simple but clean, modern and comfortable, safe and friendly. All rooms have hot water. It has a reasonable restaurant, a bar with a patio, plenty of secure parking spaces.

D Meru Safari Hotel, T064-31500, modern, attractive, well-appointed hotel, range of rooms, all with hot water. There is secure parking, laundry services, and a restaurant.

D Pig and Whistle, T064-31411, is the most charming hotel in town. It is on a hill off the road to Embu and it was here that the then Joy Bally committed adultery with George Adamson which led to her divorce from her second husband, Peter Bally, see box, page 322. There are cottages in the grounds, hot water, some of those built in the 1930s have period furnishings and fittings. The hotel has a handsome central building from the colonial period with a good restaurant (mid-range), friendly staff and excellent security.

D Rocky Hill Inn, 8 km north of town, has simple cottages for rent in a grove of pretty trees. There is a bar and they have a BBQ which is good value. If driving past you can stop here just for a drink in the garden. Notice the bizarre signposts everywhere, including one on a banda with seats named 'Cape of Good Hope for private discussions'.

E New Milimani, roughly 2 km from town on the Nanyuki road. Disco at weekends, plenty of parking space but often has water supply problems, rooms are bare but clean. Restaurant (cheap) serves wide-ranging menu including curries.

E White Star, some distance from the town centre on the road to the Meru National Park, just before the Teacher's College, T063-20989. Simple rooms in a squat block in a compound with parking, you can get basic food here but no beer as it is Muslim owned.

Meru National Park *p185*

L Elsa's Kopje, www.elsaskopje.com, no direct bookings so you will need to go through an agent, see page 86. 8 thatched stone cottages, either twin or double beds, all with en suite bathrooms and locally made furniture, 2 of the cottages have an outside bath with views over the park, and all have their own butler. Swimming pool and a gift shop. Rates are US$265-415 per person depending on the season and include food, day and night game drives, nature walks and fishing. Efforts are made to minimize the impact of the lodge on the environment and it won an eco-award for its efforts in 2003.

L Leopard Rock Lodge, reservations T020-600031, www.leopardmico.com. This is a beautiful lodge decorated with exquisite antique furniture and Persian rugs on hardwood floors, built on a 3.5-km frontage on the Murera River offering luxury full board accommodation in 15 bandas, each one with 2 bathrooms. Very fine cuisine, in a high-class restaurant with special service and a broad selection of wine and champagne. It has a small museum with library and video room, African-style open-air kitchen, pottery workshop, jacuzzi and pool bar. A simply stunning swimming pool which has a perspex wall at one end so it's actually possible to look through the clear wall at the crocodiles in the adjacent river. Rates are in the region of US$250 per person.

C **Bwatherongi Bandas**, book through the warden here, T064-20613, or **Kenya Wildlife Service**, T020-600800, www.kws.org. The 4 self-catering bandas near the park HQ are managed by the Kenya Wildlife Service. 3 have a single bed, the other has 2 single beds. They are basic, and have no kitchen as such, only an outside BBQ area that overlooks the Bwatherongi River. Bring everything you may need.

C **Murera Bandas**, reservations **Kenya Wildlife Service** (contact details as with **Bwatherongi Bandas**), 4 self-catering bandas just outside Murera Gate, they have 2 bedrooms, each with 1 double and 1 single bed, and en suite bathroom. BBQ area rather than a kitchen, and again you need to bring everything with you.

Chogoria p186

C **Meru Mount Kenya Lodge**, just inside the park at the Chogoria Gate, 25 km from Chogoria on the lower slopes of the mountain (road is hard going; a 4WD is essential). Reservations **UNIGLOBE Let's Go Travel**, Nairobi, T020-4447151, www.letsgosafari. com. Reasonable bandas, with showers and log fires, each sleeps 2-3 people and has a dining area and kitchen. There is also an additional cottage that can sleep 4. You need to be fully self sufficient here, and the only electricity is supplied by a generator.

Embu p186

C **Isaac Walton Inn**, T068-20128/9, www.izaak_waltoninn.com. This is the best hotel in Embu, situated about 2 km north of town on the road to Meru. It is an old colonial hotel apparently named after an English angler because of the proximity of good fishing spots in the mountain streams nearby. The inn is set in gardens with a comfortable lounge with a log-burning fire, the rooms, in modern cottages, all have bathrooms with hot water and each room has a balcony. The price includes breakfast

and there is a good bar and restaurant, it is very friendly and the staff are helpful.

D **Highway Court Hotel**, next door to the BP petrol station, T068-20046. Large, modern hotel with excellent views over the town from the roof, restaurant and lively bar, good security, but can be noisy.

⊖ Transport

Meru p184

The main bus and *matatu* area is behind the mosque, reached from the road going past **Barclays Bank**. There are daily buses to Meru from **Nairobi** including the luxury service. The journey to Nairobi takes about 5 hrs, to **Chogoria** about 1½ hrs and to **Embu** about 2½ hrs. **Kensilver & Akamba Bus Services** to Nairobi via Embu are cheap and reliable. *Matatus* north to **Isiolo** take about 45 mins.

Embu p186

The road from Nairobi to Embu has a very good surface but is very busy. *Matatus* are frequent, or instead take the **Kensilver** or **Akamba** bus **(Nairobi** to **Meru**, via Embu). Journey to Nairobi takes 1½ hrs.

⊕ Directory

Meru p184

Banks Barclays Bank, near the *matatu* station has an ATM that accepts Visa and Mastercard. Money can also be changed at **African Banking Corporation, National Bank of Kenya**, and **Kenya Commercial Bank**. **Internet** Scorpion Internet Café is to the north of Barclays. **Post office** Near Town Hall, with telephone and fax, and Western Union money transfer services. **Securicor** (Mon-Fri 0800-1700, Sat 0900-1200) on main road offers **DHL** courier delivery services.

Embu p186

Banks Barclays Bank is to the south of town; nearby is the **Kenya Commercial Bank**. **Co-op Bank** is near the old cinema, and **Consolidated Bank** is on Embu-Meru road. **Internet** Beatnet Cyber Café, on the second road left going south from the post office. **Post office** Towards the north of town on Embu/Meru Rd.

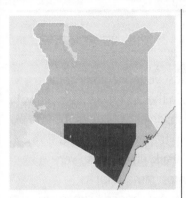

Southern Kenya

Heading south from Nairobi   **192**
Nairobi to Lake Magadi   192
Back on the Mombasa road   192
Listings   194
Tsavo National Park   **195**
Tsavo East   196
Tsavo West   197
Listings   199
Amboseli and the
Tanzanian border   **201**
Nairobi to Tanzania   201
Amboseli National Park   202
Along the Tanzanian border   204
Listings   205

⁝ Footprint features

Don't miss...   191

Introduction

Southern Kenya is one of the most visited regions of the country. The major game parks in the region are a big draw: Tsavo West and Tsavo East which, on either side of the Nairobi-Mombasa road, make up the largest park in the country, and Amboseli National Park which is also very popular. Amboseli is probably most famous for its photographs of elephants with snow-capped Kilimanjaro in the background. A picture that, above all, says 'come to Africa'. Another reason for its popularity is its closeness to the coast; visitors to this region can go on safari and also spend some time on the beach.

There are many points of interest off the Nairobi-Mombasa road leading to the coast. This is one of the most important thoroughfares in the East Africa region as it runs the length of the country to Nairobi and then to Uganda, where it continues on to Kampala. Hundreds of trucks ply this road each day carrying goods imported through the Mombasa port into the interior of the continent. Despite this, the road is in a reasonable condition except for the last 100 or so kilometres towards Mombasa, where the tar has been eaten up by the heavy traffic. An alternative to driving from Nairobi to the coast, is to take the overnight train that travels parallel with the main road. This is a splendid journey but unfortunately, although it does run through Tsavo, it does so at night so you are unlikely to see any game. Masai Mara Game Reserve in southwest Kenya, contiguous with the Serengeti National Park in Tanzania, is normally accessed via the town of Narok and is therefore included in the Rift Valley section, see page 123.

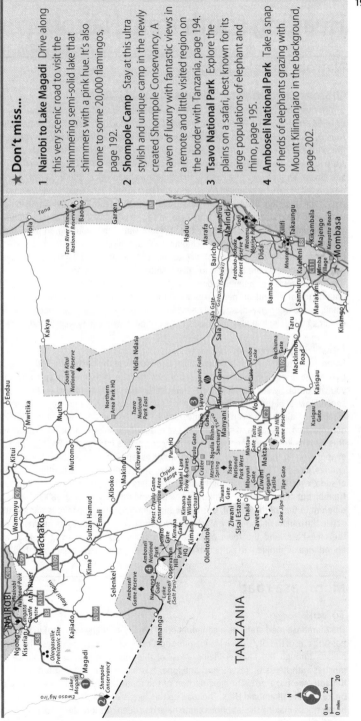

Southern Kenya

★ Don't miss...

1 **Nairobi to Lake Magadi** Drive along
this very scenic road to visit the
shimmering semi-solid lake that
shimmers with a pink hue. It's also
home to some 20,000 flamingos,
page 192.

2 **Shompole Camp** Stay at this ultra
stylish and unique camp in the newly
created Shompole Conservancy. A
haven of luxury with fantastic views in
a remote and little visited region on
the border with Tanzania, page 194.

3 **Tsavo National Park** Explore the
plains on a safari, best known for its
large populations of elephant and
rhino, page 195.

4 **Amboseli National Park** Take a snap
of herds of elephants grazing with
Mount Kilimanjaro in the background,
page 202.

Heading south from Nairobi

Nairobi to Lake Magadi

Olorgesailie prehistoric site → *Colour map 1, grid A6.*

ⓘ *You need to contact the National Museum in Nairobi, To20-3742131, www.museums. or.ke, to arrange a visit. To get there take the Langata Road out past Wilson Airport and Nairobi National Park. Soon after the park entrance take a left fork that leads through the village of Kiserian and then climbs up the Ngong Hills. It is well signposted.*

A trip to this important prehistoric site can be combined with a visit to Lake Magadi. The site covers an area of 21 ha, and is the largest archaeological site in Kenya. It was discovered in 1919 by geologist JW Gregory and later in the 1940s excavated by Kenya's most famous archaeologists, Mary and Louis Leakey. A team from the Smithsonian Institute in the USA continues to work here. In 1947 it was given national park status.

It is believed that a lake covered the present site of the mountain in prehistoric times, and that various mammals, including elephants, hippos, crocodiles and giraffes, lived near or in the lake. The abundant presence of game attracted hunters to this area. These early hunters are believed to have fashioned stone tools and axes. Fossilized remains of prehistoric animals, some gigantic compared to their descendants, and an abundance of Acheulean hand axes and other stone tools were uncovered here. A small, raised wooden walkway has been built around the display of prehistoric animal remains and tools, enabling the fossils to be exhibited where they were found.

Lake Magadi → *Colour map 1, grid A4.*

Some 30 km further south of Olorgesailie, and located at the base of the Rift Valley is Lake Magadi, a vision in pink. As you approach the lake, the views are splendid and you will probably see Masai grazing their cattle. At an altitude of 580 m, this is the second lowest of the Rift Valley lakes. It is 32 km long and 3 km wide and is the most alkaline of all the Kenyan Rift Valley lakes. The highly alkaline water, with its accumulated minerals and salts, makes the surrounding soils near the lakes alkaline. This has the knock-on effect of turning ivory and bones into fossils. The high rate of evaporation is the only way by which water escapes from the lake. Several hot springs, mostly at the southern end of the lake, bring to the surface a continual supply of soda, which evaporates forming a crust of sodium carbonate. It is only 110 km from Nairobi but the climate – semi-desert with temperatures around 38°C – is very different to that of the capital. Due to the high temperatures, the lake is particularly rich in the mineral *magadi*, the Masai word for soda. A soda factory has been built on the lakeshore, and the town of Magadi has grown up around this. There is an abundance of birdlife – in particular lesser flamingos, ibis and African spoonbills.

Mombasa road

To Voi

The Mombasa road starts as a continuation of the Uhuru Highway (A109) in Nairobi, passing one of the city's drive-in cinemas and a number of housing estates. The route passes through the Kapitiei Plains. Most of this area contains large-scale cattle ranches with herds of gazelle and antelope. It is along here that you turn right for **Kajiado**, see page 201. The next section of the route is through semi-arid country broken by the **Ukambani Hills**. The road up this long steep slope is poor, as years of heavy trucks making the laborious climb have dug deep ruts into the road. Just south of the road, by the railway line, is **Kima**, meaning 'mincemeat' in Kiswahili. Kima was so named after a British Railway Police Assistant Superintendent who was eaten by a lion. Charles Ryall, using himself as bait, was trying to ambush a lion which had been attacking railway staff and passengers. Unfortunately the ambush went horribly wrong when he fell asleep on the job.

Further on is the town of **Sultan Hamud**. It sprung up during the making of the railway at Mile 250 where it was visited by the then ruler of Zanzibar and named after him. It has hardly changed since that time and is a pleasant enough place to stop off for a soda and snack. Just south of **Emali** you can head down to **Amboseli National Park**, see page 202 for details of the route down the park and the park itself.

If you continue on the Mombasa road you will pass through Masai country, which is primarily featureless scrubland. There is a lodge at **Kiboko** that is about a third of the way through the journey (160 km from Nairobi) and a good place to stop off for some refreshment, see Sleeping for details. Another good place to break your journey is at **Makindu**, about 40 km from Kiboko where a Sikh temple of the Guru Nanak faith offers free accommodation and food for travellers (donations gratefully received). Slightly further along the road (in the direction of Mombasa) is the **Makindu Handicrafts Co-operative** where around 50 people hand-carve figures, for the tourist market.

The road continues its route passing into more lush pastures with a proliferation of the wonderful and rather grotesque baobabs, see page 251. At this stage the Chyulu Hills are visible to the south. The main trading centre at **Kibwezi** is the most important region in the country for sisal growing. Honey production is also much in evidence and you are likely to be offered some from sellers at the side of the road. Try before you buy to check its quality as sometimes it is adulterated with sugar. From Kibwezi, the road passes through heavily cultivated land to the boundary of Akamba country at **Mtito Andei** – meaning 'vulture forest' – about halfway between Nairobi and Mombasa. There is a petrol station, a few places to eat and a curio shop.

From here the road runs through the centre of the parks **Tsavo West** and **Tsavo East** for around 80 km, see page 195 for details. Many years ago, herds of elephants could be seen crossing the road in the grasslands making progress along this route slow, but this occurs less frequently these days as there are fewer elephants.

Voi → *Phone code: 043. Colour map 1, grid A6.*

The capital of this region, Voi is a rapidly developing industrial and commercial centre. It has a couple of petrol stations, a bank, a post office, a market and a supermarket. This was the first upcountry railhead where passengers would make an overnight stop but this is no longer offered as you can dine, sleep and breakfast on the train. Voi Gate into Tsavo East National Park is around 8 km to the north of town. You can buy and top up your Smartcard at this gate.

Voi to Mombasa

From Voi the road runs through the **Taru Desert** for another 150 km down to Mombasa. This area is an arid, scorched wilderness and there is little sign of life. You will see several small quarries. These supply many of the hotels on the coast with natural stone tiles used in bathrooms and patios. The next small settlement is **Mackinnon Road** with the Sayyid Baghali Shah Mosque as its only landmark. Some 30 km along the route you come to **Samburu**, a small town with no tourist facilities.

Another 30 km brings you to the busy market centre of **Mariakani**, a place of palm groves and an atmosphere quite different from upcountry Kenya. If you take the road to the right, the A107, then turn left at the junction with the A106, it leads to the **Shimba Hills**, which can also be reached from the coastal road south of Mombasa.

For the next 90 km the scenery becomes progressively more tropical, the heat increases, as does the humidity and the landscape changes to coconut palms, papaya and other coastal vegetation.

🛏 Sleeping

Lake Magadi p192

L**Sampu Camp**, reservations UNIGLOBE Let's Go Travel, Nairobi, T020-4447151, www.lets gosafari.com. On the 800 sq km Olkiramatian Group Ranch. From Magadi drive 35 km on a dirt road, the camp is 10 km after the bridge, there are signs. This European Union funded project was established to encourage tourism in the region and contribute to the incomes of the local community. The camp is built on a small hill next to a stream, 10 walk-in tents with bathrooms, main mess tent for meals and relaxation, views of Shompole Mountain and beyond. Game walks with the local Masai, mountain biking, game drives, overnight trekking and cycling safaris can be arranged.

L**Shompole**, www.shompole.com, is south of Lake Magadi on the Ewaso Ng'iro River and in the 14,000-ha Shompole Conservancy. Follow the same directions as above. Established in 2002, this is a fairly new wildlife conservancy and there are already lion, giraffe, zebra, wildebeest, buffalo and elephant within the boundaries making the additional US$20 daily conservancy fee worthwhile. Very elegant and stylish with fantastic views. As it is so hot in this region, the lodge cleverly uses channels of water throughout as a cooling system, and each airy, spacious Arabian-style tent has its own plunge pool. Tents also have his and hers compost toilets and wonderful showers that are more like small waterfalls. Built of local wood and stone, the decor is modern and imaginative. Very good fresh food is served in the open-plan dining room and activities include local day trips, game walks and drives. Expect to pay in the region of US$300 per person per night. Recommended.

Masai Camel Safaris, reservations UNIGLOBE Let's Go Travel, Nairobi, T020-4447151, www. letsgosafari.com. Off the road to the lake, 50 km (a 1-hr drive) from Nairobi. From Langata Rd, bear left at the Bomas of Kenya, and continue to Lake Magadi for 30 km, there is a camel sign on a rock pointing to the **Camel Safaris**. This is a local community enterprise with the Masai with 15 camels that can be hired daily or over the weekend on camping excursions. You need to bring all food and camping and cooking equipment with you.

To Voi p192

A**Umani Springs Camp**, in the 59- sq-km Kibwezi Forest northeast of the Chyulu Hills, near Kibwesi, reservations Nairobi, T020-520883, www.umanispringscamp.com. The 10-km approach track is suitable for high clearance vehicles (not necessarily 4WD). A raised and thatched tented camp, 8 tents are arranged to blend into the forest in a semi-circle on the edge of a lovely wetlands clearing to which birds and sometimes elephant and buffalo visit. Large bedrooms, attached bathroom with flush toilets and sunken shower cubicles. The rustic split-level central facility has a dining room (candlelit at night), a lounge and a well-stocked bar.

C**Hunter's Lodge**, Nairobi side of Kiboko, reservations Nairobi T020- 221438. The ramshackle gardens are pleasant with 100s of species of birds, and wonderful views out over the Kiboko River. Everything is rather faded but the rooms are comfortable and the staff friendly, OK food and bar.

C**Sikh Temple**, in the centre of Makindu, the Sikh temple complex of the Guru Nanak faith offers free accommodation (donations gratefully received). Secure parking, very clean rooms, very good Indian food in the dining hall which you pay for, must be well behaved and polite, alcohol is not allowed.

Voi p193

C**Tsavo Park Hotel**, near the bus stand, T043-30050, tsavoh@africaonline.co.ke. A fairly new hotel with very good modern facilities, the smart en suite rooms have satellite TV, the restaurant is reasonable. Price includes breakfast.

E**Distarr Hotel**, between the bus stand and the railway station, handy for both and centrally located, T043-30277. Basic but clean rooms, friendly staff, very good restaurant, vegetable curry is excellent.

🚌 Transport

Lake Magadi p192

It is fairly remote but not inaccessible for those with their own transport. Main road access to Magadi is directly from **Nairobi** by bus, *matatu* or private transport, via **Kiserian**. The railway line, which serves the factory, does not take passengers, but there are twice-daily *matatus* and buses (No 125) that reach Magadi town.

Voi *p193*
There are buses coming and going all day long between **Mombasa** and **Nairobi**. There are also buses that go through Voi between Mombasa, the border town of **Taveta** and on to **Moshi** in Tanzania.

This is also a major stop on the railway, although the train pulls into Voi from **Nairobi** at around 0300 and from **Mombasa** at 1200.

✪ Directory

Voi *p193*
Banks Kenya Commercial Bank, on the right on the way into town just past the railway track.

Tsavo National Park

→ *Phone code: 043. Colour map 1, grid B5/6, C5/6.*
Tsavo is the largest game park in Kenya, and its beautiful landscape and proximity to the coast make it a popular safari destination. It offers tremendous views with diverse habitats ranging from mountains, river forest, plains, lakes and wooded grassland. Because of its open spaces, the animals are fairly easy to spot and elephant are often seen wandering along every horizon. Its vastness creates a special atmosphere and on these endless plains trampled by thousands of animals it is not difficult to imagine that this is once how all of East Africa looked liked. ➤➤ *For Sleeping, Eating and other listings, see pages 199-201.*

Ins and outs
There are no scheduled flights to either Tsavo East or West, although there are several airstrips suitable for chartered light aircraft. See Transport above and the Ins and outs sections below for further transport information. Both Tsavo East and West are fairly easily navigated with a good map as all tracks are clearly defined, and junctions are numbered. Bring all your own provisions into the park including petrol and water. You should be able to eat or drink at any of the lodges if you so desire. There is a shop at Voi Gate in the east selling (warm) beers, sodas, bread and some vegetables, and another shop in Tsavo West selling basic provisions.

Background
This is the largest national park in Kenya at around 21,000 sq km. It lies in the southern part of the country, halfway between Mombasa and Nairobi and is bisected by the Mombasa-Nairobi railway and road link. For administrative purposes it has been split into two sections, **Tsavo East** (11,747 sq km) lying to the east of the Nairobi-Mombasa road/railway is the part of the park made famous by the 'Man- Eaters of Tsavo', and **Tsavo West** (9,065 sq km). The Waliangulu and Kamba tribes used to hunt in this area before it was gazetted. The remoteness of much of the park means it has had serious problems with poaching in the past. As a consequence, much of the northern area (about two thirds of Tsavo East) was off-limits to the public in an attempt to halt poaching here, which had decimated the rhino population from 8,000 in 1970 to around 100 in 1990. Recent anti-poaching laws have been particularly successful in Tsavo and the number of rhinos and elephants is increasing again, and the northern section of Tsavo East was reopened to tourists in 2002. The first European to visit this part of Kenya was Doctor Krapf, who journeyed on foot and crossed the Tsavo River in 1849 on his way to Kitui. Captain Lugards, the explorer, also passed through this area – the rapids on the Galana River are named after him.

Tsavo East

Tsavo East is the much less-visited side of the park where you will be able to see the wildlife without the usual hordes of other tourists. It mainly consists of vast plains of scrubland home to huge herds of elephants. The landscape is vast, and empty of any sign of humans, dotted with baobab trees, see page 251.

Ins and outs

The park HQ is at Voi Gate just north of Voi on the Nairobi-Mombasa road, where there is a small educational centre. Other gates off the main road are Manyani Gate, 25 km north of Voi, and Buchuma Gate at the extreme southeast corner of Tsavo East. It is also possible to enter the park on the C103 road from Malindi via Sala Gate on the eastern boundary of the park. This route which runs alongside the Galana River between Manyani Gate and Sala Gate, may be impassable during the rains. Gates are open 0600-1900 (no entry after 1815). Park entry fee is US$23 per day. Smartcards can be obtained and reloaded at the Voi Gate.

Sights

The wildlife includes all of the Big Five, plus zebra, giraffe, impala, gazelle, eland and cheetah, and there are over 500 bird species. The **Kanderi Swamp**, not far from the main entrance at Voi Gate, has the most wildlife in the area. The main attraction of this part of the park is the **Aruba Dam** built across the Voi River where many animals and bird congregate. **Mudanda Rock**, about 30 km north of Voi, is a 1.6-km long outcrop of rock that towers above a natural dam and at certain times during the dry season draws hundreds of elephants. The **Yatta Plateau**, at about 290 km long the world's largest lava flow, is also found in Tsavo East. The **Lugards Falls** on the Galana River, 40 km northeast of Voi are pretty spectacular. They are a series of rapids rather than true falls. The rocks have been sculpted into fascinating shapes by the rapid

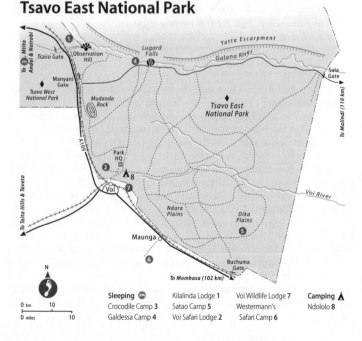

Tsavo East National Park

Sleeping
Crocodile Camp 3
Galdessa Camp 4

Kilalinda Lodge 1
Satao Camp 5
Voi Safari Lodge 2

Voi Wildlife Lodge 7
Westermann's
Safari Camp 6

Camping
Ndololo 8

Southern Kenya Tsavo National Park

South Kitui National Reserve is the
second national reserve in Kitui district. It is 1,800 sq km, adjacent to the northern
boundary of the Tsavo East National Park, but no tourism is allowed at present.

Tsavo West

Tsavo West is the more developed part of the park combining easy access, good
facilities and stunning views over the tall grass and woodland scenery. The area is
made up from recent volcano lava flows, which absorb rainwater that reappears as
the crystal clear Mzima Springs 40 km away. The environment is well watered and
this, combined with volcanic soils, supports a vast quantity and diversity of plant and
animal life.

Ins and outs
There are several entrance gates into Tsavo West. Two are on the Nairobi-Mombasa
road: Tsavo Gate, 320 km from Nairobi and 5 km north of Voi, and Mtito Andei Gate, 30
km north of Tsavo Gate, 240 km south of Nairobi and 249 km north of Mombasa. Buses
from Nairobi to Mombasa pass near both, and hitching to these gates is fairly easy, but
since walking inside the park is not allowed, visitors without vehicles may have a very
long wait. Chyulu Gate in the northwest corner of the park is used by vehicles coming
into Tsavo West from Amboseli National Park. Four-wheel drive and high clearance
vehicles are required for this route, especially in wet weather. Other entries are at
Ziwani Gate, Jipe Gate and Kasigau Gate all to the south of the park. Buses also run
between Voi and Taveta on the Tanzanian border (and then on to Moshi) through the
south of the park via Maktau and Mbuyuni gates. Gates are open 0600-1900 (no entry
after 1815). Park entry fee is US$23 per day. Smartcards can be reloaded (but not
obtained) at the Mtito Andei Gate.

Sights
The main attractions at Tsavo West are the watering holes by **Kilaguni** and **Ngulia**
lodges that entice a huge array of wildlife particularly in the dry season. During the
autumn the areas around **Ngulia Lodge** are a stopover for hundreds of thousands of
birds from Europe in their annual migration south.

Not far from the **Kilaguni Lodge** is the **Mzima Springs**, a favourite haunt of hippos
and crocodiles. There is an underwater viewing chamber here, but the hippos have
obviously decided against being studied too closely by moving to the other side of the
pool. Also around the lodges are the spectacular **Shaitani lava flow** and cones, as
well as caves that are well worth visiting. You will need to bring a good torch to explore
them. **Chaimu Crater** to the south of **Kilaguni Lodge** can be climbed and although
there is little danger of animals here, it is best to be careful.

Chyulu Hills National Park was established recently as an extension to Tsavo
West. Previously a game conservation area, the park is virtually untouched by man.
The long mountain range is home to lion, giraffe, zebra and oryx. Described as being
the youngest mountain range in the world, it is made up of intermingled volcanic
cones and lava flows that are considered only to be around 500 years old. Many of the
cones are covered with grass and there are extensive forests, allowing scope for hill
walking. There is no permanent water supply in this mountain range except for a small
spring at Ngungani. Kilimanjaro is clearly visible from the crest of the Chyulu Hills.

At the extreme southwest of the park, bordering Tanzania, is the beautiful **Lake
Jipe**, see page 204, which is fed by underground aquatic flows from Mount
Kilimanjaro. Here are found pygmy geese and the black heron along with many other
species of birds.

Wildlife you are likely to spot include: hyrax, agama lizards, dwarf mongooses, marabou storks, baboons, antelope, buffalo, zebra, giraffe, jackals and hyenas, crocodiles, hippos, leopards, lions, cheetahs. This part of Tsavo has some black rhino although most have been moved to the **Ngulia Rhino Sanctuary**. This is close to the Mzima Springs and is a fenced area of 75 sq km containing about 50 rhinos. You can visit daily 1600-1800.

In the south Tsavo West more or less surrounds the privately run **Taita Hills Game Sanctuary**, which is actually south of the Taita Hills about 15 km west of Mwatate.

Tsavo West National Park

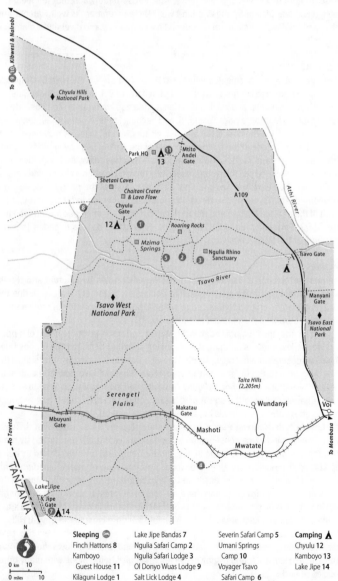

Sleeping
Finch Hattons **8**
Kamboyo
  Guest House **11**
Kilaguni Lodge **1**

Lake Jipe Bandas **7**
Ngulia Safari Camp **2**
Ngulia Safari Lodge **3**
Ol Donyo Wuas Lodge **9**
Salt Lick Lodge **4**

Severin Safari Camp **5**
Umani Springs
  Camp **10**
Voyager Tsavo
  Safari Camp **6**

Camping
Chyulu **12**
Kamboyo **13**
Lake Jipe **14**

There is a wide variety of game present including lion, cheetah, elephant and plains game. Prolific bird life includes the extremely rare Taita Falcon, a bird recorded in early Egyptian hieroglyphics. Mount Vuria at 2,205 m is the highest point in the Taitas, and from the summit there are excellent views of the plains of Tsavo below. The Taita are in fact three groups of hills, the Dabida, Sagalla and Kasigau. The Chyulu Hills can be seen if it is not misty. The **Taita Hills** are quite beautiful, densely cultivated and highly populated – in total contrast to the vast empty plains below. The fertile hills have made the Taita-speaking population relatively prosperous compared to other parts of the region. Road access to Taita Hills is on the road from Voi to Taveta. You'll need your own transport, or to be part of a safari, to reach this region.

● Sleeping

Tsavo East *p196, map p196*

L **Crocodile Camp**, reservations **African Safari Club**, UK T+44 (0)845-3450014, www.african safariclub.com. Overlooking the Galana River in an exceptionally fertile area. There are heavy duty fixed tents on a solid base or wooden bungalows with veranda and chairs, all covered by makuti thatched roofs. All have twin beds, a private shower and wc, a/c and hot water. Meals are served in the thatched dining room and there is a cosy bar and small swimming pool.

L **Galdessa Camp**, reservations Galdessa, Nairobi, T020-523156, www.galdessa.com. 10 km upstream from Lugards Falls on the Galana River are 8 bandas with river front-age. The camp is divided into downstream and upstream camps, with their own central facilities which can also be booked for exclusive use. The central mess areas house spacious dining areas, bars, and large, comfortable lounges. Price includes full board, game drives, walking safaris but excludes alcoholic beverages.

L **Kilalinda Lodge**, reservations **Private Wilderness**, Nairobi, T020-605349, www.kila linda.com. In 8,000 acres of private wildlife conservancy on the edge of the park. 6 cottages overlook the river, the largest of has its own plunge pool and jacuzzi. Central split-level bar, lounge, dining room and library. The highlight is the twin Victorian bath tubs in a private *boma* with open roof. Swimming pool. Game drives, Tsavo East and West National Park excursions, fishing, game walks and fly camping.

L **Patrick's Camp/Tiva River Camp**, reserv-ations **Bush and Beyond/Bush Homes of East Africa**, Nairobi, T020-600457, www.bush -and-beyond.com and www.bush-homes. co.ke. Traditional tented camp, run by safari guide Patrick Reynolds Jun-Oct. The camp is beside the seasonal Tiva River in the remote northern area of the park and is the base for game drives as well as Patrick's speciality: walking safaris. Spacious single and double tents are used on safari, each with its own toilet and shower combination. The beds in base camp are wooden with comfortable mattresses, the fly camp beds are metal and canvas with thick mattresses and pockets provided on the sides for personal belong-ings. Lighting in the tents is solar powered.

L **Satao Camp**, reservations **Southern Cross Safaris**, Mombasa T011-475074, www.satao camp.com. Permanent tented camp with 20 double tents, 2 with disabled facilities, constructed of sisal and boroti poles topped with a makuti roof, very nice bathrooms with stone features and hot showers. Overlooks a waterhole with resident hippo, where elephant, lion, zebra etc come down to drink at night. Lovely thatched bar and restaurant with atmospheric lighting, very good food, plus safari chairs out front around a bonfire. Game drives and sundowner trips into the bush on offer, although many animals come right into the camp. Well organized and professional.

L **Voi Safari Lodge**, T043-30019, www. kenya-safari.co.ke/voi. Slightly cheaper than the lodges of equivalent standard in West Tsavo and much less crowded. 52 rooms, each with 2 beds, swimming pool, and a good location. The animal hide by the waterhole gives very good close-up views at eye level. Baboons and rock hyrax wander through the hotel and gardens. Spectacular panoramic views. From here it is possible to arrange a drive to climb Mudando Rock.

L **Voi Wildlife Lodge**, reservations Nairobi, T020-3754393, www.voiwildlifelodge.com, is situated on a 25-acre site on the boundary the park, 5 km from the main highway. It has fine views of nearby volcanic outcrops and has been designed to blend into the surrounding environment. 72 rooms, some designed for the disabled and the walkways around the camp are wheel-chair friendly, restaurant, 2 bars, one on stilts overlooking a waterhole, badminton court, pool table, library, shop and swimming pool. All safari activities on offer. Safari Spa has a gym, steam bath, sauna, jacuzzi, cold bath and 5 treatment rooms, with an adjacent room designed for aerobics and yoga classes.

A **Westermann's Safari Camp**, T043-30028, www.westermannssafaricamp.com. About 29 km south of Voi, although it is not in Tsavo, it is very close to the boundary of Tsavo East on the opposite side of the Nairobi-Mombasa road, clearly signposted from the village of Maunga, 10 km from the road. Family run, there are 16 cosy wooden bandas and 5 new luxury bungalows all with en suite facilities, swimming pool, cocktail bar, restaurant, activities include walking and bird watching, there have been 84 species spotted in one single morning here.

Camping

E **Ndololo Campsite**, near Voi Gate, about 7 km into the park, has water and pit latrines.

Tsavo West *p197, map p198*

L **Finch Hattons**, reservations Nairobi, T020-553237/8, www.finchhattons.com, accessible from the Mtito Andei Gate. Award-winning luxury camp that oozes atmosphere. The camp accommodates up to 50 people, in large safari tents with twin beds, each with minibar, wooden Swahili chest, bookshelves and an antique writing desk, large deck balconies with chairs, tables and daybed. Elegantly appointed bar and restaurant and a comfortable private lounge, extensive library of books and an excellent range of classical music including Denys Finch Hatton's favourite selection of Mozart, swimming pool, dinner is a very formal affair with 6 courses, fine china and crystal glasses, airstrip.

L **Kamboyo Guest House**, reservations **Kenya Wildlife Service**, Nairobi, T020-600800, www.kws.org. 8 km from the main gate. Self-catering cottage with 3 rooms with

double beds and 1 room with a single bed, 10 people maximum permitted, must be taken as a unit for US$200 per night, towels, bed linen and kitchen utensils are provided, you just need to bring food, firewood and drinking water.

L **Kilaguni Lodge**, 20 km from the Mtito Andei Gate, T045-622471, reservations via www.serenahotels.com. Good-quality lodge from the Serena chain constructed of stone and thatch, blends well into the landscape, lots of wooden decks for game viewing, decorated with wooden sculptures of animals, a rock hewn bar, 56 spacious rooms, swimming pool, excellent buffet meals with a wide variety of choice, rates are full board. This was the first lodge to be built in any of Kenya's parks. Mt Kilimanjaro can be seen from the lodge. It was completely refurbished in 2002.

L **Ngulia Safari Lodge**, 55 km from the Mtito Andei Gate, book through an agent or at www.kenya-safari.co.ke. Slightly cheaper than the others at about US$100 per person full board, but still very good. 52 rooms, a swimming pool and in a good location. The waterhole, again, is a big draw both for the animals and tourists. Staff are very knowledgeable on the wildlife and are extremely helpful. The lodge overlooks the Rhino Sanctuary and the rhinos can be viewed through the binoculars that are set up there. A leopard visits the lodge's floodlit waterhole at dusk most nights to feed at the bait. The lodge is renowned as a haven for bird lovers every year Oct-Dec, who come to be involved in the bird 'ring' of migrating birds escaping the harsh winter conditions of the northern hemisphere. It is the only place where this activity takes place in Kenya.

L **Ol Donyo Wuas Lodge**, in the Chyulu Hills, reservations **Bush and Beyond/Bush Homes of East Africa**, Nairobi, T020-600457, www.bush-and-beyond.com and www. bush-homes. co.ke. Built in 1986 as Richard Bonham's private home, the lodge has 7 individual cottages and a beautiful, central mess/dining room. All cottages have en suite bathrooms, electric lighting, an open fireplace and a veranda with panoramic views of the plains and Mount Kilimanjaro. All-inclusive of food, drinks and activities: day and night game drives, horse riding and guided bush walks. US$500 per person.

African Wildlife

Introduction

A large proportion of people who visit Africa do so to see its spectacular wildlife. This colour section is a quick photographic guide to some of the more spectacular mammals found in east and southern Africa (it covers the countries shown on the map here). From the 'Big Nine', once thought by hunters to be the ultimate 'trophies' on safari and now most prized of all by those who shoot with their cameras, to the more everyday warthog, and from the wildebeest to the tiny Kirk's Dikdik antelope, which stands

at a mere 40 cm at the shoulder, here we give you pictures and information about habitat, habits and characteristic appearance to help you when you are on safari. It is by no means a comprehensive survey and some of the animals listed may not be found throughout the whole region (where this is the case, we have listed the areas where they occur). For further information about the wildlife of the country, see the Land and environment section of the Background chapter.

The Big Nine

■ **Hippopotamus** *Hippopotamus amphibius* (below). Prefers shallow water, grazes on land over a wide area at night, so can be found quite a distance from water, and has a strong sense of territory, which it protects aggressively. Lives in large family groups known as "schools".

■ **Black Rhinoceros** *Diceros bicornis* (bottom right). Long, hooked upper lip distinguishes it from White Rhino rather than colour. Prefers dry bush and thorn scrub habitat and in the past was found in mountain uplands. Males usually solitary. Females seen in small groups with their calves (very rarely more than four), sometimes with two generations. Mother always walks in front of offspring, unlike the White Rhino, where the mother walks behind, guiding calf with her horn. Their distribution has been massively reduced by poaching and work continues to save both the Black and the White Rhino from extinction. You might be lucky and see the Black Rhino in: Etosha NP, Namibia; Ngorongoro Crater, Tanzania; Masai Mara, Kenya; Kruger, Shamwari and Pilansberg NPs and private reserves like Mala Mala and Londolozi, South Africa.

■ **White Rhinoceros** *Diceros simus* (bottom right). Square muzzle and bulkier than the Black Rhino, they are grazers rather than browsers, hence the different lip. Found in open grassland, they are more sociable and can be seen in groups of five or more. More common in Southern Africa due to a successful breeding program in Hluhluwe/Umfolozi NP, South Africa.

African Wildlife

■ **Reticulated Giraffe** *Giraffa reticulata* (right). Reddish brown coat and a network of distinct, pale, narrow lines. Found from the Tana River, Kenya, north and east into Somalia and Ethiopia. Giraffes found in East Africa have darker coloured legs and their spots are dark and of an irregular shape with a jagged outline. In southern Africa the patches tend to be much larger and have well defined outlines, although giraffes found in the desert margins of Namibia are very pale in colour and less tall – probably due to a poor diet lacking in minerals.

■ **Leopard** *Panthera pardus* (below). Found in varied habitats ranging from forest to open savanna. They are generally nocturnal, hunting at night or before the sun comes up to avoid the heat. You may see them resting during the day in the lower branches of trees, see picture page ii.

■ **Common Zebra (Burchell's)** *Equus burchelli* (right). Generally has broad stripes (some with lighter shadow stripes next to the dark ones) which cross the top of the hind leg in unbroken lines. The true species is probably extinct but there are many varying subspecies found in different locations across Africa, including: Grant's (found in East Africa) Selous (Malawi, Zimbabwe and Mozambique) and Chapman's (Etosha NP, Namibia, east across Southern Africa to Kruger NP).

■ **Common/Masai Giraffe** *Giraffa camelopardis* (left). Yellowish-buff with patchwork of brownish marks and jagged edges, usually two different horns, sometimes three. Found throughout Africa in several differing subspecies.

■ **Cheetah** *Acinonyx jubatus* (below). Often seen in family groups walking across plains or resting in the shade. The black 'tear' mark is usually obvious through binoculars. Can reach speeds of 90 km per hour over short distances. Found in open, semi-arid savanna, never in forested country. Endangered in some parts of Africa, Namibia is believed to have the largest free-roaming population on the continent. More commonly seen than the leopard, they are not as widespread as the **lion** *Panthera leo* (see picture on front page of this section).

■ **Grevy's Zebra** *Equus grevyi* (left). Larger than the Burchell's Zebra, with bigger and broader ears and noticably narrower white stripes that meet in star above hind leg. Lives in small herds. Generally found north of the equator. A further zebra species, the **Mountain Zebra** *Equus zebra zebra*, is found in the Western Cape region of South Africa on hills and stony mountains. It is smaller than the two shown here and has a short mane and broad stripes.

■ **Lion** *Panthera leo* (page i). The largest (adult males can weigh up to 450 pounds) of the big cats in Africa and also the most common, lions are found on open savanna all over the continent. They are often not at all disturbed by the presence of humans and so it is possible to get quite close to them. They are sociable animals living in prides or permanent family groups of up to around 30 animals and are the only felid to do so. The females do most of the hunting (usually ungulates like zebra and antelopes).

■ **Buffalo** *Syncerus caffer* (below). Were considered by hunters to be the most dangerous of the big game and the most difficult to track and, therefore, the biggest trophy. Generally found on open plains but also at home in dense forest, they are fairly common in most African national parks but, like the elephant, they need a large area to roam in, so they are not usually found in the smaller parks.

■ **Elephant** *Loxodonta africana* (bottom and page xvi). Commonly seen, even on short safaris, throughout east and southern Africa, elephants have suffered from the activities of war and from ivory poachers. It is no longer possible to see herds of 500 or more animals but in southern Africa there are problems of over population and culling programmes have been introduced.

Larger antelope

■ **Gemsbok** *Oryx gazella* 122cm (below). Unmistakable, with black line down spine and black stripe between coloured body and white underparts. Horns (both sexes) straight, long and look v-shaped (seen face-on). Only found in Southern Africa, in arid, semi-desert country, though the very similar **Beisa Oryx** *Oryx beisa* occurs in East Africa. ■ **Nyala** *Tragelaphus angasi* 110cm (bottom left). Slender frame, shaggy, dark brown coat with mauve tinge (males). Horns (male only) single open curve. The female is a different chestnut colour. They like dense bush and are usually found close to water. Gather in herds of up to 30 but smaller groups more likely. Found across Zimbabwe and Malawi. ■ **Common** *Kobus ellipsiprymnus* and **Defassa** *Kobus defassa* **Waterbuck** 122-137cm (bottom right). Very similar with shaggy coats and white marking on buttocks. On the common variety, this is a clear half ring on rump and round tails; on Defassa, the ring is a filled in solid white area. Both species occur in small herds in grassy areas, often near water. Common in east and southern Africa.

■ **Greater Kudu** *Tragelaphus strepsiceros* 140-153cm (right). Colour varies from greyish to fawn with several vertical white stripes down the sides of the body. Horns long and spreading, with two or three twists (male only). Distinctive thick fringe of hair running from the chin down the neck. Found in fairly thick bush, sometimes in quite dry areas. Usually live in family groups of up to six, but occasionally larger herds of up to about 30. The **Lesser Kudu** *Strepsiceros imberis* 99-102 cm, looks similar but lacks the throat fringe and has two conspicuous white patches on the underside of the neck. Unlike the Greater Kudu, it is not found south of Tanzania.

■ **Topi** *Damaliscus korrigum* 122-127cm (below). Very rich dark rufous, with dark patches on the tops of the legs and more ordinary looking, lyre-shaped horns.

■ **Sable Antelope** *Hippotragus niger* 140-145cm (right) and **Roan Antelope** *Hippotragus equinus* 127-137cm. Both similar shape, with ringed horns curving backwards (both sexes), longer in the Sable. Female Sables are reddish brown and can be mistaken for the Roan. Males are very dark with a white underbelly. The Roan has distinct tufts of hair at the tips of its long ears. Found in east and southern Africa (although the Sable is not found naturally in east Africa, there is a small herd in the Shimba Hills Game Reserve). Sable prefers wooded areas and the Roan is generally only seen near water. Both species live in herds.

■ **Hartebeest**. In the Hartebeest the horns arise from a boney protuberance on the top of the head and curve outwards and backwards. There are 3 sub-species: **Coke's Hartebeest** *Alcephalus buselaphus* 122cm, also called the **Kongoni** in Kenya, is a drab pale brown with a paler rump; **Lichtenstein's Hartebeest** *Alcephalus lichtensteinii* 127-132cm, is also fawn in general colouration, with a rufous wash over the back and dark marks on the front of the legs and often a dark patch near shoulder; the **Red Hartebeest** *Alcephalus caama* (left), is another subspecies that occurs only throughout Southern Africa, although not in Kruger NP. All are found in herds, sometimes they mix with other plain dwellers such as zebra.

■ **Brindled** or **Blue Wildebeest** or **Gnu** *Connochaetes taurinus* (above) 132cm is found only in southern Africa; the **White bearded Wildebeest** *Connochaetes taurinus albojubatus* is found in central Tanzania and Kenya and distinguished by the white 'beard' under the neck. Both often seen grazing with Zebra.

■ **Eland** *Taurotragus oryx* 175-183cm (left). The largest of the antelope, it has a noticeable dewlap and shortish spiral horns (both sexes). Greyish to fawn, sometimes with rufous tinge and narrow white stripes down side of body. Occurs in groups of up to 30 in both east and southern Africa in grassy habitats.

Smaller antelope

■ **Bushbuck** *Tragelaphus scriptus* 76-92cm (top). Shaggy coat with variable pattern of white spots and stripes on the side and back and two white, crescent-shaped marks on front of neck. Short horns (male only) slightly spiral. High rump gives characteristic crouch. White underside of tail is noticeable when running. Occurs in thick bush, especially near water. Either seen in pairs or singly in east and southern Africa.

■ **Thomson's Gazelle** *Gazella thomsonii*, 64-69cm (above) and **Grant's Gazelle** *Gazella granti* 81-99cm. Superficially similar, Grant's, the larger of the two, has slightly longer horns (carried by both sexes in both species). Colour of both varies from bright to sandy rufous. Thomson's Gazelle can usually be distinguished by the broad black band along the side between the upperparts and abdomen, but some forms of Grant's also have this dark lateral stripe. Look for the white area on the buttocks which extends above the tail on to the rump in Grant's, but does not extend above the tail in Thomson's. Thomson's occur commonly on plains of Kenya and Tanzania in large herds. Grant's Gazelle occur on rather dry grass plains, in various forms, from Ethiopia and Somalia to Tanzania. Not found in southern Africa.

■ **Kirk's Dikdik** *Rhynchotragus kirkii* 36-41cm (top left). So small it cannot be mistaken, it is greyish brown, often washed with rufous. Legs are thin and stick-like. Slightly elongated snout and a conspicuous tuft of hair on the top of the head. Straight, small horns (male only). Found in bush country, singly or in pairs. East Africa only.

■ **Steenbok** *Raphicerus campestris* 58cm (top right). An even, rufous brown colour with clean white underside and white ring around eye. Small dark patch at the tip of the nose and long broad ears. The horns (male only) are slightly longer than the ears: they are sharp, have a smooth surface and curve slightly forward. Generally seen alone, prefers open plains, often found in more arid regions. A slight creature which usually runs off very quickly on being spotted. Common resident throughout southern Africa, Tanzania and parts of southern Kenya.

■ **Bohor Reedbuck** *Redunca redunca* 71-76cm (bottom left). Horns (males only) sharply hooked forwards at the tip, distinguishing them from the Oribi (see next page). It is reddish fawn with white underparts and has a short bushy tail. They usually live in pairs or otherwise in small family groups. Found in east and southern Africa. Often seen with Oribi, in bushed grassland and always near water.

■ **Klipspringer** *Oreotragus oreotragus* 56cm (bottom right). Brownish-yellow with grey speckles and white chin and underparts with a short tail. Has distinctive, blunt hoof tips and short horns (male only). Likes dry, stony hills and mountains. Only found in southern Africa.

■ **Common (Grimm's) Duiker** *Sylvicapra grimmia* 58cm (below). Grey fawn colour with darker rump and pale colour on the underside. Its dark muzzle and prominent ears are divided by straight, upright, narrow pointed horns. This particular species is the only duiker found in open grasslands. Usually the duiker is associated with a forested environment. It's common throughout southern and eastern Africa, but difficult to see because it is shy and will quickly disappear into the bush.

■ **Oribi** *Ourebia ourebi* 61cm (bottom left). Slender and delicate looking with a longish neck and a sandy to brownish fawn coat. It has oval-shaped ears and short, straight horns with a few rings at their base (male only). Like the Reedbuck (see previous page) it has a patch of bare skin just below each ear. They live in small groups or as a pair and are never far from water. Found in east and southern Africa.

■ **Suni** *Nesotragus moschatus* 37cm (bottom right). Dark chestnut to grey fawn in colour with slight speckles along the back, its head and neck are slightly paler and the throat is white. It has a distinct bushy tail with a white tip. Its longish horns (male only) are thick, ribbed and slope backwards. This is one of the smallest antelope, lives alone and prefers dense bush cover and reed beds in east and southern Africa.

■ **Springbuck** *Antidorcas marsupialis* or **Springbok**, 76-84cm (below). The upper part of the body is fawn, and this is separated from the white underparts by a dark brown lateral stripe. It is distinguished by a dark stripe which runs between the base of the horns and the mouth, passing through the eye. This is the only type of gazelle found south of the Zambezi River and you will not see this animal futher north. You no longer see the giant herds the animal was famous for, but you will see them along the roadside as you drive between Cape Town and Bloemfontein in South Africa. They get their name from their habit of leaping stiff-legged and high into the air.

■ **Impala** *Aepyceros melampus* 92-107cm (bottom). One of the largest of the smaller antelope, the Impala is a bright rufous colour on its back and has a white abdomen, a white 'eyebrow' and chin and white hair inside its ears. From behind, the white rump with black stripes on each side is characteristic and makes it easy to identify. It has long lyre-shaped horns (male only). Above the heels of the hind legs is a tuft of thick black bristles (unique to Impala) which are easy to see when the animal runs. There's also a black mark on the side of abdomen, just in front of the back leg. Found in herds of 15 to 20 in both east and southern Africa, it likes open grassland or sometimes the cover of partially wooded areas and is usually close to water.

African Wildlife

Other mammals

There are many other fascinating mammals worth keeping an eye out for. This is a selection of some of the more interesting, or particularly common, ones.

■ **African Wild Dog** or **Hunting Dog** *Lycacon pictus* (right). Easy to identify since they have all the features of a large mongrel dog: a large head and slender body. Their coat is a mixed pattern of dark shapes and white and yellow patches and no two dogs are quite alike. They are very rarely seen and are seriously threatened with extinction (there may be as few as 6,000 left). Found in east and southern Africa on the open plains around dead animals, they are not in fact scavengers but effective pack hunters.

■ **Brown Hyena** *Hyaena brunnea* (above). High shoulders and low back give the hyena its characteristic appearance. The spotted variety, larger and brownish with dark spots, has a large head and rounded ears. The brown hyena, slightly smaller, has pointed ears and a shaggy coat, and is more noctural. The spotted hyena is only found in east Africa and the brown hyena is only found in southern Africa. Although sometimes shy animals they have been know to wander around campsites stealing food from humans.

■ **Spotted Hyena** *Crocuta crocuta* 69-91cm (middle right).

■ **Warthog** *Phacochoerus aethiopicus* (left).
The warthog is almost hairless and grey with a very large head, tusks and wart-like growths on its face. It frequently occurs in family parties and when startled will run away at speed with its tail held straight up in the air. They are often seen near water caking themselves in thick mud which helps to keep them both cool and free of ticks and flies. They are found in both east and southern Africa.

■ **Chacma Baboon** *Papio ursinus* (opposite page bottom). An adult male baboon is slender and weighs about 40 kg. Their general colour is a brownish grey, with lighter undersides. Usually seen in trees, but rocks can also provide sufficient protection, they occur in large family troops and have a reputation for being aggressive where they have become used to man's presence. Found in east and southern Africa.

African Wildlife

■ **Gorilla** *Gorilla gorilla* (left) are not animals you will see casually in passing – you have to go and look for them. They are sociable animals living in large family groups and have a vegetarian diet. Gorillas are the largest and most powerful of the apes. Adult males reach an average height of 150-170 cm and weigh from 135 to 230 kg. They occur only in the forests in the west of the region in Uganda, Rwanda and DR Congo.

L **Salt Lick Lodge**, outside of the park in the Taita Hills, T043-30270, www.saltlicklodge. com. **Salt Lick** is noted for its strange design, basically a group of 96 rooms in huts on elevated stilts that are connected by open-air bridges over a number of water-holes. All rooms have a balcony. The lodge is resplendent with African wooden tables and batiks and rugs. The area is illuminated by floodlights to facilitate game viewing at night, and there is an underground tunnel and chamber allowing guests to watch wildlife safely at ground level. Tour packages offered range from 2-4 days and generally include transport from Nairobi or Mombasa, sanctuary fees, game-drives and full board accommodation.

A **Severin Safari Camp**, 50 km from Mtito Andei Gate, reservations Mombasa, T041-5487365, www.severin-kenya.com. Thatched central area with a good restaurant and bar, and a very nice fire pit for bonfires with traditional safari chairs overlooking the plains, spacious octagonal tents with very high ceilings and large mosquito nets under thatch with good views.

L **Voyager Tsavo Safari Camp**, reservations Nairobi, T020-4442115, www.heritage-east africa.com. A Heritage Group's Voyager resort, of good standard and aimed at families and first-time safari goers. Sited at the western boundary of the park on the edge of a small, secluded dam on the Sante River, with full-size permanent tents and excellent food available. Of the camp's 25 tents,16 sit on the southern bank of the Sante River and 9 on the northern. Offers

game drives and walks with highly qualified naturalists, and there is an Adventurer's Club for children.

C **Ngulia Safari Camp**, reservations UNIGLOBE Let's Go Travel, Nairobi, T020-4447151, www.letsgo safari.com. Offers self-service accommodation in the park in 6 fully equipped bandas, including bathrooms with hot water, veranda with chairs and table, small kitchenette with double ring gas cooker, crockery, cutlery and cooking utensils. Lighting is by gas wall lamps and kerosene lamps. Has a good friendly atmosphere and is popular with Kenyans and tourists alike. It is possible to arrange an early evening visit to one of the lodges from here for dinner and/or drinks.

D **Lake Jipe Bandas**, reservations through the Warden 045-22455, or **Kenya Wildlife Service**, Nairobi, T020-600800, www.kws.org. In total they sleep 5 people, kitchen but no utensils and you need to bring your own firewood and water. US$13 per banda.

Camping

There are also (E) campsites close to each of the gates at Tsavo; Kamboyo Campsite 8 km from the Mtito Andei Gate, and Chyulu Campsite 1 km from the Chyulu Gate. There are no facilities except water and pit latrines so you will need to be completely self-sufficient. There is another campsite available on the shores of Lake Jipe in the southwestern edge of the park. Campers share the outdoor cooking area and ablutions block with guests at the **Lake Jipe Bandas** (see above).

Amboseli and Tanzanian border

Nairobi to Tanzania

Kajiado → *Colour map 1, grid B4.*
Directly south of Nairobi is the A104 road to the Namanga border crossing to Tanzania. It is the administrative headquarters of southern Masai-land at the southwestern corner of the Kapitiei Plains which run between Machakos and Kajiado. The town is in the middle of bleak grasslands that show little sign of the abundance of zebra, wildebeest and giraffe that used to roam here. The town is typically Masai and there are many indicators of their preoccupation with cattle. Simple accommodation and food and drink are available.

Namanga is the Kenyan border town on the A104. It is the nearest town to Amboseli National Park, and is a convenient stopover between Arusha and Nairobi. Arusha is 130 km to the south and the drive between Nairobi and Arusha via Namanga takes four to five hours. The road to Nairobi (A104) is in good condition and there is a petrol station in Namanga, as well as a couple of shops selling Masai crafts, and lots of Masai street hawkers selling beaded Masai jewellery and red blankets. The prices are high but negotiable. You are advised to take great care when changing money, as there are many scams practised at the border. It is important to have a rough idea of the current exchange rates for Kenyan and Tanzanian shillings, or wait until you get to a bank in either Nairobi or Arusha. Immigration and customs at the border are quick and efficient, visas for both Kenya and Tanzania can be bought with US dollars, UK pounds and euros in cash, and the border is open 24 hours.

Amboseli National Park → *Colour map 1, grid B4/5.*

Amboseli's biggest draw is its location, with Mount Kilimanjaro providing a stunning backdrop. The whole park is dominated by Africa's highest mountain and at dusk or dawn the cloud cover breaks to reveal the dazzling spectacle of this snow-capped mountain. The downside is that its popularity (it has long been one of the most visited parks in Kenya) and the decades of tourism have left well-worn trails, and much off-road driving has made the park look increasingly dusty and rather bleak. Efforts are being made to remedy this with new roads being built to improve access.

Ins and outs

The main route into Amboseli is along the C103 from Namanga, on the Nairobi-Arusha (Tanzania) road. From Namanga to the park is 75 km down an appalling road and there are no petrol stations. The whole journey from Nairobi to Amboseli takes about four hours. It is also possible to enter via the C103 from the Chyulu Gate in Tsavo West National Park. Iremito Gate can be accessed from a road which joins the C102 road from Sultan Hamud on the main Nairobi-Mombasa road. There is a daily direct flight by **Air Kenya** from Wilson airport in Nairobi. Buses from the capital reach Namanga

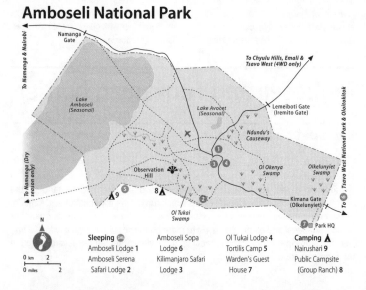

Amboseli National Park

Sleeping	Amboseli Sopa	Ol Tukai Lodge 4	Camping ▲
Amboseli Lodge 1	Lodge 6	Tortilis Camp 5	Nairushari 9
Amboseli Serena	Kilimanjaro Safari	Warden's Guest	Public Campsite
Safari Lodge 2	Lodge 3	House 7	(Group Ranch) 8

but there is no public transport from there to the park's gates. The park's tracks are
signposted and the maps are good. Both Kilimanjaro and Observation Hill serve as permanent reference points. When rains come harder than usual, some of the roads may be flooded, among them the main access to the Ol Tukai lodges from the Namanga road. In this case you will have to turn right towards Observation Hill and drive round the flooded area to the west. Gates are open 0600-1900 (no entry after 1815). Park entry fee is US$27 per day by Smartcard.

Background

This park was first established as a natural reserve in 1948, and in 1961 all 3,260 sq km of it were handed to the Masai elders of Kajiado District Council to run with an annual grant of £8,500. After years of the destructive effects of cattle grazing and tourists on the area, 392 sq km of the reserve were designated as a national park in 1973, after which the Masai were no longer allowed to use the land for grazing. The late 1980s saw the start of an environmental conservation programme to halt erosion and Amboseli now has a tough policy on off-road driving.

Sights

Amboseli is in a semi-arid part of the country and is usually hot and dry. The land is a mixture of open plains, savannah scattered with areas of beautiful yellow-barked acacia woodland, swamps and marshland and clutches of thornbush growing amidst lava debris. To the west of the reserve close to Namanga is the massif of Oldoinyo Orok at 2524 m. The main wildlife you are likely to see here are herbivores such as buffalo, Thomson's and Grant's gazelle, Coke's hartebeest, warthog, gnu, impala, giraffe, zebra and lots of baboons. One of the most spectacular sites is the large herd of elephants here. The elephant population of the greater Amboseli Basin at the base of Mount Kilimanjaro now numbers 1,000 animals in over 50 matriarchal families and associated bull groups. The Amboseli elephants have perhaps the oldest and most intact social structure of any elephant population in Africa. They are also the best known and well studied. You may also be able to see the very rare black rhino that has nearly been poached out of existence. There are a few predators: lions, leopards, cheetahs, hyenas and jackals. Birdlife is also abundant especially near the swamps and seasonal lakes.

There have been environmental changes over recent years due to erratic rainfall. Lake Amboseli, which had almost totally dried up, reappeared during 1992-1993. The return of water to the lake flooded large parts of the park including the area around the lodges. Since then, flamingos have returned, and the whole park is far greener.

Excursions

A Masai community, 25 km east of Amboseli National Park, has set up **Kimana Community Wildlife Sanctuary** – the first ever park to be owned and run by the Masai; the first project of a 'park beyond parks' set up in 1996. The idea behind the project is to manage the conflicts of interest when game rampages destroy cultivated areas. Here, the money generated by tourism goes directly to the local people. It contains elephants, lions, leopards and other game. Accommodation comprises three tented camps and one tourist lodge. The revenue generated goes to support local schools, and dispensaries and to reimburse the owners whose livestock has been killed by wild animals, or those who are particularly affected during times of drought.

Selenkei Conservation Area, 17 km north of Amboseli National Park, has also been established with local communities in mind. This 70-sq-km area has been

The movies Where No Vultures Fly, *starring Dinah Sheridan and Anthony Steel,*
and King Solomon's Mines, *with Deborah Kerr and Stewart Granger, were both shot in Amboseli.*

developed in a joint venture with a Kenyan company, **Porini Ecotourism Ltd** (PO c/o Game Watchers Safaris, Nairobi, T020-7123129, www.porini.com) and the Masai people. Roads have been created using local labour and a camp has been constructed (see Sleeping below). Again money raised from the entrance fees and rent are paid directly to the Masai. Profits are used to fund community projects such as schools and water supplies. Employment opportunities have also been provided for the local Masai people as game rangers, trackers and camp staff. The 70 km of roads in the Conservation Area were constructed using local labour so that members of the community gained employment. Where once species migrating from Amboseli were killed or driven away by the local people, wildlife conservation is now encouraged. As a result of the establishment of the Conservation Area, wildlife numbers have recovered significantly in recent years and elephants are now seen frequently after an absence of nearly 20 years. The animals are truly wild and tend to behave more naturally than those in the parks, which are often habituated to the presence of vehicles.

Along the Tanzanian border

Oloitokitok and Taveta → *Colour map 1, grid B5.*
Oloitokitok is a busy Masai town between the parks off the main road that runs from Amboseli in the southeast through to the Kimana Gate of Tsavo West. It has a busy thriving atmosphere and the best views of any town in the area of Mount Kilimanjaro. It is also a border crossing leading to the Tanzanian town of Moshi. The town has a bank and a post office, and there are market days on Tuesday and Saturday. **Taveta** is a small town on the Tanzanian border next to Tsavo West National Park. It is fairly remote and inaccessible, but there is a bank and hospital.

Lake Chala → *Colour map 1, grid C5.*
Lake Chala is just 8 km north of Taveta, part of the lake being in Kenya and part being in Tanzania. This deep-water crater lake is about 4 sq km and is totally clear with steep walls and filled and drained by underground streams. It is a tranquil, beautiful place to explore by foot and camping is possible, though you will need to bring all your own supplies. Due to the enormous depth swimming is not recommended and unfortunately, although the lake used to be popular for swimming, this is no longer recommended since a fatal crocodile attack on an English woman in March 2002. Aside from plenty of fish, there are also monitor lizards, baboons, monkeys and common snakes. Getting there is not hard, as there is a bus once a day from Oloitokitok or Taveta.

Grogan's Castle is an extraordinary construction on an isolated hill quite near the main road. It was built in the 1930s by Ewart Grogan as a resort for the sisal estate managers in the area. It has now fallen into disrepair, but retains spectacular views over Kilimanjaro and Lake Jipe.

Lake Jipe → *Colour map 1, grid C5.*
Lake Jipe straddles Kenya and Tanzania, fed from streams on the Tanzanian side and from Mount Kilimanjaro. There are a number of small fishing villages around the Kenyan side, and its southeast shores lie inside Tsavo West National Park. Again, this is a peaceful place to stop off where you will be able to see hippos and crocodiles, and plenty of birdlife. You can hire a boat to take you round the lake, but there are some vicious mosquitoes in this area, so be warned. There are some bandas on the lakeshore run by Kenyan Wildlife Service but they are accessed from Tsavo West and you will need to pay park entry fees.

● Sleeping

Kajiado *p201*

L Sirata Suruwa, 20 km to the south of Kajiado, get detailed directions before setting off, reservations **Bush and Beyond/ Bush Homes of East Africa**, Nairobi, T020-600457, www.bush-and-beyond.com and www.bush-homes.co.ke. A private wildlife estate with a tented camp for up to 10 guests. The name means 'glade of elands', and this is the home of American naturalists Michael and Judith Rainy, who are working to add wildlife conservation to the traditional pastoral economy of the local community. Increases in wildlife numbers suggest that the project is working. Game drives, bush walks, birdwatching and visits to Masai villages are offered, accommodation is in very comfortable tents with open-air showers, and the food is excellent. Rates are in the region of US$300 per person.

Namanga *p202*

D-E Namanga River Lodge is a very simple lodge and campsite in a beautiful setting in wonderful gardens with plenty of shady trees to pitch tents under. Has an excellent bar and restaurant, and accommodation is in wooden huts in the garden.

Amboseli National Park *p202, map p202*

L Amboseli Lodge, bookings **Kilimanjaro Safari Club**, PO Box 30139, Nairobi, T020-338888, ksc@africaonline.co.ke. 240 beds in colonial-style huts with pleasant gardens and a swimming pool, offers spectacular views out towards Kilimanjaro, but can get crowded. Masai dance shows but restaurant quality and the service needs a revision.
L Amboseli Serena Safari Lodge, T045-622361, reservations www.serenahotels.com. A very attractive design, drawing on elements of Masai traditional dwellings, blending into the landscape, both game and Masai cattle visit the waterhole, 96 rooms and swimming pool. A good emphasis on Masai culture. The nicest place to stay but expensive. It is near the Enkongo Narok Swamp which means there is always plenty of wildlife to see.

L Amboseli Sopa Lodge, on the road to Oloitokitok on the border with Tanzania, reservations T020-336088, Nairobi, www.sopa lodges.com. Attractive lodge set in mature wooded gardens, nice bar area from where you can sometimes spot honey badgers and hyenas, cottage-style accommodation in nicely decorated thatched huts, meals are taken in the African-themed dining room or outside on a BBQ patio, very large swimming pool, airstrip, can arrange game drives.
L Kilimanjaro Safari Lodge, bookings **African Safari Club**, UK, T+44 (0)845-3450014, www.africansafariclub.com. Sited in a pleasant setting with white thatched cottages, good views of Mt Kilimanjaro. 60 a/c rooms, with satellite TV, accommo-dation comprises chalets set in large lawns and a small forest of acacia trees, swimming pool, restaurant, bar, double room full board in high season is around US$140.
L Ol Kanju, reservations **Bush and Beyond/ Bush Homes of East Africa**, Nairobi, T020-600457, www.bush-and-beyond.com and www.bush-homes.co.ke. A traditional seasonal safari-style tented camp situated just outside Amboseli on the Kisongo Masai group ranch, with just 5 tents, this is an intimate camp and in a good location to spot elephants, game drives and bush walks with the Masai on offer. There is also the opportunity to go on guided walks with habituated baboon troops. Local conservationists and ecologists specializing in elephants work here.
L Porini Camp, in the Selenkie Conservation Area, reservations **Gamewatchers Safaris**, Nairobi, T020-523129, www.porini.com. Small and exclusive camp with 6 spacious tents, in a spot once favoured by big game hunters. No permanent structures like bar, restaurant or swimming pool, but the tents have en suite showers and toilets, meals are taken under the shade of an acacia tree and after dinner guests sit around a campfire. The camp is staffed by members of the local Masai community and there are very good walking safaris conducted here as well as game drives into Amboseli.

Southern Kenya Amboseli & Tanzanian border *Listings*

● *For an explanation of sleeping and eating price codes used in this guide, see inside the* ● *front cover. Other relevant information is found in Essentials, see pages 34-38.*

L **Tortilis Camp**, www.tortilis.com, reservations **Cheli and Peacock**, Nairobi, T020-604053, www.chelipeacock.com. 8 twin and 9 double bed tents with en suite bathrooms, raised up on a wooden deck and sheltered by makuti roofs, large verandas, excellent views of the plains and Kilimanjaro, won Top in Africa for Service, in the 2003 Condé Nast Traveller Gold Awards, also has a package available that includes game drives and visits to a Masai village. Other excursions are also available and there's a swimming pool. Rates are US$225-355 per person depending on season, excluding park fees.

A **Ol Tukai Lodge**, near the **Amboseli Serena Lodge**, 3 km east of Amboseli National Park, Nairobi T020-4445514, www.oltukailodge.com. 88 rooms in bandas have bathrooms, are equipped with electricity and occupy one of the finest viewing points in the park. Swimming pool, good value and good food. The eastern boundary is home to several families of elephants known to be amongst the best spots in the world to watch elephant.

A **Warden's Guest House**, inside the park, 2 km from Kimana Gate, reservations **Kenya Wildlife Service**, Nairobi, T020-600800, www.kws.org. 3 bedrooms one with double bed and the others with single beds, bed linen and towels provided, all kitchen utensils provided plus gas cooker. US$100 per person.

Camping

The campsites in Amboseli National Park are run by Masai communities. Although they are technically just outside of the park boundary, they can only be accessed from within the park. The public campsite in Amboseli is sometimes referred to as the Group Ranch. It is quite large but popular with low-budget camping safari companies so that it can get rather crowded and noisy at times. This site is just outside of the park boundary, southwest of Observation Hill. There are pit toilets here and a water supply which is not always reliable, so water has to be brought from one of the lodges at times. The special **Nairushari Campsite** is used by higher budget camping safari companies, located in a secluded site through the southwest corner of the park near Ilmbireshari Hill. There is firewood here, but bring your own food and water.

🍴 Eating

Amboseli National Park *p202, map p202*
If you intend to go camping or use the bandas, you will need to bring your own supplies of most things, although there is a kiosk at the campsite selling drinks. Most of the lodges allow non-residents to use their facilities and the **Amboseli Safari Lodge** is a nice place to stop off for a cold drink towards the end of the day.

🚌 Transport

Kajiado *p201*
The road to Kajiado (A104) forks right off the Mombasa highway (A109) shortly after the southern boundary of Nairobi National Park, just east of the Athi River crossing the Athi Plains. Plenty of buses and *matatus* to Kajiado run between Nairobi and Namanga.

Amboseli National Park *p202, map p202*
Air There is a daily flight from the Wilson Airport to Amboseli on **Air Kenya**. It costs US$85 one way, US$130 return in low season, and US$130 one way, US$150 return in high season. Low season is 1 Apr-15 Jun and 1 Nov-15 Dec. It leaves Nairobi at 0730, arrives at Amboseli at 0815, leaves Amboseli at 0830 and arrives back in Nairobi at 0915.

Namanga *p202*
Namanga to **Nairobi** bus takes 2½ hrs and costs US$3. The shuttle bus between **Nairobi** and **Arusha** also goes through Namanga.

Lake Jipe *p204*
There are buses and *matatus* along the road that links Oloitokitok with Taveta, running through **Rombo** (not marked on some maps), and then to **Voi**. Transport is more readily available on Tue and Sat, the market days. There are *matatus* and buses, but less frequent, east to **Tsavo** on the Mombasa Rd, and west to **Namanga**. A route south runs into **Tanzania**, crossing the border at **Kibouni**, and on to Moshi. However, it is often better to take the road through Kenya to Taveta and cross the border there.

Ins and outs	210
Mombasa	**211**
Listings	216
South coast	**223**
Likoni and Shelley Beach	223
Tiwi Beach	223
Diani Beach	224
Shimba Hills National Reserve	225
South of Diani	227
Listings	229
North coast	**237**
Mombasa to Kilifi	237
Kilifi	240
Arabuka Sokoke Forest Reserve	241
Watamu	242
Gedi Ruins	244
Malindi	246
Around Malindi	250
To the Lamu Archipelago	251
Listings	252

⁑ Footprint features

Don't miss...	209
The changing face	226
On the sea bed	239
A viewer's guide	243
Turtle watch	244
Swahili culture	249
Baobab trees	251
Fireworks at Malindi	258

Introduction

This coastal belt possesses a unique climate, a different type of people and a separate cultural history from the rest of the country. Along with the coast of Tanzania, the Swahili culture and Kiswahili language has its origins on the coast.

Built on a 15-sq-km island, and linked to the mainland by a causeway and rickety old ferry, Mombasa is Kenya's second biggest city and is East Africa's main port. It has a history dating back more than several hundred years when the Persians, Arabs, Indians and Chinese visited the East African coast to trade in slaves, skins, ivory and spices.

Today, there's a long line of top-class beachside hotels to the south of the Mombasa's Old Town centred around Diani Beach, and to the north all the way up to Malindi. More than half of the country's international hotels are based along the coast served by direct flights from Europe. Most have been constructed from thatch and local materials and are well spaced out, so despite the coast's popularity as a beach holiday destination, it never gets overly crowded even during the high seasons. The beaches are of fine white sand and there's plenty of activities on offer from the resorts including diving and snorkelling, windsurfing and jet skiing. There are marine national parks aplenty off the coast protecting the important marine life of the Indian Ocean, which can be experienced by *dhow*, glass-bottomed boat, or in a closer encounter, through a mask. Here the colourful coral reefs teem with fish, dolphins and turtles, and the aqua blue Indian Ocean provides near on perfect visibility. Away from the beach there are a number of other attractions in the dense coastal forests and undulating hills, and a safari to one of the parks can easily be combined with down time on the beach.

★ Don't miss...

1 **Fort Jesus** Visit this fort in Mombasa Old Town, built by the Portuguese in 1593 to an Italian design, and now a museum, page 213.

2 **Tamarind** Eat dinner on this romantic white-sailed *dhow* in Mombasa Harbour. Dine on delicious seafood by the light of hurricane lamps, page 218.

3 **Diani Beach** Try kite surfing along this 12-km beach, the new watersports craze to hit Kenya's coast, page 224.

4 **Shimba Hills National Reserve** Amble through this lovely forested area with a number of animals and fantastic views of the Indian Ocean and Mount Kilimanjaro, page 225.

5 **Wasini Island** Take a trip here to view the colourful coral gardens and eat a sumptuous seafood lunch at the island's famous Charlie Claw's restaurant, which has been serving up crab claws and lobster for 25 years, page 229.

6 **Watamu or Malindi marine national parks** Discover Kenya's vibrant marine life and coral reefs by snorkelling and diving here, page 244 and 250.

The coast

Ins and outs

Getting there and around
The gateway to the coast of Kenya is Mombasa, although some visitors fly directly to Malindi. The coastal highway runs north of Mombasa all the way to Kenya's northern frontier. Driving your own car or hired car as far as Malindi is very easy, and there are regular buses and *matatus*. Many hotels and resorts in this area have Mombasa shuttles or can arrange vehicle transfers. Private taxis from Mombasa will also take you to the north coast beaches for an agreed fare. Services are less regular north of Malindi, although there are daily buses to Lamu. Malindi airport has daily scheduled flights to Mombasa, Nairobi and Lamu. The airport also serves private charters. To the south of Mombasa, the Likoni ferry links the city with the coastal road that runs to the border with Tanzania. Once off the ferry there are regular *matatus* to Ukunda, the village at the turn-off for the beach road to the resorts along Diani Beach, where you can swap *matatus* or take a taxi. Again many of the resorts arrange shuttle services between Mombasa and the beach. Larger buses run daily between Mombasa and Moshi and Dar es Salaam in Tanzania, crossing the border at the extreme south of the coast road at Lunga Lunga. A popular option for reaching the coast is to take the overnight train from Nairobi to Mombasa that runs three times a week.

Best time to visit
The climate on the coast is markedly different to that in Nairobi and the Kenyan Highlands. As you drive down the main Nairobi-Mombasa road, you will feel the rise

Mombasa Island

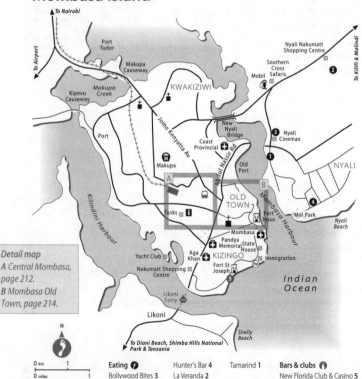

Detail map
A Central Mombasa,
page 212.
B Mombasa Old
Town, page 214.

To Nairobi

To Airport

Port Tudor

Makupa Causeway

Kipevu Causeway

Makupa Creek

KWAKIZIWI

Nyali Nakumatt Shopping Centre

Southern Cross Safaris

Mobil

To Kilifi & Malindi

Port

Jomo Kenyatta Av

New Nyali Bridge

Coast Provincial

Old Port

Nyali Cinemax

Makupa

Abdul Nassir Rd

NYALI

Kilindini Harbour

A

OLD TOWN

B

Mombasa Harbour

Moi Park

Nyali Beach

Tusks

Fort Jesus

Mombasa

Pandya Memorial

State House

Yacht Club

Aga Khan

KIZINGO

Immigration

Nakumatt Shopping Centre

Fort St Joseph

Indian Ocean

Likoni Ferry

Likoni

Shelly Beach

To Diani Beach, Shimba Hills National Park & Tanzania

N

0 km   1
0 miles   1

Eating 🍴
Bollywood Bites **3**

Hunter's Bar **4**
La Veranda **2**

Tamarind **1**

Bars & clubs 🍸
New Florida Club & Casino **5**

in temperature and humidity as you get nearer to the coast. The average temperature is 28-30°C, and days are long and sunny just about all year round, even during the rainy season. Despite this there is a down season on the coast during the rainy season from April to June, when it is often overcast and muggy, and many of the resorts and hotels offer discounts and some even close altogether out of season. If you can put up with a few afternoon showers, this is not a bad time to visit, and you are likely to have the beach to yourself. However, many facilities, such as restaurants and watersports centres, close. By contrast, during high season, especially around Christmas and New Year, the beaches are very busy with European package holiday makers.

Mombasa → *Phone code: 041. Colour map 2, grid C1. Population: 600,000.*

With a history going back 2,000 years, Mombasa is the oldest town in Kenya. Although the town is centred on an island about 4 km long and 7 km wide, it has now begun to sprawl on to the mainland. It owes its development to its location, for the island forms an ideal natural deep water harbour. Today goods are sent from the port to not only Kenya but to Uganda, Burundi, Rwanda and Sudan.

Mombasa has large communities of Indian and Arabic origin. It has the greatest concentration of Muslims in Kenya and their influence on the culture is strong. There are some ancient, Arab-inspired houses with elaborately carved doorways in narrow streets and passages, and a few other worthy distractions such as Fort Jesus and the city's most famous landmark: two pairs of crossed concrete elephant tusks created as a ceremonial arch to commemorate the coronation of Elizabeth II in 1952. Despite these, Mombasa is not a terribly attractive place and rubbish here is quite a problem, as is the traffic and pollution. Most visitors do not stay in the town itself – the city's hotels are not especially nice – and rather stay in one of the beachside locations to the north or south of Mombasa and visit on a day trip. It is now linked by causeways to the mainland at three points as well as by the Likoni Ferry. ▸▸ *For Sleeping, Eating and other listings, see pages 216-222.*

Ins and outs

Getting there
Mombasa is easily accessible. There are several direct flights from Europe (see page 23), as well as several daily flights from Nairobi on **Kenya Airways**, now the only airline to service this route. The overnight train from Nairobi runs three times a week (see page 62) and there are several bus services a day with various different companies. ▸▸ *See Transport, page 220, for further details.*

Getting around
The city is bisected by two main roads: Moi Avenue, which runs from the industrial area to the west of the island, and then becomes Nkrumah Avenue to Fort Jesus in the east, and Digo Road that crosses it in the centre of the city around the Old Town. Numerous *matatus* run up and down Digo Road going to the Likoni Ferry to the south and Nyali Beach and other points in the north. Taxis can be found all over town parked up on street corners. Tuk tuks are beginning to feature on the city's streets and are considerably cheaper than regular taxis. You can walk around the centre of Mombasa but the heat and humidity will tire you out quickly if you are too energetic. The traffic fumes are also particularly bad. Moi International Airport is located on the mainland about 10 km out of the centre of town. To get from the airport to the centre of town, you will need to take a taxi which should cost in the region of US$10-12 depending on the

time of day. Inside the airport are several taxi and shuttle bus desks that can arrange not only lifts into town but shuttles directly to most of the beach resorts. A *matatu* into town should be about US$0.20. If you are heading straight for the beach to the south of Mombasa, you will need to make for the Likoni Ferry On the otherside of the ferry there are *matatus* waiting to take people further south.

Tourist information

The tourist office ① *Moi Av, near the Tusks, T041-225428, Mon-Fri 0800-1700 and Sat 0800-1200*, sells a map of Mombasa as well as detailed guidebooks of Mombasa Old Town and Fort Jesus, and the staff are very helpful. The office is in a detached building set back slightly from the road. Mombasa has a problem in that there are a few unscrupulous tour operators, some with their offices also along Moi Avenue, which advertise their offices as tourist information centres. These may not give correct information and try and sell a tour that people don't really want. Ensure that you go into the real office.

History

The earliest known reference to Mombasa dates from AD 150 when the Roman geographer Ptolemy placed the town on his map of the world. Roman, Arabic and Far Eastern seafarers took advantage of the port and were regular visitors. The port provided the town with the basis of economic development and it expanded steadily.

By the 16th century Mombasa was the most important town on the east coast of Africa with a population estimated at 10,000. By this time a wealthy settlement, it was captured by the Portuguese who were trying to break the Arab trading monopoly,

Central Mombasa

Sleeping	Sapphire **11**	Fontanella	Recoda **12**
Castle **3**	Tana Guesthouse **13**	Steak House **3**	Shehnai **6**
Dorse **1**	Visitors Inn **8**	Galaxy Chinese **13**	Singh **2**
Excellent **4**		Little Chef **10**	Splendid View Café **7**
Hermes **5**	**Eating**	Little Chef Dinners **11**	Wimpy **1**
Manson **6**	Canton Malaysian	Mombassa Blue Room **4**	
New Palm Tree **7**	Chinese **8**	Overseas **14**	**Bars & clubs**
Royal Court **10**	Chinatown **9**	Pistacchio **5**	Casablanca **15**

N

0 metres 100
0 yards 100

particularly in the lucrative merchandising of spices. The town first fell to the Portuguese under the command of Dom Francisco in 1505. He ransacked the town and burnt it to the ground. It was rebuilt and returned to its former glory before it was sacked again in 1528. However, the Portuguese did not stay and, having again looted and razed the town, they left.

The building of Fort Jesus in 1593, the stationing of a permanent garrison there, and the installation of their own nominee from Malindi as Sultan, represented the first major attempt to secure Mombasa permanently. However, an uprising by the townspeople in 1631 led to the massacre of all the Portuguese. This led to yet another Portuguese fleet returning to try to recapture the town. In 1632 the leaders of the revolt retreated to the mainland leaving the island to the Europeans. Portuguese rule lasted less than 100 years and they were eventually expelled by the Omanis in 1698. The Omanis also held Zanzibar and were heavily involved in the slave trade. Their rule was in turn supplanted by the British in 1873.

The British efforts to stamp out the slave trade, and anxiety about German presence in what is now Tanzania, led, in 1896, to the beginning of the construction of the railway that was to link Uganda to the sea. One of the railway camps that was established before the construction of the line across the Rift Valley was at Nairobi. This town grew rapidly so that by 1907 it was large enough for the administrative quarters to move inland. The climate of Nairobi was considered to be healthier than the coast. Meanwhile, with the railway, the importance of the port of Mombasa increased rapidly and it became known as the Gateway to East Africa, serving Kenya, Uganda, Rwanda and Burundi.

In more recent history, Mombasa was the scene of a terrorist attack in 2002 when a hotel to the north of the city, popular with Israelis, was car bombed by suicide bombers, leaving 10 Kenyans and three Israeli holidaymakers dead. At the same time an Israeli plane was fired at as it was taking off from Mombasa Airport.

Sights

Old Town

The best way to see Old Mombasa is by walking around, early morning or late afternoon is preferable. The buildings in this part of town clearly reflect the Indian influences. Most of them are not actually more than about 100 years old although there are some

> ✤ Photography in the area of the old harbour is forbidden for security reasons, so take care.

exceptions. The finer buildings may have a balcony and one of the elaborate doors that are now so prized. These were once much more numerous than they are now as they were considered a reflection of the wealth and status of the family.

Fort Jesus Mombasa Old Town's major attraction, Fort Jesus was designed in the 16th century by an Italian architect called Cairati. It dominates the entrance to the Old Harbour and is positioned so that, even when under siege, it was possible to bring supplies in from the sea. For centuries it has served as an imposing bastion on the coast.

Despite this apparently secure position the Portuguese lost possession of the fort in 1698 following an uprising by the townspeople who had formed an alliance with the Omanis. The fort had been under siege for 15 months before it finally fell. During the battle a Portuguese ship named *Santo Antonio de Tanna* sank off the coast and the museum displays some of the relics that were recovered. The British took control of the fort in 1825 and from then it served as a prison until 1958 when it was restored and converted into a museum.

In the late 18th century the Omanis built a house in the northwest corner of the fort in what is known as the **San Felipe Bastion**. Since then this has served various purposes including being the prison warden's house. The Omanis also razed the walls of the fort, built turrets and equipped it with improved guns and other weaponry to increase its defensive capabilities. At the main gate are six cannons from the British ship the *Pegasus* and the German ship *SS Konigsberg*. The walls are particularly impressive being nearly 3 m thick at the base. Close to the Omani house you'll see one of the trolleys that used to be the mode of transport around town. There is also an excellent view over Fort Jesus and the Old Town from here.

There are many mosques on the island, some of which date back over 150 years. Before you enter any be sure you are appropriately dressed, ask for permission to enter and remove your shoes.

The **museum** ① *Nkrumah Rd, T041-312839, www.museums. or.ke, 0800-1830, US$3*, is situated in the southern part of the fort and has an interesting collection. Exhibits include a fair amount of pottery as well as other archaeological finds from other digs on the coast. The diversity of the exhibits is a good illustration of the wide variety of influences that this coast was subject to over the centuries. Within the fort are wall paintings and some of the oldest graffiti in Mombasa.

In season a sound and light show is held weekly. After a sunset *dhow* cruise of the old port, a guide takes you to the fort, where guests are welcomed by fire carriers and a sound and light show before dinner, taken within the ramparts of the fort. Contact **Jahazi Marine** ① *T041-5485001, www.severin-kenya.com, US$70*.

Ndia Kuu (Great Way) Leading from Fort Jesus into the Old Town, this road is one of the oldest in Mombasa. It existed during the Portuguese period and formed the main street of their settlement. **Mzizima Road** was the main route between the Portugese town and the original Arab/Shirazi town. **Mlango Wa Papa** marks the wall of the Arab town. One of the older buildings on the island is **Leven House** located just off the top end of Ndia Kuu. This was built around the beginning of the 19th century and has served many different purposes since then. It was originally occupied by a wealthy trading family and later was the headquarters of the British East Africa Company. It also housed a German Diplomatic Mission and more recently has been used by the Customs

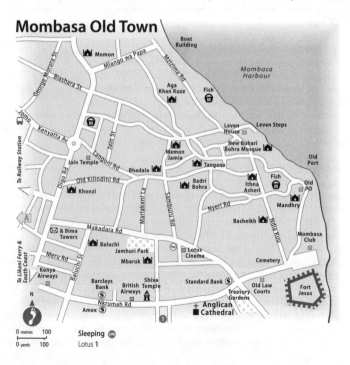

Mombasa Old Town

Boat Building

Memon

Mlango wa Papa

George Morra St

Blashara St

Mzizima Rd

Aga Khan Kuze

Fish

Mombasa Harbour

Jomo

Kenyatta Av

Jain St

Langoni Rd

Leven House

Leven Steps

New Buhari Bohra Mosque

Memon Jamia

Jain Temple

Bhadala

Tangana

Old Port

Digo Rd

Old Kilindini Rd

Khonzi

Mariakani La

Samburu Rd

Badri Bohra

Ithna Asheri

Fish

Old PO

Mandhry

Nyeri Rd

Basheikh

Ndia Kuu

Makadara Rd

& Bima Towers

Baluchi

Jamhuri Park

Mbaruk

Lotus Cinema

Cemetery

Mombasa Club

Meru Rd

Bauchi St

Kenya Airways

Barclays Bank

British Airways

Shiva Temple

Standard Bank

Old Law Courts

Fort Jesus

To Likoni Ferry & South Coast

To Railway Station

N

Nkrumah Rd

Amex

Treasury Gardens

Anglican Cathedral

0 metres 100
0 yards 100

Sleeping 🛏
Lotus 1

Department. Among its most famous visitors were the explorers and missionaries
Burton, Jackson and Ludwig Krapf. In front of Leven House are the Leven steps – here
a tunnel has been carved through to the water's edge where there is a freshwater well.
Burton actually mentions climbing up through this tunnel but you do not need to
follow his example; there are steps nearby. Close to the Leven Steps and the Fish
Market is **New Burhani Bohra Mosque** with a tall minaret, built in 1902, and is the
third mosque to have been built on this site. On Mbarak Ali Hinawy Street, to the east
of Ndia Kuu, close to the Old Port is **Mandhry Mosque**, with a white minaret. This is
thought to be the oldest mosque on the island dating from around 1570.

Old Law Court and around The court ① *US$0.40 a day*, is located close to Fort
Jesus on Nkrumah Road. The building, which dates from the beginning of this century,
is well worth a visit. It is now a library and also a gallery of Fort Jesus Museum, where
there are often historic photograph exhibitions. It also houses the collections of some
scholars who have studied the Swahili Coast. Near the Law Court on Treasury Square
is another building of approximately the same age. This was the **District
Administration Headquarters**. The roof is tiled and there is a first-floor balcony.

Mackinnon Market This lively, bustling and colourful market on Digo Road was
named after Dr W Mackinnon, a colonial administrator, at the turn of the 20th century,
who was transport officer for the route between Mombasa and Uganda. The main
section of the market is situated in an enormous shed but numerous stalls have spilt
out on to the streets. Obviously the number of tourists has affected the prices and the
market no longer has the bargains it used to. However, if you are prepared to haggle
and bargain in a good-natured manner you can usually bring the price down quite
considerably. Apart from fresh fruit and vegetables, you will be able to buy baskets,
jewellery and other souvenirs. For *kikois* and *kangas* (brightly coloured cloth squares)
the best place is **Biashara Street**.

Moi Avenue
This is Mombasa's main road and is about 4 km long. Along it are many shops that
the tourist will want to visit including souvenir shops, travel agencies and the tourist
information office. The **Tusks** are found on Moi Avenue and were built in 1952 to
commemorate the coronation of Queen Elizabeth (Princess Elizabeth as she was
then). They are actually rather disappointing close to. There are curio shops for
about 50 yards in both directions – the goods are not very good quality and are
rather expensive, although do look out for the fabulous beaded sandles.

Mzizima
The Old Town is probably not the oldest part of Mombasa – the earliest settlement
was probably around what is known as Mzizima to the north of the Old Town. The
evidence for this is the discovery of pottery dating from the 11th-16th centuries. There
is, however, very little left of this early settlement.

Mbaraki
On the other side of the island at Mbaraki is the **Mbaraki Pillar** believed to have been
built largely of coral as a tomb in the 14th century. There was a mosque next to it which
was used by a nearby village. The village has long since been abandoned, but people
still visit the pillar, pray to the spirits of the dead, burn incense and leave offerings.

Kizingo
Kizingo area, in the southern part of the island around the lighthouse, has some very
fine buildings, whose style has been called **Coast Colonial**. These buildings are
spacious and airy with wide balconies and shutters designed to take advantage of

every breeze. Hardwoods were used and many of the building materials were imported from Europe and Asia. Along Mama Ngina Drive it is possible to look over the cliffs that rise above Kilindini Channel and out towards the sea.

At the western end of Nkrumah Road is the administrative centre of the British colonial period. The main buildings surround **Treasury Square**, with the handsome **Treasury** itself on the east side. In the square is a bronze statue of Allidina Visram, born in 1851 in Cutch in India. In 1863, at the age of 12, he arrived in Mombasa and became a prosperous merchant and planter, encouraging education and prominent in public life. He died in 1916.

Proceeding west from Treasury Square, on the left is the **Anglican Cathedral**, built in 1903 and with a plaque to mark 150 years of Christianity in Mombasa, celebrated in 1994. The cathedral itself is a mixture of European and Mediterranean influences, whitewashed with Moorish arches, slender windows, a dome reminiscent of an Islamic mosque, with a cross, and two smaller towers topped by crosses. On the right, just behind the main road, is the spectacular, modern, Hindu **Lord Shiva Temple**.

Before the intersection with Moi Avenue is the **Holy Ghost Cathedral**, an elegant structure of concrete rendered in grey cement. Cool and airy inside, it has a fine curved ceiling of cream and blue, *fleur de lis* designs and stained-glass windows.

Going west on Haile Selassie Road, on the right-hand side is the **Ismaili Cemetery**, well tended, with frangipani trees and long green concrete benches. Adjacent is the **Islamic Cemetery**, with well-kept gardens, inscribed concrete benches and a small mosque. Finally, there is the **War Memorial** with bronze statues dedicated to the African and Arab soldiers who served with the East African Rifles in the First World War. On the corner of Haile Selassie and Aga Khan is the **Swaminarayan Temple** an exotic confection in powder blue and pink. In front of the Railway Station, are the **Jubilee Gardens**, laid out to mark the 60th anniversary of Queen Victoria's reign in 1897. They are neglected.

Near the Tusks are **Uhuru Gardens**. It is difficult to get in from Moi Avenue as curio kiosks block most of the entrance. Inside are some handsome trees, a fountain (not working), a café, and a brass cannon worn smooth from serving as a makeshift seat.

Nyali

One of the wealthier suburbs of Mombasa. There are a number of good restaurants here as well as the Ratna Shopping Centre, the Nyali Cinemax Centre, and the Nyali Nakumatt Complex, which has a number of shops, restaurants and a very large branch of **Nakumatt Supermarket**. It was in this area that newly freed slaves settled, and a bell tower is erected in memory. Across the bridge there is a fork in the road. On this corner is a huge and cheap second-hand clothes market. The right fork goes towards the village of **Kongowea** which is believed to date back to the 11th century. It is a fishing village and the influence of the missionaries in the 19th century remains strong. These days the Nyali area is dominated by large houses where many of Mombasa's expat community live. Only a few kilometres to the north of Nyali along the main coast road begins the strip of north coast hotels and restaurants.

● Sleeping

Mombasa *p211, map p210, p212, p214*
There is little reason to stay in Mombasa itself and it is much better to stay at a far more attractive beach hotel and visit Mombasa Old Town for the day.
B **Castle Hotel**, reservations, Nairobi, T020-315680, www.680-hotel.co.ke. Lovelywhite colonial building and historic hotel that was completely refurbished and

reopened in 2005 after lying derelict for several years. All 48 double, single and family rooms have nice modern furniture, cool tiled floors, satellite TV, electric safes, a/c, sound proofing, the front ones have balconies, another 10 twin rooms are due to be completed. Very good terrace restaurant and bar (see under Eating). Recommended as the best place in the city centre to stay.

B **Royal Court Hotel**, Haile Selassie Rd, T041-223379, royalcourt@swiftmombasa. com. Spacious and luxuriant entrance hall decorated in Swahili style, central position, 6-storey modern hotel with modern rooms, a/c, en suite bathrooms, hot water and balconies. Good Indian restaurant, excellent curries, rooftop bar/restaurant, downstairs bar with slot machines, and a swimming pool. Well run and offers good value.

B **Sapphire Hotel**, Mwembe Tayari Rd, T041-494841, hotelsapphire@africaonline. co.ke. Has 110 comfortable modern rooms with marble decor, a/c, balconies and satellite TV. **Mehfil** restaurant, terrace BBQ, buffet lunch, also has a swimming pool and a gym. Relatively expensive for the facilities.

C **Hotel Dorse**, Kwashibu Rd, T041-222252, hoteldorse@africaonline.co.ke. Very modern block, all rooms have a/c, bathroom, phone and TV, secure parking around the side, nothing unique but high quality for the area, everything is very new and fresh, standard hotel dining room and conference hall.

C **New Palm Tree**, Nkrumah Rd, T041-311756. Rather striking whitewashed old building, reception area has a high ceiling and gallery with comfy sofas, simple, quiet but rather faded hotel, fans, bathrooms but no hot water, there is a cosy relaxed bar and the restaurant serves basic dishes.

C-D **Lotus**, Cathedral Lane off Nkrumah Rd, close to Fort Jesus, T041-313207, F220673. Recently renovated, it has a charming central courtyard and a lovely atmosphere with wood panels and Oriental arches, single, double or triple rooms, all have a/c and hot water. There is a good bar and restaurant that serves buffet lunches. Recommended.

C-D **Manson Hotel**, Kisumu Rd, T041-222356, vnmulji@africaonline.co.ke. Some of the 80 rather dark rooms in this modern hotel have fans, others a/c, all rooms have hot water. Restaurant, TV lounge with pool table, massage, reasonable value.

D **Hermes**, Msanifu Kombo St, T041-313599. All rooms have bathrooms attached, there is a very good restaurant, a/c, great value.

D **Visitors Inn**, corner of Haile Selassie and Shibu rds. Price includes bathrooms and breakfast, some rooms are noisy and rooms are very basic.

D-E **Excellent Hotel**, Haile Selassie Rd, T041-311744. This is a very popular hotel with a central location, just a short walk from the train station or moderate walk to bus terminals. Advised to arrive early on in the day to secure a room. Rooms (with fans) have bathrooms with lots of hot water. Friendly staff, well run, clean with good security and the price includes breakfast. The restaurant serves good pastas. One of the best budget options and deservedly popular.

E **Beracha Guest House**, near Haile Selassie and Digo rds, T041-224106. Fans, 1st-floor caféteria, inexpensive and secure. Under new management.

E **Tana Guesthouse**, Mwembe Tayori Rd, T041-490550. Fans, mosquito nets, some rooms have balconies, freshly painted, well run, but in a busy and noisy area, exercise caution here at night.

● Eating

Mombasa *p211, map p210, p212, p214*
There are a number of eating places to choose from apart from hotel restaurants. With its large Indian population there is a lot of excellent Indian food as well as fresh fish and shellfish. At the budget end of the scale there are numerous canteens around the city centre that sell sausage or chicken and chips, samoosas and pies, especially popular during the day with office workers.

African

♦♦♦ **Little Chef Dinners**, Moi Av. Everything is painted green and there are lots of plants. African stews, plus reasonable steaks and snacks, fresh juice, busy bar that livens up considerably in the evening, but a hang out for prostitutes.

♦ **Little Chef**, Digo Rd. Centrally located, very busy canteen open all day until 2300, African food, burgers, chicken and chips on plastic tables, no booze, popular at lunchtime.

♦ **Recoda**, Nyeri St in the Old Town and another branch on Moi Av opposite the tourist office. This serves Indian and African food and is popular with locals as well as budget travellers, the food is basic but cheap with large portions, it is only open in the evenings. Closed Ramadan.

Chinese

♦♦♦ **Canton Malaysian Chinese Restaurant**, in the car park behind the Castle Hotel,

T041-227977. An upstairs formal restaurant, though the decor is rather plain, bar with some wine and spirits, good food including crispy duck with pancakes and deep fried crab claws, vegetarian dishes and litchis for dessert. Daily 1100-1500 and 1800-2300.

Chinatown, Digo Rd, look for the big red sign. Standard Chinese but with good service and a large menu.

Galaxy Chinese Restaurant, Archbishop Makarios St, T041-226132. Popular Chinese restaurant and is probably one of the best in town, it has especially good seafood dishes.

Overseas, Moi Av just north of the Tusks, T041-227801. Popular Chinese and Korean with a bar, it is family-run, friendly and the food is pretty good. Look out for the red lanterns hanging outside. It is next door to a Chinese herbal clinic.

Indian

Roshani Brasserie, in the Royal Court Hotel, Haile Selassie Rd, T041-223379. High-quality food in balcony restaurant with pleasant decor with green plants, specializes in tandoori dishes.

Shehnai, Fatemi House, Maungano St, T041-222847. Superb cuisine, specialities are mughlai and tandoori dishes, very professionally run where the quality and taste of food is paramount, elegant furniture, soothing music, pleasant decor, although no alcohol, open 1200-1400, 1930-2230, closed Mon. Recommended. There is a terrace bar at the Jambo Casino a few doors along if you want to have a drink before or after.

Bollywood Bites, at the Nyali Cinemax in Nyali opposite Ratna Sq, on the way to the Tamarind, T041-470000. Authentic vegetarian Indian cuisine, modern restaurant uniquely decorated in a Bollywood theme, a wide selection of mughlai and tandoori dishes, specialities include Indian ice cream, *kulfi*, Indian milkshake, *faluda*, and freshly squeezed juice. Go and see a Bollywood movie at the cinema and eat here for rather a different night out. Open Mon-Sat 1800-2300, Sun for lunch only 1200-1500.

Singh, Mwembe Tayari Rd, T041-493283. Good modern a/c restaurant with chunky furniture, although the menu is not very

extensive the food is authentic, freshly prepared and very tasty. Open 1230-1500, 1900-2200, closed Mon.

Splendid View Café, very good, cheap Indian meals, plus some prawns and steaks – huge portions. Nice variety of dishes for US$2-5 in a clean canteen environment, look out for the daily lunchtime specials.

International

Castle Terrace, at the Castle Hotel, T041-315680. Lovely refurbished terrace but rather unfortunately it looks straight at the traffic on Moi Av. Nevertheless this is a social place for a drink and the food is very good. Inventive menu, steaks and grills, some pasta, African specials such as 1 kg of fillet beef served with *ugali*, seafood platters for 2, sandwiches and ice cream. Recommended.

Hunter's Bar, near the Tamarind in Nyali. Small, secluded international restaurant popular with Nyali's expats, with a wide variety of seafood and meat dishes, but its speciality is its mouth-watering steaks. Other popular items offered include game meat, chicken Kiev and even apple pie.

La Veranda, Mwea Tabere St, Nyali, T041-5485452. Good traditional Italian restaurant and bar, home-made pasta with a variety of sauces, pizza oven, homely atmosphere, wide range of drinks including Italian wines. Open daily 0900-late.

Siesta, out of town on the Nyali Rd, T041-474896. Authentic Mexican food, popular with tourists staying at the north beach hotels, fajitas, nachos, guacamole, salsa etc, as well as other continental and vegetarian dishes, good atmosphere and service, outside tables overlooking the creek, lively bar, Happy Hour 1700-1900. Open daily 1700-2300 except for Sat when there is a disco 2200-late.

Tamarind, Silo Rd at Nyali, a 15-min drive from central Mombasa, over the Nyali Bridge, T041-474600-2, www.tamarinddhow.com. It is well worth the journey as the restaurant has marvellous views overlooking a creek that flows into the ocean. The Moorish design of the building is well thought out, cool and spacious with high arches, the food and service are both excellent. It specializes in seafood. It also offers cruises around Tudor Creek on the luxurious Nawalikher Dhow, where you can sip *dawa* cocktails (vodka, lime, honey and crushed ice) and eat lobster, whilst watching the moon rise over Mombasa Old Town and Fort Jesus, and listening to the strains of a traditional Swahili band. The set meals on the *dhow* include oysters or seafood or asparagus salad to start, followed by grilled lobster or seafood in coconut sauce. Seafood is freshly caught everyday, and you even have the option of picking your own crab or lobster from the tank. There are 2 sailings a day for lunch and dinner. Reservations are essential. **Carnivore** in Nairobi is also part of the Tamarind group. This is a memorable eating experience and thoroughly recommended for any visitor to the coast. Open daily 1230-1430, 1900-2230.

♟ **Books First** is an excellent chain of bookshops. There are branches at the Nakumatt Complex near the Likoni Ferry, and at the Nyali Shopping Centre. They also double up as very good cafés for coffees, pizza, snacks, some Indian and Mexican dishes, the branch at Nyali also has live bands on Fri and Karaoke on Sat 0800-late.

♟ **Fontanella Steak House**, on corner of Moi Av and Digo Rd. Nice relaxing garden in a courtyard off the street surrounded by plants, red and white checked tablecloths, attentive service, popular meeting place, very large menu with daily specials, everything from chicken masala to fried liver, juice, ice cream and plenty of cold beer.

♟ **Mombasa Blue Room Restaurant**, Haile Selassie Rd. Excellent bright, clean cafeteria style, tile floor and tables. A self-service restaurant strategically located in the heart of town, it offers Indian snacks, such as samosas, bhajias, kebabs, as well as fish and chips, chicken, burgers and pizzas. It also offers a wide variety of ice cream and doubles up as a video and DVD hire shop. Popular with locals and a good place to meet people. Here is also one of the nicest and quickest internet cafés in town. Recommended.

♟ **Pistacchio Ice-Cream and Coffee Bar**, Msanifu Kombo St. Wonderful ice cream and fruit juices, home-made cakes and excellent coffees, it serves snacks and you can also have proper meals – including a buffet lunch, pleasant decor, well-run. Thoroughly recommended.

♟ **Wimpy**, next to the **Tusks**. Standard burgers and shakes, Wimpy breakfasts are not that bad actually if you are looking for a traditional fry-up.

♥ Bars and clubs

Mombasa *p211, map p210, p212, p214*
Casablanca Club, Mnazi Moja, bar and disco, open courtyard bar on ground floor, disco and bar upstairs, fairly new, pleasant decor, very lively in evenings, no entrance fee.
New Florida Club and Casino, Mama Ngina Drive, T041-313127. Huge premises, several bars and dance floors, gets absolutely packed and men will get a lot of attention from prostitutes, on the beach with ocean views, also casino, and cabaret live shows at 0130, disco open from 2100 daily, casino and bars 24 hrs, pizza restaurant.

☻ Entertainment

Mombasa *p211, map p210, p212, p214*
In the city **Wonderland Casino**, is on Aga Khan Rd, T041-221291. **The Jambo Casino** is on Maungano St, and the **Golden Key Casino** is at the Tamarind.
Lotus Cinema, Makadara Rd, and the **Kenya**, opposite the Social Security House on Moi Av, both have fairly up to date Hollywood and Bollywood movies.
Nyali Cinemax, located in Nyali opposite Ratna Square, this ultra-modern Cinemax offers state-of-the-art viewing with a fully air-conditioned and surround sound screens, plays the latest box office releases. There is also the Scorpian Sports Bar here and a ten pin bowling alley and a casino.

☼ Shopping

Mombasa *p211, map p210, p212, p214*
Avoid buying seashells. As a result of killing the crabs, molluscs and other sea life that live inside the shells to sell them to tourists, populations have declined dramatically and many are seriously threatened. Vendors may tell you they have a licence, but if you want these species to survive don't encourage this trade.

In Nyali is the **Ratna Shopping Centre**, the **Nyali Cinemax Centre**, and the **Nyali Nakumatt Shopping Centre**, which has a number of shops, restaurants and a very large branch of Nakumatt Supermarket. There is also another vast branch of Nakumatt, with a number of other shops and cafés near to the Likoni Ferry.

Souvenirs and curios

The souvenirs that you will find in Mombasa are wooden carvings including Makonde carvings from Tanzania, soapstone carvings and chess sets, baskets, batiks and jewellery. There are lots of stalls in and around the market and around the junction of Digo Rd and Jomo Kenyatta Av. There are also lots along Msanifu Kombo St; along Moi Av from the Castle Hotel and down to the roundabout with Nyerere Av; and around Fort Jesus. For *kikois*, *kangas* and other material or fabric go to Biashara St which runs off Digo St parallel to Jomo Kenyatta Av. The bundles of sticks you see for sale on Kenyatta Av are chewed and used to clean teeth. The darker sticks are chewed for stomach upsets.

▲ Activities and tours

Mombasa *p211, map p210, p212, p214*
Mombasa Sports Club, Mnazi Mosi Rd, offers a fairly wide range of activities. **Yacht and Rowing Club**, in the southwest of the island close to the **Outrigger Hotel**, has a busy programme (both races and social events).

Tour operators

Mombasa's tour operators act as booking agents for the beach hotels and most can also organize safaris to the parks close to the coast such as Tsavo or Simba Hills. Some also offer car hire and transfers to the beach. There are dozens of tour operators here. The following ones are recommended, or go to the tourist office and get a current recommendation from the staff there.
Across Africa Safaris, Moi Av, T041-314395 www.acrossafricasafaris.co.ke.

African Route Safaris, 2nd floor, Old Cannon Towers, Moi Av, T041-230322, www.africanroutesafaris.com.
African Quest Safaris, Palli House, Nyerere Rd, T041-227052, www.africanquest.co.ke.
Bunson Travel Service, Southern House, Moi Av, T041-311331, www.bunson.co.ke. A good, reliable, well-established travel and tour agent. Flight and rail bookings, safaris and hotel bookings, agent for **Avis Car Hire**.
Ketty Tours and Camping Safaris, Diamond Trust House, Moi Av, T041-2315178, ketty@africaonline.co.ke.
Marajani Tours, Moi Av, T041-225924, www.marajani.com.
Pollman Tours and Safaris, Moi Av, T041-228308, www.pollmans.co.ke.
Rhino Safaris, Nkrumah Rd, T041-231141, rhinomsa@africaonline.co.ke.
Southern Cross Safaris, Nyali Bridge Rd, T041-475074, www.southerncrosssafaris. com. Established award-winning operator with over 40 years' experience, runs a daily trip to its own camp in Tsavo East, **Satao Camp**, operates safaris on 3 levels of service, Connoisseur, Premier and Tracker, and has a fleet of safari vehicles and its own plane, specialist for safaris for disabled clients, agents for beach resorts, this company is also involved in the annual East Africa Motor Rally. It also runs the excellent www.kenya lastminute.com, where you can pick up some bargain last-minute holidays to Kenya. Highly recommended.
Uniform Travel Centre, Makadara Rd, T041-229420/1, uniform@ikenya.com.
United Touring Company, Moi Av, T041-2229834, www.unitedtour.com. Another professional operator, the office is near the tourist office.

☉ Transport

Mombasa *p211, map p210, p212, p214*
Air
Moi International Airport is on the mainland about 10 km out of the centre of town, enquiries T041-433211. Airport tax is US$4. Mombasa is served mainly by **Kenya Airways** as well as by chartered planes for safaris etc. There are several tour and travel desks in the arrivals hall meeting clients that are heading to the coastal resorts, as well as desks for the car hire companies, and desks for various taxi

firms that offer transfers into town, and further afield such as Malindi and Diani Beach. Most prices are fixed and vary depending on whether you choose a small private car or minibus. There are banks at the airport with ATMs. At the time of writing only **Kenya Airways** were operating services between Nairobi and Mombasa, though **Air Kenya** still have a desk at the airport and may resume their service in the future.

Kenya Airways, reservations, Nairobi, T020-32074747, www.kenya-airways.com, has about 8 flights a day in both directions between Nairobi and Mombasa between 0730 and 2200, taking 1 hr. Prices vary between US$40-70 one way depending on availability. **Kenya Airways** also flies daily from Mombasa to **Zanzibar** in Tanzania, at either 1325 or 1555 depending on the day of the week, and **Kilimanjaro**, also in Tanzania at 1035 or 1250, again depending on the day of the week. At the time of writing neither **Air Kenya** or **Kenya Airways** were operating flights betweem Mombasa and **Lamu**.

Mombasa Air Safari, at the airport, T041-433061, www.mombasaairsafari.com, offers a charter service in small planes between Mombasa, **Amboseli**, **Tsavo**, and **Diani Beach**. It also has daily scheduled flights between Mombasa, **Malindi** and **Lamu**. The flight departs Mombasa at 0800, arrives at Malindi at 0845, departs again and arrives in Lamu at 0915. On the return leg it departs Lamu at 1700, arrives in Malindi at 1730, departs Malindi at 1750, and arrives in Mombasa at 1810. Mombasa-Lamu, one way US$63; Mombasa-Malindi, US$35 one way; Malindi-Lamu, US$45 one way. Other airlines with offices in Mombasa, though they fly to Nairobi and not Mombasa, include **Emirates**, Nkrumah Rd, T041-316966, www.emirates. com. **Gulf Air**, Baluchi Complex, Makadara Rd, T041-228616, www.gulfairco.com.

Bus

On all buses seats can be booked and there is no overcrowding with standing passengers anymore. There are lots of bus companies that go to **Nairobi** and their kiosks are on Jomo Kenyatta Av opposite the Islamic Cemetery and near the market. They usually leave early morning and evening and take 8-10 hrs. Fares vary and are about US$10 for the basic to US$16 for the luxury

service. **Akamba Bus**, T041-490269, is on Jomo Kenyatta Av. Buses and *matatus* depart for **Malindi** frequently throughout the day and take about 1½ hrs, costing US$2. They leave Mombasa when full from Abdel Nasser Rd outside the **New People's Hotel**. There are daily buses to **Lamu**, which also pick up in **Malindi**, 7 hrs, US$8, the **Pwani Tawakal Bus Company**, T041-222975, is recommended for the Lamu service. The bus will take you to the jetty on the mainland from where you get a ferry across to Lamu.

The bus service to Lamu has been targeted by bandits in past years, with some fatalities, and for many years the service was not recommended. However, there has not been an incident for quite some time and it is reasonably regarded to be safe. Despite this, armed escorts get on the bus on the last stretch of the road to Lamu at either Garsen or Witu. Heading south to **Tanzania**, Scandinavian Express, is a very good Tanzanian bus company, Arrow Plaza, Jomo Kenyatta Av, T041-490975, www.scandinaviangroup. com. It runs a daily service at 0800, which takes about 4 hrs to Tanga, US$10 and 10 hrs to Dar es Salaam, US$16. Other buses to Tanzania also go from Jomo Kenyatta Av. From Tanga there are connections on to Moshi and Arusha. Other companies serving the route to Tanga and Dar es Salaam include **Tawfiq** and **Takrim**, both have early morning and overnight services. The **Mombasa-Lunga Lunga** road is reasonable. Note that the border post near Lunga Lunga is fairly efficient, and visas for Tanzania and Kenya can be purchased. **Hood Buses** also operates a daily service to **Moshi**, US$12, at 0900, via the border at Taveta, and again visas can be obtained at the border.

Car

For hire: **Avis**, Moi Av, T041-311331, www.aviskenya.com; **Budget**, Associated Motors Complex, Kenyatta Av, T041-221281, airport, T041-434887, www.budget-kenya. com; **Europcar**, Makena House, Nkrumah Rd, T041-311994, www.europcar.com; **Glory Car Hire**, next to Tourist Information, Moi Av, T041-313561, www.glory carhire.com.

Ferry

Local Likoni ferry docks at the southeast of the island. The ferries depart about every 15 mins and run 24 hrs and are free for pedestrians and cyclists (cars US$0.40 and motorbikes US$0.20). There is always a throng of people waiting to board or disembark from the boat – keep an eye on your possessions and beware of pickpockets and thieves. The waters are said to contain sharks although this is debatable. *Matatus* to the ferry leave from outside the post office on Digo Rd – ask for Likoni. In fact it is possible to get a *matatu* to the Likoni ferry from just about anywhere in the city even if the taxi drivers tell you otherwise. When the ferry docks, the *matatus* for Diani Beach are located at the top of the slipway from the ferry and turn left.

Long distance Hydro-foils from Mombasa to **Tanga**, **Zanzibar** and **Dar es Salaam**, have been suspended for a while now.

Train

Mombasa Railway Station, T041-433211, is at the end of Haile Selassie Av at Jubilee Sq. You can leave luggage at the railway station for a small fee. The overnight train that runs between Nairobi and Mombasa is an historic and authentic rail experience and is an excellent way of getting to the coast. It departs Nairobi at 1900 on Mon, Wed and Fri and arrives in Mombasa at 0830. In the other direction it departs Mombasa on Sat, Tue and Thu at 1900 and arrives in Nairobi at 0900. Bear in mind delays do occur and sometimes the train may be a few hours late, so do not arrange onward travel arrangements too close to the scheduled arrival times. First class is in cabins that sleep 2 people in bunks, which includes bedding and a sink, 2nd class 4 people in bunks but with no bedding, and 3rd class is seating in carriages that take up to 80 people. First class is very comfortable and well recommended. There is a good restaurant car where 1st- and 2nd-class passengers can have dinner and drinks, although you may want to bring additional drinks and snacks with you. Tickets; 1st class, US$40; 2nd class, US$30; and 3rd class, US$6. It is essential to make reservations in advance and this can be done personally at the stations or through a tour operator or travel agent.

⊙ Directory

Mombasa *p211, map p210, p212, p214*
Banks There are many banks on Nkrumah Av. Most have ATMs. **Barclays Bank**, Moi Av, changes TCs 0900-1630 on week-days and 0900-1400 on Sat. There is another branch on Nkrumah Av, both have ATMs that accept most cards. **Commercial Bank of Africa**, Moi Av, **Kenya Commercial Bank**, Moi Av, has an ATM, **National Bank of Kenya**, Nkrumah Av, **Standard Chartered Bank**, Moi Av, **Stanbic Bank**, corner of Digo Rd and Nkrumah Av.
Bureau de change There are many on Nkrumah Av. **Pwani Bureau de Change**, opposite Mackinnon Market on Digo Rd, fast, efficient, good rates offered. **Fort Jesus Forex**, near entrance to Fort Jesus on Nkrumah Rd, **Leo Forex Bureau** on Nkrumah Av. **Coast Forex Bureau** is on the corner of Moi Av and Digo Rd on the opposite corner to the Stanbic Bank. **Internet** There are several cybercafés or small businesses offering email and internet access in Mombasa. However, access is compromised by frequent interruptions to the power supply. The best are the **Info Café**, Ambalal House, opposite the Kenya Airways office on Nkrumah Av, which also serves snacks and juices, and the internet café at the back of the **Mombasa Blue Room Restaurant**, Haile Selassie Rd, which is also an agent for DHL. **Blue Fin Cyber Cafe**, Meru Rd, also sells fresh sugarcane juice. **Cultural centres Alliance Française**, Freed Building, Moi Av. **British Council**, Jubilee Insurance Building, Moi Av just west of the Tusks. **German Institute**, Freed Building, Moi Av. **Medical services** **Aga Khan Hospital**, Vanga Rd, T041-312953. **Mombasa Hospital**, Mama Ngina Rd, T041-312190. **Pandya Memorial Hospital**, Dedan Kimathi Av, T041-312190. **Coast Provincial General Hospital**, Kisauni Rd, T041-314201. There are plenty of well-stocked pharmacies in the city centre. **Post office** Digo St, Mon-Fri 0800-1800, Sat 0800-1200. **Useful addresses** Police station: Mama Ngina Rd, T041-222121. **Immigration**, if you need to extend your visa, the office is on Mama Ngina Rd next to the police station, T041-311745.

● *Each of the Likoni ferries can carry 1,600 foot passengers and 60 vehicles. In a single year they carry around 50 million people and 1 million vehicles.*

South coast

The beaches on the south coast are some of the best in the world. The sand – coral that has been pounded by the waves over the centuries – is fine and very white. There are a few well-developed areas, but you don't need to go far to find a quiet spot. Running south from Mombasa, the main beaches are Shelley, Tiwi and Diani. The most popular beach is Diani – it is also the most built up and not surprisingly is now the most expensive. However, most of the buildings are well designed and local materials have been used so they do not intrude too much. The hotels all have their own restaurants and bars and most of them arrange regular evening entertainment such as traditional African dancers and singers. They also organise day trips to sights in the region so it is feasible to stay in one hotel for your entire holiday. ▶▶ *For Sleeping, Eating and other listings, see pages 229-236.*

Ins and outs

Once across the Likoni Ferry the A14 heads south on a reasonably good tarred road. It runs parallel to the coast, although you cannot see the sea from the road. The turn-off to Tiwi Beach is about 20 km south of the ferry and the turn-off to Diani Beach is at Ukunda about 22 km. There are plenty of *matatus* running up and down between the township of Likoni where the ferry docks and Ukunda, but these are less frequent south of Ukunda. About 12 km from Likoni is the turn-off to the right to Kwale and the Shimba Hills National Reserve and Mwaluganje Elephant Sanctuary.

Likoni and Shelley Beach → *Phone code: 040. Colour map 2, grid C1.*

Likoni is a sprawling (and none too clean with piles of unsightly rubbish everywhere) township on the southern side of the Likoni Ferry. The road that leads from the ferry is lined with market stalls. Shelley Beach is the closest beach to Mombasa, and is ideal for a day trip if you are staying in the town and are not too bothered by the proximity of the urban sprawl. Swimming here can be problematic due to excessive seaweed.

Tiwi Beach → *Phone code: 040. Colour map 2, grid C1.*

The next resort, Tiwi Beach, is about 20 km from Likoni Ferry and 3 km off the main coastal road down a very bumpy track (turn left at the supermarket). This beach is wider than that at Shelley but not as nice as Diani and for a number of years was particularly popular with families and with budget travellers. Its popularity has waned in recent years, however in favour of the hotels at Diani, and **Twiga Lodge**, once a firm favourite on the backpacker circuit through East Africa, is a shadow of its former self.

> ‡ *Avoid walking down the track from the main road to the beach as there have been several muggings in the past. Get a taxi ($2.50) to your hotel, there are no matatus.*

However, the beach is ideal for children; the waves are smaller than those at Diani, and hundreds of rock pools are exposed when the tide is out, all with plenty of marine life in them. There is also some quite good snorkelling here and it is possible to scuba dive too. However, it is prone to large amounts of seaweed in April-May. If you walk up the beach in the direction of Shelley Beach for about 1½ km you come to **'Pool of Africa'**, a rock pool in the shape of the African continent where you can swim, and even dive through a small tunnel to another pool aptly named **Madagascar**.

Before you go exploring on the reef check up on the tides (they are published in the local papers) and set out with plenty of time. It is very easy to get cut off when the tide comes in and it turns quite rapidly. Also be sure you have a good pair of thick rubber-soled shoes to protect your feet against the coral and sea urchins. It is possible to walk south to Diani Beach at low tide, but again it is important to ensure you check the times of the tides to avoid getting stranded.

Diani Beach → Phone code: 040.
Colour map 2, grid C1.

This is the longest beach in Kenya with about 20 km of dazzling white sand, coconut trees, clear sea and a coral reef that is exposed at low tide. It has acquired a whole string of hotels over the years, although these have been sensitively built, often out of thatch and local materials. Diani is the place to come if you want a traditional beach holiday. The climate and scenery are marvellous, accommodation and food is of a very high standard, and activities on offer include windsurfing, sailing, snorkelling and scuba diving. You can also go waterskiing or parascending, or hire a bike or motorbike and there is the additional option of combining time on the beach with a safari to one of the closer national parks and game reserves inland, such as Tsavo or Simba Hills, and a visit to Mombasa on a day tour.

It is geared to big-spending package tourists (usually German and English) which generates some disadvantages: intrusive beach touts that hound visitors trying to sell curios, camel rides along the beach or trips on glass-bottomed boats, as well as offering themselves as models for photos (some of the Masai who come round are not Masai at all but are of other tribes). Most of the goods are of poor quality hugely overpriced, although you can try bargaining the quoted prices down. Over the years Diani has gained a reputation as a bit of a pick-up place for European female tourists looking for sex with Kenyan men. Even if no payment for

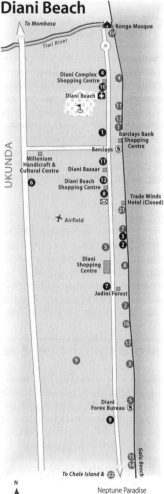

Diani Beach

To Mombasa
Kongo Mosque
Tiwi River
UKUNDA
Diani Complex Shopping Centre
Diani Beach
Barclays Bank Shopping Centre
Barclays
Millenium Handicraft & Cultural Centre
Diani Bazaar
Diani Beach Shopping Centre
Trade Winds Hotel (Closed)
Airfield
Diani Shopping Centre
Jadini Forest
Diani Forex Bureau
Galu Beach
To Chale Island &

N
0 metres 800
0 yards 800

Neptune Paradise Village 15
Nomad Beach 16
Ocean Village Club 17
Pinewood Village 22
Vindigo Cottages 21

Sleeping
Alfajiri Beach Villa 1
Baobab Beach Resort 3
Diani Beachalets 5
Diani Marine Divers Village 7
Diani Reef Beach Resort & Spa 4
Diani Sea Lodge 8
Forest Dream 9
Indian Ocean Beach Club 10
Jadini Beach 2
Leisure Lodge Resort 11
Leopard Beach 12
Neptune Beach Resort 14

Eating
African Pot 1
Ali Barbour's 2
Asin's 11
Forty Thieves 3
Galaxy 4
Hollywood 6
Komba 7
Legend 8
Shan-e-Punjab 10
Sundowner 9
Tropicana 12

Bars & clubs
Shakatak 5

'company' is exchanged, there are many hopeful young men in the area that seek to befriend a European woman in the hope of a passage to Europe.

Sights

It is worth going out to the reef at **low tide** at least once when the very top is exposed to look at the myriad of fish. You'll need to take a boat if you want to go out to the main reef, although you should be able to wade out to the sand bank which is not too far. Of course this depends on the tides. At full moon there are **spring tides** which means high high tides and low low tides, while a fortnight later there will be **neap tides** with low highs and high lows. Windsurfers can go out for longer at neap tides, while those wanting huge waves will do better at high tide.

At the far north of Diani beach just past **Indian Ocean Club**, is the **Kongo Mosque** (also known as the Diani Persian Mosque). It is rather a strange place, very run-down but not really a ruin, that still has some ritual significance. The mosque is believed to date from the 15th century and is the only remaining building from a settlement of the Shirazi people who used to live here. There are a number of entrances and you should be able to push one of the doors open and have a look inside.

Excursions

Jadini Forest ① T040-3203519, www.colobustrust.org, close to the Papillion Beach Bar, Mon-Sat 0800-1700, US$5 entry, US$5 walk, US$7 night walk, is a small patch of the forest that straggles the main beach road and used to cover the whole of this coastal area. This area is good for birding, but especially good for primates. The forest is home to troops of baboon, a large population of vervet monkeys and the endangered Angolan black and white colobus monkey. There are only an estimated 1,800 colobus in Kenya 450 of which are at Diani. A local group the **Colobus Trust** which started in 1997 is devoted to the conservation of these rare primates and their habitat. Many of the primate species of this area are threatened both by traffic on the main coastal road, and by hand-feeding by tourists which encourages anti-social and unnatural behaviour. The **Colobus Trust** works to build aerial bridges, known as 'colobridges' across the roads to prevent traffic casualties, and works to educate tourists against feeding monkeys. Another major problem is that the creatures get electrocuted on the many uninsulated power lines around Diani. The main electricity lines can carry up to 22,000 volts which can be fatal, whilst the domestic power lines, which carry around 240 volts, can severely stun an animal and cause loss of a limb and/or secondary infections. Trees that gain access to the power lines have been cut back so that the monkeys have reduced contact with them. The trust sends a team out weekly to keep the vegetation trimmed back. It has also been involved with rehabilitating vervet monkeys that were kept as pets and re-releasing them back into the wild at Shimba Hills. It has a centre called Colobus Cottage with plenty of information, nature trails, and can give good advice on local wildlife. It also offers a one-hour guided primate walk and a 1½-hour night walk to see bush babies as well as the monkeys.

Shimba Hills National Reserve → *Colour map 2, grid C1.*

This small reserve, 56 km southwest of Mombasa, is very easy to access on a day trip from the coast as it is less than an hour's drive from Diani Beach. The 300 sq km are covered with stands of coastal rainforest, rolling grasslands and scrubland. Due to strong sea breezes, the hills are much cooler than the rest of the coast making it a very pleasant climate. The rainforest itself is totally unspoilt and opens out into rolling downs and gentle hills. Two of Kenya's exquisite orchids are found here.

⁞ The changing face

The appearance of the region around Shimoni and the south coast of Kenya is set to change over the next few years. A Canadian mining company, Tiomin Resources, plan to rip apart the hills of Kwale (an area of natural forest 12 km inland from Shimoni) to extract the valuable titanium ore deposits and then truck it down to Shimoni at the rate of four lorries an hour. Here it will go into a storage depot, which will be built at the expense of acres of prime coastal forest, from where it will be conveyor-belted onto ships. These vessels will be so large that it is believed some of the coral reefs may have to be dynamited in order for the ships to turn around. In 2004 Tiomin Resources signed a 21-year mining license for its Kwale titanium project with the Kenyan government. It is estimated that the Kwale property has a mineral resource of 254 million tonnes, and once in production, the region will produce 330,000 tonnes of ilmenite, 77,000 tonnes of rutile and 37,000 tonnes of zircon during the first six years. This represents 6%, 18% and 3% of global annual output respectively. Both ilmenite and rutile are titanium-bearing minerals used in the production of titanium dioxide pigment and titanium metal. At the time of writing, construction of the plant was due at the end of 2005, with production due to commence by 2007. Whilst the project has obvious benefits for the revenue of the government and will hopefully provide jobs at a local level, it will certainly change the environment around Shimoni and possibly damage some of the coral reefs so there are very mixed feelings about how the new titanium mine will affect the region.

Ins and outs

The main route to Shimba Hills and Mwaluganje is through the small town of Kwale, on the C106, which branches off the main A14 coast road 12 km south of the Likoni ferry. The main gate is 3 km beyond Kwale. The road is well tarred as far as Kwale. It is also possible to enter the park through the Kivunoni (eastern) Gate which is located about 1 km south of the C106 3 km from Kwale. It is possible to take a half-day trip from Mombasa and Diani for around US$35 through one of the tour operators.

Sights

There are a number of Roan antelope, waterbuck, reedbuck, hyena, warthog, giraffe, leopard, baboon and bush pig in the reserve. The altitude and the damp atmosphere also attract countless butterflies and birds around the grassy hills and on the edges of the forest. However, it is famed for being the only place in Kenya where you might see the Sable antelope found in the same habitats as several large herds of buffalo. There are also elephant in the reserve who favour the refreshing fruit of the borassus palm which is abundant here. The best place to see the wildlife is near the spectacular **Sheldrick Falls** and on the **Lango Plains** close to Giriama Point. Picnic sites on either side of the escarpment provide an entrancing view of the Indian Ocean to the east, and on a clear day, the imposing mass of Mount Kilimanjaro rising behind the Taita Hills to the west.

Adjacent is the **Mwaluganje Elephant Sanctuary** set up to provide access for the elephants between the Shimba Hills and the Mwaluganje Forest Reserve. There are approximately 200 elephants, mainly large bulls. Close-range elephant viewing is virtually guaranteed. The sanctuary protects 2,500 ha of the traditional migratory route. The flora ranges from baobab trees on the coast to deciduous forests on the hills and vestigial rainforest along the watercourses. The sanctuary is an innovative concept due to the fact that the local cultures, the Duruma and Digo people, have become involved along with other local landowners, the Kwale County Council, local politicians and the Kenya Wildlife Service, and a fee is payable to the local community from every visitor to the reserve. This has helped to build school classrooms and improved the water supply in the region. You can either visit here on a day or overnight trip arranged with the hotels on the coast.

South of Diani

Chale Island → *Colour map 2, grid C1.*

About 10 km at the southern end of Diani is a small bay and Chale Island, which lies about 600 m offshore. During February and March, giant turtles lay their eggs on the sandy beaches. When they are hatched, the baby turtles are helped back to sea by the local people and staff at the only hotel on the island. This is a popular spot for day trips from Diani – boats take you out for swimming, snorkelling and beach barbecues on the island. There are many coconut plantations in this area.

Gazi → *Colour map 2, grid C1.*

A village at the southern end of Diani, once significantly more important than it is now as it was the district's administrative centre. Here you will see the **House of Sheik Mbaruk bin Rashid**. There are said to be the bodies of eight men and eight women buried in the foundations of the house to give the building strength. He was also notorious for torturing people, and suffocating them on the fumes of burning chillies. In the Mazrui Rebellion of 1895 Mbaruk was seen arming his men with German rifles and flying the German flag. British troops did eventually defeat him and he ended his days in exile in German East Africa (Tanzania). The rather run-down house is now used as a school. It once had a very finely carved door but this has been moved to the Fort Jesus Museum. Ask directions for Gazi as it is not signposted on the main road.

Msambweni → *Colour map 2, grid C1.*

About 50 km south of Likoni is the village of Msambweni which is home to what is one of the best hospitals on the coast as well as a famous leprosarium. The beach is really lovely with coral rag-rock cliffs and there are some ruins in this area that are believed to have been a slave detention camp. **Funzi Island** is located just off the coast from here where there is a luxury lodge.

South Coast

Mombasa
Port Reitz
Likoni
Mwaluganje Elephant Sanctuary
Ngombeni
Kwale
Waa
Shimba Hills National Reserve
Tiwi
Tiwi Beach
Ukunda
Diani Beach
Mwabungu
Galu Beach
Gazi
Gazi Beach
Msambweni
To Tanzania
Indian Ocean
Funzi Island
Shimoni
Wasini Island
♦ Kisite-Mpunguti National Marine Park

N
0 km   5
0 miles   5

Sleeping
Betty's Camp **1**
Chale Island Paradise **2**
Coral Cove Cottages **5**
Funzi Keys **7**
Graceland **4**
Mukurumuji Tented Camp **8**
Mwazaro **9**
Pemba Channel Fishing Club **10**
Sable Bandas **13**
Sand Island Cottages **14**
Shimba Lodge **15**
Shimoni Reef Fishing Lodge **12**
Travellers Mwaluganje Elephant Camp **16**
Travellers Tiwi Beach **17**

A small fishing village whose name means 'Place of the Hole'. This name is derived from the method of entry to the system of **Slave Caves** ⓘ *nominal entry fee (collected directly by the local people to help pay for the dispensary and educate the children)*, to the west of the village. *Shimo* means cave in Kiswahili. The vast network opens directly on to the beach. There are several caves, once joined together and reputed to extend some 5 km inland. Due to siltation, the floor has risen, blocking off access to the further caves, and what you now see is only the main entrance cavern. The next cavern, immediately behind this one, which is now only accessible via a hole in the roof of the cave, has a spring of completely fresh water in it. It is said that the caves were used by slave traders to hide the slaves, before they were sold and shipped out to overseas markets. In the caves there are well-preserved examples of the wooden crates used to transport the slaves. The other story associated with these caves is that they were used as a secret place of refuge by the Digo people during their intermittent battles with various marauding tribes, including the Masai, through the ages. Archaeological findings indicate that these coral caves, with their lovely stalactites, have been inhabited for several centuries. The caves have a thriving population of bats. A torch is required if you want to explore them.

To reach the caves take the path that begins opposite the jetty and walk up through the forest. When you get to the entrance take a ladder down through a hole in the ground. Immediately opposite the entrance to the cave are the remains of the Imperial East Africa Company's old headquarters. It is now unfortunately a ruin.

Kisite Marine National Park → *Colour map 2, grid C1.*

To the far south is this marine park which has superb coral gardens and lots of sea life. It covers 39 sq km on the southernmost part of the Kenyan coastline and is managed and protected by the Kenya Wildlife Service. This is said to be the best snorkelling in Kenya. The protected areas have a high diversity of marine life with fringing reef, channels, islands and offshore reefs. Hard and soft corals are a common feature. Green and Hawksbill turtles and seven species of dolphins have been recorded in the Shimoni complex, and both turtles and dolphins are sighted by visitors virtually on a daily basis. Humpback whales are sighted regularly on their yearly migration in October/November, sometimes as early as July. This stretch of the coastline is also a birdwatchers' paradise. The small islands dotting the coastline have old established trees including baobabs with their thick gnarled trunks. Untroubled by elephants, they dominate the island shelves in abundance. Coral seas of turquoise and dark green stretch away. Mountains rising straight up in the south over the ocean mark the Tanzanian/Kenyan border. Kisite is a flat little marine park, an atoll, with a dead coral shelf in the middle rising up off it like a table. The rest is worn to rough granular sand that is hot and uncomfortable to walk on. Unremarkable on the surface, what is truly amazing is what is in the waters around Kisite. The little convoy of *dhows* string out in a line and drop anchor. The water is pure, warm and turquoise in colour, and is so salt-saturated that it is difficult to swim in initially, as it seems to suspend you. There are thousands of fish, in a dazzling array of sizes, shapes and colours, just below the surface. There are several dive spots here. The reefs are excellent for drift diving. The bottom is a combination of sand flats and reef outgrowths. Sting rays and turtles are commonly seen, as are parrot fish, trumpet fish, bat fish, grouper, Napoleon wrasse, clown fish and Spanish dancers. One of the better reefs is **Nyulli Reef** which lies at 30 m and drops to over 80 m. This reef is spectacularly long and a large quantity of large pelagics as well as reef fish are found here. This is also home to a family of very large groupers up to 150 lbs in size.

There is no shade or protection from the burning sun and wearing a shirt/long sleeved T-shirt whilst snorkelling is a wise precaution. Masks and snorkels are available but fins are not permitted to minimize damage to the reef.

Most people visit the park on a tour. They depart daily from all the hotels along the north coast, Mombasa and Diani Beach. Included is transport, boat tours with snorkelling and lunch at the **Wasini Island Restaurant** (or **Charlie Claw's**). The day begins with collection from the hotels and a transfer to Shimoni. Then guests go snorkelling by *dhow*, or glass-bottomed boats are available for those who do not wish to swim. Lunch at **Charlie Claw's** includes steamed sea crabs in ginger with claws the size of your fist, along with fresh lime and baked coconut rinds for dipping in salt, followed by barbequed fish and rice steamed in coconut, and a fresh fruit platter and sim sim (ginger spiced coffee with balls of sugared sesame seed). This goes down well with cold Kenyan beer, but the wise drink water first. This restaurant has been going for 25 years. The afternoon is spent lazing away on day beds in the restaurant gardens, or there are optional visits to the Wasini Village, the Shimoni Caves or diving. There is not much of a beach on Wasini Island, as it gets covered by the incoming tide. Prices for the full day trip are around US$100 from the north coast and US$90 from the south, although these prices come down depending on the season.

To get to Wasini Island under your own steam either hire a taxi or take a *matatu* to Lunga Lunga and ask to be let off at the turning for Shimoni, which is about 15 km off the main road. From here you will have to hitch. The last *matatu* back to Mombasa leaves between 1500 and 1600. Boats from Shimoni to Wasini Island cost around US$4 per person one way.

Wasini Island → *Colour map 2, grid C1*
Wasini Island falls within the Kisite Marine National Park. It is a wonderful place, 1 km wide and 6 km long, totally undeveloped with no cars, no mains electricity and no running water. There is no reliable freshwater supply on the island, only rainwater. Some of the proceeds of the tourist trade have been used to build large culverts where they can store rainwater. A small village on the island includes the remains of an Arab settlement. There are also the ruins of 18th- and 19th-century houses as well as a pillar tomb with Chinese porcelain insets that have, so far, survived. The beach is worth exploring as you might well find bits of pottery and glass. Also interesting are the dead coral gardens behind the village. They are above the sea although during the spring tide they are covered as they are linked to the sea 30 m below through a series of caverns. Some of the coral formations are said to resemble animal shapes (they call one the elephant).

Lunga Lunga → *Colour map 2, grid C1.*
About 95 km south of Mombasa, Lunga Lunga is the nearest village (5 km) to the border with Tanzania and can be reached by bus from Mombasa. Buses between Mombasa and Dar es Salaam or Tanga go daily in both directions taking about 10 hours to Dar and four hours to Tanga. The border post is reasonably efficient and you can buy visas for both Kenya and Tanzania.

● Sleeping

Hotel prices vary with the season. Low is Apr-Jun; mid is Jul-Nov; high is Dec-Mar.

Tiwi Beach *p223, map p227*
A Tiwi Beach Resort, T040-3202801, www.tiwibeachresort.com. 210 rooms, all with queen size bed and 1 single bed, a/c, TV, wooden floors, arranged in 2-storey blocks with either balcony or patio, 3 restaurants, the Indian one **Shere e Punjab**,

is one of the best on the coast, several bars and cafés, swimming pools, business centre, all watersports can be arranged, full board.
B Travellers Tiwi Beach Hotel, T040-485121, www.travellersbeach.com. Opened in 1997, well designed and in keeping with the local environment. Over 200 a/c rooms, 3 restaurants, 5 bars, 24-hr coffee shop, disco. It has an exceptional swimming pool, 250 m long, connected by channels and slides.

B-C Coral Cove Cottages, T040-3205195, www.coralcove.tiwibeach.com. 9 self-catering bandas that vary in price – the 6 most expensive 2-bedroomed cottages have bathrooms but no a/c, and cost about US$40 per night. The other 4 bandas are cheaper and more basic, with outside toilets and no fans. All are attractively decorated. It is a lovely location, a beautiful white-sand beach, with swaying palm trees in a private cove and is probably the best place here. The 2-bedroomed cottages supplied with a personal cook/house-help/laundry-man at the inclusive rate of US$57 for 4 people per day. Excellent value.

C-D Graceland Hotel, T/F040-3251048, gracelandhotel@myrealbox.com. Under the new management of Yadranka, a Croatian doctor, this is a friendly clean relaxed hotel. Simple but very good rooms – some with a/c, others have fans – all with private shower. Good service. Facilities include internet access, disco, a swimming pool, bar and restaurant serving very fresh locally caught fish.

C-D Sand Island Cottages, T040-3300043, www.sandislandtiwi.com. Quiet and a little remote, 1-to 3-bed self-catering low rise thatched cottages in a grove of palms, 30 m back from the beach, similar set-up to the Maweni cottages above, you can hire a cook and a maid at extra cost.

Diani Beach *p224, map p224*

There are several private cottages and houses that can be rented along the beach: visit www.georgebarbour.com, www.kenya holidayvillas.com, www.kenyasafarihomes. com or www.dianibeach.com.

L Alfajiri Beach Villa, T040-3202630, www.alfajirivillas.com. An exclusive retreat aimed at families or groups, 2 beautiful Italian-owned double-storey thatched villas with wide verandas and balconies. Each has 2 en suite bedrooms with additional rooms under the *makuti* roof for children, vast beds swathed in mosquito nets, rim flow pool almost on the beach. Mediterranean influenced food with olive oils, parma ham and some cheeses flown in weekly from Europe. With 14 staff Alfajiri won the 2002 *Harpers and Queen* magazine award for the private villa providing the best service. The house is owned and hosted by Fabrizio

Molinaro and his wife Marika. They have collected objet d'art from around the world to decorate the villas and Marike is one of Kenya's leading interior designers. Very stylish but at a price, full board rates start from US$500 per person, half for children. Included is a vehicle for excursions and trained nannies for children. Closed Apr-Jul.

L Diani Reef Beach Resort and Spa, T040-3202723, www.dianireef.com. Newly refurbished in 2005, a super luxurious and comfortable hotel with 300 m of beach frontage, all the 300 rooms are a/c with satellite TV, mini bars, and safes. The hotel has a full range of facilities including a craft shop, doctor, 5 bars, 6 restaurants, 2 swimming pools, kids' club, casino and disco, floodlit tennis courts, squash courts, a diving school, golf-putting course, and landscaped lagoons with boating facilities and sun bathing islands. Spa, gym, steam rooms, jet baths, saunas, treatments etc.

L Indian Ocean Beach Club, overlooking the Tiwi River estuary at the northernmost point of Diani Beach, T040-3203730, www.jacarandahotels.com. Moorish-style arched main building with smaller *makuta* thatched-roof buildings in secluded 10-ha grounds with old coconut and baobab trees. 100 rooms, en suite bathrooms, a/c, fans, phones, 3 restaurants, 3 bars including the **Bahari Cover Bar**, reputed to have the best view on Diani Beach. Has a 200-m swimming pool and 3 smaller pools. Tennis, wind-surfing, sailing, snorkelling, scuba diving, glass-bottomed boat trips, deep-sea fishing.

L Leisure Lodge Resort, T040-3203624, www.leisurelodgeresort.com. Over 200 rooms in standard hotel block with balconies or in villas clustered around private pools, many restaurants, casino, several swimming pools, tennis courts, health club, dive school and windsurfing school. The 18-hole, 72 par championship golf course, home to the Diani Beach Masters, is recognized as one of the best golf courses in East Africa.

L Leopard Beach, T040-3202721, www. leopardbeachhotel.com. A popular newly refurbished luxury resort, set amidst 25 acres of lush tropical gardens, 114 standard rooms and 35 superior rooms, most of which have ocean views and private terraces. Buffet restaurant, boutiques, diving, disco and live music, and swimming pool.

L **Shambani Cottages**, www.shambani.com. 6 self-catering cottages under impressive *makuti* thatch, whitewashed interiors and traditional furniture, the rates are weekly and vary widely from US$190-1,400 depending on the size of the cottage and the season, and include cleaning service and laundry. There is a swimming pool set in mature gardens.

A **Baobab Beach Resort**, T040-3202623, www.baobab-beach-resort.com, on the cliff at the southern end (to get to the beach you have to climb down the steep steps). A large resort popular with Germans, 79 standard rooms in the main block and another 70 rooms in bungalows in the gardens, all a/c. Swimming pool, open-air disco, bars and restaurants, TV lounge, fitness centre, loads of activities from bicycle hire to windsurfing.

A **Forest Dream**, near Baobab Beach Resort, T040-3203224, www.forestdreamcottages. com. 7 large 5- to 6-bedroomed cottages with kitchen, cook and cleaner, ideal for groups and families of between 4-12 people, some have jacuzzis and a/c, all set in established gardens and each cottage is quite private, though they are some walk from the beach, very hi-tec swimming pool with underwater music, massage jets, a nice waterslide and a waterfall which cascades from a huge rock.

A **Neptune Beach Resort**, T040-3203061, www.neptunehotels.com. Together with its sister hotel (below) these are the most southerly of the large hotels, more than 2 km south of **Baobab Beach Resort** and actually on Galu Beach. 78 newly refurbished en suite rooms with balconies, set in attractive large gardens, all-inclusive watersports. Similar facilities as Neptune below.

A **Neptune Paradise Village**, T040-3203061, www.neptunehotels.com. 259 rooms set in 25 acres, organized in 2-storey cottages with 4 rooms in each, 2 restaurants serving buffet meals and 2 à la carte restaurants, several bars, rates include all meals. Watersports available, and there's a kiddie's club and a very large swimming pool.

A **Ocean Village Club**, T040-3202188, www.paladien.com. One of the smaller hotels with 69 a/c en suite rooms situated amidst a luxurious rainforest garden, each has its own private terrace overlooking the gardens to the ocean beyond, 2 restaurants, 1 serving buffet meals the other seafood, bars, boutique. Part of a French hotel group.

A-C **Nomad Beach Hotel**, T040-3202155, www.nomadhotel.tripod.com. Small family owned hotel with 21 bandas and cottages, price includes breakfast, good value and probably one of the cheapest of the resorts to stay on Diani. There is a very good seafood restaurant here and a relaxed low key bar that does a good and popular Sunday lunch with a live band (see under Eating). Watersports including good diving facilities are available.

B **Diani Marine Divers Village**, just to the north of **Forty Thieves restaurant**, T040-3202367, www.dianimarine.de. The rooms are spacious and airy, with large Swahili style beds with mosquito nets and overhead fans. The Village offers B&B and in the vicinity there are many restaurants. The dive centre is based here and most people stay on a dive package, see Activities and tours.

B **Diani Sea Lodge**, T040-322114. dianisea@ africaonline.co.ke. A/c self-catering cottages ideal for families and popular with expats. They vary in size and price, but you hire the cottage and can get in as many people as you want. They all have a balcony and are simple but very pleasant and offer excellent value. On offer is a special pool for children as well as 2 bars, boutiques, a health and fitness centre, a floodlit tennis court, mini golf, table tennis and a surf and diving school. (1 km north is **Diani Sea Resort** owned by the same group – same contact numbers – with similar facilities but apartments rather than cottages.)

B **Pinewood Village**, T/F040-3203131, www. pinewood-village.com. Good accommodation in cottages with en suite bathrooms, lounge, dining area and kitchen, on Galu Beach, almost as far south as Chale Island and therefore at one of the quietest stretches of beach. Each cottage has a cook, the guests provide the food, though rates can include breakfast if you so wish and there is an additional restaurant and bar. Facilities include attractive swimming pool, a dive base, tennis court and shop.

● *For an explanation of sleeping and eating price codes used in this guide, see inside the*
● *front cover. Other relevant information is found in Essentials, see pages 34-38.*

C-D Vindigo Cottages, T040-3202192, www.navtrader.com/vindigo. 7 self-catering bandas, sleeping 2-8 people work out very cheap if shared by a family or group, the banda sleeping 8 is only US$55 a night. All of the cottages are basically equipped with bed linen, mosquito nets, crockery, cutlery and saucepans but no towels. Set in 4 ha of gardens, a little way away from any other development, giving the cottages a more secluded feel than many other places in Diani. **C-E Diani Beachalets**, T040-3202220, www.dianibeachalets.com. A range of chalets from fully equipped houses with bathrooms and kitchens suitable for families or groups, to cheap backpackers' bandas with shared facilities, the larger units overlook the beach. Tennis court but no pool, restaurant or shop so you will have to stock up before you get here, although there is a supermarket in walking distance, fishermen come round in the mornings with fresh seafood and you can buy cold beers at reception. This is one of the most affordable options on the south coast and accommodation can work out as little as US$7 each sharing.

Shimba Hills National Reserve *p225*
L Shimba Lodge, reservations **Aberdare Safari Hotels**, Nairobi, T020-4452095, aberdaresafarihotels.com. Well-designed timber lodge overlooking a waterhole illuminated at night for viewing, children under 7 are not allowed. A boardwalk has been constructed at tree level giving good views of the forest canopy and you can walk to the Sheldrick's Falls where there is a natural pool for swimming. The rooms are comfortable with small verandas, the dining room is open air, and there is a pleasant bar. Rates are in the region of US$180 per person.
A Travellers Mwalumanje Elephant Camp, Mombasa, T041-485121, travellersshtl@swiftmombasa.com. Luxury tented accommodation in the Elephant Sanctuary, 20 tents, each with 2 beds, though there is room for a third bed to be added, bathroom and private veranda with views over the traditional elephant trail. Rates include escorted game drives and all meals.
A-C Mukurumuji Tented Camp, reservations **Diani House Hotel**, T040-3203487, www.dianihouse.com. The camp is near a village called Majimboni just outside the

southeast corner of the Shimba Hills National Reserve. The best access is via Ukunda, but it can also be accessed through Kidongo gate of the Shimba Hills National Reserve. 4 traditional comfortable double tents and 1 honeymoon suite, each covered with palm thatch with its own veranda and flush toilets and camp showers. Full-board, half-board, B&B or self-catering.
E Sable Bandas, Kenya Wildlife Service, Nairobi, T020-600800, www.kws.org, at a site 3 km from the main gate to the reserve. 4 bandas with 2 double beds in each, shared showers and toliets, solar power, shared kitchen with gas cooker and tap (not drinking) water. Drinking water, firewood and food must be brought, US$15 per person.

Camping
E At the banda site, well maintained and peaceful with excellent views over the surrounding forested areas. KWS as above.

Chale Island *p227, map p227*
L Chale Island Paradise, T040-3203235, www.chaleislandparadise.com. Luxury all-inclusive resort, 55 rooms centered around a white sandy beach, comprising roomy and elegant tented bungalows, or apartments and penthouses in round multi-storey blocks topped with thatch, all furnished with African/Arabic antiques. 2 restaurants offer local and international cuisine, and a teppanyaki Japanese restaurant. Diving and deep-sea fishing and there's a swimming pool.
L Funzi Keys, Funzi Island, south of Msambweni, T0722-204946 (mob), www.thefunzikeys.com. Very exclusive tented camp situated on a beautifully secluded island, furnished to a very high standard, 10 spacious cottages set along the high-water line and constructed of stone and thatch with large netted windows and hand-carved king-sized 4-poster beds, a perfect honeymoon venue. Facilities for all watersports are available and included in the price, as are all meals, drinks (except champagne) and transport. Rates are US$375-575 per person depending on season. Closed Apr-Jul.

Shimoni *p228, map p227*
L Pemba Channel Fishing Club, T0722-205020 (mob), www.pembachannel.com. Simple white bandas set in tropical gardens,

with many trees indigenous to the Shimoni area. Each banda has a small veranda – all with sea views. The Clubhouse has an attractive, homely lounge filled with wicker sofas and overstuffed cushions, marlin trophies and fishing photos adorn the walls. There is a great camaraderie amongst the fishermen around the very 'Hemingway-esque' bar at the end of the day. The fishing club has a reputation as Africa's premier marlin destination and has attracted many illustrious guests including Billy Pate, one of the world's top fly fisherman and holder of 110 fly records, Jeremy Paxman, BBC Newsnight presenter, and Matt Hayes, the UK's most popular fishing TV presenter. Closed Apr-Jun.

L Shimoni Reef Fishing Lodge, beyond Funzi Beach, reservations, Mombasa, T041-471771, www.oneearthsafaris.com. Wonderful location, overlooking Wasini Island, high standards catering almost exclusively to keen anglers, 14 open plan cottages with ocean views and private verandas, each is on 2 levels and accommodates 4 people. There is a sea water swimming pool made up of multi levels which is good for kids, and diving tuition. Open-air terrace restaurant overlooking the ocean, seafood a speciality, fishing, diving and snorkelling on offer.

A Betty's Camp, near the jetty, T040-52027, www.bettys-camp.com. Choose between tented rooms with own shower / toilet or en suite rooms within the main house, can accommodate 10-12 people in total, swimming pool, dining room in the house, poolside terrace restaurant and bar open to all with a good range of seafood, can arrange fishing.

B-C Mwazaro, T0722-711476 (mob), www. keniabeach.com. About 8 km north of Shimoni, there is a sign to Mwazaro Beach, turn right there and the camp is another 1 km. Run by a friendly German man Hans, accommodation is in either thatched bandas on the beach with sand floors and lit by hurricane lamps, or en suite rooms with electricity. Restaurant serving excellent affordable food, there's a comfy lounge and bar where you can play chess or backgammon, and tea is served all day. A guide will take you on an interactive tour to a local fishing village.

❶ Eating

Diani Beach p224, map p224
Apart from the hotel restaurants there are a number of others. All restaurants do very good fish and seafood and you can rely on it being very fresh. Many of the hotels do special buffet lunches and dinners and these are usually very good value.

♥♥♥ Ali Barbour's, by Diani Sea Lodge, T040-3202033. One of the most popular, you can either eat in the open air or else in a sort of underground cave that has various chambers that go 10 m below ground level, a stone floor has been fitted and a sliding roof that comes across if the weather is bad, it does excellent seafood as well as French food. If staying on Diani Beach they will provide free transport. A unique experience. Open daily from 1900.

♥♥♥ Forty Thieves, next door to Ali Barbour's, T040-3203003. Lively bar and restaurant serving good food and snacks, pool tables, live entertainment and satellite TV. A popular night spot and meeting place for many of the local residents, with discos on Wed, Fri and Sat nights. Also good live music and buffet lunch on a Sun. Open daily from 1000.

♥♥♥ Nomads Seafood Restaurant, at Nomads Beach Hotel, T040-3202155. Right on the beach on wooden decks and under canvas with good service and atmosphere. Probably one of the best restaurants on Diani, it does a very popular Sunday buffet lunch with live music, which is good value. Pizzas, excellent and imaginative pastas and risottos, seafood and grills.

♥♥♥ Shan-e-Punjab, Diani Complex, opposite Diani Reef Hotel, T040-3202116. Good-value Indian dishes, specializes in Punjab and tandoori cuisine, tikka and masala with a full range of seafood, more expensive continental dishes available, open-air beer garden and cocktail menu, provides free transport from the hotels, open daily 1000-midnight.

♥ Asin's, Diani Bazaar, Beach Rd, T040-3204075. Informal restaurant and bar under a conical thatched roof, plus rooftop terrace, varied menu including burgers, pizzas, pastas, steaks and seafood and some Japanese teppanyaki dishes, also a supermarket next door with a good selection of wines and spirits. Both open daily 0800-2300.

¶¶ **Galaxy**, opposite **Diani Reef Hotel**, T040-3202529. Tasty Chinese cuisine, small menu but quality items such as grilled lobster, roast duck, and ginger crab, open daily for lunch and dinner.

¶¶ **Legend**, T040-3202554. Large complex near the post office, originally with casino, but now pared down to restaurant, bar and disco, also with vast swimming pool. Pianist or floor shows accompany the food, rotisserie and ice-cream parlour in the landscaped grounds.

¶¶ **Sundowner**, a 5-min walk from the **Diani Beach Chalets**, T040-3202138. Serves excellent Kenyan food and local beers at low prices, one of the best-value places to eat, curries, grilled and fried fish, very good English breakfasts, sometimes has seafood such as lobster, simple decor in outside thatched bar and restaurant but nice atmosphere. Recommended.

¶¶ **Tropicana**, Diani Shopping Centre, T040-3202303. Offers a small selection of seafood, pizza, friendly bar, adjacent to the car park is also a delicatessen and supermarket selling pasta from Italy, fresh bread and home-cooked pastries.

¶ **African Pot**, T040-3203890, in front of **Coral Beach Cottages**, there is another branch at the Sanjay Building in Ukunda. Good value, tasty local food, served in the traditional way, charcoaled meat, masala curries, chipati, matoke, ugali, pilau rice. Daily 1030-2400.

¶ **Hollywood**, T040-3202562, Ukunda opposite the **Total** petrol station. Tasty Kenyan food at good prices, chicken, fish and chips and the like, fresh juices.

¶ **Komba**, T040-3203111. Open-air restaurant serving basic Swahili dishes with good fresh fish. Later on in the evening it develops into a disco and usually has quite a lively crowd. Closed Mon.

◑ Bars and clubs

Diani Beach p224, map p224
Almost all the hotels have nightclubs which are of varying quality. Along the Diani Beach Rd there are also a number of discos not run by hotels. These include **Shakatak**, www.shakatak-kenya.com, on the opposite side of the road and just south of Ali Barbour's, German-run with a restaurant and beer garden, entrance fee US$2. This is very popular, expect to queue to get in, large disco and floor shows that start daily at 2100, prostitutes abound but it's lots of fun. The website (which is in German) very generously explains that in Kenya, men over 40 go to nightclubs! They make their ice from mineral water and there are plenty of taxis outside.

Casablanca, located at the very southern end of Diani Beach Rd, run by the **Neptune Paradise Hotel**, shuttle bus will pick up guests at certain times and bus stops, entrance fee US$1.

◒ Shopping

Diani Beach p224, map p224
Curios
Millennium Handicraft and Cultural Centre, on the road between Ukunda and the beach road, just south of Ukunda village. A co-operative with 5 handicraft groups, wood carvings, kionda baskets, soapstone and Masai beadwork, you can watch the artists at work, traditional dancing is held at 1100, 1230, 1430 and 1600, there are also occasional football matches in the afternoon. Open daily, transport can be arranged from the hotels.

Food
If you are self-catering it is worth buying most of your supplies in Mombasa where it is cheaper. Try the large **Nakumatt Supermarket** there just near the ferry – it sells everything imaginable. There are a number of places closer to the beach. Firstly there is the small village of Ukunda which is on the main road close to the Diani turn-off. You can get most things here. Off the main road, on the road with all the hotels, are now four shopping centres. Opposite Diani Reef Grand Hotel is **Diani Complex**, the smallest of the 4. **Barclays Bank Shopping Centre** is next to Barclays Bank. **Diani Shopping Centre** and **Diani Beach Shopping Centre** are close to each other to the north of Diani Beach post office. Each shopping centre has a supermarket and several souvenir shops and boutiques. **Muthaiga Mini Market** in Diani Shopping Centre is a very well-stocked supermarket. If you are staying in self-catering accommodation they can arrange to have groceries ready for when you arrive,

T040-3203056, mmm@dianibeach.com.
For fresh fruit, vegetables and fish you will be able to buy off the vendors who come round all the self-catering places with their stock on their bicycles.

▲ Activities and tours

Diani Beach *p224, map p224*
Many of the hotels will help organize *dhow* trips, safaris and diving. Kite surfing along the 12-km Diani Beach is the latest craze on the Kenyan coast. For more information visit www.kitebeachkenya.com.

Deep-sea fishing
Blue Marlin Fishing Club, to the south of the beach close to the Neptune hotels, T040-3203478, www.bluemarlinfishingclub.com.
Nomad Boats, T040-3202156, nomad@ africaonline.co.ke. Peter Hutchence has been involved in big game fishing since 1968, and is also a renowned boat builder. His company is a member of the International Game Fish Association, and the Kenya Association of Sea Angling clubs, expect to pay in the region US$275-350 a day for a boat that carries 5-6 people, including crew and all fishing gear.

Golf
Leisure Lodge, T040-3202620, www.golfing inkenya.com, has an 18-hole championship course open to all guests of Diani Beach hotels and resorts. Expect to pay in the region of US$50 for 18 holes with club hire. There's a club bar and restaurant, lessons available in English, German or Italian, the par 72 course has 85 bunkers and a large lake, and golfers may spot monkeys around the course. To play the course men must have a handicap of at least 28 and ladies 36, or a playing certificate from a recognized club. Beginners are welcome on the driving range at any time. The course is home to the Diani Beach Masters.

Tour operators
There are many tour agencies at Diani Beach, mainly in and around the shopping centres. A few of these specialize in *dhow* trips.
Dolphin Dhow, Barclays Shopping Centre, T040-3202144, www.dolphindhow.com. Full day trip to Kisiti Marine Park and to the slave

caves at Shimoni (see below). There is a 95% success rate of spotting dolphins, and it is possible to get into the water with them, although not too close. Also a 2-day safari to the Shimba Hills, which includes canoeing in mangrove forests in search of crocodiles.
Dolphin Express, Diani Shopping Centre, T040-3202604, www.seahorsesafaris.co.uk. Offers boat trips to the Kisite Marine Park.
Funzi Sea Adventures, T040-3202044, funzicamp@africaonline.co.ke. Organizes trips to Funzi Island and around Funzi Bay including food and chilled drinks.
Kinazini Funzi Dhow Safaris, Diani Shopping Centre, T040-3203221. Day-long trips stop at Funzi Island to see a fishing village, snorkelling or swimming off a sand-bar, and then an afternoon on Kinazini Island, including lunch.
Malibu Tours & Safaris, Diani Shopping Centre, T040-3203164. A large fleet of taxis and other vehicles, can arrange day trips and safaris.
Pilli Pipa Dhow Safaris, T/F040-3202401, www.pillipipa.com. All-inclusive day trip, snorkelling or scuba diving in Kisite Marine Park, dinner at Wasini Island, US$90, pick-ups from all the hotels. Also offers diving, PADI Open Water Course from US$280, individual dives from US$30.

Tour to Kisite Marine National Park
This excursion is offered by **Dolphin Express**, Diani Shopping Centre, T040-3202604, www.seahorsesafaris.co.uk. **Pilla Pipa**, T040-3202401, www.pillipipa.com. **Wasini Ndogo Econotour**, T040-3202331, www.wasini-island.com.

Watersports
Aqualand, Pinewood Village, T0733-787336 (mob), www.southerncrossscuba.com. Watersports centre at Galu Beach offering kite and windsurfing courses, sailing, kayaking, banana boats, snorkelling, very professional and a whole range of activities.
Baracuda Diving, dive centre at Tiwi Beach Resort and booking office at the Diani Shopping Centre with Malibu Tours and Safaris, www.baracudadiving.com. Organizes all dives and courses and kite surfing, will pick up from any hotel.
Diani Marine, T040-3202367, www.diani marine.com. Several dive packages including

PADI Open Water course charged in euros, €490. Also has a unique 'bubble maker', which is a special pool for introductory dives for children over 8. Clients stay in the Diver's Village (see under Sleeping).

Diving The Crab, at Nomad Beach Hotel, T040-3203400, www.divingthecrab.com. Established operator with over 20 years' experience on the Kenya coast with a very comprehensive website, has over 150 sets of dive equipment and cylinders, 8 custom-built dive boats, and 16 PADI instructors.

H2O Extreme, offices at **Leisure Lodge** and **Nomad's Beach Hotel**, T0721-495876 (mob), www.h2o-extreme.com. Windsurfing, pedalos, kayaking and kite surfing.

Ocean Diving and Safaris, T040-3203379, oceandive@africaonline.co.ke. A Swiss company with dive bases at most of the larger hotels, PADI courses and dives in English, German and French, day trips to the attractions along the coast.

Shimoni *p228, map p227*
All the lodges can arrange fishing and diving. **Sea Adventures**, T040-52204, www.bigame. com, is run by experienced skippers Pat and Simon Hemphill. It offers deep-sea fishing charters into the Pemba Channel plus 4- to 8-day safaris to Pemba Island for small groups of up to 4 people. It also takes children over 8 years old and Simon's son and daughter both caught their first marlin under the age of 11.

⊖ Transport

Diani Beach *p224, map p224*
Most of the hotels at Diani will collect you from the airport or train station for a charge of around US$25.

Air
A small airfield at Ukunda is used for small planes – usually charters for safaris.

Bus and *matatus*
Matatus run frequently from Likoni to the south coast. For **Tiwi Beach** ask to be dropped off at its turn-off. It is about 3 km from the main road to the beach and unless there is a fairly big group of you then it is advisable to get a taxi or wait for a lift as there have been several muggings on

people walking down this road. It is not worth the risk of going alone. Taxis are available on the junction at the main road, and if there is not one there you should not have to wait too long.

For **Diani** by *matatu* you have to change at Ukunda village. The fare from Likoni to **Ukunda** costs US$0.60 and from from Ukunda to Diani US$0.20. There is also a large fleet of brightly coloured tuk tuks operating between Ukunda and all along the beach road that you simply flag down, if the drivers themselves do not drive right up to you. These cost little more than a US$1 for any journey and take up to 3 people. There used to be a number of places along the beach to hire cars, but the tuk tuks have replaced the need for car hire. Rather amusingly the Diani tuk tuks have wobbly arms and hands that wave at you as they drive along and some even have giant hats on their roofs!

Car
By car, take the Likoni Ferry from Mombasa Island. From Likoni drive south on the A14, the main Kenya-Tanzania coastal road. All the turnings off are well signposted. For Diani, go as far as Ukunda village (about 22 km) where there is the turning off to the smaller road that runs along Diani beach. At the T-junction, some hotels are to the left, while all the others are to the right.
Hire from: **Glory Car Hire**, Diani Beach Shopping Centre, T040-3203076, www.glorycarhire.com. Saloon cars start from US$40 per day, plus US$0.20 per km. Also can arrange motorbikes and bicycles.

⊕ Directory

Diani Beach *p224, map p224*
Banks Kenya Commercial Bank, main road in Ukunda, **Barclays Bank of Kenya**, Diani Beach, at the head of the road to Ukunda, ATM. Diani Forex Bureau, in a white building near Diani Beachalets. **Internet** Good but expensive café in the Barclays Bank Shopping Centre and many of the hotels offer access. **Medical services** Diani Beach Hospital, south of Diani Complex Shopping Centre, T040-3202435, www. dianibeachhosoital.com. South End Pharmacy, Diani Beach Shopping Centre, T040-3203354.

North coast

There is a whole string of beaches along the north coast, Nyali, Kenyatta, Bamburi, and Shanzu, with lots of hotels on the seashore immediately north of Mombasa. North of Mtwapa Creek are Kikambala and Vipingo beaches. The major attractions of Watamu Marine Park, Malindi and Lamu are further north. At these latter places there is much more choice for the budget traveller and anyone who wants to avoid the package tours. There are major historical sites at Kilifi, Malindi and Lamu. The north coast is also the location of the Malindi Marine Biosphere Reserve. This strip along the coast is 30 km long and 5 km wide and was gazetted in 1968, and covers an area of 213 sq km. It lies about 80 km north of Mombasa, and includes the Malindi Marine Park, the Watamu Marine Park and Mida Creek. The vegetation includes mangrove, palms, marine plants and various forms of algae that are home to crabs, corals, molluscs, cowrie and marine worms. Coral viewing is popular here, as are boat trips and watersports.
▸▸ For Sleeping, Eating and other listings, see pages 252-260.

Mombasa to Kilifi

Mamba Village and around
→ Colour map 2, grid C2.
Mamba Village is a **Crocodile Farm** ① adult non-resident US$6, feeding is at 1700, a habitat for over 10,000 crocodiles of all ages and sizes from newborns to huge fully grown adults. A film explains some of the conservation efforts as well as the financial side of the venture. You can go for camel and horse rides here around the village and on the beach and it is a day trip in a pleasant setting that children in particular will enjoy, though the display of 'deformed' crocodiles is not a pleasant sight. There is also a restaurant serving, among other dishes, crocodile meat. It is open all day during the week and on Saturday afternoons. A **Botanical Garden** and **Aquarium** has been added to Mamba Village.

Across the road from the crocodile farm is the 18-hole **Nyali Golf and Country Club**, T041-471589. Monty Lowry was the golfer behind the course's design. Some 160 acres of land were set aside for its construction, and in 1956 the first nine holes were completed, with

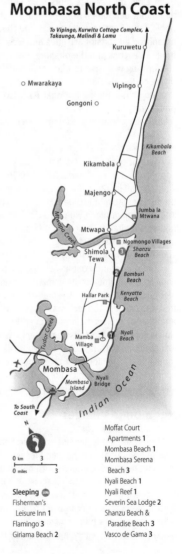

Mombasa North Coast

To Vipingo, Kurwitu Cottage Complex, Takaunga, Malindi & Lamu

Kuruwetu

Mwarakaya

Vipingo

Gongoni

Kikambala Beach

Kikambala

Majengo

Jumba la Mtwana

Mtwapa

Ngomongo Villages

Shimola Tewa

Shanzu Beach

Bamburi Beach

Hallar Park

Kenyatta Beach

Mamba Village

Nyali Beach

Mombasa

Nyali Bridge

Mombasa Island

To South Coast

Indian Ocean

0 km 3
0 miles 3

Sleeping 🛏
Fisherman's
  Leisure Inn 1
Flamingo 3
Giriama Beach 2

Moffat Court
  Apartments 1
Mombasa Beach 1
Mombasa Serena
  Beach 3
Nyali Beach 1
Nyali Reef 1
Severin Sea Lodge 2
Shanzu Beach &
  Paradise Beach 3
Vasco de Gama 3

The coast North coast

the second nine completed in 1980. This particular course is said to be challenging as the winds influence playing conditions. There is a branch of the **Minar Restaurant** here, a very good chain for superb north Indian food.

Further north along the main road is the **Bombolulu Workshops and Cultural Centre** ① *T041-471704, www.apdkbombolulu.com, Mon-Sat, 0800-1700, the shop stays open until 1800, US$5,* where you might want to do some souvenir shopping. Founded in 1969, the crafts are produced by a team of 150 local handicapped people and are generally of reasonable quality and good value. A cultural centre, demonstrating traditional dance, music and theatre, was added in 1994. You can do a tour of the workshops and Swahili food is available in the Ziga restaurant.

Nyali and Bamburi beaches → *Phone code: 041. Colour map 2, grid C2.*
Nyali and Bamburi beaches are well developed and there are lots of hotels. Most of them cater for package tours from Europe and usually each hotel caters for one nationality or another. None of them are cheap. All have facilities such as swimming pools, tennis courts, watersports and they tend to look after their guests very well, organizing all sorts of activities and trips. Here the coast is lined with pristine palm fringed beaches and the offshore reefs. Both outer and inner reef walls offer world class diving with spectacular coral gardens and drop offs, and Kenya's best wreck diving on the *MV Dania*.

Mombasa Marine National Park (10 sq km) was established in 1986 for the protection of the area's coral reefs. It can be accessed by snorkelling trips from the resorts along Nyali and Bamburi beaches and there are also good diving sites.

Hallar Park
① *T041-5485901, www.baobabfarm.com. The trail is open Mon-Fri 1000-1800, Sat 1000-1700, Sun 1200-1700. Adults US$6, children US$4.*
There are all manner of things to do in this 'Baobab Adventure': there is a fish farm producing tilapia, a luxuriant palm garden, 3.6-km forest trails with exercise points and equipment along which you can either walk, jog or cycle, a feeding centre for Rothschild giraffes, a crocodile farm and a butterfly house. There are also various antelope, monkeys, wart hog, buffalo and lots of different birds reared on the farm, some of which find their way in time on to the menu in the **Whistling Pines** restaurant.

The park started out life as the Bamburi cement factory which began quarrying coral to make lime for the cement around Mombasa in the 1950s. When quarrying stopped in 1971 an effort was made to reclaim the land by reafforestation and a nature trail was created. The reclamation scheme was ahead of its time and it attracted the attention of ecologists from all over the world. The nature park has been renamed Hallar Park after the Swiss agronomist who turned the lunar quarry landscape into luxuriant tropical forest. Part of the process included the introduction of hundreds of thousands of millipedes that helped convert the infertile sand into soil, able to support the forest in which the centre is now situated. Despite this, the whole area is still dominated by the Simbarite Ltd Quarry.

Ngomongo Villages
① *www.ngomongo.com.*
Set in 6½ ha of a reclaimed quarry in Shanzu, this might be described as a theme park of traditional rural Kenyan lifestyles. There are 10 villages, one for each of the tribes represented, complete with hut, cultivated crops, domestic and wild animals, village witch doctor and villagers. Walk around the site to see anything from subsistence farming methods to Akamba wood carving. There is an emphasis on participation, thus you can plant a tree or try many of the activities yourself, such as maize pounding or harpoon fishing whilst trying to balance on a raft. There is also a market selling jewellery and other ethnic items. **Kienyenji Restaurant**, built in

On the sea bed

The 80-m ship *MV Dania* spent 45 years plying the waters off the African coast, mainly as a live cattle transporter. In 2002 her life on the waves ended as she was sunk below the ocean just north of Mombasa. But the *Dania* has a new life as one of Africa's finest wreck dives and Mombasa's newest reefs, and the cattle pens and cabins already have become home to all kinds of sea life. The ship now lies in around 30 m of water just off Bamburi Beach and when she was sunk landed perfectly upright. She was fully prepared for sinking and had her engines removed and hull cleaned to negate any environmental impact. The interior was fully cleared for safe penetration by divers, and all potentially dangerous objects, such as wiring and doors were removed, as have all but three of the original brass portholes, allowing divers and marine life to move freely in and out of the control room and the hull with ease. Many artificial reefs have been created around the world from wrecks; some as a result of natural disaster and some, as in Dania's case, intentionally. A variety of materials, ranging from military tanks to naval ships, have been used and over the years, extensive research has been carried out to monitor and quantify the success of these artificial reefs.

The result has been that artificial reefs develop into thriving coral communities, almost indistinguishable from their natural counterparts. The solid structure that an artificial reef provides facilitates the attachment of algae, sponges, benthic organisms and gorgonia to its surface, organisms that would otherwise float around aimlessly, which are vital for coral production. Over time the vessel slowly transforms into a functioning reef; coral is produced, sea turtles and pelagic fish seek refuge amongst the protective overhangs, and as the reef matures it attracts larger sharks, groupers and moray eels. Artificial reefs also enhance the development of rare coral species that are not often found in natural reefs. In addition to the environmental relief that artificial reefs bring, coral reefs, both natural and artificial, are also taking on an increasingly important role in supplying compounds for use in medicines. AZT is used in the treatment of HIV-infected patients and its chemical composition is derived from that of a Caribbean reef sponge. Furthermore 50% of all new cancer drug research is conducted upon marine organisms.

With thanks to Bruce Phillips from Buccaneer Diving, www.buccaneer diving.com.

traditional style, serves a range of African dishes and you can sample the local beer. It has a different tribal theme each night (currently Luo on Wednesday, Kikuyu on Friday, Mijikenda on Saturday and Masai on Sunday), finished off by a display of traditional African music and dance. This won an award from the United Nations Education Programme in 2001. Highly recommended.

Mtwapa and Shanzu Beach

Mtwapa is a small, bustling, chaotic and extremely friendly town, and is the main service point for Shanzu Beach. The main settlement is just north of the creek, which is busy with boats serving the big-game fishing industry. The beach itself is sheltered and bordered by palms and glass-bottomed boat rides out to the reefs are on offer. There are a number of resorts, most interlinked with one another so guests can use all the facilities.

Jumba la Mtwana

ⓘ *0800-1800, US$4. You can buy a short guidebook to the site or hire a guide.*

About 13 km from Mombasa is this national monument, north of the Mtwapa Creek. The name means the 'house of the slave' and may have been a slave-trading settlement in the 15th century, although it was not mentioned in this capacity in either Arab or Portuguese sources. It is a lovely setting, close to the beach with shade provided by baobabs. To reach the site ask to be dropped off at the sign about a kilometre beyond Mtwapa Bridge and from there it is a walk of about 3 km. However, you will probably be offered a lift as you walk down the track. Many of the houses have been rebuilt and undergone frequent changes and it has been suggested that Jumba la Mtwana could have been a meeting place for pilgrims on their way to Mecca. The site is one of Kenya's least-known sites and has only fairly recently been excavated. It is now run by the National Museums of Kenya. Within the site, which is spread over several hectares, there are three mosques, a number of tombs and eight houses. You will notice that architecturally they look little different from the houses of today in the area. This is due to it being a successful design so no need to change. The people appear to have been very concerned with ablutions for there are many remains showing evidence of cisterns, water jars, latrines and other washing and toilet facilities. Building with coral rag (broken pieces of coral) was something reserved for the more privileged members of the community, and it is their houses that have survived. Those that belonged to the poorer people would have been built of mud and thatch.

Kilifi → *Phone code: 041. Colour map 2, grid C2.*

The town of Kilifi is situated to the north of the Kilifi Creek, 60 km north of Mombasa, while Mnarani village is to the south. In the time of the Portuguese, the main town was located to the south of the creek at Mnarani. This popular boating and sailing centre is in an absolutely glorious location – the shore slopes steeply down to the water's edge and the view from the new bridge is spectacular. Until 1991 you had to cross the creek by ferry; a bridge, complete with street lights, has now been built with Japanese funding. The town has an interesting mix of people with quite a number of resident expatriates. The main industry in the town is the cashew nut factory which employs about 1,500 people. To the south there are the Mnarani Ruins. It is an easy-going town with an attractive beach, untroubled by the hassle associated with some of the beaches closer to Mombasa.

Mnarani Ruins ⓘ *0800-1800, US$3,* were first excavated in the 1950s but renewed interest in the site has led the British Institute in Eastern Africa to work here again. It was the place of one of the ancient Swahili city-states that are found along this coast. It is believed that the town was inhabited from the latter half of the 14th century until about the early 17th century, when it was ransacked and destroyed by a group of Galla tribesmen. The inhabitants of the town are thought to have locked themselves into the Great Mosque as they were attacked.

Kilifi

To Malindi
Kobil
Masjid-ul-Noor
Kaya Gardens
Agip
Kenya Commercial
Top-Life Gardens
Coast Rd
To 2
Old Ferry
Jetty
Mnarani Ruins
Kilifi Creek
Old Ferry Rd
Kitoka Ruins
To Bridge Toll Booth & Mombasa

N

0 metres 500
0 yards 500

Sleeping
Dhows Inn **3**

Kilifi Bay Beach Resort **2**
Mnarani Club **6**
Seahorse **7**

Eating
Boat Yard **1**

The ruins include one of the deepest wells (70 m) along the coast, two mosques, part of the town wall and city gates and a group of tombs including a pillar tomb decorated with engravings of a wealthy sharif. Note particularly the tomb of the doctor that is easily the most ornate. At the ruins of the larger or **Great Mosque** can be seen the *mihrab* (which points towards Mecca) surrounded by carved inscriptions. There are many niches in the walls. To the left of the entrance, the smaller mosque is believed to date from the 16th century. There is a huge baobab tree nearby with a circumference of over 15 m. The ruins are best known for the inscriptions carved into them – many of them remaining untranslated. However, in general they are much smaller and less impressive than the ones at Gedi.

To get to the ruins, turn left off the main road to the south of the creek (signposted Mnarani Ruins) by the toll booth and go through Mnarani village. Turn right when you reach the tarmaced road and stop when you can see the creek. There is a signposted path to the left, and the ruins are a few hundred metres down this path and then a climb of about 100 steps. You also get a wonderful view of the creek from the ruins.

About 3 km south of Kilifi is the smaller site of **Kitoka**, where the ruins include a small mosque and a few houses.

Arabuko Sokoke Forest Reserve → *Colour map 2, grid C2.*

① *T042-32462, sokoke@africaonline.co.ke, 0630-1800, US$10.*
Don't expect tropical rainforest as you approach the Arabuko Sokoke Forest Reserve – from the road the only discernible difference is that the scrub disappears and the trees are noticeably closer together. The forest runs for about 40 km north from Kilifi and is 20 km wide at its widest point. It is home to many species of rare birds, and is the most important bird conservation project in Kenya.

Clarke's weaver is endemic to this area, and the 16-cm Sokoke Scops owl is only found here and in a small area in eastern Tanzania, in the Usambara Mountains. The reserve also contains rare species of amphibians, butterflies and plants. It is said to be the largest surviving stretch of coastal forest in East Africa and covers an area of 400 sq km. The forest is home to rare mammals too, such as the very small Zanzibar duiker (only 35 cm high and usually seen in pairs), the Sokoke bushy-tailed mongoose and the rare golden-rumped elephant shrew. There are four endemic plants and five endemic butterflies. The forest was gazetted as a Forest Reserve in 1943 and managed by the Forest Department until 1991 when the Kenya Wildlife Service became a partner in its management and opened it up for tourists. Kenya Forest Research Institute and the National Museums of Kenya joined the management team more recently and, in recent years projects such as butterfly pupae production and bee keeping, have been started in an effort to help local people make a legitimate living from the forest. Local farmers harvest butterfly pupae, for sale to the Kipepeo project in Gede, and for live export to overseas exhibitions. Efforts to prevent the forest being cut down completely are being made, but the constant needs for fuel and land in a country where the population is increasing so rapidly makes this difficult.

The wardens are very well informed about the wildlife and will also be able to advise whether the tracks which join the Tsavo National Park road to the north are passable. From Tsavo East to Malindi the distance is 100 km but a four-wheel drive is necessary during the rainy season. Main road access to Arubuko Sokoke is off the Mombasa-Malindi road and *matatus* can drop at the main gate. The gate to the reserve is to the left of the main road, 1.5 km before the road to Watamu and Gedi. The Arabuko Sokoke Kenya Wildlife Service's office is located nearby. There is limited vehicle access into the reserve itself. Mountain bikes can be hired. You can organize a guide at the visitor centre, specialist bird guides can be booked in advance.

Watamu → *Phone code: 042. Colour map 2, grid C2.*

Watamu Village

In recent years this small fishing village has been seeing some fairly rapid tourist development and is certainly feeling the impact. The atmosphere is mixed, but Watamu still maintains quite a lot of traditional village charm and remains reasonably hassle free, despite the proximity of the tourist hotels. The village has several small supermarkets, a number of curio and souvenir dealers, a butchers, fishmongers, a bureau de change and a post office. Watamu is known for its spectacular coral reef, and the coast splits into three bays: Watamu, Blue Lagoon and Turtle Bay. Apart from the beach and the sea, the attractions of staying here are the nearby Watamu Marine Park and the Gedi Ruins. The setting is attractive as there are a number of small islands just offshore, and Turtle Bay is quite good for snorkelling (but watch out for speed boats ferrying fishermen to the large game boats. The water is much clearerhere than at Malindi during the wet season. The most exciting way to the reef, 2 km offshore, is to go in a glass-bottomed boat, which will cost US$15-20 but is well worth it. The beach is relatively free of seaweed and at low tide, and especially Spring low tide, a number of eroded corals protrude from the surface. These resemble giant Swiss cheeses. Due to the high concentration of plankton in the sea around Watamu, the marine life is superb and it's also an excellent place for scuba diving. In particular manta rays and whale sharks are common. If you can't afford deep-sea fishing, be at **Hemingways** at 1600-1700 when the days' catch is recorded and the fishermen photographed. Tagged fish are apparently returned to the sea. Watamu is also a good place to hire bikes as an alternative way of exploring the surrounding area, including the Gedi Ruins. There are a number of shops in the village, with reasonable rates. Look out for the new village school building that was completed by five unpaid British builders within a fortnight in early 1999; they were rewarded by being appointed as elders of the Giriama tribe and given Swahili names.

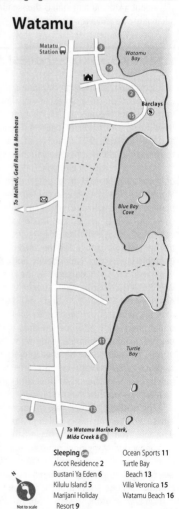

Watamu

Matatu Station

Watamu Bay

Barclays

To Malindi, Gedi Ruins & Mombasa

Blue Bay Cove

Turtle Bay

To Watamu Marine Park, Mida Creek &

Sleeping
Ascot Residence **2**
Bustani Ya Eden **6**
Kilulu Island **5**
Marijani Holiday Resort **9**
Ocean Sports **11**
Turtle Bay Beach **13**
Villa Veronica **15**
Watamu Beach **16**

Not to scale

Mida Creek

ⓘ *US$10.*

There is good birdwatching at Mida Creek. To reach the head of the creek, leave the Mombasa-Malindi road opposite the entrance to the Arabuko-Sokoke Forest and make your way down to the creek's shores. The creek is composed of

⁑ A viewer's guide

Manta Place This dive site is one of the most distant and it takes about 45 minutes to reach by boat. The chances of seeing manta rays and whale sharks are high, and there are a very large number of moray eels. Depth varies between 15 and 24 m.

Black Coral This location is only suitable for experienced divers. At a depth of 30-40 m is the famous black coral. Its appearance is very unobtrusive and only a few divers recognise it. Another attraction is the blue and golden cucumaia or sea cucumber, which is very rare, plus huge basket sponges reaching up to 1 to 1.5 m in height. This whole reef is overgrown with whip wire corals.

Shakwe Wreck During a storm in 1990 the 25-m fishing trawler *Shakwe* capsized and sank. She lies at a depth of only 12 m, almost undamaged on her starboard side, but within a short period of time her hull has become overgrown with small coral heads in which there are many small crabs of different kinds. A shoal of batfish has established its home here, and there are large groupers, stingrays, and octopus. Only the wheelhouse of the wreck is accessible. The wreck is an ideal destination for beginners.

Soldierfish Place This dive site is only suitable for experienced divers due to its depths of 30-40 m. This spot is covered with many soft corals which provide shelter for hundreds of soldier fish, nudibranchs, groupers, stingrays and many other coral fish.

Canyon, Canyon North, Deep Place and Brain Coral These four dive areas are located on the northern reef and drop from 10 to about 27 m from where they turn into sandy bottom. In the Canyon the reef rises again after a 25-m-wide ditch. In this channel, where you sometimes experience a current, reef sharks or large stingrays can be spotted. The Brain Coral is a very old coral hill, now partly collapsing, which hosts a diversity of coral fish. All these dive locations are suitable for beginners.

South Reef, Canyon East, Dolphin Corner and Lion Fish These dive spots are also found on the outer reef and the descents are from 10 to 30 m and then end in sandy ground. As the name suggests, the Lion Fish is inhabited by a large number of various lionfish. At Dolphin Corner you may see dolphins with a bit of luck. On all these dive areas beginners can dive on the reef top.

extensive mudflats and mangrove forests that attract a wide variety of flora and fauna. The best time for birdwatching is the incoming tide, when all creatures are busy feeding. A telescope is very useful. You are likely to see crab plovers, curlews, sandpipers, stints, terns, spoonbills and flamingos. There is a suspended walkway that leads 260 m through a progression of mangrove species and a bird hide here.

Bio-Ken Snake Farm

ⓘ *To733-290324 (mob), 0900-1200 and 1400-1700, US$4.*

Some 3 km north of the village is a research centre primarily dealing with reptiles, especially snakes and snake-bite venom. Bio-Ken is a registered international advisor on the handling of snake-bite victims and holds snake-bite seminars which are attended by experts from all over the world. There are over 200 snakes at the farm and a variety of species. Bio-Ken also offers a free 'remove-a-snake' service for people in the Watamu area. Any snakes removed from a property are relocated or brought back to the farm depending on the species. It also runs a snake spotting day safari with a

⁑ *There are 126 different snake species in Kenya. Of these six can kill you, 17 can cause death if not treated promptly, another 10 could cause a lot of pain and the remaining 93 are not venomous or dangerous.*

⁞ Turtle watch

Watamu Turtle Watch was formed in 1997 to continue and further develop the marine turtle conservation efforts of a local naturalist Barbara Simpson, which she had been undertaking in the area since the 1970s. Watamu has a small but nationally important nesting population of sea turtles, with 60 nests a year. There is a nest protection programme, which works in co-operation with local people and Kenya Wildlife Services to protect all nests laid on Watamu and Malindi beaches. Daily patrols check for nesting turtles and tracks in the sand that indicate new nests. Nests are allowed to incubate in situ unless they have been laid in an area threatened by sea wash, in which case they are carefully relocated to a safe area. Watamu Turtle Watch is also involved in a project to encourage fishermen to release, rather than slaughter, turtles that get accidentally caught in their fishing gears. For more information about visit www.watamu turtles.com. There are placements on offer for volunteers.

picnic lunch for visitors to show snakes and reptiles in their natural habitat. The project is run by James Ashe who was appointed Curator of Herpetology at the National Museum of Kenya in Nairobi in 1964.

Watamu Marine Park

ⓘ *US$10*. Along this coast close to Watamu village there is an excellent marine park which has been made a total exclusion zone. Obviously this change of status met with mixed feelings by some fishermen, but they seem to have adapted well, and the influx of tourists has increased the income of the village. The park headquarters are someway south of Watamu at the end of the peninsula that guards the entrance to the creek. Unfortunately the road goes a little inland, hiding views of the sea. The park covers 30 km of coastline, with a fringing reef along its entirety, as well as numerous patch reefs. The fringing reef forms several lagoons, some of which are rich in coral and fish species, while part of the beach within the park is a key turtle nesting ground. It all encompasses Mida Creek, a diverse and rich ecosystem consisting of mangroves, coral, crustacea, fish and turtles (see above). There are approximately 700 species of fish in the marine park and there are estimated to be over 100 species of stony coral. You go out in a glass-bottomed boat to the protected area and some of the hundreds of fishes come to the boat to be fed. The boats may seem rather expensive but are really well worth it. Trips can be arranged at any of the hotels, or else at the entrance to the actual park. You can also swim or snorkel amongst the fish, which is a wonderful experience. There are lots of shells and live corals that are a splendid range of colours. The water temperature ranges from 20-30°C. If you are short of time, try the islands just offshore from **Hemingways**.

Gedi Ruins → *Colour map 2, grid C2*

ⓘ *0700-1800, US$4, children US$2. If you come by* matatu *you will have to walk the last 1 km. You can hire a taxi from Malindi for about US$8.*

The Gedi Ruins are about 4 km north of Watamu and are signposted from the village of Gedi. This is one of Kenya's most important archaeological sites and is believed to contain the ruins of a city that once had a population of about 2,500. It was populated in the latter half of the 13th century, and the size of some of the buildings, in particular the mosque, suggests that this was a fairly wealthy town for some time. However, it is not mentioned in any Arabic or Swahili writings and was apparently unknown to the Portuguese although they maintained a strong presence in Malindi just 15 km away. It is believed that this was because it was set away from the sea, deep in the forest. Possibly as a result of an attack from marauding tribesmen of the Oromo or Galla tribe, the city was abandoned at some time during the 16th century. Lack of water may have also been a contributing factor as wells of over 50 m deep dried out. It was later reinhabited but never regained the economic position that it once had held. It was finally abandoned in the early 17th century and the ruins were rediscovered in 1884. The site was declared a national monument in 1948 and has been excavated since then. It has been well preserved.

There is a beautifully designed new **museum** that includes a restaurant and library. Visitors are made to feel welcome. You can buy a guidebook and map of the site at the entrance gate. There are also informative guides. Ali, the curator for the past 20 years, will show you around personally if available.

The site was originally surrounded by an inner and outer wall (surprisingly thin). The most interesting buildings and features are concentrated around the entrance gate, although there are others. Most that remain are within the inner wall although there are some between the two walls. Coral rag and lime were used in all the buildings and some had decorations carved into the wall plaster. You can still see the remains of the bathrooms – complete with deep bath, basin and squat toilet. There are a large number of wells in the site, some being exceptionally deep. The main buildings that remain are a sultan's palace, a mosque and a number of houses and tombs, a water system and a prison. Other finds include pieces of Chinese porcelain from the Ming Dynasty, beads from India and stoneware from Persia – some are displayed in the musuem, others in Fort Jesus, Mombasa.

The **palace** can be entered through a rather grand arched doorway which brings you into the reception court and then a hall. This is the most impressive building on the site. Off this hall there are a number of smaller rooms – including the bathrooms. You can also see the remains of the kitchen area that contains a small well.

The **Great Mosque** probably dates from the mid-15th century, and is the largest of the seven on this site. It is believed that substantial rebuilding was undertaken more recently. The *mihrab*, which indicates the direction of Mecca, was built of stone (rather than wood) and has survived well. As you leave, note the carved spearhead which is located above the northeast doorway.

A great deal of trade seems to have been established here – silk and porcelain were exchanged for skins and, most importantly, ivory. China was keen to exploit this market and in 1414 a giraffe was given to the Chinese Emperor and shipped from Malindi. It apparently survived the trip. There was also trade with European countries and a Venetian glass bead has been found here too.

In all there are 14 houses on the complex which have so far been excavated. Each one is named after something that was found at its site – for example House of Scissors, House of Ivory Box. There is also one named after a picture of a *dhow* that is on the wall. In the houses you will again be able to see the old-style bathrooms. Deep pits were dug for sewage, capped when full and then used for fertilizer. Such techniques are still used in the Old Town district in Malindi.

The tombs are located to the right of the entrance gate and one of them is of particular interest to archaeologists as it actually has a date engraved on it – the Islamic year 802 which is equal to the year AD 1399. This is known as the Date Tomb and has enabled other parts of the site to be dated with more accuracy. There is also a tomb with a design that is common along the Swahili Coast – that of a fluted pillar. Pillar tombs are found all along the coast and were used for men with position and influence.

The site is in very pleasant surroundings – it is green and shady but can get very hot (cool drinks are available at the entrance). There are a spectacular variety of trees including combretum, tamarind, baobab, wild ficus and sterculia, a smooth-barked tree inhabited by palm nut vultures and monkeys because snakes cannot climb up the trunk. You may hear a buzzing noise. This is an insect that lives only for three or four days until it literally blows itself to pieces! There are usually monkeys in the trees above that are filled with the noise of many different types of birds.

It is in fact also a wildlife sanctuary and is home to the magnificent, and now sadly rare, black and white colobus monkey. This monkey has suffered at the hands of poachers for their splendid coats but a few remain and you may see some here. Also in the sanctuary are the golden-rumped elephant shrew (only seen at dawn and dusk) and various birds such as the harrier hawk and palm tree vulture.

Kipepeo Project

Just inside the entrance to the ruins is a community-based **butterfly farm** ① *0800-1700, US$1.50 non-resident adults*. This project has trained local farmers living on the edge of the Arabuko-Sokoke Forest Reserve, see page 245, to rear butterfly pupae for export overseas. The project aims to link forest conservation with income generation for local communities and at present is the only butterfly farm in Africa of this kind. The project has led to a large increase in household incomes of those participating in the project and, since butterflies are shortlived and hard to breed abroad, the market is quite reliable.

Malindi → *Phone code: 042. Colour map 2, grid C2. Population: 250,000.*

Malindi is the second largest coastal town in Kenya after Mombasa. It has a pleasant laid-back atmosphere compared to Mombasa, and retains a village feel, especially along the shore road. The streets are also cleaner and the people much friendlier. In the narrow streets of the Old Town are bazaars and shops selling antique furniture and textiles. The beach is excellent and popular and, although seaweed can be a problem (especially before the spring equinox), it is less so than on the beaches around Mombasa. A great attraction is the Malindi Marine Park, with clear water and brilliantly coloured fish. It is also one of the few places on the East African coast where the rollers come crashing into the shore, there is a break in the reef, and it is possible to surf.▸▸ *For Sleeping, Eating and other listings, see pages 252-260.*

Ins and outs

Getting there Malindi is well served from Mombasa by air and bus/*matatu* services (there is no train service).▸▸ *For details, see Transport, page 259.*

Getting around You can either organize day trips through the hotel, or else try the public transport in the way of tuk tuks and *boda bodas* (bicycle taxis). Both these are surprisingly efficient, cheap and easy to find in Malindi at anytime of day or night.

Tourist information Tourist Office ① *Lamu Rd, T042-20747, Mon-Fri 0800-1600, although it closes out of season*, is very helpful and the staff friendly. The main parts of town are safe, even at night. Exercise caution elsewhere, however, and take a taxi if going further afield.

Background

The earliest known reference to Malindi is found in Chinese geography in a piece published in 1060 written by a scholar who died in AD 863. The first accurate description of the town is believed to have been written by **Prince Abu al-Fida** who lived from 1273 to 1331. Archaeological evidence supports the theory that the town of Malindi was founded by Arabs in the 13th century. In any event, locals claim that there was a big Chinese trading influence. This belief is supported by the fact that many of the local people still retain traces of Chinese features.

In 1498 **Vasco da Gama**, having rounded the Cape of Good Hope, stopped off at various ports along the coast. At Mombasa he was not made welcome – indeed attempts were made to sink his ships. At Malindi he found a much warmer reception. The good relations between Malindi and the Portuguese continued throughout the 16th century. The town was governed by Arabs, who were the wealthiest group. The wealth came from the trade with India and the supply of agricultural produce grown in the surrounding plantations.

The town went into a period of decline in the 16th century and in 1593 the Portuguese administration was transferred from Malindi to Mombasa. Although Malindi continued to suffer as Mombasa expanded and took more trade, the town's prosperity did improve during this period and the use of slaves was an important factor. In the first year of resettle- ment in 1861 there were 1,000 slaves working for just 50 Arabs. Malindi had a bad reputation for its treatment of slaves.

The period under the **Imperial British East Africa Company** (IBEAC) began in 1887 when the Company acquired a 50-year lease from the Sultan of Zanzibar for territories in East Africa. The company administered the area, collected taxes and had rights over minerals found. Bell Smith was sent to the town as officer for the Company and he began to lobby for the abolition of the slave trade. From around 1890 slaves who wished and were able to, could buy their freedom. For those who could not, the company offered jobs, or found paid employment. Relatively few took up the opportunity and the process was a gradual one. With the Protectorate government abolishing the status of slavery in 1907, merchandise trade developed, and in the early 20th century the most important exports were rubber, grain, ivory, hides and horns. During the second half of the British period the foundations were laid for what is now Malindi's most important industry – tourism. The first hotel, **Brady's Palm Beach Hotel**, opened in 1932, and famous visitors included Ernest Hemingway in 1934. These days Malindi is popular with Europeans, especially Italians. The many retirement villas that have been built has not been altogether welcomed by the local people.

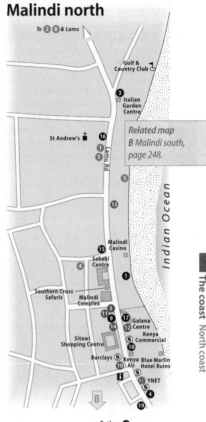

Malindi north

To ② ⑧ & Lamu

Golf & Country Club

③ Italian Garden Centre

St Andrew's ✝ ⑯

Related map B Malindi south, page 248.

⓪ ⑤

③

⑬

Malindi Casino ⑮

Sabaki Centre ⑥

Southern Cross Safaris — Malindi Complex

Sitawi Shopping Centre

⑤ ⑨ ⑭

⑰ Galana Centre ⑫ Kenya Commercial ⑤ ⑱

Barclays ⑤ Kenya Blue Marlin Air Hotel Ruins ⑩ ⑤ @ YNET ⑤ ④

ℹ️

B ⑲

Indian Ocean

The coast North coast

Eating 🍴
Bling Café 18
Carni Africane alla Brace 1
Hermann's Beer Garden 9
Karen Blixen Café 17
Lorenzo's 3
Mabeste 16
Palm Garden 4
Stars & Garters 19
Trattoria 15

Bars & clubs 🍸
Casino Black & White 10
Casino Disco 14
Fermento 12
Putipui Disco Bar 5
Stardust Club 11
Tropicana Club 28 13

N

0 metres 100
0 yards 100

Sleeping 🛏️
Auberge du Chevalier 8
Eden Roc 3
Lutheran Guest House 4
Malindi Cottages 5
Sabaki River Camp & Cottage 2
Vasco da Gamas Campsite 1

Although the history of the town dates back to the 12th century there are few remains of the ancient town. Two remains that are worth seeing, in the oldest part of the town, clustered around the jetty, are the **Jami Mosque** and two striking **Pillar Tombs**. These are thought to date from the 14th century. Malindi Curios Dealers Associations have a huge **market** here. Behind the Jami Mosque lies a maze of small streets that form the Old Town district. The oldest surviving buildings are the mosques of which there are nine (including the Jami Mosque) that date from before 1500. Contemporary accounts from the 14th century remark on two-storeyed houses with carved wooden balconies and flat roofs constructed from mangrove poles, coral and zinc mortar. None of these have survived. The smaller dwellings had timber and latticed walls covered with mud and mortar and woven palm frond roofs, called *makuti*. The density of the housing and the materials made old Malindi very vunerable to fire, and periodic conflagrations (the most recent in 1965) destroyed all the older dwellings. The mosques survived by virtue of having walls of coral blocks and mortar.

The two buildings of note from the British period are the **District Officers' House** in front of Uhuru Gardens, and the **Customs House** behind the jetty. Both have

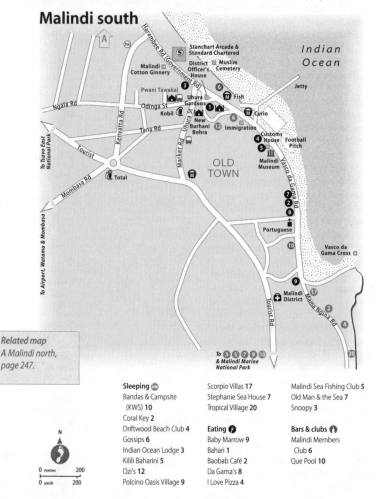

Malindi south

*Related map
A Malindi north,
page 247.*

0 metres 200
0 yards 200

Sleeping
Bandas & Campsite (KWS) **10**
Coral Key **2**
Driftwood Beach Club **4**
Gossips **6**
Indian Ocean Lodge **3**
Kilili Baharini **5**
Ozi's **12**
Polcino Oasis Village **9**
Scorpio Villas **17**
Stephanie Sea House **7**
Tropical Village **20**

Eating
Baby Marrow **9**
Bahari **1**
Baobab Café **2**
Da Gama's **8**
I Love Pizza **4**

Malindi Sea Fishing Club **5**
Old Man & the Sea **7**
Snoopy **3**

Bars & clubs
Malindi Members Club **6**
Que Pool **10**

Swahili culture

The coastal region is the centre of this distinct and ancient civilization. The Swahili are not a tribe as such – they are joined together by culture and language – Kiswahili – which is the most widely spoken language in East Africa. It is one of the Bantu languages and was originally most important as a trading language. It contains words derived from Arabic and Indian as well as English and Portuguese.

The Swahili civilization emerged from the meeting of East Africa, Islam, the classical world and eastern civilizations. Traders, as well as immigrants, from Asia and Arabia have had a gradual influence on the coast, shaping society, religion, language as well as literature and architecture. These traders arrived at the ports of the east coast by the northeast monsoon winds which occur in March and April (the Kaskazi wind) and left around September on the southerly wind (the Kusi wind). Inevitably some stayed or were left behind and there was intermarriage between the immigrants and the indigenous people.

Slavery was important to the coastal region and was not entirely an alien phenomenon. For long before slaves were being rounded up from the interior and shipped overseas, there was an important

although rather different 'slave trade'. This involved a family 'lending' a member of the family (usually a child) to another richer family or trader in exchange for food and other goods. That child would then live with the family and work for them – essentially as a slave – until the debt had been paid off. However, in the same way as with bonded child labourers in India today, the rates of interest demanded often ensured that the debt could never be paid off and the person would remain effectively a slave. Later slavery became an important part of trade and commerce and the old system was replaced with something much more direct. Many slaves were rounded up from the interior (some of them 'sold' by tribal chiefs and village elders) and taken to the coast. Here they would either be sold overseas to Arabia via Zanzibar or put to work on the plantations that were found all along the coast. Successive measures by the British formally ended the slave trade by 1907 although it did continue underground for many years. When slaves were released they were gradually absorbed into the Swahili culture although their antecedents are known it means it is almost impossible to be rid of the stigma associated with being a slave.

verandas, and neither is in particularly good repair, but the District Officers' House is a handsome and imposing structure. Close to the Customs House is the new **Malindi Museum** ⓘ *0800-1800, US$3, children US$1.50*, which is housed in an attractive 19th-century former house of an Indian trader. It was opened in 2004 and has a library on the top floor, where you can browse through local books of the region. The building was originally built in 1891, and in more recent years it has served as the office for Kenya Wildlife Service and is now a National Monument that was lovingly restored by National Museums of Kenya thanks to funding from the German Embassy. The house is on three floors with cool high rooms, intricate staircases and wooden shutters. At present there are very few exhibits but this will change, and what is there is very clearly labelled. These include some sacred wooden carved grave posts of the gohu people, which are traditionally used as a link between the living and the dead. Sacrifices are made to them in preparation for harvesting and planting. There are a few boards about Vasco de Gama and his arrival on the coast in the 15th century, and a room of posters dedicated to 'Discover Islam' with information about how Muslim men and women live their lives. On the ground floor are some interesting early photographs of Mombasa, with corresponding modern photos on what the various areas look like today. There is a football pitch opposite the museum where you can watch teams of teenagers in respective coloured T-shirts play in the late afternoon.

In the centre of town, the **Uhuru Gardens** has been relaid and the streets around here have been paved in new brick. Close to the bus and *matatu* stand is the **Malindi Wood Carvers** located off Kenyatta Road, which is run as a co-operative. Ask to visit the workshops that are behind the shop. Many of the society's 350 members work in very poor conditions on a variety of wood. You will be able to see how some of the finely carved pieces are manufactured from the most unlikely looking material. Also in this area is the main market where, apart from clothing, vegetables and charcoal, you can see old cars being converted into pots and pans and other hardware.

There are a couple of monuments that date from the Portuguese period, in particular the **Vasco da Gama Cross**, which is situated on the promontory at the southern end of the bay. It is one of the oldest remaining monuments in Africa and was built in 1498 by the great Portuguese explorer, Vasco da Gama, as a sign of appreciation for the welcome he was given by the Sultan of Malindi, and to assist in navigation. The actual cross is the original and is made of stone from Lisbon. You can reach it by turning down Mnarani Road. The small **Catholic church** close to the cross is also believed to date from the Portuguese period and is thought to be the same one that St Francis Xavier visited in 1542 when he stopped off at Malindi to bury two soldiers on his way to India. It is one of the oldest Catholic churches in Africa still in use today and the walls are original, although the thatched roof has been replaced many times.

Malindi Falconry ① *T042-31240, 0930-1800, US$4*, is a small rehabilitation centre for injured or sick birds as well as a breeding programme for falcons. It is located a little to the north of the town behind Malindi Complex on the Lamu Road. Said to be the only falconry in the country, there are eagles, hawks, buzzards, kites and owls as well as falcons. You can also be treated to a bird safari to see the falcons at close range and watch them perform exciting flight shows.

Around Malindi

Malindi Marine National Park

Situated within the Malindi Marine Biosphere Reserve is this small marine national park. Gazetted in 1968 this is an area of only 6 sq km that offers wonderful diving and snorkelling on the coral reefs off Casuarina Point. This park is popular and with good reason. The water is brilliantly clear, and the fish are a dazzling array of colours. There are two main reefs with a sandy section of sea bed dividing them. You can hire all the equipment that you will need and a boat here, but it is advisable to check your mask and snorkel before accepting. The fish are very tame as they have been habituated by being fed on bread provided by the boatman. If you see any shells be sure to leave them there for the next visitor – the shell population has suffered very severely from the increase in tourism. Try and go at low tide as the calmer the sea, the better; also be sure to take some sort of footwear that you can wear in the water. You may also be taken to one of the sand bars just off the reef so take plenty of sun protection. Some of the hotels organize this excursion, many of which seem to have arrangements with local glass-bottomed boat owners, as does the Kenya Wildlife Services headquarters at Causuarina Point, T042-20845, www.kws.org. Expect to pay around US$12 for the boat plus US$8 park entry fee.

⦂ Baobab trees

These huge trees have enormous girths which enable them to survive during long dry patches. They live for up to 2,000 years. You will see some extremely large ones – at Ukunda there is one with a girth of 22 m which has been given 'presidential protection' to safeguard it. During droughts people open up the pods and grind the seeds to make what is known as 'hunger flour'.

The legend has it that when God first planted them they kept walking around and would not stay still. So He decided to replant them upside-down which is why they look as if they have the roots sticking up into the air.

Tana River National Primate Reserve → *Colour map 1, grid B2.*

Situated 120 km north of Malindi on the Tana River between Hola and Garsen, the Tana River National Primate Reserve (TRNPR) is a highly diversified riverine forest, that has at least seven different types of primates. It was gazetted in 1976 to protect the lower Tana riverine forests and two highly endangered primates, the crested mangabey and the Tana River red colobus monkey. This is the sole habitat of these endangered primates. A number of other animals roam here including elephant, hippo, baboon, gazelle, duiker, lesser kudu, oryx, river hog, giraffe, lion, waterbuck, bush squirrel and crocodiles. The TRNPR is located on the lower reaches of the meandering course of the Tana River, covering an area of 171 km of forest, dry woodland and savanna habitat on the east and west of the river. The forest here is of high diversity with nearly 300 tree species recorded. There is a research station for study of the primates. It is possible to go boating down the swirling Tana River. This reserve has been under threat by human demands for its resources. Clearing and cultivation have been problematic, along with the damage resulting from the pastoralists bringing their animals here for water.

The reserve is accessible via the Malindi-Garissa road. There are buses running between Lamu and Garissa, and some of them detour to Mnazini village just to the south of the reserve, from where it is possible to walk north along the river (there is a small boat ferry just before Baomo Village). However, most people visit as guests of the **Tana Delta Camp**, the upmarket lodge on the Tana River, see Sleeping.

To the Lamu Archipelago

After leaving Malindi you cross the Sabaki River, and then the turning for the village of **Mambrui**. This village is believed to be about 600 years old and all that remains of the ancient Arab City is a mosque, a Koran school and a pillar tomb, which has insets of Ming porcelain. Further on you will eventually pass **Garsen**, a small town at the crossing of the Tana River where you can get petrol and drinks. Just south of Garsen on the Tana River there is a **Birdlife Sanctuary**, home to many herons. From here the road turns back towards the coast and Witu, another small Old Town. As you drive in this area you may see people of the Orma tribe as well as Somalis, for this is getting close to the border. Both groups are pastoralists, and you will see the cattle that represent their wealth. Finally, about five hours after leaving Malindi, you will get to **Mokowe** and you will see the Makanda channel which separates Lamu from the mainland. Here there is a small café and if you are in your own vehicle you can park it up here and arrange and pay for an askari to look after your car whilst you visit Lamu. This is also the point where the buses get to.

⬤ Sleeping

Low season on the Kenya coast is usually 1 Apr to 30 Jun, when many of the hotels discount their rates considerably. If you are staying in one of the big hotels then the chances are that you will eat there most evenings. If you wish to try other places, you will usually need to have your own transport or else take a taxi.

Nyali and Bamburi beaches *p238*
L **Mombasa Beach Hotel**, Nyali Beach, T041-5471861, www.mombasabeachhotel. kenya-safari.co.ke, is set up on a cliff looking over the beach and the sea. 150 rooms all of which are a/c with balconies. It is very well managed and includes business facilities, tennis courts, swimming pool, crazy golf, watersports, basketball court, bar and restaurant. **Palm Beach Annex** is a more recent addition. Cottages and self-catering apartments, some have a/c, most have balconies, the 6 suites have butler service.
L **Nyali Beach Hotel**, T041-474640, nyali sales@africaonline.co.ke, opened in 1948, with a newer and more expensive addition called the **Palm Beach Annex**. All 170 rooms are a/c and most have balconies, there are also some self-catering cottages, set in 20 acres of gardens. Facilities include meeting rooms, 5 restaurants, 7 bars, nightclub, tennis courts, and 2 swimming pools. A kite surfing centre is based here (see below).
A **Nyali Reef**, T041-471771, www.african meccasafaris.com. Recently renovated, the 160 rooms all have a/c and balconies. Facilities include meeting rooms, swimming pool, tennis court, sauna, 3 restaurants and several bars. There is lively night life here with a casino, disco and shows.
A **Severin Sea Lodge**, Bamburi Beach, T041-485001/2, www.severin-reservations. com, consists of about 180 imaginatively designed Makuti thatched rondavels all of which are a/c and are very comfortable, facilities include 2 swimming pools, tennis courts, excellent watersports and sailing. There is a choice of international restaurants including the award-winning **Imani Dhow**.
C **Giriama Beach Hotel**, Bamburi Beach, T041-486720. 2-bedroom apartments which are very comfortable, a/c with either balcony or terrace, surrounded by lush tropical

gardens of coconut trees, large swimming pool, cheerful restaurant.
D **Fisherman's Leisure Inn**, T041-471274, www.fishermans.visit-kenya.com, next to **Nyali Reef Hotel**. Very clean and great value, 5 mins from the beach, choice of double hotel rooms or 2-bedroom apartments with kitchenette, all with a/c and TV. Also has a decent restaurant, a billiards table, swimming pool and a jacuzzi.
D **Moffat Court Apartments**, T041-473351, jgithere@africaonline.co.ke, offers self-catering budget accommodation within striking distance of the beach in Nyali, and is probably the best value in this price bracket. 18 simple apartments have balconies, TV, fridge, cooker and utensils, or you can arrange local dishes to be cooked for you.

Shanzu Beach *p239*
With the exception of the Serena, most of the hotels at Shanzu Beach are managed by African Safari Club and are very similar. As they are all in a long line next to each other, guests are free to use facilities at all of them regardless of which one they are staying at and there is a central watersports centre. They are all popular in particular with German and Italian holidaymakers and all rates are weekly, roughly US$680-800 per week, with 2nd and 3rd weeks coming down in price considerably. Rates are all-inclusive.
L **Flamingo**, reservations **African Safari Club**, UK T+44 (0)845-3450014, www.africansafari club.com. 138 a/c rooms housed in 6 separate 4-storey buildings, surrounding the huge lagoon-shaped swimming pool that is so big it has its own island and palm-shaded gardens. The spacious restaurant offers hot and cold buffets at breakfast and lunch, and a table d'hôte menu at dinner and there are several bars.
L **Mombasa Serena Beach Hotel**, T041-485721, reservations www.serenahotels. com. A very pleasant luxury hotel carefully designed to resemble Lamu architecture. About 120 a/c rooms and full facilities. Superior to the others.
L **Vasco de Gama**, reservations **African Safari Club**, UK T+44 (0)845-3450014, www.african safariclub.com. No direct beach access, a short walk through the tropical

grounds and down a steep flight of steps takes you to the beach. 88 rooms with views of either the pool or ocean, buffet meals in the restaurant, bars and entertainment.

A **Shanzu Beach and Paradise Beach**, reservations **African Safari Club**, UK T+44 (0)845-3450014, www.africansafariclub.com. Winding paths lead through the tropical gardens, several 2- or 3-storey buildings set around the swimming pools, not all of them have a/c. An airy circular restaurant built in traditional Makuti style with 30-m high conical thatched roofs, also the **Le Gourmet** à la carte restaurant in the Paradise, open air discos are held nightly.

Kilifi *p240, map p240*

L **Kilifi Bay Beach Resort**, Coast Rd, about 5 km out of Kilifi, T041-522511, www.mada hotels.com. Well designed by an Italian, the complex accommodates guests in cottages with private balconies. Activities include windsurfing, canoes, snorkelling and diving. It has well-tended surroundings, located on cliffs with path down to beach, and there is a swimming pool.

A **Mnarani Club**, T041-22318-20, www. mddm.co.uk/mnarani. Overlooking Kilifi Creek on Malindi Rd, this hotel is one of the oldest in the country. It has been beautifully restored, with 84 guest bedrooms in natural wood finishes and smaller creek cottages. All rooms have a/c, mosquito nets and phones. It is set in marvellous gardens and has wonderful views, facilities include watersports (sailing, windsurfing and waterskiing), a bar, and restaurant overlooking the creek, a swimming pool, a beauty therapist and evening entertainment. Children are not permitted. The restaurant is open to non guests and is of a very high standard, with superb seafood, excellent atmosphere and speciality nights.

A **Seahorse**, reservations **African Safari Club**, UK T+44 (0)845-3450014, www.africansafari club.com. Looks out across Kilifi Creek on the northern side of the creek, has good views and is a popular drinking spot for resident expatriates. 40 detached bungalows overlook well-tended tropical grounds, many have a/c and all are spacious, simply furnished and have a large terrace. Facilities

include tennis court, swimming pool, PADI dive school, and a variety of watersports.

D **Dhows Inn**, this small hotel is located on the south side of the creek on the new road leading to the bridge, T/F125-22028. Rooms have bathrooms and mosquito nets, are clean and fairly basic but good value, the hotel has nice gardens and there is a popular bar and restaurant. Can arrange watersports and game safaris and there is secure parking.

Watamu *p242, map p242*

There are a number of resort hotels but not much in terms of budget accommodation. As an alternative to the resorts, families or groups of friends may want to consider renting a house or cottage, many of which are very nice near the beach and sometimes have a pool. Visit www.discoverwatamu.com under lettings. You can eat at all the big hotels which do various set menus and buffets.

L **Kilulu Island**, 3 km from Watamu Beach, reservations www.vladi-private-islands.de. De luxe villa with 3 elegant bedrooms, a large lounge with satellite TV, private bar, separate dining room, guest bath, covered sun terrace and a private swimming pool with marvellous views of the ocean and private beach. You can arrange all meals with the cook, or dine at one of the nearby hotels. €1,800 per day for 6 people all-inclusive, with a staff of butler, cook, stewards, gardeners and chauffeur.

A **Ocean Sports**, T042-32008, www.ocean sports.net, a little further south, has a series of cottages set in gardens, there is a large bar and restaurant and all the other usual facilities. Sunday lunch is a huge buffet, popular with expatriates and particularly good value. Will arrange big-game fishing, PADI and BASC diving courses, snorkelling, tennis and squash, friendly atmosphere. Well recommended. Good dive shop/school, with British staff.

A **Turtle Bay Beach Hotel**, T042-32003, www.turtlebay.co.ke, has a variety of rooms some a/c. A mixed clientele, very relaxed and with all facilities including watersports. Organized as a club, encouraging residents to eat all their meals and take all their entertainment at the hotel, it looks after

For an explanation of sleeping and eating price codes used in this guide, see inside the front cover. Other relevant information is found in Essentials, see pages 34-38.

guests very well. A windsurfing course for beginners costs US$50, a 5-day PADI diving course costs US$300. Tennis, basketball, massage, excellent beach and restaurant.

B Ascot Residence Hotel, T042-32326, www.ascotresidence.com. Not on beach, but good central location, bar, tennis, pizzeria, grill, boutique. Civilized Italian management, clientele include many retired Italians. Has spacious grounds and a pool, friendly staff, large rooms. Excellent value.

B Watamu Beach, reservations **African Safari Club**, UK T+44 (0)845-3450014, www.african safariclub.com. The northern-most of all the Watamu hotels, behind the village on the northern cove. It is a large hotel, popular with Germans, 155 terraced bungalows and detached chalets are scattered around lush grounds. Facilities include swimming pool, bar and restaurant. The beach is lovely and there are lots of fishermen offering to take you out to the reef.

D Bustani Ya Eden, T042-32262. 6 small, very pleasant rooms available at a very good rate for 2 sharing a room, s/c, fans. 300 m to beach, speciality African and seafood restaurant, friendly Dutch/Kenyan couple run the place.

D Marijani Holiday Resort, T/F042-32448, www.marijani.bei.t-online.de. Ocean-front resort north of Watamu. A Kenyan/German enterprise offering fully furnished cottages available for short and long rentals. Each has a kitchen so you can choose B&B or self catering, dinner can be arranged with notice. Rooms have nets, fans, hot water, fridge, sun-loungers. Bicycle and surfboard rental.

E Villa Veronica (Mwikali Lodge), T042-32083, is one of the best of the budget hotels in Watamu. Rooms have bathrooms attached, mosquito nets provided and are clean. It is a friendly family-run place, and the price includes breakfast.

Malindi *p246, maps p247 and p248*
Tourism in Malindi is very seasonal, being packed into Jun-Aug. Outside these months you should bargain and can often pay as little as a third of the high-season rate. However, off-season, the large shopping complexes are empty, and about half of the large hotels are shut. Malindi has expanded enormously in the past decade, and is geared mostly to Italian and German tourists.

There are a clutch of basic local lodgings in the town centre near the bus stand. Most charge little more than US$5 for a bed with or without bathroom but are mostly run-down and pretty grim. They often suffer from having more mosquitoes and being hotter as they do not get the sea breezes. They can also be noisy. Far better to stay near the beach.

L Indian Ocean Lodge, reservations **Savannah Camps**, Nairobi, T020-331684 www.savannahcamps.com. A very exclusive hotel with just 8 rooms and a private beach, it has been built of local materials in the Lamu Arab style and tastefully decorated and is set in marvellous colourful gardens. Full board, also trips arranged such as fishing, snorkelling, bird watching and Gedi Ruins. The property actually forms the northern boundary of the Marine National Reserve. Around US$300 per person.

L Kilili Baharini, Tourist Rd, 4 km from town centre toward Casuarina Point, T042-20169, www.kililibaharini.com. Exclusive hotel in thatched banda style, 25 exquisitely decorated rooms, almost entirely white with some antique furniture, pool, restaurants, bars, a/c, Italian-run Wellness Centre using expensive Italian products, the food is Italian too. Very stylish.

L Tropical Village, south of Malindi, T042-20442, reservations **African Mecca Safaris**, www.africanmeccasafaris.com. High-standard hotel catering largely for package tours, with good facilities: swimming pools, gym, bars and restaurant, all rooms are a/c with bathroom and veranda, the disco at the former Coconut Village is right on the beach, the bar is most unusual as it's cleverly sculpted into a tree.

A Eden Roc, T042-20480/1/2, www.eden rockenya.com. On a clifftop overlooking the bay in generous grounds containing lily ponds. Large hotel which has been recently renovated and looks fresh and clean, 150 rooms, all a/c with bathrooms as well as some cottages. It tends to cater to German package tours. It has its own beach, although it is a long walk through the gardens and the sea is 100 m away. Also 2 swimming pools, tennis courts, watersports, scuba diving, deep-sea fishing, golf, disco, massage and hair plaiting. Log on for special offers.

A Stephanie Sea House, Casuarina Point, close to marine park, 6 km south from Malindi, T042-20720, www.stephaniesea house.com. Run by Italians, with mostly Italian guests, 50 thatched cottages set in tropical gardens, Lamu-style furnishings, swimming pool and restaurant, mostly Italian food but once a week a Swahili dinner is held next to the pool.

B Coral Key, T042-30717, www.coralkey malindi.com, 2 km south of town. Very attractive layout, the 150 rooms have wide verandas with comfortable furniture, 5 swimming pools, tennis, beach bar, restaurant, videos, boutique. Italian managed, 10% discount for online bookings, rates drop significantly in low season.

B Polcino Oasis Village, T042-31995, www.holidays-kenya.com, on Silver Sands Beach, 3 km from town. Constructed in a U shape with white walls and *makuti* roofs, disco, large swimming pool, 130 1-3 bed apartments with kitchenettes, internet café, restaurant and bar. Good value for groups or families of 4 when rates work out at about US$20 per person.

B Scorpio Villas, T042-20194, www.scorpio villas.co.ke, (websites in Italian), 2 km from town on Mnarani Rd. 25 villas is set in magnificent gardens, 3 swimming pools, a restaurant and bar and the beach is very close. The cottages are all fully furnished with enormous Zanzibar beds and day couches on the terraces and balconies, an excellently managed complex with friendly service. Rates are B&B, full or half board. Rates drop significantly during low season.

B-C Driftwood Beach Club, 3 km to the south of town, T042-20155, www.driftwood club.com. One of the older hotels in Malindi, this has managed to retain a clubby but informal character. It has a range of rooms including luxury cottages, doubles and singles, 2 2-bed cottages share their own pool, a/c, breakfast is included in the price and some of the rooms work out at very good value. Facilities include what is probably the best restaurant in Malindi (the seafood in particular is spectacular), watersports including fishing, diving and windsurfing, and a squash court. Temporary membership is very cheap, so a lot of people drop in to use the facilities. The service is friendly, often boozy, and ex-pat orientated.

C Auberge du Chevalier Hotel, Lamu Rd , north of town, T042-20003, www.galanariver camp.com. Cottage-style accommodation, rather charmingly laid out, 15 a/c whitewashed rooms with big Zanzibar-style beds and veranda, comfy bar and restaurant, swimming pool, organizes horse riding.

C Malindi Cottages, Lamu Rd, T042-20304, malindicottages@yahoo.com. Self-contained cottages, fully furnished with excellent facilities, each sleep 5 so work out very cheaply per person, and everything is provided. Swimming pool and a restaurant in the complex and a bar next door.

C-E Sabaki River Camp & Cottage, T0722-861 072 (mob), www.sabakirivercampand cottage.com. Head north from Malindi, cross the bridge over the river, then immediately turn right to go through the village. Ask here for directions to the home of Rodgers Karabu, which is about 1 km further on. Cottage on a hill overlooking the mouth of Sabaki River, where thousands of birds, including flamingos, gather, about 8 km north of Malindi. This region has been earmarked as an important bird site for Kenya. Only 2 rooms, they are large and have en suite bathrooms, no electricity and lanterns are used, basic meals can be arranged for US$5 a day. The campsite is located on a breezy dune under cashew nut trees 150 m from the cottage, washing and drinking water is provided in tanks, shower, flush toilet, fireplace and cooking grill. Rooms cost US$25 and camping costs US$5. Good value in scenic location and very different to the huge resorts.

E Lutheran Guest House, T042-21098, north of the town off the Lamu Rd, behind Sabaki Centre. Good value and popular, a range of rooms singles and doubles with or without own bathroom, also a self-contained cottage. Clean and very friendly staff, no alcohol is allowed on the premises.

D Gossips, see under Eating, predominantly a restaurant but has 14 clean rooms with fans, with or without bathrooms on shore road near jetty. The cheapest double is US$14, a single US$10, including breakfast.

D Ozi's, T042-20218, ozi@swiftmalindi.com. Situated overlooking the beach very close to the jetty, this hotel has a range of 16 rooms mostly with shared bathrooms. It is simple, but clean and good value and is one of the most popular of the budget hotels, and the price includes a very good breakfast. Tends to be noisy at night because of the proximity of the bus garage. Special offer is washing 5 items of clothing per day for free!

E Bandas and Campsite, Casuaria, adjacent to Malindi Marine Park. Run by the Kenya Wildlife Service, there are simple bandas with mosquito nets and a camping area. Utensils and crockery are provided but you must bring all food. Very good value. Bandas must be booked in advance with the warden T042-20845, or **Kenya Wildlife Service**, Nairobi, T020-600800, www.kws.org.

E-F Vasco da Gamas Campsite, Lamu Rd, T042-31700, mugambina@yahoo.com. New place run by a friendly lady, site seems secure with *askaris* and big fence, very simple banda accommodation under thatch with new mosquito screens, some self-contained and some with kitchens, the **Mabeste** restaurant and disco are next door.

Tana River National Primate Reserve p251

L Tana Delta Camp, reservations Bush and Beyond/Bush Homes of East Africa, Nairobi, T020-600457, www.bush-and-beyond.com and www.bush-homes.co.ke, is a small and remote exclusive tented camp with large airy tents and cottages situated in groves of indigenous trees on top of dunes with good ocean views. Situated on the estuary of the Tana River it is a 3-hr drive from Malindi. Meals are enjoyed in a mess tent which is home to a resident family of genet cats. Expeditions down the river to the local villages may be arranged, or a 3-hr excursion to the Tana River Primate Reserve. It is expensive but you will be very well looked after and the food is excellent. The price includes all food, transport and day trips. You can be picked up from the airport or from Malindi, and will be taken there by 4WD.

⊘ Eating

Kilifi p240, map p240

Ψ The Boat Yard, on Kilifi Creek, serves very good food and cold beer. It's a working yard with boats all over the place ranging from yachts to ski boats and sail boats. Every Sat is when all the local sailing fraternity meet up for lunch, a real social gathering.

Malindi p246, maps p247 and p248

Most of the restaurants in the hotels are open to non-residents; their set menus and buffets are especially good value.

ΨΨΨ Baby Marrow, south of town near the hotels, located under the arms of an enormous tree and under a thatched roof, very intimate with huge lampshades, terrace and lovely atmosphere, rustic decor with chunky wooden furniture, all lit up at night by delicate lights in the garden out front, very good continental food and service. Recommended.

ΨΨΨ Carni Africane alla Brace, just south of casino, T042-20552. Pleasant layout of tables under awnings in a courtyard, with a big open-air charcoal grill, serving game meats, gazelle, zebra, giraffe, crocodile.

ΨΨΨ Malindi Sea Fishing Club, T042-30550. Temporary membership available for US$1.50, and well worth it, as is the food: grills, seafood including a very good prawn curry, plus cheaper burgers and chicken and chips. Comfortable club decor including giant stuffed fish on the wall, bar, excellent views out over the ocean. Members congregate for lunch and sundowners.

ΨΨΨ The Old Man and the Sea, beachfront, north of the Portuguese chapel, T042-31106. Very stylish and the best place to eat in town, named after the Hemmingway book, romantic, set in a lovingly restored low Arabic house with stone seats and arches, only a few tables so reservations are essential, impeccable service and gourmet food. Starters include lobster pâté and smoked sailfish, followed by whole crab, or the recommended Indian Ocean seafood platter. Daily 1200-1430, 1830-2300.

ΨΨ Baobab Café, T042-31699. On the sea front with good views, close to the Portuguese church. Has a wide ranging menu, you can have breakfast here, snacks and a beer or fruit juice, as well as full meals such as chicken or fish curry, red and white checked tablecloths and friendly staff.

ΨΨ Da Gama's, close to Portuguese church on Vasco da Gama Rd, T042-30295. Lots of seafood dishes and good, affordable Indian curries, omlettes, grills, fixed price menu, pleasant decor, stone floor, outside terrace, views of the lighthouse.

ΨΨ Driftwood Club, T042-20155. This is a nice way to spend a lazy day, you need to join as a temporary member – then you can eat here and use the pool and loungers. The excellent restaurant has a set menu, an à la carte menu and serves snacks at the bar.

Gossips, on shore road near jetty, is predominantly a restaurant but has some budget rooms upstairs. Full bar, Italian pasta and then choose from a variety of sauces, antipasta and bruschetta bread. Good and cheap with main courses at around US$3.50.

I Love Pizza, Vasco da Gama Rd, T042-20672. A good-value Italian restaurant serving pizza, pasta, seafood dishes and other food. Located in an atmospheric Arab house, lobsters, crabs, giant prawns combine themselves very well with pappardelle or spaghetti, rice or trenette.

Lorenzo's Restaurant, Italian Garden Centre, north of town, 800 m off the main road, T042-31750. Good standard Italian food, bar, upstairs deck, quiet out of season.

Mabeste, Lamu Rd, is a small restaurant set back from the road. High chairs and tables and modern bar, small wooden dance floor, African and some western food, pizza and pasta, main courses good value at US$3-4, good selection of alcoholic drinks, things liven up in the evening and the disco sometimes goes on to 0400-0500.

Trattoria, opposite **Malindi Casino**. Informal bistro, bar, fans and TV, large cocktail list, pizzas, burgers, Italian hams and cheeses, relaxed and not unreasonably priced, all under thatch roof.

Bahari Restaurant, close to the Juma Mosque. Popular local café with excellent chapatis, beef stew, good value, very busy at breakfast and lunch, closed in the evenings.

Bling Café, on the main road opposite Barclays Bank, very good breakfasts, juices, coffee and teas, tables under thatch, at the back is a very new and swish cyber café with quick and cheap internet access, and you can take your drinks in. Exceptionally friendly.

Hermann's Beer Garden, opposite Galana Centre, north of the shopping centre, is good for snacks and a beer, the open-air bar is popular in the evenings. Cheap food such as burgers and chicken and chips from US$3.

Karen Blixen Café, Galana Centre, Lamu Rd. Imaginatively designed, sandwiches, juices, coffee, parasols and outside tables, photos of Karen Blixen and Denys Finch-Hatton.

Palm Garden Restaurant, Lamu Rd, T042-20115. You can sit in the shade of bandas, the food is fine – curries, chicken, seafood and so on – and it is very good value. There is also a lively bar that has live music at the weekends and an ice-cream parlour (rather run-down).

Stars and Garters, opposite **Kenya Commercial Bank**. Grills, seafood, good coffee and ice cream, thatched informal bar, big screen TV for watching sport, gets busy when there is an important match on.

Snoopy, ice cream, milkshakes, sausage and chips, samoosas, tea and coffee, quick service and good white tiled environment.

Bars and clubs

Malindi *p246, maps p247 and p248*
There is plenty to do in the evenings. The bigger discos are found at the larger hotels. There is also occasionally live music – ask around. There is a particularly dense crop of bars and discos in the northern part of town around the Galana Shopping Centre where it's easy enough to walk from one to the next until you find one that suits. They make for a lively night out in high season. See also Eating.

African Pearl, north end of town. Pleasant gardens, live band on Sun during high season (Jun-Aug).

Casino Black and White, opposite the (closed) **Blue Marlin**. Open air with thatched bandas, local bar popular for watching football on TV, ice cold beer and also coffee, ice cream and basic food including grilled meat with chips or *ugali*.

Casino Disco, next to **Stardust Club**. Attractive bar with thatched cover and dance area, no entry charge.

Fermento Bar, Galana Centre, T042-31780. Serves Italian food and grills, very large disco, karaoke and occasional live music, opens at 2200 and things gets underway at about 2300. Also here is Morgan's cocktail bar with an extensive range of cocktails although they don't come cheap at US$4-6. Open Wed, Fri, Sat out of season, more nights in season if there is the demand.

Malindi Members Club, large open-air local bar on beach side of Government Rd beneath a grove of pine trees, tables under thatched shelters, nyama choma, lots of cold

⁞ Fireworks at Malindi

In 1498 Vasco da Gama, sailing north up the East African coast had met with a hostile reception both in Sofala (now in Mozambique) and Mombasa. He needed to establish good relations with a town at the coast so that he could load fresh water and victuals and engage an experienced mariner to guide his fleet to the Indies. The bales of cotton cloth and strings of beads the fleet had brought with them to trade had proved useless – the coastal people had gold from Sofola, ivory from the interior, silk from the east.

Vasco da Gama decided to present some unusual items to the King of Malindi – a jar of marmalade, a set of decorated porcelain dishes and a candied peach in a silver bowl. He then invited the king and his people to witness a firework display on the shore. The king had a brass throne with a scarlet canopy brought down to the shore and with a court of horn players, flautists and drummers gazed out to the *San Gabriel* and da Gama's fleet. In quick succession the ship's canons fired shells into the air which burst over the King and his townsfolk on the shore. It was spectacular and exciting, and the king was impressed. At last the Portuguese had an ally for their conquest of the mainland.

beer gets very lively. It is not necessary to be a member.

Palm Garden, at intersection of Kenyatta and Government Rd. Very pleasant atmosphere, with several bar areas, live bands at weekends.

Putipui Disco Bar, opposite Galana Centre. Serves Italian food, grills. Wicker furniture and dance area. Noticeable for the Italian-style red-tiled roof and lots of Italian flags.

Que Pool Bar, south of the Portuguese church. Very cheap local bar with fluorescent lights and plastic tables, but hugely popular with basic snacks.

Stardust Club, T042-20388, big white building opposite the Galana Centre, starts fairly late in the evenings but is nevertheless very popular. Open until at least 0400 in season, Sat is the big night.

Tropicana Club 28, near Eden Roc Hotel, T042-20480, is small, friendly and popular.

○ Shopping

Malindi *p246, maps p247 and p248*
Handicrafts
Most of the craft shops are close to the beach and the jetty in the Malindi curio market. A number of stalls are grouped together, and in general the quality is reasonably good as are the prices –

although you must expect to bargain. During the low season when there are not many tourists about, you may pick up some good bargains. There are also a number of quality shops on the roads lining the Uhuru Gardens, and the back streets around here selling very good cloths and items such as bags, clothes and cushions made from *kikois*. Many of these also sell Swahili antiques, presumably to decorate the Italian villas in the area. One of these is **Mimmos Gallery**, on Harambee (Government) Rd, with another nameless antique shop next door. Both are high-class establishments with antique items in wood and metal, including many pieces from Ethiopia.

Shopping centres
Galana Centre has the Karen Blixen Café, the Fremento nightclub, a bureau de change and a supermarket.

▲ Activities and tours

Watamu *p242, map p242*
Hemingways Fishing Centre, Hemingway's Hotel, T042-32624 , www.hemingways.co.ke. For deep-sea fishing.
Malindi Scuba Diving Kenya Ltd, next to the Blue Bay Village Hotel, T042-32099, www.scuba-diving-kenya.com. 6 diving

boats, 3 Bauer air compressors and 150 diving tanks (INT and DIN). It offers a workshop and storage for personal diving gear.

Malindi *p246, maps p247 and p248*
Deep-sea fishing
Academia Safaris, T042-30243, www.academiasafariskenya.com, all round safari operator for Kenya and deep-sea fishing in the region.
Kingfisher, T042-21043, kingfisher@swift mombasa.com.
Malindi Sea Fishing Club, south of the jetty, T042-30550. Has notice board for fishermen.
Peter Ready, T042-21292.

Golf, climbing, squash, tennis
Coral Key has an artificial climbing wall, supervised by qualified staff.
Driftwood Beach Club, daily membership available for squash.
Golf and Country Club, north end of town, right fork off Lamu Rd, T042-20404, www.golfinginkenya.com. Very unusual 11-hole and 15-tee course spreads out on 133 acres, inexpensive daily membership available. Tennis and squash too.

Scuba diving
Most of the hotels can organize watersports.
Crab Diving, at Tropical Village and **African Dream Hotels**, T042-20443.
Riki Diving, at Coral Key, T042-30717.
Tropical Diving Club, Tropical Village, T042-20256.

Surfing
The surf is good during Jul-Aug but silt from the Galana River can make the water a rather red, muddy colour during the rainy season.

Tour operators
Southern Cross Safaris, Lamu Rd, T042-20493, www.southerncrosssafaris.com. Helpful agent that can organize safaris away from the beach.

Transport

Kilifi *p240, map p240*
Kilifi is about 50 km from **Mombasa**, and 45 km from **Malindi**. The buses that go between the 2 towns do pick people up here although only if there is space as they may

be full. It might be easier to get a *matatu* (US$1 from Mombasa). **Tana Express** and **Tawfiq** have booking offices near bus station. To get to and from **Nairobi** from Kilifi the **Tana Bus Company** goes twice a day taking about 9 hrs. The buses leave at 0730 and 1930.

Watamu *p242, map p242*
Watamu is about 50 km north of Kilifi, and 3 km off the main road. From Malindi to Watamu, 15 km, takes about ½ hr, there are plenty of *matatus* and it will cost you about US$0.50. Hotel taxi from **Malindi** US$18; from **Mombasa** US$90. Note these taxis can seat 7, and on this basis cost US$2.50 and US$13 a head. You can organize these through a hotel or on arrival at either airport with the taxi companies in the arrivals hall.

Malindi *p246, maps p247 and p248*
Air
The airport at Malindi is served by 3 airlines, as well as by chartered planes for safaris. About 3 km south of the town, a taxi to the centre costs about US$3 and the hotels to the south will be about US$6. **Kenya Airways**, on Lamu Rd opposite Barclays Bank, T042-20237, at the airport: T042-20192, www.kenya-airways.com, flies daily between Nairobi-Malindi-Lamu. The flight departs Nairobi at 1100, arrives in Malindi at 1210, departs again at 1240 and arrives in Lamu at 1310. It then departs Lamu at 1340, arrives at Malindi at 1410, and departs for Nairobi at 1440, where it arrives at 1550. It is a popular route so be sure to book well ahead and confirm your seat.

Air Kenya, airport T/F042-30646, www.airkenya.com, has daily flights between **Malindi** and **Nairobi** (1¼ hrs) on Wed, Fri and Sun at 1900, single US$85, return US$150. Baggage allowance is only 10 kg, and check in time is 30 mins before take off. Airport tax is around US$1.

Mombasa Air Safari, Moi International Airport, Mombasa, T042-433061, www.mombasaairsafari.com, has daily flights between **Mombasa**, **Malindi** and **Lamu**. The flight departs Mombasa at 0800, arrives at Malindi at 0845, departs again at 0845 and arrives in Lamu at 0915. On the return leg it departs Lamu at 1700, arrives in Malindi at 1730, departs Malindi at 1750, and arrives in

Mombasa at 1810. Mombasa-Lamu, one way US$63; Mombasa-Malindi, US$35 one way; Malindi-Lamu, US$45 one way.

Bus

There are plenty of buses between **Malindi** and **Mombasa**. The bus companies all have offices in Malindi around the bus station, but booking is not usually necessary. They mostly leave early in the morning and take about 2½ to 3 hrs and cost about US$1. Non-stop *matatus* are faster, and take under 2 hrs. They leave when full throughout the day and cost about US$2.

You can also get the bus to **Lamu** but you should book in advance and check out the current security situation (see below). The trip takes about 5 hrs and costs about US$4. They leave in the morning between 0800 and 0900. If you miss these you might be able to get onto one of the Mombasa buses that get to Malindi about 0830 and go on at 0930 – but there is no guarantee that you will get a seat. **Pwani Tawakal Bus Company** is recommended for the **Lamu** service and the office is opposite the **Kobil** petrol station near the market. Buses depart daily at 0900 and 1200 having come from Mombasa first, and on the return leg they depart from Lamu at 0700 and 1300, US$6 each way. Try and buy the ticket the day before you want to travel to guarantee a seat. The bus will take you to the jetty on the mainland from where you get a ferry across to Lamu (see page 276). **Safety** There have been security problems, including fatalities, with armed bandits known locally as *shifta* on the road to Lamu over the past few years. On the last stretch of road towards Lamu, vehicles are accompanied by armed guards. There hasn't been an incident for a number of years and these days it is considered safe to travel by bus from Malindi to Lamu, though it is advisable to check the situation locally before finalizing your plans.

Train

There is no train to Malindi, but your hotel or a travel agent will reserve a sleeper on the **Mombasa-Nairobi** train for you (they will charge). Just as easy, and about a tenth of the price, is to ring and do it yourself, Mombasa Railway Station, T011-433211

Tuk tuks and *boda bodas*

All over Malindi are cheap tuk tuks that cost no more than US$1.50 from one end of town to the other. There are also plenty of bicycle taxis known as *boda bodas* with a single seat on the back that will cost no more then US$0.50. There used to be car hire companies in Malindi, and indeed bicycle hire, but with the introduction on what is excellent public transport, they have become defunct.

● Directory

Kilifi *p240, map p240*
Banks Two banks in Kilifi are open Mon-Fri 0830-1300 and Sat 0830-1130. **Medical services** Dr Bomo has a clinic on the old Kilifi Rd in Mnarani. **Post office** Next to the market.

Watamu *p242, map p242*
Banks There is a small branch of Barclays Bank open on Mon, Wed and Fri morning. The big hotels will change money but the rate will not be very good.

Malindi *p246, maps p247 and p248*
Banks There are a number of banks in Malindi. **Barclays** is on the main coastal road (the Lamu road) opposite the (closed) Blue Marlin Hotel and is open Mon-Fri 0830-1700, and Sat 0830-1200. It has an ATM. There is also a **Standard Chartered Bank**, just to the south of here. **Kenya Commercial Bank** is also on Lamu Rd on the opposite side to Barclays. There are several forex bureaus in town including one in the Galana Centre and **Dollar**, next to the Standard Chartered Bank. **Internet** Bling Café, near the Kenya Commercial Bank on Lamu Rd, very quick, lots of new terminals, US$1 per hr, also serves juices and snacks such as doughnuts and you can have these whilst you surf. **Intercommunications**, and **YNet**, both on Lamu Rd, also offer email access. **Medical services** Malindi District Hospital, Tourist St, T042-20490. Buhani Pharmacy, Uhuru St, near Uhuru Gardens. **Useful information** Tidal information: posted at Customs and Excise, just near jetty. **Immigration**, opposite the curio market T042-30876.

Lamu	264
Lamu Town	266
Lamu Island	270
Listings	271
Nearby islands and mainland	**277**
Manda Island	277
Pate Island	277
Kiunga Marine National Reserve	279
Dodori and Boni national reserve	280
Listings	280

Lamu Archipelago

✂ Footprint features

Don't miss...	263
Alley cat	265
Shela stash	269
New's Year Day Dhow Race	270
Maulidi	281

Introduction

In the extreme north are the intriguing islands of Lamu which make for a fascinating excursion into the old Swahili way of life. Here visitors can experience the coast's cultural heritage at its most evocative and it is often said that Lamu is similar to what Zanzibar in Tanzania used to be like 30 years ago before the onset of mass tourism.

In Lamu town, Shela and the small settlements on the other islands, the alleyways are barely wide enough to pass an oncoming donkey, and you can shake hands with the neighbour in the house opposite. Whitewashed walls and Arabic arches contribute to some of the most elegant architecture on the continent. Without the sounds of traffic, the atmosphere is pleasantly peaceful interrupted only by the low rumblings of electric juicers in the waterfront cafés as they pound the limes and mangoes and the infectious chatter of Swahili. The evenings are enchanting, when the dimly lit alleyways are full of warm shadows and fragrant hues. The islands have some wonderful deserted beaches, very atmospheric places to stay and the seafood to die for. Whilst embracing tourism, the people of Lamu want to retain the islands' mystic, religious sanctity and cloak of medieval romance. It should not be forgotten that they belong to another, older Africa.

★ Don't miss...

1 **Lamu Old Town** Get lost in the back streets and meet the friendly people, page 266.

2 **Lamu Museum** Visit this museum where the spacious, refreshingly cool hallways are decorated with 18th-century Kidaka plasterwork and filled with the finest examples of Lamu antiques, page 267.

3 **Peponi's** Eat seafood on the terrace at this lovely restaurant in Shela and watch donkeys being washed in the sea on the beach below, page 273.

4 **Takwa Ruins** Visit these ruins on Manda Island by *dhow* through the watery mangrove swamps, page 277.

5 **Manda Beach Club** Spend the afternoon relaxing here and enjoy the sail over there by *dhow*, page 282.

Lamu → *Phone code: 042. Colour map 2, grid B3.*

Lamu Island is a laid-back sort of place that makes the quieter spots of Kenya's east coast seem like throbbing metropoli. Little has changed here since the 18th century, and Lamu Town is packed with aged stone and coral covered buildings and narrow streets. It is the only coastal town to retain its original character and is the oldest living settlement in East Africa. Indeed there is a sign posted for the benefit of tourists at the airport – "Please remember that Lamu is a conservative Muslim town with a heritage of peace and goodwill. This is our home. Please tread gently here for our children are watching. Please respect this, and enjoy the unique atmosphere of our enduring yet fragile culture." And yet, at the same time, it is one of the most cosmopolitan few square miles of Kenya, where you are as likely to bump into stockbrokers from Wall Street and Hugh Grant look-alikes from Notting Hill Gate as you are Aussie backpackers. The island takes tourism seriously – it is, after all, the main source of income – but does it with a style that is often lacking in other parts of the country. With a fast-growing local population of about 12,000 people – the vast majority of whom are Muslim – and the expansion in tourism, pressure of numbers on the island is becoming a problem. But Lamu really is a paradise; it is so serene and beautiful that you are likely to want to stay forever. ▶▶ *For Sleeping, Eating and other listings, see pages 271-276.*

Ins and outs

Getting there

Air Kenya and **Kenya Airways** both have flights to the airstrip on Manda Island. Flying to Lamu is a fantastic way to get a handle on the geography of Kenya's coast: tarmaced roads become dirt tracks criss-crossing each other and leading to tiny rural settlements shrouded in palmy forest, sand spits stretch tentacles out into the blue Indian Ocean, and after less than an hour you the island of Lamu comes into view. The plane lands on the airstrip on Manda island, just to the north, from where you need to catch a boat across to Lamu. Some of the more expensive hotels will ferry you and your luggage over from the airstrip, otherwise there are always dhows to meet the planes at the jetty that will take you across for a few shillings. Alternatively, buses go to Lamu from Mombasa and Malindi. In previous years these buses have been targeted by armed robbers, and consequently armed guards ride on the bus for the last few kilometres to Lamu. However, the buses are regarded as safe these days. The bus will take you as far as the jetty at Makowe on the mainland from where you get a ferry, about 7 km, taking about 40 minutes, across to Lamu. If you are in your own vehicle it is also possible to park it up at the Makowe jetty, which is effectively Lamu's nearest carpark, but you will have to pay for an askari to look after your car. See page 251 for detail of the journey from Malindi to Lamu. ▶▶ *See Transport, page 276, for further information.*

Getting around

● *There is rumoured to be about 2200 donkeys on Lamu – take extra care about where you are stepping, especially at night when a torch might be a good idea!*

There are no vehicles on the island except for the District Commissioner's Land Rover. Donkeys and bicycles dominate. The two main thoroughfares in Lamu Town are the waterfront, also known as Kenyatta Road, and the Main Street, which runs parallel and is one block back from the waterfront, also known as Harambee Avenue. The maze of streets mean that it is easy to get lost; just bear in mind that Harambee Avenue runs parallel to the waterfront and the all the streets leading into town from the shore slope uphill slightly.

⁝ Alley cat

With their long necks and saucer like eyes, narrow bodies and straight legs, the cats of Lamu are the only cats on earth to bear the same physiques as the cats depicted in Egyptian hieroglyphics. One popular theory suggests that these cats may be the only remaining descendant of a breed of cats that were once found in ancient Egypt and now extinct in North Africa.

Traders may have carried the cats to Lamu on dhows hundreds of years ago. Other breeds of cat have since been brought to the island, and as a result the local gene pool has been distilled, yet the distinctive looking Lamu cats still survive among the winding streets. There is a cat clinic to the north of the Donkey Sanctuary where a resident vet treats injured animals.

Safety

Safety is not a major problem in Lamu, however, there have been a number of incidents over the last few years. Avoid walking around alone after dark in secluded areas of town and don't go to remote parts of the island unless you are with a group. Stay within shouting distance of other people on the beach. The increase in tourism has led to an inevitable rise in the number of touts or 'beach boys'. If they accompany you to your hotel, a substantial 'commission' (33-50%) will be added to your daily rate. To avoid using their services, carry your own bags to a seafront restaurant first, have a drink and look for accommodation later. You will have no problem finding a room.

Tourist office

Lama Tourist Information Centre ① *on the harbour front to the north of the landing jetty, just north of the Donkey Sanctuary, T042-633132,* and next door the **Lamu Tour Guides Association** ① *T0720-971412 (mob),* have friendly staff, can organize walking tours of the town and *dhow* trips for fishing or snorkelling, or trips to surrounding islands. Both are closed on Sundays and public holidays. A three-hour walking tour of the town costs in the region of US$20 for one to three people. Other excursions that can be arranged are *dhow* trips to Matondoni which include a BBQ fish lunch, or *dhow* fishing excursions in the Manda Channel followed by a barbecue on Manda Beach.

Background

The town of Lamu was founded in the 14th century, although there were people living on the island long before this. Throughout the years, and as recently as the 1960s, the island has been a popular hide-out for refugees fleeing the mainland.

The original settlement of Lamu was located to the south of the town, and is said to be marked by Hidabu hill. There was also another settlement between the 13th and 15th centuries to the north of the present town. By the 15th century it was a thriving port, one of the many that dotted the coast of East Africa. However in 1505 it surrendered to the Portuguese, began paying tributes, and for the next 150 years was subservient to them, and to the sultanate of the town of Pate on the nearby island, part of the Omani Dynasty that ruled much of the East African coast.

By the end of the 17th century Lamu had become a republic ruled by a council of elders called the Yumbe, who were in principle responsible to Oman. In fact the Yumbe were largely able to determine their own affairs, and this period has been called Lamu's Golden Age. It was the period when many of the buildings were constructed and Lamu's celebrated architectural style evolved. The town became a thriving centre of literature and scholarly study and there were a number of poets who lived here. Arts and crafts flourished and trade expanded. The main products exported through Lamu were mangrove poles, ivory, rhino horn, hippo teeth, shark fins, cowrie shells, coconuts, cotton, mangoes, tamarind, sim sim (oil), charcoal and cashews. Rivalries betweenn the various trading settlements in the region came to a head when Lamu finally defeated Pate in the battle of Shela in 1813. However, after 1840 Lamu found itself dominated by Zanzibar which had been developed to become the dominant power along the East African coast. At a local level there were factions and splits within the town's population – in particular rivalries between different clans and other interest groups.

New products were developed for export including beche de mère (a seafood), mats, bags, turtle shell, leather, rubber and sorghum. Despite this, toward the end of the 19th century Lamu began a slow economic decline as Mombasa and Zanzibar took over in importance as trading centres. The end of the slave trade dealt a blow to Lamu as the production of mangrove poles and grains for export depended on slave labour. Additionally, communications between the interior and Mombasa were infinitely better than those with Lamu, especially after the building of the railway. Many of the traditional exports still pass through Lamu, particularly mangrove poles that contain an extract that resists termites and are used for traditional buildings as roof rafters along the Indian Ocean coast and in the Middle East. Poles can be seen stacked on the Promenade, just south of the main jetty, waiting to catch the *dhows* sailing north on the September trade winds. In recent decades the tourist trade has helped improve Lamu's economic prospects.

Lamu Town

A wonderful old Muslim stone town known to locals as Mkomani, Lamu Town has distinctive architecture, carved doors, narrow streets, an absence of vehicles, donkeys, many mosques, a bustling jetty where fishermen pull up in *dhows* as well and motorboats and women dressed in black and wearing the *bui bui* who chat in the street. It is the largest (and oldest) stone town on the East African coast, but is still easy to walk around.

Sights

The town dates back to the 14th century although most of the buildings are actually 18th century, built in Lamu's Golden Age. The streets are very narrow, and the buildings on each side are two or three storeys high. The streets are set in a rough grid pattern running off the main street which is called the Usita wa Mui (formerly Main Street) now known as **Harambee Avenue**. Usita wa Mui runs parallel to the harbour and used to open out to the sea, although building from the mid-1800s onwards has cut it off from the quayside. The narrow waterfront stretches the length of the town where cannons still point seaward. Touts offer *dhow* rides and white billowing sails occupy every inch of shoreline. The smaller ones serve as local taxis for Manda or the nearby Shela Beach, and the large ocean-going vessels are stacked high with mangrove poles and sand. Muscled sailors with *kikois* hoisted around their waists heave wooden carts from the docks or slumber on deck amongst charcoal burners and grain sacks.

Mkomani is a very secluded place where the houses face inwards and privacy is carefully guarded. The families who live in these houses are mainly the patrician *wangwana* who keep themselves to themselves. The non-patricians who reside in Mkomani live there as clients of the patricians, employed or providing services and are often descendants of their patron's slaves. At the edges of the town live people of slave and immigrant ancestry.

Carved doors are one of the attractions for which Lamu has become known. The artesanal skill continues to be taught, and at the north end of the harbour you can see them being made in workshops by craftsmen and apprentices. There are over 20 mosques on the island, but mostly they are usually not very grand affairs and some are little different from other buildings. You will need to seek permission before entering to look around.

The oldest mosque in Lamu is believed to be the **Pwani Mosque**, near the fort, which dates back to 1370. The **Jumaa** (or Friday) **Mosque** is at the north end of town and is the second oldest in Lamu, dating from 1511. Then comes the **M'na Lalo Mosque** (1753), more or less in the centre of town, just a little to the north of the museum and set back from Harambee Avenue. This mosque was built in Lamu's Golden Age, and it was followed by **Muru Mosque** (1821) on Harambee Avenue, **Utukuni Mosque** (1823), well into the interior part of the town, and **Mpya Mosque** (1845), in the town centre. **Mwana Mshamu Mosque** (1855) is in the northwest area of the town; **Sheikh Mohamed bin Ali Mosque** (1875), in the town centre, and the **N'nayaye Mosque** (1880) on the northwest fringe of town. Two mosques have been built in the 20th century, the **Riyadha Mosque** (1901), to the south of the town, and the **Bohora Mosque** (1920), which is fairly central, just inland of Harambee Avenue. The **Mwenye Alawi Mosque** (1850) at the north end of Main Street was originally for women, but it has since been taken over by the men. The small Ismaili community did have their own **Ismaili Mosque**, on the Kenyatta Road at the south end of town, but this is now in ruins. Adjacent to the Riyadha Mosque is the **Muslim Academy**, funded by Saudi Arabia, and which attracts students from all over the world.

> ❗ *The Old Town of Lamu was declared a World Heritage Site in 2001 for its cultural importance and for being the best preserved Swahili settlement on the East African coast.*

Lamu Archipelago Lamu

Lamu town north

To Mwenye Alawi Mosque, Mnazi Moja & Dhow Boatyard

Related map B Lamu town south, page 268.

Wood-carving Workshops

Jumaa

Mwana Mshamu

Lamu Social Hall

N'nayaye

Cat Clinic

Promenade

Swahili House Museum

Lamu Tour Guides Association

Lamu Craft

To Coast Cinema

Utukuni

MKOMANI

Donkey Sanctuary

Whetstone

Yumbe

M'na Lalo

Sheikh Mohamed bin Ali

Mwana Hadie Famau Tomb

Harambee Av Usita wa Mui Main St

Kenyatta Rd

Mpya

Bohora

Lamu Museum

St Mary's

Jetty

Standard Chartered $

A

Sleeping
Amu House 5
Bahari 6
Casuarina Rest
House 2
Hal-Udy Guest
House 3
Jannat House 4

Lulu House 11
Petley's Inn 13
Pole Pole 14
Sunrise Guest
House 21
Yumbe House 22
Yumbe Villa 23

N

0 metres 50
0 yards 50

Lamu Museum ① *Kenyatta Rd, www.museums.or.ke, 0800-1800, US$3*, is run by the National Museums of Kenya and plays an important role in the conservation of old Lamu. The ground floor has a good bookshop and the entrance has some photographs of Lamu taken by a French photographer, Guillain in the period 1846-1849. In a lobby to the right is a Swahili kitchen with pestles and mortars and vermicelli presses. Also on the ground floor are examples of decorative 18th-century *Kidaka* plasterwork, carved Lamu throne chairs with wicker seats and elaborately carved Lamu headboards. To the rear are displays on the archaeological excavations of the Takwa Ruins (see page 277) on Manda Island, and at Siya and Shanga on Pate Island (see page 277). On the first floor, the balcony has a display of large earthenware pottery. The balcony room has photographs and models of seagoing vessels, mostly *dhows*, and the various types and styles in use. Just behind the balcony room is a display of musical instruments used in festivals and celebrations, including drums, cymbals, rattles, leg rattles. The most celebrated exhibits are the two **Siwa horns**. These are in the shape of elephant tusks, with the mouthpiece on the side. The Lamu horn is made of brass, the horn from nearby Pate is of ivory. They date from the 17th century, are elaborately decorated, and are thought to be the oldest surviving musical instruments in black Africa. Local tribes are featured in a side-room, and there are displays on the **Oroma** from around Witu, Garsen and southwest of Lamu; the **Pokot** from west of the Tana River, and the **Boni** from the north of Lamu. The jewellery includes nose rings, earrings, anklets and necklaces in bead designs and in silver. There are some illustrations of hand and feet painting, in henna, in black and red. The two end rooms are examples of typical Swahili bridal rooms with furniture and dresses on display.

Inland from the museum is the small **Swahili House Museum** ⓘ *0800-1800 daily, small entrance fee*, a traditional Swahili house, restored, with all the traditional furniture. There are three areas on the main floor. A centre aisle has beds off to the left and right. The beds are wooden with rope and raffia forming the base. The main room has a particularly fine **kikanda** plaster screen on the wall. Furnishings include a clock with an octagonal frame and a pointed pendulum case, a style found all along the East African coast. Outside is a well and a garden with frangipani.

The construction of **Lamu Fort** was begun in 1809 and completed in 1821. The tile awning over the veranda at the front was originally of makuti, a thatch made from banana leaves. Inside is a central courtyard surrounded by internal walkways and awnings. The construction is of coral blocks, covered with mortar that has a yellowy-orange hue marked by black patches. It is possible to walk round the battlements, and they afford a good view of the nearby area. The fort initially faced over the quayside, but there are now buildings between it and the sea. In the past it has served as both a fort and as a prison. Now it contains an exhibition on the

Lamu Archipelago Lamu

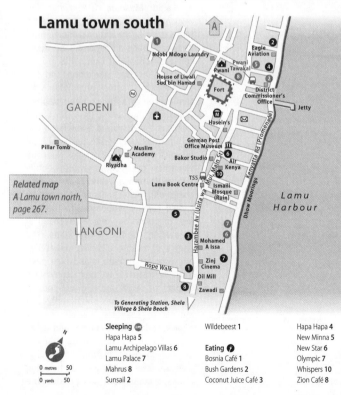

Lamu town south

Ndobi Mdogo Laundry
Eagle Aviation
Pwani Tawakal
Pwani
House of Liwali Sud bin Hamad
Fort
District Commissioner's Office
Jetty
GARDENI
Husein's
Pillar Tomb
Muslim Academy
German Post Office Museum
Riyadha
Bakor Studio
Air Kenya
TSS
Lamu Book Centre
Ismaili Mosque (Ruin)

Related map
A Lamu town north,
page 267.

Lamu Harbour

LANGONI

Mohamed A Issa
Zinj Cinema
Rope Walk
Oil Mill
Zawadi

To Generating Station, Shela
Village & Shela Beach

N

0 metres   50
0 yards   50

Sleeping		
Hapa Hapa **5**	Wildebeest **1**	Hapa Hapa **4**
Lamu Archipelago Villas **6**		New Minna **5**
Lamu Palace **7**	**Eating**	New Star **6**
Mahrus **8**	Bosnia Café **1**	Olympic **7**
Sunsail **2**	Bush Gardens **2**	Whispers **10**
	Coconut Juice Café **3**	Zion Café **8**

Shela stash

In 1915 a man called Albert Deeming was convicted of the murder of a woman and two children in Melbourne, Australia. He was sentenced to death but before his execution he prepared a document detailing the whereabouts of 50 kilos of gold bars buried on Lamu Island.

In 1901, Deeming had boarded the bullion train from Pretoria to Laurenco-Marques, shot two guards and forced a third to open the bullion compartments. Grabbing as many bars as he could carry he jumped the train and made his way to the coast. At Delgoa Bay, he sailed by *dhow* to Lamu, but locals were suspicious, and he hid the gold at a small European graveyard at Shela, in the grave of William Searle, a British sailor who died after falling from the rigging of his ship.

Deeming's belongings were eventually returned to his relatives in South Africa, and one of them made a visit to Lamu in 1919, but was unable to locate the grave.

In 1947 the documents passed to a Kenyan farmer, who with a couple of companions travelled to Lamu and found the Shela graveyard. Four graves were marked, but none of them had the name of William Searle. Convinced that this must be the graveyard described by Deeming they began probing the sands. They located a solid object and removed the covering of sand. It was a gravestone with a well-weathered crack. Deeming's instructions were that the gold was in a small wooden box at the head of the grave, at a depth of two feet. Despite extensive excavations they found nothing. They were curious over the fact that an area of sand appeared less compacted than that of its surroundings. Also, when they examined the gravestone it had some cracks that looked quite recent. They made discreet enquiries in Lamu Town. Four weeks earlier a party of three Australians from Melbourne had visited Lamu and had spent two days at the Shela sand dunes.

environment, a shop and a library, plus a pleasant café overlooking the busy square at the entrance. Wedding parties take place inside the fort – women only are allowed to attend the celebration. The invited guests sit downstairs and the town women stand up behind them. The bride sits on a bed, not participating in the dancing. There is a wedding banquet for the guests.

In the southwest part of town is a fluted **Pillar Tomb**, thought to date from the 14th century. It can be reached by going south, turning inland just after the Halwa Shop, towards the Riyadha Mosque, and continuing beyond the mosque. Alternatively one of the children will be happy to show you the way – just say *nara* and a payment of US$0.25 (20KSh) is reasonable.

Another tomb is the **Mwana Hadie Famau Tomb**, a local woman believed to have lived here in the 15th or 16th century. This is situated a little inland from the museum. The tomb had four pillars at the corners with inset porcelain bowls and probably a central pillar as well. A hermit took up residence in the hollow interior of the tomb, and became a nuisance by grabbing the ankles of passing women at night-time. The solution was to wall up the tomb while the hermit was not at home.

Behind the fort is the **House of Liwali Sud bin Hamad,** a fine example of Swahili architecture. A Liwali was a governor appointed by the Sultan of Zanzibar. The house has now been subdivided, but it is still possible to appreciate how it looked when it was a single dwelling.

On Main Street, just next to the **New Star** restaurant, is the site of the offices of the German East Africa Company. Originally the Germans thought that Lamu would make a

New Year's Day Dhow Race

The people of Lamu are fiercely proud of their maritime tradition and there is an annual *dhow* race on New Years Day at Shela Beach. This event is an important event on the island, and winning the race is a great honour among *dhow* captains. Like the annual donkey race, it brings the island to life and the shorelines throng with supporters. Individual *dhows* are brightly decorated, and festivities on race day last well into the night. Local captains and their crews compete on a course that tests their skills and prowess, and race day is one of showmanship and celebration. Until recently *dhows* were built entirely without nails – sewn with coconut cord and pegged by wooden dowels. All *dhows* have eyes painted on the bows for protection and to see dangerous rocks. A poignant, well-used Kiswahili proverb 'You cannot turn the wind, so turn the sail' originates from the sailors of Lamu.

suitable secure base for their expansion into the interior (much in the same way as the British used Zanzibar). The agreement regarding British and German 'spheres of influence' in 1886 caused the Germans to turn their attention to Bagamoya, although they opened a post office in Lamu in 1888. The site is now the **German Post Office Museum**. Towards the rear of the town is the **whetstone** for sharpening knives, said to have been imported from Oman as local stone was not suitable.

South of the jetty is the **Dhow Harbour**, and mangrove poles are stacked on the waterfront ready for loading on *dhows* catching the trade winds north to the Gulf.

St Mary's Church, next to the museum on the promenade, is the only church on the island, with walls of coral blocks, small tower, bell, roof of mangrove pole rafters and a fine Swahili door. At the **Oil Mill** on Main Street at the south end of town, the owner will be happy to show you around to observe the antique presses extracting coconut and sesame seed oil. At the extreme south end of town, the doors are always open to let out the heat of the **Generating Station**. There are four huge diesel generators, three working and one stripped down for maintenance. The engineer happy to show you around. **Bakor Studio**, at the southern end of Main Street, has an interesting collection of old photographs of Lamu and of Lamu residents, including the visit of Sultan Khalifa from Zanzibar. The Sultan was too infirm to come ashore, and meetings took place aboard ship. Purchase of any of the photographs requires great patience as the shopkeeper is highly eccentric.

In the northern part of the town close to the waterfront is the **Donkey Sanctuary**, run by the International Donkey Protection Trust, based in the UK. There is a small enclosure where sick donkeys receive care. The remainder of the donkeys roam the town (though there is fodder for them at the sanctuary) and the rubbish tip at the north of the town, near the abbatoir (which they share with some marabou storks) and on the tip in front of Salama Lodge.

Lamu Island

Lamu Island is 16 km by 7 km, with a third covered by sand dunes. The best beach on the island stretches for 12 km at Shela. Elsewhere, the coast of the island is covered with crawling mangroves attracting a number of birds. It is possible to walk all over the island, and there are many tracks into the interior. Alternatively *dhows* make the short hop between Lamu town and Shela and Mantondoni.

Here, on the western side of the island, about 8 km from town, you can see *dhows* being built and repaired. The easiest way to get there is to hire a *dhow* between a group – you will have to negotiate the price and can expect to pay around US$30-40 for the boat. Alternatively you can hire a donkey – ask at the **Pole Pole Lodge** (up near the Jumaa Mosque – turn inland at the **Pole Pole Restaurant**). A third option is to walk, although you should leave early as it gets very hot. The walk will take a couple of hours and is quite complicated. You want to turn-off the main street roughly opposite **Petley's** and keep walking west inland. Ask for directions from there; you want to keep going in the same direction of the telephone wires which go to Matondoni – if you follow these you should get there eventually.

Shela

Sticking out on the southeastern tip of Lamu, this village is a smaller duplicate of Lamu town and is the upmarket end of the island. It is a tangle of narrow, sandy lanes, tall stone houses, some smaller thatched dwellings, and a spacious square ringed with a few market stalls and small shops. Here in the cool of the evenings the elders gather to talk, while women come out to shop. In the town are a number of old buildings including several wonderfully restored houses that you can rent (at a price). The people of Shela were originally from the island of Manda and speak a dialect of Swahili that is quite different to that spoken in Lamu. The **Friday Mosque** was built in 1829 and is noted for its slender, conical minaret. The 12-km Shela Beach starts a five-minute walk from the village. Shela is just 3 km or a 40-minute walk from Lamu, go down to the end of the harbour and then along the beach. There is also a route inland: you need to head southwest and hug the shore. If you don't want to walk you can catch a *dhow* taxi.

Southern shores

The southern shores have the best beach, which begins just to the south of Shela – 12 km of almost deserted white sand which back onto the sand dunes. As there is no reef the waves get fairly big. Here you can stroll for miles along the deserted shoreline littered with pansy shells, otherwise known as sand dollars, where foamy waves sweep bare feet and cormorants attempt balancing acts on the sea breeze.

● Sleeping

Price varies with the season. Peak periods are Dec and Jan for upmarket travellers, and Jul-Sep for families and budget travellers. Most of the more expensive hotels are around the island or on nearby islands. At the lower end of the price range the hotels in Lamu tend to be hot and suffer from frequent problems with the water supply (expect cold buckets). Apart from those listed, during season there are several private houses that rent out the odd room, or even a mattress on the roof. Ask at the tourist office. If you are planning to stay here for a longer holiday and are in a group then it is worth renting a house. Many are holiday homes of Kenya residents and offer high-quality accommodation at a very modest price. People post details of houses to rent on notice board at the museum.

Lamu Town *p266, maps p267 and p268*
A-C Wildebeest, T042-632261, wildebeest @hotmail.com. Several lovely traditional apartments in 2 houses, sleeping between 2-7 people, each has a small kitchen, the floor level beds are draped with mosquito nets, fantastic stone terraces dotted at various levels with comfortable day beds for lounging, steep stone steps around courtyard gardens, *makuti* roofs, downstairs is an art shop and gallery. Larger apartments are in the region of US$130, so for groups the cost per person is very reasonable, rates include a house boy.
B Lamu Palace Hotel, T042-633272, www.chaleislandparadise.com. Located on the harbour front at the south end of town, now managed with **Petley's Inn** and **Chale Island Paradise** resort. 22 a/c rooms, very attractively decorated, pleasant patio

restaurant, the buffet set meals are average and bland, but the à la carte seafood is very good, possible to negotiate a better rate off season, Oct-May, one of few places that sells alcohol in Lamu. Friendly and helpful set up, can organize all excursions including day trips to the Manda Beach Resort. Easily the best place to stay in town.

B Petley's Inn, Kenyatta Rd, reservations through Lamu Palace above. A historic hotel founded by an Englishman called Percy Petley in 1962 who fell in love with Lamu whilst recovering from a safari accident. The hotel has 11 rooms and a swimming pool on the 1st floor, it has recently been thoroughly renovated after a fire in 2003. The rooms are very pleasant, in traditional Swahili style, the 2 front rooms have a private terrace. The restaurant no longer exists, but the bars survive and remain popular, one of the few places that serves chilled beers.

B-C Jannat House, north end of town, near Mwana Mshamu mosque, T042-633414, www.jannathouse.com, dates from the 18th century and was built as a merchant's house, the 16 rooms have Swahili furniture, have warm (not hot) water and mosquito nets, offers Kiswahili language courses. Good food in pleasant garden atmosphere, serves alcohol. 1 of only 2 hotels with a swimming pool. Rates are B&B or half board, expect pay in the region of US$60 for a double but this drops in low season considerably.

C Amu House, T042-633420, www.amu house.com, near the **Paradise Guest House**. This is very central and a charming place, owned by an American lady, being a reworked 16th-century Swahili house with plaster carvings and niches, complete with pretty Swahili furniture and canopy beds, some rooms with veranda, breakfast included but other meals only available on request.

C Hal-Udy Guest House, T042-633001. Located in the heart of the Old Town, back from the harbour, this is a small hotel with 4 suites, each has a bedroom, sitting room, with some lovely furniture, a good terrace, and cooking facilities including a freezer. There is also a house boy, and this is particularly popular with expatriate families, it is especially good value if you are planning

on staying for a few weeks.

C Yumbe House, T/F042-33101. This is a wonderful hotel full of atmosphere and excellent value, it is located in the heart of the Old Town next to the Swahili House Museum and is a traditional house of 4 storeys that has been skilfully converted into a hotel. It has a courtyard, and is airy and spacious, clean, friendly, has a good water supply and the price includes breakfast. Highly recommended.

C Yumbe Villa, see Yumbe House for contact details, is a traditional house with Zidaka niches in the ground floor room, located near the fort, clean, tidy, with traditional Lamu beds, mosquito nets, en suite shower and toilet, a/c or fan, some have fridges.

D Bahari Hotel, on Main St, to north end, T042-633172. New establishment, pleasant and peaceful internal courtyard, 20 singles or doubles arranged around a central courtyard on 3 floors, 8 rooms have sea views, Zanzibar beds, fans, mosquito nets, 24-hr water, some rooms have fridges, popular, well run and nice atmosphere.

D Casuarina Rest House, T042-633123. Great location on the waterfront, veranda overlooking harbour, on top of **Kenya Commercial Bank** (now closed), curious bell that sounds like a budgerigar. It is very clean, the 10 rooms are spacious, 6 have their own bathroom while 4 have shared bathrooms, mosquito nets and fans, it used to be the Police station and is well run and friendly, there is a large rooftop area but no breakfast. Family run and they claim that they do not give commission to touts, so go alone.

D Hapa Hapa, to rear of **Hapa Hapa** restaurant on Main St. Fairly simple but spacious, with clean shared bathroom, some rooms look out over harbour.

D Lamu Archipelago Villas, on waterfront at southern end, T042-633247. Good location, 12 rooms in an imposing white building, includes breakfast, fans, nets, efficiently run, though rooms are a little grubbier than others in town.

D Lulu House, inland of town centre, close to Sheikh Mohamed bin Ali Mosque, T042-633539. New establishment fashioned from a Swahili house around a charming centre courtyard with bougainvillea and a waterfall, roof restaurant with excellent views, table tennis.

D Mahrus, T042-633354. This has a range of 13 rooms on 3 storeys, basic but clean with mosquito nets and fans, some upper rooms have sea views, rooftop restaurant with plants and thatched roof, the price includes breakfast, though rooms are cheaper if you don't want breakfast.

D Sunsail Hotel, on the waterfront near the District Commissioner's Office, T042-632065, sunsailhotel2004@hotmail.com. 18 double rooms in a fully restored 100-year-old building that was once the sugar depot, with whitewashed walls and an impressive large carved front door. Smart rooms with fans and Lamu beds, tiled bathrooms, each room is rather uniquely named after a world city, restaurant under thatch on the roof with new windows and views of the busy jetty, big discounts during low season, very friendly management.

E Pole Pole, just inland, north end of town, T042-633204. Highest building in Lamu, with good views from roof, some s/c, mosquito nets, fans, can arrange donkey transport for excursions.

E Sunrise Guest House, inland of town centre, near Sheikh Mohamed bin Ali Mosque, T042-633175. Good value but very basic, 5 rooms for little more that US$8, plus kitchen and terrace.

Shela p271

L Johori House, T042-633460, or reservations www.kenyasafarihomes.com. Well-restored 18th-century house, sleeps up to 6 on 3 floors, with excellent views. It was built by a wealthy nobleman for his daughter on her marriage, and has a harem – now one of the bedrooms! The top floor features a covered rooftop with hammocks and day beds, lovely outside area for al fresco dining, fully equipped kitchen, staff includes houseman and cook, US$250 per night but this is for up to 6 people.

L Shela House, www.shelahouse.com, manages 3 luxury houses in the village: Shela House, Beach House and Palm House. In all 3 houses the decor is very luxurious with lots of dark wood and cream walls, floors and furniture, and each house has 3 staff including a cook. Shela (US$4200 per week) is built on 3 floors around an open courtyard, the house well and an ancient gardenia. The entrance hall leads into the courtyard, edged by a *baraza* sitting and eating area, the upper rooms comprise 5 en suite bedrooms, nursery room, and a dayroom and terrace, also hammocks on the rooftop. Beach house (US$8400 per week) is a large house with 4 double and 1 triple en suite bedrooms, an edgeless, fresh water swimming pool, bar area and low comfortable *baraza* seats. Up the first flight of stairs is a large dining and living room, leading on to a terrace. Palm House (US$4200 per week) is designed around an open courtyard, with 2 doubles and 1 twin bedroom, all en suite with private balconies. There is a panoramic view from the covered rooftop, with a bar, sun beds and *baraza* lounging area.

L Peponi's, Shela beach, T042-633421-3, www.peponi-lamu.com, facing the channel that runs between Lamu and Manda, this is a really wonderful setting with about 500 m of private beach. The hotel is made up of a series of cottages each with a veranda and full facilities. There is an excellent restaurant which is for residents only, as well a bar and grill for non-residents. The hotel provides full watersports facilities, probably the best and most extensive on the island and organizes excursions. Very efficiently run, booking well ahead is advised, it is closed mid-Apr to end of Jun. Highly recommended.

L-B Kijani House, on water's edge between Peponi's and Shela beach, T042-633235-7, www.kijani-house.com. Old Swahili house, fine gardens, traditional furniture, 2 small swimming pools, selection of seafood, Swahili dishes, and a touch of Italian cuisine in the Kijani restaurant, excellent standards. Well recommended. Room rates vary from a single for US$90 to a double with all meals for US$250. Offers fishing and snorkelling and guided tours of Lamu town.

B Shela Rest House, close to Peponi's and run by the family that own the Casuarina Rest House in Lamu Town, see for details. It is a wonderful small converted house and there are 4 self-contained apartments that are let out on a weekly or monthly basis, good if you want to be self-catering. Each has 2 verandas, 2 bedrooms, bathroom and kitchen with toaster, cooker, fridge and utensils and rates include a house boy.

D Shela Pwani Guest House, very close to **Peponi's** and the jetty, T042-632046, has 4 double rooms and 1 triple, the top double room is the best, though all have bathrooms, fans and mosquito nets, well managed. There is a small dining room downstairs, where it is possible to organize meals that include seafood and Swahili dishes.

D Stop Over Guest House, on the beach. Reservations, Nairobi T020- 4446384, lamu homes@swiftkenya.com. Newly renovated and locally owned, 5 clean rooms, simply furnished with fans and mosquito nets and have good views of the sea and plenty of sea breeze. 3 rooms on the first floor can be rented as an apartment with access to kitchen facilities on the same floor. Bathrooms do not have hot water. On the ground floor is a restaurant serving Swahili dishes, fresh juices, soft drinks and seafood, and a shop.

D White House, T042-633091, on the waterfront, good value, but as it's a modern building it doesn't have quite the same atmosphere as the older traditional architecture, 5 rooms with or without bathrooms, roof terrace, rates include breakfast.

Rest of Lamu Island

L Kipungani Explorer, reservations **Heritage Hotels**, Nairobi, T020-4442115, www.heritage -eastafrica.com. The first of Heritage Group's highest standard 'Explorer' resorts. This lodge, with just 15 *makuti* thatched cottages made from local palm leaf mats with coconut thatched roof, is located at the southern tip of Lamu Island. All extremely spacious and comfortable and each has a veranda. It organizes various excursions and snorkelling trips, sailing, windsurfing, sea water pool, there is a good restaurant and bar outside, non-residents can visit for lunch, boats to get there depart from **Peponi's**. The property has an extremely close bond with the people of neighbouring Kipungani Village, who will show you their ancient boat-building and mat-weaving techniques, or take you fishing or prawn-netting in the remote Dadori Nature Reserve.

L Kizingo, T0733-954770 (mob), www.kizingo.com, is a small eco lodge situated at one end of Shela Beach that stretches from Kizingo (which means 'the point' in Swahili) to the village of Shela,

30-min boat ride from the airport on Manda Island. 6 thatched cottages, set well apart from each other, with unrivalled sea views. Room rates include all meals as well as afternoon tea with homemade cake. Fine wines from South Africa, Chile and Italy and cocktails are extra. Supports a local turtle conservation project. Activities include fishing and bird and bush walks.

B Gillis Yoga Tower, newly built in the dunes, you can make a reservation through Monika Fauth, T/F042-632044, banana@ africaonline.co.ke. There is a great communal atmosphere. Yoga lessons and massage are available. Excellent meals at table d'hote – one large table shared by all the residents. This complex has 6 rooms. The development attracts lots of interesting people and the owner Mr Gillis is an interesting man.

❼ Eating

You will find lots of yoghurt, pancakes, fruit salads, and milk shakes as well as good value seafood. If you are looking for the traditional food that you find in upcountry Kenya, such as *ugali*, beans, curries, chicken and chips, there are a number of places that do these mainly on Harambee Av – particularly in the southern end of town. Bear in mind that Lamu is a predominantly Muslim society, so during Ramadan – the month of fasting – many of the restaurants and cafés will remain closed all day until after sunset. Stomach upsets are fairly common. Stick to bottled water and avoid ice.

Lamu Town *p266, maps p267 and p268*
❦❦❦ Lamu Palace Hotel, T042-633272, southern end of waterfront. Pleasant restaurant looking out over the harbour with some tables on a very attractive terrace, seafood, grills, Indian food, serves alcohol including wine. Set meals at dinner are rather bland but presented nicely, the à la carte dishes although more expensive are far superior. Towards the back of the restaurant is an extremely comfortable bar area.

❦❦ Bush Gardens, on the waterfront with good view over harbour and is a very good seafood restaurant, specialities include lobster cooked in coconut sauce, poached monster crab, jumbo prawns and oysters, good fresh juices, cheaper briyanis and stews, it is friendly but can be extremely slow, especially when full.

Hapa Hapa Restaurant, on the harbour front. Pasta and pizza, good fruit juices and snacks, lots of fish including an overloaded seafood platter for US$10, jumbo prawns, occasionally they have barracuda, shark and tuna on the menu, very simple decor under thatch but a lively place with excellent food.

Whispers, Main St, in a lovely coral rag built house. High quality café with juices, cappuccino, ice cream, spaghetti, pizzas, sandwiches and serves wine. Has a pretty flower-filled courtyard to the rear.

Bosnia Café, south end of Main St. Originally set up by soldier who served with the UN forces in Yugoslavia, hence the name, local food such as pilau with chapatis, and cold juices, though in grubby surroundings.

Coconut Juice Café, 1 street back from the waterfront, southern end. Specialist juices, freshly made, with combinations of lime, peanut, chocolate, avocado, papaya, mango, coconut, banana, also juice and yoghurt.

New Minna, just off the Main St, to the south end of town. Upstairs cafeteria, very popular and cheap, clean plastic tables, local stews and specials such as biryani on a Fri, try *mkata wa nyama* (local pizza) or *maharagwe* (beans in coconut sauce).

New Star Restaurant, southern end of town is reasonable and is very cheap, it has good breakfasts and opens very early – 0530.

Olympic Restaurant, south of the town also on the harbour front. Excellent pancakes and seafood, *makuti* roofed eating area.

Zion Café, south end of Main St. Upstairs simple restaurant under a thatched roof with very good music belting out of the speakers, African food, plus chicken or fish and chips and curries, friendly set up.

Shela *p271*

Barbecue Grill, at Peponi's. Excellent and open to non-residents, the food is very good value and is probably the best on the island. It serves alcohol, is comfortable and has a bar on the terrace, superb seafood, try the giant prawns cooked in chilli and lime.

Stop Over Restaurant, which serves simple, basic but good value food, including grills and some seafood, fresh fruit juices, it also has a great location right on the beach.

Bars and clubs

Only 7 places serve alcohol:
Lamu Palace Hotel, at the southern end of the waterfront, has a very attractive bar and you can get drinks with your meals.
Peponi's, in Shela, for an ice-cold beer.
Petley's, on the waterfront north of the museum, has an uninviting bar.
Police Post, on the high ground inland from the fort, serves beer in the Mess – the guardians of the law are a friendly group. Has fine views out over the harbour, and there are 2 brass cannons in the front.
Whispers, only offers wine to accompany your food.
Elsewhere on the island the **Kipungani Explorer**, and the **Kizingo** resorts have bars.

Activities and tours

Watersports organized from **Peponi's** in Shela (see Sleeping). Including windsurfing, surfing, snorkelling, deep-sea fishing, sailing, and scuba diving.

Shopping

Books
The museum has a very good collection of books on Lamu, its history and culture.
Lamu Book Centre has a reasonable selection as well as the local newspapers.

Gallery
Wildebeest, see under Sleeping for details, sells contemporary paintings as well as wall hangings made from goat hair and other fabrics. The gallery is on the ground floor and the workshop on the second floor.

Souvenirs
Hand-built model *dhows* are not too easy to carry around so get them at the end of the trip. Chests, siwa horns, Lamu candlesticks and furniture are also good value. You will be able to get jewellery – silver in particular – as well as curios. You can get things made for you but be prepared to bargain.
Baraka, Main St. Expensive, high-quality carvings, Lamu chests, jewellery, clothing.
Casuarina Gift Shop, behind **Casuarina Hotel**, on Main St, just north of museum. Good selection of Lamu crafts and clothing.

Husein's, Fakrudin Gulom Husein and brother, splendid carved door, copperware from Oman, jewellery.

Lamu Craft, behind Donkey Sanctuary, Lamu carving, signs, candlesticks.

Maasai Studios, waterfront, southern end, some very good, original design, clothing.

Zawadi (Lamu Gift Shop), waterfront, southern end. Excellent, original design clothing and accessories, particularly skirts and patchwork waistcoats and bags.

⊖ Transport

Air

Kenya Airways, on the waterfront, on the ground floor of Casuarina Rest House, T042-632040, www.kenya-airways.com, and flies between **Nairobi**, and Lamu daily with a stop in **Malindi**. Flights depart Nairobi at 1100, arrive in Lamu at 1310, depart Lamu 1410, arrive Malindi 1340. Depart Malindi at 1440, and arrive back in Nairobi at 1550. **Air Kenya**, Baraka House, T042-633063, near the Whispers Restaurant, or reservations at Wilson Airport, Nairobi, T020-605745, www.airkenya.com, has a daily flight between Lamu and Nairobi. It departs Nairobi at 1315, arrives in Lamu at 1500, departs again at 1600, and arrives back in Nairobi at 1745, one way US$135, return US$270.

For **Air Kenya** baggage allowance is just 15 kg. There is no airport tax when you leave Lamu (although there is from Malindi). **Mombasa Air Safari**, Moi International Airport, Mombasa, T042-433061, www.mombasaairsafari.com, has daily flights between Mombasa, Malindi and Lamu. The flight departs Mombasa at 0800, arrives at Malindi at 0845, departs again at 0845 and arrives in Lamu at 0915. On the return leg it departs Lamu at 1700, arrives in Malindi at 1730, departs Malindi at 1750, and arrives in Mombasa at 1810. Mombasa-Lamu, one way US$63; Malindi-Lamu, US$45 one way.

Check in time is 30 mins before take off from the Manda airstrip. Allow plenty of extra time to arrange a boat transfer or *dhow* taxi to get to Manda, the crossing itself takes about 15 mins.

Bus

Buses to Lamu go fairly regularly but the route is popular so you should book in advance. The trip takes about 4-5 hrs from Malindi and costs US$6. They leave in the morning at between 0700 and 0900, and there is usually more buses in the early afternoon at about 1300-1400. These buses will usually have come from Mombasa with departures approximately 2 hrs earlier which cost US$8. If possible sit on the left side of the bus (in the shade) and keep your eyes open for wildlife. There is tarmac to Malindi, a rough track to Garsen then a further 20 km of tarmac after which there is a good graded coral and sand section to Makowe. The bus will take you as far as the jetty at Makowe on the mainland from where you get a ferry, about 7 km, taking about 40 mins, across to Lamu which costs about US$0.50. Rather uniquely all the bus companies put their passengers on the same boat and there's plenty of help with your luggage. The **Pwani Tawakal Bus Company**, on Main St near the fort in Lamu, T042-633380, is recommended. Buses depart daily from Malindi at 0900 and 1200 having come from Mombasa first, and on the return leg they depart from Lamu at 0700 and 1300.

Again, like the airport, the buses are on the mainland. Allow plenty of extra time for the *dhow* from the main jetty to Makowe which is 7 km or a roughly 40-min ride away. For the early buses you need to be at the jetty before sunrise, but there are boats waiting to connect with the buses.

❶ Directory

Banks Few on the island, a Standard Chartered was being built on the harbour front at the time of writing. **Commercial Bank of Kenya**, on the seafront, will change foreign currency and TCs, and accept Visa cards for cash withdrawals (but not Mastercard), service slow, open 0900-1500 on weekdays, and 0900-1100 on Sat.

Internet It is possible to email from the post office and at **Shemanga**, opposite New Star Restaurant. However the internet is sparodic on Lamu and is often down.

Medical services Hospital, located in the southern end of the town to the south and inland from the fort. **Post office** Just to the south of the jetty Mon-Fri 0800-1230 and 1400-1700; Sat 0900-1200. There is a poste restante service.

Nearby islands and mainland

Manda Island is quite close, Pate Island about 20 km away, and Kiwayu Island 50 km off. You will see notices advertising trips and will, undoubtedly, be offered trips from various people who usually act as a go-between for the dhow owners. Day trips are popular and because competition is tough the prices are almost standard. Other possible excursions are to Dondori National Reserve, Kiunga Marine National Reserve and Boni National Reserve. ▶▶ *For Sleeping, Eating and other listings, see pages 280-282.*

Manda Island → *Colour map 2, grid B3.*

This island is just to the north of Lamu and has the air strip on it. It is very easy to get to and is a popular day trip to see the ruins at Takwa. The island is approximately the size of Lamu but has only a small permanent population – partly because of a shortage of fresh water and also because of the shortage of cultivable land. About a fifth of the island is made up of sand dunes and sandy flat land with just thorn bushes and palms. Another three fifths of the island is mangrove swamps and muddy creeks. Thus only about a fifth of the island's surface area is suitable for agriculture.

Ins and outs
Access to Manda Island and the towns is by way of motorized ferry as well as by *dhow*. However *dhow* is the easiest as it will take you closer to the ruins, otherwise you will have to walk across the island. The *dhow* will cost you about US$15 for a party of up to eight. If you are on your own ask at the hotels and they will arrange a trip with a *dhow* owner, who will also ask around to get a group together for the trip. Be sure you know what is included in the price. It takes about 1½ hours and is dependent on the tides. You may have to wade ashore through the mangrove swamp.

Sights
The **Takwa Ruins** are those of an ancient Swahili town which is believed to have prospered from the 15th to the 17th centuries, with a population of between 2,000-3,000 people. It was abandoned in favour of the town of Shela on Lamu, probably because salt water contaminated most of the town's supplies of fresh water. The ruins consist of the remains of a wall that surrounded the town, about 100 houses, a mosque and a tomb dated from 1683. As with many of the other sites on the coast, the remains include ablution facilities. The houses face north toward Mecca as does the main street. There is a mosque at the end of the street that is thought to have been built on the site of an old tomb. The other feature of the ruins is the pillar tomb. It is situated just outside the town walls. The ruins have been cleared but little excavation has been done here. Entrance fee of US$3. The creek that Takwa is located on almost cuts the island in half during high tide. The main port is **Ras Kilimdini** that is located on the northern side of the island.

Pate Island → *Colour map 2, grid B3.*

Pate Island is about three times the size of Lamu and located about 20 km to the northeast. Unlike both Lamu and Manda, it does not have a large area taken up by dunes. The island is divided into two parts – indeed it may have once been two islands but the channel dividing them is so shallow that only the smallest boats can go down it. The land is very low lying and the towns are situated on shallow inlets that can only be reached at high tide. The only deep water landing point is at Ras Mtangawanda in the west of the island, but as it is not a sheltered harbour it has never had a major settlement. Although it is fairly easily accessible it does not receive many visitors.

Pate Town

The town of Pate is only accessible from the sea at the right tide – otherwise you will have to walk from the landing place. It is situated in the southwest corner of the island and is one of the old Swahili towns that dot the coast. The town shows strong Arabic and Indian influences, and was once most famous for the silk that was produced here. The old stone houses are crumbling and tobacco has been planted amongst the ruins. The main ruins are those of **Nabahani** which are found just outside the town. Although they have not yet been excavated you should be able to make out the town walls, houses, mosques and tombs.

The age of the town is disputed – the earliest remains that have been found are from the 13th century – although according to some accounts the town dates back to the eighth century. The town was reasonably prosperous up to 1600, although by the time the Portuguese first arrived it had begun to decline. The Portuguese did not have much success and by the 17th century had withdrawn to Mombasa. The final decline of Pate was the war with Lamu. There had been an ongoing dispute between the two islands. Over the years the port at Pate silted up, so Lamu was used instead by the bigger *dhows*, and the tensions increased. The situation reached a climax in 1813 when the army from Pate was defeated at Shela and the town went into a decline from which it has never recovered.

Siyu

A stone-built town dating from about the 15th century. It became most well-known as a centre for Islamic scholarship and is believed to have been an important cultural centre during the 17th and 18th centuries. At one time is said to have had 30,000 inhabitants. Today there are probably fewer than 5,000 people living in the town and the inhabited part of the town is slightly apart from the ancient ruined area. A creek separates the residential part of the town from the fort, built by Seyyed Said, believed to date from the mid-19th century when the town was occupied by forces of the Sultan of Zanzibar. The fort has some impressive canons and has been partly renovated. The town itself is fairly dilapidated and outside the town are coconut plantations. It is a small fishing village that has a thriving crafts industry – you will be able to see leather goods being made as well as doors, furniture and jewellery.

About one hour's walk from Siyu there are the **Shanga Ruins**. There have been excavations in recent years and they show signs of unearthing impressive remains. There are buildings from the 13th and 14th century and many artefacts have been found dating back to the eighth and ninth centuries. There is a pillar tomb, a large mosque, a smaller second mosque, about 130 houses and a palace. The whole town was walled with five access gates and outside the wall is a cemetery containing well over 300 tombs. If you are visiting the islands by *dhow* and would rather not walk you can ask your boatman to take you to Shanga direct.

The channel which Siyu is sited on is so silted up that only the smallest boats can reach Siyu. It is therefore necessary to approach the town by foot – either from Shanga (about an hour), from Faza (about two hours), or from Pate (about 8 km). In the case of the latter two, unless you are happy to get lost and therefore walk for hours, you would be advised to take a guide, as the route (particularly from Pate) is complicated.

 In the 19th century this deep-water harbour on Pate Island was considered to be superior to Lamu and was used by ocean-going vessels that would then take dhows *across to Lamu.*

About a two-hour walk to the northeast of Siyu is the town of **Chundwa** which is situated in the most fertile part of the island. Being agriculturally productive the island is perhaps the most capable of self-sufficiency of all the islands in the archipelago; however, it does suffer from problems with the supply of fresh water.

Faza

About 20 km from Pate Town, and 10 km northeast of Siyu. Although the town of Faza is believed to date from the 13th century and possibly as early as the eighth century, there is little in the way of ruins left here. However the town is important in that it is the district headquarters of Pate Island and some of the mainland. It therefore has a number of modern facilities that are not found elsewhere on the island – such as post office, school, telephone exchange, a police station (where the police force has nothing to do) and some shops, restaurants and simple guesthouses. There's even a Land Rover ambulance donated by Saudi Arabia, the only vehicle on the island.

The town is believed to have been completely destroyed in the 13th century by the nearby town of Pate, rebuilt, and destroyed again in the late 16th century this time by the Portuguese. It was again rebuilt and joined forces with the Portuguese against Pate. However, its significance declined until recently when, being the district headquarters, it resumed its position of importance.

Close to where the ferries anchor are the ruins of the Kunjanja Mosque. You can see some the Mihrab which points to Mecca and which is a beautiful example with fine carvings. There are some rather splendid Arabic inscriptions above the entrance. Outside the town there is the tomb of Amir Hamad, the commander of the Sultan of Zanzibar's army who was killed here, in action, in 1844. Faza makes an interesting place to walk around and you're almost certain to have plenty of time to fill before the boat leaves. One part of the village is devoted exclusively to cattle stalls, but goats run everywhere, ruining the efforts of the primary school headmaster to prevent soil erosion on the badly rutted and sloping football field. From Faza you could, if you wanted, walk on to the other villages on the island, all within 40 minutes of Faza; Kisingitini, Bajumwali, Tundwa, and the closest, Nyambogi.

Kiunga Marine National Reserve → *Colour map 2, grid B3.*

The marine national reserve, opened in 1979, has a reputation for having some of the best coral reefs interspersed with limestone islands in Kenya. Leatherback turtles, dugongs and nesting migratory sea birds are to be found here. In the far northern part of the Kenyan coast, stretching from Boteler Islands to 20 km north of Kiunga, this park suffers from being rather remote. Sadly, this area has suffered from the problems to the north in Somalia, and so visitors are fewer than in previous years. It is 250 sq km from the northeast coastal border of mainland Kenya to the Pate Island. The park has a chain of about 50 calcareous offshore islands and coral reefs running for some 60 km parallel to the coastline off the northern most coast of Kenya and adjacent to Dodori and Boni National Reserves on the mainland. Composed of old, eroded coral, the islands mainly lie inland around 2 km offshore and inshore of the fringing reef. They vary in size from a few hundred square metres to 100 ha or more. The coastal area is made up of scrublands and mangroves surrounded by microscopic marine plants and dugong grass. The coral here is extensive. As you would expect, there is a good variety of marine birds with colonies of various gulls and terns. Poaching of the turtles and their eggs has been greatly reduced thanks to the efforts of the game wardens of Lamu.

Kiwayu Island is located on the far northeast of the Lamu Archipelago and is part of the reserve. The Island itself is 19 km long and roughly 1.5 km wide. There are lots of caves and coves to explore, and there two villages on the island, **Kiwayu** and **Chandani**. The highlight here is the 10-km long virgin beach and the spectacular snorkelling on the unspoilt coral reefs. There is an airstrip which serves the two luxury lodges below, as well as a launch which takes an hour to Lamu.

To get here you can take a regular boat or an easier option is to get a group of five or six together and charter a *dhow*. This should include food and water as well as snorkelling gear and should work out at around US$15 per person. The journey is dependent on the winds and the tides and so be prepared for the journey in each direction to be anything between eight and 36 hours. Alternatively if you are staying at the lodges, they can organize transport.

Dodori and Boni national reserves

Dodori and Boni national reserves are in the far north of the Kenyan coast close to the Somali border. Gazetted in 1976 they cover an area of 2,590 sq km. Dodori National Reserve is in Coastal Province and is 877 sq km extending from northeast Lamu District up to Kiunga. It is named after the river ending in the Indian Ocean at Dodori Creek, a breeding place for dugongs. The vegetation consists of mangrove swamp, lowland dry forest, marshy glades and groundwater forest and is bisected by the Dodori River. Dodori Reserve was established to protect an antelope called the Lamu topi, as this area is a major breeding ground. There are also elephant, lions, buffalo, giraffe, duikas and lesser kudu in the reserve. In addition the area is rich in birdlife. Pelicans are particularly common birds here.

Boni National Reserve is one of the large, remote parks in the northeast of the country, contiguous with the Somali border down to the coast in Northeastern Province. It is 1,340 sq km, and contains the only coastal lowland groundwater forest in Kenya. The diversity of the vegetation consist of coastal and riverine forests, mangroves, swampy grasslands and savannah. Away from the rivers and channels, impenetrable thornbush is scattered with gigantic baobabs.It has large concentrations of elephant and Harvey's and Ader's duiker in the dry season. Dugongs resemble large sea lions and have been almost hunted to extinction, making them one of the rarest sea mammals. Dugongs give birth to live pups, that suckle on teats situated high on the female's chest wall. They are believed to be the origin of sailor's mermaid sightings as it was thought that they had 'breasts'.

To reach the reserves, from Mokowe opposite Lamu, take the road D568 inland and turn right at Bodhei. This track leads to Kiunga, on the northern limit of the Kenyan coast, passing between both reserves. Along the road, at the town of Mangai, a track allows for wildlife observation at both banks of Dodori River. Once in Kiunga, the road to Mkokoni borders the coast and provides access to some waterholes amongst the bush. However, the area is only passable in the dry season. The easiest access is by sea, specially if you wish to watch the rich sea wildlife at Dodori. You can travel by boat or *dhow* to Dodori Creek and from there sail the channels and mangroves. However, because of the recent troubles in Somalia most parts of this national reserve have been out of bounds to tourists for a while. If you want to go up here be sure to check with the local authorities and tour agencies before departure, given its proximity to the Somali border. There are no camp sites or facilities at these reserves.

● Sleeping

Manda Island *p277*
There is no fresh water on Manda Island; it is brought over from Lamu daily. Consequently water is used carefully at the lodges and water conservation is encouraged.
L Diamond Village, www.diamondbeach village.com. Very comfortable bandas on the

beach with thatched roofs, 1 for families that sleeps 4-8 people, and the others with a double bed downstairs and a single bed mounted in the roof, each has a front porch and en suite shower and sink. Because of the lack of water, toilets are pit latrines. There is also a rather unique treehouse in the arms of

Maulidi

Maulidi is the prophet Mohammed's birthday, and this religious festival has its origins in Egypt from the eighth century, but the unique Lamu version is believed to have been developed by Habib Swaleh Jamal Lely, an Arab from the Comoros Islands who came to Lamu in 1866 and established the Riyadha mosque. It attracts pilgrims from Zanzibar, Somalia, Uganda, and the Comoros Islands, when the population of Lamu doubles. Maulidi celebrations take several different forms and are normally held in early June. The main religious celebrations take place in and around the Riyadha Mosque, when the central square outside the mosque is partitioned into areas for men and women for traditional dancing accompanied by drumming groups. The best known of these dances is the Goma, which involves lines of men standing together holding long walking sticks known as Bakora. Swaying gently to the rhythm of the drums, the men extend the sticks forward or interlink them among their drums. At the same time, other men pair off and arm themselves with traditional curved Arab swords. More solemn are the all night prayer vigils when the townspeople gather around the illuminated mosque for group prayer and contemplation. On the last day of Maulidi, the men of Lamu gather at the town cemetery and following quiet prayers, begin a procession into town. The colourful, energetic procession winds along the seafront towards the centre of town, with the crowds singing and dancing together.

During the festival there are also a number of sporting events. These include a donkey race along the waterfront, running the entire length of the town. For the donkey jockeys, victory in this annual race is a much coveted title. The race attracts most of the townspeople, who gather along the waterfront or anchor offshore in *dhows* to watch the action. Other events include a swimming race, a cross country race and football matches. There's also a bao competition in the large open square in front of Lamu's fort. Bao is probably the oldest known board game in human history, with archaeological evidence suggesting that the game has been played throughout Africa and the Middle East for thousands of years. The game is based around a basic board of four lines of shallow holes, and involves beads, seeds or stones being placed in the holes, and each player then redistributing these objects around the board by following a simple set order. The winner is the one who places theirs in a set pattern before the other can.

a baobab tree which has a wooden deck all the way around the trunk. Very good food in the open air restaurant. A rather special feature of the lodge are the giant clam shells that act as bird baths and attract a colourful array of birds at both dawn and dusk.

L **Manda Bay**, www.mandabay.com, has been renovated and reopened under new management. An exclusive resort offering watersports and *dhow* safaris, all the buildings are constructed with local materials in traditional coastal style, with palm thatch roofs and woven matting covering the floors. 10 cottages are spacious and comfortable with their own bathrooms and verandas. Meals, seafood and Italian, are relaxed and casual, served in the dining room, on the beach, or on board a *dhow*.

E **Camping** is available close to the Takwa Ruins, though there are few facilities and you will need to be completely self sufficient. Bring plenty of water as non is available on the island. During the rainy season elephants can be sighted from the campsite.

Every few years a lodging house opens in Faza, but the lack of visitors forces them to close sooner or later. There's a very unprepossessing council guest house which is available in theory. Private accommodation, though, is easy to find and you can ask around to stay at a family house. In Siyu it is possible to rent rooms in local houses – there are no formal guesthouses.

Kiunga Marine National Reserve *p279*
L Kiwayu Safari Retreat, reservations, Nairobi, T020600107, www.kiwayu.com. To the north of Lamu on the Kiwayu Peninsula, in a beautiful bay on the mainland, opposite the island. 18 luxurious, traditional-style thatched bandas, restaurant, bar and shop. The hotel has a fleet of deep-sea fishing vessels and game fishing, boat trips into the mangrove swamps and water skiing are on offer, the beach is also wonderful. The food is excellent, non-seafood dishes available on request. The honeymoon suite is so intimate and secluded it's a boat ride away on the opposite beach nestled amongst some baobab trees. Closes for 2 months from mid-Apr during low season.
L Munira Island Camp, reservations Nairobi, T020-512213, www.kiwayuisland.com. This camp is totally eco-friendly running on solar and wind power, the water is brought in by a team of donkeys from a nearby well. 7 comfortable and spacious bandas, built of makuti and *jambies* (local matting made from palm fronds), each with panoramic views of the ocean, rates are US$140 per person full board, the food is predominantly seafood, which is served in a communal mess tent. Game fishing on a deep-sea fishing boat, diving, water skiing and windsurfing are available.

Eating

Manda Island *p277*
♦♦♦ **Manda Beach Club** is a popular day trip from Lamu, and the options here are to get the daily boat transfer at 1000 from **Lamu Palace Hotel** with the barman, or be transferred at 1330. The transfer back is between 1700-1800. This is a relaxing afternoon for sunbathing and lunch with loungers and a bar.

Pate Island *p277*
You will probably be offered food at the place that you are staying – otherwise there is a simple restaurant in the village.

Transport

Pate Island *p277*
The inlet is very shallow, and sea-going *dhows* and the motor launch from Lamu bypasses Siyu en route to Faza. It may be possible to persuade a small boat to sail or pole you round to **Siyu** from Pate or Faza. Otherwise it is about a 10-km hike from each of these places, and you may need a guide.

To get to Faza from **Lamu** take the motor launch which goes 3 times a week (on Mon, Wed and Fri) and takes about 4 hrs. To get back to Lamu the boat leaves Faza at about 0600 on Tue, Thu and Sat. You have to take a small boat out to the launch so be sure to get there early. The journey to Lamu takes about 4 hrs and will cost you about US$3. Generally when visiting Pate Island the best thing to do is to start at Pate Town, and walk through Siyu to Faza from where you will be able to get a boat back to Lamu.

To get to Pate from Lamu, you will have to take the motor launch to Faza or to Mtangawanda and walk from there. To Faza the boat goes 3 times a week, Mon, Wed, and Fri and takes about 4 hrs. To Mtangawanda the trip takes about 3 hrs. Once you get to Mtangawanda the walk will take you about an hour – the track is clear, and you will probably be accompanied by other people from the boat. To get back to Lamu the boat leaves Faza on Tue, Thu and Sat. It does not always call at Mtangawanda so you may have to walk to Faza via Siyu (quite a hike) and catch it from there. You would be advised to take a guide (at least as far as Siyu).

Kiunga Marine National Reserve *p279*
Air Kenya, Wilson Airport, Nairobi, T020-605745 (reservations), www.airkenya.com, has a daily flight from Nairobi to Kiwayu which runs on demand and is an extension of the Lamu service. It departs from Nairobi at 1315, arrives on Kiwayu at 1520 and departs again at 1530, arriving in Nairobi at 1745. (return US$325).

Ins and outs	286
Kitale to Lake Turkana	**287**
Listings	291
Isiolo and around	**293**
Listings	295
Isiolo to Lake Turkana	**298**
Listings	302
Marsabit to Moyale	**304**
Listings	305

Northern Kenya

⁝ Footprint features

Don't miss...	285
Onwards and upwards	292
Maralal International	
Camel Derby	299

Introduction

This is a vast area of forested and barren mountains, deserts and scrubland occasionally broken by oases of vegetation and the huge Lake Turkana. Northern Kenya accounts for almost half of the country and yet only a fraction of the population live here and the region is infrequently visited by tourists. The people who do inhabit the area – the Samburu, Rendille, Boran, Gabbra, Turkana and Somali – are semi nomadic peoples that cross between their villages in the region using ancient migration routes, existing as they have done for generations, hardly affected by the modern world. The main reason tourists come here is to see the wonders of Lake Turkana – the Jade Sea – however inspite of the barren environment, there are also plenty of national parks in Northern Kenya, most of which are relatively unknown. On the northeastern shores of Lake Turkana is the Sibilois National Park, and just north of Isiolo you will find Samburu, Buffalo Springs and Shaba national reserves, all three along the banks of the Ewaso Ng'iro River covering an area of some 300 sq km. Further north still are the parks at Maralal, Losai and Marsabit. Travelling in the northern regions can be rough and uncomfortable; the roads are far from good, distances between places are vast, and there are very few facilities. However, a safari up to the frontier lands of Kenya makes for an adventurous and rewarding excursion, a long way from the comfort of the game lodges and beach hotels in the rest of the country. Be prepared though, this is not a region suitable for visitors who want a relaxing holiday.

★ Don't miss...

1 **Marich Pass Field Studies Centre** Base yourself here, the best place from which to explore the remote northwest, page 287.

2 **Lake Turkana** Although very remote and inhospitable, its wild and dramatic beauty makes the journey well worthwhile, pages 290 and 300.

3 **Samburu and Buffalo Springs national reserves** Go game viewing on the hunt for Grevy's zebra, reticulated giraffe and Beisa oryx, page 294.

4 **Elephant Watch Safari Camp** Stay at this wonderful luxurious camp in Samburu from where you can track elephant, page 296.

5 **Annual camel derby** Try and catch this event at Maralal. It's fun to watch, but becomes hilarious if you take part and enter the race, page 299.

6 **Camel safari** Go into the wilderness on a camel safari. A number of places offer this excursion, but try the Desert Rose Lodge, page 303.

Ins and outs

Travelling in Northern Kenya is a real adventure as there is almost no public transport in this desolate region. In fact, there is little traffic of any kind making hitching an unadvisable option. Although there has not been a security incident since 2003 in this region, there have been armed hold ups and robberies in the past. The recent problems in Sudan and Somalia, and the subsequent influx of refugees into Kenya from these

> ❣ Travellers are currently advised against travel into the far northeast of Kenya from Isiolo towards the Somali border because of safety concerns.

countries, means there is a high military presence in the north. Vehicles usually travel in convoys, and are in some cases are escorted by armed guards. Road blocks are common and vehicle searches are a part of everyday life. However on the A2 – Trans-East African Highway – that passes through Isiolo, Marsabit and on to Moyale at the Ethiopian border, the situation has improved greatly since 2003 and, whilst the convoy still occurs, it

is now not obligatory (though advised). On the whole the area is reasonably safe to travel in, with only the occasional skirmish reported, and you are assured a warm welcome wherever you go. However, the area north of Isiolo into the far northeast towards the Somali border, including the town of Garissa, has had a number of incidents, resulting in injuries and fatalities, and travel here is still not advised. Communities in the region dispersed because of cattle rustling and problems with Somali and Sudanese refugees, and though there are still problems, villages have largely regrouped along the main roads. In the extreme north, there are very few defined roads around Lake Turkana. The east and west shores of the lake are accessed completely separately, and are physically separated by the vast uncrossable Suguta Valley south of the lake. The east shore is reached via Maralal and Marsabit with the central point of access being the small oasis town of Loiyangalani. The west shore is

accessed via Kitale and the central point of access is Lodwar. There are airstrips on both shores for chartered aircraft. Turkana and much of the north is best visited as part of a professionally organized safari. Most operators offer an eight- to nine-day tour heading up the Rift Valley to stop at Lake Baringo going on to Maralal and then to Lake Turkana via Baragoi and South Horr. The return journey goes via Samburu National Reserve and Buffalo Springs National Reserve. Some go via the Marsabit National Reserve crossing the Chalbi Desert. Most use open-sided four-wheel drive trucks, not built for comfort but they are sturdy and reliable. If you have a bit more money to spend, some companies arrange flying safaris, and there is a scattering of upmarket lodges. See page 88 for tour operators specializing in the region. Jade Sea Expedition, offered by **Bush and Beyond/Bush Homes**, Nairobi, T020-600457, www.bush-and-beyond. com and www.bush-homes.co.ke, if you've got the money, is easily the most upmarket and comfortable method of

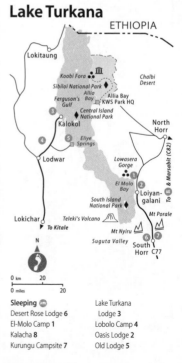

Lake Turkana

Sleeping 🛏️
Desert Rose Lodge 6
El-Molo Camp 1
Kalacha 8
Kurungu Campsite 7

Lake Turkana
Lodge 3
Lobolo Camp 4
Oasis Lodge 2
Old Lodge 5

exploring northern Kenya. The expedition starts and finishes at Lobolo and also includes fly camping on Central Island and boat trips all the way up Lake Turkana to the border with Ethiopia. Driving yourself is a possibility if you are experienced in wilderness driving (a four-wheel drive is imperative), though this is not exactly trouble free. You will need to bring a number of tools in case of breakdown or getting stuck in the sand, such as a jack, sand ladders, a shovel and a rope, and a GPS is a good idea. You'll need plenty of petrol too, as it is in particularly short supply.

Kitale to Lake Turkana

If you are coming up into Northern Kenya from Kitale, you travel a glorious route through the highlands, close to the Saiwa Swamp National Park, see page 154. Continuing through the northern gorges of the Cherangani Hills, will bring you to the desert plains through the Marich Pass. This is a dramatic deep rocky cleft at an altitude of 3,000 m carved by the Moruny River between the heavily wooded Cherangani Hills, opening out to the arid plains of the Lake Turkana basin below. The views are incredible, looking down onto the plains from the lush highlands. At intervals the road passes close to the Morun River, and at two points crosses it. The river is permanently flowing and during the wet season the local Pokot people can often be seen panning for gold. The first glimpse of Lake Turkana, at the end of the road, doesn't disappoint. ➤➤ For Sleeping, Eating and listings, see pages 291-293.

Ins and outs
The Marich Pass is about 70 km from Kitale and the most direct route is going north along the spectacular sealed tarmac A1 road, via Kapenguria towards Lodwar. You can also reach it from Eldoret or Kabarnet via Iten and then on through the upper Kerio Valley joining the Kitale-Lodwar road near Kapenguria. The third way is via the unmade road from Lake Baringo through the Kito Pass, across the Kerio Valley to Tot, although this route involves travelling a track through the northern face of the Cherangani Hills that becomes impassable after heavy rains, when the streams that cross the track flood the road. This route is only manageable with a four-wheel drive. The centre itself is off the main Kitale-Lodwar road to the north. It is clearly signposted 1 km north of the Sigor-Tot junction at Marich Pass. There is no public transport.

Ortum and Marich Pass Field Studies Centre
Although the scenery is stunning, there isn't much happening around here, the only town in these parts is Ortum where you should be able to find accommodation though it is pretty basic. If you do intend to stop and explore the area, the best place to stay is the **Marich Pass Field Studies Centre** (see also Sleeping below). It's a lovely spot on the banks of the Moruny River and Pokot guides can be hired to explore the region. The centre is primarily an education establishment, catering for school and university groups on academic field study courses, but tourists and independent travellers are also welcome to stay. It is located 2 km downstream of the pass in a forest clearing. The compound comprises 12 ha of virgin forest leased from the Pokot County Country. Four hectares have been used to build the centre on the banks of the Moruny River and there are bush trails through the remaining 8 ha of virgin forest. Baboons, vervet monkeys and monitor lizards are permanent residents and are easily viewed, elephants and antelopes visit occasionally and the forests abound with birds. The centre has been built using local labour and traditional materials and a percentage of its takings are donated to the local development fund. Pokot guides, many of whom are English speaking, are used for all walks and treks in the region. There is a strong eco-tourism ethos. There are a variety of excursions including treks

to visit local villages giving travellers an insight into Pokot culture. Further away, three-day trips to climb Mount Sekerr can be organized, or you can explore the Cherangani Hills to the south over several days.

Elgeyo Escarpment

Elgeyo Escarpment presents one of the most astonishing panoramic views in the Rift Valley. About 1,000 m below the sheer cliff face south of the village of **Tot**, stretches the hazy scrublands extending as far as the eye can see north to Turkana and Pokot. This region is not easy to access: you'll need a four-wheel drive and calm nerves to drive up the escarpment road. It is probably easier to walk from Tot (about 25 km). If you intend to stay in the area, Tot offers a delightful peaceful atmosphere with small local hotels.

To explore these hills a good map is required.

The Elgeyo Escarpment has been inhabited for centuries. **Marakwet**, who live here, arrived around 1,000 years ago and claim they took over existing irrigation systems which zigzag all over the escarpment from the Cherangani Hills over 40 km away. The waterways make this area a lush land of agriculture with back-to-back *shambas* (small farms) everywhere.

Cherangani Hills

These wild, thickly forested hills are miles away from the popular tourist circuit with fine mountain landscapes. They offer some of the best walking in Kenya and are a good place to base yourself to explore the area. This is the fourth highest mountain range in Kenya and includes rolling hills as well as dramatic mountain peaks, and forms the highest, most breathtaking and spectacular escarpments of the Rift Valley. Unlike most of Kenya's mountains and ranges, the Cherangani Hills are not volcanic in origin. They are centred upon a forested escarpment and surrounded on three sides by sheer cliff faces. They are criss-crossed by walking paths, and ease of direction and undemanding slopes make this excellent country for relaxing hill walking. The paths cross open farmland, pass through sheltered valleys and wind their way up to forested peaks. All the main routes cross the 3,000 m contour, with decreased oxygen supplies. Car engine performance may be adversely affected by the altitude, and it is essential to carry extra supplies of fuel as consumption is heavy. The northern ranges are the most dramatic and least populated, but getting to them takes time if hitching, as there is no public transport. There are two approaches, from the Kapenguria-Marich Pass road, past a terrifying deep valley, or through the Kito Pass and up the Tot Escarpment. The main road is known as the Cherangani Highway, and is one of the most terrifying and challenging roads in Kenya. Grave mounds are concealed on top of the Kaisungur Range, venerated and closely guarded by the local people. There are occasional sightings of the lammergeyers here, drifting on the thermal currents. The highlands are malaria free, but the lowlands are not. Tours (including ornithological) can be arranged through **Sirikwa Safaris**, see page 158.

Mount Sekerr and Mount Koh

Mount Sekerr, also known as Mtelo Mountain or Sigogowa, is a few kilometres from the Study Centre and is a fairly easy climb over a couple of days. Climbing Mount Sekerr starts from the thornbush covered plains of Turkana to the lush upper reaches inhabited by the Pokot people. As you ascend the flora changes from woodlands to heathland near the summit. The views from the top (3,326 m) are great looking down on to lush green forest glades and in the far distance the open thorn bush-covered plains of Turkana. Mount Sekerr is located to the north of the Cherangani Hills, and is an area where gold-panning is widespread.

Mount Koh, 2,608 m, is very steep, with almost vertical rock rising for 300 m from a northerly spur of the Cheranganis. Should you feel inclined to climb it there are footpaths almost all the way, with just a couple of rough areas where scrambling is

required. There are wonderful views overlooking the Weiwei Valley. The Marich Pass
Field Studies Centre is a good local base and Pokot guides can be arranged from here.

About 1½ hours from the Marich Pass Field Studies Centre, the **Elgeyo Escarpment** rises to over 1,830 m with spectacular views out over the Kerio Valley. **Nasolot National Reserve** is also close by – see below.

South Turkana National Reserve → *Colour map 3, grid B6.*

① *Kenya Wildlife Service, Nairobi, T020-600800, www.kws.org. 0630-1830, US$15 plus vehicle entry.*

South Turkana National Reserve is just northeast of the Marich Pass Field Studies Centre. Situated in the Rift Valley in Turkana District this is remote, rarely visited and has no tourist facilities. It is 100 km north of Kitale and is located between 900-2,720 m. The Kerio River borders the reserve to the southeast. If you do venture up here you are likely to see elephant or lesser kudu in the dense thorn bush, riverine forest and scattered forest that make up its 1,000 sq km area. There are two small mountains in the reserve with forests on their summits, home to the larger mammals in the reserve. The local Turkana people have a warlike reputation, and will kill wild animals for food unlike the other groups in this region. The nearest town to the reserve is **Chepterr,** west of the main road close to Nasolot National Reserve (see below). There are many caves in the hills, of which some have a great significance to the Pokot people. The area is rich in archaeological findings. There are a number of permanent rivers and the Pokot people, farmers in the hills and semi-nomadic pastoralists on the arid northern plains, have traditionally panned the rivers in the reserve for gold.

The reserve is 50 km north of the Marich Pass to the east of the main A1 road. Bush walks with an armed ranger can be organized in conjunction with Kenya Wildlife Services. Since 2002 KWS have been upgrading the roads in the reserve so it is now possible to drive here as well as walk, though a four-wheel drive is required. Camping is permitted near the ranger's post but there are no facilities.

Nasolot National Reserve → *Colour map 3, grid B5/6.*

① *Kenya Wildlife Service, Nairobi, T020-600800, www.kws.org. 0630-1830, US$15 plus vehicle entry. Marich Pass Field Studies Centre (see under Sleeping) is 30 km away and offers half day tours.*

Nasolot National Reserve lies on the Kitale-Lodwar road and was gazetted in 1979. Because of its remote location and limited game resources, Nasolot receives very few visitors. It covers 92 sq km, ranging in altitude from 750-1,500 m, and is bounded to the east by the seasonal Weiwei River. The habitat is predominantly thicket and dry bushland, with many succulents and acacias bordering the seasonal streams and rivers that criss-cross the reserve. There are elephants in the reserve but they are well camouflaged by the flora, though you are quite likely to spot their dung. Other mammals include the greater and lesser kudu, buffalo, lion, leopard, dikdik, warthog and bushbuck. The birdlife is rich and varied and includes the white-crested turacos, Abyssinian ground hornbills, superb starlings and Abyssinian rollers.

A good road bisects the reserve and leads to the Turkwell Dam, a hydro-electric dam at the head of a gorge harnessing the waters of the Turkwell River. The dammed waters have formed a large artificial lake that stretches westwards between the hills, home to a large variety of birdlife.

It is located to the west of the A1 road which goes from Wabuye on the A104 to Lodwar, Lokchogio and on to the Sudanese border in the extreme northwest of the country. It can be reached from a turn-off to the left approximately 80 km north of Kapenguria. Access within the park is by foot, as there are very few roads and the rocky terrain makes most of the park inaccessible to vehicles. There are no formal camping facilities at Nasolot, though camping is permitted virtually anywhere in the reserve. One nice area could be by the Turkwell Gorge to the north-east of the reserve.

The only town of any size in the northwest of the region is Lodwar, the administrative centre. Historically it was an important colonial outpost where frequent Ethiopian raids were countered. Jomo Kenyatta was held here briefly whilst in detention. It is not nearly so isolated as in the past due to the opening of a surfaced road from the highlands and air connections to Nairobi, but it is still very much a backwater town with a pleasant enough atmosphere. It is currently the boom town in the region because of the possibility of oil discoveries, the development of the fishing industry at the lake, and the extension of a surfaced road from Kitale. This is a useful base if you intend to explore the lake from the western side. There is both a bank (though do not rely on it taking travellers' cheques) and a post office in town. The local people, predominately Turkana, are persistent in attempts to sell their crafts, but it is generally done in a friendly spirit. You can buy very large, beautiful baskets made by local women. Take good care of your possessions here.

Lake Turkana (western shore) → *Colour map 3, grid A4.*

The largest lake in the country, Lake Turkana runs about 250 km from the Ethiopian border in a long thin body of water which is never more than 50 km wide. It stretches into the Ethiopian Highlands where the Omo River enters its waters. Giant Nile perch are reported to grow from 90-180 kg in the lake, but Nile tilapia are a more commercial option as they are more palatable and are either dried or frozen before being marketed all over Kenya. There is also a profusion of birdlife including many European migratory species. The environment in Northern Kenya supports many species not seen in other parts of the country such as the Grevy's zebra and reticulated giraffe.

Count Sammuel Teleki Von Szek is believed to have been the first white man to see the lake in 1888. In honour of his patron, Von Szek named it Lake Rudolf, after the Austrian Archduke. President Jomo Kenyatta changed the name to Lake Turkana in 1975. This lake used to be far larger than it is today. Around 10,000 years ago it is believed the water level of the lake was about 150 m higher and considered to be one of the sources of the Nile. At that time it supported a far greater number and diversity of plant and animal life. Now a combination of factors including evaporation and major irrigation projects in southern Ethiopia have brought the water level to its lowest in memory. As a result, the water is far more alkaline than in the past. The lake still supports a huge number of hippos and the largest population of Nile crocodiles in the world, estimated to number about 20,000.

Do not be fooled by the lake's calm appearance, the lake's waters are highly unpredictable; storms build up out of nowhere and are not to be dismissed lightly as they are capable of sinking all but the most sturdy craft. The climate up here is extraordinary. It can easily reach 50°C during the day with not a cloud in sight, then out of nowhere a storm will break whipping up a squall on Lake Turkana. For most of the year, the area is dry but when the rains do come, the rivers and ravines become torrential waterways sweeping over the parched plains. It is quite a sight, and it can leave you stranded until the water levels drop.

Ins and outs Seeing the western side of Lake Turkana by road involves a long rough trip. It is best to spend one or two nights at Marich Pass and access the lake from there. It is possible to get a *matatu* from Kitale to Marich Pass via Kapenguria. At Marich Pass transport on to Lodwar passes through around midday. It is then possible to get a *matatu* from Lodwar to Kalokol, of which there are about four daily. From Kalokol it is a one hour's walk or 4 km to the lake and you will need to walk out to the abandoned fish processing plant. The local boys will offer to be your guide. You are advised to walk either in the early morning or evening as it gets extremely hot. Plenty of water and a good sense of direction are both vital. For access to the lake from the eastern side see page 298.

Kalokol Only 35 km from Lodwar, this is a small, simple town lying just a few kilometres from the lakeshore and the heat is quite oppressive. From this side of the lake it is possible to access Central Island National Park. Getting water supplies in the dry season poses major problems here and the women walk 3 km to extract water from the riverbed. Although you can drink the lake water after boiling it, it is brackish and tastes unpleasant.

Ferguson's Gulf Some 64 km northeast of Lodwar, this is the most accessible part of the Lake Turkana, but not the most attractive. However, here the lake is fringed with acacias, doum palms and grass, in marked contrast to the moonscape appearance with a mass of volcanic lava around Teleki's Volcano, at the south of the lake. There are loads of birds here particularly flamingos and it is the only place in Kenya where, in the springtime, black-tailed godwits and spotted redshanks can be seen. Birds of prey can also be spotted, and the number of hippos and crocodiles make swimming a fairly exciting activity. If you do intend to swim, ask the local people where to go.

En route to or from Kalokol look out for the standing stones of **Namotunga** which have a spiritual meaning to the Turkana who gather here in December.

Eliye Springs Eliye Springs are a far more pleasant place to see the lake from and the springs themselves under the palm trees bubble up warm water. However, you will need a vehicle to get here. There is a small village nearby where you can get some food and drink and no doubt some of the local people will want to sell you their handicrafts. The turn-off for Eliye springs is about halfway along the Lodwar to Kalokol road. As it is 70 km from Lodwar, your best bet would be to base yourself there, and travel up to the Springs. The last 10 km is very sandy.

Central Island National Park This national park was established as a 5 sq km national park in 1983, in order to protect the breeding grounds of the Nile crocodile. Formed as a result of volcanic activity, the island is an old volcano with three immense crater lakes that lie in the basins of a series of volcanic vents. A university research team suspects that there is still a tiny active volcano situated on the tip of the island. The crater lakes are also connected through sub-terrain ducts with the main lake, and are renowned for the differing shades of jade, green and blue at various times of the day. The island is a favorite haunt for breeding crocodiles as well as migratory and resident birds. If you arrive around April-May, you can witness crocodiles hatching and sprinting off down to one of the crater lakes. The island has black lava sand beaches. It was designated as a World Heritage Site by UNESCO in 1997 and is approximately a 45-minute boat ride from **Lake Turkana Lodge**. It is possible to negotiate with a local fisherman to take you out on his craft, though remember that the lake's unpredictable sudden squalls are a real danger, and there are crocodiles.

● Sleeping

You will need a room with both a fan and mosquito protection to get any sleep.

Marich Pass Field Studies Centre *p287*
D-E Marich Pass Field Studies Centre,
Dr David Roden, Director, Marich Pass Field Studies Centre, PO Box 564, Kapenguria, West Pokot. Fully inclusive tours with flights, transport, accommodation and insurance can be made for groups from the UK through, Kuoni Schools, Kuoni House,

Dorking, Surrey, RH5 4AZ, UK, T01306 744285, kuoni.schools@kuoni.co.uk. 19 African bandas sleeping 2-3 people with or without bathrooms, and 4 larger cottages that sleep up to 6. There are also larger dormitories housing 5-25 people. The ablution block, about 140 m from the bandas, has toilets and showers (cold). Hot bucket showers can be arranged. Facilities include firewood, a laundry service and fresh, pure drinking water from the well. There is a

Onwards and upwards

Isiolo is 50 km north of Meru, which is why it is included in this section, though strictly speaking it is located in the Central Highlands. Although Isiolo is safe enough, travel further north requires caution, especially towards the northeast. The town is at the end of the tarmac road heading north, which quickly becomes Samburu country. Up to

Isiolo, the road is paved but in bad condition north of Nanyuki. North from Isiolo it becomes a broad dusty track to Archers Post and beyond. Depending on the safety status of the area, you may be retained by the police at the Isiolo barrier to wait for a convoy to be formed for the stretch north to Marsabit.

restaurant offering a buffet of fresh locally grown produce prepared in both African and western style, and a small bar serves beer and cold sodas (no spirits). If preferred guests may eat outside their bandas. Local shops sell provisions, there is a guidebook for sale, but there is no petrol available.

Camping
F Camping is also available here for US$3.50 per person at a shady spot.

Nasalot National Reserve *p289*
D-E Kenya Power and Lighting Company, the owners of the dam in the reserve and the company town, have comfortable cottages for rent. Pre-booking is necessary and there is a small entrance fee to the compound. Contact Turkwell Dam, T054-20602. Facilities include a swimming pool, bar and restaurant. Some of the small birds like starlings and weavers in the compound are unusually tame.

Lodwar *p290*
Most available accommodation is currently at the bottom end of the market.
D Turkwel Lodge, in the centre of town near the bus stand, T054-20166. Best in town, rooms come with a fan and bathroom, for slightly more you can hire a larger self-contained cottage with a full breakfast included in the price. The restaurant serves some western dishes like simple chicken and chips and the bar is popular with Lingala music playing into the small hours, and it can get quite noisy.
E-F Nawoitorong Guest House & Conference Centre, just outside of town to

the south, 2 km off the main road. The centre was set up to support single mothers and drought victims but will take travellers. Clean dormitories, well maintained, showers and toilets, there are also bandas sleeping 2-4, some with small kitchens. Mosquito nets, breakfast and dinner are provided. Camping is allowed in the grounds.

Lake Turkana *p290*
L Lobolo Camp, Bush and Beyond/Bush Homes, Nairobi, T020-600457, www.bush-and-beyond.com and www.bush-homes. co.ke. Quality camp in Lobolo with 6 individually designed tents overlooking the lake, with showers and short drop toilets, boats can be hired for US$250 a day for fishing and trips to Central Island, closed April. The camp is hosted by the Sheuermans who are very knowlegable about the region.
C-D Lake Turkana Lodge, on a spit at the mouth of Ferguson's Gulf, www.ivorynet. com/laketurkana, is surrounded by water on 3 sides and access is by boat across the gulf to its sandy beach. 18 rustic timber cabins with verandas affording a magnificent view of the lake. The water in the bathrooms is alkaline and untreated and is pumped directly from the lake. Usually meals are available and there is a well-stocked bar, however at the time of writing this was semi closed for refurbishment. You can still stay here but need to bring everything with you including kerosene for the lamps. It is also possible to camp at designated points on the lodge site.
Old Lodge, Eliye Springs, is the one place to stay, but facilities are virtually non-existent. Follow the main sandy road straight to the

lake, where the palm leaves are on the road. This used to be a fishing lodge but it is now closed down. You can still negotiate with the local people to camp here but you will have to be completely self sufficient.

○ **Transport**

Lodwar *p290*
Buses go between here and **Kitale** daily, taking around 7 hrs. There are also a few *matatus* which work the route though whether they reach their final destination

depends on the number of passengers. The bus leaves from Kitale at 1500 and leaves Lodwar for Kitale at 0700. It is wise to take water and food for the trip as breakdowns and delays are common. Book your seat on the return to Kitale the night before as the bus gets very full. The petrol station at Lodwar is the last place to buy fuel and food on the way to Eliye Springs.

Lake Turkana *p290*
Matatus go between **Lodwar** and Kalokol and take 1½ hrs.

Isiolo and around

Isiolo is an interesting little frontier town, very different from the rest of the Central Province towns around Mount Kenya. It is a small town north of Meru inhabited mostly by the descendants of Somali people who were resettled there after the First World War. It is also the nearest town to explore the national reserves at Samburu, Buffalo Springs and Shaba, all grouped together 40 km to the north. These national parks are the most accessible of the northern wildlife sanctuaries. ▸▸ *For Sleeping, Eating and listings, see pages 295-297.*

Isiolo → *Phone code: 064. Colour map 4, grid C2.*

There's a busy goat, cattle and camel market here, in addition to the fruit and vegetable market, though security problems with nomadic bandit groups operating to the north, up to the Ethiopian border have disrupted livestock raising, leading to a fall in prosperity. Petrol is available and there is a branch of Barclays Bank (though no ATM) and a post office (the last town to have these facilities until you reach either Maralal or Marsabit). It is also the last place to have a good supply of provisions, including an excellent fruit and vegetable market. At the **Frontier Bar and Disco** you can drink and dance with the locals. George Adamson who was later to become internationally famous along with his wife, Joy, for hand-rearing Elsa, the lioness featured in *Born Free*, was a game warden in Isiolo prior to becoming a celebrity.

For travelling to Lake Turkana's eastern shores the best route is likely to be from Isiolo, and it is the town closest to the entrance of the **Lewa Wildlife Conservancy**, situated about 15 km to the southwest, see page 181.

Archers Post

About one hour's drive north of Isiolo, or 35 km, this is a very small and hot outpost bordered by the Samburu and Buffalo Springs National Reserve to the west and the Shaba National Reserve to the east. There are a couple of small shops and cafés, as well as curio sellers hoping to catch the traffic into the Samburu, Buffalo Springs and Shaba national parks.

The Samburu people inhabit this region. Every 14 years their circumcision rite is enacted when a new group of boys are officially initiated into manhood. For the next 14 years this group become warriers, while the preceding group are elevated to become junior-elders. As the boys are rarely circumcized prior to puberty, the group includes many men. They can be easily identified because they wear goatskins, dyed black and worn draped over one shoulder. These black goatskins are worn prior to and for one month after circumcision.

Samburu, Buffalo Springs and Shaba parks → *Colour map 4, grid C2/3.*

Just north of Isiolo and around 325 km north of Nairobi, are the Samburu, Buffalo Springs and Shaba national reserves, some of the more remote and least visited of Kenya's game parks. They are located in Kenya's hot and arid northern region, and when you see a camel train walking single file along a dry riverbed, you know you're in a pretty parched area. The three reserves cover around 300 sq km in total and are

> In all the campsites at the parks, the baboons are a real nuisance, stealing anything not nailed to the ground. Don't leave food, or anything else for that matter, in your tent.

separated by the Ewaso Ng'iro River, which provides water for the animals including the local goats and sheep, and some relief from the equatorial sun. They are some of the most pleasant national parks in Kenya, are not too crowded, and are usually visited on a combined safari of all three. There are a number of lodges and campsites in the reserves, but think carefully when to go – daytime temperatures regularly reach 40°C between January-October, even when it rains.

Ins and outs A couple of hours drive north of Nanyuki, they are accessible by road via Isiolo and Archers Post. There are airstrips in both Samburu and Buffalo Springs reserves. Samburu and Buffalo Springs are contiguous reserves, while the separate Shaba, which is often also included in safari itineraries in this region, is a short drive to the east. At Archer's Post the entrance to Shaba is at the right side, while the main gate to Samburu, Archer's Post Gate, is found 5 km on the left. Samburu also has another gate at its western end, but it is seldom used. Access to Buffalo Springs is either through Samburu or 20 km north of Isiolo, there is a detour left which leads to Isiolo Gate, formerly known as Ngare Mara Gate. Some 10 km ahead, 3.5 km before Archer's Post, a second detour leads to the Buffalo Springs Gate. Park entry to all three parks is US$15 per day, plus vehicle costs.

Samburu This national park was opened in 1965 in the hot, arid lowland area just to the north of Mount Kenya. Vegetation is made up of narrow stretch of palms and woodland along the Ewaso Ng'iro River, away from this is acacia woodland and hot, dusty scrubland. This desolate landscape is the face of the less hospitable Africa, but is the preferred habitat for some mammals well adapted to this harsh environment,

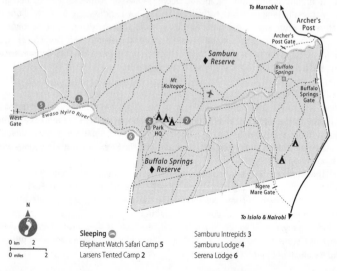

Samburu/Buffalo Springs National Reserves

Sleeping ⏺
Elephant Watch Safari Camp 5
Larsens Tented Camp 2

Samburu Intrepids 3
Samburu Lodge 4
Serena Lodge 6

some of them rarely seen in milder climates. Among these are Grevy's zebra, reticulated giraffe and Beisa Oryx, species found only north of the equator and not found in other parks. There are also elephant, cheetah, vervet monkey, and hippo and crocodile habituate the river. The long-necked gerenuk, also known as the 'giraffe necked antelope', is an unusual animal that spends much of its time on its hind legs reaching up to the withered bushes. Leopards are regularly spotted. The birdlife is unusually numerous in this park, and large flocks of guinea-fowl can be seen in the afternoons coming to drink at the riverbanks. Doves, sandgrouse and the pygmy falcon are frequently seen. The area north of the Ewaso Nyiro River is very attractive with plains and low hills that are rocky in places. The dry watercourses are fringed with acacias, and the blue-grey mountains fringe the view in silhouette. After a downpour the arid countryside turns green overnight, and a short time later flowers and sweet smelling grasses are abundant.

One of the highlights of the area are the 'Sarara Singing Wells'. Samburu warriors bring their cattle to these watering holes on a daily basis during the dry season. Some of the wells are up to 10 metres deep. The warriors strip off, descend to form a human chain and chant traditional Samburu songs as they pass water up by hand for the cattle.

Buffalo Springs Buffalo Springs is south of the river from Samburu, and a bridge over the Ewaso Ng'iro River linking the two reserves was built in 1964. Elephant, zebra, giraffe, oryx, cheetah and crocodile can be found in the riverine forest of acacia and doum palm in this reserve 85 km north of Mount Kenya in Eastern Province, adjoining Samburu to the south. In the park is a crater, made when an Italian bomber mistook buffalo for targets in the Second World War. It is now a spring and is reportedly safe to swim in. Unlike Samburu, Buffalo Springs has populations of the common zebra as well as the Grevy's zebra – it's an unexplained phenomenon why the common zebra is not found on the north side of the river.

Shaba National Reserve Lying to the east of Archers Post is the Shaba National Reserve in Isiolo District of Eastern Province, which is to the south of the Ewaso Ng'iro River. It is home to a number of gerenuk, gazelle, oryx, zebra, giraffe, cheetah, leopard and lion which roam around acacia woodlands, bushlands and grasslands. Shaba got its name from the volcanic rock cone in the reserve. The riverine areas are dominated by stands of acacia and doum palms. This is an extension of Buffalo Springs and Samburu National Reserve that lies to its west, and is often visited during game drives during organized safaris incorporating the other two. The martial eagle can often be spotted here, alert for its prey the guinea-fowl, or the occasional dik-dik. The naturalists Joy and George Adamson who hand-reared lions and leopards and later returned them to the wild (the subject of *Born Free*, a book and film) had a campsite in Shaba Reserve. Joy's last project was the release of Penny the leopard, who subsequently mated and reared a cub in the eastern part of the reserve, near a swamp. It was here that Joy was murdered in 1980, and there is a simple memorial plaque commemorating Joy's life and work erected by Isiolo County Council at her campsite under the shade of umbrella acacias, adjacent to a swamp in eastern Shaba. The reserve was the location of some parts of *Out of Africa* and *Born Free*, and also the US TV show *Survivor Africa* in 2001.

◉ Sleeping

Isiolo *p293*
Plenty of cheap rooms, those preferring a little more comfort should move on.
D **Bowmen**, T064-2389, best in town, a little expensive by Isiolo standards, but neverthe-

less good value. Well furnished with a bar, TV room, pool table and a good restaurant. Friendly staff, secure parking. Hot water.
F **Jamhuri Guest House**, T064-2065, is one of the better cheap hotels. Popular with

travellers for years, it has undergone recent renovations. The clean rooms have mosquito nets and the communal showers have hot water. You are ensured a warm welcome by the hosts. Small, clean restaurant attached.

F **Mashallah**, T064-2142, is good value, very friendly and safe with a variety of rooms, hot water in the mornings. Has great views of Mt Kenya summit on a cloudless day from roof. Limited secure parking.

F **Mocharo Lodge**, T064-2385. Best of the cheaper hotels, obliging staff, rooms functional and clean with mosquito nets, hot water (although the supply can be erratic). Secure parking, moderate food.

F **Silver Bells**, T064-2251. Good value, safe parking for cars and motorcycles, some rooms s/c or shared bathrooms, hot water mornings and evenings, attached restaurant is reasonable and cheap.

Samburu p294, map p294

L **Elephant Watch Safari Camp**, west of Samburu Intrepids, on the banks of the Ewaso Ng'iro River, www.elephantwatch safaris.com. An eco-friendly camp with 5 tents draped with colourful cloth and unusual furniture: huge cushioned sofas, woven local mats and special beds and furniture made from fallen trees, the bathrooms are built around trees. Very good gourmet food and the whole camp is lit by torches at night. An elephant tracking day excursion is offered which can also be booked from the other lodges. This camp is owned by the acclaimed Iain and Oria Douglas-Hamilton who have been involved in elephant conservation for more than 30 years. They wrote the books *Among the Elephants* and *Battle for the Elephants* and Dr Iain Douglas-Hamilton is the founder and president of the registered charity, **Save the Elephants**. He has without doubt played a leading roll in stopping elephant poaching in Kenya. Elephant Watch was selected as a world 'hot spot' by *Conde Nast Traveller* magazine in 2002. Rates including everything except park fees and champagne are US$465 per person. Thoroughly recommended.

L **Larsens Tented Camp**, reservations African Mecca Safaris, www.africanmecca safaris.com. By the river, 17 tents with en suite bathrooms, the dining tent is open on 3 sides and tables are adorned with silver and fine china. There is an animal-viewing platform in a tree. Very elegant colonial style, highly recommended. Offers game drives and excellent food and the use of **Samburu Lodge** pool. Children under 10 excluded.

L **Samburu Intrepids**, reservations Heritage Hotels, Nairobi, T020- 4442115, www.heri tage-eastafrica.com. 27 luxurious tents overlooking Ewaso Ng'iro River, with large 4-poster beds and en suite bathrooms. Swimming pool and activities on offer include camel safaris, and rafting when the river level is high enough. Education is very much a focus and there are special safaris for children and nightly talks and slide shows on wildlife and culture in the lounge and bar.

L **Samburu Lodge** (A in low seasons), reservations **African Mecca Safaris**, www.african meccasafaris.com, is the oldest lodge in the reserve built in 1963 situated in the bend of the river. This is a wonderful place to stop off for a drink at the **Crocodile Bar** even if you do not stay. Each night bait is put out for leopard and crocodile that can be viewed from the bar. Relaxed atmosphere in a beautiful setting, swimming pool, shop, open-sided dining area, a wide range of accommodation along the river bank in 60 cottages and bandas, each with 4-poster beds with mosquito nets.

L **Serena Lodge**, lodge T064-30800, for reservations go to www.serena hotels.com. Located at the south bank of the river, west of **Samburu Lodge**. Technically, this lodge is outside the reserve, though it must be accessed from the inside and there's no gate to cross for accessing the lodge. Facilities include swimming pool, restaurant and bar, in addition to the usual bait for the leopards. The verandas in front of the rooms allow for the observation of crocodiles in the river. Both here and at **Samburu**, it is a good idea not to leave the floodlit paths after dusk, since leopards sporadically drop by.

Camping

E The campsites in Samburu are scattered along the Ewaso Ng'iro River near the Samburu Lodge and the West Gate. All sites are flat cleared spaces under trees with limited facilities. Those nearer to the lodge tend to be more secure. At **Butterfly Public Campsite**, it is possible to walk to the lodge for a cold drink and a look at the crocs. This is not advisable after 1900 as the lodge gates are locked and the leopard bait is laid. Another site is the **Vervet Campsite**, also near the lodge which is popular with camping safari companies. Kenya Wildlife Service, Nairobi, T020-600800, www.kws.org.

Buffalo Springs *p295, map p294*
There is no formal accommodation in Buffalo Springs and most people stay at the lodges in Samburu and visit on game drives.

Camping
E Buffalo Springs has 5 campsites with bad or no facilities at all. The public camp sites along Champagne Ridge, close to the Isiolo Gate, are seldom used, mainly due to the fact that their vicinity to the main road makes it an unsafe area with the threat of robbery. The lack of use has allowed vegetation overgrowth to such an extent that they are even difficult to find. Kenya Wildlife Service, Nairobi, T020-600800, www.kws.org.

Shaba National Reserve *p295*
L **Sarova Shaba Lodge**, reservations, Nairobi T020-2714444, www.sarova.co.ke/shaba. The luxury lodging facility of the Sarova group is the only accommodation in Shaba. It offers 85 rooms, restaurant, bar, petrol station, a magnificent swimming pool that curves around a natural rock formation, and a game viewing deck from which you can watch and feed crocodiles. Inspired by the *Survivor TV* show that was filmed in Shaba, the lodge runs adventure style team building courses.

Camping
E In theory there are 3 campsites in Shaba but they are infrequently used and have no facilities. Kenya Wildlife Service, Nairobi, T020-600800, www.kws.org.

⊙ Eating

Isiolo *p293, map p*
℉ **The Bomen Restaurant** has the widest choice and the best food. Excellent place for a beer in the evening.
℉ **Salama Restaurant**, T064-2229, is the best of the cheap restaurants, the simple fare includes Somalian dishes.
℉ **The Silver Bells** is a decent basic restaurant and the curries are to be recommended.

⊙ Transport

Isiolo *p293*
Isiolo is an important transport hub for travel north to **Marsabit** and **Moyale**, and northeast to **Wajir** and the very remote town of **Mandera** close to both the Somali and Ethiopian border in Kenya's far northeast. Travel to northeastern Kenya is currently advised against on grounds of safety. Transport services are erratic and availability varies.

Akamba runs buses twice daily (0700 and 2000), 6 hrs to **Nairobi**, stopping at **Nanyuki**, **Nyeri** and other towns for US$6. There are also numerous *matatus* on this route.

Babie Coach, a converted Isuzu truck, runs up and down between **Maralal** and **Isiolo** via Wamba, leaving each town on alternate days, US$6. It leaves 1100-1300 depending on the passenger numbers and takes 5-8 hrs, depending on load and road conditions.

It is possible to arrange a lift on a truck (you may have to travel in the back on top of the cargo) to **Marsabit** (8 hrs) and **Moyale** (12 hrs from Marsabit). It is a hot, dusty journey. The people in **Mashallah Lodge** are very helpful with this. Trucks leave in convoy at 0530 from near **Barclays Bank**. There are regular *matatus* to **Meru** and other nearby Central Province towns.

Samburu *p294, map p294*
Reasonably regular buses and *matatus* run from **Isiolo** to **Archer's Post**. The gate to Samburu is 5 km to the east of Archer's Post so feasibly it is walkable. However, this would be a very hot walk and you are unlikely to encounter any traffic that will give you a lift into the reserve. Same goes for the **Shaba Gate** to the east of Archer's Post. Most people visit on an organized safari. **Air Kenya**, Wilson Airport, Nairobi, T020-605745 (reservations), www.airkenya.com, has daily flights from Wilson Airport, Nairobi, US$115 one way, US$175 return. The first one is at 0745 (1 hr), though some of these also stop at Meru, making the journey time slightly longer. This flight continues on to the Masai Mara (1 ½ hr) at 0915. There is another daily flight that leaves Nairobi at 0915 and arrives Samburu at around 1030, on the way back they leave Samburu for Nairobi at about 1050, arriving back at 1215.

Isiolo to Lake Turkana

Exploring the lake from the east is far more exciting than the west, and you pass through a number of national reserves. Driving here takes skills and steel nerves and you will need a four-wheel drive vehicle. Few of the roads are surfaced, and the main A2 road is tricky to say the least. Avoid the rainy season as some routes become impassable. Public transport is available for most of the way, though it is not as easy as on the west. The following route is taken: north from Isiolo to Archers Post on the A2 road, also known as the Trans-East-African Highway, then looping west along the C79 to Wamba and Maralal, before travelling north along the secondary road to Baragoi, South Horr and the eastern side of Lake Turkana including the remote Sibiloi National Park. ▸▸ *For Sleeping, Eating and other listings, see pages 302-304.*

Ins and outs

There are regular *matatus* from Isiolo to Maralal. There are also larger buses running between Maralal and Nyahururu where you can swap on to a bus to Nairobi. Then from Maralal to Baragoi there are *matatus* that cost about US$6 to cover the 150 km. But Baragoi is really the end of the road as far as public transport is concerned and nothing else except trucks head north from here to South Horr. Without your own transport, going north to the lake or Marsabit requires putting the word out (and paying) and waiting, possibly for several days for a lift.

Wamba and the Mathew's Mountains → *Colour map 4, grid C2.*

Wamba is a small town 90 km northwest of Isiolo and 55 km from the Samburu National Reserve. Northeast of Wamba are the Mathew's Mountain Range, where the peaks are covered in cycads and podocarpus forest. The best view of the mountain is to be seen from the road going up to **Kitich Camp**. The highest peak in the range is Mount Warges at 2,688 m. Other peaks are Mathew's peak at 2,374 m, Mathew's South Peak at 2,284 m, Lolokwe at 1,852 m, Lesiolo at 2,475 m and Poror at 2,581 m. These mountains offer pleasant walking opportunities in the shade but views tend to be restricted by the flora. The Ngeng River has a couple of big rock pools suitable for swimming. Guides and Askaris are needed to visit this area. Wamba is a useful place to stock up on fresh meat and other provisions. Near Wamba, in lush forest at the southern end of the Mathew's Mountains, are two luxury lodges (see Sleeping below).

Maralal → *Phone code: 065. Colour map 4, grid C1.*

High up in the hills, Maralal looks down onto the Lerochi Plateau, 240 km from Meru and 160 km from Nyahururu. Long before the British administrators moved in, this was a spiritual site for the Samburu. The route from Isiolo passes though a wildlife haven and from the road you will be able to see zebra, impala, eland, buffalo, hyena and warthog roaming a lovely area of gentle hills and forests. There is also the small **Maralal Game Sanctuary** with a small waterhole that can be accessed from the **Maralal Safari Lodge**. Maralal was until recently home to Wilfred Thesiger, explorer and travel writer.

❦ *You can arrange to join a safari to Lake Turkana from here taking about eight days.*

One of your first meetings with Maralal, if you stop here, will be with 'The Plastic Boys', an unendearing nickname for the local guides, touts and curio sellers, who have been organized into a co-operative. It is not clear whether this has done them any good. If you are polite to them they will happily show you around Maralal. In return you are encouraged to visit their little shop on the town's outskirts and buy a little token. It is through them that excursions within this area can be organized – by camel or donkey. You can also arrange a trek to Lake Turkana from here through the **Yare Safari Club and Camp**.

⦂ Maralal International Camel Derby

The annual Maralal International Camel Derby has been operating since 1990, and from 1998 the event has been coupled with the Kenya Amateur Cycling Association Race, which offers rating points in the international cycling circuit for winning participants. These races are held over the first weekend of August each year, beginning with the Amateur Camel Race on the Saturday morning, followed by a Semi Professional Camel Race on the Saturday afternoon, and the Professional Camel Derby on the Sunday. The camel races can be hilarious events for amateurs, and an exciting one for professionals, and no matter what your experience, you can join in. All proceeds go to charity. The derby is centred at Yare Club and Camp. Yare Safaris, www.yaresafaris.com, usually arrange transport to and from Nairobi for the weekend. The amateur/novice camel and cycling events are over 12 km and run round Maralal town once, starting and ending outside Yare Club, and take about 1 hour to complete. There is a small entry fee in addition to hiring the camel and handler which is about US$30. In the amateur race the handler accompanies the rider and runs along side the camel, but not so in the semi professional race, when the rider must have sufficient experience to handle a camel independently over the distance. The professional Camel Derby is over 42 km and goes through the town and surroundings, again starting and ending outside Yare Club, and it takes about 3 to 4 hours to complete. Apart from having lots of fun, the aim of the derby has also been to promote an interest in better camel breeding among the people of northeastern Kenya and for them to understand the benefits that such animals can bring to these desert and arid land inhabitants. The Kenyan national herd of over one million animals is rapidly growing, and there is an ongoing overflow from Somalia, which has estimated herds of 5.6 million camels, many of which have filtered into Kenya.

The town itself has all basic amenities, including a number of good cheap hotels as this is the preferred route of safaris going up to Lake Turkana. If you are heading north Maralal is the last town with a bank. Both the Kenya Commercial Bank and the post office are near the market and bus station, and there are also several petrol stations in town. Traditionally garbed Samburu are still very much in evidence here, brightening up the surroundings with their skins, blankets, beads and hair styles.

Baragoi → Colour map 4, grid B2

This next settlement on the route up to the eastern shores of Lake Turkana marks the end of the Elbarta Plains, climbing into the mountains. Baragoi is very easy to reach from Maralal, with many hitches and *matatus* available. It's an awful road in parts, particularly as there are a fair few steep climbs and descents. It takes from three to six hours depending on conditions. About 40 km before Baragoi you will see what looks like an almost lunar landscape of semi-arid mountains and plains. It is a sight well worth a stop before the descent into the plain that takes you to Baragoi.

Baragoi is an important and expanding centre in this wilderness area. The locals jokingly say that the road is the 'International dividing line' between the Samburu and

⦿ *Some of the Samburu warriors in this region fought in Bosnia in the early 1990s as UN*
⦿ *peace keepers as part of a 900-strong Kenyan battalion.*

NorthernKenya Isiolo to Lake Turkana

Turkana, and you will notice the design differences in their homesteads – the dome shape of the Turkana and the flatter wider Samburu *manyattas*. The nearby Baragoi secondary school produces an amiable bunch of English speakers, knowledgeable about the area. There are a few general stores here and you should be able to get petrol (sold out of barrels). However, at present there is no electricity or running water in Baragoi.

South Horr → *Colour map 4, grid C2*

The nearest village to the southern end of Lake Turkana. The village itself is set in a beautiful canyon and is an oasis of green between two extinct volcanoes (Mount Nyiru and Mount Porale). The Samburu regard Mount Nyiru as being a place sacred to N'kai, their god, at the flat top of the mountain and take their cattle there to graze during the dry season where there is a plentiful supply of water. If you want to climb the mountain, the shortest approach is via Tum, and an early morning start allows the ascent to be made in the mountain's shadow. On the summit a great pile of rocks marks the grave of a famous *laibon*, and there are excellent views of Lake Turkana and the Sugutu Valley. There are some great walks in the mountain forests all around you and you could either hike through (it's a good idea to take a guide) or go on a camel trek. It would appear there is no petrol for sale in South Horr.

Lake Turkana (eastern shore) → *Colour map 4, grid A1/B1.*

The region around the eastern shores of Lake Turkana has been made into one of Kenya's four biosphere reserves, the 7,000 sq km **Mount Kulal Biosphere Reserve**. The area includes many different types of environments ranging from mountain forest about 2,400 m above sea level to desert with grasslands, dry evergreen forest, woodlands, bushlands and saltbush scrublands in between. It covers most of Lake Turkana, its volcanic southern shores, the South Island National Park, and the Chalbi Desert. The latter is a shimmering and seemingly endless expanse of sand stretching for 300 km to the south of North Horr to the shore of the lake of which it was once part. Even today, perhaps once in every decade, in one of the torrential downpours that occur during a rare rainy season, it will again come into flood to form a vast but shallow lake. Animals likely to be found in this region include giraffe, zebra, dik-dik, gazelle, elephant, cheetah, lion, black rhino, leopard, ostrich and crocodile, as well as less common species such as gerenuk and greater kudu.

Loyangalani One of the biggest villages on the eastern lake shore, Loyangalani is a collection of traditional huts, with thatched grass and galvanized-iron roofs. This is home to the dwindling numbers of El Molo people, a group of hardy fishermen. Believed to be of Cushitic origin from the northeast, this is Kenya's smallest ethnic group (according to ethnologists the 'pure' El Molo only number about 40, whereas others have traces of Samburu or Turkana ancestery). They are believed to have lived to the north of Lake Turkana, but were driven south by other warring tribesmen, seriously depleting their numbers in the process. They took refuge from their enemies by living on the small offshore islands. However, some of the small communities now live along the shoreline. An El Molo village overlooks the bay, perched above it on a hillside. The water level of Lake Turkana is declining at a rate of 30 cm per annum, in a region where the annual rainfall is estimated to be only 50-60 mm. The lake is estimated to be 150 m lower than in the last century. This dramatic change in the lake's water level is attributed in part to the increased volume of water withdrawn for irrigation purposes from the River Omo by the Ethiopians.

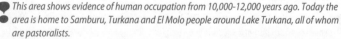 *This area shows evidence of human occupation from 10,000-12,000 years ago. Today the area is home to Samburu, Turkana and El Molo people around Lake Turkana, all of whom are pastoralists.*

North of El Molo Bay there is a stretch of metamorphic rocks dating from the preCambrian period, leading to Lowasera Gorge. Excavations here, initially by DW Philipson in 1975, indicate that this is a very important archaeological site, rich in stone tools, weapons, pottery and bones.

The barren lava beds at the southern end of Lake Turkana peter out into the waters of the lake itself. The high salinity and soda mean nothing much grows around the shores.

South Island South Island is 39 sq km and was established as a national park in 1983 again for the protection of the Nile crocodile's breeding ground. South Island is also home to several species of venomous snakes, including vipers, puff adders and cobras. It is also an important breeding ground for hippos and is home to a flock of feral goats. The terrain of South Island is rugged, access is difficult and there is no permanent human settlement on the island, making it one of Kenya's most inhospitable parks. Only well equipped travellers should consider making the trip out to the island. To get there from the mainland, you will need to hire a boat and guide from Loiyangalani.

Teleki and Mount Kulal There are two outstanding volcanoes in the reserve, **Teleki**, that bounds the southern end of the lake, and **Mount Kulal**, that stands at 2,285 m high, an extraordinary much-eroded tertiary volcanic mountain with its ridge running parallel to Lake Turkana, 24 km to the east. Both mountains are a pretty straightforward climb if you are suitably equipped. Mount Kulal is covered by thick lush green forest in marked contrast to the desolate lava moonscape of the southern shores of Lake Turkana. Its ridge runs in a north-south direction, with deep gorges radiating to the east and west. **El Kajarta**, a great gorge with vertical walls rising over 300 m, located to the southeast of Kulal, appears to almost split the mountain in two. El Kajarta Gorge can be accessed with difficulty around the east side of the mountain.

Sibiloi National Park Lying on the eastern shores of Lake Turkana in the far north of Kenya, just 30 km to the border with Ethiopia, it is one of the less well known of Kenya's national parks, despite its large size of 2,575 sq km. It is now designated a World Heritage Site though it has no tourist facilities because of its isolated geographical location.

The landscape is relatively verdant lake side terrain with grassy plains with yellow spear grass and doum palms, extending to dry semi-desert. Within the national park is **Central Island** that contains the world's largest crocodile population of about 12,000. Despite the fact that this park is windblown and arid, it has a surprising variety of wildlife including the reticulated giraffe, Grevy's zebra, Grant's gazelle, oryx, hartebeest, *tiang* (topi), ostrich, gerenuk, lion and cheetah. The golden jackel is found near Allia Bay. Birdlife is prolific with over 350 recorded species of bird. Sibiloi National Park extends well into Lake Turkana in the process encompassing a large portion of Lake Turkana's huge population of Nile crocodile.

Within the park stands a petrified forest which serves as a reminder that 7 million years ago, this area was lush and densely populated. The national park was originally established by the National Museum of Kenya to protect the unique prehistoric archaeological sites. In 1960-70s the Leakeys made many remarkable fossil finds of humans from 10,000-12,000 years ago. These finds included *Homo Habilis* and *Homo Erectus*, which dated man's origin to 3,000,000 years ago. **Koobi Fora palaeontological site** is located here, as is a museum near the park's headquarters which houses the remains of prehistoric elephants among other things. Over 4,000 fossil specimens have been found in this area. Important finds include the homanid remains, the shell of a giant tortoise believed to be over 3,000,000 years of age, the fossilized remains of the elephant's forebear – the behemoth with massive tusks, and crocodile jaws measuring over 1.5 m (which equates to an overall length of over 14 m). The discovery of these fossils has resulted in a greater understanding of the environment one to 3,000,000 years ago.

Sibiloi is very remote and only fully equipped expeditions should attempt the drive there. The two main routes to the park headquarters at Alia Bay are from Loyangalani and from Marsabit. It is about 120 km from Loyangalani along an unpaved trail through the desert to North Horr and then northwest to Allia Bay, the park HQ. This is only passable by four-wheel drive. No public transport vehicles run to Sibiloi, but occasional supply vehicles do make the journey between Marsabit and the park. Alia Bay is Sibiloi Park's Headquarters with some official buildings, an airstrip and a campsite. The campsite is located beside a dry river bed about 4 km from the airstrip. You will need to bring all your own supplies, and it must be stressed that sufficient supplies of fuel and water must be carried by any travellers who visit this area.

◉ Sleeping

Wamba and the Mathew's Mountains *p298*

L **Sarara Tented Camp**, north of Wamba in the Mathew's Mountains, reservations **Ker & Downey Safaris**, Nairobi, T020-890754, www.kerdowneysafaris.com, is the first tourist lodge to be wholly owned and run by the local Samburu people, with the assistance of the Lewa Wildlife Conservancy. The lodge is on the Namunyak Wildlife Conservation Trust, an area of 75,000 ha home to the Samburu. Namunyak means '*place of peace*'. Set up in 1995 to promote wildlife conservation and to assist the local community to benefit from tourism, in return for protecting the wildlife species living on their land, this has been hugely successful – after the severe ivory poaching crisis of the mid 1970's and early 1980's, there were no recorded elephants remaining in the Mathew's Mountains by 1985, today there are several thousand. The tented camp has 5 luxury tents, each with its own flush loo and open-air bush shower. The lounge/dining banda overlooks a natural swimming pool and waterhole with views of the mountains. L **Kitich Camp**, www.kitichcamp.com or **Bush and Beyond/Bush Homes of East Africa**, Nairobi, T020-600457, www.bush-and-beyond.com and www.bush-homes.co.ke. 6 twin-bed tents with bush showers and long drop loos in an attractive setting beside a seasonal river, game walks, bird watching and a natural pool nearby suitable for swimming. The camp is hosted by Giulio Bertolli, who left Italy over 30 years ago to live in Kenya. Very good food and 3 courses meals are traditional Tuscany cuisine, the olive oil still comes from the owner's farm in Tuscany, house wines are included, bar and sitting room with fireplace. Kitich means 'place of happiness' in Samburu. E **Saudia Lodge**, off the main street in Wamba, where you can get sound food and lodging in a family run establishment, very simple rooms with shared facilities, this is the only place to stay in town.

Maralal *p298*

L **Maralal Safari Lodge**, in the Maralal Game Sanctuary, about 3 km out of town towards Baragoi, T065-2060, www.angelfire.com/jazz/maralal. A classy country retreat with a/c, en suite cottages with verandas, main bar and restaurant, swimming pool, terraces for game viewing and bird watching, and there is also a souvenir shop. The lodge is by a waterhole which attracts a wide range of wildlife, and it is a nice place to go and have a beer (you don't need to be staying to eat or drink here). Rates are in the region of US$200 for a double, full board.

C-E **Yare Club and Camp**, 3 km out of town on the road towards Isiolo, T/F065-62295, www.yaresafaris.com. The Isiolo-Maralal bus will drop you at their gate. Quiet place, though it can get raucous in the evening once the bar gets going, the camping facilities are excellent, with lots of toilets and showers. Costs US$4 a night for the pitch, there are also 10 charming bandas, all s/c (only cold water) and roomy for US$28. Also a games room with a dart boards, table tennis and a pool table in the making. A token membership is required for their use. Camel safaris and mountain bike trips can be organized from here. A 7-day camel safari costs US$510 per person fully inclusive, except for sleeping bag. Shorter treks can be arranged for US$45 per person per day including camels, Moran or Samburu guides, food, tents and the client's cooks for themselves. To have an additional cook and support vehicle, it's US$100 per day per person.

E **Impala Lodge**, T065-62290, quiet and clean local board and lodgings, out of town next to the stadium, rooms don't have bathrooms but there is hot water in the shared showers, and you can park here.

E **Jamaru Hotel**, the best of the budget options to stay and eat in town with a choice of clean rooms, walk through the restaurant which serves basic African meals.

Baragoi p299

There's a campsite about 4 km north of town, cross the River Baragoi and take first right, with water, toilets and Samburu warriors who will guard your possessions for US$3 a night. It is often referred to as the Pump Station as it is located close to the main Baragoi water pump, so it gets busy.

South Horr p300

L **Desert Rose Lodge**, T0722 638774 (mob), www.desertrosekenya.com. On the southern slopes of Mount Nyiru, below the tree-covered peaks of Mowongosowon to the north of South Horr. A remote and secluded lodge with 5 sympathetically designed luxury guesthouses, a notable feature being the open-air en suite bathrooms. Fantastic views, a stunning rock swimming pool, bar and restaurant and wooden decks. There are a number of walks around the lodge and leopard can sometimes be spotted as well as abundant birds, nearby is a unique waterfall that provides a rock slide. Profits from the lodge have been used to build the local primary school and medical centre. Camel safaris from a 2-day ride to a 14-day trek, departing on the first Sat of every month. You walk alongside the camels and they carry everything needed and there are 2 options: a very simple camel train with no ice or meat at a cost of US$120 per person per day, or something slightly more luxurious with chilled wine and three-course meals, at a cost of US$220 per day. This is a unique experience and comes thoroughly recommended. On top of all this, the lodge has its own workshop for making unique and stylish wooden furniture, including wooden wash stands and bath tubs, you can commission a piece and they can arrange for shipping home.

E **Kurungu Campsite**, Safari Camp Services, Nairobi, T020-891348, www.safaricampserv. com. About 5 km north of South Horr, to the right of the road. In a nice spot surrounded by trees, with askaris for security, showers, long drop loos and firewood is available.

Chalbi Desert p300

C **Kalacha**, www.tropicair-travel.com. Situated in the Chalbi Desert, North Eastern Kenya, on the edge of a permanent oasis. The only way to get here is by air safari arranged by **Tropic Air Travel**. Kalacha Camp has been set up as a community based project for the Gabbra people of this area, providing them with a further source of income, and is managed by **Tropic Air**. The oasis provides water for vast numbers of their livestock, including cattle, sheep, donkeys and camels. A very simple camp, built using local materials, including dhom palm trunks for the poles, and leaves woven into mats which have been used for the roofs and walls. 4 bandas with twin beds, flush toilet and cold shower. The mess area is a circular building designed around a kidney shaped swimming pool. You need to bring your own food and drink, but the cook will prepare it.

Loyangalani p300

L **Oasis Lodge**, Nairobi, on the lakeshore, T020-503267, www.oasis-lodge.com. Primarily a fishing lodge, German run, 24 wooden cottages with electricity, very good meals based on fresh fish from the lake. Non-residents are charged US$9 entrance to use the facilites, restaurant and bar. Can organize boat trips to South Island National Park and sport fishing for tiger fish, tilapia and the giant Nile Perch. It can arrange flights from Wilson Airport in Nairobi.

E **El-Molo Camp**, located next to **Oasis Lodge**, Nairobi, T020-724384. Pleasant campsite, well equipped with a swimming pool and a bar, there is also a restaurant that appears to open when you want, showers and long drop loos. Gametracker safaris also have a campsite in the region but you can only stay there if you are on one of its (recommended) tours.

Marsabit to Moyale

Travelling north on the Trans-East-African Highway from Archers Post the A2 heads north through very dry country to Marsabit and beyond to Moyale on the Ethiopian border. For many years this road was considered dangerous and there were several incidents of armed robberies on vehicles by Shifta poachers from Somalia. Vehicles travelled along this road in armed convoy from Isiolo all the way through to Moyale. This is still the case, though the armed convoy is now not obligatory. Check the situation locally if driving in this region. The Mathew's Mountain Range lies to the west of the Isiolo to Marsabit road, just north of Wamba.

Losai National Reserve → *Colour map 4, grid B2/C2.*

The road travels through this reserve, with the majority of reserve located west of the road. This is 1,800 sq km of thorny bushland situated in the Losai Mountains southwest of and adjacent to Marsabit National Reserve and about 175 km north of Mount Kenya, in northern Kenya. The reserve was gazetted in 1976 to give protection to elephant, greater and lesser kudu, lion and a few black rhino. It is a lava plateau with scattered volcanic plugs. There is a landing strip at a missionary post but no tourism is allowed at the moment as the reserve is trying to rehabilitate its elephant and black rhino populations that have been decimated by poachers. It is also unlikely tourism will develop for in the near future as it is virtually impenetrable even with a four-wheel drive.

Marsabit → *Colour map 4, grid B3.*

Rising to 1,000 m above the surrounding plains, Marsabit is permanently green. The hills around the town are thickly forested making a nice change to the desert which surrounds the area. Marsabit is in Kenya's Eastern Province 560 km north of Nairobi and 280 km from Isiolo. There is a bank and post office here, as well as shops and three petrol stations. This is also the administrative capital of the district and a major trading centre. The main inhabitants of the town are the Rendille who dress in elaborate beaded necklaces and sport wonderful hairstyles. They are nomadic people keeping to their traditional customs of only visiting the town to trade. Marsabit National Park is nearby. During periods of drought Marsabit has had no running water. Like northeastern Kenya, the region has witnessed security problems in recent years. In 2005, a reported 66 people were killed in the remote village of Turbi 150 km to the north of Marsabit near the border with Ethiopia, 22 of them school children, an attack by the Borana clan on the rival Gabra clan. The attackers were armed with AK47s, machetes and bows and arrows. Cattle, sheep and goats, and camels were also taken in the raid.

Marsabit National Park → *Colour map 4, grid B3.*

Marsabit National Park covers 2,088 sq km and contains the cloud-capped Mount Marsabit rising from an empty desert, undoubtedly the most attractive of North Kenya's extinct volcanic mountains. It is a large massif covered with lush, verdant growth that offers a welcome change from the desert that surrounds it. Its altitude stretches from 420 m, where thorny bushland dominates the scenery, to 1,700 m above sea level. There are several craters in the forest. The upper reaches are covered in forest, merging into acacia grasslands. The mountain is covered in a thick morning mist that dissipates by midday, after which it becomes warm and sunny.

Marsabit used to be famous for its large stocks of elephants, but these have sadly become depleted. They included the famous Ahmed, the bull-elephant whose long pointed tusks weighed over 45 kg each. Jomo Kenyatta designated him a national monument, and accorded him 24-hour protection. Ahmed died aged 55 years and his preserved remains can be viewed in Nairobi National Museum.

A number of birds are found here including 52 different types of birds of prey and it houses a wide variety of animals such as elephant, greater kudu, various species of monkeys, baboons, hyena, aard-wolf, caracal, cheetah, lion, gazelle, oryx and the reticulated giraffe though it is difficult to see much through the thick forest. The volcanic craters are a special feature of Mount Marsabit, several of which contain freshwater lakes. **Gof Sokorte Guda** (Paradise Lake) is a wonderful spot to observe elephant and buffalo in the late afternoon, when they congregate for water. To visit the park you really need to be on an organized trip with the **Marsabit Lodge** (see below).

Moyale → *Phone code: 0185. Colour map 4, grid A4.*

About 250 km north of Marsabit, Moyale is on the Kenyan-Ethiopian border. There have been differing reports on the time at which the Kenyan side of the border closes (either at 1800 or 1600 hours so get there before 1600 to make sure). The Ethiopian border is closed all day Sunday, as well as on public and religious holidays. It is possible to cross freely during daytime hours into Ethiopian Moyale to do some shopping, or even stay in the Ethiopian part of the town overnight, leaving the car behind on the Kenyan side, prior to completing the border formalities. This is a small town with a post office, basic shops and a police station that has only recently been supplied with electricity. It is developing slowly and there is now a bank here and two petrol stations.

● Sleeping

Marsabit National Park *p304*
B-C Marsabit Lodge, reservations, Nairobi, T020-604781, www.marsabitlodge.com. Wonderfully situated in front of the crater lake, Gof Sokorte Dik, within the Marsabit National Park, 24 fully refurbished guest-rooms all with private bathrooms and back doors giving access to the balcony, which enjoys uninterrupted views, restaurant and bar, offer half and full board rates, flights can be organized from Wilson Airport in Nairobi and packages including return flight, a game drive and 2 nights accommodation and meals are in the region of US$400 per person (minimum 3 people for the flight). Walking safaris outside Marsabit National Park accompanied by armed rangers and experienced guides can be arranged.

Camping
There is a site (E) near the main gate of the national park. There are no facilities. KWS, Nairobi, T020-600800, www.kws.org.

Moyale *p305*
D Medina Hotel, central but a bit off the main road, clean and friendly hotel, nice balconies, bucket baths, no restaurant.
F Barissah, where you can rent a bed for the night in an unlockable room for less than US$2, there are no showers, but you can have a bucket wash.

● Transport

Marsabit *p304*
It is possible to charter a **plane** from Wilson Airport, Nairobi or take one of the small private airlines directly to Marsabit.

There is no longer a **bus** service to Marsabit and Moyale from Isiolo. Trucks and private vehicles travel in convoy, with an armed guard, usually passing through during the afternoon or early evening in either direction. All vehicles travelling around Marsabit, Isiolo and Moyale must travel in convoy to minimize the likelihood of being attacked. The journey to Moyale can take up to 9 hrs passing through the Dida Galgalu Desert. The roads become virtually impassable when it rains.

Moyale *p305*
There is no longer a bus service to Marsabit and Moyale from Isiolo. Convoys leave for the south at around 0800, the lorries tend to congregate near the police station, so staying on the Ethiopian side (definitely the civilized preference), carries the risk of not clearing both immigration posts in time. The bus going north to Addis Ababa leaves at around 0500, so it is not possible to leave Moyale by bus on the day of entry. The bus northwards leaves from **Brothers Hotel** courtyard on the Ethiopian side of this border town.

Northeast Kenya

The most remote part of the country is the northeast, a vast wilderness with almost no sign that humans have ever been here. Part of the attraction is the immense scale and vast emptiness of this remote wilderness. Endless blue skies and flat landscapes produce a sense of solitude that is hard to experience anywhere else. The landscape is made up of tracts of desert and semi-desert barely broken by settlements and with almost no public transport. Its inaccessibility combined with security problems around the Somali border make this area unappealing to even the most intrepid travellers – no tour companies operate in this region.

Grouped together adjacent to Meru National Park (see page 188) are a chain of reserves: Bisanadi National Reserve, Kora National Park and North Kitui National Reserve. Rahole National Reserve is north of Kora National Park. There are no facilities for visitors in any of these reserves. A new park headquarters is to be built near Adamson's Falls on the Tana River, with a bridge linking Kora to Meru National Park, enabling visitors to Meru to cross over into Kora.

Ins and outs

There is an airstrip with several flights a day transporting *miraa*. A flight costs US$50-100 to Nairobi, depending on demand, and is negotiated with the *miraa* charterer.

Background

Physically, the area is very flat with two important rivers flowing through, the Tana River and the Ewaso Ng'iro. As you would expect, it is around these waterways that settlement is greatest and the national parks are based. Tana River Primate National Reserve, is based near Garsen though it is hard to reach. It was set up to protect the red colobus and crested mangabey monkeys (both endangered species). The reserve is more easily accessed from the coast, north of Malindi, so details are given on page 255.

❣ *Poachers pose a real threat to tourists, being heavily armed and quite willing to attack if they feel it is justified. In recent years the government has had some success in combatting them.*

The majority of people living in this area are Somali and before the creation of country boundaries pastoralists roamed the area freely. In fact in colonial days, the area was known as Somali country. As countries in the region gained Independence, Somalis unsuccessfully tried to claim this area as part of Somalia. Shortly after, the area was closed to visitors by the Kenyan authorities who wished to drill for oil. Years of neglect and almost no development leave it one of the poorest areas of the country. These problems have been exacerbated more recently by the civil war in Somalia resulting in a huge influx of refugees into northeast Kenya. There are a number of refugee camps now set up for them (and for Somali-Kenyans who can no longer support their way of life in this barren area). Somalis are blamed for most of the poaching in the region.

Bisanadi National Reserve → *Colour map 3, grid C3.*

This is adjacent to the northeast boundary of Meru National Park and is about 600 sq km. The area is mainly thorny bushland and thicket merging into wooded grasslands with dense riverine forests of raffia palm along the watercourses. You are likely to see the same sort of wildlife as in Meru National Park because it acts as a dispersal area during the rains. It is a particularly good place to find elephant and buffalo in the wet season. Bisanadi National Reserve forms a protective screen to the east of Meru National Park, allowing the latter's wildlife more freedom of movement at the same time restricting human encroachment. The reserve is underdeveloped, roads are virtually non-existent, and travelling to the reserve is difficult and can only be achieved in a four-wheel drive vehicle from the neighbouring Meru National Park or from the Tana River, at the reserve's south border. In any case and mainly due to the safety problems in the area access is restricted. If you want to arrange a visit, you will have to ask for a permit at Kenya Wildlife Service's Headquarters in Langata, Nairobi, next to Nairobi National Park, T020-600800, www.kws.org.

Kora National Park → *Colour map 4, grid C3.*

On one of Kenya's most important waterways, the Tana River, the Kora National Park is 125 km east of Mount Kenya in Coastal Province and covers 1,787 sq km. It was gazetted in 1973 and was upgraded to a national park just three days before the death of George Adamson. Meru National Park and the Tana River mark its northern boundary for 65 km. The eastern boundary is the Mwitamyisi River. The land is mostly acacia bushland with riverine forests of doum palm and Tana River poplar. On Tana River are the spectacular Adamson's Falls, the Grand Falls and the Kora Rapids.

Rocky outcrops or inselbergs are a local feature. These are domed hills or hard rocks rising steeply from the surrounding area. Their cracks have filled with soil and a wide variety of shrubs, herbs and small wind-blown trees have become established in the crevices. The highest of the inselbergs is Mansumbi, 488 m, followed by Kumbulanwa, 450 m, and Kora Rock, 442 m. There is also a wide variety of animal species here including elephant, hippo, lion, leopard, cheetah, serval, caracal, wildcat, genet, spotted and striped hyena, and several types of antelope. The rivers hold lizards, snakes, tortoises and crocodiles. This area has had serious problems with poachers in recent years. George Adamson and two of his assistants were murdered here in 1989 by poachers. His Kora camp, Kampi ya Simba, is where George's grave is flanked by that of his brother Terence, and the one of the lion he called Boy.

Rahole National Reserve → *Colour map 4, grid C3/4.*

Situated to the northeast of Kora National Park, this reserve is an enormous stretch of dry thorny bushland in the Garissa district of Northeastern Province about 150 km northeast of Mount Kenya. It is home to elephant, Grevy's zebra and beisa oryx. The reserve is located on the north bank of the Tana River at the western extreme of North Eastern Province. The reserve is a vast expanse of unspoiled wilderness, accessible only by four-wheel drive vehicles, as tracks are few and far between in the park. Even where tracks do exist, they are extremely rough and in generally poor condition. Rahole, like neigbouring Kora National Reserve to the south and Bisanadi and North Kitui reserves further west, serve as protective areas for migrating animals from Meru National Park. The closest approaches to the reserve are at the south, near the Tana River. One track leads north-west from Garissa to the village of Mbalambala on the Tana near the eastern edges of both Kora National Park and Rahole. From Mbalambala, there is a road heading north into the eastern section of Rahole. Alternatively, there are tracks leading to the western sections of the reserve from the town of Garba Tula off the main Isiolo-Wajir road (B9). Again, if you want to arrange a visit, you will have to ask for a permit at Kenya Wildlife Service's Headquarters in Langata, Nairobi, next to Nairobi National Park, T020-600800, www.kws.org.

North Kitui National Reserve → *Colour map 3, grid C3.*

Adjacent to and southeast of Meru National Park is North Kitui National Reserve in Eastern Province. It measures 745 sq km and is mainly bushland and riverine forest. The Tana River runs through the reserve and you are likely to see crocodiles and hippos. There are no good roads leading to North Kitui National Reserve. The main route into the reserve would be from Meru National Park, across the Tana River, but bridging the Tana River is difficult if not impossible for vehicles.

This is the town in the northeast that is closest to Nairobi both geographically and culturally. It is on an alternative route back from Lamu to Nairobi. It is the administrative centre for the district, and there are shops for provisions, petrol and a bank. The heat is fierce and there is high humidity making it an unpleasant climate to stay in for long. The town is mostly populated by Somalis, as well as a few of the original riverine people. The Somalis claim that much of what was then known as the Northern Frontier District (NFD), had originally been part of Somalia following the redrawing of the border between Kenya and Italian Somaliland by the British in 1925, a fact much disputed by the Kenyans. The Laikipiak Masai lived in this area as far north as the Juba River and over the years have fought incessantly with the Somalis. Travellers are advised not to travel east of Garissa towards the Somali border, as there have been many incidents of armed robbery with fatalities by heavily armed *shiftas* (bandits) in recent years.

Wajir → *Colour map 4, grid B5.*

Some 300 km from Isiolo, along the most remote route in the country, the area is a vast scrubland that seems to go on forever. Due to security problems in this area following the Somali War, this unappealing journey is ill advised.

The town of Wajir itself is growing. The population and atmosphere of the place has more Arab than African influences and is far more interesting to visit than Garissa. The settlement developed around wells that have been fought over by rival clans for generations, water being such a valuable commodity in this area. In 1984, the rivalry between clans became fiercer than usual, forcing the regional administration to act. An amnesty was announced for all those who surrendered their arms, but thousands of men and boys of one of the clans, the Degodia, did not avail themselves of this opportunity. They were rounded up to be interned by the government authorities in a military airstrip with no facilities, where many died of exposure or dehydration. This tragedy has made the relationship between local people and the administration poor to say the least.

The **market** here is quite different from anything else you are likely to see in Kenya. It consists of a section of grass huts with a wide assortment of produce. Fruit and vegetables are uncommon, but you will find some beautiful pottery. A visit to the wells just outside of town to the north would also be quite interesting. A popular pastime among Somali men is to chew *miraa*, an appetite suppressant and mild stimulant (see page 185).

Mandera → *Colour map 4, grid A6.*

This is the furthest point in Kenya, 370 km northeast beyond Wajir on the Ethiopian, Somali and Kenyan border. The war has made this a particularly foolhardy expedition at the moment with marauding rival Somali clans. The main line of contact is on the private aircraft who fly in shipments of *miraa*. In the past, trade and communication with Somalia was more important than with Kenya as Mandera is far closer to Mogadishu, the capital of Somalia, than to Nairobi.

Until recently Mandera was a fairly small border town servicing the local community. Since the Somali civil war, it has become home to literally tens of thousands of Somalians putting an impossible strain on resources. The lack of water, always a problem, has become critical. Also, the stability of the place is severely tested by the prevailing conditions. *Miraa* (see page 185) is the big business in town. There is a post office, police station and bank.

Background

History   310
Modern Kenya   314
Economy   316
Culture   318
Land and environment   324
Books   334

Footprint features

A real tear jerker   322

History

Earliest times

There is evidence that the forefathers of *Homo sapiens* lived in this part of East Africa 10,000-12,000 years ago. In the 1960s Louis Leakey, a Kenyan-born European, and his wife Mary, began a series of archaeological expeditions in East Africa, particularly around Lake Turkana in the north. During these excavations they traced man's biological and cultural development back from about 50,000 years to 1,800,000 years ago. They discovered the skull and bones of a 2,000,000-year-old fossil which they named *Homo habilis* and who they argued was an ancestor to modern man. Since the 1970s, Richard Leakey, son of Louis and Mary Leakey, has uncovered many more clues as to the origins of mankind and how they lived, unearthing some early Stone Age tools. These findings have increased our knowledge of the beginnings of earth, and establish the Rift Valley as the Cradle of Mankind. Many of the fossils are now in the National Museum of Nairobi. Little evidence exists as to what happened between the periods 1,800,000 and 250,000 years ago except that *Homo erectus* stood upright and moved further afield, spreading out over much of Kenya and Tanzania.

Very recently there have been two significant discoveries. In March 2001 it emerged that a team including Richard Leakey's wife Meave had found an almost complete skull of a previously unknown creature near Lamekwi River in the north. The skull of *Kenyanthropus platyops* has a flat face, much like modern humans and has been dated at between 3,200,000 and 3,500,000 years old. This is about the same time as the famous 'Lucy' – *Australopithecus afarensis* – found in Ethiopia in 1974, was living and suggests that modern humans evolved from one of several closely related ape-like ancestors of that period.

A potentially more remarkable find was also announced in 2001. Fourteen fragments of a 6,000,000-year-old 'Millennium Man' were discovered in the remote Tugen Hills west of Lake Baringo. The fossils from four bodies of *Orrorin tugenensis* are among the oldest remains of ape-like ancestors ever found, about twice as old as Lucy. They appear to be more human-like than could have been imagined for a creature that lived so long ago and could be the remains of the oldest known direct ancestor of humans. If this controversial finding is confirmed it could force a major revision in current understanding of the history of human evolution.

In more recent times, from 5,000-3,000 BC Kenya was inhabited by hunter-gatherer groups, the forefathers of the Boni, Wata and Wariangulu people.

Bantu expansion

Later still began an influx of peoples from all over Africa which lasted right up until about the 19th century. The first wave came from Ethiopia when the tall, lean Cushitic people gradually moved into Kenya over the second millennium BC settling around Lake Turkana in the north. These people practised mixed agriculture, keeping animals and planting crops. There is still evidence of irrigation systems and dams and wells built by them in the arid northern parts of Kenya. As the climate changed, getting hotter and drier, they were forced to move on to the hills above Lake Victoria.

The Eastern Cushitics, also pastoralists, moved into central Kenya around 3,000 years ago. This group assimilated with other agricultural communities and spread across the land. The rest of Kenya's ancestors are said to have arrived between 500 BC and AD 500 with Bantu-speaking people arriving from West Africa and Nilotic speakers from Southern Sudan attracted by the rich grazing and plentiful farmland.

The Kenyan coast attracted people from other parts of the world as well as Africa. The first definite evidence of this is a description of Mombasa by the Greek Diogenes in AD 110 on his return to Egypt. He describes trading in cloth, tools, glass, brass,

Ptolemy included details of this part of the coast in his Map of the World. It was to be
another few centuries before the arrival of Islam on the coast and the beginning of its
Golden Age.

Arab and Persian settlers developed trade routes extending across the Indian
Ocean into China establishing commercial centres all along the East Africa coast.
They greatly contributed to the arts and architecture of the region and built fine
mosques, monuments and houses. Evidence of the prosperity of this period can be
seen in the architecture in parts of Mombasa, Malindi and Lamu, and particularly in
the intricate and elegant balconies outside some of the houses in the old part of
Mombasa. All along this part of the coast, intermarriage between Arabs and Africans
resulted in a harmonious partnership of African and Islamic influences personified in
the Swahili people. This situation continued peacefully until the arrival of the
Portuguese in the 16th century.

Portuguese and Arab influence
Mombasa was known to be rich in both gold and ivory, making it a tempting target for
the Portuguese. Vasco da Gama, in search of a sea route to India, arrived in Mombasa
in 1498. He was unsuccessful in docking there at this time, but two years later
ransacked the town. For many years the Portuguese returned to plunder Mombasa
until finally they occupied the city. There followed 100 years of harsh colonial rule
from their principal base at Fort Jesus overlooking the entrance to the old harbour.
Arab resistance to Portuguese control of the Kenyan coast was strong, but they were
unable to defeat the Portuguese who managed to keep their foothold in East Africa.

The end of Portuguese control began in 1696 with a siege of Fort Jesus. The
struggle lasted for nearly 2½ years when the Arabs finally managed to scale the
fortress walls. By 1720, the last Portuguese garrison had left the Kenyan coast. The
Arabs remained in control of the East African coast until the arrival of the British and
Germans in the late 19th century. In this period the coast did not prosper as there
were destructive intrigues amongst rival Arab groups and this hampered commerce
and development in their African territories.

The Colonial period
The British influence in Kenya began quite casually in 1823 following negotiations
between Captain Owen, a British Officer, and the Mazruis who ruled the island of
Mombasa. The Mazruis asked for British protection from attack by other Omani
interests in the area. Owen granted British protection in return for the Mazruis
abolishing slavery. He sent to London and India for ratification of the treaty, posted
his first officer together with an interpreter, four sailors and four marines and thus
began the British occupation of Kenya. At this time, interest in Kenya was limited to
the coast and then only as part of an evangelical desire to eliminate slavery. However,
50 years later attitudes towards the country changed.

In 1887 the Imperial British East Africa Company (IBEAC) founded its
headquarters in Mombasa with the purpose of developing trade. From here it sent
small groups of officials into the interior to negotiate with local tribesmen. One such
officer Frederick Lugard made alliances with the Kikuyu en route to Uganda.

The final stage in British domination over Kenya was the development of the
railway. The IBEAC and Lugard believed a railway was essential to keep its posts in the
interior of Kenya supplied with essential goods, and also believed it was necessary in
order to protect Britain's position in Uganda. Despite much opposition in London, the
railway was built, commencing in 1901, at an eventual cost of £5 million.

Nairobi was created at the centre of operations as a convenient stopping point
midway between Mombasa and Lake Victoria where a water supply was available.
Despite many problems, the railway reached Nairobi in 1899 and Port Florence (now

Kisumu) in 1901, and was the catalyst for British settlers moving into Kenya as well as for African resistance to the loss of their lands.

From 1895 to 1910 the government encouraged white settlers to cultivate land in the Central Highlands of the country around the railway, particularly the fertile Western Highlands. It was regarded as imperative to attract white settlers to increase trade and thus increase the usefulness of the railway. The Masai bitterly opposed being moved from their land but years of war combined with the effects of cholera, smallpox, rinderpest and famine had considerably weakened their resistance. The Masai were moved into two reserves on either side of the railway, but soon had to move out of the one to the north as the white settlers pressed for more land. Kikuyu land was also occupied by white settlers as they moved to occupy the highlands around the western side of Mount Kenya.

By 1915 there were 21,400 sq km set aside for about 1,000 settlers. This number was increased after the Second World War with the Soldier Settlement Scheme. Initially the settlers grew crops and raised animals, basing their livelihood on wheat, wool, dairy and meat, but by 1914 it was clear that these had little potential as export goods so they changed to maize and coffee. Perhaps the most famous of the early settlers was Lord Delamere. He was important in early experimental agriculture and it was through his mistakes that many lessons were learnt about agriculture in the tropics. He tried out different wheat varieties until he developed one that was resistant to wheat rust. The 1920s saw the rapid expansion of settler agriculture – in particular coffee, sisal and maize – and the prices for these commodities rose, giving the settlers reason to be optimistic about their future.

However, when the prices plummeted in the Depression of the 1930s the weaknesses of the settler agriculture scheme were revealed. By 1930 over 50% by value of settler export was accounted for by coffee alone, making them very vulnerable when prices fell. Many settlers were heavily mortgaged and could not service their debts. About 20% of the white farmers gave up their farms, while others left farming temporarily. Cultivated land on settler farms fell from 644,000 acres in 1930 to 502,000 acres in 1936, most of the loss being wheat and maize.

About one-third of the colonial government's revenue was from duties on settlers' production and goods imported by the settlers. Therefore the government was also seriously affected by the fall in prices. In earlier years the government had shown its commitment to white agriculture by investment in infrastructure (for example railways and ports) and, because of its dependence on custom duties, it felt it could not simply abandon the settlers. Many of the settlers were saved by the colonial government who pumped about £1 million into white agriculture with subsidies and rebates on exports and loans, and the formation of a Land Bank.

Following the Depression and the Second World War the numbers of settlers increased sharply so that by the 1950s the white population had reached about 80,000. As well as dairy farming, the main crops they grew were coffee, tea and maize. However, discontent among the African population over the loss of their traditional land to the settlers was growing. In order to increase the pool of African labour for white settler development (most Africans were unwilling to work for the Europeans voluntarily) taxes and other levies were imposed. Furthermore, Africans were prevented from growing coffee, the most lucrative crop, on the grounds that there was a risk of coffee berry disease with lots of small producers. Thus many Africans were forced to become farm labourers or to migrate to the towns in search of work to pay the taxes. By the 1940s the European farmers had prospered in cash crop production.

As the number of Europeans moving into the country increased, so too did African resistance to the loss of their land and there was organized African political activity against the Europeans as early as 1922. The large number of Africans, particularly Kikuyu, moving into the growing capital Nairobi formed a political community supported by sections of the influential Asian community. This led to the

formation of the East African Association, the first pan-Kenyan nationalist movement 313
led by Harry Thuku. His arrest and the subsequent riots were the first challenge to the
settlers and the colonial regime.

Jomo Kenyatta, an influential Kikuyu, led a campaign to bring Kikuyu land grievances
to British notice. In 1932 he gave evidence to the Carter Land Commission in London
which had been set up to adjudicate on land interests in Kenya, but without success.
During the war years, all African political associations were banned and there was no
voice for the interests of black Kenyans. At the end of the war, thousands of returning
African soldiers began to demand rights, and discontent grew. Kenyatta had remained
abroad travelling in Europe and the Soviet Union and returned in 1946 as a formidable
statesman. In 1944 an African nationalist organization, the Kenya African Union (KAU)
was formed to press for African access to settler occupied land. The KAU was primarily
supported by the Kikuyu. In 1947 Kenyatta became president of KAU and was widely
supported as the one man who could unite Kenya's various political and ethnic factions.

Mau Mau era

At the same time as the KAU were looking for political change, a Kikuyu group, Mau
Mau, began a campaign of violence. In the early 1950s the Mau Mau began terrorist
activities, and several white settlers were killed as well as thousands of Africans
thought to have collaborated with the colonial government.

The British authorities declared a state of emergency in 1952 in the face of the
Mau Mau campaign and the Kikuyu were herded into 'protected villages' surrounded
by barbed wire. People were forbidden to leave during the hours of darkness. From
1952 to 1956 the terrorist campaign waged against the colonial authority resulted in
the deaths of 13,000 Africans and 32 European civilians. Over 20,000 Kikuyu were
placed in detention camps before the Mau Mau finally were defeated. The British
imprisoned Kenyatta in 1953 for seven years for alleged involvement in Mau Mau
activities, and banned the KAU, though it is debatable as to whether Kenyatta had any
influence over Mau Mau activities.

The cost of suppressing the Mau Mau, the force of the East African case, and world
opinion, convinced the British government that preparation for Independence was the
wisest course. The settlers were effectively abandoned, and were left with the prospect
of making their own way under a majority-rule government. A number did sell up and
leave, but many, encouraged by Kenyatta, stayed on to become Kenyan citizens.

The state of emergency was lifted in January 1960 and a transitional constitution
was drafted allowing for the existence of political parties and ensuring Africans were in
the majority in the Legislative Council. African members of the council subsequently
formed the Kenya African National Union (KANU) with James Gichuru, a former
president of KAU, as its acting head, and Tom Mboya and Oginga Odinga, two
prominent Luos, part of the leadership. KANU won the majority of seats in the
Legislative Council but refused to form an administration until the release of Kenyatta.

In 1961 Kenyatta became the president of KANU. KANU won a decisive victory in
the 1963 elections, and Kenyatta became prime minister as Kenya gained internal
self-government. Kenya became fully independent later that year, the country was
declared a republic, and Kenyatta became president. Kenya retained strong links with
the UK, particularly in the form of military assistance and financial loans to
compensate European settlers for their land, some of which was redistributed among
the African landless.

Kenyatta

The two parties that had contested the 1963 elections with KANU were persuaded to
join KANU and Kenya became a single-party state. In 1966 Odinga left KANU and formed
a new party, the Kenya People's Union, with strong Luo support. Tom Mboya, was
assassinated by a Kikuyu in 1969. There followed a series of riots in the west of the

country by Luos, and Odinga was placed in detention where he remained for the next 15 months. At the next general election in 1969 only KANU members were allowed to contest seats, and two-thirds of the previous national assembly lost their seats.

The East African Community (EAC) comprising Kenya, Tanzania and Uganda, which ran many services in common such as the railways, the airline, post and telecommunications, began to come under strain. Kenya had pursued economic policies which relied on a strong private sector; Tanzania had adopted a socialist strategy after 1967; Uganda had collapsed into anarchy and turmoil under Amin. In 1977, Kenya unilaterally pulled out of the EAC, and in response Tanzania closed its borders with Kenya.

Kenyatta was able to increase Kenya's prosperity and stability through reassuring the settlers that they would have a future in the country and that they had an important role in its success at the same time as delivering his people limited land reform. Under Kenyatta's presidency, Kenya became one of the more successful newly independent countries.

Moi

Kenyatta died in 1978 to be succeeded by Daniel arap Moi, his vice president. Moi began by relaxing some of the political repression of the latter years of Kenyatta's presidency. However, he was badly shaken by a coup attempt in 1982 that was only crushed after several days of mayhem, and a more repressive period was ushered in. Relations between Kenya and its neighbours began to improve in the 1980s and the three countries reached agreement on the distribution of assets and liabilities of the EAC by 1983. At this time the border between Kenya and Tanzania was reopened. In 1992 political parties (other than KANU) were allowed. Moi and KANU were returned (albeit without a majority of the popular vote) in the multiparty elections late in 1992. In the 1997 presidential elections Moi was again victorious, with an increased share of the vote. In the elections for the National Assembly KANU achieved a slender overall majority with 107 seats out of 210.

Modern Kenya

Politics

Daniel arap Moi was elected to the Presidency in October 1978 following the death of Jomo Kenyatta, and began a programme to reduce Kenya's corruption and release all political detainees. Moi, a Kalenjin, emphasized the need for a new style of government with greater regional representation of tribal groups. However, he did not fully live up to his promises of political freedom and Oginga Odinga (the prominent Luo who had been a voice of discontent in KANU under Kenyatta) and four other former KANU members who were critical of Moi's regime were barred from participating in the 1979 election. This led to an increase in protests against the government, mainly from Luos. Moi began to arrest dissidents, disband tribal societies and close the universities whenever there were demonstrations. This period also saw the strengthening of Kenya's armed forces.

On 1 August 1982 there was a coup attempt supported by a Luo-based section of the Kenyan Air Force supported by university students. Although things initially appeared to be touch-and-go, the coup was eventually crushed, resulting in an official death toll of 159. As a result of the coup attempt, many thousands of people were detained and the universities again closed. The constitution was changed to make Kenya officially a one-party state.

Moi decided to reassert his authority over KANU by calling an early election in which he stood unopposed. Inevitably he was re-elected but less than 50% of the electorate turned out to vote.

Subsequent measures have served to centralize power under the presidency, and to reduce the ability of the opposition to contest elections. The president acquired the power to to dismiss the attorney-general, the auditor-general and judges, while control of the civil service passed to the President's Office. Secret ballots were abandoned, and voters were required to queue behind the candidate of their choice. This severely reduced willingness to be seen voting against the government. Secret ballots were restored in 1990.

In 1990, Dr Robert Ouko, a Luo and Minister for Foreign Affairs and International Cooperation, was murdered. British police were asked to investigate, and named Nicholas Biwott, a Kalenjin and Minister for Energy, as being implicated in the killing. Biwott was dropped from the cabinet, but has subsequently returned.

International pressure in 1991 succeeded in persuading Moi to introduce a multi-party system. The opposition was fatally split, however, and in the 1992 elections Moi was returned as president with 36% of the popular vote. However, the opposition did secure 88 seats of the 188 contested, and the democratic process was significantly strengthened as a result.

The 1997 election was similar, with the opposition again split, and Moi again returned with 40% of the vote. In the Parliament the opposition made gains, with nine opposition parties securing 103 seats between them, while KANU obtained a slender overall majority with 107. Attention now centres on the successor to Moi, who cannot stand again under the present constitution in the next election, expected in December 2002. Within KANU there appear to be two main contenders, the Vice-President, George Saitoti, who styles himself as a Masai, but who is thought to be Kikuyu, and Musalia Mudavadi, a Luhya, who is Minister for Information Transport and Communications.

Moi's relationship with his neighbours was not an easy one. Although he offered full co-operation with Museveni and the National Resistance Army (NRA) when they came to power in 1986, relations between Kenya and Uganda have often been strained. Moi was at one stage nervous that Uganda might supply arms to dissident elements in Kenya. In 1987 the Kenya/Uganda border was temporarily closed as the two armies clashed, although later they both signed a treaty for co-operation. There have been problems with banditry and cattle raiding across the border with Ethiopia, and traffic has been moving in convoys with armed escorts north of Isiolo on the route to Moyale and Addis Ababa. In 2005, 76 people were killed in a north eastern village by raiders of a rival clan over water and land rights. The influx of refugees from Somalia, Sudan, and Ethiopia has also placed a heavy burden on the government. Many of the Somalians have recently returned to Somalia, though the northeast region close to the border and the northwest region near the Sudanese border are still today regarded as no go areas because of safety issues.

There were three incidents in early 1998 where tourists were killed during robberies. Later in 1998 the US Embassy was destroyed by a bomb in an attack mounted by Middle East anti-American terrorists. Although these incidents are very alarming, Kenya overall continues to be a safe holiday destination provided precautions are taken to avoid unnecessary risks.

Moi was in total re-elected five times over 24 years. His term ended when the KANU candidate who replaced him as head of the party, was beaten at the polls in a landslide victory in the 2002 election by Mwai Kibaki of the opposition party – only the third president of the country. Initially he pledged to attack corruption and proposed an anti corruption commission. As a result of this the IMF resumed loans to Kenya over a three year period. But some international donors estimate that US$1 billion has been lost to corruption through government departments between

2002-2005. In 2003, the government also decided to grant immunity of prosecution to Moi over corruption charges. Other pressing challenges for the new government has been unemployment, crime, which has significantly risen in Nairobi in recent years, and poverty; most Kenyans live on the poverty line of below US$1 a day. However, Kenya has been applauded as one of the more politically stable countries in Africa and it has been a leading force in peace negotiations in neighbouring troubled Sudan and Somalia.

Economy

Kenya's economic strategy maintains reliance on a strong private sector in manufacturing and services as well as in the farming sector. Foreign investment is encouraged, although the regulations have recently been uncertain, and there are periodic efforts to increase local participation in foreign-owned enterprises. In the East African context, Kenyan economic management has been successful, and has achieved as much as can reasonably be expected of a country with no oil and without any major mineral deposits.

Economic structure

Population in 2001 was estimated at 31,000,000, and it continues to grow rapidly at 3.3% a year. This implies an increase in population of just over 1,000,000 each year. Most people live in the rural areas, with only a quarter in the towns. Overall population density is high by African standards, over double the average. Given that a large proportion of the country is arid, the pressure on the land in the fertile areas, particularly in the central highlands and around Lake Victoria, is intense.

Income levels are modest. Converting the value of output to US dollars, indicates Kenya is a low-income economy, and among the 20 or so poorest in the world. Most families rely on agriculture for their livelihood, and 81% of the labour force is engaged in farming. However, incomes in agriculture are low, and the sector generates only 29% of GDP. Industry contributes 18% of output, but it must be remembered that there is little contribution from mining which boosts industrial output in many other African countries. Services is the largest sector at 53%, and it contains tourism, which is Kenya's largest source of foreign exchange.

Expenditure is reasonably well balanced, with 72% of income going on consumption, a reasonable investment rate of 16%, and a modest level of government spending at 17%.The economy is very dependent on foreign earnings, and 25% of output is exported. The main sources of export earnings are tourism which generate 27% of receipts, tea 16%, coffee 8% and horticulture 8%. Spending on imports is 30% of all expenditure. The main components of imports are machinery 24%, fuels 21% and vehicles 9%.

Economic performance

Kenya managed to expand output slightly faster than the rate of population increase in the 1980s. However, performance slipped in the 1990s and GDP grew at 2.2% 1991-95 while population expanded at 3.3%. Good coffee prices in 1996 and 1997 boosted performance, but current growth rates have slipped to around 2 per cent a year and living standards are falling.

The main impetus for growth has come from the services sector. Industry, too, has performed well. Agricultural growth has not kept pace with population expansion, and the main constraint is the limited amount of fertile land. Kenya is gradually changing to higher value, intensively cultivated crops such as vegetables and flowers, but the process is slow and limited to areas in the central highlands.

Export volume performance has been good, with a 3.3% rate of annual expansion, but lower world prices have more than offset the increased production and export earnings have fallen. Consequently, import volumes have fallen being limited by the lower export earnings and the need for increasing payments to service external debts. Currently debt service takes up over a quarter of export earnings.

Aid receipts per head are about average for Africa – they would be higher if the international community were more confident about the government's intention to tackle corruption.

Inflation averaged 10% a year in the period 1980-1993. This fairly good performance faltered in 1991 and 1992, when prices increased by over 20% thought to be the result of irresponsible spending by the government in the run-up to the 1992 election. Subsequently there has been rather erratic inflation performance, but in 1995 prices seemed more under control with an increase of under 5%. Alas, with the heavy government spending prior to the election in 1997, inflation increased to 12%, but is now averaging around 9% a year.

Recent economic developments

Kenya has been in receipt of structural adjustment loans from the World Bank. Policy changes involve gradual amendments to bring domestic prices in line with world prices. Moves to privatize parastatal enterprises have been resisted (although most agricultural marketing monopolies have now been ended), and the donor community is beginning to lose patience over this issue.

A series of financial scandals led to a suspension of IMF support in 1994, but a new agreement was signed in April 1996. The programme anticipated continued liberalization, more privatization, civil service reform and a campaign against corruption. It subsequently ran into difficulties and payments were suspended pending better performance in controlling inflation and implementing the privatization programme. A new agreement with the IMF and the World Bank was concluded in 2000.

The financial sector has been subject to a series of failures by privately-owned domestic institutions. There have been collapses of five financial groups, where three have shown evidence of irregularities, and two have suffered from the ensuing lack of confidence. Banking regulations have been tightened, and banks with foreign ownership and control, namely Barclays and Standard Chartered, have increased their share of banking business, realizing higher profits.

Efforts are being made to reform and improve the performance of the parastatal sector with changes in management personnel. The grain purchasing body, the National Cereals and Produce Board (NCPB), provides a continuing problem as maize is bought at well above the world price, and in recent years of good harvests, the Board is accumulating stocks and runs at a continual loss. Kenya seems inclined to solve problems in the parastatal sector by reforms rather than privatization, although the monopoly of the NCPB has been terminated by making it a purchaser of last resort.

The government claims that 105 enterprises have been sold under the privatization programme. Two big developments in this area is the reorganization of Kenya Posts and Telecommunications into three units (one to be a regulatory body) prior to privatization. Kenya Power and Lighting is to have the distribution network separated from generation.

Some US$7 billion of external debt is estimated outstanding. Debt service takes up just under a third of export earnings and at present this is within Kenya's ability to service, providing export revenues can be maintained.

Kenya's exchange rate policy involves periodic adjustments such that the official rate responds to the market rate. The black market in foreign exchange is not particularly vigorous, but there is evidence of some measure of currency over-valuation. The exchange rate has depreciates each year against the dollar at somewhere between 5% to 10%.

Economic outlook

Despite the good economic performance since Independence, and the avoidance of major stability problems, there are reasons to be cautious about Kenya's prospects. The tourism sector is now the main source of foreign exchange earnings, and this is very vulnerable to perceptions of deterioration of law and order in the country. The political situation has undoubtedly improved with the introduction of a multi-party system and a large contingent of opposition MPs in the national assembly. However, the outbreaks of violence before elections are worrying, and it remains to be seen if the present political system can deliver stability and security on a long-term basis.

Social conditions

Literacy rates are good at 71%, and noticeably better than the African average. There is almost universal primary education with 95% enrolments. Secondary enrolments are also good, with almost 30% of children receiving education at this level. Tertiary education opportunities are limited, despite the fact that Kenya has expanded its university enrolments substantially since 1980.

Life expectancy at 58 years is better than the Africa average. Food availability with 86% of minimum requirements being met, give cause for concern. Population per doctor is high, but medical delivery is good, given the low income level, with the infant mortality rate significantly lower than the African average.

Females have good access to primary education, with the enrolment rate just a little below that of males. Female access is less good at the secondary level, with enrolments a quarter below those of males. Low income levels place heavy demands on women to contribute to family income by working outside the home, and female employment is almost 40% of the total. With such a high population growth rate, the fertility rate is lower than might be expected – at 3.7 children per woman, it is below the Africa average. Contraception usage is high, with a third of women participating, and this will continue to reduce fertility rates and the population growth rate.

Culture

Tribal identity is still important in Kenyan life though this is changing as more people move into towns and tribal groups become scattered. Polygamy is still practised, though it is not officially condoned. The custom of a man taking more than one wife is only recognized in the traditional systems, and not by official Kenyan family law. There is much resistance to western censure of polygamy. However, the practice is dying under the twin influences of economic realities and social pressure. Few men can now afford to take more than one wife. Among the better off, it is frowned upon for anybody in public life as it causes embarrassment when mixing with the international community. The Christian churches strongly disapprove.

People

Kenya has long been a meeting place of population movements from around the continent. This has resulted in there being as many as 70 different tribes living in Kenya with an estimated overall population of 29,000,000 people. There are three main groupings based on the origins of these groups. The Bantu came from West Africa in a migration, the reasons for which are not clearly understood. The Nilotic peoples came from the northwest, mostly from the area that is now Sudan. They were mainly pastoralists, and moved south in search of better grazing on more fertile land. Finally there is the Hamitic group, made up of a series of relatively small communities such as the Somali, Rendille, Boran, Ogaden and others, all pastoralists, who have spread into Kenya in the north and northeast from Ethiopia and Somalia.

Kikuyu (Bantu) Primarily based around Mount Kenya, this is the largest ethnic group with 21% of the total population. They are thought to have originated in East and Northeast Africa around the 16th century. Land is the dominant social, political, religious and economic factor of life for Kikuyus and this soon brought them into conflict with colonial interests when settlers occupied their traditional lands.

The administration of the Kikuyu was undertaken by a council of elders based on clans made up of family groups. Other important members of the community were witch doctors, medicine men and the blacksmiths. The Kikuyu god is believed to live on Mount Kenya and all Kikuyus build their homes with the door facing the mountain. In common with most tribes in Kenya, men and women go through a number of stages into adulthood including circumcision to mark the beginning of their adult life. It is not so common for women to be circumcized today.

It is said the Kikuyu have adapted more successfully than any other tribe to the modern world. Kikuyu are prominent in many of Kenya's business and commercial activities. Those still farming in their homelands have adapted modern methods to their needs and benefit from cash crop production for export, particularly coffee and tea. They have a great advantage in that their traditional area is very fertile and close to the capital, Nairobi.

Kalenjin (Nilotic) Kalenjin is a name used by the British to describe a cluster of tribes, the main being the Kipsigis (4% of total population), Nandi (2%), Tugen (1%), Elgeyo (1%), Keiyo, Pokot, Marakwet, Sabaot, Nyangori, Sebei and Okiek, who speak the same language but different dialects. They mainly live in the western edge of the central Rift Valley and are thought to have migrated from southern Sudan about 2,000 years ago. Most Kalenjin took up agriculture though they are traditionally pastoralists. Bee-keeping is common with honey being used to brew beer. Administration of the law is carried out at an informal gathering of the clan's elders. Witch doctors are generally women, which is unusual in Africa.

Kamba (Bantu) The Kamba (more correctly the Akamba) traditionally lived in the area now known as Tsavo National Park. They comprise 11% of the total population. Originally hunters, the Kamba soon adopted a more sedentary lifestyle and developed as traders because of the relatively poor quality of their land. Ivory was a major trade item as were beer, honey, ornaments and iron weapons which they traded with neighbouring Masai and Kikuyu for food. Kamba adolescents go through initiation rites at around 12, including male circumcision. In common with most Bantu tribespeople, political power lies with clan elders.

The Kamba were well regarded by the British for their intelligence and fighting ability and they made up a large part of the East African contingent in the British Army during the First World War.

Kisii (Bantu) The Kisii are based on the town of the same name in the west, south of Kisumu. Traditional practices have been continued, with soothsayers and medicine men retaining significant influence, despite the nominal allegiance of most Kisii to Christianity. Trepanning, the drilling of a hole in the skull, has been a time-honoured remedy for mental illness and headaches, and is still used occasionally today.

Luo (Nilotic) The Luo live in the west of the country on the shores of Lake Victoria. The second largest ethnic group with 14% of the total. They migrated from the Nile region of Sudan in around the 15th century. Originally the Luo were cattle herders but the devastating effects of rinderpest on their herds compelled them to diversify into fishing and subsistence agriculture. The Luo were also prominent in the struggle for Independence and many of the country's leading politicians, including Tom Mboya and Oginga Odinga, were Luos. The Luos have a different coming of age ritual to other tribes in the region which involves extracting the bottom four or six teeth, though this practice has fallen into disuse.

Luyha (Bantu) The Luhya are based on Kakamega town in western Kenya, and make up 14% of the total population. They are Kenya's third largest grouping after the Kikuyu and the Luo. They are cultivators, and small farmers are the mainstay of sugar-cane growing in the west. They occupy a relatively small area, and population densities are the highest anywhere in Kenya's countryside, with plot sizes becoming steadily smaller with the passing of each generation.

Masai (Nilotic) The Masai are probably the best-known tribe to people outside Kenya with their striking costume and reputation as fierce and proud warriors. They comprise 2% of Kenya's people. The Masai came to central Kenya from the Sudan around 1,000 years ago, where they were the largest and one of the most important tribes. Their customs and practices were developed to reflect their nomadic lifestyle and many are still practised today, though change is beginning to be accepted. The traditional basic Masai diet, is fresh and curdled milk carried in gourds. Blood tapped from the jugular vein of cattle is mixed with cattle urine and this provides a powerful stimulant. Cattle are rarely killed for meat as they represent the owners' wealth.

Meru (Bantu) Arrived to the northeast of Mount Kenya around the 14th century, following invasions by Somalis in the coast, this group is not homogenous being made up of eight different groups of people, accounting for 5% of Kenya's population. Some of the Meru were led by a chief known as the *mogwe* until 1974 when the chief converted to Christianity and ended the tradition. A group of tribal elders administer traditional justice along with the witch doctor.

The Meru occupy some of the country's richest farmland which is used to produce tea, coffee, pyrethrum, maize and potatoes. Another highly profitable crop grown by the Meru in this region is *miraa*, a mild stimulant particularly popular amongst Islamic communities and Somalis, see page 185.

Swahili (Bantu) The Swahili dwell along the coast, and make up less than 1% of the total population. Although they do not have a common heritage, they do share a common language, religion and culture. Ancestry is mainly a mixture of Arabic and African. Today the majority of coastal people are Muslims.

Turkana (Nilotic) Like the Masai, this group has retained its rich and colourful dress and has a reputation as warriors. They comprise 2% of the total population. They are mainly based in the northwest part of Kenya living in the desert near the Ugandan border. This is the most isolated part of the country and as a consequence the Turkana have probably been affected less by the 20th century than any other tribe in Kenya.

The Turkana are pastoralists whose main diet consists of milk and blood. Cattle are important in Turkana culture, being herded by men. Camels, goats and sheep are also important and are looked after by boys and small girls. Recently some Turkana have begun fishing in the dry season.

The traditional dress of the Turkana is very eye-catching and is still fairly commonly worn. Men cover part of their hair with mud which is then painted blue and decorated with ostrich feathers. The main garment is a woollen blanket worn over one shoulder. Women wear a variety of beaded and metal adornments many of which signify different events in a woman's life. Women wear a half skirt of animal skins and a piece of black cloth. Both men and women sometimes insert a plug through the lower lip. Tattooing is still fairly common. Men are tattooed on the shoulders and upper arm each time they kill an enemy. Witch doctors and prophets are held in high regard.

Most traditional Kenyan music and dance are centred on drums (*ngomas*), and there is a variety of drums used throughout the country that are played for people to dance to. Other instruments include reed flutes and basic stringed instruments, such as the nyatiti, which is similar to a medieval lyre and is usually played by a solo singer. Inland, the colonial period gave rise to Beni singing; very long narrative songs with strong elements of social commentary and political criticism. On the coast, the Swahili culture saw the growth of a unique style of music called Taarab, which fuses African percussion with Arabian rhythms and is performed by a large group of musicians playing violins, ouds and singing in Kiswahili. It was thought to have its origins from the 19th century when the Omanis traded on the coast. In modern times, these instruments are being replaced by electric guitars and keyboards but the scales of the notes are still distinctively Arabian. Most of the singers are female and the songs these days are very similar to the music that accompanies Bollywood movies. Since the 1970s pop music has been popular in Kenya, especially imported West African music such as makossa or highlife, or Congolese rumba, which are all very infectious and danceable. Today Congolese music (Lingala) is extremely popular and the type you are most likely to hear on matatus, in the streets, in bars and clubs, in fact anywhere and everywhere. Many of the musicians that play this music have actually relocated to Nairobi because of their success there. Also today, thanks to FM radio, young Kenyans are listening and dancing to, as well as playing, the same sort of chart topping music as their contemporaries in the rest of the world. Rap has become increasingly popular among young Kenyans, and there are several Kenya based rap bands. Whilst the style of music is virtually indistinguishable from US based rappers, the lyrics are most definitely Kenyan and have much to say about life in modern Kenya. Since the late 1990s, two young Kenyan musicians, Joseph Ogidi and Jahd Adonijah who call themselves Gidi Gidi Maji Maji, have become one of Kenya's most successful rap bands, not only in Kenya but in South Africa. Their style of music is a fusion of contemporary rap and African music in Dholuo, their mother tongue. One of their most famous songs is Unbwogable (Unbeatable) a danceable and politically flammable song that became an anthem for opposition politics and reached its peak during the 2003 change of government in Kenya. The rise of Christianity greatly increased the popularity of gospel and choral music and many Kenyans sing in church each Sunday. Acrobatics have also become increasingly popular in Kenya. A growing number of young performers have taken to this art of traditional dance combined with modern gymnastic technique. In Nairobi's poorest suburbs, acrobatics has become a popular form of exercise, entertainment, and a low cost and accessible form of performance art, and these acts are beginning to feature as entertainment in the tourist hotels.

Art

Although Kenya has less formal art galleries than many other countries, it has an invaluable artistic wealth easily seen in the many curio and craft markets and shops. Going right back in time there are a few locations in the country with examples of rock art painted by early man when they still lived in caves. Many of Kenya's tribes have traditionally held a great significance on decoration of both functional objects such as pots and baskets, weapons, and musical instruments, and also the body. You only have to see a proud Masai or Samburu warrior wrapped in vivid robes and intricate jewellery to see evidence of how important adornment is in these societies. In fact the Samburu who pay a great deal of attention to their appearance with their ochre stained skin and elaborate hairstyles, were named, perhaps a little scornfully, by the other tribes – Samburu means butterfly.

For the Masai, the use of decorative beading is very significant as it is used to emphasise social status and to record stages of initiation and passage. Wood carving

⁝ A real tear jerker

Joy and George Adamson were one of the 20th century's most famous champions of wildlife. Their relationship with Elsa the lioness in the 1950s and 1960s is one of the best-known animal stories ever told – immortalized in the book and film *Born Free*. The public image of their lives in the inhospitable bush lands of Kenya was of romantic safaris and tireless commitment. Joy with her tight knit of blond curls and easy laugh was a colonial queen and George with his suntanned chest, khaki shorts and white beard, a legend of the bush. George grew up in India but moved to Kenya as a child, and after working on farms in the Rift Valley, he turned his hand to hunting but had a change of heart about killing lions when he came across one sitting on a rock: "She was sculptured by the setting sun, as though she were part of the granite on which she lay. I wondered how many lions had lain on the self-same rock during countless centuries while the human race was still in its cradle." This passage from his diary was read by Bill Travers, the actor who played George in *Born Free*, at his 1989 memorial service in London. He decided on a career as a game warden and got a job in the remote and unexplored Northern Frontier of Kenya on the border with Somalia and arrested 25 poachers in the first few months.

Joy was born Friederike Gessner in 1910 in what was then, the Austro-Hungarian Empire (later to become part of Austria). She set sail for Africa in 1937 and met Peter Bally, a botanist, on the boat between Cairo and Mombasa. They married in Nairobi in 1938 and he renamed her Joy, after the joy that she had bought into his life. Ironically, the marriage was unhappy and didn't last long. Joy met George on safari and seduced him in the Norfolk, the famous hotel in Nairobi a month later. She shared his passion and respect for the Northern Frontier and

demonstrated compatibility for adventure and a love of wildlife. She was also a fine artist and was commissioned to paint a collection of the tribes of Kenya (which today hang in the Kenya State House and the National Museum). Successful in her own right, she became increasingly promiscuous and her frequent affairs were legendary amongst the tight knit community of colonial Kenya. But George still loved her and recognized their compatibility, especially when on safari.

Their next safari in 1955 was the one that changed their lives forever. After shooting a dangerous man-eating lioness, George found her three newborn cubs in a cleft of rock and took them home to Joy. When they opened their eyes a few days later, they immediately imprinted on her as their mother. For the first few months, she raised all three, but they grew big and boisterous and two were sent to a zoo in Rotterdam. Elsa stayed and was doted on by Joy who showered her with all the affection and attention she had never been able to give a child. The lioness went everywhere with the Adamsons and Joy adored her. Despite their affection for the lioness, they both agreed she must be set free. George taught her to hunt and kill, which involved dragging a carcass behind his Land Rover for Elsa to chase. When she could fend for herself, she was released in the bush but visited the Adamsons almost daily and retained her old friendship with Joy. Elsa's unique rehabilitation became the success it was, when she mated with a wild male and bore three cubs, which she introduced to Joy. Only once before had captive lions successfully been released in the wild but with no contact, it was never known if they reproduced. She took her story to London and the publishing house of Collins. *Born Free* became an instant success and sold over 5 million copies in 12 languages. Her publisher Billy Collins came to Kenya to meet Elsa, where he was seduced by the then 50-year-old Joy. In January 1961, whilst Joy was away on business with Billy, Elsa became ill from tick bite fever and died with her feverish head resting in George's lap. Joy returned grief-stricken and buried Elsa next to the Tana River at Meru causing a worldwide reaction of condolence never before seen for an animal. In 1964 Columbia Pictures started filming *Born Free*, and George was hired as the technical adviser on lion handling. George selected the lions (over 20 were needed); they came from zoos and circuses, and he made them do what was needed in front of the cameras. Virginia McKenna and Bill Travers who played the parts of Joy and George (married in real life), refused to use doubles in their scenes with the lions but the crew worked from within cages. After the film was finished, George was able to keep three of the lions and Joy agreed to finance their rehabilitation at Meru Reserve. She had been given a cheetah cub to set free, so by curious arrangement they both set up camps 15 miles apart where they lived for over four years. Cheetah and lion cannot share the same territory. Bill Travers returned to Kenya to make a documentary on the Adamsons, but Joy withdrew because she was jealous of the amount of coverage of George. Travers apologised, but she never spoke to him or Virginia McKenna again. An audience of 35 million saw the finished film, *The Lions are Free*. George earned royalties for the first time, and made money from his autobiography, aptly entitled *My Pride and Joy*. In 1969, Joy moved to Elsamere, her new house on Lake Naivasha, which is today a museum. George's pride of 15 lions was faring well for themselves in the bush and in 1970, George moved to the isolated wilderness of Kora on the Tana River where he spent the rest of his life.

He re-released Boy and another young cub that had been found by Bill Travers in a furniture shop at the bottom of the Kings Road in Chelsea. Over the next seven years George released a further 17 lions, and became known as 'baba ys simba' – father of the lions. Despite being awarded the Austrian Cross of Honour for Science and the Arts from her country of birth and contributing to wildlife projects throughout the world (and her celebrity status increasing), Joy resented George's obvious contentment at Kora, his activeness, deep concern for his lions, and success with supporters such as the actress Ali McGraw. Her mood was revived when she was given another leopard cub, Penny, in 1977, which she raised and released at her camp at Shaba, and in 1979 she invited George to come to her camp and celebrate Christmas. At the last minute, he couldn't make it due to problems with his plane. On the 3 January 1980, Joy Adamson was found in a pool of blood after being stabbed. One of her ex-workers later confessed to her murder in retaliation for being sacked. He buried his wife's ashes beneath the graves of Elsa and Pippa at Meru. Nine years later George was killed by Somalia Shifta poachers carrying automatic weapons at his beloved camp in Kora. On the Sunday morning of 20 August 1989 after his usual eleven o'clock gin, a 50-year ritual, he rushed in his battered Land Rover to investigate a commotion in the bush. Poachers were ambushing a female German guest and threatening her with rape, and he charged forward in the vehicle firing his pistol. George and two of his employees were shot dead in a hail of bullets. He was 81. Hundreds of people came to his funeral at Kora and he was buried alongside Boy. A bottle of gin was placed beneath his coffin, and after the funeral, a wreath was dragged away by a lion – evidence that his pride had visited the grave of the father of the lions.

all over Kenya was at first used for decoration of personal items, but today of course every African animal or image that might be attractive to tourists is carved out of wood and this is a lucrative trade that employs a number of talented carvers in Kenya. Some of the best carvers are found on the islands of Lamu, who produce excellent doors, brass inlaid boxes, picture frames and small replica dhows.

The Kisii of western Kenya are also well known for their carving in stone, using locally quarried soapstone in various pastel shades. Most are small items such as goblets, chess pieces or ash trays. Sisal baskets usually produced in Kikuyu areas are usually used as handbags, although their traditional use is being carried by Kikuyu women behind the head, with the strap across the forehead. Painting and drawing in the formal European sense was introduced in Africa by colonialism. Probably the best known artist in Kenya was Joy Adamson, who as well as being known for her work with the conservation of cats (see box, page 265) she was also commissioned by the Kenya government to pay a series of portraits of Kenya's tribes in the 1940-1950s. Even today these are a great testament to the people of Kenya, especially as these days younger people are choosing not to follow their tribal traditions. Today Kenya has a number of young modern artists and the Nairobi galleries exhibit contemporary art, whilst the curio markets continue to find a steady stream of customers for crafts.

Religion

The Constitution of Kenya guarantees freedom of worship and there are hundreds of religious denominations and sects in the country. The population in Kenya generally follows three major, modern religions. 38% is Protestant, 28% Roman Catholic, and 6% are Muslim. The remaining people are followers of various tribal religions and there are a few Hindus and Sikhs. Most of the Christian population lives in western and central Kenya, while Islam is the main religion for most of the communities along the coast and the Somali community. Islam arrived along the East African coast some time in the eighth century, as part of the trade routes from the Persian Gulf and Oman. Kenya's Christian churches are the outcome of early missionary activities, which assisted in the administrative of the country during colonial times and were mostly founded in the 1920-1930s. In Kenya today there are still many mission churches and many worldwide religious groups have a strong presence. Although traditional beliefs and practices vary in detail among Kenya's ethnic groups, they share many general characteristics. Almost all involve belief in an eternal creator. For example the Kikuyu's god is named Nagi, who is represented in the sun, moon, thunder and lighting, stars, rain, the rainbow and in large fig trees that serve as places of worship and sacrifice. In many traditional religions, ghosts of ancestral spirits are thought to return to seek revenge on the living so they too must be paid homage.

Land and environment

Geography

Kenya is 580,367 sq km in area with the equator running right through the middle. Physically, the country is made up of a number of different zones. It lies between latitude 5° North and 4° 30' South and longitude 34° and 41° East. The Great Rift Valley runs from the north to the south of the country and in places is 65 km across, bounded by escarpments 600-900 m high. This is probably the most spectacularly beautiful part of the country, dotted with soda lakes teeming with flamingos. To the east of the Rift Valley lies the Kenya Highlands with Mount Kenya, an extinct volcano, which at 5,199 m is Africa's second highest mountain. This is the most fertile part of southern end of the Central Highlands. The north of Kenya is arid, bounded by Sudan and Ethiopia. To the west lies Uganda and the fertile shores around Lake Victoria. Further south, the land turns into savannah, and is mainly used for grazing.

The Indian Ocean coast to the east of the country runs for 480 km and there is a narrow strip of fertile land all along it. Beyond this, the land becomes scrubland and semi-arid. Somalia borders Kenya in the northeast, and this is also a fairly arid area.

Climate

Kenya's different altitudes mean that the climate varies enormously around the country. Probably the most pleasant climate is in the Central Highlands and the Rift Valley, though the valley floor can become extremely hot and is relatively arid. Mount Kenya and Mount Elgon both become quite cool above 1,750 m and the top of Mount Kenya is snow-covered. Mount Kenya and the Aberdares are the country's main water catchment areas. Western Kenya and the area around Lake Victoria is generally hot, around 30-34°C all year with high humidity and rainfall evenly spread throughout the year. Most rain here tends to fall in the early evening. The country is covered in semi-arid bushland and deserts throughout the north and east of the country. Temperatures can rise to 40°C during the day and fall to 20°C at night in the desert. Rainfall in this area is sparse, between 250 mm and 500 mm per annum.

The coastal belt is hot and humid all year round, though the heat is tempered by sea breezes. Rainfall varies from as little as 20 mm in February to 240 mm in May. The average temperature varies little throughout the year but is hottest in November and December, at about 30°C.

Vegetation

Kenya is justifiably famous for its flora and fauna. In areas of abundant rainfall, the country is lush, supporting a huge range of plants, and the wide variety of geographical zones house a corresponding diversity of flora. The majority of the country is covered in savannah-type vegetation characterized by the acacia. The slopes of Mount Elgon and Mount Kenya are covered in thick evergreen temperate forest from about 1,000 m to 2,000 m; then to 3,000 m the mountains are bamboo forest; above this level the mountains are covered with groundsel trees and giant lobelias. Mangroves are prolific in the coastal regions.

Wildlife

Mammals

Practically everyone travelling around Kenya will come into contact with animals during their stay. Of course there is much more than the big game to see and you will undoubtedly travel through different habitats from the coast to the tropical rainforests but the mammals are on the top of most people's 'to see' lists.

Big Nine The 'big five' **Elephant** (*Loxodonta africana*), **Lion** (*Panthera leo*), **Black Rhino** (*Diceros bicornis*), **Buffalo** (*Syncerus caffer*) and **Leopard** (*Panthera pardus*), was the term originally coined by hunters who wanted trophies from their safaris, but nowadays the **Hippopotamus** (*Hippopotamus amphibius*) is usually considered one of the Big Five for those who shoot with their cameras, whereas the Buffalo is far less of a 'trophy'. Equally photogenic and worthy to be included are: **Zebra**, **Giraffe** and **Cheetah** (*Acinonyx jubatus*). Whether they are the Big Five or the Big Nine these are the animals that most people come to Africa to see, and, with the possible exception of the Leopard, you have an excellent chance of seeing all of them.

They are all unmistakable and when seeing them for the first time in the wild you will find that they are amazingly familiar and recognisable. The only two that could possibly be confused are the Leopard and the Cheetah. The **Leopard** is less likely to be seen as it is more nocturnal and more secretive in its habits than the Cheetah. It frequently rests during the heat of the day on the lower branches of trees, and, as you drive round the parks, your best bet is to look for the animal's tail, which hangs down below the branches, and can be quite easily spotted while the rest of the animal remains well concealed. If you are lucky you will see one with its kill, which it may have hauled up into the lower branches.

Cheetahs are often seen in family groups walking across the plains or resting in the shade. They are slimmer and longer legged than Leopards, with a characteristic sway back. The black 'tear' mark on the face is usually obvious through binoculars. (If all else fails you can identify Cheetahs by the accompanying mini buses.)

Lions (*Panthera leo*), usually found in open savanna in Africa, are, after tigers, the second largest carnivorous members of the cat family. They live in prides or permanent family groups, numbering up to around 30 animals, and are the only felid to do so. The prides are usually composed of a group of inter-related females and their cubs, led by a dominant male, or occasionally, a group of males. There is no dominant lioness. They communicate with one another with a range of sounds that vary from roaring, grunting and growling to meowing. Roars, more common at night, can reach sound levels of over 110 decibels and be heard from distances of up to 8 km. The females do most of the hunting (usually ungulates like zebra and antelopes), while the males are mostly involved in protecting their pride from other lions and predators. Lions are very sociable except when eating, when aggressive fighting can break out. Although the females kill most of the prey the males are first to feed, followed by the lionesses, the cubs just getting the leftovers. (The main cause of cub death is starvation.) Lions augment their diet by scavenging prey killed by other predators.

Elephants are awe-inspiring and it is wonderful to watch a herd at a waterhole. Although they have suffered terribly from the activities of poachers in recent decades they are still readily seen in many of the game areas.

The other animals which have suffered badly in recent times are the two Rhinos. The **White Rhino** (*Diceros simus*) is now probably extinct in much of its former range in eastern Africa though it flourishes in places. The **Black Rhino** has also diminished in number in recent years. The two rhinos may be distinguished by the shape of their mouth. The White Rhino has a square muzzle, whereas the Black has a long upper lip (the difference is in fact quite easy to see). The Black Rhino is a browser, that is to say it feeds usually on shrubs and bushes. It achieves this by using its long, prehensile upper lip which is well adapted to the purpose. If you see rhino with their young you will notice that the White Rhino tends to herd its young in front of it, whereas the Black Rhino usually leads its young from the front. See also box, page 68.

The **Buffalo**, considered by hunters to be the most dangerous of the big game, can be seen everywhere, sometimes in substantial herds in many areas. Beware: these animals, cut off from the herd, can become bad-tempered and easily provoked.

The **Hippo** is another animal which appears harmless, even comic (from a safe vantage point). During the day it rests in the water and you can get excellent views and interesting photographs, particularly if there are displaying males active in the area. These Hippos will 'yawn' at each other and two animals will sometimes spar. At night the Hippo leaves the water and ranges very far afield to graze (a single adult animal needs up to 60 kilos of grass every day). Should you meet a Hippo on land by day or night keep well away. If you get between it and its escape route to the water, it

The names of the Rhino have no bearing on the colour of the animals as they are both a rather nondescript dark grey. The name White Rhino is derived from the Dutch word 'weit' which means wide and refers to the shape of the animal's mouth.

may well attack. These animals are now considered as dangerous as buffalos, once thought to be the most dangerous of all the big mammals. In many ways the most stunning of the Big Nine is the **Giraffe**. It may not be as magnificent as a full-grown Lion, nor as awe-inspiring as an Elephant, but its elegance is unsurpassed. To see a small party of Giraffe galloping across the plains is seeing Africa as it has been for hundreds of years. Although the Giraffe itself is unmistakable and easily identified, there are in fact several sub-species which differ from each other. Authorities, though, are not always agreed on the exact division into species and races, as there seems to be much overlap of the types.) Extending from about the Tana River northwards and eastwards into Somalia and Ethiopia is the almost chestnut coloured **Reticulated Giraffe** (*Giraffa reticulata*) which is sometimes considered a separate species. This is the most handsome of the various forms, its reddish brown coat being broken up by a network of pale, narrow lines, like the outlines of crazy paving stones. Found further south than the Reticulated Giraffe the **Common Giraffe** (*Giraffa camelopardalis*) which has two forms, or races: one is the **Masai Giraffe** which occurs in southwest Kenya (and Tanzania). This has a yellowish-buff coat with the characteristic patchwork of brownish markings with very jagged edges. In most animals there are only two horns, though occasionally animals are seen with three horns. The other form of the Common Giraffe is known as **Rothschild's Giraffe** and accurs west and north of the Masai Giraffe and into Uganda as far west as the Nile. It is usually rather paler and heavier looking than the Masai Giraffe and can have as many as five horns, though more commonly three. The lolloping gait is very distinctive and it produces this effect by the way it moves its legs at the gallop. A horse will move its fore and hind legs diagonally when galloping, but the giraffe moves both hind legs together and both fore legs together. It achieves this by swinging both hind legs forward and outside the fore legs. It is not a dumb and voiceless animal as many believe but can produce a low groaning noise and a variety of snorts.

The **Zebra** is another easily recognized animal. It forms herds, often large ones, sometimes with antelope. As with giraffe, there is more than one sort of zebra in eastern Africa, and, again, the relationship between the types is complex, but they can be considered as two main types: **Grevy's Zebra** (*Equus grevyi*) and the **Common** or **Burchell's Zebra** (*Equus burchelli*). Grevy's is the larger of the two and has much narrower white stripes which are arranged in such a way as to meet in a sort of star-shaped arrangement at the top of the hind leg. Burchell's, on the other hand, has broad stripes which cross the top of the hind leg in unbroken oblique lines. The ranges of the two animals overlap to a certain extent and they can be seen in mixed herds in some northern areas. Generally though, Grevy's Zebra prefers the more arid areas and seems less dependent on water, and occurs mainly north of the equator, whereas Burchell's ranges to the south.

Larger antelope The first animals that you will see on safari will almost certainly be antelope. These are by far the most numerous group to be seen on the plains. Although there are many different species, it is not difficult to distinguish between them. For identification purposes they can be divided into the larger ones which stand at 48 inches (about 120 cm) or more at the shoulder, and the smaller ones at 36 inches (about 90cm) or less.

For the record, it is worth pointing out here that antelope are not 'deer', which do not occur in Africa, except in parts of the very north, but you will undoubtedly hear many people refer to them as such. There are many differences between the two groups. For example, deer have antlers, which are solid, boney, branching outgrowths from the skull and which are shed annually. Antelope, on the other hand, have horns, which are hollow, unbranched sheaths made of modified skin, rather like finger and toe nails. They are not shed seasonally and if a horn is lost it is not replaced.

The largest of all is the **Eland** (*Taurotragus oryx*) which stands 175-183 cm (69-72 inches) at the shoulder. It is very cattle-like in appearance, with a noticeable dewlap and shortish spiral horns, present in both sexes. The general colour varies from greyish to fawn, sometimes with a rufous tinge, with narrow white stripes on the sides of the body. It occurs, usually in small herds, in a wide variety of grassy habitats.

Not quite as big, but still reaching 140-153cm (55-60 inches) at the shoulder, is the **Greater Kudu** (*Tragelaphus strepsiceros*) which prefers fairly thick bush, sometimes in quite dry areas. Although nearly as tall as the Eland it is a much more slender and elegant animal altogether. Its general colour also varies from greyish to fawn and it has several white stripes running down the sides of the body. Only the male carries horns, which are very long and spreading, with only two or three twists along the length of the horn. A noticeable and distinctive feature is a thick fringe of hair which runs from the chin down the neck. Greater Kudu usually live in family groups of not more than half a dozen individuals, but occasionally larger herds of up to about 30 can be seen. Its smaller relative, the **Lesser Kudu** (*Strepsiceros imberis*), looks quite similar, with similar horns, but stands only 99-102cm (39-40 inches) high. It lacks the throat fringe of the bigger animal, but has two conspicuous white patches on the underside of the neck. It inhabits dense scrub and acacia thickets in semi-arid country, usually in pairs, sometimes with their young.

The **Roan Antelolope** (*Hippoptragus equinus*) is a rare species in Kenya. Roan associate in herds of up to 20 individuals with a very characteristic social structure. Amongst the females, the more dominant is the leader. There is only one adult bull in each herd, and the juvenile males are evicted at the age of about three years. All the female calves remain within the herd, and when it becomes too big, it divides into smaller groups of cows and their young, with once again only one adult bull. The young males evicted from the herd, form bachelor groups of up to about 12 individuals. Amongst these, the most dominant is the first one in line to join a new group of females. Roan are fairly courageous amongst antelopes. If threatened by predators, including lion, they will confront them, and lion have been known to be gored to death by the scimitar-shaped horns of a roan. Adults attain a mass of up to 270 kg and they can live to about 15 years.

Another large antelope with a black and white face is the **Oryx** (*Oryx beisa*). This occurs in two distinct races, the **Beisa Oryx** which is found north and west of the Tana River, and the **Fringe-eared Oryx** which occurs south and east of this river. Both these animals stand 122cm (48 inches) at the shoulder and vary in colour from greyish (most Beisa Oryx) to sandy (most Fringe-eared Oryx), with a black line down the spine and a black stripe between the coloured body and the white underparts, rather like that on found on the much smaller Thomson's Gazelle. They both also have very long straight (not curving) horns, present in both sexes, and which make identification of this animal quite easy. The two races may be distinguished by the long dark fringe of hair on the tips of the ears in the Fringe-eared Oryx, absent in the Beisa Oryx. The Beisa Oryx is found in herds in arid and semi desert country and the Fringe-eared Oryx, also in herds, in similar habitat, but also sometimes in less dry habitats.

Common Waterbuck (*Kobus ellipsiprymnus*) are about 122-137cm (48-54 inches) at the shoulder with shaggy grey-brown coats which are very distinctive. The males have long gently curving horns which are heavily ringed. They are distinguished by the white mark on the buttocks, on this species of waterbuck this forms a clear half ring on the rump and round the tail. This animal occurs in small herds, in grassy areas, often near water. They are fairly common and widespread.

The **Wildebeest** or **Gnu** (*Connochaetes taurinus*) is well-known to many people from published photographs of the spectacular annual migration through Masai Mara. It is a big animal about 132cm (52 inches) high at the shoulder, looking rather like an American bison from a distance, especially when you see the huge herds straggling across the plains. The impression is strengthened by its buffalo-like horns (in both sexes) and humped appearance. The general colour is greyish with a few darker stripes down the side. It has a noticeable beard and long mane.

The four remaining large antelope are fairly similar. Three of these four are **Hartebeest** of various sorts and the fourth is called the **Topi**. All four antelope have long, narrow horse-like faces and rather comical expressions. The shoulders are much higher than the rump giving them a very sloped back appearance, especially in the three hartebeest. Again all four have short, curved horns, carried by both sexes. In the three hartebeest the horns arise from a boney protuberance on the top of the head and curve outwards as well as backwards. One of the hartebeests, **Jackson's Hartebeest** (*Alcelaphus buselaphus*) (about 132cm, 52 inches) is similar in colour to the **Topi** (*Damaliscus korrigum*) (about 122-127cm , 48-50 inches) being a very rich dark rufous in colour. But the Topi has dark patches on the tops of the legs, a coat with a rich satiny sheen to it, and more ordinary looking lyre-shaped horns. Of the other two hartebeest, **Coke's Hartebeest** (*Alcephalus buselaphus*) (about 122cm, 48 inches), also called the **Kongoni**, is usually considered to be a race of Jackson's Hartebeest, but is a very different colour being a more drab pale brown with a paler rump.

Smaller antelope The remaining common antelopes are a good deal smaller than those described above. The largest is the **Impala** (*Aepyceros melampus*) which is 92-107 cm (36-42 inches) at the shoulder and a bright rufous in colour with a white abdomen. From behind, the white rump, with black lines on each side, is characteristic. Only the male carries the long, lyre shaped horns. Just above the heels of the hind legs is a tuft of thick black bristles, unique to the Impala, which are surprisingly easy to see as the animal runs. Also easy to see is the black mark on the side of abdomen, just infront of the back leg. Another two are **Grant's Gazelle** (*Gazella granti*), about 81-99cm (32-35 inches) at the shoulder, and **Thomson's Gazelle** (*Gazella thomsonii*), about 64-69cm (25-27 inches) at the shoulder. They are superficially similar. Grant's, the larger of the two and has longer horns, but this is only a good means of identification when the two animals are seen together. The general colour of both varies from a bright rufous to a sandy rufous. In both species the curved horns are carried by both sexes. Thomson's Gazelle can usually be distinguished from Grant's by the broad black band along the side between the rufous upper parts and white abdomen, but not invariably, as some forms of Grant's also have this dark lateral stripe. If in doubt, look for the white area on the buttocks which extends above the tail on to the rump in Grant's, but does not extend above the tail in Thomson's. This is the surest way to distinguish them. The underparts are white. Thomson's Gazelle or 'Tommies', are among the most numerous animals that inhabit the plains of Kenya and Tanzania. You will see large herds of them often in association with other game. Grant's Gazelle, occurs on rather dry grass plains, in various forms.

The last two of the common smaller antelopes are the **Bushbuck** (*Tragelaphus scriptus*) which is about 76-92cm (30-36 inches) at the shoulder, and the tiny **Kirk's Dikdik** (*Rhynchotragus kirkii*) only 36-41cm (14-16 inches). Both are easily identified. The Bushbuck's colour varies from chestnut (probably the most common) to a darkish brown. The coat has a shaggy appearance and a variable pattern of white spots and stripes on the side and back. There are, in addition, two white crescent shaped marks on the front of the neck. The horns, present in the male only, are short, almost straight and slightly spiralled. The animal has a curious high rump which gives it a characteristic crouching appearance. The white underside of the tail is noticeable when it is running. The Bushbuck tends to occur in areas of thick bush especially near water. They lie up during the day in thickets, but are often seen bounding away when disturbed. They are usually seen either in pairs or singly. Kirk's Dikdik is so small it can hardly be mistaken for any other antelope. In colour it is a greyish brown, often washed with rufous. The legs are noticeably thin and stick-like, giving the animal a very fragile appearance. The snout is slightly elongated, and there is a conspicuous tuft of hair on the top of the head. Only the male carries the very small straight horns.

Finally, mention must be made of a rare antelope which fairly frequently seen in the Aberdare National Park. This is the **Bongo** (*Boocercus eurycerus*) , a large and handsome 112-127cm (44-50 inches) forest antelope.

Other mammals Although the antelope are undoubtedly the most numerous animals to be seen on the plains, there are others worth keeping an eye open for. Some of these are scavengers which thrive on the kills of other animals. They include the dog-like Jackals, of which there are three main species, all being similar in size, (about 86-96cm, 34-38 inches in length and 41-46cm, 16-18 inches at the shoulder). The **Black-backed Jackal** (*Canis mesomelas*) , which is the most common and ranges throughout the area, is a rather foxy reddish fawn in colour with a noticeable black area on its back. This black part is sprinkled with a silvery white which can make the back look silver in some lights. In general colour the **Side-striped Jackal** (*Canis adustus*) is greyish fawn and it has a variable and sometimes ill-defined stripe along the side. It is most likely to be seen around Lake Victoria and in Tanzania.

The other well known plains scavenger is the **Spotted Hyaena** (*Crocuta crocuta*). It is a fairly large animal, 69-91cm (32-36 inches) at the shoulder. Its high shoulders and low back give it a characteristic appearance. It is brownish with dark spots and has a large head. It usually occurs singly or in pairs, but occasionally in small packs.

A favourite and common animal is the comical **Warthog** (*Phacochoerus aethiopicus*). This is unmistakeable being almost hairless and grey in general colour with a very large head with tusks and wart-like growths on the face. They are often seen in family parties. The adults will run at speed with their tails held straight up in the air.

In suitable rocky areas, such as *kopjes*, look out for an animal that looks a bit like a large grey-brown guinea pig. This is the **Rock Hyrax** (*Heterohyrax brucei*), an engaging and fairly common animal that lives in communities in rocky places.

The most common and frequently seen of the monkey group are the Baboons. The most widespread species is the **Olive Baboon** (*Papio anubis*), which occurs almost throughout the area. This is a large (127-142 cm, 50-56 inches), heavily built animal olive brown or greyish in colour. Adult males have a well-developed mane. In the eastern part of Kenya and Tanzania, including the coast, the Olive Baboon is replaced by the **Yellow Baboon** (*Papio cynocephalus*) (116-137 cm, 46-54 inches) which is a smaller and lighter animal than the Olive Baboon, with longer legs and almost no mane in the adult males. The tail in both species looks as if it is broken and hangs down in a loop. Baboons are basically terrestrial animals, although they can climb very well. In the wild they are often found in acacia grassland, often associated with rocks, and are sociable animals living in groups called troops. Females are very often seen with young clinging to them. In parts of East Africa they have become very used to the presence of man and can be a nuisance to campers. They will readily climb all over your vehicle hoping for a handout. Be careful, they have a very nasty bite.

The smaller monkey that makes a nuisance of itself is the **Vervet or Green Monkey** (*Cercopithicus mitis*), which is the one that abounds at camp sites and often lodges. This has various forms, the commonest and most widespread having a black face framed with white across the forehead and cheeks. Its general colour is greyish tinged with a varying amount of yellow. The feet, hands and tip of the tail are black.

At dusk in Africa you will notice many bats. The most spectacular of them is the **Straw-coloured Fruit Bat** (*Eidolon helvum*) which has a wing span of 76 cm (30 inches).

Birds

East Africa is one of the richest areas of birdlife in the world. The total number of species is in excess of 1,300, and it is possible, and not too difficult to see 100 different species in a day. You will find that a pair of binoculars is essential. The birds described here are the common ones and, with a little careful observation, you will soon find that you can identify them. They have been grouped according to the habitat.

certainly be the large numbers soaring overhead. Early in the morning the numbers are few, but as the temperature warms up, more and more are seen circling high above the buildings. Many of these will be **Hooded Vultures** (*Neophron monachus*) 66 cm, 26 inches and **Black Kites** (*Milvus migrans*) 55 cm, 22 inches. They are both rather nondescript brownish birds which are superficially similar. They are, however, easily distinguished by the shape and length of the tail. The tail of the Hooded Vulture is short and slightly rounded at the end, whereas the Black Kite (which incidently is not black, but brown) has a long, narrow tail which looks either forked when the tail is closed or slightly concave at the end when spread. Also soaring overhead in some cities (notably Kampala) you will see the **Marabou Stork** (*Leptoptilos crumeniferus*) 152 cm, 60 inches. Although this bird is a stork it behaves like a vulture, in that it lives by scavenging. Overhead its large size, long and noticeable bill and trailing legs make it easily identified. The commonest crow in towns and cities is the **Pied Crow** (*Corvus albus*) 46 cm, 18 inches. This is a very handsome black bird with a white lower breast which joins up with a white collar round the back of the neck. It is a slender, shiny black bird with a grey neck. In gardens and parks there are a number of smaller birds to look out for. The **Dark-capped or Common Bulbul** (*Pycnonotus barbatus*) 18 cm, 7 inches, can be heard all day with its cheerful call of "Come quick, doctor, quick". It is a brownish bird with a darker brown head and a slight crest. Below, the brown is paler fading to white on the belly, and under the tail it is bright yellow.

There are a large number of Weaver birds to be seen, but identifying them is not always easy. Most of them are yellow and black in colour, and many of them live in large noisy colonies. Have a close look at their intricately-woven nests if you get the chance. The commonest one is probably the **Black-headed Weaver** (*Ploceus cucullatus*) 18 cm, 7 inches, which often builds its colonies in bamboo clumps. The male has a mainly black head and throat, but the back of the head is chestnut. The underparts are bright yellow, and the back and wings mottled black and greenish yellow. When the bird is perched, and seen from behind, the markings on the back form a V-shape.

Birds of open plains Along with the spectacular game, it is here that you will see many of the magnificent African birds. In particular, there are two large birds which you will see stalking across the grasslands. These are the **Ostrich** (*Struthio camelus*) 2 m, 7 ft and the **Secretary Bird** (*Sagittarius serpentarius*) 101 cm, 40 inches. The Secretary Bird is so called because the long plumes of its crest are supposed to resemble the old time secretaries who carried their quill pens tucked behind their ears. The bird is often seen in pairs as it hunts for snakes, its main food source. The Ostrich is sometimes seen singly, but also in family groups. There are other large terrestrial birds to look out for, and one of them, the **Kori Bustard** (*Otis kori*) 80 cm, 35in, like the Secretary Bird quarters the plains looking for snakes. It is quite a different shape, however, and can be distinguished by the thick looking grey neck (caused by loose feathers). It is particularly common in Serengeti National Park and in the Masai Mara. The other large bird that you are likely to see on the open plains is the **Ground Hornbill** (*Bucorvus cafer*) 107 cm, 42 inches. When seen from afar, this looks for all the world like a turkey but close up it is very distinctive and cannot really be mistaken for anything else. They are very often in pairs and the male has bare red skin around the eye and on the throat. In the female this skin is red and blue.

Soaring overhead on the plains you will see vultures and birds of prey. The commonest vulture in game areas is the **African White-backed Vulture** (*Gyps africanus*) 81 cm, 32 inches. This is a largish, brown bird with a white lower back, and it has, of course, the characteristic bare head of its family. Because they are commonly seen circling overhead the white rump is sometimes difficult to see. So look out for the other diagnostic characteristic – the broad white band on the leading edge of the undersurface of the wing. The **Bateleur** (*Terathopius ecaudatus*) 61 cm, 24 inches, is a magnificent and strange looking eagle. It is rarely seen perched, but is quite commonly seen soaring very high overhead. Its tail is so short that it sometimes appears tailless. This, its bouyant flight and the black and white pattern of its underparts make it easy to identify.

Where there is game look out for the Oxpeckers. The commonest one is the **Red-billed Oxpecker** (*Buphagus erythrorhynchus*) 18 cm, 7 inches. These birds are actually members of the starling family although their behaviour is not like that of other starlings. They associate with game animals and cattle and spend their time clinging to, and climbing all over the animals while they hunt for ticks, which form their main food. There are other birds which associate with animals in a different way. For example the **Cattle Egret** (*Bubulcus ibis*) 51 cm, 20 inches, follows herds and feeds on the grasshoppers and other insects disturbed by the passing of the animals. Occasionally too, the Cattle Egret will perch on the back of a large animal, but this is quite different from the behaviour of Oxpeckers. Cattle Egrets are long legged and long billed white birds which are most often seen in small flocks. In the breeding season they develop long buff feathers on the head, chest and back

Birds of dry, open woodland The two habitats of open plain and dry open woodland form a vast area of Africa and most of the game parks come into these categories. As well as being quintessentially African, this dry open woodland with acacia thorn trees is an extremely rewarding area for bird watching. It supports an enormous variety of species and it is relatively easy to see them.

The Guinea Fowls live in flocks and if you surprise a group on the road they will disappear into the bush in a panic. There is more than one sort of Guinea Fowl, but they are rather similar, being a slaty grey with white spots.

The tops of the thorn trees are used as observation perches by a number of different species. Specially noticeable is the **Red-billed Hornbill** (*Tockus erythrorhynchus*) 45 cm, 17 inches, which has blackish-brown back, with a white stripe down between the wings. The wings themselves are spotted with white. The underparts are white and the bill is long, curved and mainly red. As the bird flies into a tree the impression is of a black and white bird with a long red bill and a long tail. Another striking bird which perches on tree tops is the **White-bellied Go-away Bird** (*Corythaixoides leucogaster*) 51 cm, 20 inches. This gets its strange name from its call "Go-away, go-away". It is a basically grey bird with a very upright stance. The top of the head carries a long and conspicuous crest. The belly is white and the long tail has a black tip. It is usually seen in small family parties.

The strange looking, brightly coloured bird **d'Arnaud's Barbet** (*Trachyphonus darnaudii*) 15 cm, 6 inches, is common in the dry bush country. The impression you get is of a very spotted bird, dark with pale spots above, and pale with dark spots below. It has a long dark tail which again is heavily spotted. Its call and behaviour is very distinctive. A pair will sit facing each other with their tails raised over their backs wagging them from side to side, and bob at each other in a duet. All the while they utter a four note call over and over again. "Do-do dee-dok". Another brightly coloured bird is the **Lilac-breasted Roller** (*Coracias caudata*) 41 cm, 16 inches, which is very easy to see as it perches on telegraph poles or wires, or on bare branches. The brilliant blue on its wings, head and underparts is very eye catching. Its throat and breast are a deep lilac and its tail has two elongated streamers. It is common in open bush country. Also often seen sitting on bare branches is the **Drongo** (*Dicrurus adsimilis*) 24 cm, 9 inches, but this is an all black bird. It is easily identified by its forked tail, which is "fish-tailed" at the end. It is usually solitary.

There are many different species of starling to be seen in eastern Africa, and most of them are beautifully coloured. Two of the most spectacular are the **Golden-breasted Starling** (*Cosmopsarus regius*) 32 cm, 13 inches, and the **Superb Starling** (*Spreo superbus*) 18 cm, 7 inches. Both are common, but the Superb Starling is the more widespread and is seen near habitation as well as in thorn bush country. Tsavo East is probably the best place to see the Golden-breasted Starling. Look out for the long tail of the Golden-breasted Starling, and the white under tail and white breast band of the Superb Starling. Both are usually seen hopping about on the ground. Another long- tailed bird quite commonly seen in bush country is the **Long-tailed Fiscal** (*Lanius cabanisi*) 30 cm, 12 inches. Unlike the Golden-breasted Starling, however, it is a black and white bird which is usually seen perched on wires or bare branches. It can be identified by its very long all-black tail and mainly black upperparts, which are grey on the lower back and rump.

Finally look out for three birds which though small are very noticeable. The **Red-cheeked Cordon-bleu** (*Uraeginthus benegalus*) 13 cm, 5 inches, is a lovely little blue bird with a brown back and bright red cheek patches. They are seen in pairs or family parties, and the females and young are somewhat duller in colour than the males. They are quite tame and you often see them round the game lodges. In the less dry grasslands you can see the beautiful red and black Bishop birds. There are two species both of which are quite brilliant in their colouring. The brightest is the **Red Bishop** (*Euplectes orix*) 13 cm, 5 inches, which has brown wings and tail, and noticeable scarlet feathers on its rump. The almost equally brilliant **Black-winged Bishop** (*Euplectes hordeaceus*) 14 cm, 5.5 inches, may be distinguished from the Red Bishop by its black wings and tail and rather less obvious red rump. Both species occur in long grass and cultivation, often, but not invariably, near water.

Water and waterside birds The inland waters form a very important habitat for both resident and migratory species. A lot can be seen from the shore, but it is especially fruitful to go out in a boat, when you will get quite close to, among others, the large and magnificent herons which occur here. The king of them all is the aptly named **Goliath Heron** (*Ardea goliath*) 144 cm, 58 inches, which is usually seen singly on mud banks and shores, both inland and on the coast. Its very large size is enough to distinguish it, but the smaller **Purple Heron** (*Ardea purpurea*) 80 cm, 34 inches, which frequents similar habitat and is also widespread, may be mistaken for it at a distance. If in doubt, the colour on the top of the head (rufous in the Goliath and black in the Purple) will clinch it, also the Purple is much more slender with a slender bill.

The Flamingos are known to most people and will be readily identified. However, there are two different species which very often occur together. The **Greater Flamingo** (*Phoenicopterus ruber*) 142 cm, 56 inches, is the larger and paler bird and has a pink bill with a black tip. The **Lesser Flamingo** (*Phoenicopterus minor*) 101 cm, 40 inches, is deeper pink all over and has a deep carmine bill with a black tip. They both occur in large numbers in the soda lakes of western Kenya, but are also seen in several lakes in Tanzania. The magnificent **Fish Eagle** (*Haliaeetus vocifer*) 76 cm, 30 inches, has a very distinctive colour pattern. It often perches on the tops of trees, where its dazzling white head and chest are easily seen. In flight this white and the white tail contrast with the black wings. It has a wild yelping call which is usually uttered in flight. Try and watch the bird as it calls: it throws back its head over its back in a most unusual way.

There are several different kingfishers to be seen, but the most numerous is the black and white **Pied Kingkisher** (*Ceryle rudis*) 25 cm, 10 inches. This is easily recognized as it is the only black and white kingfisher. It is common all round the large lakes and also turns up at quite small bodies of water. It hovers over the water before plunging in to capture its prey.

Marine wildlife

The fish and coral here are wonderful and can be observed without having to dive. Many of the fish do not have universally recognized English names, but one that does is the very common **scorpion** or **lion fish** (*Pterois*), which is probably the most spectacular fish you can see without going out in a boat. It is likely to be wherever there is live coral, and sometimes it gets trapped in the deeper pools of the dead reef by the retreating tide. It can be up to 26 cm long and is easily recognized by its peculiar fins and zebra stripes. Although it has poisonous dorsal spines it will not attack if left alone.

While most visitors naturally want to spend time diving and snorkelling on the live reef and watching the brilliant fish and many coloured living corals, do not bypass the smaller, humbler creatures which frequent dead as well as living coral. These can be seen on most of the beaches, but one of the best places is Tiwi beach by **Twiga Lodge** in Kenya. Here a vast area of dead coral is partly exposed at low tide and you can safely paddle. Be sure to wear shoes though, because there are many sea urchins. These **sea urchins** (*Echinoidea*) are usually found further out towards the edge of the reef, but can be found anywhere. There are two forms, the more common **short-needled sea urchin** and the much less common **long-needled** variety. Their spines are very sharp and treading on them is extremely painful. Look out also for the common **brittle stars** (*Ophiuroidea*) which frequent sandy hollows. They vary considerably in size, but are usually 10 cm across. They are so called because the arms break off very readily, but they will grow again. These are not sea urchins, though they are related, and can safely be picked up for a closer look, but handle them carefully.

Other living creatures which can be seen crawling along in the shallows include the **sea slug** (*Nudibranchia*) and the **snake eel** (*Ophichthidae*). Both are quite common in sandy places. The unlovely sea slug is blackish brown and shaped a bit like the familiar garden slug, though much bigger. It often has grains of sand sticking to it. Don't be put off by the name of the snake eel, it is quite harmless. It looks a bit like a snake and has alternating light and dark bands on its body. What are beautiful, without doubt, are the **starfish** (*Asteroidea*) which are best seen by going out in a boat, but some can be seen nearer in shore.

The commonest shells are without doubt the **cowries**. Many dead ones can be found on the beach. The two most common are the **ringed cowrie** (*Cypraea annulus*) and the **money cowrie** (*Cypraea moneta*). Of these the ringed is especially plentiful and is a pretty grey and white shell with a golden ring. The money cowrie, once used as currency in Africa, varies in colour from greenish grey to pink according to its age. The big and beautiful **tiger cowrie** (*Cypraea tigris*) is also seen occasionally. This can be up to 8 cm in length. There is quite a lot of variation in colouring, but it is basically a very shiny shell with many dark round spots on, much more like a leopard than a tiger.

Books

History
Hibbert C, *Africa Explored: Europeans in the Dark Continent 1769-1889*, London: Penguin 1984, describes the exploits of the main explorers, including the search for the source of the Nile.

Miller C, *Lunatic Express*, highly readable history of East Africa, centring around the building of the railway.

Monbiot G, *No Man's Land*, Macmillan 1994, tells how the nomadic tribes in Kenya and Tanzanian were forced off their land.

Murray Brown J, *Kenyatta*, biography of the man who became the first president of Kenya.

Huxley E, *Flame Trees of Thika*, stories of the lives of early pioneers.

Memoirs
Blixen K, *Out of Africa*, wonderfully written, impressions of the author's life in Kenya.

Markham B, *West with the Night*, marvellous autobiography of the woman who made the first solo east to west Atlantic flight.

Fiction
Hemingway E, *Green Hills of Africa*, masterly short stories based on the author's African visits in 1933-1934.

Mwangi M, *Going Down River Road*, grim but entertaining story of African urban life.

Footnotes

Language	336
Index	337
Complete title listing	340
Map index	342
Advertisers' index	342
Map symbols	343
Credits	344
Acknowledgements	345
Author biography	345
Colour maps	347

Language

Here are some useful words and phrases in Kiswahili. Attempting a few words will be much appreciated by Kenyans.

Good morning	*Habari ya asubuhi*
Good afternoon	*Habari ya mchana*
Good evening	*Habari ya jioni*
Good night	*Habari ya usiku*
Hello!	*Jambo!*
A respectful greeting to elders, actually meaning: "I hold your feet"	*Shikamoo*
Their reply: "I am delighted"	*Marahaba*
How are you?	*Habari yako?*
I am fine	*Nzuri / Sijambo*
I am not feeling good today	*Sijiziki vizuri leo*
How are things?	*Mambo?*
Good/cool/cool and crazy	*Safi / poa / poa kichizi*
See you later	*Tutaonana baadaye*
Welcome!	*Karibu! (Karibu tena!)*
Goodbye	*Kwaheri*
Please	*Tafadhali*
Thank you	*Asante*
Sorry	*Pole*
Where can I get a taxi?	*Teksi iko wapi?*
Where is the bus station?	*Stendi ya basi iko wapi?*
When will we arrive?	*Tutafika lini?*
Can you show me the bus?	*Unaweza ukanioyesha basi?*
How much is the ticket?	*Tiketi ni bei gani?*
Is it safe walking here at night?	*Ni salama kutembea hapa usiku?*
I don't want to buy anything	*Sitaki kununua chochote*
I have already booked a safari	*Tayari nimeisha lipia safari*
I don't have money	*Sina hela*
I'm not single	*Nina mchumba / siko peke yangu*
Could you please leave me alone?	*Tafadhali, achana na mimi*
It is none of your business!	*Hayakuhusu!*
One	*moja*
Two	*mbili*
Three	*tatu*
Four	*nne*
Five	*tano*
Six	*sita*
Seven	*saba*
Eight	*nane*
Nine	*tisa*
Ten	*kumi*

Index

A

Aberdare Forest 164
Aberdares National
  Park 166
accommodation 34
activities 40
Adamson, Joy 186
adventure sports 40
airport information 26
Amboseli National
  Park 202
animals 325
Arabuko Sokoke Forest
  Reserve 241
Archers Post 293
Aruba Dam 196

B

Baden-Powell 162,165
ballooning 40
Bantu expansion 310
baobab trees 251
bargaining 27
bars 38
begging 27
birds 330
birdwatching 40
Bisanadi National
  Reserve 306
boda boda 33
Boni 268
Boni National
  Reserve 280
books 334
border crossings 25
budgets 22
Buffalo Springs 295
bungee jumping 40
Bungoma 153
bus 31
Busia 153

C

camping 35
car hire 32
Carnivore, Nairobi 80
caving 40
Central Island National
  Park 291
Chagaik Dam and
  Arboretum 146
Chaimu Crater 197
Chale Island 227
Chandani 279
Chepterr 289
Cherangani Hills
  121, 288
Chetambe's Fort 153

children, travelling
  with 18
Chogoria 186
Chogoria trail 186
Chundwa 279
Church of St James and
  All Martyrs 164
Chyulu Hills National
  Park 197
cinema 38
CITES 29
climate 13, 325
climbing 41
clubs 38
consulates 20
Crater Lake Game
  Sanctuary 102
credit cards 22
Crescent Island Game
  Sanctuary 101
cuisine 36
culture 318
currency 22
customs 20, 26

D

dance 38, 321
David Sheldrick Trust 72
Diani Beach 224
diarrhoea 52
disabled travellers 18
diving 42
Dodori National
  Reserve 280
drinks 38
Dunga 135
Dunga Swamp 135

E

East African
  Community 314
economy 316
ecotourism 27
Eldoret 150
elephants 72
Elgeyo Escarpment 288
Eliye Springs 291
Elsamere 101
Emali 193
embassies 20
Embu 186
events 39

F

Faza 279
Ferguson's Gulf 291
festivals 39
fishing 41

flamingos 111
flights 23, 30
food 36
Fort Jesus, Mombasa 213
Fourteen Falls 163
Funzi Island 227

G

Gambles Cave 107
game drives 49
Garissa 308
Garsen 251
gay travellers 18
Gazi 227
Gedi Ruins 244
geography 324
Gof Sokorte Guda 305
golf 41
Got Ramogi 153
Great Mosque 245
Grogan's Castle 204

H

Hallar Park 238
health 51
Hell's Gate National
  Park 102
history 310
Hobley's 102
homestays 34
horse racing 41
hostels 35
hotels 34
House of Sheik Mbaruk
  bin Rashid 227
Hyrax Hill Prehistoric
  Site 111

I

immigration 19
Impala Sanctuary 136
Imperial British East
  Africa Company 311
insurance 21
internet 57
Isiolo 293
itinerary 12

J

Jumba la Mtwana 240

K

Kabarnet 121
Kaisagat Desert
  Garden 154
Kajiado 192, 201
Kakamega 148

Kakamega Forest
  National Reserve 148
Kakamega Show 148
Kalenjin 121
Kalenjin (Nilotic) 319
Kalenjin runners 120
Kalokol 291
Kamba (Bantu) 319
Kanderi Swamp 196
Kaputiei Plains 192
Karatina 164
Karen Blixen Museum 70
Kariandusi 107
Kendu Bay 141
Kenya African National
  Union 313
Kenya National
  Museum 67
Kenya People's
  Union 313
Kenyatta 313
Kenyatta, Jomo 313
Kericho 145
Kerio Valley 121
Kerio Valley National
  Reserve 121
Kiambethu 99
Kiambu 98
Kiboko 193
Kibwezi 193
Kigoi Wildlife
  Conservancy 102
Kikuyu 319
Kilifi 240
Kima 193
Kimana Community
  Wildlife Sanctuary 203
Kipepeo Project 246
Kisii 144
Kisili (Bantu) 319
Kisite Marine National
  Park 228
Kisumu 134
Kisumu Bird
  Sanctuary 136
Kiswahili 18
Kitale 153
Kitale Nature Reserve 154
kite surfing 41
Kitoka 241
Kiunga Marine National
  Reserve 279
Kiwayu 279
Kiwayu Island 279
Kizingo 215
Kongoni Wildlife
  Conservancy 101
Kongowea 216
Kora National Park 307

L

Laikipia Plateau 179
Lake Baringo 119
Lake Bogoria National
    Reserve 118
Lake Chala 204
Lake Elmenteita 107
Lake Jipe 197, 204
Lake Magadi 192
Lake Naivasha 99
Lake Nakuru National
    Park 109
Lake Turkana 290, 300
Lambwe region 142
Langata 71
Lango Plains 226
language 18
laws 26
Leakey, Louis 310
Leakey, Mary 310
Leakey, Richard 310
Lewa Wildlife
    Conservancy 181
Likoni 223
Likoni ferry 221
literacy 318
Lodwar 290
Losai National
    Reserve 304
Loyangalani 300
Lugard Falls 196
Lunga Lunga 229
Luo (Nilotic) 319
Luyha (Bantu) 320

M

Magadi 192
magazines 58
Makindu 193
Malaba 153
malaria 54
Malindi 246
Malindi Marine National
    Park 250
Mambrui 251
mammals 325
Manda Island 277
Mandera 308
maps 33
Maralal 298
Maralal Game Sanctuary
    298
Mariakani 193
Marich Pass 287
marine life 333
Markham, Beryl 74
Marsabit 304
Marsabit National Park
    304
Masai (Nilotic) 320

Masai Mara National
    Reserve 123
matatu 31
Mathew's Mountains 298
Matondoni Village 271
Mau Mau 313
Mbaraki Pillar 215
Mboya, Tom 142,313
media 58
medicines 51
Menengai Crater 113
Meru 184
Meru (Bantu) 320
Meru National Park 185
Mfangano Island 143
Mida Creek 242
Millennium Man 310
miraa 185
Mitchell's Farm 99
Mkomani 266
Mnarani Ruins 240
Mnazini village 251
Moi 314
Moi University 150
Mokowe 251
Mombasa 211
    sights 213
money 21
Mount Elgon National
    Park 155
Mount Elgon NP (K)
    climbing 155
Mount Kenya 172 - 173
Mount Kenya Biosphere
    Reserve 172
Mount Koh 288
Mount Longonot 103
Mount Sekerr 288
Mount Suswa 98
mountain climbing 41
Moyale 305
Msambweni 227
Mtito Andei 193
Mtwapa Creek 239
Mudanda Rock 196
Mugeka 163
Murang'a 163
music 38,321
Mwaluganje Elephant
    Sanctuary 226
Mwea National Reserve
    186
Mzima Springs 197
Mzizima 215

N

Nabahani 278
Nairobi 59
    airport 62
    climate 63
    eating 80
    history 64

orientation 62
    sights 65
    sleeping 76
    transport 90
Nairobi National Park 71
Naivasha 98
Nakuru 107
Namanga 202
Namotunga 291
Nanyuki 172
Naro Moru 172
Nasolot National Reserve
    289
national parks 43
National Resistance Army
    315
Ndere Island National
    Park 136
newspapers 58
Ngomongo Villages 238
Ngong Hills 76
Ngulia Rhino Sanctuary
    198
nightclubs 38
nightlife 38
North Kitui National
    Reserve 307
Northern Rift Valley 121
Northrup MacMillan, Sir
    William 163
Nyahururu 114
Nyali 216
Nyali Beach 238
Nyeri 163 - 164

O

Odinga, Oginga 313
Ol Doinyo Sapuk National
    Park 163
Ol Pejeta Game Reserve
    183
Olkaria 102
Oloitokitok 204
Oloololo Escarpment 125
Oloor Karia Masai Cultural
    Centre 102
Olorgesailie Prehistoric
    Site 192
Oroma 268
Ortum 287
Ouko, Dr Robert 315

P

packing 21
park beyond parks 203
parks 43
Pate Island 277
Pate Town 278
people 318
Pokot 268
politics 314

population 316
Portuguese influence 311
post 58
Prince Abu al-Fida 246

R

Rahole National Reserve
    307
Ras Kilimdini 277
Ras Mtangawanda 278
reading 334
Religion 324
reserves 43
responsible tourism 27
rhino conservation 68
rhinos 72
Rift Valley 95
Rongai 112
Ruma National Park 141 -
    142
Rusinga Island 142

S

safari 43
safari lodges 36
safari operators 33
Sagana 164
Saiwa Swamp National
    Park 154,287
Samburu 193,294
scuba diving 42
Sea Slug 334
Selenkei Conservation
    Area 203
self catering 34
Shaba National Reserve
    295
Shaitani lava flow 197
Shanga Ruins 278
Shanzu Beach 239
Shela 271
Sheldrick Falls 226
Shelley Beach 223
Shimba Hills 193
Shimba Hills National
    Reserve 225
Shimoni 228
Simbi Nyaima Lake 141
Sirikwa Safaris 158
Siyu 278
sleeping 34
Solio Game Ranch 165
South Horr 300
South Kitui National
    Reserve 197
South Turkana National
    Reserve 289
sport 40
stomach upsets 52
student travellers 18
Sultan Hamud 193

Swahili (Bantu) 320
Swahili culture 249
Sweetwaters Game
  Reserve 181

T

Tabaka 144
Taita Hills Game
  Sanctuary 198
Takwa Ruins 277
Tana River National
  Primate Reserve 251
Tana River Primate
  National Reserve 306
Taru Desert 193
Taveta 204
taxis 33
telephone 58
The Norfolk, Nairobi 65
The Rift Valley 95
Thika 163
Thimlich Ohinga 143
Thomson's Falls 114
Timau 184
tipping 27,50
Tiwi Beach 223
Tot 288

tour operators 15
train 30
transport 23,30
  air 23,30
  boda boda 33
  bus 31
  car 32
  matatu 31
  taxi 33
  trucks 33
  tuk tuks 33
travellers' cheques 22
Treetops 165,167
tribes 318
truck safaris 33
trucks 33
Tsavo East 196
Tsavo National Park 195
Tsavo West 197
tuk tuks 33
Turkana (Nilotic) 320

U

Uganda border 153
Uhuru Gardens 70
Ukambani Hills 192
Ukunda 234

V

vaccinations 20
Vasco da Gama 247
vegetation 325
visas 19
Voi 193

W

Wajir 308
Wamba 298
Wasini Island 229
Watamu 242
Watamu Marine Park 244
water hyacinth 137
watersports 42
Webuye 153
Webuye Falls 153
Weeping Stone 149
Western Highlands 144
Western Kenya 131
whitewater rafting 43
wildlife 43,325
Witu 251
women travellers 19
working 19

Y

Yatta Plateau 196

Complete title listing

Footprint publishes travel guides to over 150 destinations worldwide. Each guide is packed with practical, concise and colourful information for everybody from first-time travellers to travel aficionados. The list is growing fast and current titles are noted below. Available from all good bookshops and online www.footprintbooks.com

(P) denotes pocket guide

Latin America & Caribbean
Antigua & Leeward Islands (P)
Argentina Barbados (P)
Belize, Guatemala & Southern
Bolivia
Brazil
Caribbean Islands
Central America & Mexico
Chile
Colombia
Costa Rica
Cuba
Cusco & the Inca Trail

Dominican Republic (P)
Ecuador & Galapagos
Havana (P)
Jamaica (P)
Mexico
Nicaragua
Patagonia
Peru
Peru, Bolivia & Ecuador
Rio de Janeiro (P)
St Lucia (P)
South American Handbook
Venezuela

North America
New York (P)
Vancouver (P)
Western Canada

Africa
Cape Town (P)
East Africa
Egypt
Kenya
Libya
Marrakech (P)
Morocco
Namibia
South Africa
Tanzania
Tunisia
Uganda

Middle East
Dubai (P)
Israel
Jordan
Syria & Lebanon

Australasia
Australia
East Coast Australia
New Zealand
Sydney (P)
West Coast Australia

Asia
Bali
Bangkok & the Beaches
Bhutan
Cambodia
Goa
Hong Kong (P)
India
Indian Himalaya
Indonesia
Laos
Malaysia & Singapore
Nepal
Northern Pakistan
Rajasthan
South India
Sri Lanka
Sumatra
Thailand
Tibet
Vietnam
Vietnam, Cambodia & Laos

Europe
Andalucía
Barcelona (P)
Belfast & the north of Ireland (P)
Berlin (P)
Bilbao (P)
Bologna (P)
Britain
Cardiff (P)
Copenhagen (P)
Costa de la Luz (P)
Croatia
Dublin (P)
Edinburgh (P)
England
Glasgow (P)
Ireland
Lisbon (P)
London
London (P)
Madrid (P)
Naples & the Amalfi Coast (P)
Northern Spain
Paris (P)
Reykjavík (P)
Scotland
Scotland Highlands & Islands
Seville (P)
Siena & the heart of Tuscany (P)
Spain
Tallinn (P)
Turin (P)
Turkey
Valencia (P)
Verona (P)
Wales

Lifestyle guides
Surfing Britain
Surfing Europe

Also available
Traveller's Handbook (WEXAS)
Traveller's Healthbook (WEXAS)
Traveller's Internet Guide (WEXAS)

Map index

Aberdares National Park   166
Amboseli National Park   202
Diani Beach   224
Kakamega   148
Kakamega Forest Reserve   149
Kericho   145
Kilifi   240
Kisumu   136
Laikipia Plateau   180
Lakes Bogario & Baringo   119
Lake Naivasha &
  Hell's Gate National Park   100
Lake Nakuru National Park   110
Lake Turkana   286
Lamu town north   267
Lamu town south   268
Malindi north   248
Malindi south   247
Masai Mara National Reserve   124

Mombasa Island   210
Mombasa Old Town   214
Mombasa, central   212
Mount Elgon National Park   156
Mount Kenya region   173
Nairobi   64
Nairobi centre   66
Nakuru   108
North coast   237
Nyeri   165
Rongai   112
Samburu/Buffalo Springs
  National Park   294
South coast   227
Tsavo East   196
Tsavo West   198
Watamu   242

Advertisers' index

Acacia Adventure Holidays, UK   16
The Africa Travel Centre, UK   15
Easy Travel & Tours Ltd, Tanzania   14
Hoopoe Safaris, Kenya   16
Kenya Airways, UK   Inside back cover

Predators Safari Club, Tanzania   17
Safari Drive, UK   15
Shoor Safaris, Kenya   129, 352
Travel Africa Magazine, UK   17
UNIGLOBE Let's Go Travel, Kenya   87

Map symbols

Administration

- □ Capital city
- ○ Other city/town
- International border
- Regional border
- Disputed border

Roads and travel

- Motorway
- Main road (National highway)
- Minor road
- Track
- Footpath
- Railway with station
- ✈ Airport
- Bus station
- Ⓜ Metro station
- Cable car
- Funicular
- Ferry

Water features

- River, canal
- Lake, ocean
- Seasonal marshland
- Beach, sandbank
- Waterfall

Topographical features

- Contours (approx)
- Mountain
- Volcano
- Mountain pass
- Escarpment
- Gorge
- Glacier
- Salt flat
- Rocks

Cities and towns

- Main through route
- Main street

- Minor street
- Pedestrianized street
- Tunnel
- One way-street
- Steps
- Bridge
- Fortified wall
- Park, garden, stadium
- Sleeping
- Eating
- Bars & clubs
- Building
- Sight
- Cathedral, church
- Chinese temple
- Hindu temple
- Meru
- Mosque
- Stupa
- Synagogue
- Tourist office
- Museum
- Post office
- Police
- Bank
- Internet
- Telephone
- Market
- Hospital
- Parking
- Petrol
- Golf
- Detail map
- Related map

Other symbols

- Archaeological site
- National park, wildlife reserve
- Viewing point
- Campsite
- Refuge, lodge
- Castle
- Diving
- Deciduous/coniferous/palm trees
- Hide
- Vineyard
- Distillery
- Shipwreck
- Historic battlefield

Credits

Footprint credits

Editor: Stephanie Lambe
Editorial assistant: Angus Dawson
Map editor: Sarah Sorensen
Picture editor: Rob Lunn
Proof reader: Sarah Chatwin

Publisher: Patrick Dawson
Editorial: Alan Murphy, Sophie Blacksell, Sarah Thorowgood, Claire Boobbyer, Felicity Laughton, Nicola Jones
Cartography: Robert Lunn, Claire Benison, Kevin Feeney
Series development: Rachel Fielding
Design: Mytton Williams and Rosemary Dawson (brand)
Sales and marketing: Andy Riddle
Advertising: Debbie Wylde
Finance and administration: Sharon Hughes, Elizabeth Taylor

Photography credits

Front cover: Images of Africa (Flamingos)
Back cover: Alamy (Hot-air balloon over the Masai Mara)
Front colour section: Images of Africa, Ben Winston, Alamy
Wildlife colour section: NATUREPL (Karl Ammann, Ingo Arndt, Peter Blackwell, Nigel Bean, John Cancalosi, Philippe Clement, Richard Du Toit, Laurent Geslin, Tony Heald, Eliot Lyons, Pete Oxford, Andrew Parkinson, Constantinos Petrinos, T J Rich, Jose B Ruiz, Francois Savigny, Anup Shah, Mike Wilkes)

Print

Manufactured in Italy by LegoPrint
Pulp from sustainable forests

Footprint feedback

We try as hard as we can to make each Footprint guide as up to date as possible but, of course, things always change. If you want to let us know about your experiences – good, bad or ugly – then don't delay, go to **www.footprintbooks.com** and send in your comments.

Publishing information

Footprint Kenya
1st edition
© Footprint Handbooks Ltd
November 2005

ISBN 1 904 777 52 X
CIP DATA: A catalogue record for this book is available from the British Library

® Footprint Handbooks and the Footprint mark are a registered trademark of Footprint Handbooks Ltd

Published by Footprint

6 Riverside Court
Lower Bristol Road
Bath BA2 3DZ, UK
T +44 (0)1225 469141
F +44 (0)1225 469461
discover@footprintbooks.com
www.footprintbooks.com

Distributed in the USA by

Publishers Group West

Every effort has been made to ensure that the facts in this guidebook are accurate. However, travellers should still obtain advice from consulates, airlines etc about travel and visa requirements before travelling. The authors and publishers cannot accept responsibility for any loss, injury or inconvenience however caused.

Author biography

Originally from London, **Lizzie Williams** has worked and lived in Africa for 12 years, starting as an expedition leader on trips across the continent on overland trucks, including the Istanbul to Cape Town run. She is now something of an expert on border crossings and African beer, and has sat with a gorilla, slept amongst elephants, swam with a hippo, and fed a giraffe. Lizzie has travelled independently to over 20 African countries and could feasibly have driven many hundreds of thousands of kilometres through Africa. She has spent lengthy periods working in Zimbabwe running an overland stop and tour company specialising in Mozambique and in South Africa as manager of a backpacker's lodge equipped to receive overland trucks. She is co-author of *Footprint South Africa*, author of *Footprint Kenya*, and has updated both *Footprint Namibia* and the *Rough Guide to Turkey*. She is also the author of the first country-specific guidebook to Nigeria, the *Bradt Guide to Nigeria*. She has written www.overlandafrica.com a leading website on the overland industry in Africa, contributed Africa destination guides to US websites, including iexplore and yahoo, and written *Africa Overland*, a souvenir coffee-table book on the Kenya to Cape overland route. Lizzie writes full time and, when not on the road, lives in Cape Town.

Acknowledgements

Lizzie would like to thank Bulawayo Bruce and Dutch Pete in Mombasa and Graham and Rosemary Thompson in Nairobi for their exceptional hospitality. Thanks to Stu Hodge at Global Village, a leading travel agent in London specializing in Africa, for organizing flights. For car hire thanks to Alan and all at UNIGLOBE Let's Go Safaris in Nairobi, an excellent African tour operator. Tour operators in Kenya that were especially helpful include Jerome Jones of Southern Cross Safaris in Mombasa, the staff at Gametrackers Safaris in Nairobi, and Netta Ruthmann of Kwa Kila Hali Safaris in Nairobi and Eldoret. In Lamu thanks to the staff at the Lamu Palace Hotel and Ziwa Abdallah from the Lamu Guides Association, in Mombasa the staff at the excellent tourist office, and again at Diani Beach the very helpful tourist office. Thanks to Simon Lewis for helping me find 'somewhere to watch sport' at Diani Beach in the run up to his beloved Liverpool winning the 2005 European Championships. Thanks to the staff at Footprint for their back up and to Stephanie Lambe for making it all make sense. Thanks must also go to Mike Hodd, the author of *Footprint East Africa*, for his excellent text. Finally thanks for all the input from my friends in East Africa, it was a great pleasure to catch up and hopefully it won't be as long next time.

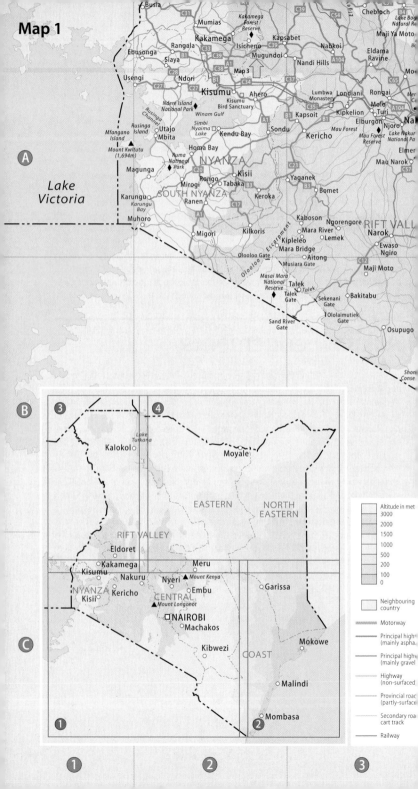

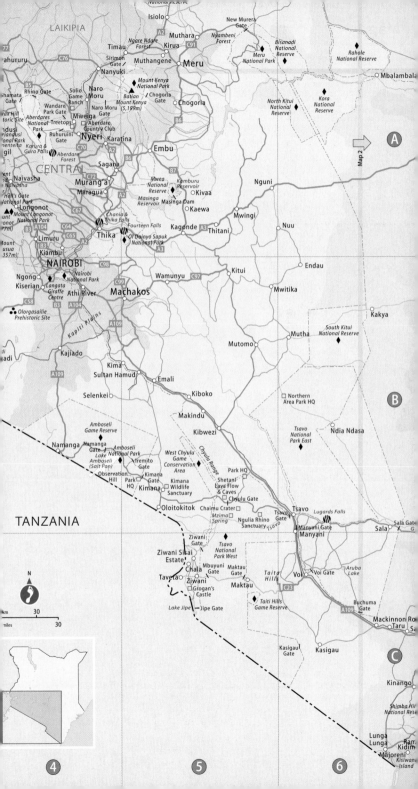

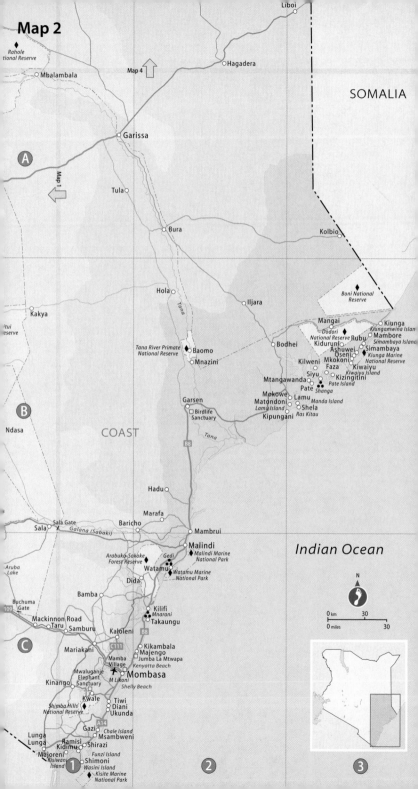

Map 2

Map 4
Map 1

Rahole
tional Reserve

Mbalambala

SOMALIA

A

Garissa

Tula

Bura

Kakya

Kolbio

Hola

Iljara

Boni National
Reserve

Mangai

Kunga
Kiungamwina Island

Tana River Primate
National Reserve

Baomo

Bodhei

Dodori
National Reserve

Rubu
Kiduruni

Mambore
Simambaya Island

Mnazini

Ashuwei
Oseni

Simambaya
Kiunga Marine
National Reserve

Kilweni

Mkokoni

B

tui
Reserve

Ndasa

COAST

Garsen

Birdlife
Sanctuary

Tana

Mtangawanda

Mokowe
Matondoni
Lamu Island

Faza
Siyu

Pate

Kiwaiyu
Kiwaiyu Island

Kizingitini
Pate Island

Shanga

Lamu
Manda Island

Shela
Ras Kitau

Kipungani

Hadu

Marafa

Indian Ocean

Sala Gate
Galana (Sabaki)

Sala

Baricho

Mambrui

Malindi

Aruba
Lake

Arabuko-Sokoke
Forest Reserve

Gedi

Malindi Marine
National Park

Watamu

Watamu Marine
National Park

Dida

Bamba

Buchuma
Gate

Mackinnon Road
Taru

Samburu

Kaloleni

Kilifi
Mnarani
Takaungu

N

C

Mariakani

Mamba
Village

Kikambala
Majengo
Jumba La Mtwapa
Kenyatta Beach

0 km   30

0 miles   30

Mwaluganje
Elephant
Sanctuary

M Likoni

Mombasa

Shelly Beach

Kinango

Kwale

Shimba Hills
National Reserve

Tiwi
Diani
Ukunda

Gazi

Lunga
Lunga

Ramisi
Kidimu

Msambweni

Funzi Island

Shirazi

Majoreni
Kisiwani
Island

Shimoni

Wasini Island

Kisite Marine
National Park

1   **2**   **3**

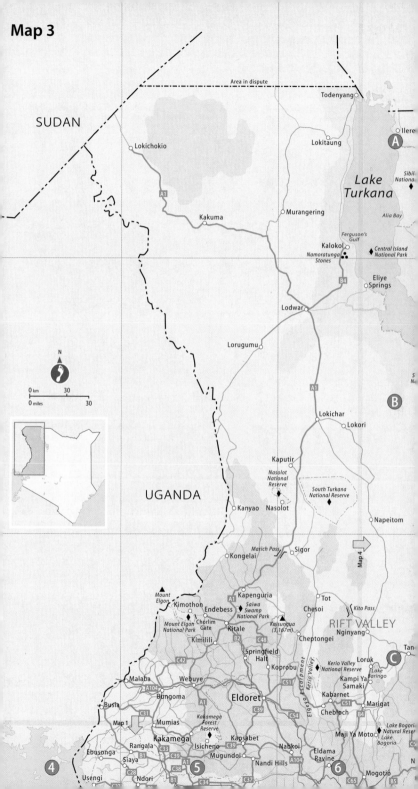

Map 3

SUDAN

Area in dispute

Todenyang

Ilere

Lokichokio

Lokitaung

A

Lake Turkana

Sibil
Nationa

A1

Kakuma

Murangering

Alia Bay

Ferguson's
Gulf

Kalokol

*Namoratunga
Stones*

Central Island
National Park

B4

Eliye
Springs

Lodwar

Lorugumu

N

0 km   30
0 miles   30

A1

Lokichar

Lokori

S
Ne

B

Kaputir

*Nasolot
National
Reserve*

South Turkana
National Reserve

UGANDA

Kanyao

Nasolot

Napeitom

Marich Pass

Sigor

Map 4

Kongelai

Mount
Elgon

Kimothon

Kapenguria

Endebess

*Saiwa Swamp
National Park*

Tot

Chesoi

Kito Pass

RIFT VALLEY

Chorlim
Gate

*Mount Elgon
National Park*

Kitale

*Kaisungua
(3,167m)*

Nginyang

Tan

Kimilili

B2

C48

Cheptongei

Loruk

C

Springfield
Halt

Koprobu

*Kerio Valley
National Reserve*

*Lake
Baringo*

C42

Kampi Ya
Samaki

Malaba

Webuye

Kerio Valley

Kabarnet

A104

Bungoma

A1

C51

C54

Chebloch

Marigat

B4

Busia

Eldoret

C39

Maji Ya Moto

*Lake Bogoria
Natural Reser*

*Lake
Bogoria*

C31

Mumias

*Kakamega
Forest
Reserve*

Kapsabet

Nabkoi

Map 1

Rangala

B1

Kakamega

Isicheno

Mugundoi

Nandi Hills

A104

Eldama
Ravine

6

Ebusonga

C28

C39

C33

5

C37

Mogotio

B5

Siaya

Ndori

A1

C34

C65

Usengi

4

B1

Map 4

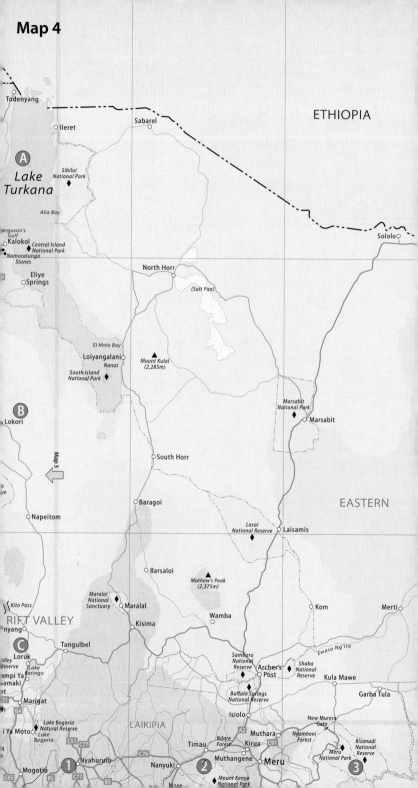

ETHIOPIA

Todenyang

Ileret

Sabarel

Sololo

A

Lake Turkana

Sibiloi National Park

Alia Bay

Ferguson's Gulf

Kalokol

Central Island National Park

Namoratunga Stones

Eliye Springs

North Horr

(Salt Pan)

El Molo Bay

Loiyangalani

Nanat

Mount Kulal (2,285m)

South Island National Park

Marsabit National Park

Marsabit

B

Lokori

South Horr

Map 3

Baragoi

EASTERN

Napeitom

Losai National Reserve

Laisamis

Barsaloi

Mathew's Peak (2,375m)

Kom

Merti

Kito Pass

Maralal National Sanctuary

Maralal

RIFT VALLEY

nyang

Kisima

Wamba

C

Tangulbel

Ewaso Ng'iro

Loruk

Lake Baringo

alley Reserve

ampi Ya amaki

Samburu National Reserve

Archer's Post

Shaba National Reserve

Kula Mawe

Marigat

Buffalo Springs National Reserve

Garba Tula

i Ya Moto

Lake Bogoria Natural Reserve

Lake Bogoria

Isiolo

New Murera Gate

LAIKIPIA

Muthara

Nyambeni Forest

Bisanadi National Reserve

Mogotio

Nyahururu

Timau

Ndare Forest

Kirua

Meru National Park

Nanyuki

Muthangene

Meru

Mount Kenya National Park

①

②

③

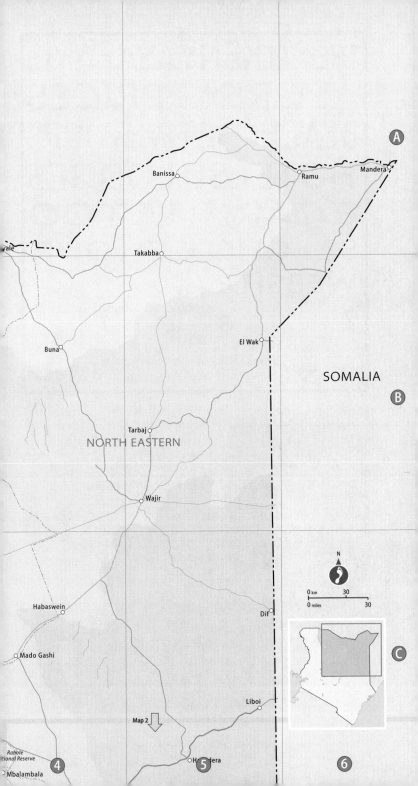

A

Banissa

Ramu

Mandera

vale

Takabba

Buna

El Wak

SOMALIA

B

Tarbaj

NORTH EASTERN

Wajir

N

0 km   30
0 miles   30

Habaswein

Dif

Mado Gashi

C

Liboi

Map 2

Rahole
tional Reserve

Mbalambala

4

H   dera

5

6

352